MANAGING
ENERGY PRICE
RISK

MANAGING ENERGY PRICE RISK

RISK PUBLICATIONS

ENRON CAPITAL & TRADE RESOURCES

Published by Risk Publications
104-112 Marylebone Lane
London W1M 5FU
Tel +44 (0)171 487 5326; fax +44 (0)171 486 0879

© Financial Engineering Ltd
London 1995; reprinted with minor amendments 1995
ISBN 1 899332 05 7 – Hardback
ISBN 1 899332 10 3 – Softback

Designer: Judith Charlton
Editor: Robert Jameson
Production Editor: Miles Smith-Morris

PREFACE

The aim of this book is to provide a comprehensive review of energy risk management. It's a rapidly growing area, with few reliable sources of information. We hope that *Managing Energy Price Risk*, produced by Risk Publications in association with Enron Capital & Trade Resources, will become a standard text on both theory and practice in this sector.

We have focused the volume on the more advanced concerns of providers and end-users of risk management products, while striving to make even the most technical chapters accessible to those unfamiliar with the concepts and the jargon. The latest energy derivative products are explained and analysed in detail, along with consideration of how these instruments are used by customers; the fundamentals of the producing, refining and processing, distribution and consuming industries; and a host of legal and regulatory issues.

To cover all these angles, the book is divided into four major sections.

The first section is devoted to the technical issues behind energy derivatives: the term structure of the forward curve; volatility; correlation; and the adaptation of valuation models to energy-sector requirements.

The next section reviews the full range of instruments now employed in the industry – from swaps and options to the more exotic options and cross-market products. Supplementing this review is a series of worked examples.

The third section concentrates on the impact of the fundamentals of the world's energy markets on energy risk management: the connections between the global oil markets, the booming natural gas market in the United States, electricity derivatives in the United Kingdom and the potential of emerging markets.

In the final section, the focus is on structural and legal problems – and recent regulatory changes. The book concludes with a glossary.

Lou Pai, Managing Director, Enron Capital & Trade Resources
Peter Field, Publisher, Risk Publications

CONTENTS

AUTHORS

Kaushik Amin is currently a vice-president at Lehman Brothers. Previously, he was an associate professor of finance at the School of Business Administration of the University of Michigan. He has published various articles on option pricing in leading journals. He has also been an advisor of Merrill Lynch and a consultant for Susquehanna Investments Group.

Frédéric Barnaud has been responsible for Risk Management and Research and Development at Elf Trading SA, the international supply, trading and shipping division of Elf Aquitaine, since April 1992. Frédéric qualified as an Ingénieur at the École Nationale des Ponts et Chaussées, Paris, where he specialised in civil engineering, applied maths and finance. He subsequently spent a fifteen-month secondment period from Elf to the Oxford Institute for Energy Studies, where he researched oil economics, and to the London University City Business School, where he studied the financial and commodities markets.

Alban Brindle recently joined Trafalgar Commodities Ltd, a specialist energy broker in London, as marketing manager. While writing Chapter 13 for this book, however, he worked for the International Petroleum Exchange (IPE) in London. Alban had been associate director for business development and research at the IPE since August 1993, and had worked in research at the IPE since June 1989. Alban began his career with

Gill & Duffus Plc, a major London-based commodity dealer trading in soft commodities, metals, energy and financial futures, after graduating from university in 1984.

Colin Bryce is executive director and head of the European Commodities Department of Morgan Stanley & Co International Ltd in London. After graduating from Glasgow University in 1978, Colin worked for the British National Oil Corporation (BNOC) in various supply and pricing functions. From 1982 until 1986, he served as the senior crude oil trader with Britoil. He joined Morgan Stanley in 1987 to set up oil trading operations in London. Colin also serves as a Director of the International Petroleum Exchange of London.

Shannon Burchett is a vice-president of The Chase Manhattan Bank in New York and is responsible for derivative product origination for global commodities. Prior to joining Chase, Shannon worked for Salomon Brothers' Phibro unit, where he headed Structuring and Origination for the United States for all commodity derivatives. He has managed various derivative product areas including foreign exchange, interest rate and commodity units while holding positions at PepsiCo, Aetna and Bankers Trust. He is a former professor of finance and economics at New York University, and holds an MBA degree in finance from Tulane University and a bachelors degree

in electrical engineering from Texas Tech University.

Stijn Claessens is a senior financial economist with the World Bank in Washington, working in the Private Sector and Finance Division of the Technical Department for East Europe, Central Asia and Middle East regions. He holds a PhD in Business Economics from the Wharton School of the University of Pennsylvania. His assignments at the Bank have included operational work on debt management in various countries and policy work on external debt. Prior to coming to the Bank, Stijn taught at New York University.

Jean Dabouineau, based in Geneva, is general manager in charge of Economics and Risk Management for Elf Trading SA - the international supply, trading and shipping division of Elf Aquitaine. Before joining Elf Trading in 1986, he held a number of positions in the refining and marketing division of Elf Aquitaine, and was technical director of the Elf refinery in Donges, France.

Darrell Duffie is Professor of Finance at The Graduate School of Business, Stanford University, and is the author of several texts on finance, including *Dynamic Asset Pricing Theory*, as well as articles for journals in economics, finance and mathematics. Darrell has acted as a consultant to, among others, Shell Oil Company, Mobil Corporation, Morgan Stanley and Enron.

William Falloon is the US editor for *Risk* magazine, and a leading contributor to Risk Publication's specialist newsletter, *Energy Risk*. He has reported on the derivatives market since graduating from the University of Chicago in 1983. He is also co-author of *Strategic Risk Management: How Global Corporations Manage Financial Risk for Competitive Advantage* (1991).

Jay Fitzgerald is vice president in charge of the Industrial Services Group of Enron Capital & Trade Resources (ECT), the merchant services operation of Enron Corp. Prior to his current position, he was responsible for building and developing ECT's derivatives marketing effort. Jay joined Enron in 1992 after spending five years marketing capital markets products at UBS Securities and Credit Lyonnais New York.

Jacques Gabillon is head of research and development in the Commodity Derivatives Group of Banque Indosuez in London. Previously he was a partner and manager of Alternative Energy, a commodity derivative institution affiliated to Caisse Nationale de Crédit Agricole. Before that, he was an oil trader with Elf Trading, and visiting research fellow at the Oxford Institute for Energy Studies. He has an engineering degree from Ecole Centrale des Arts et Manufactures, Paris.

Stinson Gibner is a vice-president with Enron Capital & Trade Resources (ECT), working in the research group of Enron Risk Management and Trading in Houston, Texas. His responsibilities include the valuation of exotic options and customised contracts, analysis of hedging strategies, and helping to develop state-of-the-art portfolio risk measurement systems. Stinson holds a BA in

Physics from Rice University and a PhD in Physics from Caltech.

Jeffrey Golden is a partner in the London office of the law firm of Allen & Overy. Jeffrey has acted as one of the International Swaps & Derivatives Association's legal advisors since ISDA's inception and has participated since 1984 in the preparation of ISDA's standard master agreement forms and other documentation for energy-linked and other derivatives. He has written and lectured on various legal issues relating to international capital markets. Jeffrey was educated at Duke University, the London School of Economics and Political Science, and the Hague Academy of International Law, and at Columbia University School of Law (from which he received his JD degree in 1978).

Stephen Gray is assistant professor of finance at the Fuqua School of Business, Duke University. Stephen's research interests include asset pricing and econometrics, particularly modelling volatility in financial markets. He has Honours degrees in commerce and law from the University of Queensland, Australia, and a PhD in finance from Stanford University.

Alison M. Gregory is an associate in the Commodities, Futures and Derivatives Group of the law firm Sullivan & Cromwell. After graduating from the University of Virginia, Alison traded derivatives for Morgan Stanley & Co Inc from 1987 until 1989, before attending Stanford Law School. Upon graduation from law school, she served as a law clerk to the Honorable Ralph K Winter in the United States Court of Appeals for the Second Circuit. She is currently Secretary of the Committee on Commodities and Futures Law of the New York State Bar Association's Business Law Section.

Michael Hampton is responsible for commodities and shipping-related transactions at Cedef Finance Ltd in London. Prior to joining Cedef, Michael was executive director at Swiss Bank Corporation in Chicago, where he was co-head of SBC's commodity derivatives unit. Before that, from 1987-91, he set up and ran the commodity derivatives operation of The Chase Manhattan Bank in Europe, where he was involved in Chase's pioneering effort to introduce oil swaps. His 16 years at Chase also encompassed an eight-year period working in the global shipping division. He is a frequent lecturer on applying derivatives and economic cycles to the shipping industry, and has written a short book entitled *Long and Short Shipping Cycles*, as well as numerous magazine articles.

James Hoare is manager of the Electricity Forward Agreement (EFA) department at GNI Ltd in London, and has been involved in the international commodity markets for over 10 years. He has managed the EFA department for GNI since the market began in 1991, having joined GNI as a futures broker in 1990. Before this, he spent seven years as a physical sugar trader.

Steve Jones is the distillates trader for Credit Lyonnais Rouse Derivatives. After graduating from Middlesex Business School in 1989, he joined Credit Lyonnais Rouse as a graduate trainee. Shortly afterwards, CLR developed their commodity derivatives business, which later evolved into a separate company, Credit Lyonnais Rouse Derivatives. Initially, Steve was responsible for operations. He then adopted a marketing role, developing CLRD's customer base on the distillates book for three years before moving to his present role.

Vincent Kaminski is a vice president and head of research in Enron Risk Management and Trading, a unit of Enron Capital & Trade Resources (ECT), based in Houston, Texas. Vince is responsible for developing analytical tools for pricing commodity options and other commodity transactions, hedging strategies, and the optimisation of financial and physical transactions. Vince joined Enron in June 1992, having previously been vice president in the research department of Salomon Brothers in New York (Bond Portfolio Analysis Group), and a manager in AT&T Communications. Vince holds an MS degree in international economics and a PhD degree in mathematical economics from the Main School of Planning and Statistics in Warsaw, Poland, and an MBA from Fordham University in New York.

Ewan Kirk is executive director of Commodity Strategies in the J Aron division of Goldman Sachs. He is responsible for developing risk management strategies for customer and proprietary business in London. He is a graduate of the universities of Glasgow, Southampton and Cambridge. Before joining J Aron he completed a PhD in General Relativity, and worked as a management consultant.

Louise Kitchen is natural gas trading manager of Enron Capital & Trade Resources – Europe. Louise joined the company in the spring of 1994 and is currently responsible for the physical and financial trading of natural gas in the United Kingdom. Prior to joining Enron, Louise was employed by PowerGen, where she worked in electricity trading before moving to take responsibility for PowerGen's gas trading activities. Louise is a graduate in Economics and holds honours degrees from

universities in England and France.

Chris Mason joined Credit Lyonnais Rouse in 1990 to set up the Credit Lyonnais group's business in OTC commodity derivatives, having previously spent ten years with the London branch of another French banking group, managing first their specialist commodity finance group and, subsequently, their interest rate and currency trading activities. Since being appointed managing director of Credit Lyonnais Rouse Derivatives Plc in 1993, Chris has been closely involved in widening the scope of the business from the trading and marketing of OTC derivatives to include commodity structured finance.

Jean-François Maurey has been with Société Générale since 1989, when the bank first started trading and market making in oil options. He is a senior trader on the commodities derivatives desk in Paris, where he is responsible for structured products and exotic warrant or bond issues, and for the development of exotic option risk-management instruments.

James MeVay is a managing director of Chase Securities in New York, where he heads the corporate Derivatives Origination and Structuring Group. Prior to joining Chase in 1985, he held a variety of domestic and international treasury positions at General Foods Corporation, including European treasurer. James holds an MBA from the University of Connecticut.

Victor Ng is currently an economist at the capital market and financial studies division of the International Monetary Fund. He is also an associate editor of the *Journal of Business and Economic Statistics*. Previously, he was an assistant professor of finance at the School of Business

Administration of the University of Michigan. He has published numerous articles in leading journals on volatility modelling, option pricing, commodity futures and econometric techniques.

Patrick Perfetti is a technical analyst with Société Générale's energy and commodities team in Paris, which deals with oil, precious and base metals. His experience in the commodities markets includes trading and making markets in both classic and Asian energy derivatives (options and futures).

Craig Pirrong is an assistant professor of business economics and public policy at the School of Business Administration of the University of Michigan. He is the author of "Grain Futures Markets: An Economic Appraisal"; "Corners and Squeezes: The Economics, Law and Public Policy of Derivative Market Manipulation"; and eleven articles on pricing and regulatory issues in futures markets. He has also consulted extensively in the derivatives area.

Joseph T. Pokalsky is vice president, Global Risk Manager for Enron Capital & Trade Resources (ECT). He is responsible for the natural gas, crude, products, gas liquids, power, interest rate and currency trading and risk management activities, both domestically and internationally. Prior to joining Enron in 1991, he held positions with Manufacturers Hanover and Chemical Bank in currency and interest rate derivatives trading and product development. Joseph graduated from SUNY Buffalo and received Masters' degrees in Finance and Transportation from the Wharton School and the University of Pennsylvania. He is a Chartered Financial Analyst (CFA) and a member of the Association for Investment Management & Research (AIMR), the Society of

12

Financial Engineers, and the Energy Risk Management Association (ERMA).

David Quarmby is a member of Credit Lyonnais Rouse Derivatives' structured finance team based in London. David graduated in economics from the University of East Anglia, Norwich, joining Midland Montagu in 1989. He worked in various departments, including corporate finance, treasury and capital markets before moving to Credit Lyonnais Rouse. His responsibilities include the design and provision of commodity-linked finance, structured notes and over-the-counter hedging.

Kenneth M. Raisler is a partner in Sullivan & Cromwell's New York office, and co-head of the firm's Commodities, Futures and Derivatives Group. Kenneth is a graduate of Yale University and New York University School of Law. He joined the Commodity Futures Trading Commission as Deputy General Counsel in 1982, and was the General Counsel of the Commission from 1983 to 1987. From 1988 to 1991, he was Chairman of the Association of the Bar of the City of New York Committee on Futures Regulation, and is currently a member of the Board of Directors of the Futures Industry Association and a member of the Working Group of The Group of Thirty Derivatives Project.

Ted Robson has worked for the last three years for BZW in London, marketing oil hedging instruments to clients in the UK and Europe. He completed the first oil swap by the Barclays Group worldwide in Australia in July 1990. Prior to moving to the UK in early 1991 he worked for the Barclays Group in Australia for four years, marketing treasury products and financial derivatives. Before that he worked for the

Australian subsidiary of Bank of America for seven years in a similar role, and prior to that for the ANZ Bank in various general banking roles. Ted contributed an article to the first edition of *Energy Risk*, Risk Publications' specialist newsletter, and has lectured at various London conferences on energy price risk management.

Sara Sullivan is a vice-president with The Chase Manhattan Bank in London, and heads up the FX Options Marketing Team for Europe. Her responsibilities include the structuring of FX options related transactions for corporate and investor clients. Prior to joining Chase in early 1992, Sara worked on the Specialist Option Sales team at Midland. Sara holds an honours degree in Chemistry and Anthropology from the University of Durham.

David Tolley is the commercial manager of National Power, the largest generating company in the United Kingdom. His responsibilities include administration of the company's contracts with the Regional Electricity Companies and negotiation of contracts with the National Grid Company. David began his career working with electricity distribution companies. In 1979 he joined the Electricity Council, where he was concerned with electricity pricing. In 1987 he joined the Central Electricity Generating Board as their business planning manager, and was later closely involved in the development of the electricity Pool during the transition of the industry to a market basis.

Christopher Turner is second vice-president at The Chase Manhattan Bank and conducts research on risk-management related issues. He has published in the *Journal of Financial Economics* and the *Journal of*

Finance as well as in several trade journals. Chris received his bachelor degree from Loyola College in Baltimore, Maryland, and his PhD from the University of Washington in Seattle, Washington.

Panos Varangis is an economist in the Commodity Policy and Analysis Unit of the World Bank, dealing primarily with commodity risk management, research in the area of commodity price behaviour, and agricultural markets. He has worked extensively on projects for several developing countries in Latin America and Africa, and has written various papers and journal articles on the above topics. Panos holds an MA degree in economics from Georgetown University, and a PhD degree in economics from Columbia University.

John Woodley joined Morgan Stanley & Co Inc in their New York commodities department in 1994 in order to help develop their electricity trading operations in the United States. He gained his knowledge of the electricity market with The Southern Company of Atlanta, first market planning for their subsidiary, The Georgia Power Company, and then as Assistant to the Chief Financial Officer of The Southern Company.

Liz Wright joined Southern Electric in 1990 to head the team managing the price risk associated with buying electricity from the electricity Pool. She was instrumental in setting up the Electricity Forward Agreements (EFA) market. She is a graduate of Exeter University (1981), and began her career as a chemical engineer with BP. Following assignments in various locations, she joined BP Chemicals, where she purchased naphtha and LPG feedstocks for their United Kingdom sites and traded oil derivatives.

INTRODUCTION

A Market is Born

William Falloon[1]
Risk Magazine

With Cathay Pacific Airways Ltd in Hong Kong, and Koch Industries in Wichita, Kansas as counterparties, Chase Manhattan Bank entered into the world's first oil-indexed price swaps in October 1986. These back-to-back swaps, with Chase in the middle, represented the first time that hedging concepts developed for the interest rate and currency swap market had been successfully transferred to the energy markets.

The first historic transaction, in the form of a cash-settled, four-month swap on 25,000 barrels of crude oil per month, took place just after the price of oil had collapsed to around $14 per barrel. Koch agreed to pay the average spot price of oil over the period, while Cathay Pacific hoped that by agreeing to pay a fixed price of $14–15 per barrel of oil, it would gain an effective hedge against any rise in the price of jet fuel in the coming months.[2] The success of the deal prompted Koch to make swap transactions with a notional value of more than 1 million barrels over the next 24 months, including deals in which oil prices were swapped for as much as five years into the future.

The original stimulus for these back-to-back swaps came from Chase, which quickly attracted Cathay Pacific's interest by explaining to the airline how it might manage energy price volatility and its overall impact on fuel consumption costs through a swap.[3] Unfortunately, Chase had not been able to find an oil company willing to take the "other side" of this new-fangled instrument. After a couple of months searching, Chase's enthusiasm sparked interest at privately-held Koch Industries. Assisting Koch Industries to assess the worth of these pioneering transactions were Corky Nelson, treasurer, and Lawrence Kitchen, a well-known energy derivative expert who later switched to the dealer side of the market. Charles Koch, the chief executive officer and primary owner of Koch Industries, gave them the green light to go ahead with this initial deal. His degrees in

mechanical (nuclear) and chemical engineering from MIT were invaluable in helping him to understand the implications of this new hedging instrument – and perhaps also made him more receptive to using it than other oil producers and refiners.

Prior to Koch's deal, the concept of "commodity swaps" had been brainstormed in a series of seminars attended by senior managers at Chase.[4] Leading the way in turning these ideas into commercial deals were Chase's Gaylen Byker and Ron Liesching.[5] Byker remembers having long talks with Liesching about the concept; in turn, Liesching frequently discussed which energy indices might be appropriate benchmarks for swaps with Colin Carter, an oil analyst at Chase who has since died. Although Liesching had been toying with the idea since 1984, he became seriously interested in applying the concept after a meeting with Amerada Hess Corporation, which was considering funding some of its activities in British pounds and Norwegian kroner. The sensitivity of those currencies to oil prices jogged a wild thought in Liesching's mind: given the close links these currencies have to oil prices, why not fund yourself in another currency – oil?

The gregarious Byker, in contrast, seemed willing to take Liesching's conceptual notions and hammer them into a project on which he could focus his entrepreneurial energies. "I was rotating through the interest rate and currency swap area at the time, after doing my doctorate in foreign exchange risk management," recalls Byker. "I had practiced law and taught finance, but I didn't really have any practical experience. Frankly, I don't think Chase knew quite what to do with me. I had some long talks with Ron. If this was such a good idea, I told him, then why don't we do it?"

Byker found a loyal internal sponsor in the form of Chase's chief operating officer at the time, Richard Urfer.[6] Over the months following the first Koch-Cathay Pacific deal, Chase executed two sizeable oil price swaps with Canadian and US railways, so that within a short period of time deals had been booked in the bank's New York, Toronto and London offices.

In the same period, some of Chase's competitors such as Bankers Trust, Citibank and Phibro Energy (owned by Salomon Brothers) were tinkering with their own ideas. Through a subsidiary that was allowed to trade in the physical market, Citibank International Trading Co (Citco), Citibank had begun to offer six-month hedging protection against energy cargoes coming from the Middle East and the Far East. The bank's initial short-term programmes met with minimal success, but they predated Chase's first transactions and seem to represent the first attempt by a bank to get involved with risk transfer in the energy markets. Citibank's efforts lasted only a few months, as the bank found it very difficult to manage basis risk – the uncertain relationship between Citco's forward contract price on these cargoes and the price of the futures contracts at the New York Mercantile Exchange (Nymex) that the bank then used as a way of hedging this obligation. The problem was that the bank was trying to hedge the price of energy cargoes arriving outside the United States with exchange-traded instruments whose prices reflected directly only what was happening in the New York Harbor market.

The pioneering efforts to market energy swaps prompted one of the first media references to the nascent energy derivatives industry in the April 9, 1987 edition of the *Wall Street Journal*. This identified Chase and Phibro Energy as two intermediaries getting involved in new-fangled hedging instruments linked to commodity prices. Journalist Ann Monroe wrote: "A handful of banks and investment banks are betting that if corporations liked interest rate swaps, they'll love oil price swaps." The article explained that the idea was to give producers, refiners, marketers and consumers of oil products a longer-term and more customised hedge than they could achieve in the futures market. Rather than using an interest rate benchmark to determine the exchange of cash-flows, payments on an oil price swap would be determined by the average spot market price of oil.

Bankers Trust began playing with ideas about energy derivatives in late 1986, and from that date received occasional queries from interested customers. By late 1987, Allen Levinson, then a Bankers Trust managing director (now a

vice-president at Goldman Sachs in New York) had proposed a formal business plan to Bankers Trust president Eugene Shanks. The thrust of this proposal was to make energy and other commodity derivatives an official line of products at the bank. Over the next decade, Bankers Trust would become one of the most important providers of energy-based derivative instruments.

However, unlike Chase, Bankers Trust would emphasise OTC option-based hedging instruments and would later become the first bank to successfully apply average rate option pricing methodologies.[7] According to Mark Standish, formerly a vice-president in interest rate derivatives at Bankers Trust and currently managing director–equity derivatives at Kidder, Peabody & Co in New York, Bankers Trust started to see interest from end-users in options at about the same time that Chase began to market swaps. "During the latter half of 1987, I started spending my time looking at the potential for commodity derivatives," explains Standish. "We had a couple of enormous trades come in. One European customer was interested in buying put options on Brent [crude oil] to the tune of 250 million barrels over a period of five years. It was an enormous trade, just totally outrageous. And who had a clue at that time what the price of five-year Brent was?"

As a result of this query, Standish flew to Tokyo in search of an eligible counterparty. In his mind, "as massive consumers of oil, the Japanese were the only ones who would sell put options of that type." While the transaction proved too large for anyone to handle at the time, it was during his trip to Tokyo that Standish came upon David Spaughton (formerly with Bankers Trust International and now a managing director of new product development with Credit Suisse Financial Products in London). Together, the men were to create the first commercially used option-pricing methodology to be based on the average price of crude oil over time.

Spaughton had already started using this exotic option technology in some long-term currency warrant issues that Bankers Trust had devised for Svensk Exportkredit (SEK); in these warrants the stipulated settlement price was an average exchange rate, not one discrete price, at maturity. However, as Standish points out, "There was really no compelling reason to have an average price option model until commodity derivatives came along. Whereas in financial markets you have explicit risk on a particular day or at the end of the year, a standard physical contract in crude is typically based on an average price over the month." As for the name, "We were in Tokyo at the time we developed this pricing methodology, so we called it the 'Asian option'. It's as simple as that."

This option-pricing innovation made it possible for dealers to cope with the historical volatility of the crude oil market, which is far greater than that found in the interest rate or currency markets (Fig. 1). Without the breakthrough, the price of offering option-based hedges to end-users, and managing the associated risks, might have slowed down the development of OTC commodity options.

Bankers Trust first applied the idea in March 1989, to 18-month WTI oil-linked average price warrants and to gold-indexed notes with embedded four-year gold options.[8] The warrants were launched in two series: the first issue cost $2.58 and gave the holder the right to buy oil at $17 a barrel, 18 months ahead. This issue was aimed largely at corporate treasurers who wanted to manage oil price exposures, and at bond portfolio managers interested in an inflation hedge. The second issue was an "up and in" warrant: if the closing price of the WTI contract reached $21.50 at least once over the next two months, the warrants automatically became fungible with the first issue. This second issue was aimed at speculators and investors looking to gain more leveraged exposure to the energy markets.

These deals were early predecessors of the rash of commodity-linked warrants and structured notes that appeared in 1994, as the commodity markets again seemed to offer a good inflationary hedge, and many dealers followed in Goldman Sachs' footsteps to launch proprietary commodity-based indices.

The regulatory rollercoaster

When Chase began to develop energy swaps, the bank was keenly aware that it was wading into uncharted legal and regulatory waters. As a first step, Byker made use of his legal training to begin to convert an interest rate swap document into a user-friendly oil swap document. With the help of Schuyler Henderson, formerly with Sidley & Austin and now a partner with Baker & MacKenzie in London, Chase polished a final draft of a legal document that would be used by its original four-man commodity index and swap financing team for its initial groundbreaking deals.

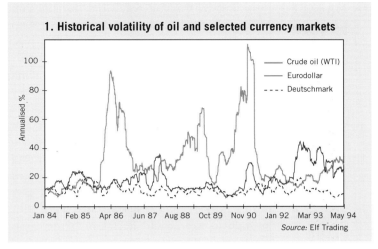

1. Historical volatility of oil and selected currency markets

Source: Elf Trading

The concept of commodity derivatives received a major boost on July 20, 1987, when Chase's attorney, Margery Waxman at Sidley & Austin, received a "no-action" letter from the Office of the Comptroller of the Currency – the regulator of US commercial banks (Fig. 2). The letter stated that Chase's commodity price index swaps represented both a traditional banking function and "a modern concept of banking as funds intermediation". Henderson notes that since Chase was operating as a credit intermediary and not involving itself in commodity mar-

2. First page of the "no-action" letter sent by the Office of the Comptroller of the Currency, which seemed to give Chase Manhattan the regulatory "green light" for its commodity swaps

kets directly, banking regulators saw only one major difference between commodity swaps and interest rate swaps: a commodity price index was being used as a pricing reference.

"That was truly an amazing letter," admits Byker. "Up until that point there had never been one shred of paper in which a federal government entity had explicitly approved the legality of any kind of swaps. So even our interest rate and currency swap people were ecstatic when we got it. We had already made some pretty good money and were basically all alone in this market. After that letter, we were about as high as you could get from being at the threshold of a new industry."

That emotional high did not last long. On August 1, 1987, not long after printing up a glossy blue brochure to promote its expertise in energy derivative instruments, Chase received a subpoena from the Commodity Futures Trading Commission (CFTC) and was threatened with enforcement actions – including possible criminal charges. Ironically, the glossy brochure became the basis for the CFTC's queries. "If you look at their original questions to us," says Byker, "it's as if the CFTC staff went through the brochure line by line to form its questions." Implicit in this regulatory action was the accusation that Chase was marketing and trading off-exchange futures contracts – an activity outlawed by the Commodity Exchange Act of 1974. According to the CFTC, this act of law specifically required that all futures contracts be traded on a designated exchange by a member of that contract market, and that all commodity-linked forward contracts be settled with physical delivery.

The critical debate was about to begin. In the view of the CFTC, oil price swaps posed a jurisdictional challenge to the CFTC because they possessed characteristics of both futures contracts and forward contracts. Prodding the CFTC to take this view were the US futures exchanges – notably the two Chicago exchanges. The exchanges had watched the interest rate swap market grow to $313 billion in notional principal contracts outstanding by the end of 1986, and were unconvinced at that time by the argument that a major OTC energy market would complement, rather than compete with, their own activities. They therefore dropped a few sharp tacks on the commodity swap market's road to Washington – it was even suggested to the CFTC that the familiar Chase corporate logo resembled a futures trading pit.

Chase was not alone in running into this regulatory quicksand. The legality of a gold-linked certificate of deposit (CD) offered by Wells Fargo Bank in July had been challenged by the CFTC on November 17, 1987, in the Central District Court of California. Wells Fargo subsequently closed down its offering and returned money to investors to appease the CFTC (which, in its legal suit, likened the offering to commodity options), but the legally conservative Chase seemed willing to take up the fight. "Chase did not go into this market blind," explains Henderson. "They were very aware of the legal issues involved and comfortable that their activities in this market were defensible."

While the CFTC proceeded in its attempt to pigeonhole commodity swaps as "off-exchange futures", Chase took its commodity swap business offshore and continued its legal battle to conduct such activities in the United States. On December 11, 1987, the CFTC issued an advance notice of proposed rulemaking as prepared by the CFTC's Off-Exchange Task Force. The notice, entitled "Regulation of Hybrid and Related Instruments", established the Commission's hard-line position on the regulation of hybrid instruments, including oil-index price swaps.

Lauren S. Klett summarised the CFTC's position in the *Dickinson Law Review* in Winter 1989, in an essay she wrote about oil price swaps:[9]

> Specifically, the Commission takes the position that, in all likelihood, the swaps are illegal. The CFTC, however proposes a blanket no-action position with respect to transactions solely involving commercial participants, such that oil producers and consumers are permitted to participate in the transactions. The CFTC's proposal, however, prohibits intermediaries, such as Chase Manhattan Bank, from participating in the swaps. In proposing to prohibit swap transactions involving intermediaries, the CFTC states that these types of transactions "substantially depart from the context in which the forward contract exclusion has historically operated".

The battle was hardly over, however. That advance notice for public comment resulted in 61 responses to the CFTC's rulemaking proposal, with the overwhelming majority opposing them.[10] The only support for the proposed rule came from exchanges such as the Chicago Board of Trade, Chicago Mercantile Exchange, Coffee, Sugar & Cocoa Exchange, Commodity Exchange and the New York Mercantile Exchange. Quite legitimately, many of the exchanges also questioned the CFTC's authority even to make a legal ruling on this complex issue.

On July 17, 1989, under the helm of CFTC chairwoman Wendy Gramm, the CFTC released Safe Harbor provisions for commodity swaps and hybrid instruments. "Wendy Gramm and her staff finally made the rational decision," explains Byker. "An overly literal interpretation of the Commodity Exchange Act would have brought down not only our business but the whole interest rate swap market, which by that time had hundreds of billions of dollars in notional contracts outstanding."

Ironically, soon after it exempted swaps and hybrid instruments, the CFTC's legal authority to interpret and enforce the Commodity Exchange Act in this way was itself questioned. Those concerns were heightened when, in 1990, another OTC market – Brent Oil forward contracts – suffered a major disruption as a result of a federal district court holding that those contracts were unenforceable futures.[11] The CFTC promptly issued yet another regulatory interpretation seeking to give legal sanction to such contracts. However, many US participants in the Brent Oil market complained that foreign firms remained reluctant to deal with them.

Only in 1992 was the legality of the CFTC's decisions made official, when Congress passed the Futures Trading Practices Act. "It's fascinating to look back on those early days," says Byker, "I just negotiated another swap contract with Enron recently and, to be honest, the substance of that original commodity swap document hasn't changed all that much. Sure there's a lot more 'boilerplate' in the ones we use now, but the substance is exactly what we came up with at Chase in 1986." (Chapter 14 of this book follows the story of the regulation and documentation of the industry up to the autumn of 1994.)

One thing that has changed is the number of participants in the market. At last count, over 50 swap and derivative dealers around the globe were offering a wide variety of over-the-counter instruments to manage energy price risk in oil, refined products and natural gas. While 25.5 billion barrels of oil (worth $382.5 billion) were consumed in 1993,[12] energy derivatives repre-

senting over 3 billion barrels of crude oil (10,000 deals) were outstanding by the end of 1993. According to OTC dealer estimates, 70% of this volume was crude oil derivatives, 20% refined products and 10% natural gas. Within these categories, 75% were swaps, 20% options, and 5% were structured transactions (such as prepaid swaps or volumetric production payments). In the case of the exchanges, volume for energy contracts in 1993 amounted to over 70 million contracts – an increase of 70% in the four years since 1989, just before the Gulf War.

Meeting of the markets

Since those early days, energy swap dealers and futures exchanges have come to regard their respective markets as mutually beneficial. The first evidence of this came when Chase and others began pushing their commodity swap business offshore when oil was fluctuating consistently at around $20 per barrel in 1987–88. At this price, the bank was not always able to match up producers with consumers "back-to-back" because of the different views in the market about the ideal price levels at which to transact. Unfortunately, there were not as many consumers of oil looking to manage price risk as there were producers and refiners.

By that time, however, some derivative participants had started to use the futures markets and physical markets to intermediate energy risk in ways that banks, legally, could not. Phibro Energy, for example, had started to use the energy futures market to offset the risk of one leg of a swap while waiting for a price level in which an opposing counterparty would be willing to take the other side. In this way, swaps could be "warehoused" for short periods. Phibro would do so by going "long" a strip of energy futures to offset the risk of an unmatched swap position, and closing out the "long" position once a natural counterparty had taken the other side. Being allowed to take physical delivery of oil – and to do this flexibly at different delivery points through the exchange of futures for physicals (EFPs)[13] – gave the major oil and natural gas companies an early competitive advantage. (The Federal Reserve only started to allow selected US commercial banks, such as Bankers Trust and JP Morgan, this facility from around 1992.)

Indeed, between 1987 and 1991, a "second wave" of cutting-edge energy derivative teams entered the market in Europe as the CFTC controversy drove business outside the United

States. It included the likes of Elf Aquitaine, British Petroleum, Phibro Energy and later J Aron, Morgan Stanley and Shell International Trading Company (Sitco). Unlike counterparties such as Chase, these oil companies and so-called "Wall Street refiners" represented a class of counterparties that was willing to run unmatched positions on their books, or assume calculated levels of basis risk, on behalf of their derivative customers. Elf and Phibro, in particular, aggressively marketed to sectors such as shipping companies and airlines. "Very few firms were willing to take on oil yield curve risk," explains Scott Marinchek, director of global commodity derivatives for Merrill Lynch in London and a one-time member of Phibro Energy's team in London. "The market liquidity was limited because the banks' propensity for risk was limited. The banks were some of our biggest customers."

Marinchek, for example, remembers selling Chase six-month $50 call options on WTI crude oil when the market price shot up to $43 per barrel during the Gulf War. "The bid/offer spreads at that time could sometimes be exorbitant," he says. "I recall volatilities at that time of 210–215%. Only a few days later, volatilities dropped 100% and the oil price was down $10–15. But we were happy to assume risks when it fitted our outlook on market fundamentals."

Another key development in the market during this critical period was the arrival of inter-bank brokers. These companies were able to facilitate two-way prices among the wholesale participants in the energy derivative markets and their customers. In particular, Intercapital Brokers and Tradition Financial Services built a handsome business while creating greater price transparency and liquidity for all involved. "A two-way market really only started to develop in 1990," says Paul Newman, managing director of commodity swaps for Intercapital in London. "The first deals were brokered in August 1990, and what was a field for a privileged few suddenly became more of a public forum."

The importance of energy futures exchanges to the OTC market cannot be underestimated – in the early days or at present. Futures contracts such as No. 2 Heating Oil, to cite just one example, can be used as a "proxy" hedge against swap contracts that dealers offer in refined product markets such as jet fuel. But the differential between the price of the product that has to be risk managed, and its proxy on the exchanges, is never absolutely predictable –

indeed, one of the main reasons the OTC market exists is the desire on the part of end-users to isolate themselves from this basis risk.

Sometimes even the banks and oil majors themselves get bitten by basis risk. For a three-month period in December 1988, and during the Gulf Crisis, a sharp spike in the price for jet fuel was not matched in the No. 2 heating oil market. This meant that energy risk managers who had relied on close-fitting "proxy" hedges in the futures markets, or who ran mismatched books that relied on their trading skills in the physical markets, lost millions.

In general, however, highly liquid contracts of this sort on the exchanges have allowed swap dealers to warehouse positions, manage portfolio imbalances, and to assume and manage basis risk. Partly because of the demand from the OTC sector, Nymex has been able to push the expiration dates for the contracts that it offers as far as 36 months into the future in the cases of crude and natural gas, and out as far as 18 months in the case of refined product futures contracts. The International Petroleum Exchange (IPE) and the Singapore International Monetary Exchange (Simex) have become the other key hubs of managing energy price risk for dealers and end-users, as described in Chapter 13.

Barry Schaps, business manager of risk management at Shell Oil Co in Houston, explains why an EFP (the exchange of a futures position for a physical position in the underlying cash market, or vice versa) is so important to participants in OTC energy derivatives:[14]

Suppose a bank is writing a swap for an independent crude oil producer. The producer promises to deliver to a bank a physical volume of oil, so many barrels per month for so many months. In exchange, he may get an immediate inflow of cash. In essence, the independent is selling his product forward at a fixed price and is getting paid for it today.

What does the bank do with the stream of crude? More than likely, the bank will turn around and try to entirely lay off the risk in the futures market. It may wish to place the physical oil with a refiner in exchange for a futures contract. Essentially, it will do an EFP on the opposite side of the swap. It will offer to a refiner a one-year physical supply of 100,000, 200,000 or 300,000 barrels per

月 in exchange for an equal volume of
futures contracts at a price to be determined today. The banker just unwinds an
entire year's strip of EFPs at that one time.
The refiner, who needs the wet barrels,
has the flexibility of locking in his supply
without committing a price. It's a flexible
tool for a refiner, and helps the bank
unwind the swap position it has entered
into with the producer.

Although a futures markets in energy is taken
for granted today, launching exchange-traded
contracts was not easy. Nymex first introduced
heating oil and residual oil futures with a
Rotterdam delivery point in the early 1970s. But
trading in those contracts was patchy at best,
and died away soon after the contracts were
launched.

However, after two potato delivery failures at
Nymex in the mid-1970s, the CFTC refused to
approve any new contract submissions from the
exchange. Nymex was forced to develop products from a list of contract markets that had
already been approved by the CFTC, including
apples, silver coins, nickel, currencies and oil
(from the Rotterdam days). Joel Faber, president
of Faber's Futures Inc, has remarked of Nymex's
entrance into the energy markets: "The revival
of the Nymex energy contracts wasn't obvious,
and it wasn't some brilliant brainstorm, it was a
matter of circumstance. Because of the potato
problems, the exchange was in danger of losing
its franchise. The days of potato trading were
numbered, platinum was essentially the only
viable commodity traded."[15]

Despite these haphazard beginnings, the
alchemy of launching a new heating oil contract
on November 14, 1978 proved fortuitous. It
would later give Nymex its identity as a leader
in energy-related futures and options, and pave
the way for other successful contract launches
in leaded gasoline (1981), unleaded gasoline
(1984), West Texas Intermediate crude oil
(1983), propane (1987) and natural gas (1990).

To create the successful heating oil futures
contracts for the energy industry (and ultimately
a successful complex of energy futures and
options), Nymex broke ranks with futures
industry convention and the preferences of its
local members. The contract was launched with
a $4.20 minimum tick per contract at a time
when virtually no-one in the futures industry
used a minimum tick move of less than $5. This
mechanism, which equated one tick to 1/100th

of a cent per gallon, would later turn out to be
a key factor when overcoming challenges from
competing contracts launched by the Chicago
Board of Trade (CBOT) and Chicago Mercantile
Exchange (CME).

Steven Errera, one of the creators of the heating oil contract at Nymex and a 25-year veteran
in energy futures, explains:[16]

> In 1978, I rewrote the contract and
> changed it to a 42,000-gallon contract from
> 30,000 gallons because 42,000 gallons was
> equal to 1,000 barrels, and I wanted the
> ability to talk about "barrels" in heavy oils
> and "gallons" in gasoline and heating oil,
> which is how they are sold in the physical
> market.
>
> When I sat down to work out the mini-
> mum price fluctuation, I bumped into a
> particular problem. A minimum fluctuation
> of $0.0001, which reflected the way the oil
> industry calculated its pricing for refined
> products, meant the minimum tick would
> be $4.20 per contract... Many of the locals
> [on the exchange] wanted a $5 minimum
> tick [which would] cover their commis-
> sions. They didn't like $4.20, because they
> might have had to trade through two ticks.
>
> We didn't listen to the locals. Today,
> we have a 1,000-barrel (42,000-gallon)
> contract in crude oil and we have a
> 42,000-gallon (1,000-barrel) contract in
> heating oil, gasoline and propane. It
> worked out to connect the markets better
> and obviously assisted in the development
> of crack spreads.

Errera notes that, a few years later, the Chicago
Board of Trade wrote a crude oil contract with a
tick of $0.00025, giving a minimum fluctuation
of $10.50 per contract; the contract failed
because the oil industry did not trade in halves
(five decimals) and thus could not relate to it.

Nymex would ultimately be rewarded hand-
somely for carefully thinking through the logic
of its contract specifications. Heating oil futures
volume began to pick up in October 1979. By
that time, prices were strong and frequently
moved "limit up" – the maximum that contract
prices are allowed to move over one day of
trading, as specified by the CFTC – after a period in the United States in which energy consumption had actually declined for a number of
years after the 1973 oil embargo. As a result,
many companies started to buy as many barrels

as possible on both the spot and futures market to assure themselves of adequate supply, while traders sold futures as part of their arbitrage strategy.

By November 14, 1980, the second anniversary of the contract, open interest was more than 10,000, while average daily volume often exceeded 3,000 contracts. During the Iran-Iraq war, which broke out in September 1980, the heating oil contract became a refuge of risk transfer for oil price risk managers and speculators. From that point, trading volume and liquidity rapidly grew, reaching a trading volume of 8,625,061 contracts and 185,425 open interest by the end of 1993.

By the time Nymex launched the light sweet crude oil futures contract on March 30, 1983, the exchange was becoming a hub of trading and risk transfer for the oil industry. "The industry's successful transfer of risk from the cash crude oil market onto the floor of the exchange through heating oil futures made it easier for the oil industry to accept crude futures," explained former Nymex chairman Lou Guttman, on the 10th anniversary of the crude oil contract.

By the mid-1980s, market conditions were ripe for both OTC and exchange-traded markets to grow synergistically. One reason for this was the dramatic price collapse of crude oil from $31.75 per barrel in November 1985 to $9.75 on April 1, 1986, which spurred on trading in all of the exchange energy contracts. Heating oil volume for that year finished 48.3% ahead of the previous year, with a total volume of 3,275,044 contracts, an average of 13,100 per day. Crude oil futures, in contrast, traded 8,313,529 contracts that year, 2472.6% more than they did in their first year of trading in 1983.

At the same time, the banks involved in OTC energy derivatives were encroaching on the turf of major oil companies and refiners. Products such as energy price swaps meant that purchasing decisions made by airlines, mass transit authorities, chemical companies, shipping and trucking companies, refiners and marketers, and other industrial companies could be decoupled from risk-management decisions.

This put pressure on major oil companies – first in Europe, and later in the United States and Canada – to offer many of the same risk management services that were being offered by major commercial and investment banks. "That definitely was important," says Standish. "BP started getting more aggressive. Shell did.

The French started coming in. It was a matter of necessity. And then brokers in London such as Intercapital started making pricing in short-dated product derivatives such as jet fuel very plain vanilla. That was a milestone in the European market – when you could start to see one-, two-, three-month swaps in products like jet quoted on the screen."

It is now estimated that energy swap dealers account for anywhere from 25–60% of the open interest in energy futures and options contracts traded at Nymex, IPE and Simex. Likewise, oil and natural gas producers such as British Petroleum, Chevron, Enron, Mobil, Texaco and Shell Oil now play an essential role in the OTC energy derivative markets – and, as a result, 23 major oil producers are presently listed as Nymex members.

Enron, in fact, provides an excellent example of how intertwined the exchange-traded and OTC energy derivative markets have become with the underlying physical business activities of many energy firms. As the largest US integrated natural gas company, Enron embarked on a strategy of creating a "gas bank" in March 1989, shortly before the Nymex natural gas contract began to be traded on April 3, 1990. Enron's idea had been to intermediate between buyers and sellers of gas, earning a spread in the same way that a traditional bank earns a spread when intermediating. In this instance, however, the spread earned by standing in the middle of producers and consumers would be a function of natural gas prices, not interest rates.

The benefits of decoupling physical gas delivery from pricing issues through a swap structure – even though it was not called this at the time – became obvious in 1989 when Enron was attempting to negotiate a fixed-price gas deal with a Louisiana-based aluminium producer. The producer was not interested in a long-term fixed-price deal because the cost of physically transporting gas made the deal economically inefficient. To solve the problem, Enron entered into a "financial" contract in which the aluminium producer agreed to pay Enron fixed sums whilst Enron paid the producer's floating prices. With hindsight, this deal can be seen as one of the market's first natural gas swaps.

As a result of these sorts of derivative activities, Enron eventually complemented its "gas bank" with a risk management services group designed to manage the credit and price risk exposures created by the array of financial settlement contracts that Enron was building up with natural gas producers and consumers. Enron's commodity risk management team now comprises more than 100 people.

The key to running a natural gas book, which potentially represents large credit and market risk exposures, is to match it off. To do this for fixed-price contracts with local distribution companies, which are shorter in term, Enron makes use of the exchange-traded futures and options markets out to 18 months. For fixed-price contracts of three to five years, which are of interest to industrial users and cogeneration plants, Enron is obliged to find offsetting transactions in the OTC market.

Meanwhile, certain business deals such as the volumetric production payments (VPPs) discussed below create long-term exposures for Enron that also have to be managed. The counterparties to these longer-term commitments are usually other major oil and gas companies, or the energy derivative groups at major financial institutions.

It is this interconnection between the markets when managing a broad spectrum of risks that causes many dealers to suggest that the success of the exchange market is becoming reliant upon the success of the OTC market. As recent proof, OTC principals have estimated that they account for as much as 25% of overall open interest in natural gas futures; during peak periods, such as in 1992 when hurricanes hit the US Gulf Coast, they may account for as much as 60% of open interest.

Intermarket activities between the exchange and OTC markets continue to grow. As one example of this, Canadian utilities typically bought gas on a fixed-price basis before 1993. But, in October 1993, Canadian utilities like Centra Ontario, Consumers Gas, Union Gas and Centra Manitoba all negotiated procurement contracts priced at a differential to Nymex-based natural gas futures prices. In addition, utilities in the United States such as San Diego Gas & Electric, Southern California Gas Company and Pacific Gas & Electric, and New Jersey Natural Gas Company have all introduced gas cost procurement incentive programmes that aim to share lower costs with customers and shareholders.

Many dealers believe that contracts of this sort and incentive-based procurement programmes linked to Nymex natural gas prices will encourage producers and consumers in Canada and the United States to make use of futures, options and swaps to manage their exposure to volatile natural gas prices. They believe it will lead to the further integration of the underlying physical and energy derivative markets.

Back to the future

In terms of volume, the energy risk management market is likely to remain dominated by standard products of one- to two-years' duration, as the core business is driven by corporate budgetting and opportunistic investment. However, the range of products that the market feels familiar with is continually expanding. An interesting development at the end of 1994 was Nymex's launch of crack spread option contracts on heating oil and unleaded gasoline – an apparently successful attempt to offer in a standardised form a type of instrument that has become familiar in the OTC market (see Panel 5, Chapter 9).

Although "plain vanilla" instruments will continue to dominate in terms of volume, new instruments more carefully tailored to the needs of end-users are likely to be an important growth sector. Chapter 5 demonstrates how, even within the swaps market, an increasingly wide range of instruments is now in common use, while Chapters 6 and 7 chart the huge advances in modern option technology. As the authors of those chapters are aware, however, end-users are unlikely to be tempted by "black boxes" – they will want to know the risks that exotic instruments entail and to be able to value them accurately.

In the past, some end-users have suspected that the more exotic instruments are simply a way for intermediaries to keep margins high – but Chapter 8 makes clear that, as part of a carefully planned strategy, these more sophisticated instruments can act to reduce the cost of hedging. Although integrated hedging is still in its infancy, it may well represent an important growth sector in the medium term.

Another important growth sector, and one which has made increasing use of innovative structures, is project financing. The most important instrument type here is perhaps the prepaid swap, whereby the fixed payments of a classic swap are brought forward and paid upfront. In effect, this sort of swap creates a synthetic financing which is amortised as the proceeds from energy production are realised.

Many variations of this prepaid swap theme have been applied in the market already. As described in Chapter 10, in the natural gas risk management market this type of structure is often called a volumetric production payment (VPP). In a VPP deal, actual physical gas or oil production is committed as payment to a counterparty. On the other side of the deal, a counterparty such as Enron calculates the net present value of the future commodity flows to be realised from the reserves financed under the VPP contract. The buyer of the gas secures the contract by securing its rights to the physical gas, or by obtaining a financial guarantee such as a letter of credit, to avoid potential complications resulting from a counterparty that goes into default. In the event of bankruptcy, a VPP entitles a counterparty to receive a predetermined volume of produced gas over a certain time period, and provides it with a direct legal claim on the reserves.

In what is believed to have been the first VPP, Enron Gas Services, recently renamed Enron Capital & Trade Resources, paid Forest Oil Corporation, a gas producer struggling to avert bankruptcy, $44.8 million upfront to acquire approximately 32 billion cubic feet of future gas production over a period of five years. This represented roughly half of Forest Oil's gas reserves. The potential of this market is immense – since its first deal, it is estimated that Enron has transacted over $1 billion in VPPs.

Other versions of the VPP structure have been linked to oil production. In 1993, *Institutional Investor* named a similar derivatives-linked financing as one of its "deals of the year". The prepaid financing structure involved Shell Oil Company, which was hoping to finance the development of a deep-water oil field in the Gulf of Mexico. To lock in favourable long-term economics for Shell, while leaving it potential equity upside if the price of oil rose, Bankers Trust teamed up with Shell to structure a financing package that included a prepaid forward contract, oil and interest swaps, and a syndicated loan. The whole deal gave Shell Offshore Inc, a wholly-owned subsidiary of Shell Oil, a total of $700 million to develop the field. It also locked in the project's economics for a period of seven years – regardless of oil price and interest rate volatility. As Bankers Trust reported: "The $700 million credit was made available to CEO Inc, a special purpose corporation designed by Bankers Trust and Shell, to sell oil forward on an off-balance sheet basis while entering into a series of derivative transactions to lock in an oil price and interest rates. The derivatives strategy allowed Shell to

shed the financial risks that are beyond its control while maintaining exposure to the operating risks within its control."[17]

One striking feature of the market is the degree of customisation that is now available. The variable face value (VFV) option now offered by certain derivatives providers, such as Bankers Trust, may suit an oil producer which has to cope with great uncertainty about the value of the "home" currency of the company. When oil prices move through an agreed strike level, the VFV option allows the producer to reduce the level of cover in line with drops in the level of the spot exchange rate. In general, the greater the move in the spot rate over the life of a VFV option, the greater the advantage of using the VFV option compared to normal options.

This book focuses on energy risk management, but many uses are now being found for energy derivative technology that do not involve altering risk profiles. Prepaid commodity swaps, for example, are now starting to be used to manage liability and tax positions – a development driven by the fact that such a swap may not be eligible for withholding tax and may not be recorded on the balance sheet as debt.

The investor side of the market also could prove to be a growth area for energy derivative providers. In January 1994, for example, Pacific Mutual Life Insurance, with $14 billion in fixed-income assets, entered into an oil swap with Merrill Lynch to take advantage of the fact that the oil market was in contango (that is, the forward curve was sloping upwards). Since the market typically trades in backwardation (where future prices are lower than spot prices, and the curve slopes downwards), Pacific Mutual entered into a forward oil swap with a "spread lock" that would allow it to profit from any shift out of contango into backwardation.[18] According to Peter Lee, vice-president and fixed-income portfolio manager at Pacific Mutual, the swap was unwound early at a slight profit.

The Pacific Mutual deal was a carefully customised play on the energy markets. But during 1994 many dealers active with asset managers started to promote structured note investments and derivative structures with embedded energy option and swap characteristics. These "structured notes" are traditional fixed-income instruments that are indexed to the performance of oil or gas prices. They typically offer investors a guaranteed minimum rate of return, along with the potential for enhanced yields. The full principal can be guaranteed so that, regardless of energy price moves, the investor will not lose any of its principal investment. Or for more aggressive investors, some portion of principal, such as 80%, can be guaranteed. The structured note pays the investor a fixed coupon, plus an additional payout linked to the value of energy prices above some specific energy price level.

In 1994, a lot of the enthusiasm for structured notes of this kind arose out of short-term interest in the commodity markets. It has yet to be seen whether the longer-term attractions of investor-oriented energy-linked derivatives (inflation hedging, diversification, repeated strategic investment in the "commodity cycle") allow the market to mature.

The technology for pricing and trading hybrids of this type is quite similar to the technology needed to produce hybrid hedges for energy producers or users with multiple exposures – a subject that is described in detail in Chapter 8. Both the structured note market and the nascent market in integrated hedging instruments involving energy price exposures share a common problem – developing a market of users that feel confident in their ability to value and manage the complex instruments that they are being offered. In fact, many corporate hedgers espouse a preference to unbundle their interest rate, foreign exchange and commodity price risks. And most end-users – be they corporates or investors – are now aware of the specific recommendations made by the Group of Thirty concerning the overall management of derivative activities. They know that they may be criticised if they use instruments that they cannot price or monitor directly themselves.

The problem is not one of simply understanding the technical complexities of pricing an exotic swap or option whose payoff profile is simultaneously indexed to two variables such as interest rates and oil prices. As Chapters 4 and 8 make clear, if an investor is to make use of a structured note that involves some complex derivative play on energy prices, or a hedger is to make use of an integrated hedge product, a significant amount of time must be spent on understanding the correlation of risks between market variables, and how that correlation may change over time. The sophistication of these instruments makes the educational efforts of dealers, and increased resources devoted to their prudent use on the part of end-users, absolutely critical.

One difficulty in looking to the future of the energy risk management market is that there are few reliable indicators even of the present size of the market, still less statistical evidence of sector growth. However, it seems probable that there was more than $50 billion–75 billion worth of OTC derivative contracts outstanding at the end of 1993, and traders point to the fact that a 100,000–200,000 barrel per month crude oil swap can be priced out to two or three years (some would say even five to 10 years). Anecdotal evidence suggests that sufficient liquidity is available in both the OTC and exchange-traded markets for even the largest of corporate energy participants to hedge a significant portion of its price exposure.

While the energy risk management market is certainly only a fraction of the size of the OTC interest rate and currency derivative market – now estimated to represent $14.5 trillion in notional contracts outstanding – dealers are keen to point out that many potential hedgers remain on the sidelines. These include entities such as American Airlines, which consumes more energy (jet fuel) than all but five of the world's industrialised economies; oil producing or consuming state governments and municipalities; and even the odd multinational oil company. The potential of the emerging markets is still also largely untapped, for reasons confronted in Chapter 12. However, if the World Bank succeeds in its programme of raising the awareness of developing countries to their exposure to energy prices, and the costs and benefits of using risk management instruments, the participation of these countries could add hugely to the size and liquidity of the market.

One important development for the future is that some quite conservative potential counterparties have started to weigh the risk of getting involved in energy derivatives against the risk of not using these instruments. The state of Alaska, for example, which derives 85% of its tax revenue basis from oil production, introduced a resolution in April 1994 to establish an oil hedging task force – the first step toward a full risk management programme. It is interesting that for many of these larger potential users, their perception of the ability of the market to handle their risk management needs is a critical factor. An aide to the Alaska State Senator (and co-chairman of Alaska's Finance Committee), Steve Frank, noted that the Senator had "been considering a hedging programme since 1988, but frequently questioned whether the market could stand it. Now the market has grown and matured."[19]

Another source of growth for energy risk management is the development of wholly new sectors. Until recently, few commentators would have mentioned the electricity industry in the United States, or the natural gas industry in the United Kingdom, in connection with price risk management. The nature of risk management in both these sectors is only just starting to take shape, as described in Chapters 10 and 11 – but is evolving fast.

As noted earlier in this introduction, one major brake on the growth of the market in its early years was the uncertain legal and regulatory environment. Although the risk management and derivative industry hit the headlines throughout 1994, and attracted the attention of regulators, the final chapter of this book reveals that in some ways the legal environment has become less problematic, at least in the United States. As detailed in a separate panel in that chapter, the industry may even be moving toward a more standardised means of documentation.

So far, this introduction has talked about market growth in terms of technical innovation, regulatory evolution and the increasing sophistication of market participants. But no introduction to the history of energy price risk management should conclude without mentioning the role of "event risk". In the short history of the industry, energy-related calamaties and the price volatility they bring have arguably proven as important in market growth and change as any of the factors discussed above. The Gulf War, for example, played a key role in increasing oil and refining product derivative volumes, while the havoc wreaked by Hurricane Andrew along the US Gulf Coast helped fuel the dramatic growth of the natural gas derivative market in 1993. In a risk management industry, the importance of these events largely speaks for itself. As Julian Barrowcliffe, director in commodity derivatives at Merrill Lynch, points out, "There's only one predictable aspect of such event-induced chaos. The more disruptive it is, the more fertile its effect on the energy risk management market overall."

1 *This introduction could not have been written without the advice and views of numerous experienced risk management practitioners. In particular I would like to thank Gaylen Byker, Nachamah Jacobovits, Ron Liesching, Jennifer Modesett, Kate Smith, Jon Wheeler and Mildred Ford for directing me to many sources of information that I could not have found without their help. I would also like to thank the larger cast of energy derivative participants – both those named in the introduction and those who are not – who freely gave their time in contributing to this whirlwind history. Paul Newman of Intercapital Commodity Swaps Ltd was kind enough to read, and offer useful comments on, the finished draft.*

2 *As discussed below, later in the market's development it became clear that hedging exposure to jet fuel prices by fixing the price of crude oil left hedgers badly exposed if the price of jet fuel rose much faster and further than crude prices.*

3 *The negotiations with Cathay Pacific were conducted by Van Lessig of Chase Hong Kong, who began talking to Cathay Pacific after attending one of the Advanced Financial Risk seminars described in Note 4.*

4 *Chase's headstart in oil swaps grew out of a series of Advanced Financial Risk seminars held at the bank from 1984. These AFR seminars were designed to bring together a critical mass of ideas and people to stimulate new product development. Ironically, they were also designed as a "mind-stretcher" for corporate clients: if an oil producer considered the possibility of swapping oil cash flows for Libor flows, then more conventional interest rate caps and currency swaps might start to seem almost old-fashioned. The seminars were organised by Sykes Wilford, now with Bankers Trust in*

London. Other key figures included Bruce Smith, a some-time lecturer at the seminars, who took the first swap proposal to Chase's senior management, and Michael Hampton, author of Chapter 6 of this book, who helped to build the energy swaps concept and to start up Chase's commodity swaps business in Europe.

5 *Gaylen Byker is now with Offshore Energy Development Corporation and is a frequent end-user of natural gas price swaps to hedge that company's own gas exploration and production activities. Liesching is now with Pareto Partners in London.*

6 *Also backing up his efforts were Peter Foggin and Michael Hampton (who pushed the commodity swap concept to airlines, shipping companies and utilities), Mark Harrison (head of Chase commodities), Michael Hudson (head of Chase's project finance group), Yoram Kimberg (a new products specialist who served on Chase's risk management committee) and Bob Lichten (head of North American capital markets at Chase).*

7 *Market sources say that Howard Sosin and Drexel Burnham Lambert were also hot on the trail of average price options at this time. In an academic setting, the concept of an average price option, or Asian option, was first developed by David Emanuel, now professor of finance at the University of Texas at Dallas, and Phelim P. Boyle, now the J. Page R. Wadsworth chair in finance in the School of Accountancy at the University of Waterloo in Waterloo, Ontario. Boyle says they first had a conversation on this topic in the foyer of the Faculty Club at the University of British Columbia in Vancouver (where both of them were professors in the faculty of commerce) in the autumn of 1979. In working papers, they* subsequently generalised the average price option concept to include different types of averages as well as the arithmetic average: notably the geometric average and the harmonic average. They demonstrated how to value these options using the Monte Carlo method, and in later research, showed how to use the geometric mean as a control variate to increase the accuracy of the answer.

In a recent interview, Prof. Boyle shared this interesting anecdote about the perceived value of their discovery early on: "When we submitted our paper, the Journal of Finance rejected it, mostly on the grounds that the proposed new options did not then exist and would have limited practical interest. We put the paper in a drawer and went on to work on other topics. Our general approach was rediscovered several times in the 1980s by Ton Vorst and Angelien Kemna, as well as Peter Ritchken and many others. I had always wanted to develop a closed-form solution for the European Asian option with continuous averaging and spent several hours on this problem. I posed this problem while visiting UC Berkeley in 1989. Eric Reiner's roommate was in my class and he gave it to Eric. At the time, Eric was completing his doctorate in Chemical Engineering. I recall first meeting Eric in a coffee shop on Telegraph Avenue and discussing the problem with him. Eric was the first person to solve this problem with a closed-form solution; unfortunately, he did not publish it. The problem has also been solved by Marc Yor, the eminent French probabilist."

8 This is not to claim that Bankers Trust devised the first examples of oil-linked financial engineering. This accolade belongs to Standard Oil of Ohio (Sohio), a semi-independent subsidiary of British Petroleum, which in 1985 became the first company to develop and market oil-indexed securities. Sohio issued $300 million in oil-linked notes to raise money in the debt markets at sub-Libor rates. These notes included two tranches of embedded oil call warrants.

9 "Oil-Price Swaps: Should These Innovative Financial Instruments Be Subject to Regulation by the Commodity Futures Trading Commission or the Securities and Exchange Commission?", by Lauren S. Klett. Dickinson Law Review, Winter 1989, p. 398.

10 Including responses from the American Bankers Association, Federal Reserve System Board of Governors, the Comptroller of the Currency, the Securities and Exchange Commission, Chase, Citicorp, JP Morgan, Morgan Stanley, and oil companies such as BP America, Chevron, Exxon, Koch Industries and Mobil.

11 Transnor (Bermuda) Limited v. BP North America Petroleum, 783 F. Supp. 1472 (S.D.N.Y. 1990). This case is discussed in more detail in the final chapter of this book.

12 Figure supplied by the Petroleum Industry Research Foundation.

13 EFPs are discussed in detail in Chapter 13 of this book.

14 "10th Anniversary of Crude Oil Futures", Energy in the News, New York Mercantile Exchange, Spring 1991, p. 21.

15 "15th Anniversary Edition", Energy in the News, New York Mercantile Exchange, Fall/Winter 1993, p. 5.

16 "15th Anniversary Edition", Energy in the News, New York Mercantile Exchange, Fall/Winter 1993, p.7.

17 Bankers Trust New York Corporation Annual Report, 1993, pp. 8 and 13.

18 At the time the deal was done, crude spot levels were at $15 per barrel, and the price one year forward was $17 per barrel. Pacific Mutual's $15 million (1 million barrels of oil) forward swap compared the difference between the price of WTI two and one half years forward and the WTI price in the current month one and a half years forward. This spread was then compared to the spread in the market when the transaction was first executed. Pacific Mutual received a payment if the differential of the future spread turned out to be less than that of the preset spread when the swap started. This smaller spread represents a flattening in the oil forward curve and a move back towards a state of backwardation. Of course, if the curve became steeper, Pacific Mutual could have ended up making a swap payment. "In reality, this structure turns out to be a play on near months being cheap to the back months. It wasn't a play on the price so much as it was a play on the price relationship," notes Peter Lee, vice-president and fixed-income portfolio manager at Pacific Mutual.

The deal is also described in "Pac Mutual Enters into 1st Oil Swap, Augurs Year of the Commodity", by Janine Schultz, Derivatives Week, vol. 3, no. 3, pp. 1, 9–10.

19 "Alaskan Lawmaker Proposes State Study Use of Hedging to Cut Oil-Revenue Losses", by Laurie Lands, The Oil Daily, vol. 44, no. 81, April 28, 1994.

RISK
ANALYSIS

1

Analysing the Forward Curve

Jacques Gabillon
Banque Indosuez

One of the most important ways in which the commodity markets differ from the financial markets is that trading in the underlying physical products varies so considerably from one commodity to another. The identity and strength of market participants, the nature of the commodity itself, the mechanisms of production, the means of transportation and storage and the supply/demand equation shape each market in a very different way. Forward curves of prices and volatilities play an essential role in commodity markets, and are probably as important as the absolute level of prices. When conducting hedging operations, it is crucial that market participants understand the circumstances that determine why the market is in backwardation or contango; forward prices also comprise the most vital decision parameters when planning energy-linked projects.

In this chapter, we will look at the determinants of forward curves in the case of oil products (and especially crude oil), and examine whether futures prices succeed in forecasting the future price of oil correctly. We will study in some detail the impact of the so-called "convenience yield" and the mean reversion of oil price, and also look at the effect that the typology of hedging participants has on forward curves. Finally, we will critically analyse the persistence of structural backwardation in the oil markets and, in a separate panel, look at the insights that financial theory may provide for analyses of the forward curve.

Is the futures price of oil a forecast for the spot price?

To consider the futures price of an energy commodity as the forecast for the spot price prevailing at maturity constitutes the first and most natural approach to the term structure of prices. In this case, a market in backwardation (contango) means that the anticipated value of the spot price in the future is lower (higher) than the current one. In backwardation (contango), market participants expect the spot price to go down (up).

Figures 1 and 2 can be used to compare the evolution of crude oil and heating oil spot prices since 1983,[1] and the term structures of their futures prices at selected dates. These graphs seem to indicate that term structures anticipate in a satisfactory way the changes occurring to spot prices when large price movements are experienced. It is not surprising to discover – indeed, it is well known – that the oil markets were in a uniquely steep contango during June 1990. Market participants forecast that this configuration of low oil prices would not last more than a few months – although they could hardly have forecast the invasion of Kuwait by Iraq. In October of the same year, as

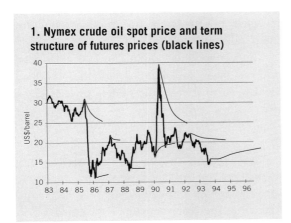

1. Nymex crude oil spot price and term structure of futures prices (black lines)

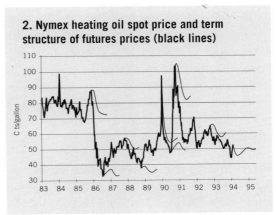

2. Nymex heating oil spot price and term structure of futures prices (black lines)

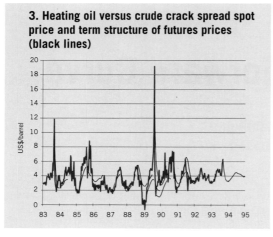

3. Heating oil versus crude crack spread spot price and term structure of futures prices (black lines)

oil prices began to approach US$40 per barrel, the expectation of lower prices in the near future was reflected in a strong backwardation.

However, one must not be misled by the apparent, if approximate, forecasting power invested in futures prices. Many historical studies have shown that the futures price of oil for a given maturity, taken at a given date, is as bad a predictor for the spot price prevailing at maturity as is the spot price of oil taken at the same initial date. In other words, if today's spot price of oil is US$15 per barrel, and the futures price for delivery in one year's time is US$17, then statistically US$15 is not a worse guess for the value of the spot price at one year from now than is US$17.

So, if the term structure is an interesting indicator of market expectations, it has little forecasting power of the absolute level of prices. However, the situation appears to be slightly different when price differentials are examined. Figure 3 charts the evolution of the spot price of the crude oil versus heating oil crack spread since 1983, and compares this with the term structure of the relevant futures prices at selected dates. The graph indicates that the term structures are reasonably successful in anticipating the changes in the crack spread spot price.

When analysing the forward curve, the futures price of oil must be understood for what it is: an equilibrium price derived from the expectations of market participants, which may be locked in by means of a hedging strategy. It should not be regarded as an accurate forecast of the spot price. While bearing this in mind, it is useful to examine the determinants of the term structure of energy commodities.

Introducing the convenience yield

Imagine for a moment that a market for the future delivery of oil did not exist. In this cir-

cumstance, how could one establish the expected value of the price of oil in the future? In the financial markets, the future value of an asset can be calculated using the current value of this asset and its cost of carry. No-arbitrage models of this kind seem to offer a direct valuation of futures prices. However, we can readily demonstrate that most of the situations experienced in the oil markets cannot be described by so simple a model. If we assume that the only source of uncertainty is the spot price denoted S, then the futures price F at the present time t for delivery at maturity time T is a function of S, t and T and is given by:

$$F(S,t,T) = Se^{(r+C_s)(T-t)}$$

where r is the riskless interest rate and C_s is the marginal cost of storage of oil. The interest rate r is constant and positive. The cost of storage C_s, supposed constant, is strictly positive. Therefore, the cost of carry, comprising the interest rate and the cost of storage $(r+C_s)$, is strictly positive. The result is that F should be higher than S, and oil markets should be permanently in contango. However, since backwardation situations commonly occur in oil markets, the cost of carry of oil is obviously not the only determinant of the term structure of futures prices.

Indeed, when oil markets are in backwardation, one may wonder why some market participants continue to hold physical inventories of oil and thus support a seemingly positive cost of carry (since they could purchase oil for future delivery at a discount to the spot price). Actually, in those circumstances, some participants benefit from holding physical oil instead of holding a contract for future delivery. This is because such action results in an extra yield for the owner of oil inventories. Known as the "convenience yield", this gain has been usefully defined by Brennan (1989) as "the flow of services which accrues to the owner of a physical inventory but not to the owner of a contract for future delivery".

The convenience yield can be introduced into our basic model as a continuous dividend yield C_y. In that case, the futures price is given by:

$$F(S,t,T) = Se^{(r+C_s-C_y)(T-t)}$$

Thus, depending on whether the convenience yield of holding inventories is higher or lower than the implicit costs of storage and financing, the term structure will either be in backwardation or contango. In the oil markets, inventory holders are mainly refiners, distribution companies and end-consumers. The convenience for these companies in holding inventories arises from the fact that they cannot afford to be short of physical oil – especially those companies in the last category.

Naturally, the size of the convenience yield is related to the level of inventories that companies are holding. Figures 4 and 5 chart the evolution of levels of crude oil and heating oil inventories[2] and compare these to the term structures of short-term futures prices.[3] These graphs clearly illustrate the inverse relationship between the level of inventories and the convenience yield. This inverse relationship has been evidenced many times, and for most commodity markets.

In fact, the level of inventories is a key determinant of the shape of term structures. Contangos are limited by storage and financing costs, since market participants can make "cash-and-carry" arbitrages. Indeed, if the futures price is much higher than the spot price, people can purchase the commodity at the spot price, store it, finance it and sell it forward at a futures price which locks in a profit for the entire operation. By this action, market participants tend to ease the contango situation by putting upward pressure on the spot price, and downward pressure on the futures price.

The possibility of this kind of action should give rise to a theoretical limit value for the difference between the futures price and the spot price for any given maturity. However, contango limit values form, in effect, a series of "steps", depending on which stocks are being used. That is, once the cheapest available means of storage is filled up with cash-and-carry arbitrages, the contango will tend to widen to take into account the value implied by the cost of the second-cheapest means of storage, and so on. In practice, the cost of the marginal storage capacity tends to be continuous, and therefore the evolution of the term structure is also continuous. (There have even been situations in which, with all inland storage facilities full up, the contango in the market became so steep that setting up cash-and-carry arbitrages by storing oil on ships began to be profitable.)

In the real world, then, the relationship between stocks and term structures is neither clear nor simple. Moreover, different kinds of stocks vary in their effect on the market, due to the identity of the holders and the degree of

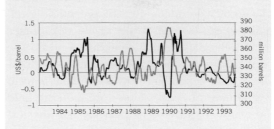

4. Crude oil 1st versus 2nd nearby time differential (black lines) and inventories

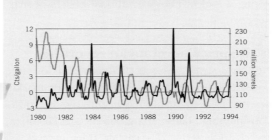

5. Heating oil 1st versus 2nd nearby time differential (black lines) and inventories

availability. Also, in commodity markets such as crude oil or refined petroleum products, where the cost of trading inventories is relatively high, it is important to take into account all the implied costs when determining the theoretical limits of contangos.

The limits to backwardation are much more difficult to ascertain. In some circumstances, market participants are ready to pay virtually any premium for prompt availability – in the oil industry, nothing is more damaging than a disruption of supply. It follows that if stocks are low, or are held mainly by end-users, then there is a great reluctance to make reverse cash-and-carry arbitrages. Even if such arbitrages are possible in theory, in effect one may consider backwardation situations as no-arbitrage situations.

Backwardation, ie high convenience yield, may be described as the preference shown by market operators for ensuring present supplies. This structural preference, which is historically a strong feature of the oil markets, arises from both the physical nature of the commodity and from its strategic and political importance. Since oil cannot be produced or transported instantaneously, and since production centres are distant from refining and consuming centres, a shortage of supply can have a dramatic effect. This means that the elasticity of demand for refined petroleum products is close to zero in the short term. Which, in turn, means that buyers put a constant upward pressure on physical prices.

This technical configuration is worsened by the strategic nature of energy. It is well known that OPEC produces 40% of the world's oil, while about 60% of world production comes from politically unstable countries or areas. The oil market is thus hardly a free market, and risk-averse spot-dependent buyers naturally tend to ensure their physical supply, and prefer to hold either inventories or to overpay for physical supplies.

While the fundamental factors of the physical markets, briefly outlined above, are the essential determinants of forward curves, it is also worth taking a look at the less rational beliefs of market participants.

Is the price of oil mean reverting?

Hedging strategies are dictated by economic considerations, but the expectations of market operators also influence company decisions considerably. These expectations are based on the operator's own forecast of price evolutions, which – apart from projected offer/demand patterns and guesses about moves by OPEC – tends to be based on historical prices. Some consumers adopt systematic hedging policies, but most of them tend to conduct hedging operations when they consider that the price of oil is low. At the same time, however, producers are reluctant to cover their exposure when the price

6. Crude oil term structure of nominal and constant (black line) futures prices

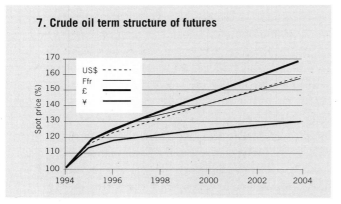

7. Crude oil term structure of futures

reaches historically low levels.

These considerations have a direct impact on the shape and the dynamics of term structures. If the marketplace considers that US$20 per barrel is the "right" price for oil – and this has been the case until recently – futures prices tend to be fairly stable at around this value, and the spot price goes up or down according to the physical situation. As long as people think that, for instance, the configuration of a depressed spot price is temporary, consumers will enter into hedging operations as soon as the forward price is lower than their expectations. The pressure that this buying puts on the forward price maintains the forward price at this relatively higher level, and the contango widens rapidly as the spot price falls. At some stage, if the physical situation is such that the low spot price begins to look as if it will last, then the short-term forward prices also start to move down, as expectations converge towards the spot price. Also, theoretically, the flow of information affecting the physical situation is much greater than the flow that acts to create the long-term price equilibrium. This results in a pattern of decreasing volatilities along the forward curve. Indeed, taking crude oil as an instance, the movements of short-term prices are large and erratic, while the prices of longer maturities tend to remain relatively stable. In the minds of most market participants, over a horizon of several years, oil is a "mean reverting" asset; that is, the spot price might be temporarily depressed or strong, but never for long enough to alter the long-term futures prices to a significant extent.

To sum up, the perception of relatively low or high prices is crucial to the analysis of forward curves. However, the dependence of this perception on historical prices must be analysed cautiously. It is well known that the price of oil, expressed in constant terms, is currently at about the same level as in 1970 – or even, in fact, as in 1870 – but, of course, this apparently constant term price has fluctuated wildly in between these dates. Figure 6 shows the term structures, as of March 1994, of both nominal and constant crude oil futures prices.[4] While, at that time, the nominal term structure was in contango, the constant term structure appeared to be in backwardation after a few years. This meant that the futures prices for oil for the next 10 years could be locked in, on average, at a price (expressed in 1994 US dollars) that was lower than the prevailing spot price. At the time, this situation may have lightened the hearts of those investing in projects that were dependent on oil as an energy source, but was rather depressing for oil producers.

However, the perception of the relative cheapness of oil varies, depending on the currency in which the price is analysed. This is because oil is a US$-denominated commodity; therefore, foreign exchange rates influence the relative position of the spot price when compared to historical or futures prices. Figure 7 shows the term structures of crude oil, again as of March 1994, expressed as a percentage of the spot price, and in different currencies. In such a situation, Japanese consumers might have looked more favourably at hedging their consumption than English consumers, while for American and French companies the situations were very similar.

To sum up: the price of oil is mean reverting, at least in the medium term. However, perceptions of the average price in the long run are liable to be influenced by the particular situation of the evaluator.

Evaluations of physical demand, supply, inventories and operator expectations constitute the key determinants of the short- to mid-term part of the forward curve of energy prices. However, in recent years there has been a massive development of energy derivatives. While exchange-based futures and options markets provide satisfactory mechanisms for the discovery of short-term prices, derivative instruments with maturities of up to 15 years are now commonly traded for the most liquid products.[5] This extension of the horizon of the oil markets gives rise to a number of interesting questions. What are the determinants of the complete forward curve of prices? Which type of operator influences which part of the curve? And how do these variables react together?

Who is doing what and why?

When examining the profile of participants in the market, it seems logical to start with the upstream operators. Since producing companies or countries hold reserves, they are exposed to a drop in prices, and are consequently natural "short" hedgers. In the case of existing oil fields, for which investments may have been amortised, producers are often eager to hedge their expenditure budget, typically at a horizon of one year. To develop new oil fields, producers may also lock in the market valuation of the reserves which they expect to recover. Besides this, producers use hedging operations to cover the short-term exposures (typically under three months) that are derived from their formula-based sale contracts and their inventories. In all cases, this causes producers to exert a downward pressure on futures prices.

While most producers use hedging for short-term risk management, probably only a very small proportion trade in cover for longer maturities. This situation results from a number of factors:

❏ poor expertise in sophisticated financial instruments;
❏ the desire of governments or shareholders to receive profits whenever the market moves up;
❏ the absence of a sufficient liquidity for large hedging operations (for instance, those necessary to cover a significant part of OPEC production).

While expertise in derivatives is growing among producers, a willingness to remain unhedged, and a general lack of liquidity, seem likely to keep most world production out of the derivatives market for some time yet. This problem is discussed in greater detail in Chapter 12.

The physical operations of refiners are numerous; they involve both crude oil and all refined petroleum products, and result in complex price exposures. By nature, refiners tend to be "long" hedgers for crude oil and "short" hedgers for refined products. As a result, refiners are "short" hedgers of their refining margins, even if structural time delays exist between the pricing of incoming crude oil and the pricing of the outflowing products. A growing number of refiners hedge their price exposure on short-term inputs, outputs or stocks and also look at the forward refining margin over a time horizon of about one year. Through their hedging operations, refiners play an increasing and important role as arbitragers between the forward curve of crude oil and the curve of refined products. They provide a transfer of financial risk between the two curves. (Indeed, just as producers push down forward crude oil prices, refiners push down forward product prices through the hedging of refining margins.) Therefore the net effect of refiners on forward curves is fairly neutral, since the absolute level of prices is not crucial to their economics. The hedging of refining margins or inter-product margins is fairly well developed, but does not extend beyond a couple of years for a significant proportion.

Traders or distribution companies also conduct hedging operations. These companies are keen to lay off their price risk, since their commercial margins are generally thin. Like refiners, the hedging operations of these intermediaries address price differential risks rather than absolute prices. Unlike refiners, however, these operators are generally structurally exposed to a single product (although for various maturities). Typically, a distribution company that purchases a physical product at a fixed price is exposed until it sells the product to its customers at a later time. As a result, these operators are holding stocks for short periods of time and are consequently "short" hedgers; their operations have an average horizon of under three months. Even so, their influence on futures prices is important, since most of these companies actively conduct hedging operations. Some companies also adopt more sophisticated long-term hedging strategies, in order to take advantage of their structural forward sales. A distribution company knows that it will benefit from contango situations because, structurally, it sells forward its flow of physical product; therefore it will try to lock in attractive time differentials for specified quantities and maturities. Overall, the net result of the hedging operations of distribution and trading companies is a downward pressure, mainly concentrated on the short-term part of the term structure.

Consumers are exposed to an upward movement of prices, and therefore are structurally "long" hedgers. Consumers tend to lead the way in expanding the time horizon of hedging operations. First, consumers analyse their true exposure to oil prices by removing the exposure which can be passed on to their customers, and by looking at what their competitors are doing. Then, customers tend to concentrate on a budget horizon ranging typically between one and two years. Apart from the consumers of refined products such as gasoline (where the set of customers is highly fragmented), most oil consumers are aware of hedging techniques and cover a significant part of their consumption. This results in a strong upward pressure on forward prices for maturities of up to several years. Like producers, in the case of new projects dependent on the price of energy, consumers may conduct long-term hedging operations to lock in the return on their investments and to secure their choice of energy.

Investors who speculate on the evolution of oil prices also influence the term structures. They can, for instance, try to take advantage of the backwardation in oil markets by holding

futures contracts and rolling them forward before expiration. Even when the spot price of oil remains constant, rolling forward a futures contract in a market experiencing backwardation may produce a profit – but the strategy also arbitrages itself, since rolling forward long positions tends to reduce backwardation.

Last but not least, arbitrageurs play an important role at the centre of the derivative markets insofar as financial risk transfer and liquidity are concerned. All the market participants mentioned hitherto have interests pointing in opposite directions. However, these people do not hedge at the same time or with the same type of instruments and futures contracts, and at any given moment the markets are not necessarily adequate or sufficiently liquid for their operations. The need for arbitrageurs, who in effect assume or warehouse maturity, differential, volatility and credit risks, is therefore obvious. The presence of arbitrageurs tends to ensure that the term structures of prices (but also of volatility and differential prices) are homogeneous and do not allow either obvious risk-free arbitrages or operations which are too obviously profitable. Arbitrageurs may also offer transactions for very long maturities (up to 15 years), as they are ready to accept the inherent risk in exchange for embedded remunerations. The influence of arbitrageurs and speculators on forward curves is complex, and this group cannot be classified as straight "long" or "short" hedgers.[6]

The net result of all these hedging and speculative operations depends upon which category of market participant is the most willing to hedge. An analysis of market behaviour over recent years suggests a typical pattern for the term structure of crude oil futures prices. The forward curve can be divided into two separate parts: the first part consists of maturities below 18 months, and the second part consists of maturities above 18 months. These two parts differ not only through the maturities that they embrace, but also because the factors influencing them are of a different nature and origin.

The first part of the forward curve is linked to the physical market and to short-term expectations. The offer/demand equilibrium, the level of inventories and the fear of supply disruptions or limitations determines the state of the short- to mid-term forward curve: backwardation or contango. Hedging decisions are closely linked to these factors and are also closely connected to expectations about price. Hundreds of companies worldwide, most of them producers, refiners, distribution companies or traders, and consumers, play an active role in the market, and it is reasonable to regard the first part of the forward curve as a genuine equilibrium resulting from the actions of all market participants. Since the Gulf war, backwardation and contango situations have presented themselves alternately, depending on the configuration of the market.

As far as the long-term part of the forward curve is concerned, the situation is very different. This part is much more closely connected to finance than it is to the physical market for oil. Since most of those conducting long-term hedging operations are motivated by investment and project financing, factors such as interest rates, anticipated inflation or concurrent energy price forward curves are determinant. Also, for maturities of beyond a couple of years, the number of market participants drops to under fifty companies worldwide – with a large proportion of arbitrageurs among them. As a result, arbitrageurs have a dramatic influence on the shape of the long-term forward curve. For the last four years, this part of the forward curve has been in contango as a result of pressure from "long" hedgers. However, the lack of transparency and liquidity raises some doubt as to whether the current term structure is a genuine equilibrium resulting from the actions of all those who would benefit from entering the market.

Arbitrageurs operate on the term structures of prices and volatilities in a such a way as to "homogenise" the different parts. If, for instance, long-term volatility is "too" low, they might try to carry long volatility positions to benefit from the increase in volatility as expiration approaches. If the long-term contango is "relatively" high, and backwardation is prevailing in the short-term, arbitrageurs might also be willing to carry short positions of long-term time differential until expiration (when the market should be in backwardation). Recently, a contango market persisted for some considerable time; one might wonder whether this hints that backwardation should no longer be considered as "structural" in the oil markets.

Is short- to mid-term backwardation structural in the oil markets?

The evidence for asserting that the structural configuration of oil markets has shifted may seem largely circumstantial, but perhaps the two factors outlined below, and the theoretical argument developed above, give credence to the idea. There has been plenty of conjecture about why the contango experienced in the markets in 1993 and in the first quarter of 1994 prevailed for so long. My own tentative suggestion is simply this: that the "fear factor" that used to create a strong and structural convenience yield may have begun to decline.

First, it may be that the oil markets are metamorphosing from quasi-monopoly to quasi-free market. As the market share of the OPEC countries has decreased, the cartel has begun to lose its grip on supply. For years, OPEC managed to maintain the price of oil at well above the marginal cost of production. But, as the political shocks of the 1973 and 1979 oil crises have receded into history, one of the main fear factors has lessened – though it must be remembered that OPEC's market share is expected to recover in a few years.

The seeming asymmetry of oil demand elasticity to price traps OPEC in a vicious circle. A price drop does not cause a large increase in consumption, since consumers prefer not to increase their dependence on oil. However, a price surge reduces demand, especially during a world recession. If OPEC ceases to act as a cartel, that is, if it lacks the political will to cut supply on a large scale when prices fall, then the price of oil should eventually find an equilibrium somewhere near the high end of the marginal costs of production (that is, about US$10 per barrel at the present time). If market participants continue to consider the oil price as mean reverting, it might be some time before market participants adjust their price forecast downward even in the case of low spot prices. In such circumstances, the oil markets could conceivably remain in contango for a prolonged period before expectations fall – or OPEC revises its political strategy.

One could also speculate as to whether structural backwardation is simply a feature of unsophisticated commodity markets. One must remember that, unlike other commodity markets, oil trade was almost non-existent before 1980. Hedging on a large scale has developed only in the last few years, with the growth of derivative markets. International oil companies are now more efficient in the allocation of resources, traders are less present on the crude oil markets, and refiners may feel generally more relaxed about their supply of crude oil. Concurrently, hedging instruments permit the management of large-scale inventories. This is particularly true of refined products, since refin-

THE TERM STRUCTURE OF OIL PRICES:
A THEORETICAL APPROACH

In the main text, a basic model of the term structure of futures prices is created in order to introduce the notion of convenience yield.

This basic model, with the spot price as the only source of uncertainty, and a convenience-yield function, describes situations characterised by both backwardation and contango. In order to develop a general framework for the valuation of oil futures and derivative products, a second state variable is needed.

The discussion in the main text about the stability of futures prices for long-term maturities hints at the existence of a long-term price of oil that would arise out of the equilibrium level of the long-term expectations of market participants. Although this long-term price is not the price of a traded asset, it can still be used as a state variable to introduce a second source of uncertainty in the term structure of futures prices.

In the following, we make the assumption that the price of oil futures depends only upon these two state variables. We note S as the spot price; L as the long-term price; t as the present time; T as the maturity time; and F as the futures price. We assume that both S and L follow a diffusion process and that their joint stochastic process is specified as follows:

$$dS = \mu_S(S,t)dt + \sigma_S(S,t)dz_1$$
$$dL = \mu_L(L,t)dt + \sigma_L(L,t)dz_2$$

where dz_1 and dz_2 are two correlated processes such that $dz_1 dz_2 = \rho(t)dt$.

By using Itô's lemma, we can derive the instantaneous change of the futures price. By constituting a riskless portfolio of futures contracts, it can be shown that the futures price satisfies the following partial differential equation:

$$(r - C_Y)SF_S + \mu LF_L + \frac{1}{2}\sigma_S^2 S^2 F_{SS}$$

$$+ \frac{1}{2}\sigma_L^2 L^2 F_{LL} + \rho \sigma_S \sigma_L SLF_{SL} + F_{t=0}$$

subject to the limit condition $F(S,L,T,T) = S$ and where C_Y is the convenience-yield function defined so that it includes all yields and costs resulting from holding physical oil (except the financing cost).

S and L have been assumed to have a log normal stationary distribution, and the following parameters have been set:

$$\sigma_S(S,t) \equiv \sigma_S(t)S$$
$$\mu_L(L,t) \equiv \mu_L(t)L$$
$$\sigma_L(L,t) \equiv \sigma_L(t)L$$
$$\mu(t) = \mu_L(t) - \lambda_L \sigma_L(t)$$

where L is the market price per unit of long-term price risk. This parameter cannot be removed since L is not the price of a traded asset. We may then specify the form of the marginal convenience yield:

$$C_Y(S,L,t) = \beta(t)\ln\frac{S}{L} + \delta(t)$$

The futures price can then be written:

$$F(S,L,t,T) = A(t,T)S^{B(t,T)}L^{1-B(t,T)}$$

if the functions A and B satisfy the following partial differential equations and the associated conditions. With some arithmetic, it can be shown that:

$$A_t + (r - \delta(t))AB + \frac{1}{2}v(t)AB(B-1)$$

$$+ \mu A(1-B) = 0$$

$$B_t - \beta(t)B = 0$$

where $v(t) = \sigma_s(t)^2 + \sigma_L(t)^2 - 2\rho(t)\sigma_s(t)\sigma_L(t)$, and with the associated limit conditions:

$$A(T,T) = 1$$

$$B(T,T) = 1$$

B(0,T) can be computed for all T from the current term structure of futures prices volatilities.

ers increasingly anticipate seasonal episodes of high demand by hedging stocks. This tends to reduce the convenience yield of carrying inventories, and it therefore reduces backwardation. It is interesting to note that the heating oil futures contract on the Nymex is, on average, less backwardated than the gasoil futures contract on the IPE (which is much more recent and less used than its American equivalent).

Also, the long-lasting contango situation may

A(O,T) can be determined from B(O,T) and the current term structures of futures prices. The implied time-dependent convenience-yield function can then be extracted from the market data, and all kinds of securities can be valued in a consistent framework of prices and volatilities.

However, such a model shows a poor dynamic behaviour. By reducing the degree of freedom of the parameters, the model loses its ability to fit exactly market prices and volatilities, in exchange for enhanced dynamic properties. If r, ν, β, δ and μ are constant, the formulation of the futures price becomes:

$$F(S,L,\tau) = A(\tau)S^{B(\tau)}L^{1-B(\tau)}$$

$$A(\tau) =$$

$$\exp\left[\frac{r-\mu-\delta-\dfrac{\nu}{4}}{\beta} + \mu\tau + \frac{\mu-r+\delta+\dfrac{\nu}{2}}{\beta}e^{-\beta\tau} - \frac{\nu}{4\beta}e^{-2\beta\tau}\right]$$

$$B(\tau) = e^{-\beta\tau}$$

where τ denotes the time to maturity $T-t$. μ has a large impact on the shape of the term structure.

Let us define:

$$\lambda^* = \frac{\mu_L}{\sigma_L}$$

λ^* equals the value of the market price of long-term price risk if L were the price of a traded asset.

The relative position of λ_L and λ^* induces long-term backwardation or contango. Indeed, this model shows that if there is a long-term contango, market participants holding long futures positions accept a lower expected rate of growth of futures prices.

In such a market, people holding long futures positions overpay for futures contracts in comparison with a market in which there exists a contract for delivery at an infinite time. Long hedgers are more willing to cover their exposure against long-term price risk than are short hedgers. The first group outnumbers the second group or is more risk-averse.

If there is a long-term backwardation, market participants holding long futures positions enjoy a higher than expected rate of growth in futures prices. In such a market, people holding long futures positions underpay for futures contracts. Short hedgers outnumber long hedgers or are more risk-averse.

This model gives a theoretical support to the discussion in the main text concerning the short- to mid-term, as well as the long-term, parts of the forward curves.

On the one hand, the convenience yield C_Y (physical considerations) and the relative position of S and L (market expectations) determines the shape of the short- to mid-term part of the curve. On the other hand, the market price of long-term price risk λ_L (the most numerous or most risk-averse category between long and short hedgers) influences the shape of the long-term part of the curve.

This model also provides explicit American option valuation, term structures of futures price volatilities and term structures of futures price intercorrelations. It can also be adapted to describe petroleum products that have a strong seasonal pattern.

The construction of exactly the same model can be achieved with a completely different set of hypotheses. If we assume that oil is not a traded asset, since it is held primarily for consumption, then the market price of spot price risk is also connected to the pricing of derivative securities.

Under this assumption, we can suppose that the spot price S follows a mean-reverting diffusion process in which L now represents the long-run average value of the spot price. It is then easy to derive a model that is similar to the one above.

This shows that the role of the expected rate of growth of the spot price, ie expectations about the spot price, is more important than the notion of convenience yield. Again, the theory supports the qualitative discussion about the links between the short-term part of the term structure of futures prices and the mean-reverting nature of the price of oil.

have been perpetuated by more complex effects induced by the derivative markets. For instance, some market participants are said to have been rolling forward long futures positions on the Nymex on a very large scale, and as hedges for long-term short exposures. Large operations linked to the term structure of futures prices, and designed for risk management or investment purposes, may also have exercised a constant downward pressure on futures prices.

Due to the nature of the demand for oil, as outlined earlier in this chapter, there will always be extended periods of backwardation – even of strong backwardation. In the second quarter of 1994, for example, the market reverted to backwardation for quite specific reasons:
❑ the strong US economic recovery and the resulting demand and supply shortage;

❑ the upward pressure on prices from speculators focusing on all commodities;
❑ and the fear that supplies (from Nigeria, in the first instance) might be disrupted.

However, it seems probable that contango situations will become more frequent, and last longer, and that on average backwardation will become less pronounced.

1 *The proxies used for crude oil and heating oil prices are, respectively, the first nearby contract of Nymex light sweet crude oil futures and the first nearby contract of Nymex heating oil futures.*

2 *The proxies used for crude oil and heating oil inventories are stocks in the United States published by the American Petroleum Institute.*

3 *The term structures of short-term futures prices for crude oil and heating oil are represented by the differential between the first nearby futures contract and the second nearest futures contract, and constitute proxies for the convenience yields of crude oil and heating oil.*

4 *The term structure of prices expressed in constant terms is calculated by deflating the futures prices with current zero-coupon interest rates.*

5 *As far as futures prices for maturities of over 18 months are concerned, Nymex long-dated futures contract prices and OTC long-term prices for crude oil swaps (available from derivatives houses and specialised brokers) constitute a reliable source of information.*

6 *A recent discussion of "commercial" versus "non-commercial" trading can be found in Edward Krapels, "The Profit Motive",* Energy Risk, *vol. 1, no. 10, pp. 15-16.*

BIBLIOGRAPHY

Black, F., and M. Scholes, 1973, "The Pricing of Options and Corporate Liabilities", *Journal of Political Economy*, vol. 81, no. 3, pp. 637-54.

Brennan, M. J., 1989, "The Price of Convenience and the Valuation of Commodity Contingent Claims", working paper, University of British Columbia.

Brennan, M. J., and E. S. Schwartz, 1985, "Evaluating Natural Resources Investments", *Journal of Business*, vol. 58, no. 2, pp. 135-57.

Cox, J. C., J. E. Ingersoll and S. A. Ross, 1985, "A Theory of the Term Structure of Interest Rates", *Econometrica*, vol. 53, no. 2, pp. 385-407.

Fama, E. F., and K. R. French, 1988, "Business Cycles and the Behaviour of Metal Prices", *Journal of Finance*, vol. XLIII, no. 5, pp. 1075-93.

Gabillon, J., 1991, "The Term Structure of Oil Futures Prices", Oxford Institute for Energy Studies, working paper (WPM17).

Gibson, R., and E. S. Schwartz, 1990, "Stochastic Convenience Yield and the Pricing of Oil Contingent Claims", *Journal of Finance*, vol. XLV, no. 3, pp. 959-76.

Hull, J., and A. White, 1990, "Valuing Derivative Securities Using the Explicit Finite Difference Method", *Journal of Financial and Quantitative Analysis*, vol. 25, no. 1, pp. 87-100.

Hull, J., and A. White, 1990, "Pricing Interest-Rate Derivative Securities", *Review of Financial Studies*, vol. 3, no. 4, pp. 573-92.

Hull, J., and A. White, 1990, "One-Factor Interest-Rate Models and the Valuation of Interest Rates", working paper, University of Toronto.

Vasicek, O., 1977, "An Equilibrium Characterisation of the Term Structure", *Journal of Financial Economics*, no. 5, pp. 177-88.

Working, H., 1977, *Selected Writings of Holbrook Working*, Chicago Board of Trade.

2

Volatility in Energy Prices

Darrell Duffie and Stephen Gray
Stanford University and Duke University[1]

Prices in the energy markets are marked by a volatility that is both high and variable over time. These characteristics mean that the energy markets are an ideal testing ground for volatility models – our primary concern in this chapter – and that the ability to track and forecast volatility is of paramount importance when trading and hedging energy-related portfolios of derivatives.

When making markets, for example, a trader will need to track the exposure of a book of positions to market changes of various types, including volatility. What is a 95% worst case mark-to-market on a given position? What is the risk (standard deviation) of the current book? Which desk is above its risk limit, and how should such limits be set? Which traders have shown acceptable or superior performance, in the light of the volatility of the markets in which they trade? The answers to all these questions rely on estimates of past or future volatility.

A model of stochastic volatility is also useful when estimating a fair price for a given option, cap or other volatility-dependent derivative. Or when calculating the delta of a given portfolio of energy-related securities – and the option positions that would make a reasonable delta hedge against that portfolio.

We hope that this chapter will provide a useful review of the modelling and empirical behaviour of volatility in energy prices. As a point of departure, we first review the standard constant-volatility model. Then we describe stochastic volatility models of a Markov variety, in which current volatility is a function of the past level of volatility and a new "shock", which may or may not be correlated with the current return on the underlying price. We move on to examine simple regime-switching models, and then some of the ARCH-based models.

Throughout the chapter, we refer to a series of tests that we performed in order to discover which of the most commonly used and discussed models of volatility was the most effective forecaster. For the purposes of this experiment, we used historical data supplied by the energy industry to compare the forecasts of the models, at a given point in time, to the level of volatility that was subsequently realised in the markets. In our conclusion, we highlight our most important findings and suggest some directions for future work.

In this chapter, we shall not address the term-structure of volatility. The principal components of changes in the forward curve of energy prices have been discussed in some detail in the previous chapter, with reference to the oil markets. However, it would also be useful, in the future, to determine how much risk is accounted for by each principal component, and the standard deviations of changes associated with these principal components.[2]

We will also avoid discussing the estimation of the correlation of price changes across related markets; this is obviously an important issue when determining risk-minimising hedging positions and risk exposures, and it is discussed in detail in Chapters 4 and 7.

A few preliminary comments are necessary on the different applications of volatility estimation. Some investors speculate on energy volatility, attempting to predict changes in volatility before those changes are impounded into generally available market prices. This is perhaps as much of an art as it is a science. Changes in volatility are not generated by a mathematical model, but rather by real-world events that have a significance which may at first only be apparent to engineers, geologists, economists or geopolitical analysts. Armed with a solid understanding of the Black-Scholes formula, a well-informed trader with advance knowledge of volatility-related events (or a superior ability when analysing the implications of such events) would not need the modelling approaches we offer here in order to be successful.

Instead, this chapter is aimed at the managers of systems that are designed to cope with energy *portfolios*. A buyer of long-term natural gas contracts for an electric power utility, a heating oil supplier, a major oil refiner and marketer, or a market maker in energy derivatives would naturally rely on the sort of models that we present here.

Constant volatility

For a given asset, "volatility" is the standard deviation of return, conditional on all available information. The starting point for almost any model of volatility is the constant volatility model exploited by Black and Scholes (1973), in which the volatility is a constant over time.

The constant-volatility model can be presented in a simple form. The return on an asset, say on a daily basis, is the percentage payback on a dollar investment. We will ignore dividends or storage costs, since, being comparatively small and predictable over limited time horizons, they have a relatively minor effect on volatility in energy markets over the time horizons that we study here. Instead, we will concentrate on price returns. On a continuously compounding basis, the price return over a given period can be computed as the logarithm of the ending price less the logarithm of the beginning price.

For example, if the price of a barrel of oil at the close on Monday is \$16.00, and at the close on Tuesday is \$16.20, then the close-to-close price return is $\log 16.20 - \log 16.00 = 0.0124$. On an annualised basis ($365 \times 0.0124 = 4.53$), this results in an annual return of 453%.

Whether in a discrete or continuous time setting, the constant volatility model assumes that the underlying prices $S_1, S_2, \ldots$ of the asset in question have returns $R = \log S_t - \log S_{t-1}$ given by:

$$R_t = \mu + \sigma \in_t \qquad (1)$$

where μ is a constant mean return coefficient, σ is a constant volatility parameter, and $\in_1, \in_2 \ldots$ is *white noise* (by which we mean independent, normally distributed random variables of zero mean and unit variance). Sticking to daily frequency (mainly for expositional reasons), the annualised volatility is the standard deviation of $R_1 + \cdots + R_{365}$, which is $\sqrt{365}\sigma$ in our constant-volatility model (1).

In the continuous-time setting of Black and Scholes, it is well known that the price of an option at time t, say a European call, is given explicitly by the famous Black-Scholes formula $C_t = C^{BS}(S_t, \tau, K, r, \sigma)$, given the strike price K, the time τ to expiration, the continuously compounding constant interest rate r, and the volatility σ.

It is also well known that this formula is strictly increasing in σ, so that, from the option price C_t, one may theoretically infer, without error, the volatility parameter $\sigma_t = \sigma^{BS}(C_t, S_t, \tau, K, r)$. The function σ^{BS} is known as the Black-Scholes implied volatility.[3] While no explicit formula for σ^{BS} is available, one can compute implied volatilities readily with a simple numerical search routine such as Newton-Raphson. For these and many other details on the Black-Scholes model and extensions, one may refer to Cox and Rubinstein (1985), Stoll and Whaley (1993) and Hull (1993), among many other sources.

If an option price is not available, one may estimate σ from returns data. The *historical* volatility $\hat{\sigma}_{t,T}$ implied by returns $R_t, R_{t+1} \ldots, R_T$ is the usual maximum likelihood estimator for σ given by

$$\hat{\sigma}_{t,T}^2 = \frac{1}{T-t} \sum_{s=t+1}^{T} \left(R_s - \hat{\mu}_{t,T}\right)^2 \qquad (2)$$

where $\hat{\mu}_{t,T} = (R_{t+1} + \cdots + R_T)/(T-t)$. If, as in the Black-Scholes setting, the constant-volatility returns model (1) applies at arbitrarily fine data frequency (with suitable adjustment of μ and σ for period length), then one can learn the volatility σ within an arbitrarily short time interval from the historical volatility estimator.[4]

In reality, price data frequency is limited, and in any case returns at exceptionally high frequency have statistical properties that are heavily dependent on institutional properties of the market that are of less importance over longer time periods. Given a fixed number of observations over a given period, the optimal sampling times for estimation of σ are not necessarily evenly spaced, as shown by Genon-Catalot and Jacod (1993).

When estimating σ in the Black-Scholes setting, one can also take special advantage of additional financial price data, such as the high and low prices for the period, as shown by Garman and Klass (1980), Parkinson (1980) and Rogers and Satchell (1991).

For energy prices, and indeed for many other assets, historical volatility data strongly indicate that the constant-volatility model does not apply. For example, the returns of heating oil, crude oil and natural gas shown in Figure 1 appear to indicate that volatility is changing, in some manner, over time.

Even in the constant-volatility setting, one

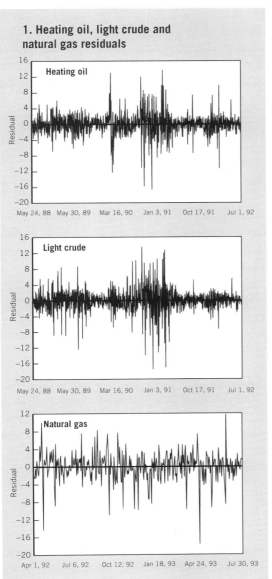

1. Heating oil, light crude and natural gas residuals

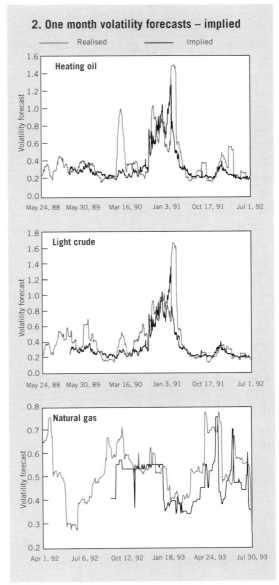

2. One month volatility forecasts – implied

— Realised   — Implied

expects the historical volatility estimate to vary over time, sometimes dramatically, merely from random variation in prices. (This is sometimes called "sampling error".) One can perform various tests to find out whether changes in historical volatility are *so* large as to cause one to reject the constant volatility hypothesis at a given confidence level. For example, under the constant volatility hypothesis, the ratio $F_{a,b} = \hat{\sigma}^2_{t(a),T(a)}/\hat{\sigma}^2_{t(b),T(b)}$ of squared historical volatilities over non-overlapping time intervals has the F distribution (with degrees of freedom given by the respective lengths of the two time intervals). From standard tables of the F distribution, one can then test the constant-volatility hypothesis, rejecting it at, say, the 95% confidence level, if $F_{a,b}$ is larger than the associated critical F statistic. (One should take care not to select the time intervals in question in the light of one's impression, based on observing prices, that volatility

apparently differs between the two periods. This would introduce a selection bias that tends to make such classical tests unreliable.)

In any case, most energy price data, including those considered in this chapter, generate rejections of the constant volatility hypothesis in tests such as this, and it seems inappropriate here to go into the subtleties designed to refine such tests. Although rejections in such classical tests are, by nature, subject to random errors, the Black-Scholes implied volatility trajectories shown in Figure 2 certainly suggest that options traders do not believe that the constant-volatility model applies to heating oil, crude oil or natural gas.

In other words, when buying or selling options, each trader has in mind a fair price that reflects the likelihoods for that trader of each possible level of the underlying price. If the constant-volatility model were correct and *believed by traders* to be correct, then the prices paid for options would have constant implied volatilities. That is not what we see in Figure 2. Of course, it is theoretically possible that volatility is constant and that the evidence in Figure 2 is due to failures of one or more assumptions in the Black-Scholes model other than constant volatility, but it seems unlikely that the extent of the failure of these other assumptions could be responsible for the dramatic variation of the implied volatilities shown in Figure 2, especially given the alignment of sharp changes in implied volatility with identifiable market events such as the Gulf War.

If traders have in mind something other than constant volatility, then one can learn something about their forecasts of volatility from the prices at which they buy and sell options. For example, even if the Black-Scholes model is incorrect, the Black-Scholes implied volatilities could have forecasting power for volatility. Indeed, Figure 2 shows that this seems to be the case, as the plot of Black-Scholes implied volatility "leads" historical volatility.

That is, we can view $\sigma^{BS}(C_t,S_t,T-t,K,r)$ as a useful predictor of $\hat{\sigma}_{t,T}$ the former known at time t, the latter only at the expiration date T of the option. Even though Figure 2 plots historical volatility for 25-day periods, regardless of the expiration dates of the options underlying the implied volatility, the ability of implied volatility to forecast changes in historical volatility is apparent. Later, we will compare the forecasting quality of implied volatility with that of other volatility predictors.

The seasons of the year play an important role in the markets for energy products. For example, the demand for heating oil depends on winter weather patterns, which are obviously only determined in the winter. The demand for gasoline is greater, and shows greater variability, in the summer, and gasoline prices therefore tend to show greater variability during the summer months. There is even a day-of-the-week effect in the volatility of most futures markets that reflects institutional market features, including the desire of market makers to close out their positions over weekends.

One can "correct" for seasonality, for example by estimating volatility separately by season. Even after correcting volatility for seasonality, however, there are still persistent and random changes in volatility. That is, a model in which volatility is constant, but in which the constant level of volatility depends on the season in some regular way such as this, can also be safe-

ly ruled out. This is not to say that seasonality is not important. Indeed, one would probably want to include seasonality in a detailed model of volatility, but seasons alone do not adequately account for the patterns of volatility that we see in the energy markets.

It seems safe to conclude that, at least for energy markets, we can benefit by moving beyond the constant volatility model.

Stochastic volatility

The word "stochastic" simply means "random". It is reasonable, and has become popular, to treat "volatility" as a stochastic process. A reasonably large class of extensions of the constant-volatility model can then be built on a "stochastic-volatility" model of returns, given by

$$R_t = \mu + \sigma_{t-1}\varepsilon_t \qquad (3)$$

where the constant[5] mean return and random return shocks ε_1, ε_2, ... are as above, and where σ_{t-1} is the standard deviation of the return R_t, conditional on information available at time $t-1$.

Knowledge of the *stochastic volatility* process σ_1, σ_2, ... would, under certain conditions, allow us to handle the applications described in the introduction. For example, if we knew the random manner in which σ varies over time, we could estimate the risk (standard deviation) of a portfolio of energy positions simply by Monte Carlo simulation of σ and of the returns process R from (3). Likewise, from such a simulation, we could estimate the position in an energy derivative, such as a futures contract, that minimises the risk of a portfolio of energy market commitments. As we shall see, with a model of σ, depending on the technical assumptions that one is willing to make, one can price an option-embedded derivative on the underlying energy price. Other applications, such as trading performance evaluation, can be improved if we can estimate a stochastic model for volatility, since that would allow one to estimate the level of volatility that existed over an historical period.

While the current return R_t is normally distributed in the stochastic-volatility model (3), conditional on information available at time $t-1$, the unconditional distribution of returns can be thought of as a mixture of normal distributions. In particular, the unconditional distribution of returns would typically be skewed and leptokurtic, consistent with the distribution of returns typical in most markets, including the energy markets.[6]

The basic objective here is to model the stochastic volatility process, and from such a model, forecast future volatility from past returns data, options prices, and perhaps prices from related energy markets. Before getting into the details, it may help to focus on what it is about "volatility" that one wants to estimate. Ideally, we want to specify completely the joint behaviour of returns and volatility, as stochastic processes. For comparison purposes, however, and given the sorts of applications one may have in mind, it makes sense to consider forecasts of volatility.

We will concentrate especially on forecasting the average future squared volatility:

$$v_{t,T}^2 = \frac{1}{T-t}\left(\sigma_t^2 + \cdots + \sigma_{T-1}^2\right) \qquad (4)$$

This is a reasonable objective, for, as one can show by the law of iterated expectations, an unbiased forecast of $v_{t,T}^2$ is the same as an unbiased forecast of

$$\frac{1}{T-t}\sum_{s=t+1}^{T}\left(R_s - \mu\right)^2$$

which in turn is almost identical to the historical volatility measure $\hat{\sigma}_{t,T}^2$. (These differ only by the replacement of the estimated mean return $\hat{\mu}_{t,T}^2$ with the true value μ and this substitution has a negligible effect in practice.)

Another advantage of concentrating on $v_{t,T}^2$ is that, under well-understood conditions that we review below, it is straightforward to convert Black-Scholes implied volatilities into unbiased forecasts of $v_{t,T}^2$, and vice versa. Finally, from forecasts of $v_{t,T}^2$, one can estimate risk exposures (such as standard deviations or 95% worst-case scenarios), and more generally feed the needs of a risk-management system.

Markovian models of stochastic volatility

One can envision a model for stochastic volatility in which the current level of volatility depends in a non-trivial way on the path that volatility has taken in the past. For example, one might say that volatility tends to decline if it is currently higher than its average level over some period in the past. It is also realistic, in energy markets, to believe that volatility depends on the quantities of the asset, say heating oil or crude oil, currently held in readily accessible inventory. See, for example, Ng and Pirrong (1994) for such a model in the context of metals markets. While we advocate the consideration of volatility models that include

potential path dependencies, dependencies on inventory levels, and other potential determinants of volatility, for simplicity of illustration we will focus here only on the simplest forms of volatility models that have commonly appeared in the literature. These models are mainly of the Markovian form:

$$\sigma_t = F\left(\sigma_{t-1}, z_t, t\right) \qquad (5)$$

where F is some smooth function in three variables and $z_1, z_2, \ldots$ is a white noise. The term "Markovian" means that the probability distribution of the next period's level of volatility depends only on the current level of volatility, and not otherwise on the path taken by volatility. This form of volatility also rules out, for reasons of simplification, dependence of the distribution of changes in volatility on other possible state variables, such as inventory levels (as mentioned above) and macro-economic factors. Later, we do consider Markov models in which other state variables, such as price levels or volatilities in related markets, play a role. Moreover, we do not necessarily assume that the volatility shock z_t and the return shock ε_t are perfectly correlated.

In the following sections, we will consider several basic classes of the Markovian stochastic volatility model (5). Each of these classes has its own advantages, both in terms of empirical reasonability and tractability in an option-pricing framework. The latter is particularly important, since option valuation may, under certain conditions, provide volatilities implicitly – as in the Black-Scholes setting.

REGIME-SWITCHING VOLATILITY
A relatively simple version of (5) that one can take as an illustration of stochastic volatility is given by a Markov chain. For example, if one takes two possible levels, v_a and v_b for volatility in a given period, we can take the transition probabilities of σ_t between v_a and v_b to be given by a matrix

$$\Pi = \begin{pmatrix} \Pi_{aa} & \Pi_{ab} \\ \Pi_{ba} & \Pi_{bb} \end{pmatrix}$$

so that, for example, if $\sigma_t = v_a$ then the conditional probability[7] that $\sigma_{t+1} = v_b$ is Π_{ab}. This simple model of stochastic volatility is often called a *regime-switching* model.

A key empirical property of volatility that one can pick up from the charts of squared returns for crude oil, heating oil and natural gas shown in Figure 1 is *persistence*, by which we

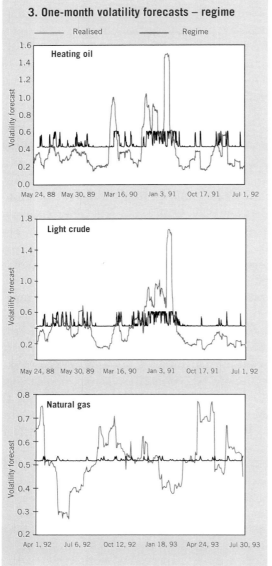

3. One-month volatility forecasts – regime

——— Realised ——— Regime

Heating oil

Light crude

Natural gas

shocks $\in_1$, $\in_2$, the expected average squared future volatility is given by

$$\bar{v}_{t,T}^2 \equiv E_t\left(v_{t,T}^2\right) = \frac{1}{T-t}\sum_{s=t}^{T-1} p_s v_a^2 + \left(1-p_s\right)v_b^2 \quad (6)$$

where the probability p_s of volatility v_a at time s is given by

$$\begin{pmatrix} p_s \\ 1-p_s \end{pmatrix} = \left(\Pi^T\right)^{s-t}\begin{pmatrix} p_t \\ 1-p_t \end{pmatrix} \quad (7)$$

where Π^T denotes the transpose of Π.

Table 1 illustrates the estimates of this regime-switching model, indicating high degrees of persistence at daily frequency for crude oil, heating oil and natural gas. For example, for all three products, the higher volatility level v_b is estimated at roughly three times the lower level v_a. The daily persistence probabilities for heating oil and light crude are estimated at 90% or greater.

But for natural gas the estimated persistence of high volatility is much lower; instead the estimate is characterised by long periods in the low-volatility regime, with occasional and brief sojourns in the high-volatility regime. To make the example more general, we have departed slightly from our original model (3) by allowing the mean returns μ_a and μ_b to vary with the level of volatility.[8]

Figure 3 shows the forecasts of the regime-switching model for the 25-day future average squared volatilities for heating oil, light crude oil and natural gas, as well as the ultimately realised volatilities. As one can see, the model is limited by the number of levels of volatilities that are actually permitted. Gray (1993) develops generalisations of the regime-switching model that include switching from one form of stochastic volatility model (such as GARCH, described below) to another, and cites related literature in this area.

AUTO-REGRESSIVE VOLATILITY
A standard Markov model of stochastic volatility is given by the log-AR(1) model:

mean that relatively high recent volatility implies a relatively high forecast of volatility in the near future. Likewise, with persistence, recent low volatility is associated with a prediction of lower volatility in the near future. The diagonal probabilities Π_{aa} and Π_{bb} of the regime-switching model can be treated as measures of the persistence of volatility.

Taking the evolution of this Markov chain for volatility to be independent of the returns

Table 1. Markov regime-switching estimates

1a Heating oil			1b Light crude oil			1c Natural gas		
Coefficient	Estimate	t-Statistic	Coefficient	Estimate	t-Statistic	Coefficient	Estimate	t-Statistic
μ_a	0.0239	(0.346)	μ_a	0.0437	(0.407)	μ_a	0.431	(2.70)
v_a	1.511	(16.7)	v_a	1.602	(14.5)	v_a	2.19	(17.4)
μ_b	0.131	(0.509)	μ_b	−0.070	(−0.150)	μ_b	−1.12	(−1.11)
v_b	4.642	(11.8)	v_b	5.870	(4.77)	v_b	6.17	(9.34)
Π_{aa}	0.969	(91.9)	Π_{aa}	0.971	(111)	Π_{aa}	0.891	(27.1)
Π_{bb}	0.909	(32.3)	Π_{bb}	0.893	(17.2)	Π_{bb}	0.506	(3.32)

$$\log \sigma_t^2 = \alpha + \gamma \log \sigma_{t-1}^2 + \kappa z_t \qquad (8)$$

where α, γ and κ are constants. We always assume that z_t and ε_s are independent for $t \neq s$, and that z_t and ε_t have some constant correlation ρ. Volatility persistence is captured by the coefficient γ. A value of γ that is near zero implies low persistence, while a value that is near one implies high persistence. We always assume that $-1 < \gamma < 1$, otherwise volatility becomes "explosive".

From (3) we may write

$$\log(R_t - \mu)^2 = \log \sigma_{t-1}^2 + \log \varepsilon_t^2 \qquad (9)$$

Harvey, Ruiz and Shepard (1992), and Harvey and Shepard (1993), have shown that one can estimate the coefficients of (8) – (9) by quasi-maximum likelihood,[9] which is indeed consistent under certain technical restrictions. We have not estimated this volatility model for energy prices, but for completeness we provide the calculation by Heynen and Kat (1993) of the expected average squared future volatility associated with (8):

$$\overline{v}_{t,T}^2 = \frac{\overline{\sigma}^2}{T-t} \sum_{k=1}^{T-t} \sigma_t^{2\gamma^k} \exp\left(\frac{-\alpha\gamma^k}{1-\gamma} - \frac{\kappa^2\gamma^{2k}}{2(1-\gamma^2)}\right) (10)$$

where $\overline{\sigma}^2$ is the steady-state[10] expectation of σ_t^2.

OPTION-IMPLIED AND FORECASTED VOLATILITY

A natural continuous time version of the Markov model (5) is given by the stochastic differential equation

$$d\sigma_t = a(\sigma_t, t)dt + b(\sigma_t, t)dZ_t \qquad (11)$$

where a and b are continuous functions in two variables and Z is a Standard Brownian Motion. (Regularity conditions on a and b are required. See, for example, Karatzas and Shreve, 1988.) The associated continuous-time model for the underlying asset price, analogous to (3), is

$$dS_t = \mu S_t dt + \sigma_t S_t dB_t \qquad (12)$$

where B is a Standard Brownian Motion. With (11) and (12), we can extend the Black-Scholes approach to option valuation, and obtain a generalisation of the notion of implied volatility.

For example, we can follow Hull and White (1987), Scott (1987) and Wiggins (1987) in assuming that, after switching to risk-neutral probabilities, a stochastic differential equation of the form (11) – (12) still applies, in which the innovation process Z^*, driving stochastic volatil-

ity, is independent of the returns innovation process B^*. With this, one obtains the option pricing formula

$$
\begin{aligned}
C_t &= C^{SV}(S_t, \sigma_t, T, K, r) \\
&\equiv E^*\left[C^{BS}(S_t, v_t, T-t, K, r)\big|S_t\sigma_t\right]
\end{aligned} \qquad (13)
$$

where E^* denotes risk-neutral expectation and

$$v_{t,T}^2 = \frac{1}{T-t}\int_t^T \sigma_s^2 ds \qquad (14)$$

The fact that (13) – (14) is a valid option-pricing model follows from the fact that, if volatility is time-varying but deterministic, then one can substitute $v_{t,T}$ in place of the usual constant volatility coefficient to get the correct option price $C^{BS}(S_t, v_{t,T}, T-t, K, r)$ from the Black-Scholes model.

With the independence assumption above, one can simply average this modified Black-Scholes formula over all possible (probability-weighted) realisations of $v_{t,T}$ to get the result (13). One may note that we use the same notation $v_{t,T}$ in (4) and (14), as these two definitions of $v_{t,T}$ coincide in the limit as the length of a time period goes to zero.

It is known that, as with any stochastic differential equation, an increase in σ_t implies an increase in σ_s for all $s \geq t$.[11] Thus, under mild technical conditions on a and b, expected future average squared future volatility $\overline{v}_{t,T}^2$ is strictly increasing and continuous in σ_t. Since the Black-Scholes implied volatility σ^{BS} is likewise strictly monotone and continuous in volatility, each of the following is a strictly increasing continuous function of the other (in particular, knowledge of any one implies knowledge of the others):
i) the current option price $C_t = C^{SV}(S_t, \sigma_t, t, T, K, r)$,
ii) the current volatility σ_t,
iii) the expected average squared future volatility $\overline{v}_{t,T}^2$ and
iv) the Black-Scholes implied volatility $\sigma^{BS}(C_t, S_t, T-t, K, r)$.

Neither the current volatility σ_t, nor the expected average squared volatility $\overline{v}_{t,T}^2$, are directly observable, but there may be traded options from whose prices they can be inferred.[12]

Knowing how to convert the option price or Black-Scholes implied volatility to the current or forecasted volatility depends on knowledge of the functions a and b determining the random behaviour of volatility in (11) – and these functions must themselves be estimated from data.

This programme has been carried out by Renault and Touzi (1992), who also point out that, in this setting, one can synthetically replicate (and therefore perfectly hedge) a given option with positions in the underlying asset, riskless borrowing and lending, and positions in any other option. In other words, stochastic volatility risk is *spanned* in this setting. We revisit this spanning property later in our discussion.

For many specifications of (11), and with empirically fitted parameters, one obtains from (13) the well-documented "smile-shaped" dependence of the Black-Scholes implied volatility on the strike price.

There are several methods for computing option prices under the continuous-time model (11) – (12), such as Monte Carlo simulation, or numerical solution of the associated partial differential equation.[13] Hull and White (1987) and Lu and Yu (1993) point out that option valuation with this stochastic volatility model can be well approximated by a Taylor-series expansion in the moments of volatility, given by:

$$C^{SV}(S_t, \sigma_t, T, K, r) = C^{BS}(S_t, \overline{v}_{t,T}, T - t, K, r)$$

$$+ \frac{1}{2} \frac{\partial^2}{\partial \sigma^2} C^{BS}(S_t, \overline{v}_{T-t}, T - t, K, r) \, var_t(v_t, T) + \frac{1}{6} \ldots \quad (15)$$

where $var_t(\cdot)$ denotes conditional variance.

While the Black-Scholes option-implied volatility $\sigma^{BS}(C_t, S_t, T - t, K, r)$ is generally a biased forecast of $v_{t,T}$ the bias can be corrected when one knows the functions a and b in (11). In fact, as we have already seen from Figure 2, the bias is not large for our data set. (For the purposes of that figure, the well-documented "smile" aspect of the bias is mitigated by taking as the "Black-Scholes implied volatility" the average of the implied volatility for several near-to-the-money puts and calls.)

Several special cases of (11) have been analysed. The log-AR(1) model of discrete-time volatility given by (8) has the continuous-time counterpart $\log \sigma_t^2 = v_t$ where

$$dv_t = (\alpha + \gamma v_t)dt + \kappa Z_t \quad (16)$$

for constants α, γ and κ. With $\gamma < 0$, we have "mean reversion", by which we mean that the expected rate of change of log-volatility is negative when v_t is above its steady-state mean $\overline{v} = -\alpha/\gamma$ and is positive when $v_t = \overline{v}$. The special case with $\alpha = 0$ (no mean reversion) was considered by Hull and White (1987), Scott (1987) and Wiggins (1987).

For a closely related model, Lu and Yu (1993) proposed the special case of (11) given by $\sigma_t = \sqrt{V_t}$ where

$$dV_t = (\alpha + \gamma V_t)dt + \kappa V_t dZ_t \quad (17)$$

where the coefficients α, γ, and κ have interpretations similar to those for (16). When $\alpha = 0$, the two volatility models, (16) and (17) both have the standard log-normal volatility assumed by Hull and White (1987).

The Lu-Yu model has the expected average squared future volatility:

$$\overline{v}_{t,T}^2 =$$

$$\frac{1}{\gamma^2(T - t)} \left[\left(\gamma \sigma_t^2 - \alpha \right) \left(1 - e^{-\gamma(T - t)} \right) + \alpha \gamma (T - t) \right] \quad (18)$$

Other continuous-time Markovian models for stochastic volatility have been considered. For example, Heston (1992) uses a stochastic volatility of the "square-root" style, and incorporates the impact of risk premia for volatility.

GARCH VOLATILITY
Many modellers have turned to ARCH (autoregressive conditional heteroscedasticity) models of volatility, proposed by Engle (1982), and the related GARCH and EGARCH formulations, because they capture volatility persistence in a simple and flexible way.

For example, the GARCH[14] model of stochastic volatility proposed by Bollerslev (1986) assumes that

$$\sigma_t^2 = \alpha + \beta(R_t - \mu)^2 + \gamma \sigma_{t-1}^2 \quad (19)$$

where α, β, and γ are positive constants.[15] Here, γ is the key persistence parameter: a high γ implies a high carry-over effect of past to future volatility, while a low γ implies a heavily damped dependence on past volatility.

One can estimate the parameters α, β, and γ from returns data. For example, Table 2 illus-

Table 2. GARCH estimates

Heating oil
$$\sigma_t^2 = 0.235 + 0.228 \, (R_t - \mu)^2 + 0.771 \, \sigma_{t-1}^2$$
$$(4.98) \quad (8.17) \qquad (32.2)$$

Light crude
$$\sigma_t^2 = 0.155 + 0.292 \, (R_t - \mu)^2 + 0.724 \, \sigma_{t-1}^2$$
$$(3.95) \quad (9.31) \qquad (30.1)$$

Natural gas
$$\sigma_t^2 = 0.000470 + 0.212 \, (R_t - \mu)^2 + 0.395 \, \sigma_{t-1}^2$$
$$(3.80) \qquad (3.10) \qquad (3.30)$$

47

VOLATILITY
IN ENERGY
PRICES

trates the estimated GARCH parameters associated with crude oil, heating oil and natural gas, obtained by maximum likelihood estimation. The data indicate a relatively high persistence of daily volatility, with γ estimated at over 75% for heating oil and light crude oil. The volatility process for natural gas appears to be much less persistent. (Another explanation is measurement error, which may be greater in natural gas due to the lower liquidity and greater volatility.)

As shown by Heynen and Kat (1993), provided $\delta \equiv \beta + \gamma < 1$, which is a condition for "non-explosivity", the forecasted (expected average squared future) volatility associated with the GARCH model is given by

$$\overline{v}_{t,T}^2 = (T-t)\overline{\sigma}^2 + \left(\sigma_{t+1}^2 - \overline{\sigma}^2\right)\frac{1-\delta^{T-t}}{1-\delta} \quad (20)$$

where $\overline{\sigma}^2 = \alpha/(1-\delta)$.[16] Figure 4 compares the 25-day GARCH forecast of volatility, and the ultimately realised historical volatility for the same 25-day period, in the cases of heating oil, light crude oil and natural gas. While a casual review of the figures shows some apparent forecasting ability for the GARCH model, one might also notice a potential disadvantage of the GARCH model, in that the impact of the current return R_t on σ_{t+1}^2 is quadratic; this means that a day of exceptionally large absolute returns can have a dramatic impact on forecasted volatility, and cause "overshooting" in forecasted volatility. For example, with any reasonable degree of persistence, the "Gulf War" effect could imply a sustained and major impact on forecasted volatility. (The key days of the Gulf War were in fact "dummied out" out of all of our maximum likelihood estimates.)

EGARCH VOLATILITY

A potentially more flexible model of persistence is the EGARCH model proposed by Nelson (1991), which takes the form[17]

$$\log \sigma_t^2 = \alpha + \gamma \log \sigma_{t-1}^2$$
$$+\beta_1\left(\frac{R_{t-\mu}}{\sigma_{t-1}}\right) + \beta_2\left(\left|\frac{R_t - \mu}{\sigma_{t-1}}\right| - \sqrt{\frac{2}{\pi}}\right) \quad (21)$$

Maximum likelihood estimates of the EGARCH model for crude oil, heating oil and natural gas are shown in Table 3 overleaf. Again, a strong degree of volatility persistence is evident in the heating oil and light crude oil markets. Persistence in natural gas volatility is estimated to be much lower. For the EGARCH model, some asymmetry[18] in the impact of return shocks

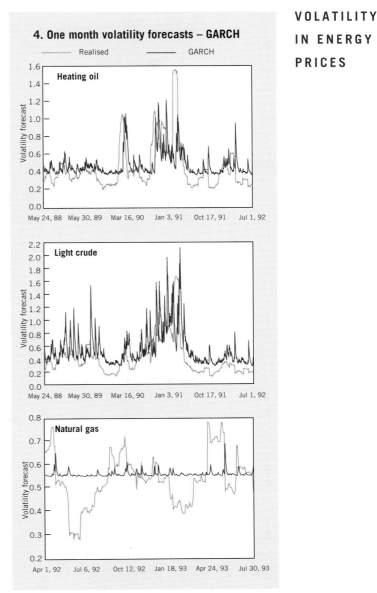

4. One month volatility forecasts – GARCH

——— Realised   ——— GARCH

to volatility is permitted, as these shocks appear in both levels, and in their absolute values.

In all three markets, the coefficient β_1 on return shocks is positive, indicating that an increase in price is estimated to increase volatility more than does a decrease in price.

Figure 5 overleaf illustrates volatility forecasts for the EGARCH model.

The expected average squared future volatility implied by the EGARCH model is

$$\overline{v}_{t,T}^2 = \sum_{k=0}^{T-t-1} C_k \sigma_t^{2\gamma^k} \quad (22)$$

where C_k is a relatively complicated constant given by Heynen and Kat (1993).

Nelson (1990) has shown that the EGARCH model (21) and the log-AR(1) model (8) converge with decreasing period length, and appropriate normalisation of coefficients, to the same continuous-time model (16).

Table 3. EGARCH estimated volatility models

Heating oil

$$\log(\sigma_t^2) = 0.0771 + 0.958 \log(\sigma_{t-1}^2) + 0.0576 \left(\frac{R_t - \mu}{\sigma_{t-1}} \right)$$
$$\quad (4.79) \quad (102) \qquad\qquad (3.92)$$

$$+ 0.347 \left(\left| \frac{R_t - \mu}{\sigma_{t-1}} \right| - \sqrt{\frac{2}{\pi}} \right)$$
$$\quad (11.3)$$

Light crude

$$\log(\sigma_t^2) = 0.0595 + 0.971 \log(\sigma_{t-1}^2) + 0.0292 \left(\frac{R_t - \mu}{\sigma_{t-1}} \right)$$
$$\quad (4.47) \quad (137) \qquad\qquad (1.62)$$

$$+ 0.411 \left(\left| \frac{R_t - \mu}{\sigma_{t-1}} \right| - \sqrt{\frac{2}{\pi}} \right)$$
$$\quad (11.1)$$

Natural gas

$$\log(\sigma_t^2) = 1.18 + 0.490 \log(\sigma_{t-1}^2) + 0.0519 \left(\frac{R_t - \mu}{\sigma_{t-1}} \right)$$
$$\quad (3.03) \ (2.97) \qquad\qquad (0.839)$$

$$+ 0.339 \left(\left| \frac{R_t - \mu}{\sigma_{t-1}} \right| - \sqrt{\frac{2}{\pi}} \right)$$
$$\quad (3.45)$$

MULTIVARIATE GARCH VOLATILITY

When, as in many energy markets, one can infer volatility-related information for one commodity from changes in the volatility of returns in another market, one can generally do better by incorporating such cross-market information rather than sticking to a model in which the volatility for the given commodity is affected only by its own past price behaviour.

A simple model that accounts for cross-market inference is the multivariate GARCH model. For example, a simple two-commodity version of this model takes

$$\begin{pmatrix} \sigma_{a,t}^2 \\ \sigma_{ab,t} \\ \sigma_{b,t}^2 \end{pmatrix} = \alpha + \beta \begin{pmatrix} R_{a,t}^2 \\ R_{a,t}R_{b,t} \\ R_{b,t}^2 \end{pmatrix} + \gamma \begin{pmatrix} \sigma_{a,t-1}^2 \\ \sigma_{ab,t-1} \\ \sigma_{b,t-1}^2 \end{pmatrix} \quad (23)$$

where
$R_{a,t}$ is the return on commodity a at time t
$R_{b,t}$ is the return on commodity b at time t
$\sigma_{a,t-1}$ is the conditional volatility of $R_{a,t}$
$\sigma_{b,t-1}$ is the conditional volatility of $R_{b,t}$
$\sigma_{ab,t-1}$ is the conditional covariance between $R_{a,t}$ and $R_{b,t}$
σ is a vector with three elements
β is a 3×3 matrix
γ is a 3×3 matrix.

With β and γ assumed to be diagonal for simplicity, a maximum likelihood estimate for the bivariate GARCH model (23) for heating oil (a) and crude oil (b) is given by

$$\begin{bmatrix} \sigma_{a,t}^2 \\ \sigma_{ab,t} \\ \sigma_{b,t}^2 \end{bmatrix} = \begin{bmatrix} .2963 \\ (1.9830) \\ .11408 \\ (1.6360) \\ .83939 \\ (1.5507) \end{bmatrix}$$

$$+ \begin{bmatrix} .15663 & 0 & 0 \\ (4.8101) & & \\ 0 & 1.3227 & 0 \\ & (3.5760) & \\ 0 & 0 & .13509 \\ & & (3.0763) \end{bmatrix} \begin{bmatrix} R_{a,t}^2 \\ R_{a,t}R_{b,t} \\ R_{b,t}^2 \end{bmatrix}$$

$$+ \begin{bmatrix} .81675 & 0 & 0 \\ (19.076) & & \\ 0 & .84643 & 0 \\ & (17.969) & \\ 0 & 0 & .86455 \\ & & (18.609) \end{bmatrix} \begin{bmatrix} \sigma_{a,t-1}^2 \\ \sigma_{ab,t-1} \\ \sigma_{b,t-1}^2 \end{bmatrix}$$

with t-statistics shown in parentheses. Note the differences between the univariate and multivariate GARCH parameters for heating oil (alone) and crude oil (alone). In principle, cross-market information can only improve the quality of the model if the multivariate model is appropriate. Figure 6 illustrates the fit of the multivariate GARCH model estimated above.

5. One month volatility forecasts – EGARCH

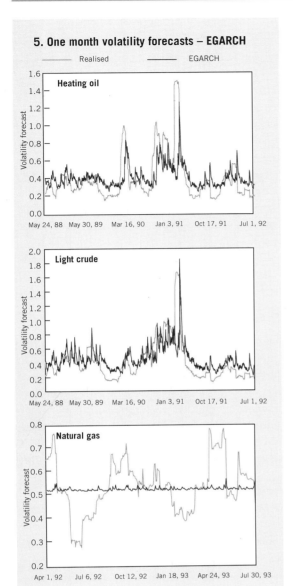

6. One month volatility forecasts – MV GARCH

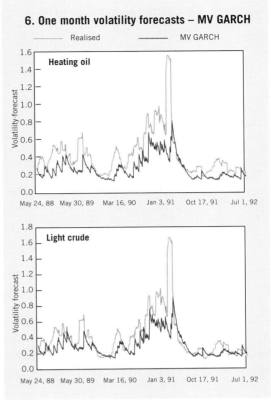

volatility settings, as shown by Duffie and Richardson (1991). The extent to which prices are martingales, however, improves the robustness of myopic hedges. See, for example, Duffie and Jackson (1990). Further progress in the ability to exploit stochastic volatility models in selecting dynamic hedging policies is reported by Schweizer (1993).

Cross-model comparisons

Table 4 overleaf provides a comparison of the performance of several stochastic volatility models as applied to heating oil, light crude oil and natural gas. Except where noted, we are comparing the quality of each of the following six models with regard to forecasting realised historical volatility:

i)   GARCH
ii)   EGARCH
iii)   bivariate GARCH
iv)   regime switching
v)   past historical volatility
vi)   Black-Scholes implied volatility.

For models (i) through (iv), the forecast $\bar{v}_{t,t+25}$ is as outlined above. For the "historical volatility" (v), we take $\hat{\sigma}_{t-25,t}$ as the forecast of its own future value, $\hat{\sigma}_{t,t+25}$. For the Black-Scholes implied volatility, we take the time series supplied to us by CRB Infotech, based on averaging near-the-money call and put implied

STOCHASTIC VOLATILITY AND DYNAMIC HEDGING POLICIES

Park and Bera (1987), Cecchetti, Cumby and Figlewski (1988), and Kroner and Sultan (1993) discuss the application of bivariate GARCH models to the choice of hedging positions. In general, there is an improvement, both within and outside of the sample period over which the model is estimated, of the quality of hedging positions suggested by the stochastic volatility model over those suggested by assuming constant covariances. These studies are limited to one-period hedges.

The dynamic-programming solution of multi-period hedges in the bivariate GARCH setting would, in general, imply different hedging coefficients, period by period, than those suggested by myopic (one-period-at-a-time) hedging. This is true even in deterministic

Table 4. Volatility forecast quality

| | Root mean squared error of forecasted volatility (%) | | | | |
| | In-sample | | | Out-of-sample | |
	Heating oil	Light crude	Natural gas	Heating oil	Light crude
GARCH	26	22	11	22	14
EGARCH	22	22	11	15	15
MV GARCH	25	23	N/A	N/A	N/A
Historical	29	26	15	15	8
Regime	24	26	11	N/A	N/A
Implied	21	17	N/A	12	4

volatilities for the next-to-expire exchange-traded options. (These implied-volatility averages are therefore usually *not* for options 25 days from expiration.) In each case, the root mean squared forecast error is in terms of annualised percentage volatility – that is, the unit normally used to quote implied volatility.

Table 4 is broken into two parts: "In Sample" and "Out of Sample". The distinction is important for those models, (i) – (iv), for which parameters must be estimated before a forecast can be calculated.

In the case of the in-sample forecasts, the parameters were estimated from the same historical period over which the forecasts were made. These "forecasts" are therefore not possible to make contemporaneously. The out-of-sample forecasts for models (i)–(iv) are based on parameters estimated during the earlier (in-sample) period. Such forecasts are therefore possible to obtain contemporaneously, and are perhaps more realistic for practical purposes.

Incidentally, one should not attempt to compare directly the out-of-sample forecast quality with the in-sample forecast quality, as these apply over different time periods, and the level of volatility appears to have been reduced during the out-of-sample period.

The distinction between in-sample and out-of-sample forecasts turned out to be important for the particular data set that we examined. As one can see from Table 4, the historical volatility estimator (which is always possible to produce contemporaneously, since there are no parameters to estimate in advance) was outperformed by models (i)–(iv) during the in-sample period, but then outperformed these same models (i)–(iv) during the out-of-sample period.

The Black-Scholes implied-volatility forecasts, which are always contemporaneously feasible, outperformed models (i)–(iv), as well as the historical volatility estimator, during both the in-sample and the out-of-sample periods. One can

also see that the forecast errors were generally much higher during the in-sample period, so this particular realisation of history treats models (i)–(iv) quite harshly.[19]

Nevertheless, it seems fair to conclude that, when available from options data, the Black-Scholes implied volatility is likely to be a more reliable method for forecasting volatility than the other methods that we examined. Somehow, implied volatility is capturing expectations of volatility held by traders, and those expectations appear to contain useful information that is not captured in a simple way by past returns.

Even when options data are not available, it seems unrealistic to conclude that models (i)–(iv) are of much assistance in improving the naive historical volatility estimator.

Of course, our empirical study is very preliminary; our principal ambition was to use this empirical test to illustrate some of the issues. In fact, we remain quite hopeful that sophisticated and carefully estimated econometric models of stochastic volatility will turn out to be much more useful when estimated with more data, and when used in conjunction with additional information (such as inventory levels, trading volume, price levels and cross-market volatility).[20]

Most promisingly, when options data are available, models of stochastic volatility can be constructed in which one uses options prices, possibly in conjunction with historical returns data, to estimate current volatility. In this case, one would estimate the parameters of a stochastic volatility model of the form (11)–(12) and apply a formula such as (13) (or extensions for more general cases) so as to infer the current level of volatility, σ_t. From σ_t and (11), one can then forecast volatility over future periods – by Monte Carlo simulation, if by no other means. The confounding effect of imperfect parameter estimation on volatility forecasts can be treated, again by Monte Carlo simulation if no more computationally efficient method can be designed.

Other volatility models and option hedging

Rubinstein (1994), Dupire (1992, 1994), and Derman and Kani (1994) have shown that one may take

$$\sigma_t = F(S_t, t) \qquad (24)$$

for some continuous function F so as to match

the modelled prices of traded options with the prices for these options that are observable in the market. For example, appropriate choice of F allows one to match the well known "smile" curve for Black-Scholes implied volatility as a function of exercise price. This is reminiscent of the idea of calibrating the parameters of a term-structure model of interest rates to the prices of bonds and option-embedded securities, as pursued earlier by Ho and Lee (1986), Black, Derman and Toy (1992), and Black and Karasinski (1993).

The Rubinstein model treats a family of options with a particular expiration date and varying strike prices, while the Derman-Kani and Dupire approach addresses options with different exercise dates and strikes. Underlying the approach is the idea that one can infer, from the family of available options prices, something about the risk-neutral probability distribution of the underlying asset or, equivalently, the "state prices", in the sense of Breeden and Litzenberger (1978).

The computation of the implied probability distribution function (or state prices) has been taken up by Banz and Miller (1978), Shimko (1993), and, in the context of crude oil markets, by Melick and Thomas (1993). Given the implied risk-neutral probability distribution function, one then determines the stochastic process for the underlying asset price, using some simple rules to construct a "tree" that is consistent with the probabilities assigned to prices at the exercise dates. The Derman-Kani and Rubinstein trees are "binomial" (two branches out of each node), while the Dupire tree is "trinomial". Dupire also has in mind a continuous-time process that is consistent with a binomial or trinomial discretisation.

An implication of the price-dependent volatility model (24) is that all options can be hedged merely by taking positions in the underlying asset, along with riskless borrowing and lending, an important distinction from the Markov models of stochastic volatility considered previously; in the latter case, hedging also calls for positions in other volatility-related positions, such as options. It seems likely that, in the energy markets, volatility is broadly affected by market-wide events of an unpredictable nature, such as wars, natural disasters and cartel discussions. The onset of such events apparently raises volatility in many markets simultaneously in a way that has little to do with the levels of individual asset prices. If this is indeed

the case, then (24) may be an inappropriate model for energy derivatives valuation and hedging.

For example, in times of dramatically changing volatility, we would guess that a hedge of a position in the energy markets with embedded options that is based on the "delta" from a model such as (24) could be improved by taking positions in the underlying commodity *as well as* positions in another option-related instrument.

It may be useful to model volatility that is both stochastic, as well as dependent on the price of the underlying commodity. For example, we may wish to replace the univariate Markovian stochastic volatility model (5) with

$$\sigma_t = F(\sigma_{t-1}, S_t, z_t, t) \qquad (25)$$

so that one combines the stochastic volatility approach with that of Rubinstein, Dupire and Derman-Kani. To our knowledge, this combined approach has not yet been explored in any practical way.

In continuous time, such a combined form of stochastic volatility might supplant the simpler model (11)–(12), under risk-neutral probabilities, with a stochastic differential equation for the volatility σ and asset price S of the form

$$d\sigma_t = a^*(\sigma_t, S_t, t)dt + b(\sigma_t, S_t, t)dZ_t^*$$
$$dS_t = rS_t dt + \sigma_t S_t dB_t^* \qquad (26)$$

where we can assume for simplicity that the riskless rate r is constant and that the risk-neutral Brownian motions Z^* and B^* have constant correlation. In this setting, the prices $C(\sigma_t, S_t, t)$ and $A(\sigma_t, S_t, t)$ of any two distinct options (having, for example, distinct strike prices or distinct expiration dates) would generally have different deltas with respect to both σ_t and S_t. These deltas (partial derivatives) are denoted $C_\sigma(\sigma_t, S_t, t)$ and $C_S(\sigma_t, S_t, t)$ for the first option and $A_\sigma(\sigma_t, S_t, t)$ and $A_S(\sigma_t, S_t, t)$ for the second option. From Ito's lemma and the absence of arbitrage, the first option price $Y_t = C(\sigma_t, S_t, t)$ satisfies

$$dY_t = rY_{dt} + C_\sigma(\sigma_t, S_t, t)b(\sigma_t, S_t, t)dZ_t^*$$
$$+ C_S(\sigma_t, S_t, t)\sigma_t S_t dB_t^*$$

This option can therefore be hedged by a dynamic trading strategy consisting of a portfolio (α_t, β_t) in the underlying asset and the second option, respectively, given by

$$\alpha_t = \frac{C_\sigma(\sigma_t, S_t, t)}{A_\sigma(\sigma_t, S_t, t)} A_S(\sigma_t, S_t, t)$$

$$\beta_t = \frac{C_\sigma(\sigma_t, S_t, t)}{A_\sigma(\sigma_t, S_t, t)} \qquad (27)$$

The residual capital necessary to finance this hedging strategy would, in theory, be obtained by riskless borrowing and lending. The option prices, deltas and trading strategies above can be computed for practical purposes using numerical methods, such as finite-difference schemes or Monte Carlo simulation, for solving the partial differential equations for C and A that arise in the usual way. See, for example, Hull (1993) or Duffie (1992) for a review. The major unknowns, of course, are the functions a^* and b in (26) – or, in discrete-time, the risk-neutral analogue of F in (25) – that determine the stochastic behaviour of volatility under risk-neutral probabilities. The simple models (25) and (26) could easily be expanded so as to allow path-dependence, or additional dependence on other state variables, as we have mentioned.

Of course, there are alternative models for volatility that go well beyond those that we have covered here. See, for example, Levy, Avellaneda and Paras (1994).

Concluding remarks

We have reviewed some of the basic approaches to modelling volatility that have been adopted for energy prices (and, in fact, most asset prices). The review above is not entirely comprehensive, but it does support the following basic conclusions.

Firstly, constant-volatility models, such as Black-Scholes, are a necessary starting point at a conceptual level, but are unreasonable for energy price data. They are, nevertheless, adequate for pricing near-to-expiration options, provided that the volatility coefficients used are consistent with contemporaneous option prices.

Secondly, stochastic volatility is persistent for energy prices. That is, when volatility is higher than "normal", it tends to stay higher for some time; when volatility is lower than "normal", it tends to stay lower for some time. This fact is apparent from market data (on squared returns and implied volatility), as well as from the esti-

mated coefficients of several standard models that we examined.

Thirdly, Black-Scholes option-implied volatility, when available, provides a more reliable forecast of future volatility than either historical volatility, or than can be obtained from the standard Markovian models of volatility that we have examined; the latter included simple regime-switching models and ARCH-based models such as GARCH, EGARCH and multivariate GARCH. (That is, although volatility is clearly stochastic, there are as yet no good models of stochastic volatility in energy prices.)

Fourthly, a reasonable test for the quality of a stochastic-volatility model is an out-of-sample measure of volatility forecast error. In-sample tests can be misleading. We also recommend, as a check of the quality of a stochastic volatility model, a measure of the accuracy of implied option hedges, such as the extent to which the payoff of a (possibly fictitious) option can be replicated by a dynamic trading strategy, such as that in (27), involving the underlying asset price and, possibly, other options for which market prices are available.

Finally, there is good reason to explore stochastic volatility models that incorporate one or more of the following features:
i) spreads between spot and forward prices;[21]
ii) inventory levels;
iii) price levels of the underlying asset;[22]
iv) the estimated level of volatility of related commodities;
v) volumes of trade;[23]
vi) implied volatilities from stochastic-volatility models.

Given the explanatory power of simple, unadjusted Black-Scholes implied volatility, the use of contemporaneous estimates of volatility based on available options prices and models of stochastic volatility – feature (vi) – seems especially promising to us.

A reasonable place to start is a model such as (26), in which the probability distribution of volatility shocks is assumed to depend on the current levels of the underlying asset price and of volatility itself. We regret that, due to lack of time and space, we have not yet pursued routes (i)–(vi) to better models of stochastic volatility. We encourage our readers to do so.

1 *Darrell Duffie can be contacted at the Graduate School of Business, Stanford University, Stanford CA 94305-5015; phone 415-723-1976. Stephen Gray is at the Fuqua School of Business, Duke University, Durham, NC 27708; phone 919-660-7786.*

We are grateful for assistance in obtaining data to Robert Jameson of Risk, Vince Kaminsky of Enron Capital & Trade Resources, and Joshua Sommer and Harold Lea of International Risk Control. We are also grateful for data from Platt's and from CRB Infotech. Support from the Financial Services Research Initiative is gratefully acknowledged. We are grateful as well for comments from Victor Ng, Jacques Gabillon, and Vince Kaminsky. Finally, we thank Robert Jameson of Risk for suggesting this chapter and for his help editing it.

2 *For such issues in the context of the term structure of interest rates, see for example Litterman and Scheinkman (1988).*

3 *This idea goes back at least to Beckers (1981).*

4 *Literally,* $\lim_{T\to\infty}\hat{\sigma}_{t,T}=\sigma$ *almost surely, and since an arbitrary number of observations of returns is assumed to be possible within an arbitrarily small time interval, this limit can be achieved in an arbitrarily small amount of calendar time.*

5 *There are of course good reasons to allow the mean return* μ *to vary with volatility, but we shall avoid this generality for expositional reasons.*

6 *For early models of this, see Clark (1973).*

7 *This fits into our general Markovian template (5) by taking* $F(v_a,z,t)=v_a$ *for all* $z\le z_a^*$ *where* z_a^* *is chosen so that the probability that* $z_t\le z_a^*$ *is* Π_{aa} *by taking* $F(v_a,z,t)=v_b$ *whenever* $z>z_a^*$, *and likewise for* $F(v_b,z,t)$.

8 *Because of this departure, equation (6) is slightly modified to account for the randomness in conditional mean returns.*

9 *Except that* $\log\varepsilon_t^2$ *is (by our assumption on* ε_t) *not normally distributed, this would be a standard setup for Kalman filtering of volatility. In such a setting, we would have access to standard methods for estimating volatility given the coefficients* α, γ, *and* κ, *and for estimating these coefficients by*

maximum likelihood. See for example, Brockwell and Davis (1992) for the consistency of the estimators in this setting.

10 *That is,* $\bar{\sigma}^2=\lim_t E(\sigma_t^2)$, *this limit existing if* $0<\gamma<1$.

11 *See for example Karatzas and Shreve (1988).*

12 *A qualification: if the underlying price process is continuously observable,* σ_t *is observable as the limit of historical volatility* $\hat{\sigma}_{t-\delta,t}$, *as* $\delta\downarrow 0$ *and the data frequency goes to infinity. This is not, however, a practical recipe.*

13 *For this equation, see for example Hull and White (1987).*

14 *This is known more precisely as the GARCH (1,1) model. For specifics and generalisations, as well as a review of the ARCH literature in finance, see for example Bollerslev, Chou and Kroner (1992).*

15 *The GARCH model is in the class (5) of Markov models since we can write* $\sigma_t=F(\sigma_{t-1},z_t)=[\alpha+\beta\sigma_{t-1}^2z_t+\gamma\sigma_{t-1}^2]^{1/2}$ *where* $z_t=\varepsilon_t$ *is white noise. Formally, this is known as a GARCH (1,1) model.*

16 *Note that* $\bar{\sigma}^2$ *is in fact the steady-state mean squared volatility,* $\lim_{T\to\infty}E(\sigma_t^2)$.

17 *The term* $\sqrt{2/\pi}$ *is equal to* $E_t[|(R_t-\mu)/\sigma_{t-1}|]$.

18 *This asymmetry was originally viewed by Nelson (1991), Schwert (1989), and Campbell and Kyle (1993) as important for stock returns.*

19 *One should also note that all of our forecast methods are subject to a bias due to Jensen's Inequality, since we are measuring forecasts of the square root of average future squared returns, whereas our models only claim to be unbiased forecasts of the squares of this quantity.*

20 *See Lamoreux and Lastrapes (1993).*

21 *See Ng and Pirrong (1992, 1994).*

22 *See Dupire (1992, 1994), Derman and Kani (1994) and Rubinstein (1994).*

23 *See Lamoreux and Lastrapres (1993).*

BIBLIOGRAPHY

R. Baillie and R. Myers, 1991, "Modeling Commodity Price Distributions and Estimating the Optimal Futures Hedge", *Journal of Applied Econometrics*, vol. 6, pp. 109-24

R. Banz and M. Miller, 1978, "Prices for State-Contingent Claims: Some Evidence and Applications", *Journal of Business*, vol. 51, pp. 653-72

S. Beckers, 1981, "Standard Deviations Implied in Option Process as Predictors of Future Stock Price Variability", *Journal of Banking and Finance*, vol. 5, pp. 363-82

F. Black and P. Karasinsky, 1991, "Bond and Option Pricing when Short Rates are Log-Normal", *Financial Analysts' Journal*, pp. 52-59

F. Black and M. Scholes, 1973, "The Pricing of Options and Corporate Liabilities", *Journal of Political Economy*, no. 81, pp. 637-59

F. Black, E. Derman and W. Toy, 1990, "A One-Factor Model of Interest Rates and its Applications to Treasury Bond Options", *Financial Analysts Journal*, January-

February, pp. 33-9

T.Bollerslev, 1986, "Generalised Autoregressive Conditional Heteroskedasticity", *Journal of Econometrics*, vol. 31, pp. 307-27

T. Bollerslev, R. Chou and K. Kroner, 1992, "ARCH Modeling in Finance: A Review of Theory and Empirical Evidence", *Journal of Econometrics*, vol. 52, pp. 5-59

D. Breeden and R. Litzenburger, 1978, "Prices of State-Contingent Claims Implicit in Options Prices", *Journal of Business*, vol. 51, pp. 621-51

P. Brockwell and R. Davis, 1987, *Time Series: Theory and Methods*, New York

J. Campbell and A. S. Kyle, 1993, "Smart Money, Noise Trading and Stock Price Behavior, Review of Economic Studies", vol. 60, pp. 1-34

S. Cechetti, R. Cumby and S. Figlewski, 1988, "Estimation of the Optimal Futures Hedge", *Review of*

Economics and Statistics, vol. 70, pp. 623-30

P. Clark, 1973, "A Subordinated Stochastic Process Model with Finite Variance for Speculative Prices", *Econometrica* vol. 41, pp. 135-55

J. Cox and M. Rubinstein, 1985, *Options Markets*, Englewood Cliffs

S. Dasgupta, 1992, *Pricing Futures Options with Stochastic Volatility: Early Exercise, Incomplete Markets, and Maximum Likelihood Estimation of Parameters*, New York

E. Derman and I. Kani, 1994, "Riding on the Smile", *Risk*, February, 1994, pp. 32-9

D. Duffie, 1992, *Dynamic Asset Pricing Theory*, Princeton University Press

D. Duffie and M. Jackson, 1990, "Optimal Hedging and Equilibrium in a Dynamic Futures Market", *Journal of Economic Dynamics and Control*, vol. 14, pp. 21-33

D. Duffie and H. Richardson, 1991, "Mean-Variance Hedging in Continuous-Time", *Annals of Applied Probability*, vol. 1, pp. 1-15

B. Dupire, 1992, "Arbitrage Pricing with Stochastic Volatility", Société Générale, Paris

B. Dupire, 1994, "Pricing with a Smile", *Risk*, January, 1994, pp. 18-20

R. Engle, 1982, Autoregressive Conditional Heteroskedasticity with Estimates of The Variance of United Kingdom Inflation, *Econometrica,* vol. 50, pp. 987-1008

M. Garman and M. Klass, 1980, "On the Estimation of Security Volatilties from Historical Data", *Journal of Business*, vol. 53, pp. 67-78

V. Genon-Catalot and J. Jacod, 1993, "On the Estimation of the Diffusion Coefficient for Multi-Dimensional Diffusion Processes", *Annales Institut Henri Poincare*, vol. 29, pp. 119-51

S. Gray, 1993, *Regime-Switching Models of Volatility*, Graduate School of Business, Stanford University

J. Hamilton, 1990, "Analysis of Time Series Subject to Changes in Regime", *Journal of Econometrics*, vol. 45, pp. 39-70

A. Harvey and N. Shepard, 1993, "The Econometrics of Stochastic Volatility", LSE Financial Markets Group Discussion Paper Number 166, London School of Economics

A. Harvey, E. Ruiz and N. Shepard, 1992, "Multivariate Stochastic Variance Models", LSE Financial Markets Group Discussion Paper, London School of Economics

S. Heston, 1993, "A Closed-Form Solution for Options with Stochastic Volatility, with Applications to Bond and Currency Options", *Review of Financial Studies*, vol. 6, pp. 327-44

R. Heynen and H. Kat, 1993, "Volatility Prediction: A Comparison of the Stochastic Volatility, GARCH(1,1) and EGARCH(1,1) Model", Department of Operations Research, Erasmus University

T. Ho and S. Lee, 1986, "Term Structure Movements and Pricing Interest Rate Contingent Claims", *Journal of Finance*, vol. 41, pp. 1011-29

J. Hull, 1993, *Options, Futures, and Other Derivative Securities*, Second Edition, Englewood Cliffs

J. Hull and A. White, 1987, "The Pricing of Options on Assets with Stochastic Volatilities", *Journal of Finance*, vol. 42, pp. 281-300

H. Johnson and H. Shanno, 1987, "The Pricing of Options when the Variance is Changing", *Journal of Financial and Quantitative Analysis*, vol. 22, pp. 143-51

I. Karatzas and S. Shreve, 1988, *Brownian Motion and Stochastic Calculus*, New York

K. Kroner and J. Sultan, 1993, "Time-Varying Distributions and Dynamic Hedging with Foreign Currency Futures", *Journal of Financial and Quantitative Analysis*, vol. 28, pp. 535-51

C. Lamoreux and W. Lastrapes, 1993, "Endogenous Trading Volume and Momentum in Stock Return Volatility", Olin School of Business, Washington University, St. Louis, forthcoming: *Journal of Business Economics and Statistics*

A. Levy, M. Avellaneda and A. Paras, 1994, "A New Approach for Pricing Derivative Securities in Markets with Uncertain Volatilities: A 'Case Study' on the Trinomial Tree", Courant Institute of Mathematical Sciences, New York University

R. Litterman and J. Scheinkman, 1988, "Common Factors Affecting Bond Returns", Goldman-Sachs, Financial Strategies Group

W. Melick and C. Thomas, 1993, "Recovering an Asset's Implied PDF From Option Prices: An Application to Crude Oil during the Gulf Crisis", Federal Reserve Board, Washington DC

A. Melino and S. Turnbull, 1990, "Pricing Foreign Currency Options with Stochastic Volatility", *Journal of Econometrics*, vol. 45, pp. 239-65

D. Nelson, 1990, "ARCH Models as Diffusion Approximations", *Journal of Econometrics*, vol. 45, pp. 7-39

D. Nelson, 1991, "Conditional Heteroskedasticity in Asset Returns: A New Approach", *Econometrica*, vol. 59, pp. 347-70

D. Nelson, 1992, "Filtering and Forecasting with Misspecified ARCH Models I: Getting the Right Variance with the Wrong Model", *Journal of Econometrics*, vol. 52, pp. 61-90

V. Ng and C. Pirrong, 1992, "The Relation between Oil and Gasoline Futures and Spot Prices", School of Business, University of Michigan, and Midamerica Institute

V. Ng and C. Pirrong, 1994, "Fundamentals and Volatility: Storage, Spreads, and the Dynamics of Metals Prices", *Journal of Business*, vol. 67, pp. 203-30

A. Park and A. Bera, 1987, "Interest Rate Volatility, Basis Risk, and Heteroskedasticity in Hedging Mortgages", *AREUEA Journal*, vol. 15, pp. 79-97

M. Parkinson, 1980, "The Extreme Value Method for

Estimating the Variance of The Rate of Return", *Journal of Business*, vol. 46, pp. 434-52

E. Renault and N. Touzi, 1992, "Stochastic Volatility Models: Statistical Inference from Implied Volatilities Working Paper", GREMAQ, IDEI, and CREST, France

C. Rogers and L. Satchell, 1991, "Estimating Variance from High, Low, and Closing Prices," *Annals of Applied Probability*, vol. 1, pp. 504-12

M. Rubinstein, 1994, "Implied Binomial Trees", Haas School of Business, University of California, Berkeley

M. Schweizer, 1993, "Approximating Random Variables by Stochastic Integrals", Working Paper, University of Bonn

W. Schwert, 1989, "Why Does Stock Price Volatility Change

Over Time?", *Journal of Finance*, vol. 44, pp. 1115-53

L. Scott, 1987, "Option Pricing when the Variance Changes Randomly: Theory, Estimation, and an Application", *Journal of Financial and Quantitative Analysis*, vol. 22, pp. 419-38

D. Shimko, 1993, "Bounds of Probability", *Risk*, April 1993, pp. 33-7

H. Stoll and R. Whaley, 1993, *Futures and Options: Theory and Applications*, Cincinnati

J. Wiggins, 1987, "Option Values Under Stochastic Volatility: Theory and Empirical Estimates", *Journal of Financial Economics*, vol. 19, pp. 351-72

Valuing Energy Derivatives

Kaushik Amin, Victor Ng and S. Craig Pirrong[1]

Lehman Brothers, The International Monetary Fund, The University of Michigan

The great expansion in the variety and the volume of trading in energy derivatives in recent years has created a need for new analytical tools to price energy-contingent claims. In this chapter, we review some of the relevant techniques available in the literature to value energy claims, and we interpret the models used to value other securities in the context of energy derivatives.

In particular, our focus will be on models that take the current term structure of futures or forward prices as given, and then value options and other types of derivatives based on this term structure. The use of the entire term structure makes the models more general than the standard Black (1976) model that is often used to price commodity-contingent claims. Moreover, the simultaneous modelling of the evolution of the entire term structure unifies the pricing and risk management of a portfolio of energy derivative positions. This is of great practical importance to the market participants who trade these claims.

Since we are interested in valuing claims that are based on the entire term structure of futures prices, we first need to understand the relationship between futures contracts of different maturities. This will provide some guidelines on how we can model the evolution of futures prices. Therefore, in the first section of this chapter, we discuss the implications of the theory of storage for the relationship between spot, forward and futures prices, and how that relationship is affected by fundamental supply and demand conditions. In particular, since supply and demand conditions for energy products have strong seasonal elements, the relationship between the spot and futures prices will be seasonal as well. These patterns need to be modelled and explicitly considered in the pricing of energy derivatives.

Furthermore, such relationships can be stochastic in nature, as supply and demand conditions change unpredictably – and this must

also be incorporated into the valuation exercise. Therefore, in the second section of this chapter, we present an extension of the framework in Black (1976) which allows for seasonality in a deterministic way. A closed-form solution for the price of a European futures option is given for a one-factor model that only permits parallel shifts in the term structure of futures prices. A binomial-tree approach for the valuation of American options is also introduced. Further, the valuation of options in a multi-factor model using a Monte Carlo approach, such as that described in Cortazar and Schwartz (1992), is discussed.

In the third section of this chapter we consider the more general case, in which the relationship between the spot and futures prices is stochastic. A two-factor model which extends the Gibson and Schwartz (1990) model is presented. However, in contrast to Gibson and Schwartz, we model the evolution of the entire term structure of futures prices.[2] The model permits non-parallel shifts in the term structure; a closed-form solution for the price of a European futures option is provided, and a tree approach to valuing American options is also introduced.

In this chapter, we will focus mainly on arbitrage-free approaches to the valuation of options. We will not discuss in any detail those models which require assumptions about investor preferences (or the market price of risk), as these are of less practical use. Furthermore, we do not discuss the pricing of futures contracts, as this pricing is exogenous to our framework.

Relationship between the spot, forward and futures prices

A distinguishing feature of the energy futures market is the behaviour of the term structure of futures prices. This term structure describes how futures prices depend upon time-to-contract expiration. For energy products, the term structure exhibits a variety of shapes. Moreover, the energy futures term structure varies substantially and unpredictably over time.

Given that the behaviour of the term structure is such a salient feature of energy prices, a contingent claim pricing model should be predicated upon a firm understanding of the factors that determine this behaviour. This section provides an analysis of the relationship between spot, forward and futures prices, and a brief discussion of the factors that determine the evolution of the term structure of energy futures prices; a more detailed discussion of the relationship between these factors can be found in Chapter 1 of this book. The sections below build upon this theory of the term structure to derive contingent claim pricing models that are applicable to energy derivatives.

Let $S(t)$ be the current spot price of a commodity and $F(t,T)$ be the forward price at date t to deliver one unit of the commodity at date T. For simplicity, we assume that the commodity can be delivered against the forward contract only on the expiration date T. In other words, we ignore the delivery option whereby the party at the short side of the contract can choose to deliver the commodity at any point in the delivery month (or week). We also assume that there exists a forward price for every maturity date T up to some finite maturity date T_m.

Since we focus on the term structure of futures prices, and its effect on the valuation of energy derivatives, we further assume that interest rates are known (deterministic). Given deterministic interest rates, forward prices will equal futures prices, as described by Jarrow and Oldfield (1981). Therefore, the futures price of the commodity at date t for delivery at date T is also equal to $F(t,T)$. This assumption of deterministic interest rates can be relaxed, as described by Amin and Bodurtha (1994), only at the expense of added complexity.

Arbitrage implies a mathematical relationship between futures prices with different maturities, and between spot and futures prices. The textbook example of such a relationship is the traditional "cost-of-carry" model, which states that the futures price must exceed the spot price by the cost of carrying inventory. Formally, let $r(u)$ be the instantaneous forward interest rate at date u, and $w(u)$ be the instantaneous storage cost at date u measured as a proportion of the spot price, which is also known at time t. Then,

$$F(t,T) = S(t)\exp\left[\int_t^T \left[r(u) + w(u)\right]du\right] \quad (1)$$

An examination of spot and futures prices

reveals that this relationship seldom, if ever, holds in the energy markets. With a few exceptions (such as occurred in 1986, or late 1993 and early 1994 when the price of oil collapsed), energy futures prices are typically lower than predicted by the simple cost-of-carry model. This is because of the phenomenon known as the "convenience yield", which is described in detail in Chapter 1.

The convenience yield affects the relationship between the energy spot and futures prices in the same way that a dividend yield affects the relation between the value of a stock index and a futures contract on that index. Specifically, it drives the futures price below the level implied by the pure cost-of-carry model because it reduces the opportunity cost of holding inventories.

Formally, one may define $y(t,u)$ as the instantaneous convenience yield, as perceived by the marginal storers at date t, arising from having a unit of the commodity in inventory at date u. The relation between the spot and futures prices is then given by:

$$F(t,T) = S(t)\exp\left[\int_t^T \left[r(u) + w(u) - y(t,u)\right]du\right] \quad (2)$$

To avoid excessive notation, we can rewrite the above equation as:

$$F(t,T) = S(t)\exp\left[\int_t^T \left[r(u) - z(t,u)\right]du\right] \quad (3)$$

where $z(t,u) = y(t,u) - w(u)$ is now the instantaneous forward convenience yield net of physical storage cost. To avoid confusion, we will still refer to $z(t,u)$ as the instantaneous forward convenience yield. Further, $z(t) \equiv z(t,t)$ will be referred to as the spot convenience yield.

Intuitively, the above relationship suggests that, in equilibrium, the marginal holder of inventories must be indifferent as to whether she holds the spot commodity or a futures contract. If this investor holds the spot, she has to finance the initial purchase price $S(t)$ at prevailing interest rates, but she also receives the convenience yield of holding the spot asset in inventory. If expression (3) holds, the payoffs to the futures contract and a position in the spot commodity are identical over the interval from t to T. Put another way, in equilibrium the convenience yield earned on stocks exactly offsets the expected capital loss on these stocks when (3) holds.

It is evident from an examination of (3) that the behaviour of the convenience yield has an important effect on the dynamics of energy futures prices, and therefore upon the prices of energy options, swaps, and swaptions as well.

An economic model called the "theory of storage" has important implications regarding the evolution of the convenience yield. These implications can be incorporated into a model for pricing energy contingent claims. Specifically, the theory predicts that the convenience yield should increase as supplies decline and/or demand increases. This is true because the convenience yield measures the marginal value of a unit of the commodity in store. Given demand, this marginal value should increase as the available supply declines. Similarly, given the available supply, this marginal value should increase as the demand for the commodity increases. This also necessarily implies a relation between the level of inventory and the convenience yield. In particular, the convenience yield should vary inversely with the level of inventory.[3]

As a concrete example, consider the heating oil and natural gas markets. During a cold snap, the demand for these products increases. This is typically associated with a decrease in the level of inventory, an increase in the overall levels of natural gas and heating oil prices and an increase in convenience yields. That is, during cold snaps the price of gas or heating oil for immediate delivery increases relative to its price for deferred delivery. In this situation, the term structure of futures prices exhibits less "carry", or a more pronounced backwardation.

Moreover, since demand for some energy products (especially natural gas and heating oil) is seasonal, this relation between demand and the convenience yield implies that the term structure of futures prices may exhibit pronounced seasonalities. For example, the ratio between the January and March heating oil futures prices is typically greater than the ratio between the March and June heating oil futures prices. This pattern reflects the fact that the demand for heating oil is high in the winter months, and low in the summer months.

Furthermore, since supply and demand vary unpredictably, the convenience yield should vary unpredictably as well. Uncertain and changing weather conditions are primary sources of convenience yield variability in some energy products. Similarly, unexpected disruption of supply, such as that caused by the Gulf War, or changes such as the explosion of refining capacity, have caused pronounced shifts in the shape of the term structure in the past. Business cycle fluctuations can also unexpectedly change the term structure. All else equal, an unexpected increase in aggregate economic activity tends to cause a rise in convenience yields.

No discussion of the supply conditions in the energy markets would be complete without mentioning the effects of the Organisation of Petroleum Exporting Countries (OPEC). The collapse of the cartel in 1986 caused an unexpected glut of oil which drove down the general level of oil prices and forced the crude oil futures price term structure into a nearly full "carry" situation. A similar glut in early 1994 had a similar effect on the level and shape of the crude oil term structure.

Finally, the convenience yield should be mean reverting. That is, if the convenience yield is unusually high (low) at time t, it should tend to decline (increase) as time progresses after t. This mean reversion reflects the ability of economic agents to adjust supply and demand over time. For example, a high convenience yield for heating oil implies that inventories are very valuable. Refiners can respond to such a situation by increasing production runs, or perhaps activating idle capacity, in order to expand output and replenish stocks. These activities tend to reduce the convenience yield, but they cannot be effected instantaneously. Thus, a large increase or decrease in the convenience yield tends to induce consumption and production responses that gradually drive the yield back towards a "normal" level. The expectation of a long-run adjustment process also tends to make the short end of the term structure more volatile than the long end.[4]

In the next section of this chapter, we will discuss the valuation of energy derivatives when the term structure of convenience yields is deterministic, but can exhibit seasonality. In the following section, we will consider the more general case when the convenience yields are stochastic and mean reverting.

Option valuation with deterministic convenience yields

The simplest framework used to value general commodity options is that of Black (1976). Some additional details on the valuation of American options in this framework are given in Brenner, Courtadon and Subrahmanyam (1985). This framework can be used to value energy options. However, Black (1976) focuses only on the valuation of options based on a single futures price.

In the first subsection immediately below, we will modify Black's framework in a simple man-

VALUING

ENERGY

DERIVATIVES

ner to incorporate the entire term structure of futures prices in the spirit of term-structure models by Ho and Lee (1986), Heath, Jarrow and Morton (1992), and Amin and Jarrow (1991). Matching the initial term structure and modelling the evolution of the entire term structure of futures prices in a consistent way are important to guarantee that the model is arbitrage free, and that it can be applied to more general types of options such as American options on the spot price or swaptions – which cannot be valued in the Black (1976) framework. The subsections after this will examine, in turn, the valuation of European-type contracts; American-type options; and the valuation of options in a multifactor model, like that in Cortazar and Schwartz (1992), using a Monte Carlo approach.

AN EXTENSION OF THE BLACK (1976) FRAMEWORK

Since futures prices of different maturities are related indirectly through the spot-futures parity relation expressed in equation (3), one approach when building a consistent model for the evolution of the entire term structure of futures prices is to specify the dynamics of the spot price and the term structure of convenience yields to preclude arbitrage.

Initially, we assume that the convenience yields are deterministic. In this case, specifying the dynamics of the spot price and the initial term structure of convenience yields completely specifies the model, since the futures prices at future dates can be determined from the spot/futures parity relation (3) and the known convenience yields. In this setup, the spot price and the futures prices of all maturities are governed by the same underlying source of uncertainty. The model is based on a single risk factor and, therefore, all the futures prices are instantaneously perfectly correlated.

Let the spot price at date t evolve over time according to the stochastic differential equation:

$$dS(t) = \mu(t)S(t)dt + \sigma S(t)dW_1(t) \quad (4)$$

where $\mu(t)$ is the deterministic drift of the spot price, σ is the constant instantaneous volatility, and $W_1(t)$ is a Brownian motion. It is possible to permit σ to be a deterministic function of time without changing the essence of the arguments to follow. For simplicity, we will initially maintain the constant volatility assumption. Writing the spot price process in stochastic integral form, we have:

$$S(t) = S(0)\exp\left[\int_0^t \left(\mu(u) - \sigma^2/2\right)du + \sigma W_1(t)\right] \quad (5)$$

Since $W_1(t)$ is normally distributed with mean 0 and variance t, the logarithm of the relative spot price $(S(t)/S(0))$ at date t is normally distributed with mean $\int_0^t (\mu(u) - \sigma^2/2)du$ and variance $\sigma^2 t$.

The theory of storage developed in the previous section implies that the forward price at date 0 for delivery at date T is given by the relation:

$$F(0,T) = S(0)\exp\left[\int_0^T \left(r(u) - z(0,u)\right)du\right] \quad (6)$$

where $z(0,u)$ is the forward convenience yield at date 0 for maturity date u and $r(u)$ is the spot interest rate at date u. Since we assume that interest rates are deterministic, $r(u)$ is equal to the current instantaneous forward interest rate for maturity u. Therefore, the current term structure of interest rates is easily incorporated. Given the current spot price and the term structure of forward or futures prices for every maturity, we can compute the initial term structure of convenience yields from equation (6).

At any future date t, if we are given the spot price within the model, then under the assumption of deterministic convenience yields and interest rates, the term structure of futures prices for all maturities can be computed using the theory of storage relation:

$$F(t,T) = S(t)\exp\left[\int_t^T \left(r(u) - z(t,u)\right)du\right] \quad (7)$$

with deterministic convenience yields, $z(t,u) = z(0,u)$.

Therefore, to compute option prices, it is sufficient to model the evolution of the spot price. All of the futures prices can be computed using the storage relation in (7).

To understand the dynamics of the futures prices implied by equation (7), we will now write down the stochastic integral representation for all the futures prices. Using (7),

$$d\log F(t,T) = d\log S(t) - \left[r(t) - z(t,t)\right]dt \quad (8)$$

Substituting for $d\log S(t)$ from (4), we obtain

$$d\log F(t,T) =$$
$$\left[\mu(t) - \sigma^2/2 - r(t) + z(t,t)\right]dt + \sigma dW_1(t) \quad (9)$$

or, in stochastic integral form,

$$F(t,T) = F(0,T)$$
$$\exp\left[\int_0^t \left(\mu(u) - \sigma^2/2 - r(u) + z(u,u)\right)du + \sigma dW_1(t)\right] \quad (10)$$

Therefore, given the futures price for maturity

T at the initial date 0, the logarithm of the relative futures price $(F(t,T)/F(0,T))$ for that maturity at any subsequent date t is normal with mean $\int_0^t (\mu(u) - \sigma^2/2 - r(u) + z(u,u))du$ and variance $\sigma^2 t$.

A crucial feature of this framework is that the futures prices of all maturities are governed by the same shock $W_1(t)$. Therefore, the model is based on a single risk factor and the futures prices of all maturities are instantaneously, perfectly correlated. If the volatility parameter σ is independent of the futures maturity date T, then it is apparent from (9) that the futures term structure is subject only to parallel shocks. In that sense, our model is analogous to the Ho and Lee (1986) model of the term structure of interest rates.

Another possible approach is to specify the model directly in terms of the different futures prices, and to simply define the spot price as $S(t) = F(t,t)$. That is, we can specify the entire futures term structure as:

$$d\log F(t,T) = \left[\alpha(t,T) - \sigma^2/2\right]dt + \sigma dW_1(t) \quad (11)$$

or

$$F(t,T) = $$
$$F(0,T)\exp\left[\int_0^t \left[\alpha(u,T) - \sigma^2/2\right]du + \sigma W_1(t)\right] \quad (12)$$

The entire term structure of futures prices is governed by the same Brownian motion $W_1(t)$. The link between the specifications specified by (12) and (9) is readily apparent if we simply redefine $\alpha(u,T)$ in equation (12) to be $\mu(u) - r(u) + z(u,u)$. In this case, the two specifications are equivalent. Further, the term structure of convenience yields in (12) is given implicitly by the relation:

$$F(t,T) = F(t,t)\exp\left[\int_t^T \left(r(u) - z(t,u)\right)du\right] \quad (13)$$

In this framework, we can also permit the futures prices of different maturities to be affected differently by the shock $W_1(t)$ by specifying σ to be a function of the futures maturity T. However, the futures prices are still instantaneously perfectly correlated. In this case, we obtain a one-factor version of the model in Cortazar and Schwartz (1992). To permit independent variation in futures prices of different maturities, we can add additional Brownian motions on the right-hand side in (11), with different volatility coefficients for different maturities. For example, consider the following specification for futures prices:

$$d\log F(t,T) = $$
$$\left[\alpha(t,T) - \sigma_1^2(t,T)/2 - \sigma_2^2(t,T)/2\right]dt \quad (14)$$
$$+ \sigma_1(t,T)dW_1(t) + \sigma_2(t,T)dW_2(t)$$

This specification permits futures prices to be affected by two independent shocks (Brownian motions) $W_1(t)$ and $W_2(t)$. Each of these shocks can impact futures contracts of different maturities in different ways. That is, the volatility corresponding to each of these shocks can be different for different maturities. Therefore, we represent each of the volatilities $\sigma_1(t,T)$ and $\sigma_2(t,T)$ as explicit functions of the futures maturity. These volatility functions can be determined by a principal component analysis or a maximum likelihood factor analysis, as in Cortazar and Schwartz (1992). Furthermore, in a more general setup, the number of independent shocks (factors) that affects the entire term structure of forward prices can also be estimated jointly with the volatility functions.

The model specified directly in terms of the futures prices, as in (14), is very general. However, for the valuation of more complicated derivatives such as swaptions or American options, it is not easily amenable to numerical computations and requires the use of tedious procedures such as Monte Carlo simulation or path-dependent models (see Amin and Bodurtha, 1994) except under restrictive specifications of the type specified in the penultimate section of this chapter. A brief description of the Monte Carlo simulation method to value European-style options is given later on in this section.

Furthermore, computing American option prices is difficult. In contrast, our simple model represented by (4) and (9) or (11) is easily amenable to computations for most kinds of derivatives, as we will show in the next subsection of this chapter.

The major innovation in our framework, as compared to Black (1976), is its simultaneous modelling of the evolution of the entire futures term structure using (10), conditional upon the initial futures term structure (or the convenience yields). This feature permits the valuation of options on futures with different maturities, options on the spot asset, commodity swaptions etc in a single unified framework. It also permits us to hedge all these claims within a single "book". This feature is in the spirit of Ho and Lee (1986) and Heath, Jarrow and Morton

(1992), who take the initial term structure of interest rates as given and then model the simultaneous evolution of the entire term structure of interest rates. The specific model developed above is a special case of the model in Amin and Jarrow (1991) which contains a stochastic term structure of interest rates, a stochastic asset and a stochastic term structure of yields. Our model obtains if we assume a deterministic yield and deterministic interest rates in the Amin and Jarrow (1991) framework. The model is similar to that proposed by Jamshidian (1992).

This completes the description of our model setup. Now we will focus on the valuation of options based on the term structure of futures prices.

RISK-NEUTRAL VALUATION OF EUROPEAN OPTIONS

We will refer to the economic model described so far as the "true model" or the "true economy". However, for the purpose of option valuation, we will transform the true economy into a risk-neutral economy. This transformation is now the standard technique for option valuation. For a description of this technique, see Jarrow and Rudd (1983).

In the risk-neutral economy, investors price all future cash flows at their expected values, discounted back to the current date using the risk-free interest rate. Alternatively, the expected return on all assets (both risky and risk-free) in this risk-neutral economy equals the riskless rate of return. Therefore, once the transformation to the risk-neutral economy is accomplished, we can value an option by computing its expected payoff when it is exercised, and then discounting this payoff to the current date using the riskless interest rate. In our model, there is only one source of uncertainty, $W_1(t)$, affecting the entire term structure of futures prices. Therefore, we can replicate the cash flows from any option dependent on the term structure of futures prices by dynamically trading a riskless bond and a single futures contract. This condition implies that our economic model is dynamically complete and permits the construction of the risk-neutral economy. We now describe its construction.

Since the futures contract does not require an initial investment and continuously pays the change in the futures price, in a risk-neutral world, the expected change in the futures price must be zero. In the risk-neutral economy, the

futures prices of all maturities therefore satisfy the equation:

$$dF(t,T)/F(t,T) = \sigma dW_1^*(t) \qquad (15)$$

where $W_1^*(t)$ is a Brownian motion in the risk-neutral economy.

Similarly, since the spot asset requires an initial investment equal to the spot price, unlike the futures contract, an investment in the spot asset must earn a return equal to the riskless return less the convenience yield earned from holding the riskless asset. That is, the spot price distribution is specified by:

$$dS(t)/S(t) = \left[r(t) - z(t,t)\right]dt + \sigma dW_1^*(t) \qquad (16)$$

or

$$d\log S(t) = \left[r(t) - z(t,t) - \sigma^2/2\right]dt + \sigma dW_1^*(t) \qquad (17)$$

Since investors are risk-neutral in this economy, options can be valued by their expected discounted payoffs. A European call option with maturity date τ on the futures contract with futures maturity T will have a price given by:

$$c[t,F(t,T)] = $$
$$E_t^*\left[\exp\left[-\int_t^\tau r(u)du\right]Max\left[F(\tau,T) - K,0\right]\right] \qquad (18)$$

where K is the strike price of the option and E is the conditional expectation given the information set at date t under the risk-neutral distributions given by equations (15) and (16).

By substituting the futures price distribution from (15) into (18) and simplifying, we obtain:

$$c[t,F(t,T)] = $$
$$\exp\left[-\int_t^\tau r(u)du\right]\left[F(t,T)N(d_1) - KN(d_2)\right] \qquad (19)$$

where $N(.)$ is the normal cumulative distribution function,

$$d_1 = \left[\log\left[F(t,T)/K + \sigma^2(\tau-t)/2\right]/\left[\sigma\sqrt{(\tau-t)}\right]\right]$$

and

$$d_2 = d_1 - \sigma\sqrt{(\tau-t)}$$

Similarly, a European futures put option has a value:

$$p[t,F(t,T)] = $$
$$\exp\left[-\int_t^\tau r(u)du\right]\left[KN(-d_2) - F(t,T)N(-d_1)\right] \qquad (20)$$

Since the futures price equals the spot price at the futures maturity, a European call (put) option on the spot commodity has the same value as a European futures call (put) option with the same maturity if the underlying futures maturity is the same as the option maturity. We can also rewrite these formulae in terms of the spot price by substituting equation (7) into the above formulae.

It is interesting to note that the formulae (19) and (20) for the European call and put options on the spot and the futures still hold even if the model for the evolution of futures prices is specified as a multifactor Cortazar and Schwartz (1992) model, as in a K-factor version of equation (14). All we require is that the volatility functions $\sigma_j(.)$ be a function only of calendar time and maturity. Then, the futures price of a given maturity is lognormal and European call and put prices at date t are given by (19) and (20) with σ^2 replaced by the average proportional variance of the futures price during the remaining life of the option, that is:

$$\int_t^\tau \text{Var}\left[dF(t,T)/F(t,T)\right]/(\tau-t) \qquad (21)$$

The key is that this variance is deterministic, and therefore can be computed at the current date t. For additional details, see Amin and Jarrow (1991).

VALUATION OF AMERICAN OPTIONS AND OTHER OPTIONS

Most listed and OTC options are of the American type, whereby the owner is permitted to exercise the option at any date prior to maturity. Further, closed-form solutions cannot be derived for other types of derivative securities such as swaptions. In this section, therefore, we show how our simple model can be discretised so that option values for which closed-form solutions are not available can also be computed.

To value an American option, we need to evaluate the expression:

$$C(t) = \max_\theta E_t^*\left[\exp\left[-\int_t^\theta r(u)du\right]g(\theta)\right] \qquad (22)$$

Where $g(\theta)$ is the cashflow to the American option if exercised at date θ and the maximum is taken over all possible early exercise strategies θ. For example, one possible early exercise strategy is to exercise the option the first time that it crosses a particular boundary in the futures price versus time state space. The standard technique to compute option values is to approximate the spot price or futures price distribution by a discrete binomial-type model. The option value at the option maturity date τ is

known as a function of the spot or futures price at that date. Given the terminal option prices, we can obtain the option price by working backwards in time through the tree representing the state space of the futures prices over time. The option value at any given node in the tree is equal to the maximum of the value if exercised at the current node, and the expected value in the next period, discounted back to the current period.

Consider an option with maturity τ years. Suppose we wish to value this option using a discrete approximation with N time steps. Therefore, the length of each time step is:

$$h = \tau/N \qquad (23)$$

The spot commodity is the primary security in our framework. All futures (forward) prices can be computed as a function of the spot price using equation (7). Therefore, to value any claim, it is sufficient to build a discrete-time model which approximates the risk-neutral spot price distribution given by:

$$S(t) =$$
$$S(0)\exp\left[\int_0^t\left[r(u)-z(u,u)-\sigma^2/2\right]du+\sigma W_1^*(t)\right] \qquad (24)$$

Over a small time interval of duration h, the commodity price change can be represented by the equation:

$$S(t+h) =$$
$$S(t)\exp\left[\int_t^{t+h}\left[r(u)-z(u,u)-\sigma^2/2\right]du\right.$$
$$\left.+\sigma\left[W_1^*(t+h)-W_1^*(t)\right]\right] \qquad (25)$$

This distribution can be approximated with a binomial distribution given by:[5]

$$S(t+h) =$$
$$\begin{cases} S(t)\exp\left[\mu^*(t)h+\sigma\sqrt{h}\right] & \text{with prob } \frac{1}{2} \\ S(t)\exp\left[\mu^*(t)h-\sigma\sqrt{h}\right] & \text{with prob } \frac{1}{2} \end{cases} \qquad (26)$$

where,

$$\mu^*(t)h = \int_t^{t+h}\left[r(u)-z(u,u)-\sigma^2/2\right]du \qquad (27)$$

is the drift of the term inside the exponent in (25). Figure 1 depicts the evolution of the commodity price using this binomial distribution (26) over three periods, each of length h.

Any option can now be valued on the state space tree depicted by Figure 1 overleaf and (26). We first compute the value of the option at each of the nodes at maturity as a function of

1. Binomial tree for commodity price evolution

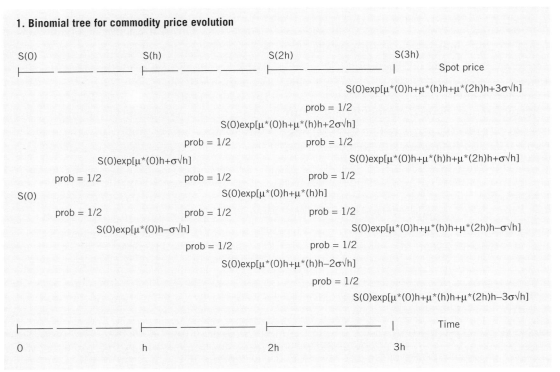

the spot commodity price at that node. If the option value depends on the futures or forward prices, then these prices can be computed using the cost-of-carry relationship in (7). Then, we step back one time-step and value the option as the expected value in the next time period, discounted back to the current time period. That is, when C(t) is the value of the option at time t, the computation of option prices is given by the equation:

$$C(t) = E_t^* \left[C(t+h) \exp\left[-\int_t^{t+h} r(u)du \right] \right] \quad (28)$$

An American-style option which can be exercised early, can be valued by using the alternative equation:

$$C(t) = Max \left[g(t), E_t^* \left[C(t+h) \exp\left[-\int_t^{t+h} r(u)du \right] \right] \right] \quad (29)$$

where g(t) is the payoff if the option is exercised at date t in the current state.

For an American call option on the spot asset with a strike price K, g(t) = Max[S(t) – K, 0]. For the corresponding American futures call option on the futures contract with maturity T, g(t) = Max[F(t,T) – K,0]. This model can now be used to value very general claims dependent on the term structure of futures prices.

VALUATION OF EUROPEAN-STYLE OPTIONS USING MONTE CARLO METHODS
The discrete-time binomial style model developed in the previous section, as well as its con-

tinuous-time limit used to compute closed-form solutions for European option prices, impose strong restrictions on the volatility of the commodity price. In particular, we required the volatility to be constant. Further, the model implies that the volatilities of the futures prices of all maturities are also identical. When we wish to incorporate more general volatility functions (for example, as a function of the levels of futures prices), then closed-form solutions for European options cannot be derived and binomial-style discrete approximations are also very difficult to build. In this situation, Monte Carlo simulation can be used to compute European-style option prices, but with significant computation effort. However, it is extremely difficult to value American options in this framework.

Consider a multifactor generalisation of the two-factor model in (14):

$$dlog F(t,T) = \left[\alpha(t,T) - \sum_{j=1}^N \sigma_j^2(t,T)/2 \right] dt + \sum_{j=1}^N \sigma_j(t,T)dW_j(t) \quad (30)$$

In this specification, the volatility functions $\sigma_j(t,T)$'s can be some arbitrary functions of time t, maturity T or even the level of futures prices.

In the risk-neutral economy, as we argued earlier, the expected change in the futures price should be zero. Therefore, for option valuation, the risk-neutral distributions of the futures prices are represented by:

$$d\log F(t,T) =$$

$$\left[-\sum_{j=1}^{N}\sigma_j^2(t,T)/2\right]dt + \sum_{j=1}^{N}\sigma_j(t,T)dW_j^*(t) \quad (31)$$

where W_j^*'s are independent Brownian motions in the risk-neutral economy. Equation (31) is the starting point of the approach in Cortazar and Schwartz (1992). In this case, the number of factors and the volatility functions can be determined by a principal component analysis or maximum likelihood factor analysis, as in Cortazar and Schwartz (1992). We describe this in a little bit more detail in the next paragraph.

Specifically, suppose $\sigma_i(t,T_j)$ is a constant for all i and maturity T_j, then $\sigma_i(t,T_j)$ can be estimated as $\beta_{ij}\sqrt{\alpha_i}$. Where α_i is the ith largest eigenvalue of the covariance matrix of the vector of futures returns: $(d\log F(t,T_1), d\log F(t,T_2), ..., d\log F(t,T_m))'$, and β_{ij} is the jth element of the eigenvector corresponding to α_i. As another example, suppose $\sigma_i(t,T_j)$ takes the functional form $\delta_{ij}\exp(-(T_j-t))$, then $\sigma_i(t,T_j)$ can be estimated as $\exp(-(T_j-t))\beta_{ij}\sqrt{\alpha_i}$, where α_i is the ith largest eigenvalue of the covariance matrix of the vector of transformed futures returns: $(w_1 d\log F(t,T_1), w_2 d\log F(t,T_2), ..., w_m d\log F(t,T_m))'$, w_j is defined as equal to $\exp(T_j-t)$ and β_{ij} is the jth element of the eigenvector corresponding to α_i. If $\sigma_i(t,T_j)$ takes a very general nonlinear functional form, then the computationally simple principal component analysis cannot be conveniently applied. In this case, a full fetch maximum likelihood factor analysis needs to be performed.

Since we are in a risk-neutral economy, the value of a European option which pays $g(\tau)$ at the expiration date τ is given by:

$$C(t) = E_t^*\left[g(\tau)\exp\left[-\int_t^\tau r(u)du\right]\right] \quad (32)$$

To compute the value of this expression, we need to compute the distribution of the futures prices at date τ and then integrate the option payoff with respect to this distribution. In general, this distribution cannot be obtained in closed form. However, we use the fact that increments to a Brownian motion are normally distributed with mean zero and variance equal to the elapsed time to build the distribution of the futures prices. Consider a discretisation of (31) to generate the distribution of futures prices at some future date. Let the time interval be discretised by: $[0, h, 2h, ..., t, t+h, t+2h, ...]$ for some sufficiently small time interval h. Suppose we consider the increment to the log of the

futures prices of all maturities over the time interval $[t, t+h]$, that is, $\log F(t+h,T) - \log F(t,T)$ for all maturities T. Then, equation (31) implies that $\log F(t+h,T) - \log F(t,T)$ can be approximated by:

$$\log F(t+h,T) - \log F(t,T)$$
$$= \left[-\sum_{j=1}^{N}\sigma_j^2(t,T)/2\right]h + \sum_{j=1}^{N}\sigma_j(t,T)\varepsilon_j^*(t)\sqrt{h} \quad (33)$$

where $\varepsilon_j^*(t)$'s are independent at date t and are also serially independent and normally distributed random variables with mean zero and variance 1.

The term $\varepsilon_j^*(t)\sqrt{h}$ approximates the increment to the jth Brownian motion from t to $t+h$. We can generate a sequence of $(\varepsilon_1^*(t), \varepsilon_2^*(t), ..., \varepsilon_N^*(t))$'s, one for each discrete date $0,h,2h,...$ and then recursively compute the value of the futures prices at future dates using (33). This yields one possible realisation (path of futures prices) in the approximation scheme represented by (33). Note that the futures prices of all maturities are simultaneously computed using the same values of $(\varepsilon_1^*(t), \varepsilon_2^*(t), ..., \varepsilon_N^*(t))$ for $t=0,h,2h,....$ Therefore, the single realisation corresponds to a path of all the futures prices of all maturities. To generate the entire distribution of futures prices, we need to repeatedly sample $(\varepsilon_1^*(t), \varepsilon_2^*(t), ..., \varepsilon_N^*(t))$ for $t=0,h,2h,...$ and generate futures prices from (33). Option prices can be computed by integrating (averaging over the different realisations) over this distribution.

For example, consider an option which has a payoff of $g(\tau)$ at date τ as some function of the realisation of the path of futures prices up to date τ. Then, the price of the option is given by:

$$C(t) = E_t^*\left[\exp\left(-\int_t^\tau r(u)du\right)g(\tau)\right] \quad (34)$$

The option being considered above can also be an Asian option or other type of exotic option, as long as the option does not permit early exercise. For example, the price of an Asian call option which is dependent on the average futures price from time s to τ is given by:

$$C(t) = E_t^*\left[\exp\left(-\int_t^\tau r(u)du\right)\right.$$
$$\left.\text{Max}\left(0,(1/(\tau-s))\int_s^\tau F(u,T)du\right)-K\right] \quad (35)$$

where K is the exercise price and τ is the expiration date of the option. To compute the option price, we need to compute the expectation in (34) as described below.

For each simulated price path, the term

inside the expectation can be computed. This yields the realised price of the option under that realisation. To compute the current price of the option today, we take the average over a large number of realisations so that the price of the option does not change if we increase the number of realisations (in most cases, 10,000 realisations will prove more than sufficient).[6]

Option valuation with stochastic convenience yields

As we discussed at the beginning of this chapter, convenience yields are affected by supply and demand conditions and hence can exhibit seasonal patterns. Our treatment above allows deterministic (but seasonal) convenience yields. However, since relative supply and demand conditions can also change unpredictably from time to time, the convenience yields are likely to have a stochastic component. Allowing the convenience yields to be random enriches the one-factor model we described in the previous section. In the one-factor model, futures prices of all maturities are perfectly correlated and the term-structure of futures prices is subject only to parallel shocks. By permitting the convenience yields to be stochastic, independent variation between the futures prices of different maturities can occur.

We will model the entire term structure of convenience yields, and then price options based on the evolution of this term structure. Our approach is arbitrage-free, as we do not require any additional assumptions except the absence of arbitrage once the dynamics of the futures prices are specified. It is worthwhile to mention an alternative modelling method in which only the evolution of the spot price and the instantaneous convenience yield is specified. Futures prices (in addition to the prices of options) in these models are endogenously determined within the model, as a function of the spot price and the instantaneous convenience yield only.

For an example of this approach, see Gibson and Schwartz (1990). Their approach requires additional assumptions on investors' preferences, and requires the specification of the market price of risk of the instantaneous convenience yield. Further, it has difficulty matching the initial term-structure of futures prices. Since our main objective in this chapter has been to price options rather than the underlying futures contracts, we do not discuss these issues in more detail. In order to price futures within the same

framework, the approach followed by Gibson and Schwartz (1990) would be necessary.

THE EVOLUTION OF THE TERM STRUCTURE OF CONVENIENCE YIELDS

For simplicity, we will focus on a model in which forward convenience yields of all maturities are subject to a single source of uncertainty. Furthermore, we will directly specify the evolution of convenience yields in the risk-neutral economy rather than in the true economy. Let the term structure of forward convenience yields $z(t,T)$ for all maturities T, in the risk-neutral economy, be governed by the stochastic differential equation:

$$dz(t,T) = \beta(t,T)dt + \delta(t,T)dW_2^*(t) \qquad (36)$$

It is worthwhile to note that the entire term structure of convenience yields is governed by the same Brownian motion $W_2^*(t)$. Further, we permit the Brownian motion $W_2^*(t)$ to have a constant correlation ρ with $W_1^*(t)$. For simplicity, we assume that $\delta(t,T)$ is a deterministic function of time and maturity. This function and the correlation parameter ρ constitute the parameter inputs. The function $\beta(t,T)$ is determined inside the model, as we will show in following paragraphs.

In the risk-neutral economy, the convenience yield drift $\beta(t,T)$ must be such that the expected change in the futures prices of all maturities is zero. As noted in the previous chapter section, a futures contract does not require any initial investment. Therefore, its expected price change in a risk-neutral economy must be zero. This condition provides the relationship between the convenience yield drifts, $\beta(t,T)$, and the volatility structure of convenience yields. The value of $\beta(t,T)$ in the true economy is irrelevant from the perspective of valuation.

The relationship between the futures and spot price derived earlier is given by:

$$F(t,T) = S(t)\exp\left[\int_t^T \left(r(u) - z(t,u)\right)du\right] \qquad (37)$$

By substituting the stochastic differential equation for $z(t,u)$ and $S(t)$ into the above equation and simplifying, we can write down the stochastic differential equation for $F(t,T)$ as:[7]

$$dF(t,T)/F(t,T) = \sigma dW_1^*(t) - \left[\int_t^T \delta(t,u)du\right]dW_2^*(t) \qquad (38)$$

Further, our Appendix to this chapter also shows that the drift $\beta(t,T)$ must satisfy the relation:

$$\beta(t,T) = \delta(t,T)\left[\int_t^T \delta(t,u)du - \sigma\rho\right] \qquad (39)$$

That is,

$$dz(t,T) =$$

$$\delta(t,T)\left[\int_t^T \delta(t,u)du - \sigma\rho\right]dt + \delta(t,T)dW_2^*(t) \quad (40)$$

From (38), the instantaneous proportional variance of the futures price of maturity T at date t is therefore given by:

$$\zeta^2(t,T) = \sigma^2 + \left[\int_t^T \delta(t,u)du\right]\left[\int_t^T \delta(t,u)du - 2\rho\sigma\right] \quad (41)$$

The volatility is given by the square root of the above expression, that is $\zeta(t,T)$. Further, the futures price is lognormal with volatility $\zeta(t,T)$. Therefore, the value of a European futures option is given by the Black (1976) formula, by substituting $\zeta(t,T)$ for the volatility.

That is, the price of a European call option with maturity date τ on the futures contract with futures maturity T is given by:

$$c[t,F(t,T)] =$$

$$\exp\left[-\int_t^\tau r(u)du\right]\left[F(t,T)N(\gamma_1) - K\,N(\gamma_2)\right] \quad (42)$$

where $N(.)$ is the normal cumulative distribution function,

$$\gamma_1 = \left[\log\left[F(t,T)/K\right] + \eta^2(t,\tau,T)(\tau-t)/2\right]/$$

$$\left[\eta(t,\tau,T)\sqrt{(\tau-t)}\right]$$

$$\gamma_2 = \gamma_1 - \eta(t,\tau,T)\sqrt{(\tau-t)}$$

and

$$\eta^2(t,\tau,T) = \left(1/(\tau-t)\right)\int_t^\tau \zeta^2(u,T)du$$

Our framework with a stochastic convenience yield term structure is therefore similar to Black's (1976) framework, except that we explicitly specify the link between futures contracts of different maturities and the link between the spot and futures prices. This link is important for valuing American options on the spot price based on the current term structure of futures prices. It is also important for valuing options whose prices depend on the entire term structure of futures prices, for example swaptions. At any date, the swap value is a function of the entire futures curve. Therefore, the theory must *simultaneously* model the evolution of futures prices of all maturities.

In actual implementation, we need to assume a parsimonious form for $\delta(t,T)$. The exact function, $\delta(t,T)$, can then be estimated from the futures returns based on (38) with the drift term included or, more appropriately, from the return on the price spread between futures contracts of different maturities. To the extent that the $\delta(.)$ functions are reasonably stable through time, these can be estimated historically using the maximum likelihood technique. The model then contains only two unestimated parameters, σ and ρ, which can be implied out from the previous day's option prices.

To the extent that the correlation parameter is reasonably stable, it can also be determined by historical data analysis. In this case, only σ needs to be determined by the implied method. Alternatively, if the function $\delta(.)$ involves only one or two parameters, which are common across all maturities, then, provided that a relatively large number of options are available, these parameters can be implied out simultaneously from the previous day's option prices.

An alternative method of constructing a two-factor model is to model the term structure of futures prices directly with two factors, as in equation (14). It is possible to show that these methods are equivalent from a theoretical perspective. However, specifying the model in terms of convenience yields is more intuitive, since it permits a better understanding of the relationship between futures contracts of different maturities. Moreover, if we choose a particular volatility structure for the convenience yields, our model permits the construction of a discrete time approximation with a lattice structure similar to Figure 1. This discretisation will be described in the following subsection.

A TREE APPROACH TO VALUING AMERICAN AND OTHER OPTIONS

Simple European-style options on the spot or futures can be valued using the Black (1976) formula with the volatility $\eta(t,T)$. To value more complicated options, such as Asian options or lookback options or European-style swaptions, we can use a Monte Carlo simulation of equations (17) and (36) or (38). It is straightforward to implement our model using this technique.[8]

American-style options can be valued with a discrete-time version of our model. With general volatility functions, the techniques developed in Amin and Bodurtha (1994) are applicable. A detailed description of the discretisation procedure is beyond the scope of the current chapter. Here, we describe a discretisation procedure when $\delta(t,T) = \delta$ is a constant (independent of t or T). Then, it is possible to build a path-independent discrete-time tree such that the discrete-time distribution of the state variables converges to the continuous-time distributions given by (5) and (38) as the discrete time interval $h \to 0$.

The tree for the state variables describes the evolution of the spot price $S(t)$ and the entire term structure of convenience yields $z(t,T)$. The futures prices at any date can be computed as functions of these state variables. Suppose the tree up to date t has already been constructed. We permit four possible states given by A, B, C, and D, to occur at the next date $t+h$. Under each of these states, the spot price $S(t)$ and all the convenience yields $z(t,T)$ can be updated for their possible values at date $t+h$, according to Table 1.

Table 1 yields a tree for the evolution of the state variables in which, given a current state, there are four possible nodes at the next date. For example, state A corresponds to both the spot price and the convenience yields increasing, whereas state C corresponds to the spot price decreasing and the convenience yields increasing. Another notable feature is that the entire term structure of convenience yields can be updated at each date using the table. Further, from a computational perspective, the tree is path independent: the order of occurrence of the different states over time is irrelevant.

For example, the occurrence of state A in the first period, followed by state D in the second period, yields the same values of all the state variables as state D in the first period followed by state A in the second period. Therefore, the number of nodes in the tree after n time steps is only $(n+1)^2$. This implies that the computational effort for computing even long maturity option values is quite manageable.

An important feature of our tree is that the probability that each state (A, B, C, or D) will occur is not the same at all nodes in the tree. The probabilities depend on the current spot convenience yield $z(t,t)$. Once the state space represented by a tree has been constructed, option values can be computed using the same procedure as described in the previous section of this chapter, using equation (27).

This completes our description of the model with stochastic convenience yields.

Applications and limitations

In this chapter, we have presented a unified approach for pricing energy derivative products. One of the salient features of energy derivative products is that the term structure of futures prices depends upon convenience yields. These convenience yields can cause the term structure of futures prices to slope upwards or slope downwards, or to vary non-monotonically with maturity. The models derived herein explicitly incorporate this convenience yield feature in order to determine how it influences the pricing of energy contingent claims. Our first, and simpler, model assumes that convenience yields are deterministic; whereas the model described in the last section considers the more complex and more realistic case in which the convenience yields vary stochastically.

In addition to the added realism arising from the incorporation of convenience yields into the pricing formulae, the valuation models presented herein offer several advantages to the practitioner. Specifically, unlike the standard Black (1976) model, these models can be used to price American options, Asian options and swaptions. Moreover, all of these various types of contingent claims can be priced within a single unified framework. Finally, and perhaps most importantly, using these models, a portfolio of energy-contingent claims can be hedged within a single "book". This last feature simplifies substantially the task of managing the risk of a portfolio of energy derivatives.

Finally, we should discuss some of the limitations of our approach in this chapter. We have assumed that the maturity of each futures contract is known and that delivery occurs only on the maturity date. However, there are delivery timing options embedded in exchange-traded futures contracts. Incorporating this feature is quite difficult since it requires an explicit framework to value the delivery option of the short.

Table 1: Single period distribution of the spot price and convenience yields

Variable	Increment over (t,t+h)	Risk-neutral probability	State
$\log[S(t+h)/S(t)]$ $z(t+h,T)-z(t,T)$	$[r(t)-\sigma^2/2]h + \sigma\sqrt{h}/2$ $\beta(t,T)h + \delta\sqrt{h}$	$[1- z(t,t)\sqrt{h}/\sigma]/4$	A
$\log[S(t+h)/S(t)]$ $z(t+h,T)-z(t,T)$	$[r(t)-\sigma^2/2]h + \sigma\sqrt{h}/2$ $\beta(t,T)h - \delta\sqrt{h}$	$[1- z(t,t)\sqrt{h}/\sigma]/4$	B
$\log[S(t+h)/S(t)]$ $z(t+h,T)-z(t,T)$	$[r(t)-\sigma^2/2]h - \sigma\sqrt{h}/2$ $\beta(t,T)h + \delta\sqrt{h}$	$[1 + z(t,t)\sqrt{h}/\sigma)/4$	C
$\log[S(t+h)/S(t)]$ $z(t+h,T)-z(t,T)$	$[r(t)-\sigma^2/2]h - \sigma\sqrt{h}/2$ $\beta(t,T)h - \delta\sqrt{h}$	$[1 + z(t,t)\sqrt{h}/\sigma]/4$	D

For long-term options, ignoring this delivery option is not likely to introduce significant valuation errors. However, for short-term options, this delivery option may be quite important.

A second limitation of our approach is the assumption that the volatility of the spot asset is constant. In the energy markets, the theory of storage implies that the volatility is higher when inventories are low, and that the volatility is lower when inventories are high. Since there is a negative relationship between the convenience yield and inventories, this implies a positive relationship between the spot volatility and the level of convenience yields. This feature cannot be incorporated in our simple framework without significantly complicating the model and making the computational task much more difficult.[9]

A final limitation of our approach is the assumption of deterministic interest rates. For long-term options (with maturities greater than three years), the stochastic nature of interest rates will also have some influence on option values. Incorporating the entire term structure of interest rates once again introduces an additional risk factor, which also makes the model more complicated.[10]

1 *Kaushik Amin, Lehman Brothers; Victor Ng, Capital Market and Financial Studies Division, The International Monetary Fund; S. Craig Pirrong, School of Business Administration, The University of Michigan. Please address all correspondence to: Dr. Victor K. Ng, Capital Market and Financial Studies Division, Research Department, International Monetary Fund, 700 19th Street N.W., Washington D.C. 20431. Tel 1 202 623 7671. Fax 1 202 623 6339. Email: vng@imf.org.*

The authors would like to thank Vince Kaminski of Enron, Frédéric Barnaud of Elf Trading SA and, particularly, the editor, Robert Jameson for very useful comments. The views expressed in this paper are those of the authors and do not necessarily represent those of the International Monetary Fund.

2 *As in Heath, Jarrow and Morton (1992) for interest rates or Amin and Jarrow (1991) for risky assets.*

3 *See Ng and Pirrong (1993) and (1994) for an analysis of the theory of storage.*

4 *See Ng and Pirrong (1993) and (1994) for evidence on the*

mean reversion of convenience yields in refined petroleum and industrial metal products, and the greater volatility of the spot than the futures prices associated with this long-run adjustment process. Also see Gabillion, in Chapter 1 of this book, for a discussion of the mean-reverting property of the oil spot and futures prices.

5 *See Amin (1991) for a similar discretisation.*

6 *For details, see Boyle (1977).*

7 *See Appendix A for details.*

8 *See Boyle (1977) for a description of Monte Carlo methods applied to option pricing.*

9 *For details on how the above issues can be accommodated, see Amin, Ng and Pirrong (1994).*

10 *Some work along these lines is given in Amin and Jarrow (1991).*

BIBLIOGRAPHY

Amin, K.I., 1991, "On the Computation of Continuous Time Options Prices Using Discrete Approximations", *Journal of Financial and Quantitative Analysis*, 26, pp. 477–96.

Amin, K.I., and J.N. Bodurtha, 1994, "Discrete-time Option Valuation with Stochastic Interest Rates", forthcoming, *Review of Financial Studies*.

Amin, K.I., and R.A. Jarrow, 1991, "Pricing Foreign Currency Options Under Stochastic Interest Rates", *Journal of International Money and Finance*, 10, pp. 310–30.

Amin, K.I., and R.A. Jarrow, 1991, "Pricing Options on Risky Assets in a Stochastic Interest Rate Economy", *Mathematical Finance*, no. 2, pp. 217–38.

Amin, K.I., V.K. Ng, and C. Pirrong, 1994, "Arbitrage Free Valuation of Commodity Options with Stochastic Volatility and Convenience Yields", technical report, University of Michigan.

Black, F., 1976, "The Pricing of Commodity Contracts", *Journal of Financial Economics*, 3 (1/2), pp. 167–79.

Boyle, P.P., 1977, "Options: A Monte Carlo Approach", *Journal of Financial Economics*, 4, pp. 323–8.

Brenner, M., G. Courtadon, and M. Subrahmanyam, 1985, "Options on the Spot and Options on Futures", *Journal of Finance*, 40, pp. 1303–17.

Cortazar, G., and E. Schwartz, 1992, "The Valuation of Commodity Contingent Claims", technical report, Anderson Graduate School of Management, University of California, Los Angeles.

Gibson, R. and E.S. Schwartz, 1990, "Stochastic Convenience Yield and the Pricing of Oil Contingent Claims", *Journal of Finance*, vol. XLV, no. 3, 959–76.

Heath, D., R.A. Jarrow and A. Morton, 1992, "Bond Pricing and the Term Structure of Interest Rates: A New Methodology", *Econometrica*, 60, pp. 77–105.

Ho, T.S.Y., and S.B. Lee, 1986, "Term Structure Movements and Pricing Interest Rate Contingent Claims", *Journal of Finance*, 41, pp. 1011–29.

Jamshidian, F., 1992, "Commodity Option Evaluation in

the Gaussian Futures Term Structure", *Review of Futures Markets*, 11, pp. 325–46.

Jarrow, R.A., and G. Oldfield, 1981, "The Relationship Between Forward and Futures Prices", *Journal of Financial Economics*, 9 (4), pp. 373–82.

Jarrow, R.A., and A. Rudd, 1983, *Option Pricing*, Irwin, New York.

Ng, V.K., and S.C. Pirrong, 1992, "The Relation Between Crude Oil, Heating Oil, and Gasoline Futures and Spot Prices", *Mid-America Institute Research Report*, Mid-America Institute, Chicago, IL.

Ng, V.K., and S.C. Pirrong, 1993, "Price Dynamics in Physical Commodity Spot and Futures Markets: Spread, Spillovers, Volatility and Convergence in Refined Petroleum Products", Mitsui Life Financial Research Center Working Paper, University of Michigan.

Ng, V.K., and S.C. Pirrong, 1994, "Fundamentals and Volatility: Storage, Spreads, and the Dynamics of Metal Prices", *Journal of Business*, vol. 67, no.2 (April), pp. 203–30.

4

Correlation in the Energy Markets

Ewan Kirk

J Aron

Many of the risks that lie at the heart of the energy business – proxy hedge risk, crack risk, cross commodity risk and refining margin risk – depend on the degree of *correlation* between two or more products or securities. By understanding and managing this *correlation risk*, energy producers and consumers can manage their risk more effectively and efficiently.

Correlation will be defined formally later in this chapter, but it can be described most simply as "the tendency of two measures to move together". It is important to stress at the outset that correlation is not the same as *causation*. Two sets of numbers that have a correlation greater than zero need not be causally related. For example, although the population in Wales is declining and the membership of Greenpeace is increasing, these two time series are unlikely to be causally related. This example is intuitive, but some apparent correlations between markets may not, in fact, be causally related.

Conversely, the price of the May 1995 IPE Brent Contract is fairly well correlated to the price of the May 1995 IPE Gasoil Contract – and this positive correlation is causal for obvious structural reasons.

In this chapter, we will be interested only in those correlations which are known to be causal. First, we will look at some of the general implications of correlation when trading in the energy markets. We will then explore how correlation is calculated and, in Panel 1, examine how traders can avoid some of the common problems encountered when deriving correlation coefficients from energy market data. We will then look at how correlation is used when proxy hedging and when dealing in spread and crack options. Finally, we will analyse how correlations are calculated and applied when constructing the most correlation-dependent of exotic options: the "basket option".

Correlation and market dynamics

There are many areas of the energy market where causal correlations are fundamental to an understanding of market dynamics. For example, it is expected that the individual months in a series of futures prices will be reasonably well correlated to each other. That is, movements in one particular future will be strongly correlated with movements in the futures that expire one month before and one month after it.

It is also true that this correlation deteriorates as the futures come closer to expiry. The reason for this is easy to see. The energy futures markets are intimately related to the market for physical cargoes of oil which are delivered by producers to consumers. Short-term effects, such as weather, industrial problems or political strife, can disrupt this short-term physical market. However, by their very nature, these disruptions can only be priced into the short-term futures market. One can be sure that a problem on a North Sea platform will cause "tightness" in the Brent market next month, but it is difficult to predict the political strife that may happen three years hence. Therefore, there is no particular reason for a future contract with 24 months until expiry to be priced radically differently from a future contract with 23 months until expiry.

Indeed, were traders in 1995 to see June 1997 WTI priced at 50 cents higher than July 1997 WTI, then they would have to see some pretty convincing reasons as to why they should not sell June 1997 and buy July 1997. However, there are numerous valid reasons as to why prompt WTI might be 50 cents over second month WTI and, indeed, might have a very low correlation to the price of the second month.

Furthermore, the spreads (or price differentials) between each commodity also show these correlation effects. If we look at the historic data in the over-the-counter (OTC) market, we can observe that the spread between Brent and WTI for the year 1997 very rarely changes. The movements in WTI are very well correlated with the movements in Brent.

What is the reason for this? As explained above, there is limited information available now with regard to events that may alter the spread between WTI and Brent in 1997. As a result, the long-dated Brent market is often priced by traders as a constant spread off WTI. One can look at this the other way round and say that traders are assuming that the correlation between Brent and WTI is very high in the long-dated market.

Of course, as time progresses it can become apparent that a correlation is not, in fact, stable. It changes in just the same way that prices, spreads and volatilities can change. This may happen because of changes in market conditions or in market fundamentals. For example, the correlation between Low Sulphur Fuel Oil and High Sulphur Fuel Oil has shown a gradual decline over the last few years, as illustrated in Figure 1.

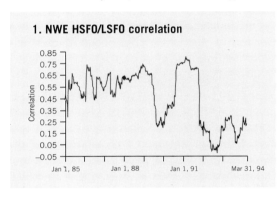

1. NWE HSFO/LSFO correlation

This correlation has reduced over time due to the reducing liquidity in the high sulphur fuel oil market; this in turn has been caused by a lessening of demand for environmental reasons.

This brings up the question of what participants in the energy markets can do if they buy a product or design a hedge that depends on correlation, only to find that the expected correlation does not materialise. This is an especial concern when dealing with energy derivatives. In other derivative markets, and particularly in the currency markets, there are many products that depend implicitly or explicitly on the correlation between two assets. Therefore, if a trader takes a position which depends on the correlation between two assets, there is a good chance of hedging the correlation exposure exactly by taking an opposite correlation position in a different financial product. In the energy markets, it is rare that this can be done and, therefore, market participants are usually exposed to an unhedgeable correlation risk.

To use a volatility analogy, if we buy an option at 24% volatility and we do not hedge our volatility exposure, there is little or nothing that we can do if the volatility turns out to be 10%. If we expect this to continue to the expiry of the option, then all we can do is mark our books accordingly.

However, this effect is only true if we are delta hedging our exposure. If we buy an option and do not delta hedge, then we are completely unconcerned with the level of volatility. We are only concerned with the volatility as it affects the absolute price of the option. To see this more clearly, consider the example of buying a call struck at the money. If the market goes up by 1% every day, the actual volatility will be zero, but the trader will end up with a handsome payout from the option if the option expires with the future above the strike plus the premium that she or he has paid for the option.

This is to be expected. If one buys an option and delta hedges it, one is making a statement about volatility. One is saying, "I think volatility will be higher than the implied volatility I bought this option at." If one buys an option and does not delta hedge it, one is making a statement about the absolute price such as, "I think the market is going up. In particular, I think the market is going up above the strike plus the premium I have to pay", or, "If the market goes below this value, I cannot run my business profitably".

As we shall see later, in pricing options which depend on correlation, the expected correlation in the future comes into the formula in the form of the *effective volatility* or the *cross volatility* between the two assets. Therefore, if you are buying or selling an option which depends on correlation because you expect that correlation to rise or fall, you must delta hedge the exposure that the option gives you.

Conversely, if you are buying or selling a spread option because you wish to protect your business from adverse movements in the spread, then the actual correlation between the two commodities over the life of the option is immaterial. The *implied correlation* from the option price is only important in that it affects the premium for that option.

How is correlation measured?

Correlation is normally measured on a scale of −1 to 1, although it may also be quoted as a percentage. If two sets of numbers have a correlation of 1, they are perfectly correlated; as one moves up, the other one moves up. If they have a correlation of −1, as one moves up, the other moves down. If two sets of numbers have a correlation close to zero, they are said to be *uncorrelated* and they have no relation to each other.

Assume that we have two time series x and y, whose means are x̄ and ȳ. The *covariance* of x and y may then be defined as:

$$Cov(x,y) = \sigma_{xy} = E((x - \bar{x})(y - \bar{y}))$$

and the correlation is:

$$Corr(x,y) = \frac{\sigma_{xy}}{\sigma_x \sigma_y}$$

where σ_x is the standard deviation of x. Note that:

$$Corr(x,x) = \frac{\sigma_{xx}}{\sigma_x \sigma_x} = \frac{E((x - \bar{x})^2)}{\sigma_x \sigma_x} = \frac{\sigma_x \sigma_x}{\sigma_x \sigma_x} = 1$$

You can use a similar derivation to the above to show that $Corr(x,-x) = -1$.

Formulae to calculate the coefficients in a variety of ways can be found in any statistics text book.[1] Like many other participants in the energy derivatives business, the author uses standard libraries for statistics such as those found with popular spreadsheets and programming languages.[2]

For the same reasons that we use the standard deviations of the returns on an asset in calculating historical volatility, we use the correlation of the *returns on an asset* on the sample. These returns are measured as:

$$r = \frac{p_1 - p_0}{p_0}$$

and correlations are taken from these.

In the case of financial time series, we often have a large number of data points. For example, we might look at Dated Brent daily prices over a period of ten years. If we wanted to estimate the correlation of Dated Brent with NWE Gasoil Cargoes CIF, how should we do it? Should we calculate this correlation over the entire sample or should we take a sub-sample? This problem is very similar to that of estimating the volatility of a commodity from historical data.

Volatility is defined as the annualised standard deviation of the returns. However, how much of the sample should be used in this estimate? In the case of volatility, practitioners often use a rolling 20-day or 60-day window. Any

point on a graph of historical 20-day volatility is the annualised standard deviation of the returns *over the last 20 days*. This changes over time and does not provide any reliable estimate of what the volatility might be over the *next* 20 days. Therefore, a graph of historical volatility does not indicate what the future volatility might be; in an option transaction, it is the volatility in the future which is of key importance.

Similarly, correlation can be measured over the previous 20, 60, 180 days – or any number of days that one chooses. The choice is normally governed by the time to expiry of the deal and the length of time for which the researcher can find the data. However, if a market participant is holding a hedge for a considerable period of time, they may also want to look at the correlation over shorter timescales to give some indication of the short-term losses or gains which may be expected. For example, for a six-month ANS hedge in WTI, a trader may look at the minimum and maximum 20-day correlation so that they have some idea of the possible slippage in any 20-day period.

In this chapter (for example, in Panel 1 where I describe some problems that can arise when measuring the correlation between Brent and WTI), we will measure correlations over a rolling 30 business days unless otherwise stated.

As with volatility, estimating the correlation between two time series by looking at the historical correlation is a potentially dangerous technique. Although it can indicate the range within which the correlation may lie, it does not indicate what the correlation will be in the future, and when buying or selling securities which depend on the correlation, it is this future correlation that one would really like to define. For all practical purposes, however, the historical correlation method is the only method currently available. For this reason, throughout this article, I have estimated future correlations using the mean of the rolling historical correlation.

Of course, it is *theoretically* possible to estimate future correlation by means of a number of "high tech" methods recently developed for estimating future volatility. Readers who are interested in ARCH and GARCH methods should consult Chapter 2 of this book and the relevant papers.[3] Although the research community has found GARCH useful and interesting, many practitioners in the energy markets do not use it, since the corrections that it offers to results generated by the "low tech" method are, in practice, swamped by other sources of error.

CORRELATING BENCHMARKS: WTI–BRENT

The spread between the benchmark crude in the United States and the benchmark crude in Europe is related to the relative supply and demand situation in each crude market, and the arbitrage opportunities that exist between both markets. This trading is made possible by the liquid futures markets on the IPE and the Nymex respectively.

There are many reasons why we might want to know the correlation between Brent and WTI. We may be hedging a Brent related deal with WTI; we might be speculating on the spread widening or narrowing (and therefore hoping to obtain a measure of our risk); we could be buying or selling an option on the spread between Brent and WTI. There are many reasons to calculate the correlation and also many ways in which this calculation can go wrong.

Our first attempt might be to take the two continuation or "front month" series of prices. These are price series which return the price of the most prompt futures contract. For example, on February 20, 1994, the front month Brent contract was the March Contract. It closed (and expired) at 13.34, while the April contract expired at 13.54. The following day, the April contract became the most

prompt month and closed at 13.50. The continuation series would thus be 13.34, 13.50. The graph of the 30-day historical correlation between Brent and WTI is shown in Figure A.

The average of this correlation over the period shown is 0.90 with a standard deviation of 0.05. However, there is a problem with this calculation. For example, on February 21 the front month Brent contract went up 16 cents and the WTI contract went down four cents. Obviously, this is because of the rolling of the Brent contract. The lack of correlation between the front month Brent and WTI contracts is an artefact caused by the rolling of the contract.

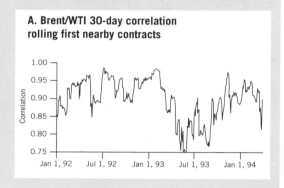

A. Brent/WTI 30-day correlation rolling first nearby contracts

Proxy hedging

In the energy markets, traders are constrained by the fact that there are a plethora of different physical commodities but only a few liquid contracts. In the United States, the WTI, Natural Gas, Heating Oil and Gasoline contracts are actively traded. In Europe the situation is worse, given the illiquid nature of the IPE gasoline contract, and there are only the Brent and Gasoil contracts. Furthermore, to take the Brent crude contract as an example, we might hope that it hedges exposure to Brent Blend physical cargoes – but there are 20 or more other North Sea crudes.

To hedge a commodity, say x, without a futures market, we must use a futures contract, say y, as a *proxy hedge*.

The *hedge ratio* or β is defined as

$$\beta = \frac{\sigma_x}{\sigma_y} \text{Corr}(x, y) \qquad (1)$$

where σ_x is the volatility of x and σ_y is the volatility of y.

To see how this works in practice, let us assume that a refinery manager is expecting to take delivery of a cargo (500,000 bbls) of Ekofisk one month from now. How would she or he hedge this exposure?

Of all the available futures contracts, it is clear that the Brent contract is likely to be the best hedge for the Ekofisk. The 30-day correlation between the roll-adjusted first nearby Brent contract and Ekofisk over the last two years is illustrated in Figure 2 opposite.

Although there is a significant variation in this number, we shall take the average of the correlation over the last two years as our best estimate of the correlation over the next 30 days. This best estimate computes to 0.90.

For the other quantities in equation (1), we use the implied volatilities, since these are easy to get from the options markets in Brent and Ekofisk. Assuming an implied volatility of 25% for Brent, and 25% for Ekofisk, we find that the hedge ratio is 90%. Therefore, we expect the most efficient hedge for our cargo of Ekofisk to

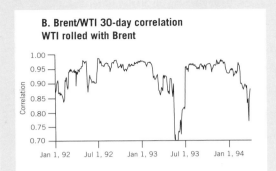

**B. Brent/WTI 30-day correlation
WTI rolled with Brent**

How might we reduce this error? First, we might artificially roll the WTI contract at the same time as the Brent contract. This gives the result illustrated in Figure B. The mean correlation here is 0.93 with a standard deviation of 0.05.

Second, we could look at the correlation between the individual contracts. That is, we could look at the correlation between the March 94 Brent contract and the March 94 WTI contract over the course of the contract's lifetime. This gives us the result illustrated in Figure C.

This graph reveals another pitfall in measuring correlation. Note that the rolling correlation is low when the contracts are very far out. This is due to inconsistent settlement prices on the exchange. The correlation then rises and finally, when the contracts are prompt, the correlation drops again. This is because the prompt Brent-WTI spread is

ultimately driven by purely physical factors, such as the availability of cargoes, and therefore is more volatile. The longer-dated spreads are less volatile due to less information in the market. The term structure model described by Gabillon in Chapter 1 of this book also predicts the same effect of low volatility in the longer term, and higher volatility as futures become prompt.

In conclusion, if we were buying a spread option on the October 95 WTI-Brent spread, we would probably be best to use the contract-against-contract graph to get an estimate of the correlation. If we were interested in hedging a rolling front month position in WTI rather than Brent, the front month/front month graph (suitably rolled) is probably better. As with all these things, there is no substitute for experience!

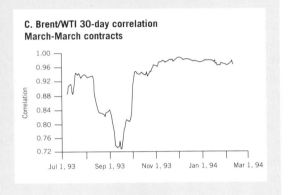

**C. Brent/WTI 30-day correlation
March-March contracts**

be 500 × 0.9 = 450 contracts of Brent. Of course, as with all these estimates based on historical data, the period of the hedge may not match the historical period.

The beta coefficient which we have called the *hedge ratio* is in fact just the statistical *coefficient of regression*. It is possible to construct proxy hedges using more than one commodity. In this case, we need to discover the coefficients of regression for each commodity against each other and use those to construct a hedge. This technique is somewhat more involved than

simple regression, with many statistical pitfalls, and will not be covered here.[4]

Spread and crack options

One of the major trading activities for participants in the energy market is trading the differences between individual commodities. These can be:

❏ *time spreads* such as the difference between first and second month Brent;

❏ *crude spreads* such as the difference between May WTI and May Brent; or

❏ *crack spreads* such as the difference between WTI and Heating Oil on the Nymex (or the difference between any other crude and refined product).

Whilst trading futures spreads is relatively easy to understand, trading options on cracks is not as widely understood or practised. We will derive some simple formulae for options on cracks, and then show some practical applications of spread options.

Using the example of Gasoil on the IPE

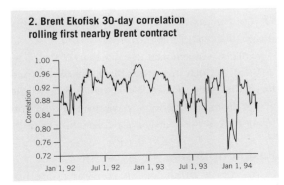

**2. Brent Ekofisk 30-day correlation
rolling first nearby Brent contract**

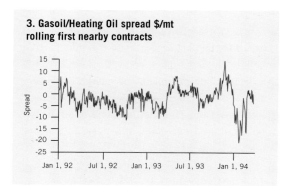

3. Gasoil/Heating Oil spread $/mt rolling first nearby contracts

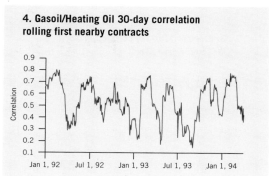

4. Gasoil/Heating Oil 30-day correlation rolling first nearby contracts

against Heating Oil on the Nymex, Figure 3 illustrates some of the features of spreads which make them fundamentally different from their underlying commodities.

First, and most important, we can see from Figure 3 that at times the spread has been less than zero. This is to say that heating oil in the United States has been worth more than gasoil in Europe. Because the time series is zero at some points, we can immediately say that the returns on the spread are not log normal, and therefore applying a simple Black-Scholes analysis to the spread is bound to fail. Note also that measuring the volatility of the spread directly results in near infinite volatilities. This seems rather high!

Mathematically, these problems arise because the difference between two log normal distributions is not log normal. The volatility of a combined distribution is given by:

$$\sigma_{12}^2 = \sigma_1^2 + \sigma_2^2 - 2\rho_{12}\sigma_1\sigma_2 \qquad (2)$$

Where σ_{12} is the volatility of the spread, σ_1, σ_2 are the volatilities of the two commodities and ρ_{12} is the correlation of the returns between Commodity A and Commodity B. We can use a standard Black-Scholes model to value the options by performing the following transformation.

We transform the payout of the call from Max(A–B–K, 0) to Max(A/(B+K)–1,0) × (B+K), where A is the price of commodity A, B is the price of commodity B, and K is the strike price of the option. It is easy to see that this is just an option on A/(B+K) struck at 1.

We can approximate the volatility of A/(B+K) with the following expression:

$$\sigma^2 = \sigma_A^2 + \left(\sigma_B \frac{B}{(B+K)}\right)^2 - 2\rho_{AB}\sigma_A\sigma_B \frac{B}{(B+K)} \qquad (3)$$

This approximation follows from an assumption that the value of K is much less than the value of B and therefore B+K is approximately log normal. There are better, analytic models for spread options[5] but this one allows the use of a simple Black-Scholes calculator with the above substitutions.

To see this in practice, let us assume that today is May 1, 1994, and then look at buying a $3 spread call option between the June 1994 IPE Gasoil contract and the June 1994 Nymex Heating Oil contract. The Heating Oil contract expires first on May 31, 1994 and, therefore, our call option will expire on that date. Other assumptions are:

	Gasoil	Heating Oil
Current price	143.50	45.10
Current implied volatility	24%	28%

Thus, converting the heating oil into $ per tonne with the conversion factor 3.1332 we arrive at an at-the-money value of $2.19.

The correlation between the first nearby Gasoil contract and the first nearby Heating Oil contract over the previous two years is shown in Figure 4.

The average of this correlation is 0.52, with a standard deviation of 0.15. Therefore, using equation (2), we can calculate the volatility of the spread to be 25.3%. We use a standard Black-Scholes calculator with the following substitutions:

Spot	= (143.50/(45.10 × 3.1332+3.00))
	= 0.994
Strike	= 1
Vol	= 0.253
Time to expiry	= 0.0833 years
Interest rates	= 4%.

The estimated fair value for this option is $3.80. Of course, market makers will probably not quote this exact price.

Once we have been given a market (say 3.60 at 4.05), we can invert the Black-Scholes formula to discover the *implied correlation*. In the above case, the market makers are selling a correlation of 46% and buying a correlation of 60%.

Basket options

Many energy producers or consumers are not

PANEL 2

PROBLEMS AND PITFALLS

Below is a table of some common pitfalls when calculating and applying correlation to energy contracts.

Pitfall	Solution
Looking at the wrong two data series when calculating correlation.	For a security which prices against the front-month contract, use the rolled nearby series (remember to roll at the same time). For a futures-futures spread, use a number of individual contract series.
Assuming correlation is fixed.	Never assume this! If today is January 1, 1995 and during the last 30 days, the correlation of Aug 95 WTI to Aug 95 Brent has been 99.9%, this does not mean that it will be 99.9% during the entire lifetime of the contract. In short, be aware of the term structure of correlation.
Hedging your entire exposure to Gasoil in Pork Bellies because the correlation happens to have been 90% over the last 30 days.	Think about causation. There are a lot of commodities out there: some of them, by chance, will be highly correlated to your risk.
Hedging your entire exposure to WTI in Brent because the correlation is high.	If there's a reasonably liquid contract, use it. There are costs associated with using an illiquid market, and there are costs associated with using a proxy hedge. You should consider both when deciding whether or not to hedge directly or with a proxy.
Worrying about correlation in pricing a spread option when you are "taking a view".	If you think the Unleaded Gasoline contract is going to rise to three cents over No. 2 Heating Oil, there is no point buying a 2.50 call for 0.5c – no matter how cheap the implied correlation looks. However, if you are delta hedging, you might be able to capture that cheap correlation.

just exposed to a single commodity or even to the spread between one commodity and another. They are exposed to a basket of commodities. An example of this is provided by the Long-Term Interruptible Gas supply contracts which are used in the United Kingdom for pricing natural gas. Often the value of these contracts depends on a number of different commodities such as gasoil, fuel oil, coal etc.

Although each portion of the basket can be hedged individually, this is often an expensive way to hedge a basket of risks. For these basket-pricing schemes, an option on the basket can take advantage of correlation or lack of correlation in the individual component to allow hedgers to hedge their risk more precisely and cheaply. The correlations between each component of the basket are the key to pricing these options correctly. But let us first consider the problem intuitively.

Consider a basket of two commodities. If these two commodities have a very high positive correlation, then as one moves up, the other will also be likely to move up. Therefore, the basket will also be likely to increase in price. However, if the two commodities have a high negative correlation, as one increases in

price, the other will reduce in price and the volatility of the basket will be very low – and so an option on the price of the basket should be cheaper.

The volatility of a basket of commodities may be defined as follows:

$$\sigma^2 = \begin{bmatrix} p_1\sigma_1 & \cdots & p_n\sigma_n \end{bmatrix} \begin{bmatrix} \rho_{11} & \cdots & \rho_{1n} \\ \vdots & \ddots & \vdots \\ \rho_{n1} & \cdots & \rho_{nn} \end{bmatrix} \begin{bmatrix} p_1\sigma_1 \\ \vdots \\ p_n\sigma_n \end{bmatrix} \quad (4)$$

where $\sigma_1 \ldots \sigma_n$ are the volatilities of each commodity, $p_1 \ldots p_n$ the percentages of each commodity in the basket, and ρ_{mn} is the correlation between commodity m and commodity n.

Every commodity is perfectly correlated to itself ($\rho_{nn} = 1$, for all n). All entries in the principal diagonal of the matrix are equal to 1 and the matrix is symmetric. It is therefore easy to see that, in the case of two commodities, this reduces to equation (2).

Using this formula, we can calculate the correlation coefficient of the basket, construct a suitably weighted sum of the individual components, and employ a Black-Scholes model.

To see this in action, let us take the example of a petrochemical company which is buying a basket of petrochemical feed stocks each month, as well as fuel oil to power the plant. The basket prices, two months forward, are:

Commodity	%	Forward price $/MT	Volatility %
Naphtha	60	135	24
Fuel oil	20	76	20
Propane	20	148.50	25

The current forward price of this basket is $126. Let us assume that the petrochemical plant risk manager wants to protect against the basket price rising above $126. She could do this by buying individual calls on each commodity.

Commodity	Forward price	ATM 2-month call premium
Naphtha	135.00	5.23
Fuel oil	76	2.45
Propane	148.50	6.00

Therefore, using the basket proportions, we get a total hedging cost of $4.85.

To price a basket option, we need the cross-correlation matrix for these three commodities. Using the techniques outlined above, we can find that a good estimate of the correlation between naphtha and fuel oil is 35%; naphtha and propane is 25%; and fuel oil and propane is 10%. As a matrix this is:

$$\rho = \begin{bmatrix} 1.00 & 0.35 & 0.25 \\ 0.35 & 1.00 & 0.10 \\ 0.25 & 0.10 & 1.00 \end{bmatrix} \qquad (5)$$

The total volatility of the basket is given by:

$$\sigma^2 = \begin{bmatrix} 0.60*0.24 & 0.20*0.20 & 0.20*0.15 \end{bmatrix}$$
$$\begin{bmatrix} 1.00 & 0.35 & 0.25 \\ 0.35 & 1.00 & 0.10 \\ 0.25 & 0.10 & 1.00 \end{bmatrix} \begin{bmatrix} 0.60*0.24 \\ 0.20*0.20 \\ 0.20*0.15 \end{bmatrix}$$

which works out at 18%.

Using this value and the forward value of the basket as $126, we can compute the premium for the ATM call as 3.65. This represents a considerable saving compared to the price of hedging each component individually.

1 *An excellent book on statistics is* The Theory of Probability *by H. Jeffreys.*

2 *For example, Microsoft Excel includes an extensive statistics package including correlations. To implement statistical calculations in a programming language the reader is recommended to look at* Numerical Recipes *by Press, Flannery et al (Cambridge, 1986).*

3 *Some useful papers on ARCH and GARCH are: Generalised Autoregressive Conditional Heteroskedasticity. Bollerslev. Journal of Economics 31 (1986) and Bivariate GARCH estimation of the Optimal Commodity Futures Hedge: Ballie and*

Mayers, Journal of Applied Economics 6 (1991) and Modelling the Persistence of Conditional Variances, Engle and Bollerslev, Econometric Reviews 5 (1986).

4 *It is documented in the previously cited statistical texts.*

5 *John Hull,* Options, Futures and Other Derivative Securities *(New Jersey, 1993); P. Wilmott, J. Dewynne and Sam Howison,* Option Pricing *(Oxford, 1993).*

6 *See* The Term Structure of Oil Futures Prices *by Jacques Gabillon (Oxford Institute of Energy Studies WPM17, 1991), and Chapter 1 of this book by the same author.*

ENERGY INSTRUMENTS

5

Swaps

Chris Mason and Steve Jones
Credit Lyonnais Rouse Derivatives

Given that the first major post-war oil shock occurred in 1973, the energy industry – that is, producers, processors and users of energy – proved slow to adopt swaps as a tool for risk management. As the introduction to this book makes clear, the first oil swaps were tentatively traded only in 1986, a full eight years after Nymex began trading heating oil futures. However, the 1 billion-barrel mark was passed in 1989, and since then the swap market has increased at a phenomenal rate.[1]

The driving force behind this growth has been the increasing involvement of financial intermediaries. Banks and trading companies that understand market-making and risk management have acted as middlemen, bridging the gap between market participants that wanted protection from falling prices and those that wanted protection from rising prices. Without the intermediaries, it is unlikely that consumers of oil would have been able to match themselves up with producers to offset risks of similar size and duration.

Another principal reason for the growth is the increase in technical knowledge about the market and the instruments available. As major end-users come to a deeper understanding of the mechanics of risk control, so their inclination to enter into complex swaps that are tailored to specific risks increases.

One of the aims of this chapter is to extend that understanding by analysing the range of energy swap structures now available. We will also review the various market sectors, and examine the role played by intermediaries. As well as surveying some of the problems of using the energy swaps market from the point of view of the end-user, we will explore some of the strategic considerations in pricing and hedging swaps faced by the intermediary. We will conclude by highlighting how we think that the energy swaps market will evolve in the near future.

The structure of energy swaps

The basic or "plain vanilla" energy swap differs little from swaps in other derivative markets, and is really a very simple financial instrument. However, several interrelated factors have combined to cause an increase in the diversity of the instruments used in the oil swap market. In particular, a more liquid and competitive market for swaps has attracted oil industry participants which are very aware of the specific price risks that they face – particularly in the low profit margin environment since 1993–94 – and are demanding more customised structures. Therefore, after briefly describing the basic building-block, we will outline the most important tailored instruments; the practical application of these structures is demonstrated throughout this chapter in a series of separate panels.

"PLAIN VANILLA" SWAP
A simple oil swap is an agreement whereby a floating price is exchanged for a fixed price over a specified period. It is an off-balance sheet financial arrangement which involves no transfer of physical oil; both parties settle their contractual obligations by means of a transfer of cash. The agreement defines the volume, duration, fixed price and floating price. Differences are settled in cash for specific periods – usually monthly, but sometimes quarterly, six-monthly or annually.

Swaps are also known as "contracts for differences" and as "fixed-for-floating" contracts – terms which summarise the essence of these arrangements.

Producers sell swaps to lock in their sales price. The producer and the intermediary agree a fixed price, for example, $18 per barrel for an agreed oil specification, and a floating price, often a reference price derived from Platt's or one of the futures markets.

For the period agreed, the producer receives from the intermediary the difference between fixed and floating if the latter is lower. If the

PLAIN VANILLA SWAP

In 1993, Rhumba Reefers A/S, a refrigerated vessel operator consuming about 400,000 tonnes of fuel per annum, decided to hedge some of the company's exposure to heavy fuel oil price risk, as the current price was low relative to the company's budget levels. It was new to the market and unfamiliar with the jargon, settlement processes, etc. It therefore chose a "plain vanilla" or straightforward swap as the simplest vehicle for its first hedge. Such a swap is a simple exchange of fixed for floating prices, whereby the consumer fixes his price today for a period some time into the future. The cash settlements under the swap mirror the ups and downs of the physical market, so Rhumba Reefers knew that the final price it would pay would be the fixed price agreed under the swap.

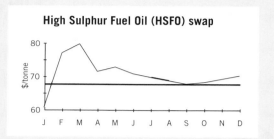

High Sulphur Fuel Oil (HSFO) swap

Fixed price buyer:	Rhumba Reefers A/S
Fixed price seller:	CLRD
Fixed price:	$68.00
Reference prices:	HSFO 3.5% Barges FOB Rotterdam
Duration:	Calendar year 1994
Volume:	5,000 tonnes per month. Total of 60,000t
Settlement:	Monthly cash settlement

On October 27, 1993, Rhumba Reefers locked into a swap at $68.00/t for calendar year 1994. By December, prices had fallen even further, but the company remained comfortable with the fixed price that it had locked in, which was some $7/t lower than its budgeted figure; it was happy to take advantage of lower prices on its remaining, unhedged consumption. In the New Year, prices rallied strongly as a result of lower stocks, cold weather and, more significantly, tight supply due to the lack of the sour crudes usually exported from Russia. On balance, the hedging strategy looked wise, and the company decided to add additional volume at a similar level if the market dipped.

floating price is higher, the difference is paid by the producer to the intermediary.

The simplest formula for calculating the difference is:

$$\text{Contracted monthly volume} \times (\text{fixed price minus floating price})$$

An example of a Brent swap for January 1994 might be:

$$50{,}000 \text{ bbl} \times (\$18.00 - \$17.20) = \$40{,}000$$

In this case, a seller of Brent crude which took on an $18 swap for 50,000 bbl per month would have received $40,000 for January. Had the average of the floating price been higher, the producer would have paid the difference to the intermediary.

The consumer of energy uses a swap in order to stabilise the buying price (see Panel 1). An airline buying jet fuel, for example, would contract to buy a jet swap with a fixed-price element of, for example, $180 per tonne. If the floating average was $190 per tonne,

then the airline would receive a monthly settlement of $10 per tonne multiplied by the volume hedged. If the floating price averaged $175 per tonne, then the airline pays out $5 per tonne.

DIFFERENTIAL SWAP

Whereas a standard swap is based on the differential between fixed and floating prices, a "diff" swap is based on the difference between a fixed differential for two products, and the actual or floating differential over time.

Some examples of energy products which might attract diff swaps include jet versus gasoil, physical (Platt's) gasoil versus futures, 3.5% fuel versus 1% fuel, and unleaded versus leaded gasoline.

Diff swaps are typically used by refiners to hedge changing margins between refined products. Refiners usually receive the fixed-price side of the swap, ensuring a known, forward relationship for the price of their various products. If they sell the diff and the diff narrows, then the refiner receives the difference; if it expands, the refiner pays out.

PANEL 2

DIFFERENTIAL SWAP

Foxtrot Flyers, a European scheduled carrier, uses a mixture of jet fuel and IPE gasoil swaps to hedge its jet fuel exposure for the immediate budget year. It tends to use gasoil swaps when it perceives the forward jet fuel premium to be too high.

Due to a sustained period of weakness in the physical jet fuel market, the forward jet-gasoil premiums have recently narrowed quite significantly. Foxtrot Flyers decides to take this opportunity to eliminate the basis risk inherent in its gasoil hedges – that is, the risk that the gasoil price would move out of tandem with the price of jet fuel – by effectively converting these hedges to jet fuel by means of a jet-gasoil differential swap.

Differential:	Jet Cargoes CIF NWE minus IPE Gasoil
Differential buyer:	Foxtrot Flyers
Differential seller:	CLRD
Differential price:	$21.00 per tonne
Reference prices:	Platt's mean quotes for Jet Cargoes CIF NWE
	IPE frontline settlements for gasoil

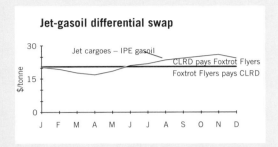

Jet-gasoil differential swap

Duration:	April to March inclusive
Volume:	10,000 tonnes per month. Total of 120,000 tonnes
Settlement:	Monthly cash settlement

If the average differential between the price of gasoil and jet fuel for each month is above $21 per tonne, then Foxtrot Flyers will receive the difference multiplied by the monthly volume. It will pay the difference if the monthly average is less than $21. Consequently, the company has eliminated the risk that jet fuel prices will increase more than gasoil prices.

Diff swaps may also be used by companies as a way of managing the basis risk assumed during their normal hedging activity. For example, an airline which prefers to hedge its jet exposure with gasoil swaps, because of the perceived value of these deals, may enter into a jet/gasoil diff swap to hedge this potential basis risk (see Panel 2).

MARGIN OR CRACK SWAP

Refiners which prefer to fix a known refining margin can construct elaborate forward and futures deals for their products. However, such constructions can be costly and rarely provide complete cover.

Alternatively, they can enter into a refining margin swap, whereby the product output of the refinery and the crude (or feedstock) input are simultaneously hedged, ie. the products are sold and the crude is bought for forward periods. At settlement, the refiner either pays or receives the difference between the margins; the calculation is based on the prices in the spot markets and those locked in (see Panel 3). In this way, the profitability of a refinery can be guaranteed for a few years forward. This kind of hedging is often integrated into development projects and upgrad-

ing schemes when the financiers are keen to ensure the viability of the project and a minimum revenue stream.

PARTICIPATION SWAP

A participation swap is similar to a regular swap in that the fixed price payer is 100% protected when prices rise above the agreed price but, unlike an ordinary swap, the client "participates" in the downside (see Panel 4). If, for example, a participation swap was agreed at a level of $80 per tonne for high sulphur fuel oil, with a 50% participation, the buyer would be fully protected against prices above $80 per tonne, but would also retain 50% of the savings generated when prices fell below $80 per tonne. If prices fell to $70 per tonne, the client would only pay out $5 per tonne rather than the $10 per tonne due under a regular swap. The level agreed determines the percentage of the participation, or vice versa.

DOUBLE-UP SWAP

By using this instrument, swap users can achieve a swap price which is better than the actual market price, but the swap provider will retain the option to double the swap volume

MARGIN SWAP

Rock 'N Roll Refiners Ltd, a refiner based in Rotterdam, wishes to protect a proportion of its exposure to oil prices. Because it is both a consumer of crude oil and a producer of refined products, its exposure is to adverse movements in the value of crude oil relative to products, typically referred to as "crack spread" risk. Refiners such as Rock 'N Roll are therefore attracted to "margin swaps", whereby the company can fix feedstock cost and sell the refined products forward in a proportion that matches the refinery's output profile in order to lock in the margin. Because refining margins can often be negative for sustained periods of time, especially in simple or hydroskimming refineries where upgrading capacity is limited, refiners tend to have a good appetite for such structures.

Crude oil leg

Fixed price buyer:	R 'N R Refiners Ltd
Fixed price seller:	CLRD
Fixed price:	$17.00/bbl (landed equivalent)

Reference prices:	IPE Brent crude oil 1st nearby contract
Duration:	Calendar year 1995
Volume:	100,000 bbls per month.
	Total of 1,200,000 bbls
Settlement:	Monthly cash settlement

Refined products leg

Fixed price buyer:	CLRD
Fixed price seller:	R 'N R Refiners Ltd
Reference prices:	Platt's European Marketscan
	mean prices

Product	Fixed Price	%
Unl. Gasoline Cargoes CIF NWE	$190.00	20%
Jet Fuel CIF Cargoes NWE	$181.50	10%
Gasoil 0.2 CIF Cargoes	$159.50	30%
LSFO 1% Cargoes CIF NWE	$101.00	37%
Losses		3%

By using the above structure, the refiner is able to lock into a margin of $1.98 per barrel for the whole of calendar year 1995.

---

before the pricing period starts. The mechanism by which this is achieved involves consumers (which are buying fixed) selling a put swaption, or producers (which are selling fixed) selling a call swaption; in either case, the premium earned from the sale is used to subsidise the swap price.

For example, an airline might be able to negotiate a swap price of $190 per tonne for the winter period. This swap price could be reduced to $185 by selling the put option on the same swap to the counterparty. On the swaption exercise date, the swap provider will decide whether or not to double the swap volume (depending on market prices at the time).

EXTENDABLE SWAP
The extendable swap is constructed on the same principle as the double-up swap, except that the provider has the right to extend the swap, at the end of the agreed period, for a further predetermined period (see Panel 5).

PRE-PAID SWAP
By means of a pre-paid swap, the fixed payment cash-flow line can be discounted back to its net present value and paid to the user. Pre-paid

swaps are often used as a source of pre-export financing, and they are discussed in detail in the section devoted to that topic below.

OFF-MARKET SWAP
In this type of swap, a premium is built into the swap price to fund the purchase of options or to allow for the restructuring of a hedge portfolio. Off-market swaps are generally used to restructure or cancel old swap/hedge deals: essentially, they simulate a refinancing package.

For example, imagine that a shipping company has entered into a three-year swap at $90 per tonne for heavy fuel oil. For the first two years, the swap proves advantageous, and provides the company with a significant positive cashflow (as market prices remain high). However, an increase in Russian crude exports then causes fuel oil prices to fall rapidly at the start of the third year of the contract.

The company believes that this price slump will not last long and, due to a lull in business, it decides it would rather not have this additional strain on its cash-flow. Consequently, it decides to extend the swap for a further year, at the price of $93. As the price of fuel oil is now

PANEL 4

PARTICIPATION SWAP

Tango Trucking Company, a small distribution company, has only a relatively small volume of gasoil (diesel) exposure. However, it sees a dip in market prices as an ideal opportunity to protect its budget for the next financial year. In the past, the company had preferred to use straightforward swaps as a hedging instrument due to their simplicity. But, in this instance, it has a strong view that prices may go lower and so it wants an instrument that allows it to benefit from any downside move without having to pay any up-front premium. To achieve these objectives, Tango Trucking opts for a 50% participation swap.

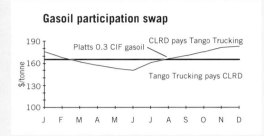

Gasoil participation swap

Fixed price buyer:	Tango Trucking
Fixed price seller:	CLRD
Fixed price:	$165/tonne
Buyers participation:	50%
Reference prices:	Platt's Gasoil 0.3 CIF Cargoes
Duration:	January to December inclusive
Volume:	5,000 tonnes per month. Total of 60,000 tonnes

Settlement: Monthly cash settlement

Tango Trucking was correct in its view that the gasoil price would drop lower for a time. With the 50% participation swap, it had only to pay out half of the normal settlement amount when the average price for the month was below $165 (that is, the price difference times 2,500 tonnes). When the average gasoil price for the month then rose above $165, Tango Truckers received the price difference times 5,000 tonnes.

lower, the price of this extension is actually $10 above the normal swap price. The discounted value of the extension is then deducted from the price of the current-year swap.

CURVE-LOCK AND BACKWARDATION SWAPS
These structures are variations on the same theme, and are basically plays on the shape of the oil price curve. By locking into a spread between different points on the curve, a market participant can lock into either backwardation or contango in the market.

For example, by buying October 1994 WTI contracts and selling March 1995 WTI contracts, a trader could lock into a spread of six cents; that is, the trader sells the forward contract at six cents below the prompter contract. If at the end of the pricing period, the average daily spread between these two contracts was 16 cents, then the trader will collect 10 cents profit. If, on the other hand, March averaged four cents above October, the trader will pay out 10 cents.

The rationale behind such a trade is that the trader believes that the backwardation in the market will become steeper (which typically reflects a bullish view of the market). A strategy such as this, therefore, is essentially speculative.

However, the strategy can be viewed as an indirect hedge in that if the market goes into contango while a market participant is locked into this kind of structure, it is because prompt prices have become very weak. And if prices are weak then obviously any consumer of fuel will benefit from cheaper physical supplies. The problem with using curve-lock swaps as a base hedge is that the user often remains vulnerable to basis risk.

BARTER SWAP
The use of barter as a form of trade has increased in the world's major commodity markets, particularly between sources with inadequate financing infrastructure and poor credit ratings. The problem with barter is that it leaves the participant exposed to fluctuating prices. This can be alleviated by using barter swaps to fix the prices: in a barter swap, one commodity is swapped for another.

The process of fixing prices on both sides of the barter is relatively easy in the case of major commodities (oil against wheat, for example). As it is only the differential between the two products which determines the profitability of the overall barter, the price-fixing element can be arranged using a standard swap. However, a

PANEL 5

EXTENDABLE SWAP

Pogo Producers, an independent Brent crude oil producer, has decided that the timing is right to enter the market to fix the revenue for a portion of its production for the next 12 months. At the current market swap price, it will comfortably beat its budget forecasts. However, the company believes that prices are unlikely to continue at the relatively high levels. To take advantage of this view, and its naturally long oil position, it decides to enter into an extendable swap. In this case, Pogo Producers will be selling the swap provider the right to extend a one-year swap into two years. The swap provider will have the right to extend the swap at the end of the first year. The price for the second year will be the same as the first year. The actual swap price which the company achieves will be an improvement on the normal market price, equating to the market price plus the premium value of the swaption (option on a swap) that they are selling.

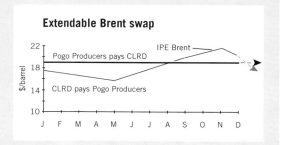

Extendable Brent swap

Duration:	January to December inclusive
Volume:	100,000 bbs per month. Total of 1,200,000 bbls
	(same for extendable swap)
Settlement:	Quarterly cash settlement

Fixed price buyer:	CLRD
Fixed price seller:	Pogo Producers
Fixed price:	$19/bbl
Extendable price:	$19/bbl
Reference prices:	IPE Brent frontline settlement prices

For the duration of the swap for the first year, Pogo Producers will be benefiting from the fact that it has a higher swap price. It will be receiving cash settlements when the average quarterly Brent price is below $19, and paying out when the market price is above $19. At the end of this first year, the swap will be extended for another 12 months if the forward swap value for the period is higher than $19. This price also complements the company's longer-term budget forecast.

barter for oil against, for example, tractors, is more awkward; while the oil price element can be fixed with some precision, the two-year forward price of Albanian tractors is problematic! Baskets of commodities may also be swapped against baskets of goods. Problems do arise, however, if the exports do not conform with the delivery schedule on which the hedge calculation was based.

Applying energy swaps: end-user benefits and concerns

The various swap arrangements described in the previous section allow companies to manage their exposure to energy price risk with considerable flexibility:

❏ producers and processors can offer fixed-price products to their consumers;

❏ refiners can fix their margins;

❏ production margins can be guaranteed in development projects;

❏ banks can offer more attractive financing when price exposure is controlled;

❏ pre-export financing can be secured on net present values of swap cash-flows;

❏ exposure to one oil product can be switched to another, for example, an airline fixing futures prices in gasoil can eliminate the inherent basis risk by using a jet-gasoil differential swap;

❏ competitive advantage can be secured by locking into high/low prices;

❏ certain limitations of the exchanges (notably liquidity, duration, the need for margin adjustments and the limited range of product specifications) can be overcome.

Despite these benefits, few companies hedge all of their price exposure, particularly in the longer term. Instead, the convention among end-users is to hedge the current financial year plus one, while the percentage of this exposure that companies seek to cover is usually somewhere between 40–60%. A growing number of companies are also using swaps to part-protect their three- to five-year budgets.

One reason why companies only hedge a fraction of their exposure is because they do

PRIVATE PLACEMENT INDEXED TO JET FUEL

Waltzing Wings, a relatively small but profitable regional carrier, has decided that, in the current circumstances, the best way to raise significant financing is in the private placement market. The best offer that its bankers achieve is from a US insurance company which is willing to invest $100 million for a return of Libor plus 50bp over 10 years. The bank has offered to swap this floating rate into a fixed rate of 8.00% for the airline. Waltzing Wings is happy with this price; however, as its business is so marginal it is concerned that the maintenance on this financing may prove excessive during periods when other costs are high.

In the past, its most significant and volatile cost has been jet fuel, which generally accounts for about 15% of operating costs. From experience, it knows that its cash flows, particularly, suffer during periods of high oil prices. Thus, it wants to ensure that, with such burdensome financing costs, this fuel exposure is appropriately managed. After weighing up the options, the company decides to enter into a structure which simply indexes the financing cost to the price of jet fuel.

This fuel-indexed financing is arranged so that, over the 10-year term, when the price of jet fuel (cargoes CIF NWE) is above $195 per tonne there is an offsetting reduction in the loan interest. Conversely, when the jet fuel price is below this level, the interest cost will rise. The net payments are bi-annual. This relationship can be expressed using the simple formula:

$$8.00\% \times (1 + (195 - FPF)/195)$$

where FPF = Future Price of Fuel, calculated as the daily average of the mean price of Jet Fuel Cargoes CIF NWE as published by Platt's for each six-month period.

not want to risk foregoing gains if the market moves favourably. Companies may also be concerned that they will be left at a relative price disadvantage compared to their competitors. But it would still appear that most companies are under-utilising the risk management potential of energy swaps.

One of the main limiting factors is a lack of knowledge about derivatives. Although growth rates in the energy sector in recent years have been strong, it should be remembered that problems in the interest rate swap market, where inadequately briefed users failed to understand the obligations associated with swaps, caused that market to falter temporarily in the early 1990s.

Another problem is that, in the past, the energy swaps market has been inefficient with regard to competition and liquidity. There is gradual improvement on these counts – particularly for longer-dated products. Swap spreads (the difference between the cost of a swap to a buyer and a seller), have narrowed, although in some of the less mainline products, and in less active geographical areas, illiquidity still leads to inconsistencies and inefficiencies.

Another specific improvement in efficiency is that the market can now generate swap prices in non-dollar currencies. Users may want only the fixed-price part of a swap in the local currency, if they buy oil in dollars. However, if they buy oil in the local currency then it is possible to arrange both the fixed and floating side in that currency. Clearly the currency risk element in a swap out of dollars into any other currency will need a certain amount of management. In the latter case, the risk rests with the swap issuer, whereas in the usual dollar-denominated case the risk will be borne by the consumer. (In most cases non-dollar swaps are sought by smaller companies with limited foreign exchange lines, such as a local charter airlines. In other cases, they may simply reflect the fact that most of the company's transactions are in the local currency, and that dollar-denominated oil is an awkward but significant element in the equation.)

The true cost of any kind of swap can be difficult to resolve, and this is of legitimate concern to end-users. Given that almost all oil swaps are executed through intermediaries, it is clear that there *must* be a cost. A transaction in which a consumer swap is directly offset by a producer swap is the ideal transaction from the intermediary's point of view: the lack of risk means that the price difference between the two can be minimised, and no additional hedging is required by the intermediary. However, precise fits are rare, and thus the swap price will reflect the intermediary's perception of the degree of

SWAPS risk that it will be obliged to assume (temporarily, at least).

Even in the case of "vanilla" swaps, users tend to be unfamiliar with the process of costing. Unfamiliarity breeds suspicion, and this in turn inhibits trading. But this disadvantage is being eroded: a cursory check by users of a range of quotes for a given swap should now produce fairly even prices. This procedure is of no use in the case of tailored swaps, of course, and most users are unlikely to possess the techniques necessary to price complex long-term swaps themselves.[2]

The structure of the swap market: a providers' perspective

COMPARISON WITH OTHER SWAP MARKETS
The mechanics of exchanging fixed-for-floating prices did not originate in the commodity markets, but in foreign currency and interest rate markets. Although commodity swaps are virtually identical to other swaps in terms of rationale and structure, providing and using them presents some quite specific problems.

Conventionally, the credit risk of commodity counterparties is regarded as greater than that of participants in the foreign exchange and interest rate market. The strains on credit-backed arrangements, such as swaps, are also stretched by the greater price volatility on commodity markets – particularly oil.

This volatility also generates different problems. The global and highly liquid markets in foreign exchange and interest rates provide an efficient medium for swaps providers to lay off their risk. There is no structural difference between the cash and the forward markets; there are virtually no geographical concerns; and the relationships between different instruments, such as government and commercial paper, are generally well-established and relatively stable.

None of this is true for energy derivatives. Markets move in and out of contango and backwardation according to shifts in the balance of demand and supply. Local shortages and surpluses cannot be overcome quickly, simply because of the cost and time of moving product into and out of these areas. And, in the short term, even the established relationships between crude and downstream product can vary considerably. It is not uncommon, for example, for Brent crude FOB Sullom Voe to be in backwardation at the same time that Mediterranean MoGas or jet is in contango.

These variations in the "normal" price relationship between crude and downstream products, additional local variations and shifts in the spot/forward price relationship mean that dealing in energy swaps is relatively complex.

Perhaps the biggest challenge for energy swap providers is the swings in oil price curves, particularly for downstream product, which require them to adopt a more flexible approach to hedging than their money-market counterparts. Such problems are exacerbated during times of uncertainty, when the psychological comfort of holding physical oil pushes up short-term buying, causing the spot premium or backwardation to rise sharply.

In the longer term, oil prices are determined by market expectations. But these expectations are themselves influenced by the amount of business being executed. This problem is analysed more formally in Chapter 1 of this book. But practitioners are well aware that a single large swap for three or four years out, for example, can influence the perception of the market.

Oil markets are also highly exposed international barometers of key political and military activity. Brent prices increased by 18% the day after Iraq invaded Kuwait. Traded option volatility soared to over 100%, and settled at 70–80% for some weeks after. The pressure on jet prices, based on expectations of a large increase in military flying activity, was even greater. Swaps providers trying to hedge in such markets faced considerable difficulty, and the provider should be cautious about being short in the short term. Supply problems can lead to a spike in near-end prices while having little effect on longer-term prices.

Finally, because of the physical/raw material nature of oil, the responsibility for hedging often falls on the purchasing or operations manager of the end-user corporations. In contrast, currency and interest rate hedging is normally undertaken by the treasury manager. While we would not want to imply that purchasing managers are less capable, it is certainly true that they are often less familiar with measuring and offsetting risk. A swap provider in the energy markets therefore needs to be able to explain the conceptual basis for hedging, as well as proving the operational advantages of particular deals.

MARKET SECTORS: A BRIEF REVIEW
Oil companies Most major oil companies main-

tain specific derivatives trading or risk management teams. In addition to dealing in forwards, futures and options, these teams also use swaps to manage physical exposure, to hedge particular deals with their own clients and, increasingly, to trade for profit.

The main application of swaps, however, is the managed hedge, which enables an oil company to offer a fixed-price deal to its client. The offer of fixed-price product often generates a competitive advantage over other suppliers, and the oil producer hedges the assumed fixed/floating risk by means of a swap.

Historically, investment in new production capacity in the oil business was directly linked to the profitability of existing production. New plant and equipment were installed or upgraded after a profits surge, and the consequent effect on supply tended to depress prices and slow down new investment. During the 1950s and 1960s, high oil consumption rates evened out this peak-to-trough pattern. In the future, swaps will provide the industry with the ability to finance new capacity in a manner that should ensure a more even development of supply.

Airlines The jet fuel sector is the most mature and developed oil product sector. Airlines were the first serious users of commodity swaps, largely because jet fuel accounts for up to 20% of airline operating costs, and is the cost that is most exposed to short- and medium-term price fluctuation.

The Iraq-Kuwait crisis reinforced the need to manage this risk, as jet prices rose even further than the 80–100% price rise in crude oil.

Most major airlines now manage their jet exposure to some extent. Tight competition in the US airline sector has discouraged airlines from adopting new exposure management practices until recently. This is now beginning to change.

Since the growth of this business in the mid-1980s, airlines have become adept at combining swaps with various option structures. Typically, an airline will concentrate on hedging the next budget year (that is, 12–18 months out). Given present, historically low, price levels, there is also a growing tendency to hedge part of the medium-term exposure (three to five years forward). The latter strategies are usually implemented using a basis of swaps, with option structures added on.

Shipping companies The variable costs of a ship-

ping company are dominated by bunker-fuel prices. In particular, fuel is often the only variable when ships are chartered for fixed terms. As with airlines, there is an increasing tendency to hedge forward with swaps, beyond annual budget periods. The shipping business is a long-term business: freight contracts of around 10 years' duration are common, and ship owners are therefore used to dealing with long-term risk. Long-term derivatives are a natural means of managing the oil price risk in such contracts, and although shipping companies tend not to hedge as large a percentage of their total consumption as airlines, they tend to hedge for longer periods. A detailed example is provided in Panel 1, Chapter 8.

Whereas airlines have no traditional alternative risk management tools, the shipping industry has used "bunker adjustment clauses" for many years to hedge oil price risk. It is only because such clauses are much less efficient and flexible that shipowners are switching to OTC derivative transactions.

Transport companies Like other sectors of the transportation sector, road haulage firms are exposed to diesel fuel prices. The biggest barrier to their participation in the OTC markets is the fragmentation of this risk. The majority of consumers are very small firms or independent truck owners working on a contract basis, and the price risk is thus spread relatively thinly.

Power companies Power generators that use gasoil or fuel oil are exposed to fluctuations that comprise a very large proportion of their variable cost base. Furthermore, the ability of generators to vary their power prices is very limited, particularly in the case of sales to the household sector. Some companies have started hedging their fuel exposure, but without an adequate reference price mechanism (for example, Platt's) it is difficult to define a settlement price.

The developing market in electricity swaps (known as contracts for differences and EFAs) is analysed in Chapter 11.

Industrial groups Firms with a high energy consumption (for example, metal smelting and refining companies, cement manufacturers, glass makers) are increasing their use of swaps to manage fuel oil exposures. Some of these firms, such as metal producers, are experienced in managing other commodity price risks.

PROJECT FINANCE: A CASE HISTORY

Ted Robson, BZW

In mid-1993, BZW was approached by International Petroleum Corporation (IPC) in relation to its interest in purchasing the Welton Field. This was an onshore UK field owned at the time by British Gas and BP.

As it was a producing field, with relatively straightforward technical requirements, BZW was able to offer competitive stand-alone project financing terms – *providing* that IPC was prepared to hedge some 2 million barrels of the first two years of production. The oil price hedge meant that, assuming production continued as expected, IPC would be able to meet all the loan principal and interest repayments and operating expenses over what would probably be the period of tightest cash flow.

Because BZW required an oil price hedge for only the first two years, and during this period for less than 100% of production, IPC maintained a fair degree of "upside" potential.

IPC decided to hedge by means of an oil price swap. This was put in place at $17.70, with settlements made quarterly against the average mean Platt's quotation for Dated Brent. This matched the price basis on which IPC sold the crude oil from the Welton Field.

During the first 11 months of the hedging programme, the average settlement price has been $15.37. At the time of writing, therefore, average payments of $2.33 per barrel have been received by IPC on a volume that has proved to be 48% of total production. Prices would need to average close to $20 for the remaining period of the hedge, for the hedge not to provide a net positive flow of income over its full maturity.

Ironically, perhaps, it would be better for IPC if the average price of oil during the term did exceed $20. In that situation, the unhedged proven and probable reserves would be likely to provide a much better return.

Instead of a swap, IPC could have chosen to hedge the oil price using oil price options. This would have required either up-front cash payments, or giving up some of the "upside". Given the outcome, it is unlikely that any option scheme would have provided as good a return as the swap.

Chemical companies Petrochemical producers are typically exposed to naphtha price fluctuations but, apart from a few companies, this sector has yet to use swaps to any significant degree.

Financing organisations Banks and institutions which provide development finance for oil projects often carry a risk that is related to oil price. This may be because repayment is linked directly to the oil output of the completed project or, less directly, because of the credit risks associated with new projects that are dependent on forward markets.

Companies may also link oil swaps directly to bonds, warrants or other securities. As described in the introduction, there is also a specialist fund management market which uses certain commodity market instruments such as oil swaps.

Below, we provide a brief summary of the financing structures associated with energy derivatives.

ENERGY SWAPS IN FINANCING STRUCTURES
There are certain forms of finance which require long-term oil price risk management. In each case, the basic principle is the same: to use a swap to fix a known forward oil price (that is, income stream or cost factor). The following sections survey the range of financing problems that can be solved using swap-based structures.

Project finance Finance for a new field, large well or refinery, for example, is often provided by banks on a limited recourse basis. The bank's recourse to the development firm, for example, may be limited by the failure of the developer to achieve set income levels according to plan. There may be a number of reasons for this (technical, political, etc.), but one risk which can be removed by a swap structure is the market risk.

If selling prices are too low, then the income generated by a new project may be insufficient to repay the loan according to agreed terms. Engaging in a fixed-for-floating swap protects the prospective oil producer from any subsequent decline in oil prices (at the same time, of course, it gives up the right to participate in higher prices should they develop). Panel 7 provides a case history example of how swaps are used in project finance.

A particular risk in the context of project finance is the danger that the project will not even have come on line by the date that the swap comes into force. However, given the generally long lead times for such projects, it is usually possible to renegotiate these arrangements.

The role of swaps in financing such developments is particularly appropriate where the project is a high-cost producer, and the projected production costs are close to market prices. In this instance, the sensitivity of producers to adverse market fluctuations will increase the risks to the lenders, and thus increase the cost of financing.

Pre-export financing Swap-based financing does not only apply to commercial operations, such as mining and refining companies. Most oil-producing countries raise a production/export levy on oil output, particularly where oil exports are the major foreign exchange earner.

This makes such countries susceptible to changes in oil prices. Governments with a two- or three-year spending programme, or fixed loan repayments, are at risk from market-driven changes in the level of royalties. Many producer countries are heavily loaded with long-term debt arising from the upgrading of oil production, or the development of downstream capacity. As oil prices fall, their ability to finance this debt diminishes in tandem with their ability to raise new loans.

By means of pre-export financing, oil-exporting countries can pledge future production as collateral against immediate cash. Banks are usually more comfortable about advancing finance on the basis of receiving future oil flows, although clearly there can be considerable "country" or political risk to be taken account of.

Pre-export financing has been around for over a decade, since the famous deal in 1982 between the United States and Mexico. In this deal, the United States offered $1 billion cash in exchange for the transfer of Mexican oil into the US Strategic Petroleum Reserve. Although this kept the oil off the market, thereby helping to maintain stable prices, the effective interest rate on this debt, payable in the form of additional oil, amounted to 30%. Repayment schedules have become considerably less burdensome since.

In the Middle East, this type of pre-export financing has been popular due to the Islamic prohibition on interest rate financing. Iran, for example, has raised $2.5 billion in pre-export credits, primarily from three French banks: Crédit Lyonnais, BNP and Paribas. Repayment was in the form of physical oil, assigned to the banks at the time of loading. Simultaneously, oil trading companies made payments directly to the banks and were, in turn, assigned the cargoes.

Since the repayment schedules have traditionally been written in the form of "oil to the value of", the market risk of this kind of deal to the intermediaries is negligible – especially as they are able to lay the risk off immediately on receipt. However, it seems only logical, now that the swaps market is large and liquid enough to handle country volumes, that the market risk element of pre-export finance will in the future be covered by a swap.

Asset finance Companies with a need to invest in new capital equipment or assets can link the cost of financing that asset to their fuel exposure. For example, aircraft or ship finance can be indexed to jet or bunker prices (see Panel 1, Chapter 8). Alternatively, refinery equipment costs can be linked to refinery margins.

Bond issues, equity issues and placements Bond and equity financing is a variation on direct financing (in the sense that it creates tradeable paper for the issuer or lender). The capital value of the debt and the income/coupon/dividend stream can be indexed to oil in much the same way as asset or pre-export finance deals.

The role of the intermediary

In theory, there is no reason why producers should not issue fixed-price swaps for purchase directly by consumers. In practice, the wide range of variables affecting oil markets – specification, geography, timing etc – would make this a choppy business.

In addition to smoothing out the flows, intermediaries have added a considerable amount of professional skill. They have, as a group, effectively assumed some of the characteristics of a clearing system. They channel trades between buyers and sellers, they absorb and flatten out some of the imbalances which occur in the market and, increasingly, they provide a greater degree of price transparency. They cannot, however, perform the clearing function of offsetting, in order to reduce bilateral credit risk.

An intermediary requires significant price making and risk management skills, an increasingly high degree of sophisticated structuring skills, and a detailed knowledge of the cash markets for energy. Perhaps most important, however, given the bilateral financial risks which swap participants incur, is that the intermediary should be well-capitalised and financially strong. Some firms in this sector, and not simply the intermediaries, have established high credit rating, big balance sheet subsidiaries, specifically in order to trade swaps.

Banks and commodity trading companies comprise the largest group of swaps intermediaries, although there is a newer breed of "pure" swaps companies developing too. Originally, banks were involved in swaps as an extension of their lending activities, while trading companies incorporated swaps into their trading activities. Some trading companies are subsidiaries of banks, however, which blurs these lines somewhat.

PRICING AND HEDGING
Swap prices are initially derived from an extrapolation of futures and OTC contract prices. Included in this extrapolation will be forward interest rates and elements of the cost of financing physical production and storage. A margin is added to allow for any basis risk, forward curve shift or hedge execution risk (the risk of not achieving the assumed hedge price for the desired volume).

Swaps for a product with no exchange-traded equivalent are priced from a curve of a related product. Heavy or sour crudes, for example, can be measured against light sweet crudes with a reasonable accuracy. By contrast, Mediterranean MoGas has no easy equivalent; although a ratio hedge with WTI is acceptable during stable periods, this leaves open a potentially high basis risk if the price relationship veers away from the historical norm.

The OTC market has begun to evolve mechanisms which signal long-term levels for nonstandard products. There is a market for long-term WTI spreads, for example, whereby the relationship of crude prices from one year to another enables product swappers to infer forward product price curves at one remove from the crude market.

Perhaps the clearest way to explain how

traders price swaps is to look at a specific example. Imagine that a trader wants to sell a jet fuel CIF NWE swap to an airline. If the term of the swap is about a year forward, then quotes are generally available from other traders or brokers; that is, the market is quite liquid and pricing is unproblematic. However, pricing is more complicated if the swap has to be priced further forward than a year. Although a specific quote could still be obtained from another trader, or brokers, it is dangerous to let the market know your intentions prior to dealing in an illiquid market (such as longer-term jet fuel). This is because other traders may try to bid the forward prices in front of you, knowing that you will still be forced to pay up to cover your position. Even so, many banks and trading companies adopt these tactics because their mandate obliges them to cover each position "back-to-back".

The alternative is to devise a price by calculating the different elements of the equation: the underlying crude oil swap; the Brent/IPE Gasoil differential; and the IPE Gasoil/jet fuel differential.

With regard to the crude oil swap, a relatively liquid market exists in WTI and Brent swaps for up to three years forward. Beyond this, as we have said, there is a market in WTI year spreads (that is, brokers will offer prices on the time spread between, say, June 199X and June 199Y). The swap price can be extrapolated from these spreads. For jet fuel CIF NWE it would be easiest to use the underlying crude price in Brent (the more common benchmark for European products). The Brent price can then be calculated from the WTI swap by subtracting the arbitrage spread; this spread can be readily obtained from brokers.

The next part of the equation is the Brent/IPE Gasoil differential (or crack). Again, it is fairly easy to get a market price for this from brokers for up to two years forward. Beyond this, traders rely on historical analysis, experience and common sense when calculating the mark-up. The Brent/IPE Gasoil crack is quoted in US$ per barrel; for ease of calculation, the sum of the Brent and the gasoil crack is therefore converted to tonnes at 7.45 barrels per tonne.

This is because the final element in the equation, the IPE Gasoil/jet differential, is quoted in US$ per tonne. Prices for this differential can be obtained through a broker for 18 months to two years forward. Beyond this, the trader must make an individual calculation.

By means of the calculations demonstrated in

PANEL 8

PRICING A SWAP: JET FUEL CARGOES CIF NWE SWAP

In this example, we assume that the client, an airline, has asked the trader to price a swap of jet CIF NWE for three years forward, starting in January 1996.

	1996	1997	1998
Brent	17.00	no quote	no quote
WTI (spreads Dec. to Dec.)		0.60	0.65
Brent/WTI arbitrage		1.30	1.30
Brent/gasoil crack	5.40	5.50*	5.55*
Jet/gasoil differential	23.50	24.00*	24.50*

* assumed

Note: Prices above are offer prices

STEP ONE

The Brent price for 1996 is obtained from a broker as $17.00. For 1997 and 1998, the WTI offer prices are extrapolated from the futures via the time spreads to $18.90 and $19.55, respectively. From the Brent/WTI arbitrage, the Brent swap prices are calculated as $17.60 and $18.25, respectively.

STEP TWO

The gasoil prices are calculated by adding the gasoil cracks to the Brent swap prices. The cracks for the last two years have been deduced:

1996: $17.00 + 5.40 \times 7.45 = 166.88$/tonne
1997: $17.60 + 5.50 \times 7.45 = 172.10$
1998: $18.25 + 5.55 \times 7.45 = 177.31$

STEP THREE

The jet fuel prices are calculated by adding the jet differential to the gasoil swap prices. The differentials for the two years furthest out have been deduced.

1996: $166.88 + 23.50 = 190.38$
1997: $172.10 + 24.00 = 196.10$
1998: $177.30 + 24.50 = 201.80$

STEP FOUR

The average offer price for this swap equates to $196.10. The trader will probably round this number up or down depending on the risk/reward assumptions built into the above prices.

Panel 8, the trader can arrive at an offer price without implying that he is likely to be a buyer of fixed-price jet fuel in the near future. Furthermore, even if the trader finds that it is impossible to hedge the impending position with a back-to-back jet fuel swap, the deal can be hedged step by step. That is, the trader can buy a crude oil swap, and then add a crude/gasoil crack and jet/gasoil differential to this at a later date. The crude should be quick and easy to purchase, as the market is quite liquid; the crack and the differential are much less volatile, and thus the trader will have more time to cover them.

Of course, it is possible that the trader will not be able to find reasonable quotes for the crack and the differential. The trader must, therefore, feel secure that the deal with the airline is sufficient to preserve a margin of profitability even if these positions have to be bought back some weeks or months into the future. The trader always has the option of running the position until it matures – but the natural desire to realise profits (and bonuses) militates against this!

The methodology described above and in Panel 8 can be applied to many other oil products, given the appropriate product differentials. These differentials, and the resulting price, will be marked up or down to reflect liquidity, volatility and basis risk.

Where structures are especially complex or difficult to hedge, swap issuers will build this risk factor into the swap price using correlation coefficients. (The technical process of measuring how closely correlated different contracts are, and of constructing proxy hedges for fuel products which lack a futures exchange contract, is explained in Chapter 4 of this book.) However, it may be very difficult for them to realise any profit – that is, to trade out of the positions.

Competitive pricing is also sometimes a feature of deals between intermediaries and new clients. A swap issuer may price the first swap to a new client more aggressively than other indicators would suggest.

Apart from assuming risk, swaps issuers also make money from market-making. In an ideal world, an intermediary would generate profits from "bid/offer" activity, where a fixed-price buyer (a consumer) receives the offered side of the swap price while producers, as fixed-price sellers, receive the bid price. As long as the swap price to the buyer is higher than the bid price to the seller then the swap issuer, the intermediary, makes a profit. The variation in bid-offer spreads is largely determined by:

❏ term (that is, it tends to be narrower for short dates;
❏ liquidity of the market (that is, the number of active traders); and
❏ the volatility of the commodity.

However, while intermediaries would like to "back-to-back" all their various deals, so that the risk in their portfolios balanced out, this is rarely possible. Differences in size, timing, product specification and geography are such that intermediaries end up with composite positions.

The ideal hedge for a long swap is a short swap at the same price levels and for similar duration. Failing that, the net exposure will need to be hedged, unless the issuer deliberately leaves a position exposed as a form of surrogate trading. Futures exchanges, with their increasing range of product and liquidity, are important risk-offset markets. However, swaps traders are often forced to warehouse certain market risks, such as product or time-spread risks. A trader's willingness to take on a position that may lead to warehousing will depend partly on its "appetite for risk", and partly on how confident it is that the position will eventually be profitable, even if kept to maturity.

Of course, each institution will try to draw a line between warehousing risk and what is, in effect, speculative trading. Most traders, like most market-makers, regard the level of risk implied in speculative trading as unacceptable – their ambition is to *minimise* their exposure to price movements.

THE LIQUIDITY PROBLEM
Equally important is the question of liquidity, which is one of the key practical issues in swaps markets. Liquidity here does not only refer to the liquidity of the swaps market itself – which has a bearing on bid-offer spreads – but to the liquidity of the wider market in oil for the purpose of risk management.

Infrequently traded or illiquid product markets will be more liable to basis risk, as hedging the exposure may be slow and difficult. Before embarking on a deal, a swap provider needs to know that further-out liquidity is sufficient to

establish some prospect of a reasonable hedge. Although basis shifts are considered to be disruptive, as far as the issuer is concerned, forward curve risks can be more damaging; this is because they can affect the whole range of swaps rather than individual products. Therefore, the trader will try to limit the number of situations where it is likely to be forced to "stack" its hedge in short-dated positions against a longer-dated swap.

This focus on further-out risk suggests that the problems are concentrated in this area. But, in practice, short-term risks also need to be managed. The need to hedge a large exposure in any given month itself generates a hedge risk, because any major trade in the futures market is liable to move the price.

Most product swaps to end-users tend to be arranged between buyers of fixed price (that is, consumers) and intermediaries. The market is thus one-sided, with sellers of fixed price potentially exposed to substantial shifts in the yield curve, execution risks on futures exchanges and local liquidity problems.

Where the degree of exposure is clear some time ahead, all these problems can be overcome. But a busy swaps issuer operates in a dynamic market. New deals change the balance of exposure, sometimes reducing overall exposure, sometimes increasing it. In practice, each new deal is weighed up for its effect on the existing net position. A swap issuer already short on fixed-price jet in a market with a steepening curve, and where the jet premium over refining margins is also growing, will not want to exacerbate this exposure by entering into additional keenly priced swaps. (Unless of course the issuer believes that these pressures are going to subside, in which case an element of market judgement may enter the equation.)

Future developments
OVERVIEW
As in most areas of the swap market, the pace of new development in energy swaps will be set by the intermediaries. Most intermediaries expect that the overall growth in energy swaps activity will continue, and that it will lead to increased liquidity, greater competition and tighter margins.

Structurally, the development of the energy swap market is likely to follow two main routes. The first is the continuing expansion of the number of participants in the markets. Banks have, until now, tended to target larger partici-

SUCCESS IN THE SWAPS MARKET: SOME CRITICAL COMMENTS

As far as the end-user is concerned, the criteria for success in the energy swap markets are often dangerously simple. The successful use of a swap seems all too evident to a crude oil producer that sold fixed for floating in a falling market. A jet-fuel hedger that bought fixed for floating in a rising market will be the first to recommend a similar strategy to his colleagues. Unfortunately, this criterion for success is essentially speculative. It necessarily leads to risk management operations taking the blame for hedges which supposedly go "wrong" – that is, when the hedge subsequently proved unnecessary or led to "opportunity loss".

As far as providers are concerned, success in the market is often confused with success in technical innovation. Pricing and administration technologies are constantly evolving, but it is important that providers use these developments to generate products which buyers want, and that they are able themselves to cope with the additional risks that the new range of products entails.

In a mature market, the ability to provide swaps with properly constructed and priced embedded options is bound to attract attention and business. But too many "whistles and bells" may be counter-productive. It is insufficient to be able to offer highly advanced concepts without being able to deliver working strategies. The practical experience of intermediary and bank providers in recent years has shown clearly that although the exotic composite is much favoured by researchers, the ability of (a) the customers to understand them and (b) the bank to hedge them, is limited.

Inevitably, users which fail to understand the true implications of a particular structure will feel that the unknown or uncertain elements in it are to their disadvantage. This is particularly true in new markets, and for smaller companies in any market.

The solution here is for the swaps provider to remain market-oriented, not product-oriented. They must remember why the user wants the swap – not why the provider wants to provide it.

pants in the fuel/oil markets – but the use of swaps will eventually filter down to the smaller industrial and transport companies.

One reason for believing this is that intermediary bank account managers are becoming familiar with the applications and operations of swap contracts and, increasingly, encourage the treasury managers of smaller companies to become involved. At the moment, bank account managers are particularly encouraging their clients to hedge interest rate and foreign exchange exposure – but the oil/fuel price swap is not conceptually different, and will surely follow.

The other main area of expansion is likely to be in the area of exotics – that is, swaps with more complex option structures attached. As with options and other OTC instruments, the ability to structure tailored flexibility into the hedge mechanism required by the client will add value, both to the client and to the swap provider (Panel 9 provides additional comment). One important factor here is the market's growing confidence in managing curve risk. Longer-term deals are becoming more frequent, particular in the context of structured finance deals.

The increase in the range of oil indices and products traded will also have an effect, as it gives swaps providers more flexibility to manage and offset basis risk.

GROWTH SECTORS

When trying to identify growth sectors, it is useful to remember the following observation. Although it might be thought that the natural development of swaps would fit closely with the availability of exchange instruments suitable for hedging, in practice the growth has been driven very largely by end-user demand. The jet fuel and fuel oil sectors are striking proof of this.

So where is demand growing fastest at present? Tapis crude, the Far East crude benchmark, is certainly one growing market for swaps, partly as a result of the fast-growing physical market for the product, and partly because of the basis risk between Tapis and the two exchange crudes: Brent and WTI. The oil product swaps business, particularly gasoil and fuel oil, is also increasing in the Singapore-based market.

US jet fuel swaps are one of the largest single

identifiable areas of potential growth in the foreseeable future. As the fuel consumption of the larger US airlines is two or three times that of their European counterparts, the potential is vast. Airlines which currently do not hedge their jet fuel can be expected to develop hedging via swaps in a more liquid, and already technically accomplished, market. The improving credit ratings of the American airlines is a supplementary factor.

Naphtha swaps represent a relatively small part of the overall market, but are expected to increase as industrial activity increases. Post-recession activity in petrochemicals will increase the marginal activity in this sector, with operating margins needing to be secured against adverse fluctuations in naphtha prices.

The effect on demand of the environmental lobby is bound to increase demand for low-sulphur fuels and unleaded gasoline, and this may also lead to an increase in swaps activity in these sectors (largely to protect against basis risk).

Crude oil and integrated producers, particularly in newly risk-aware markets such as Eastern Europe, are starting to come to the swaps market for medium-term price protection. The ability of Russia, Ukraine and other ex-USSR countries, for example, to finance new capacity investment during periods of historically low oil prices has been greatly enhanced by using swaps.

By far the largest single area of potential growth, however, is the natural gas sector. As a clean fuel, its use is growing dramatically, but outside the United States there is no futures contract and until recently there has been no market for OTC gas swaps. At the time of going to press, a futures contract is being explored jointly by IPE in London and Simex in Singapore. When this contract is launched, the additional focus on hedging natural gas will attract considerable extra interest to the swaps market in Europe and the Far East. Some natural gas swaps have already been executed, not simply by consumers wishing to fix purchase prices, but also by power generators protecting their margins on large generation projects; the maturities of these deals reportedly extend beyond ten years in some cases. The market for natural gas swaps is discussed in more detail in Chapter 10 of this book.

1 *To the extent that it is impossible to make an accurate estimate of current volumes, as discussed in the Introduction.*

2 *However, the pricing of structured deals can be "checked"* to a limited degree. For instance, the provider's underlying swap value can be compared to other quotes.

6

Options

Michael Hampton
Cedef Finance Ltd[1]

Energy options now comprise a huge global market, rivalling the energy swaps market as a means of managing exposures to energy prices. The size of the over-the-counter (OTC) options market is difficult to estimate, but it has grown at least as fast as the exchange-based options market. The two principal exchanges offering energy options, the New York Mercantile Exchange (Nymex) and the International Petroleum Exchange (IPE), report a compounded growth rate since 1987 of over 20% per annum (see Table 1, Chapter 13).

It was not always apparent that the energy options market would grow so quickly. The introduction of exchange-traded options lagged behind the successful introduction of traded energy futures by several years. Nymex began trading WTI options in November 1986, three and a half years after it introduced its first energy futures contracts. IPE followed with gasoil options in July 1987, a full six years after its gasoil contract was launched.

However, two factors greatly spurred the growth of the young energy options market: the successful launch of an OTC market in swaps from 1986; and the extreme volatility in oil prices in 1990, the year of Iraq's invasion of Kuwait.

The emergence of an energy swaps market, described in the Introduction to this book, meant that banks and oil companies hired large numbers of commodity derivatives marketing staff. Bank marketing of OTC commodity derivatives grew steadily in Europe and Asia, and took off in the United States after the CFTC issued its safeharbour ruling in 1989 (described in Chapter 14). These new marketing people were added to the marketing staff of the exchanges, who were already scouring the market for potential business opportunities. Their marketing efforts cultivated the demand for energy derivatives, preparing the ground for the new option instruments.

Even so, explaining the concept of options to end-users in a way that related directly to the energy industry was – and still is – a challenge. The first part of this chapter therefore offers an "intuitive" approach to understanding energy option technology without algebraic equations, and acts as a foundation for the more technical discussion presented in Chapter 7. (Like the other chapters in this book, it will take the OTC market, rather than the exchange market, as its primary focus.)

The rise of crude oil prices to $40 in 1990, followed by their collapse to under $18 in 1991, was also crucial in increasing the energy option market, because it illustrated so strongly to end-users the dangers of price exposure. For buyers of call options in the early days of the price rise, options provided protection against a price rise with a limited amount of risk. For those who sold call options in late 1990 – when option volatilities exceeded 100% – they also provided a way of enhancing income by selling price insurance to a very nervous market.

As the first period of extreme volatility after energy options became available, 1990–91 also taught end-users (and some derivative providers) that using options in energy markets has quite specific problematics. The second half of this chapter therefore highlights the features that make using energy options different to using interest rate and currency options, before moving on to describe the simpler option-based instruments such as caps, floors, collars and swaptions. The concluding section summarises how the various instruments suit different exposure-management strategies.

An intuitive approach to energy options

SOME TRADITIONAL DEFINITIONS
The two basic types of option are traditionally defined as follows:
❑ A *call* option is the right to buy a particular asset at a pre-determined fixed price (the strike price) at a time up to the maturity date.

❏ A *put* option is the right to sell a particular asset at the strike price up to maturity.

The problem with these conventional definitions is that they assume that the value of the option will be captured through exercise. For the call, this would mean purchasing the asset at the exercise price and then either reselling it or holding it. The traditional definitions ignore the fact that options are increasingly "settled" in cash, so that the underlying asset does not change hands.

In the oil market, OTC options are generally settled in a different way to exchange-traded options. Exchange options are exercised into futures contracts, and futures, if held to maturity, nearly always result in physical delivery of the product. (An exception is the cash-settled Brent crude oil contract offered by the IPE.) In contrast, OTC options, like OTC swaps, are generally cash-settled. Their value at settlement is normally based on the average price over a period – a calendar month is most common. The average is calculated based upon an index price derived from daily futures settlements prices or from an energy industry pricing source such as Platt's or Argus.

Cash settlement of options has advantages for many players in the market. First, it can be expensive to exercise an option and then resell the asset to capture the increase in value. This is particularly true in the case of less liquid products, but may be true even for deep-in-the-money crude oil options. For example, a refiner may hold an exchange-traded call option on crude as protection against a rise in crude prices. Selling this option at an acceptable price is usually possible. But if the options market is not liquid, the refiner would need to exercise the option by taking delivery of the underlying futures position at the strike price. However, the refiner may prefer to buy his crude from another source or for a different delivery date than the crude controlled by the futures contract. If he exercises the option and takes delivery of the future, he will need to resell it in order to capture the increase in value beyond the strike price. This may result in additional commissions to pay, or the market might move unfavourably before the futures position is disposed of.

A second reason for cash settlement of options is that many clients favour settlement against average prices. Compared to settlements based on a single point in time, they can provide a better hedge for non-specific "cash-flow type" exposures. For example, an oil trader

which is buying and selling cargoes of oil can use large "lumps" of futures to hedge its large "lump" of oil. The matching of the hedge is easy. When the trader buys cargo and wants to hedge, he can sell an equal quantity of futures. And when he sells the cargo, he can buy back his short futures to unwind his hedge. For this operation, the futures are sold at a specific moment and bought back at a specific moment within the timing constraint of the ship's voyage.

But cash-flow exposures are less precise, because they are made up of individual exposures too small to hedge individually. An airline may be fuelling its aircraft several times a day. Effectively, it will be paying an average price over the course of the month. Given the "flow" of small refuellings, the airline may prefer to settle its hedge against an average price. A shipping company may be running a fleet of ships, with its fleet taking on bunker fuel at unpredictable moments where and when the fuel can be obtained most cheaply. Given the unpredictability, the shipping company does not know ahead of time when the ships are going to take on fuel or from what location.

Averages are difficult or time consuming to replicate in the futures market, particularly for options, so many end-users of derivatives prefer to buy the averaging mechanism in the OTC market and leave the mechanics of running the hedges to the OTC market makers. (The special pricing and hedging issues created by settling against an average are discussed in Chapter 7.)

Finally, options are increasingly used to hedge cross-market risks. If the option holder does not have an interest in the underlying asset, but is merely interested in the price protection the option provides, cash settlement can be significantly cheaper. For example, a company might buy an option on gasoil as a cross-market hedge against a rise in the price of jet fuel. In this case, the option buyer is not at all interested in acquiring the underlying asset (physical gasoil or a gasoil futures contract), he merely wants a price hedge the value of which is (normally) highly correlated with his underlying price exposure. A cash-settled option is a more cost-effective solution because it does not require reselling the underlying asset, and it fits well with settlement against an average.

With the increasing tendency towards cash settlement in mind, it is possible to formulate a simple and intuitively satisfying definition of the basic options:

❏ A *call* is the "upside" in the price of a particular commodity beyond the strike price as determined by a particular settlement mechanism and limited by the maturity of the option.

❏ A *put* is the "downside" in price below the strike price with the same restrictions.

HOW DO OPTIONS RELATE TO SWAPS?

Using these definitions, the relationships between various derivatives instruments become more intuitively obvious. And the relationship between cash-settled swaps and options becomes particularly clear.

As explained in the previous chapter, a swap represents the exchange of a periodic floating payment for a fixed payment. The practice for energy swaps is that the two amounts are calculated and only the net cash difference is paid at the end of each period. Payments are required only if there is a difference, and then only one side pays. Given the settlement mechanism, the energy swap can be explained using "upside" and "downside", as illustrated in Figure 1.

The swap buyer (ie the "consumer" side of the swap which pays the fixed payment) agrees with the swap seller a fixed price for the period and a periodic quantity. Based upon this fixed price, the buyer agrees to pay the downside amount, if any, and in return receives the upside, if any. The two potential payments can be defined as follows:

❏ *upside* Amount by which the floating price exceeds the fixed price times the quantity;

❏ *downside* Amount by which the floating price is less than the fixed price times the quantity.

If the floating amount exceeds the fixed amount, then the upside difference is paid by the swap seller (floating payer) to the swap buyer (fixed payer). If the floating payment is less than the fixed amount, then the downside difference is payed by the swap buyer to the swap seller.

These payment definitions now sound very similar to the definitions of puts and calls that we provided above. In fact, a swap can be decomposed into the two options, so that being "long" a swap is the same as being "long" the upside of a strip of calls struck at the fixed swap price, and "short" the downside of a strip of puts below the swap price.

The relationship between a forward (or any individual settlement period in a swap) and its option components is illustrated in Figure 2.

There is an important relationship called put/call parity which means that a put and a call have equal (theoretical) value when they are both struck at the forward price. Similarly, a cap and a floor (option instruments described later on in Panel 5) both struck at the current market swap price have equal value.

This relationship is illustrated in Figure 2. Since a forward entered at the market price requires no upfront premium to be paid, and such forward can be decomposed into long a call and short a put with both struck at the forward price, then the two options must have equal value. The cost of the call purchased is fully covered by the value of the put sold. Otherwise a net premium would need to be paid. No logical person would pay an upfront premium for a combination of two options (long the upside through the call, short the downside through a put), when the risk characteristics of these options could be perfectly replicated through the purchase of a forward.

Another concept, called "conversion", can also be explained using Figure 2. Conversion is when one directional option is converted into an option of the opposite direction. A call can be converted into a put, or a put into a call. This can be easily explained.

If an option holder is long a call, he is long upside. If he then sells a forward at a price identical to the call strike price, he has sold the upside controlled by his call. The upward price risk inherent in the sale of the forward is therefore covered by the call, and so he has no net gain or loss if prices move higher. However,

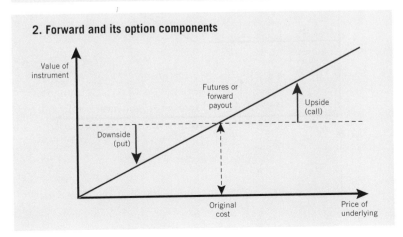

1. Fixed-for-floating is the same as upside-for-downside

Floating = Index times quantity
Fixed = Fixed times quantity
Difference only is paid

Upside = Floating – fixed (if +)
Downside = Fixed – floating (if +)
Exchange of upside for downside

2. Forward and its option components

OPTIONS

through the short created by the forward sale, he can benefit if the price falls below the strike price. Therefore, through the combination of being long the call and short the forward, he has acquired the downside below the strike price. So long as the maturities on the forward and the call are the same, the combined position is exactly equivalent to a long put.

In a similar fashion, a put can be converted into a call by purchasing a forward at the same price as the put strike. The downside exposures cancel each other, and the combined net position is pure upside.

OPTION VALUE AND OPTION EXERCISE

The value of an option, as compared with a forward or future, is in the flexibility it provides. The holder of an option has time to decide whether or not he wants to exercise it. The time value of delaying the decision until some future moment up to the final exercise date is that the market may give better opportunities along the way. The option provides a low risk way to wait for those better opportunities to arise.

As illustrated in Figure 3, the two basic components of an option's value are:

❑ *intrinsic value* The amount by which the option is "in-the-money" (that is, the amount the option would pay out if it were exerciseable immediately). For a call, this is the amount by which the price of the underlying commodity exceeds the strike. For a put, it is the amount by which the price of the underlying is below the strike;

❑ *time value* The value (above and beyond the intrinsic value) which the option attracts

3. Intrinsic versus time value

because of the possibility that, as the price for the underlying commodity fluctuates up to maturity, the option may increase in intrinsic value. All else equal, time value will be greatest when the underlying is trading at the strike price. At that point, intrinsic value is zero but can increase immediately if the price moves in the right direction. (Another way of saying this is that the flexibility provided by the option is worth most when the probability of it gaining intrinsic value is 50% – as it is when the underlying is trading at the strike price.)

Realising the value in an option is dependent upon the form of option exercise that has been stipulated. There are three basic types of option exercise:

❑ *American options* can be exercised at any time up to the maturity date;

❑ *European options* can only be exercised on the maturity date; and

❑ *Asian options* (also called average rate options) which settle in cash based upon an average price. Asian options are generally exercised automatically if they are in the money.

The exchange-traded energy options on the Nymex and the IPE are of the American type, while most OTC energy options are of the Asian variety, because of the popularity of the averaging mechanism. A few OTC options are American or European style.

Up to maturity, American and European options tend to have the same valuation except for those special cases where early exercise of an American option may enable a holder to capture more value than he could do by locking in the intrinsic value and waiting for the option to mature. (Intrinsic value can be locked in for a call by selling, and for a put by buying, the appropriate future in the same quantity.) One special case arises when options are very deeply in the money, and hence have little time value. Another occurs when the markets are very illiquid or in markets where commodities are expensive to finance or short. In this case an American option may have additional value because early exercise may enable an option holder to conclude a trade in the underlying commodity which it is impossible to achieve (cheaply) without delivery of the underlying future or commodity through early exercise.

What makes commodity options special?

Although industrial commodities may theoretically be fungible, the price for given units of an

DEFINING BASIS RISK

The term "basis risk" is used to describe the risk that the value of a hedge may not move up or down in tandem with the value of the actual price exposure that is being risk managed. Ideally, a hedge would match the underlying position in every respect, negating any chance of basis risk. But the large number of energy products, and the lack of liquid hedging markets for many of the underlying products, means that some mismatched hedges are unavoidable. The principal types of mismatch are:

❑ *Product basis* This is the most important basis risk in most risk management markets, including the energy markets. If there is a mismatch in quality, consistency, weight, or other specification then the underlying product and the hedge are not fungible. In the energy markets, there is a large number of products and only a few liquid hedging instruments (most exchange-traded futures and options and a few of the OTC indices are generally liquid). Consequently, it often happens that an illiquid underlying exposure is hedged with a liquid instrument, the price of which is linked to a different product. Even when the instrument's underlying price shows a strong historical correlation with the underlying exposure, significant basis risk can emerge if the relationship between the two products breaks down (as discussed in Chapter 4). The most famous example occurred in late 1990, after the invasion of Kuwait by Iraq: the differential between European jet fuel and gasoil quickly widened to more than five times its usual margin.

❑ *Time basis* This is a common-enough exposure in many markets. For example, in financial markets, banks will often lend money over six months, and fund this activity with one-month deposits – creating a "yield curve exposure" or "time gap". However, in energy markets, a time basis exposure can be much more dangerous, particularly when there is a sudden shift in demand or transporta-

tion bottlenecks occur. An illustration would be an electric utility needing gas in the winter time which hedges its position by purchasing January natural gas call options. If a severe cold wave were to arrive early in the winter, say in late November, then the price of December natural gas prices may surge much more than the January prices. The market knows that the price rise is likely only to last as long as the cold spell, or as long as it takes for gas pipelines to bring sufficient new supplies. In this circumstance, the January call options may not provide an efficient hedge for the December physical gas requirement.

❑ *Locational basis* As discussed in the main text, prices of exactly the same product can vary significantly from one location to another. As an illustration, Platt's reports prices for 1% sulphur fuel oil in both the US Gulf and New York Harbor, as well as a similar 1% low sulphur fuel oil in Rotterdam. An OTC swaps market has developed in trading these materials and the price differential normally shows New York Harbor at a premium which roughly reflects the cost of shipping the oil up from the Gulf. However, the trans-Atlantic differential between New York and London depends upon whether the demand for 1% fuel is greater in Europe or the United States. The premium, if great enough, will attract oil from across the ocean. But the differential is not stable and can swing with the premium on either side.

❑ Other types of basis risk can be seen in the energy markets. For example, "mixed basis" risk occurs when an underlying position is hedged with more than one type of mismatch. A January jet fuel exposure might be hedged with a February gasoil contract, leaving both time and product basis exposures. Another sort of basis risk, peculiar to the options market, arises when an option of one strike is hedged using an option with another strike.

industrial commodity at a particular place and a particular time is not. This quality, which may be termed "price specificity" in the sense that the price is specific to a particular time and location, has an important impact upon the pricing and hedging of energy options.

All commodities vary in price depending upon when and where they are valued. But this

is particularly true for energy commodities, which tend to be expensive to transport and difficult to store, relative to their value. A cargo of crude oil is thus worth significantly more in an importing country, such as the United States, than it is in an exporting region such as the Arabian Gulf. Likewise, natural gas prices will nearly always be much higher in the northeastern American cities, like Boston or New York, than they are at Henry Hub or Kingsport (which are near producing gas fields).

For financial commodities, like gold, there is little locational variation in value except where taxes and regulations have an effect. If this were not the case, gold could be moved quickly by air transport to the location of greatest value, and the extra supply would bring down the price. For most energy commodities, air transport is not practical. Cheaper but slower means of transport such as ships, trucks or pipelines are employed.

The more extreme and short-term variations in energy spot prices are not directly due to transportation costs. Instead they occur because bottlenecks and time delays in the normal method of transportation give rise to an extreme inflexibility in short-term supply, and this interacts with the short-term inflexiblity of demand for energy discussed in Chapter 1 of this book. (The price risk that this gives rise to is one form of "basis risk", as discussed in Panel 1.)

"Price specificity" is pronounced in the natural gas market because of its vulnerability to transportation bottlenecks. If, for example, cold weather in the northeastern United States causes a large drawdown of local natural gas inventories, then the local spot price may rise very quickly in the period until fresh deliveries reduce the imbalance in physical supplies. Conversely, a supply glut can cause a price to fall below replacement cost.

Through its effect on volatility, price specificity has an important impact upon option valuation. In particular, it is normal for spot energy prices to be more volatile than forward prices. This is because demand and supply disruptions which affect the physical market tend to be short-lived, while longer-term prices reflect more stable economic fundamentals.

Normally, the further forward the energy price, the lower its expected price volatility. This creates a volatility curve which is "downward sloping" as it moves forward in time. This characteristic is illustrated by Table 1.

The prices in Table 1 were sampled in a relatively quiet market and so the levels shown and the degree of fall-off in the volatility curve over time is characteristic of a market without a major disruption in supply or demand. By contrast, in late 1990 and early 1991, as oil prices surged at the time of Iraq's invasion of Kuwait, short-dated oil option volatilities exceeded 100% at times. Because of the prevailing nervousness in the market, longer-dated options were also marked up. Nevertheless, there remained a pronounced downward slope in the oil volatility curve throughout the large price shifts of 1990–91.

An intuitive explanation of option pricing

This section provides an intuitive approach to option pricing, building upon concepts introduced already.[2] The approach is deliberately "non-mathematical" but, as understanding the conventional mathematical terminology is important, the principal expressions are defined in Panel 2. (Chapter 7 uses these terms to discuss, at a more advanced level, pricing and hedging methodologies for a wide range of option structures.) Panels 3 and 4 explain delta hedging – a core tactic when actively managing option positions.

There are five key inputs to an options pricing model:
❑ price of the underlying commodity;
❑ strike price;
❑ time to maturity;
❑ volatility estimate; and
❑ interest rates.

In the following, we will examine how each of the individual pricing dimensions impact on the price of an at-the-money option (if an option has intrinsic value, or is out-of-the-money, the impact of each dimension is more complex).

Price of underlying
The "character" of the underlying price affects all the other variables, and especially the volatility estimates. In particular, as explained earlier, in the case of energy options the underlying price tends to become more volatile as it moves from being a forward price to being the price of a spot commodity for physical delivery. Nearby energy prices are thus very "whippy"; that is, they move around much more than longer-dated prices.

Table 1. Summary of Nymex WTI crude oil options prices (Dec 1994)

Contract	Future	Strike	Type	Option price	Option volatility
Nearby	$16.99	$17.00	put	$0.25	28.2%
2nd	$16.99	$17.00	put	$0.58	25.5%
3rd	$17.01	$17.00	put	$0.69	24.0%
4th	$17.05	$17.00	put	$0.75	22.5%
5th	$17.08	$18.00	call	$0.50	21.7%
6th	$17.10	$18.00	call	$0.58	21.4%
8th	$17.18	$18.00	call	$0.71	20.3%

Note: This is a selection of some of the most liquid contracts for each month

OPTION PRICING AND "THE GREEKS"

Throughout the risk management industry, letters of the Greek alphabet ("the Greeks") are used to describe the various assumptions underlying an option's price and its sensitivity to market moves. The four most important terms are:

Delta (δ) This term describes the change in the value of the option with respect to the change in the underlying price. (It can also be thought of as a measure of the probability of an option finishing in the money on the maturity date.) The "delta" of an option also has the very useful purpose of indicating what size of holding (or short holding) of the underlying is required to provide an effective hedge for (changes in) the option's value. Thus, a call option with a positive delta of 50% can be hedged with an equal but opposite position in the underlying; that is, a short position 50% the size of the overall quantity controlled by the option. Naturally, as the underlying price moves, the delta will change as well: a higher price increases the call delta and a lower price reduces the delta (the impact on put deltas is the reverse). Thus, delta hedges have to be modified as underlying prices move.

Gamma (γ) A second-order derivative, this term describes the change in delta with respect to the change in price. Essentially, this variable describes how much the underlying hedge for an option must be changed in order to remain "delta neutral" as prices move. A high gamma option requires more frequent adjustments to remain effectively hedged. An option is normally at its highest gamma when the underlying is trading at the strike price and when the option is approaching its moment of expiry. A low gamma option is one whose strike is far away from the underlying price, or one with a large amount of time remaining to expiry.

Theta (θ) This describes the change in the value of the option with respect to the change in time. As described in the main text, as a rule of thumb, the value of an option tends to change with the square root of time. The impact on the value of an at-the-money or out-of-the-money option is that the loss of value over time (the "time decay") starts slow and becomes increasingly rapid as an option approaches its expiry. However, if an option is deep in-the-money and nearly the whole of its value is intrinsic, there will be little time decay.

Vega This describes the change in the value of the option with respect to the change in volatility. For an at-the-money option, the option value tends to change proportionally with changes in volatility. Thus, a doubling of volatility should tend to double the value of an at-the-money option. However, volatility only affects the "time value" of an option, not its intrinsic value. Therefore, an in-the-money option which holds a large part of its value as intrinsic, will be proportionally much less affected by changes in volatility. The influence on out-of-the-money options is more complex. They may be proportionally more affected than at-the-money options, but the change in absolute value will be smaller (because they have a smaller absolute value to begin with). Below is an example showing one-year options, relative to an underlying price of $20.00.

Impact of volatility changes on value of call options with various strikes

Type of call option	Strike	10% vol % change	15% vol +50.0%	20% vol +100.0%	30% vol +200.0%
Out-of-the-money	$22.00	**$0.181** % change	$0.474 +161.9%	$0.814 +349.7%	$1.545 +753.6%
At-the-money	$20.00	**$0.758** % change	$1.136 +49.9%	$1.513 +99.6%	$2.265 +198.8%
In-the-money	$18.00	**$2.038** % change	$2.286 +12.2%	$2.584 +26.8%	$3.233 +58.6%

Exchange-traded options generally settle into futures contracts maturing in, at most, a few weeks. The volatility estimates for such options can shoot up dramatically as the underlying contract approaches maturity. OTC options, on the other hand, tend to settle against an average price and consequently carry a much smaller volatility estimate.

Where the underlying price is that of another instrument (as in a swaption, where the option, if exercised, settles into a swap), the volatility is likely to be relatively low. For a swaption, the longer the tenor of the swap period, the lower the appropriate volatility estimate.

Strike price Although we are describing at-the-money options, it is worth considering what happens if strike prices are shifted out of, or into, the money. Here it is important to remember that supply and demand disruptions in the physical market widen the probability distribution of price movements of energy commodities. Spot prices can move more in a few days or hours than further-out prices move over weeks. Consequently, the range of historical spot prices shows a greater deviation from the mean than would be predicted from a normal distribution. (It is sometimes said that the distribution of energy prices has a "fat tail" compared with the normal probability distribution.)

The higher probability of an extreme move, and particularly of a move upwards, creates the so-called "volatility smile" for options of varying strike prices. The traded prices of options in or out of the money, but particularly of those with higher strike prices, normally have a higher volatility estimate than options struck at the money. Implied volatility increases as the option strike gets further away from the at-the-money price. For the option with its strike price at the money, the resulting graph of implied volatilities (Fig. 4) looks like a slightly off-centre "smile" around the lower volatility estimate.

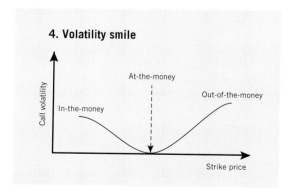

4. Volatility smile

Time As a useful "rule of thumb", other effects being equal, an option's value varies with the square root of time. A six-month option can be expected to cost 41.4% more than a three-month option (1.414 is the square root of two), and a one-year option double as much as a three-month option (the square root of four being two). As the intuitive expectation may be that it should increase *proportionally* with time (ie that a six-month option will be twice as expensive as a three-month option), long-dated options can appear "cheap".

In practice, there are some discounting effects which slightly reduce option values. Thus, in a 5% interest environment with flat volatilities, a one-year European call would be worth $1.36 when a 90-day call is worth $0.70 − a slightly smaller increase of 94.3% instead of the 100% increase expected in a zero interest rate environment with a fourfold increase in time.

Volatility All else equal, there is a direct correlation between volatility and the price of an option. This is easy to understand intuitively: the value of the flexibility offered by an option increases in proportion with the liklihood of price movements. As an example, if the volatility estimate embedded in an option jumps from 20% to 30%, an increase of half, the price of an at-the-money option will increase by 50%. For a three-month oil call struck at $18, when the forward price is $18, an increase in volatility from 20% to 30% would increase the value of the call 50% from $0.70 to $1.05.

Interest rates These have a much smaller impact than the other variables. An option effectively provides "free financing", since the holder of the option does not directly pay any carrying costs for the underlying physical commodity or futures contract. On the other hand, the option buyer must pay his option premium upfront. Generally, for options on futures, these effects tend to counteract each other. As an example, consider a European-style three-month oil call struck at $18, when the forward price is $18 and the implied volatility is 20%. Because this style of option may only be exercised at maturity, the discounting effect of interest rates is slightly more likely to outweigh the value of the free financing. Even so, an increase in interest rates from 5% to 10% would reduce the value of the call only slightly from $0.70 to $0.692.

Combination of effects Overall, certain effects

DELTA HEDGING

One way of extracting the value from an option is to hedge its value through trading in the underlying using an arbitrage strategy called "delta hedging". This strategy involves an ongoing series of trades which are designed to hedge the value of an option through frequent adjustments in the size of a commodity futures or forward position.

In the case of a call option, delta hedging involves a risk manager or trader translating the market level into a "delta equivalent" quantity of the underlying, which they then sell short. For example, an $18 call will increase in value by roughly *half a cent* if the value of the underlying rises *one cent* from $18 to $18.01. That approximate 50% "sensitivity" is the delta equivalent for an at-the-money option. As the value of the underlying increases, the percentage sensitivity, and therefore the delta equivalent, increases. (Conversely, when a trader is long a put, the delta equivalent is a negative amount such that an at-the-money put has an approximate delta equivalent of –50%.)

Having translated an options position into a delta equivalent value, a oil trader hedging an exchange-traded call can simply sell short the delta equivalent of oil futures. The amount sold short is such that any change in the underlying price will have an equal effect on both the option value and the value of the short position.

Thereafter, as the market moves up and down, the trader varies the number of contracts held short according to the delta equivalent formula. The trader thus sells at high prices and buys back (the short contracts) at lower prices. This strategy cashes a notional profit each time there is an in-and-out trade (assuming zero transaction cost and no time decay).

Normally a risk manager would use specialised option software to measure the delta exposure on a daily or a minute-to-minute basis. The program is quite complex to implement perfectly, since theoretically it requires minute adjustments in hedge positions based upon instantaneous price changes, plus adjustments for any changes in gamma, theta or vega variables. Panel 4 describes some of the problematics market makers encounter when they are delta hedging.

The table below provides a highly simplified illustration of how to hedge the value of an $18.00 call on 1,000,000 barrels (1,000 futures contracts) of crude oil. In this example, we look at the delta equivalents on $18.00 calls at two points in time: three months prior to maturity (at 24% volatility) and with one month to maturity (at 28% volatility).

In the hedging operation, the trader needs to sell short futures contracts of the same month as those controlled by the call option.

To give some idea of how the delta hedging would work over time, let us assume the starting price level for the relevant oil contract is $18.00, which means that the option being hedged is at-the-money. Using the delta-hedging formula shown above, the trader would sell short the delta equivalent, which is 517 contracts (51.7% of 1,000 cts = 517 cts), at a price of $18.00 per barrel. For the moment, let us assume that assume no further delta adjustments were made, and that the relevant contract finished $1.00 lower at $17.00 with one month yet to run. The 517 contract short position would then show a profit of $517,000, ($1.00 × 517,000). This largely offsets the fall in the value of the call

Simplified table illustrating hedging an $18.00 call option

| Underlying price | 3 months (24% vol.) | | | 1 month (28% vol.) | | | Time decay | | Change |
	option value	delta	no. cts	option value	delta	no. cts	option value	%	no. cts
$20.00	$2.203	81.8%	818	$2.055	91.2%	912	$0.148	6.7%	+94
$19.50	$1.808	75.9%	759	$1.613	85.1%	851	$0.195	10.8%	+92
$19.00	$1.446	68.8%	688	$1.209	76.3%	763	$0.237	16.4%	+75
$18.50	$1.121	60.6%	606	$0.855	64.8%	648	$0.266	23.7%	+42
$18.00	$0.840	51.7%	517	$0.564	51.4%	514	$0.276	32.9%	–3
$17.50	$0.605	42.4%	424	$0.342	37.4%	374	$0.263	43.5%	–50
$17.00	$0.416	33.2%	332	$0.188	24.6%	246	$0.228	54.8%	–86
$16.50	$0.272	24.6%	246	$0.092	14.3%	143	$0.180	66.2%	–103
$16.00	$0.167	17.3%	173	$0.040	7.3%	73	$0.127	76.0%	–100

Note: assumes 5% interest rate

option, which amounts to $0.652 per barrel ($0.840–$0.188), or a $652,000 loss for the 1 million barrel size of the calls.

Obviously, this result can be improved upon by "trading around" the starting position or "rebalancing" the deltas on a frequent basis. (It would make little sense to consider delta hedging in this fashion unless there was an intention to regularly rebalance.) For example, if prices proved highly volatile and the oil contract first rose instantaneously by $1.50 to $19.50 (and the delta hedge was increased by 242 cts to 759 cts short at an overall average price of $18.478), and then fell $2.50 to $17.00, the entire short position could be closed out for a profit of $1,122,000.

The more volatile the underlying price over the life of the option, the more value can be extracted from delta hedging. Moreover, if a trader takes profits from delta hedging, he retains any remain-

ing value in the call option.

Of course, it is possible that the market will move higher, and there will be a loss on the short futures contracts. For example, if the oil price were to reach $20.00 then there would be a loss of $2.00 per barrel on the starting 517 cts (1,000 × $2 × 517 = $1,034,000 loss). However, given our assumption of a large $2 jump in the underlying, and one month to maturity, the $18.00 call should be worth $2.055 per barrel or $2,055,000. The resulting gain of $1,215,000 more than covers the calculated loss of $1,034,000 on the starting short position.

Whatever level the underlying contract might settle at, any gains realised from "trading around" the deltas would be added to the gain or loss on the call. However, if there is little volatility then any gains from "rebalancing" might not fully offset the time decay of the call option.

interact in the energy market to create a very curious phenomenon: unusually slow time decay. The rise in implied volatility as an option approaches maturity, combined with the non-linear time effect (ie the square root of time, which is characteristic of all options) can mean substantially smaller time decay than for options on financial instruments which have a flatter volatility curve. As an example, in cases where prices move sideways, ie, where spot prices do not change, we can see some very small time decay as shown by the following illustration:

Time left (months)	1	3	6	12
Implied volatility (%)	30	26	22	18
Theoretical price ($)	0.605	0.910	1.087	1.226

Note: Underlying price at $18, $18 strike, 5% interest rate

The decline in the value of the option over the 11 months is much less than it would be if the volatility were constant. In the example, the option value declines by $0.621, or 50.7%, as it decays from being a 12-month option to a being a one-month option. If the volatility had remained at 18%, the one-month option would have been valued at $0.363, and the time decay over 11 months would have been $0.863 or 70.4%. In the example, the rise in implied volatility as the option approaches maturity reduces the time decay by $0.242 (which is 38% more slowly over the 11 months).

End-user's guide to energy option strategy

A truism discovered by those who attempt to market options is that everyone wants to buy options until they see what they cost. Corporations that use derivatives value the flexibility that energy options can provide. But because of the high volatilities, energy options "look" expensive: corporate derivatives users do not find it easy to justify premiums which might be 4–6% of the underlying for options of less than a year's duration.

This is especially true when corporate treasurers realise that to make optimal use of any plain vanilla options that they buy, they may need to become regular participants in the energy derivatives market. Often it is only by "trading around" a core options position through effective delta hedging (see Panel 3) that an option holder can extract the full value from the flexibility that options provide.

Since most corporate users have other businesses to run, becoming an active trader in the market is not usually practical. Consequently, a key issue for most corporate users is to find ways of making the options "cheaper" than the large upfront premium on a straight option purchase.

The easiest way to reduce the upfront cost of an option is to simultaneously sell another option. This is generally done by selling off potential cash inflows which may arise from the underlying commodity being hedged or from

MANAGING OIL OPTIONS USING THE BLACK-SCHOLES MODEL

Jean-François Maurey and Patrick Perfetti, Société Générale

When using oil options, end-users have the tricky task of finding the best compromise between the perfect hedge and the cost of the envisioned strategy. However, in most cases, once the hedging tool is put into place, the position is managed passively.

Players such as market-makers or volatility traders are obliged to behave differently. By their nature, these players assume "positions" with regard to price movements, and the volatility of the underlying asset, that have to be actively managed.

To be able to conserve a spread (as a market-maker), profit from an expectation about the market (when taking a position) or a market aberration (in arbitrage), the trader needs to discover the "real" price of the option, and to have available a method of arbitrage which will capture this price with sufficient accuracy. A trader who buys an at-the-money option with an implied volatility of 20% (with, for example, an option premium of $1/bbl), and who thinks that in the future the "historical" volatility will be 25% (and therefore that the option is actually worth US$1.25/bbl) should, through applying the chosen method of arbitrage, be able to gain that $0.25/bbl in whatever direction the market moves and, especially, whatever the value of the option when it expires.

The best known, and most often used, arbitrage method is that developed by Professors Black and Scholes (see Chapter 7). However, this model contains assumptions and limitations that make its application problematic – especially in the energy markets. In particular, it is based on a particular statistical hypothesis describing the

behaviour of the underlying asset: it assumes that the instantaneous relative variations of the underlying asset are distributed lognormally, so that the standard deviation (volatility) is stable over time.

In theory, if this condition is met, and if a trader buys an option at the implied volatility of the market and delta hedges his position on a continuous basis as described in Panel 3, the trader will not make either a profit or a loss on maturity (the return will only be the risk-free rate on the invested premium). The trader will have "captured" the theoretical price of the option.

In practice, transaction costs (typically one cent per barrel) and the market's bid/offer spread (on long-dated contracts, the spread may be as high as 10 or 15 cents a barrel), and the fact that a trader can only hedge "discontinuously" (close to close, for example) interfere. Despite this, if all the prices chosen for hedging are derived from a lognormal price distribution, the trader will succeed in sticking pretty closely to the theoretical arbitrage price of the option (Fig. A).

Unfortunately, the distribution of prices used for hedging is not always very close to a lognormal distribution. In the case of a short-term position, for example, the number of close-to-close prices will not be sufficient to be statistically significant; if the trader increases the hedge frequency, the problem of transaction costs reappears.

More generally, any statistically representative sample of oil data is unlikely to have a lognormal distribution, especially at times of very high volatility. Graphs showing the distribution of oil prices tend to present a narrower distribution

A. Delta hedge close to close with lognormal underlying (historical volatility = implied volatility)

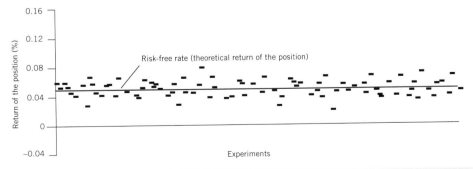

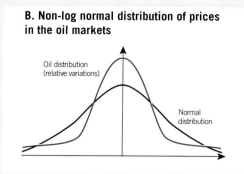

B. Non-log normal distribution of prices in the oil markets

Oil distribution (relative variations)

Normal distribution

centre and wider borders (Fig. B). This is part of the explanation for "volatility smiles" on out-of-the-money options, and reflects the very abrupt and violent price movements manifested on the commodities markets.

There is also the problem of estimating volatility. Contrary to the hypothesis of the Black-Scholes model, this volatility is not constant over time. To get as accurate a duplication as possible of the theoretical option price, the historical volatility of the management period should be used – but for obvious reasons, this is only available in retro-

spect. The calculation of historical volatility also has to be coherent with the practicalities of risk managing the option position: for example, close-to-close delta hedging and the problem posed by weekends has to be taken into account.

On the other hand, if one wants to continuously value the portfolio by marking to market, then it is necessary to use the market's implied volatilities – which change everyday! This is a problem in the financial, as well as the commodity, risk management markets. But the problem is greatly accentuated by the fact that the underlying energy markets are relatively much more volatile.

Because of these imperfections, the effectiveness of the Black-Scholes model can only be judged statistically across multiple option positions. Globally, on a very large number of positions, it will indeed prove to be satisfactory, and the trading house will be able to duplicate the theoretical price of its portfolio. But, as Figure C indicates, in a one-off operation there may be surprises!

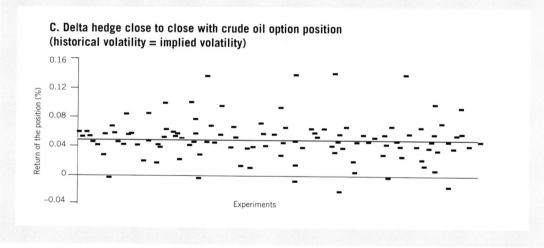

C. Delta hedge close to close with crude oil option position (historical volatility = implied volatility)

Return of the position (%)

Experiments

the option purchased. The premium received from the option sold can then be used to reduce the net cost. The key challenge for the risk manager thus becomes constructing optimal combinations of sold and bought options.

"STRAIGHT" OPTIONS
These instruments, depicted graphically in Figure 5 overleaf,[3] include individual puts and calls, as well as caps and floors (see Panel 5).

While the size of the upfront premium may be large, certain users find straight options acceptable as a core risk management tool. This is often because the options are being used as component pieces of a larger risk management

programme. Many oil producers and refiners use a variety of derivatives and like to construct customised hedging programmes around individual futures and options.

In addition, there are some companies whose credit risk is such that it is much easier for them to buy options rather than sell options. This is because the option buyer normally pays the upfront premium one or two business days after transacting, and thus poses a far lower credit risk than an option seller, who does not settle his obligations until maturity (or upon early exercise). Given the much smaller credit exposure, companies of lesser credit-standing can normally transact on equal terms with top

PANEL 5

CAPS, FLOORS AND COLLARS
Jean-François Maurey and Patrick Perfetti, Société Générale

Caps, which are simply "strips", or consecutive series, of call options with the same strike price, are some of the commonest option-based instruments in energy price risk management.

To understand how they are applied, imagine that a major European refiner has decided to protect itself against price rises in crude oil over the next financial year. The company arranges to buy a cap with a strike price of $20 per barrel, a maturity of 12 months, and monthly settlement; the volume hedged is 200,000 barrels per month, and the premium charged is 60 cents a barrel.

At the end of each month, the average price over the month (representing the cost of physical supply) is compared with the strike price of $20.00 per barrel. If the average price rises above $20.00 per barrel ($24.00 for example), the seller of the cap pays the refiner ($4.00 multiplied 200,000 times = $800,000). The cap thus assures the refiner of a supply of 200,000 barrels, at a maximum price of $20.60 per barrel, for a year (Fig. A).

A floor, composed of a strip of put options, is simply a cap in reverse. By selling a floor, a consumer fixes the *minimum* price that it will pay for energy, and thus gives up any chance of profiting from a fall in prices below a certain level. But the sum raised from the sale may be used to subsidise the price the consumer pays for energy or for risk management.

For example, imagine that the management of the refinery decide they cannot afford to pay the full price of the cap (the $0.60 per barrel premium). They therefore agree to purchase a $20.00 cap and finance it through the sale of a $17.50 floor. This provides them with a "collar" at zero cost.

If the price of the crude rises above $20, to $24.00 for example, the refinery exercises its cap at $20.00 and receives $4.00 per barrel from the

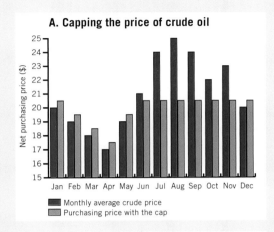

A. Capping the price of crude oil

Net purchasing price ($)

■ Monthly average crude price
■ Purchasing price with the cap

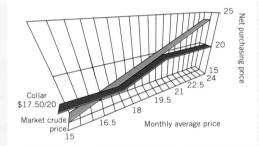

B. Controlling crude prices with a collar

Collar $17.50/20

Market crude price

Monthly average price

Net purchasing price

collar provider. If the price of crude falls below $17.50, to $15.00 for example, the collar provider exercises its floor at $17.50 and the refinery pays out $2.50 per barrel. If the crude price stays between $17.50 and $20.00, the refinery obtains its supplies at the market price.

At first sight, using a zero-cost collar may appear to be the safest course of action for the refinery: it involves no upfront cost and offers no "speculative" return. However, if oil prices fall considerably, the refinery may end up paying much more for its feedstock than its competitors – who may lower their prices aggressively as a result. The "zero-cost" collar is thus really a "zero *upfront cost*" collar – true price insurance can be secured only by purchasing a cap.

credits when they are pure option buyers.

Typical examples of companies using this kind of option strategy might be a privately-owned shipping company which buys an OTC fuel oil cap as a hedge against an increase in bunker fuel prices, or a small charter airline that buys a jet fuel cap. Typically, these would settle in cash against the monthly average price of an

appropriate index (typically Rotterdam HSFO, Singapore 180cst, 380cst, 3% NY Harbor, or 3% US Gulf in the case of fuel oil; and NWE, Rotterdam barges, or the Singapore quotation in the case of jet fuel).

Caps such as these provide a cash inflow to the option buyer if the monthly average price of the relevant index exceeds the strike price. For example, the shipping company might buy a six-month cap for 5,000 tonnes per month struck at $80 per tonne of fuel oil and pay $3 per tonne for the option. For each month that the average is above $80, they would receive the "upside" times the quantity. If the average were $87 for a particular month, they would receive $7 times 5,000, (ie, $35,000) for such month; if the index averages below $80 they pay nothing beyond the original premium.

There is a potential "risk control" benefit in the straight option. The option buyer limits his potential hedging cost to the upfront premium. Unlike some of the instruments described below, even if the price falls far below the option strike, the buyer only loses the premium – not the opportunity of benefitting from lower prices. This can be important in fiercely competitive industries: for example, a charter airline

may be forced to pass on to its customers at least a portion of any potential fuel savings if prices fall sharply.

COLLARS

This instrument (Fig. 6) involves the simultaneous purchase of a call and the sale of a put. If a series of settlements are required, a multi-settlement collar would involve a simultaneous purchase of a cap and sale of a floor. The instrument can also be constructed the other way round so that a company trying to protect against a downside move might sell the upside (call or cap) and purchase the downside (put or floor).

Collars are often constructed as "zero cost" collars, which really means zero *upfront* cost in the sense that the value of the option sold is equal to the one purchased. (It is not necessarily "zero cost" because if prices fall the buyer of a collar may have to pay out a considerable downside below the put strike price.)

This instrument can also be thought of as a forward (or a swap) with a band in the middle (the range between the put strike and the call strike) where "nothing happens". Above the call strike, the collar seller pays out the upside; below the put strike, he receives the downside. (Payments are reversed when a company buys a collar.)

With the notion of put/call parity in mind, it might be thought that the put strike and the call strike should be symmetrical around the price of a forward (or swap). This is not usually true for two reasons:

❑ As the symmetrical distance from the forward (swap) price increases, the call (cap) value increases faster than the put (floor) value due to the expected "log normal" distribution of prices. The reason is that there is a "compression effect" on potential downside prices. Because a commodity price cannot go below zero, a put has a limited potential payout. Whereas on the upside, in the case of a call, there is no theoretical limit to how high the commodity price may go. The result is that the probability of prices are distributed in an upwardly skewed distribution (a "log-normal" distribution) around the forward price. As an illustration, with forward prices at $18 and volatility at 20%, a one-year $20 call might be worth $0.68 and a one-year $16 put (also $2.00 away from the money) would be worth $0.55 (using the same volatility assumption in pricing the options). On the same assumptions, and with an $18 forward price, a

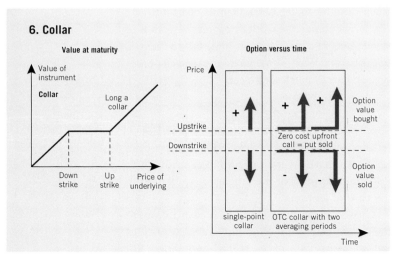

5. Straight options

Value at maturity

Value of instrument

Call or cap

Long a call

Strike price

Price of underlying

Option versus time

Price

Option value

+

American call

+ + +

OTC cap with two averaging periods

Time

Value at maturity

Value of instrument

Short a put

Put or floor

Strike price

Price of underlying

Option versus time

Price

American put

OTC floor with two averaging periods

-

- -

Option value

Time

Note 3 at the end of this chapter provides an introduction to these "option versus time" diagrams

6. Collar

Value at maturity

Value of instrument

Collar

Long a collar

Down strike

Up strike

Price of underlying

Option versus time

Price

+

+ +

Upstrike

Zero cost upfront call = put sold

Downstrike

-

- -

Option value bought

Option value sold

single-point collar

OTC collar with two averaging periods

Time

zero-cost collar might be constructed using a $16.00 put which would have equal value to a $20.56 call. (Note that this level of call strike does not take account of the market maker's profit margin, or "volatility spread".)

❏ The second reason for a lack of symmetricality on collar structures is that an options market maker will not take on the responsibility for managing the options inherent in a collar without building in a margin. Consequently, a market maker might retain a "volatility edge" of some amount (a 1–2% spread on volatility is not abnormal on energy options) for transacting a collar. For example, if the one-year forward is $18.00, and a client buys a one-year collar with $16.00 as the "downstrike", the buyer might have to accept an "upstrike" of $21.14 (which gives a 2% volatility spread to the market maker). If the client is selling the collar, he might set $16.00 as the downstrike and $20.03 as the upstrike for a zero-cost collar. Obviously, the mid-point between upstrike and downstrike is higher for the collar buyer ($18.57) than it is for the collar seller ($18.02). A market maker can rarely find a buyer and seller for the same collar structure, so this difference in bid/offer may have to cover his cost of managing the embedded option position as well as offering a profit margin.

Many companies use collars because they like the idea of "cheap insurance". An energy consumer buying a collar gets protection from an adverse upward move through the cap, pays nothing upfront, and only has a cash outflow if prices settle below the downstrike on the floor. In a rising market, the collar buyer gets a cash inflow from the upside (beyond the cap strike) without paying anything upfront.

In a falling market, the consumer will be able to buy energy more cheaply. But the energy consumer does not give away all of the benefit of lower prices. Because the collar has a "range where nothing happens", the fall in prices below the original forward price should be greater than the cash outflow he pays on the floor. The consumer therefore pays out only a portion of his savings. However, the consumer does "give away" a volatility spread to the market maker.

Any type of energy consumer might use a collar structure (an airline, an industrial user of oil, or an oil or gas burning electric utility). The structure can be reversed for an oil producer, with the oil producer selling the cap and buying the floor.

PARTICIPATING COLLARS AND PARTICIPATING SWAPS

These structures (Fig. 7) are essentially exchanges of options, offering a zero upfront cost. In the case of the participating collar, a company normally sells an option struck at-the-money and buys one that is out-of-the-money. Because an at-the-money option has greater value, if the options were transacted for the same quantity, then the at-the-money option sold would be worth more than the option purchased – and so the company would be due an upfront premium. With a participating collar, the option bought is for a larger quantity than the one sold and so the options have equal premium value but different sizes.

A participating swap is like a participating collar except that the gap between the call strike and the put strike is eliminated by moving the strikes to the same point. In order to give a larger quantity to the purchased option, the strike price on the option sold is moved into the money.

To make these two participating structures clearer, we will provide examples of both. Imagine that an oil producer wants to sell a participating collar. This would involve simultaneously selling a cap struck, for example, at the swap price and buying a lower strike floor out-of-the-money for a larger quantity. To keep the example simple, we can use a single settlement. The producer might sell a one-year call on 66,700 barrels struck at $18.00 which is at-the-forward, and this call might have a value of $1.36 per barrel or a total premium received of $90,712. A one-year put struck at $16.70 might cost $0.907 per barrel, and this could be acquired in a zero-cost exchange if it were for 100,000 barrels. With this "participating" instrument, if prices were to rise and settle at $19.12, which is above the $18 upstrike, the producer

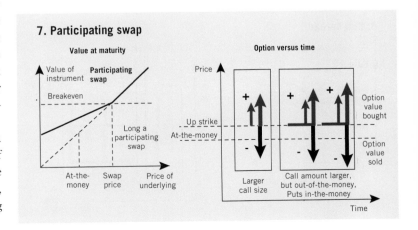

7. Participating swap

would pay a cash outflow of $1.12 per barrel, or $74,704 on the 66,700 call. On the other hand, if prices fell and settled at $14.65, below the $16.70 downstrike of the put, there would be a cash inflow of $205,000 – the downside multiplied by the larger downside quantity ($2.05 × 100,000).

Alternatively, the oil producer might sell a participating swap. To keep the quantities in the same ratio of 66.7/100, a call is sold for 66,700 barrels, and the put is bought for 100,000 barrels. If we move both strikes to $17.34, both options would have equal premia (assuming the market maker that buys the participating swap from the producer retains a 1% volatility spread). If oil prices settle at $19.12, the participating swap would cost $118,726; the cash outflow is more than the participating collar described above because of the lower call strike. If prices settle at $14.65, the cash inflow is $269,000 ($17.34–14.65 = $2.69 × 100,000), which is a greater hedge benefit because of the higher strike on the put.

These instruments are described as "participating" because the company that enters into them participates in any favourable price move in the underlying commodity. For example, the oil producer can protect 100% of its downside risk (below the floor price) while selling a call on a smaller quantity and therefore retaining some portion of the upside in the underlying above the cap price. In the participating collar example, the producer pays out 66.7% of its upside on the underlying price of 100,000 barrels of production, but protects 100% below $16.70. The cost of the "participation" is the less favourable placement of the option strike prices.

BULL & BEAR SPREADS

A bull spread is a call that is partly financed by simultaneously selling back a higher strike call. A bear spread is a put that is acquired more cheaply by selling a lower strike put. These instruments (Fig. 8) are cheaper than straight options because the size of the payout is limited. The call (or cap) payment is limited to a fixed amount of the "upside" and the put (or floor) payment is limited to a fixed amount of the "downside". For example, a bull spread might be the potential upside between a $19.00 cap and a $21.00 "supercap" so that the potential cash inflow to the purchaser is limited to a maximum of $2.00 per barrel. A bear spread might be, for example, the downside between $17.00 and $15.00, also limited to $2.00. The reason for using such instruments is that they are cheaper to buy than straight options with the same strike as the cap or floor; but the hedge protection begins to be seen at the same strike level.

An illustration of the possible cost savings for one year, single point settlement is given below. The illustration assumes a forward price of $18; other assumptions as above. The payout amounts below each instrument indicate the amount received by the holder of the instrument if the price settles at the figure indicated. For example, a $19 cap has a payout of $3 if the settlement price of the underlying is $22.

Instrument	$19 Cap	$19/21 Bull	$17 Floor	$17/15 Bear
Option premium	$0.98	$0.57	$0.90	$0.66
Payout at $22.00	$3.00	$2.00	0	0
at $20.50	$1.50	$1.50	0	0
at $15.50	0	0	$1.50	$1.50
at $14.50	0	0	$2.50	$2.00

These structures usually attract companies that would like to buy straight options, but which also want to pay a smaller upfront premium. To gain a saving they are willing to give up some of the less likely, or distant, beneficial price movements. An example might be an industrial company that wants a hedge against a rise in the price of the low sulphur fuel oil that it consumes, and which is willing to use a Brent crude oil cap as a hedge. (The company has consciously accepted the product basis risk between the price of crude and low sulphur fuel oil, because the crude option appears cheaper and is more liquid.) To make the upfront cost lower, they might agree to limit their cash inflow to $2.00 per barrel. Thus, they might buy a $19–21 bull spread at $0.57, rather than the $0.98 that a straight call option would cost. This is over 40% cheaper and yields the

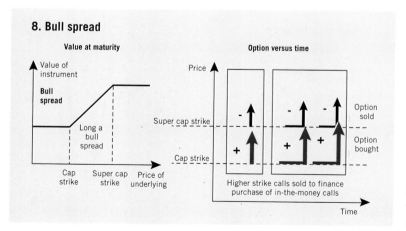

8. Bull spread

Value at maturity

Value of instrument

Bull spread

Long a bull spread

Cap strike Super cap strike Price of underlying

Price of underlying

Option versus time

Price

Super cap strike

Cap strike

Option sold

Option bought

Higher strike calls sold to finance purchase of in-the-money calls

Time

same payout for the first $2.00 of price move over the cap strike.

The range of payouts shown in the example above illustrates the value of using such an option where the energy price is expected to stay within a range limited by the supercap or superfloor. Often, companies use these "spread instruments" as part of a shorter maturity hedging strategy, and a standard collar as part of a longer-range hedge.

SWAPTION

A swaption (Fig. 9) is an option to buy (or to sell) a swap. As with any option, the swaption buyer pays an upfront premium for the right, but not the obligation, to buy an oil (or gas) swap at a fixed price. Compared to a cap covering the same period as the swap, the call swaption is cheaper because after the swaption is exercised, there is two-way risk on the swap, while the cap contains no downside risk for the buyer.

Swaptions are typically purchased by clients who need the assurance of a maximum fixed price, but feel that there is a reasonable prospect of a price fall before the expiry of the swaption. If prices do fall, then they will let the swaption expire unused and buy a swap at a lower cost. Typically, a swaption is held until maturity because there is normally no advantage in exercising prior to maturity. Logically, a holder of a swaption will only exercise it if the predetermined fixed exercise price is lower than an alternative swap purchased at the then-prevailing market price.

As an example, let us assume that a swaption, maturing in five weeks, was purchased in late December, expiring in the middle of February; the swaption controls a six-month swap at $19.00 for February through July. Such a swaption might have cost 30 cents per barrel of the swap, or $180,000 for a swap covering 100,000 barrels per month or 600,000 barrels overall. Assuming that the swaption is exercised at maturity, then the monthly payouts over the six months, February to July, for a $19.00 fixed-price swap would be as follows:

	Average price	Fixed price	Difference	Payment on 100,000 bbl
January	18.82	Not covered	0	
February	19.05	19.00	0.05	5,000
March	18.96	19.00	(0.04)	(4,000)
April	20.22	19.00	1.22	122,000
May	20.99	19.00	1.99	199,000
June	22.36	19.00	3.36	336,000
July	21.75	19.00	2.75	275,000
Feb–Jul 92	20.56	19.00	1.56	933,000

From this cash inflow, the swaption cost of

$180,000 could be subtracted, giving a net cash inflow of $753,000 for the swaption exercised prior to maturity. In this particular instance, where the swaption was cheap because of its short maturity, and where the market rose during the life of the swap, the net inflow is likely to have been more than for a straight call or for a collar.

However, the short maturity in the example does not fully reflect the flexibility inherent in the swaption. The advantage of the swaption is that the client need not exercise the swaption and can take advantage of any lower-cost opportunities which may be seen in the market during the period prior to maturity of the swaption.

Conclusion: strategy summary for end-users

From the discussion above, it should be clear that different types of energy derivative are suited to quite different exposure management strategies.

❏ If an energy consumer feels certain that energy prices are at an important low (or a producer sees a high), then a swap is likely to be the most cost-effective way of locking into a low fixed price (or high price for a producer). There are no upfront premiums to pay, and the swap increases in value as soon as the price begins to move. The disadvantage is that the swap (or forward or future) leaves the client exposed to the risk of very substantial losses if he is wrong and prices move in an unfavourable direction.

❏ The more uncertain the end-user is about the future direction of prices, and the more he desires flexibility in executing his hedging requirements, the more attractive are option-related instruments, because options bring flexibility. The issue with the option is whether the cost of the flexibility provided by the option is

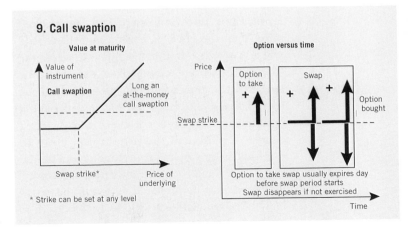

9. Call swaption

Value at maturity

Option versus time

HEDGING VERSUS SPECULATION WITH OPTIONS: SOME GUIDELINES

What is hedging and what is speculation? This question took on increasing importance during 1994 as reports emerged of large losses suffered by corporations as a result of derivatives trading. If losses from hedging do emerge, a risk management strategy should be defensible as appropriate "hedging" if the following guidelines have been followed:

❏ The *direction* of a hedging transaction should normally be the opposite of both the specific underlying position being hedged, and the overall exposure of the company.

❏ The *size* of a hedging trade will normally relate to the underlying position, but it must also be realistic – particularly where a basis exposure is involved. For example, hedging long-term oil exposure with short-term oil futures leaves a time basis exposure. If the shape of the futures curve moves "against" a hedger, so that every month when they roll over their futures contracts on the exchange (that is, when they buy the front contract and sell the next contract) there is a big loss, the hedging company may face a significant negative cashflow. A hedge that is theoretically satisfactory in the long term is of little use if the hedging company cannot withstand the monthly losses while it waits for the basis to move back into its favour.

❏ The *risk/reward* should make sense. If combina-tions of options are used, there should probably be a ratio of exposures which, if prices go the "wrong" way, remains somewhere near symmetrical exposure on both the put and call sides of the trade. In 1994, some companies got into trouble using "leveraged swaps" wherein protection bought through a call was financed by selling a vastly larger exposure on the put side. When the market moved against the hedge, the losses were magnified, and the ultimate loss was far larger than any likely gain from the hedge had prices moved the other way.

❏ There should be a clear *understanding* of the hedging transaction so that the corporation can measure, monitor and anticipate the extent of its exposure on the trade (and explain the transaction to its board, if necessary).

❏ The should be a clear *hedging policy*. For example, "trading around a hedge" (ie taking profits and modifying hedge positions) can be a good tactic so long as the amount of trading is not excessive and it fits the policies and strategies agreed by the corporation's senior management.

❏ There should be close *supervision* from the senior levels of the corporation to make sure that corporate policies are being followed, and that those responsible for risk management have the ability to understand and manage the overall risk management programme.

affordable. Many combinations of buying and selling options have been developed to reduce their upfront cost.

❏ The most "swap-like" options-related instruments are collars and participating swaps. For a collar, if the "upstrike" and "downstrike" are set at the same price and there is a single fixed price, then the collar is exactly equivalent to a swap. The greater the distance between the "upstrike" and the "downstrike", the larger the range of variation where no payments will be required and the more the collar will exhibit option-like features. For a client who wants a degree of protection similar to a cap, but who does not want to pay an upfront premium, the "zero-cost" collar can be attractive. However, the client must be prepared to accept the possibility of substantial losses if prices fall below the "downstrike". The more precisely an energy consumer can identify a suitable level for the "downstrike" (with little risk of cash outflows), which still provides a substantial reduction in the cost of a cap at the desired level, the more beneficial the collar structure. Producers should seek low-risk levels for placing the upstrike.

For a participating swap, if there is zero participation (ie the quantities on both sides are the same) then the instrument is exactly equivalent to a swap. As the quantity of the option purchased increases, then the strike on the option sold must be moved into-the-money to compensate for the smaller size. The participating swap is really two separate instruments sold as a combination: an offmarket swap entered with an immediate negative value which pays for an option in the desired direction. For a consumer, this means buying a swap with a fixed swap price "above market" to pay for an out-of-the-money cap. It follows that a participating swap should be used if a corporate feels there is a high probability that prices will move so that the embedded swap will be in-the-money.

❏ The cap provides certainty of a limited maximum loss (the same is true of the floor for an energy producer). For a standard cap, with the premium payable upfront, the potential loss is limited to the upfront premium. There is normally no limitation on the cash in-flows on the cap and so the cap provides ideal risk control in a volatile market: limited risk, and unlimited return. The disadvantage is the cost: the more volatile the market, the higher the upfront cost.

❏ The swaption is a hybrid which can provide the best of both worlds (in the right circumstances), or merely a more expensive way of entering a swap (in the wrong circumstances). For the energy consumer, the call swaption gives the assurance of protecting a maximum fixed hedge price, while allowing time for prices to drop – and it normally does this at a lower cost than a cap. However, it should only be used when there is a reasonable prospect that prices may go lower, and that there may be a fall in swap prices which is large enough to at least cover the upfront premium on the swaption.

1 *The author would like to thank Vince Kaminski and Stinson Gibner of Enron Capital & Trade Resources, and Graham Wright, consultant on futures and options and visiting lecturer at the City University Business School, for reading and commenting on this chapter. Risk would also like to thank Kosrow Dehnad of Citicorp Securities, Inc for his advice and help.*

Different option pricing models can produce different prices and delta equivalents. The figures published here are for demonstration purposes only.

2 *For the sake of clarity, the relationships described in this section are simplified and should really be regarded as approximations, or "rules of thumb".*

3 *This chapter introduces a new type of option diagram. Conventional diagrams show the option "value at maturity" with the price of the underlying on the x-axis and the option payout on the y-axis. The problem with the usual type of diagram is that it makes it impossible to compare options combinations where there are different maturities and to show how the option values are affected by time. The new type of diagram puts "time to maturity" on the x-axis and depicts an option as an arrow with the base of the arrow starting at the strike price and the length of the arrow representing the option's value. This makes it possible to compare visually the value of options of different maturities while instantly visualising how option values will change over time.*

Exotic Options

Vincent Kaminski and Stinson Gibner[1]

Enron Capital & Trade Resources

Exotic options are increasingly used as a means of controlling exposure to energy prices. One reason is the persistently high volatility of a number of energy commodities. Certain kinds of exotic options are better able to cope with the problems caused by high volatility: Asian or average price options, for example, help to mitigate the risk of price spikes.

Another factor is related to the deregulation of the US markets which, in different energy sectors, has affected both producers (natural gas) and consumers of energy (for example, airlines and utilities). Deregulation has resulted in intense competition, and a concomitant sensitivity to price fluctuations. As companies have realised how vulnerable they are to fluctuations in commodity (especially energy) prices, they have tended to create or expand risk management units. Such specialised units have proven more likely to accept novel risk management instruments such as exotic options.

One of the main reasons that exotic options have been accepted within the energy industry is that options were, in fact, embedded in many energy contracts long before they became fashionable tools of financial engineering (and even before they were analysed in academic papers). An example is provided by the "take-or-pay" contracts in the natural gas industry. Under such a contract, the buyer agreed to purchase fixed-price gas up to an annual maximum, but became subject to deficiency payments if the volume bought dropped below a minimum amount. For example, a buyer of 3,600,000 MM Btus[2] of gas per year with a minimum take of 50% could elect to purchase 1,800,000 MMBtus. But any shortfall below the 1,800,000 MMBtu level would trigger a penalty payment equal to the product of the deficiency times an agreed unit fine. In addition, many contracts allowed the buyer to vary their take amount widely from month to month – providing they bought the agreed volume over the year. The buyer effec-

tively had an option on the timing of purchases over the year, and thus could take into consideration, among other factors, the prices of alternative fuels. Until the late 1980s, these options were not explicitly recognised (or priced) by the sellers, who lacked the financial sophistication to isolate them from the other provisions of the contract.

Moreover, certain contracts in the energy industry contained, directly or indirectly, averaging provisions. For example, many contracts in the oil industry are based on the monthly or weekly averages of reference spot prices compiled by different institutions. Similarly, many natural gas contracts settle against reference prices which are, in effect, averages over some time period. This arose because the price indices compiled by newsletters in the natural gas industry – widely used as a pricing benchmark in supply contracts – represent average prices during the bid-week[3] for deliveries of gas at specified locations. It follows that the risk exposure of most producers and end-users of oil and gas is to an average price level over a period of time, and this facilitated the acceptance of Asian options.

One of the distinctive features of commodity risk management is the importance of basis risk, where basis is defined as the difference between two prices. This type of risk leads directly to another type of exotic option that is commonly traded in the energy business. Refiners are exposed to risks associated with changing crack spreads (the price differential between crude and the refined products); and producers are exposed to changing spreads between the prices of various grades of crude, or between the prices for natural gas at different geographic locations. In addition, both producers and consumers may be exposed to a "seasonal" risk (summer to winter price changes) or "annual" (year-to-year) price risk. All these types of risks have led to the prevalence of spread options in the industry.

PANEL 1

DEFINING EXOTIC OPTIONS

What are the modifications to the classical payoff definition that convert a standard option into an exotic option? We can identify a few major changes, which can be classified as follows:

1. Path dependency. The option payoff depends not only on the price of the underlying at exercise (which is simultaneous with expiration for a European option), but also on the price trajectory during the entire life of the option (or some part of it). Examples of path-dependent options include:

❏ Asian options, which have a payoff defined as $\max(\text{avg}(F)-K, 0)$ for a call and $\max(K-\text{avg}(F), 0)$ for a put. Thus the payoff is a function of the average price avg(F) of the underlying instrument, calculated over a specified time period.

❏ Average strike options, which have a payoff defined as $\max(F(T)-\text{avg}(F),0)$ for a call and $\max(\text{avg}(F)-F(T),0)$ for a put. The call payoff is equal to the price at horizon, less the average price over a certain time period.

❏ Lookback options, which offer the opportunity to obtain the best price that occurs during the life of the option. The payoff is defined as $F(T)-\min(F)$ for a call and $\max(F)-F(T)$ for a put, where max(F) and min(F) denote respectively the highest and the lowest price during the life of the option.

❏ Barrier options, which are extinguished or activated contingent upon the occurrence of a certain event defined in terms of the price of the underlying or defined in terms of the price of an entirely different asset. For example, an option on natural gas may have a barrier defined in terms of the price of residual fuel oil.

2. Multiple-commodity options with payoffs that depend on the prices of two or more commodities. Most common are the dual-commodity options. Examples include:

❏ Spread options, which have a payoff defined as $\max(F_1-F_2-K,0)$ for a call and $\max(K-(F_1-F_2),0)$ for a put, where F_1 and F_2 denote prices of commodities 1 and 2 at option expiration. The payoff of the option depends on the difference (spread) between the two prices.

❏ Options on the maximum and the minimum of two commodities with payoffs given, respectively, by $\max(\max(F_1,F_2)-K,0)$ and $\max(\min(F_1,F_2)-K,0)$ for a call, and $\max(K-\max(F_1,F_2),0)$ and $\max(K-\min(F_1,F_2),0)$ for the put.

❏ Options to exchange one asset for another or, in other words, to get the better of two assets.

3. Compound options in which the underlying instrument is itself an option.

4. Digital or binary options with pre-determined payoffs that depend on the occurrence of events usually defined in terms of one or more prices.

Note: This list of exotic options is by no means complete, but most of the options offered over-the-counter represent hybrids of the options enumerated here.

Another major reason for the increasing popularity of exotic options is that the recent period of high price volatility in energy inputs has coincided with increased price volatility in other commodities – in particular, commodities that are associated with large energy inputs such as copper and aluminium. This volatility has seemed particularly threatening to producers because the globalisation of many industries, and worldwide excess capacity, mean that it is difficult to transfer higher input costs to customers. Certain kinds of exotic options are particularly suited to the management of multiple price exposures simultaneously.

By the same token, an energy producer with debt on the balance sheet will suffer if energy prices fall and if interest rates increase. But the real danger arises if these two conditions happen to coincide. A producer may seek protection against low prices and higher interest rates independently, but it may be more cost efficient to seek remedies against the joint occurrence of two related risky situations. This creates the need for an option with a payoff that is dependent on two prices: the energy index price and interest rates. Such options tend to be referred to as either exotic or hybrid contracts. We will look at some of the technical aspects of this type of option; a more detailed discussion of their application and the concept of "integrated risk management" can be found in the next chapter.

This chapter is intended to provide a comprehensive review of the range of exotic options used in the energy industry. Our objective is to cover a rapidly expanding and highly technical area of applied finance in a way that is useful to a wide audience of professionals in the energy industry who might have had a limited prior exposure to derivatives; the chapter should also provide a useful and up-to-date summary of energy specific applications for derivative professionals. We provide the essential mathematical details and give detailed references to the most important papers; Appendix B at the back of this book lists many of the standard formulae for pricing exotic options.

We begin by defining what exactly an "exotic" option is, and then move on to discuss modelling and pricing. This overview is followed by sections describing each of the different types of contracts that have gained popularity in the energy industry: path-dependent options; dual-commodity options; compound options; digital options; and natural gas daily options. In our concluding section, we offer a resumé of some of the most pressing practical issues facing the providers and major end-users of exotic options.

What are exotic options?

The term *exotic option* is generally applied to those derivative contracts, detailed in Panel 1, that diverge from the assumptions inherent in the early models developed by Black-Scholes (1973), Merton (1973) and Cox, Ross and Rubinstein (1979). These early models apply to call and put options with payoffs that are defined as the difference between the price of the underlying instrument $(F(T))$ at the time that the option is exercised (T) and the strike price (K), or zero if it makes no sense to exercise.

To be more precise, the payoff of the option is defined as $\max(F(T)-K,0)$, in the case of a call, or $\max(K-F(T),0)$ in the case of a put. In the case of a European option, exercise is allowed only at expiration; in the case of an American option, early exercise is possible. To price an option, one has to make assumptions regarding the dynamics of the price of the underlying instrument. A standard assumption in option pricing is that the price of the underlying instrument (F) follows a geometric Brownian motion process, defined by:

$$dF = \mu F dt + \sigma F dz \qquad (1)$$

where

μ = drift (instantaneous expected return)
σ = volatility
dz = Wiener's variable ($dz = \varepsilon\sqrt{dt}$, ε being the standard normal random variable) and dt is an infinitesimally small step in time.

Black and Scholes (1973) proposed a formula for pricing European options on a stock that does not pay dividends. Their formula, one of the most important contributions to applied economics, reads as follows (for a call):

$$C = S(t)N(d_1) - e^{-r(T-t)}KN(d_2) \qquad (2)$$

with

$$d_1 = \frac{\ln(S(t)/K) + (r+0.5\sigma^2)(T-t)}{\sigma\sqrt{T-t}}$$
$$d_2 = d_1 - \sigma\sqrt{T-t}$$

where
t = valuation time
$T-t$ = life of the option in years
r = risk-free interest rate
K = strike price
$S(t)$ = stock price at time t
$N(.)$ = cumulative normal distribution function
and
C = call option value.

The use of the risk-free interest rate in formula (2) is based on the principle of risk-neutral valuation. Risk-neutral valuation uses the notion of a riskless portfolio, which is formed by combining an option with a position in the underlying. Since this portfolio has a predictable value under any circumstance, it is risk free and should earn the same rate of return as other risk-free securities. Information about the cost of creating a riskless portfolio allows us to price the option.

Note that the riskless hedge can be created even if the expected rate of return on the underlying instrument is unknown. This means that the price of an option can be determined without reference to investors' preferences regarding the rate of return that they would require to hold the underlying. If investors' risk preferences do not affect option prices, one can value the options under any type of risk preference – and it makes sense to assume the simple case of risk neutrality.

The Black-Scholes formula given by equation (2) must be modified if the standard assumption of geometric Brownian motion for the evolution of the underlying asset price is changed. Incorporation of a time-dependent or stochastic volatility is one example of a modified price evolution process. Another possibility is the selection of a different type of stochastic process altogether – for example, the jump diffusion process. Modifications to the Black-Scholes formula are also required if the option payoff definition diverges from the original specification in Black and Scholes. Asian options and lookback options are examples of options with other payoff definitions.

In this chapter, we focus on options that have a payoff definition that is different from the standard Black-Scholes framework, and focus on variations that are popular within the energy industry. Unless otherwise stated, none of the options discussed here allow for early exercise (that is, all are European-style options). We assume that the underlying instrument is a forward contract on a physical commodity, such as crude oil or natural gas, and that the price follows the geometric Brownian motion process described by equation (1).

One of the consequences of using a forward contract as the underlying is that the drift coefficient μ in equation (1) equals 0. The drift of a forward price (or, technically speaking, the certainty equivalent) must be equal to zero, since the zero initial cost of entering into a forward contract is incompatible with an assumption of positive expected return (Black 1976). The use of futures prices is followed consistently in all the pricing formulae used in this chapter. It is important to stress that the formulae apply to options on financial contracts; they are not applicable to options on physical commodities. The call option on a forward contract has a premium given by

$$C = \exp[-r(T-t)]\,[F(t)N(d_1) - KN(d_2)] \quad (2a)$$

where

$$d_1 = \frac{\ln(F(t)/K) + 0.5\sigma^2(T-t)}{\sigma\sqrt{T-t}}$$

$$d_2 = d_1 - \sigma\sqrt{T-t}$$

and $F(t)$ is the forward price at time t.

Pricing and hedging exotic options

A natural question asked by a potential buyer or writer of exotic options is how to price such contracts and also, in the case of a seller, how to hedge them. In response, we shall offer a few general comments and give some specific examples for different types of exotics.

To price an exotic option, one should first attempt to replicate it with a package of standard options or simpler exotics. If this is possible, then

each component option should be priced individually, and the sum of all the long and short positions will give the desired price. As a bid-offer spread for volatility is usually included in the option valuation, one should be careful not to artificially inflate the premium by including the volatility spread for each component option.

If the replication approach does not work, one should try to find a closed-form expression for the option price that is comparable to the Black-Scholes formula. Such solutions are available for many exotic options. We shall discuss some of them here and give references for some others. Even if an exact closed-form solution cannot be found one may be able to find an approximation method which gives acceptable accuracy in pricing.

If neither a closed-form solution nor a good approximation method can be found it is necessary to use one of the numerical methods. The numerical methods used for option valuation fall into three categories: Monte Carlo (simulation) methods; tree (binomial or multinomial) methods; and finite difference or numerical integration methods. Hull (1993) discusses in detail the implementation of Monte Carlo, tree and finite difference methods for option valuation.

PRICING METHODOLOGY
Monte Carlo methods The Monte Carlo approach for valuing options was first described by Boyle (1977). The Monte Carlo approach simulates the prices of the instruments underlying the option, and allows us to compute the option payoff for each simulated scenario of price movement. The simulations are repeated several times (typically, at least a few thousand times), and the option payoffs for the different paths are discounted to the present time and then averaged. This average payoff represents an estimate of the option value.

A single price is often simulated over time using the assumption of geometric Brownian motion – the assumption that underlies the Black-Scholes equation. The following formula for the price at time $t + \Delta t$ follows from equation (1) and can be used to produce a path for a single price:

$$F(t+\Delta t) = F(t)\exp\left[\left(\mu - \frac{\sigma^2}{2}\right)\Delta t + \sigma\varepsilon\sqrt{\Delta t}\right] \quad (3)$$

where ε represents a drawing from the standard normal distribution. The time increment may be taken as one calendar or trading day (or week or month), with an appropriate scaling of the other parameters (which are conventionally quoted on an annual basis). The drift coefficient μ, which is usually set to the risk-free interest rate for a stock that does not pay dividends, is made zero when modelling forwards and futures prices. Volatility, σ, is usually quoted as an annualised number, and should be adjusted according to the simulation frequency.

Although geometric Brownian motion is a common assumption for price behaviour, virtually any type of price evolution can be simulated using the Monte Carlo approach. Monte Carlo may be the method of choice for price processes that are difficult or impossible to implement using binomial or finite-difference methods. Because of the simplicity of implementation, the Monte Carlo approach is also useful as a way of validating pricing models that are based on other approaches.

The two main drawbacks of the Monte Carlo method are its relatively slow speed, and its inability to properly cope with American-style options. Since the standard error of the result from a Monte Carlo simulation is inversely proportional to the square root of the number of price path simulations, a large number of price simulations may be required – resulting in a long "run time" for the model. Of course, in a trading environment it is critical to produce precise option premium estimates within a short period of time. As a result, variance-reduction techniques are often used to improve the convergence of simulation results, and to keep the number of price scenarios within acceptable limits. One such technique, known as the "method of control variates", is discussed later in the section on Asian options. Curran (1994) discusses stratified sampling, another variance reduction technique.

Monte Carlo methods may also be used to value options that have payoffs which are dependent on two or more underlying instruments. In this case, the simulation should take into account the correlation between the underlying prices. An even more difficult problem is represented by options with payoffs that are dependent on the shape of the forward price curve and the yield curve (options on swaps). To price such claims it is necessary to model the entire curve. One approach to solving this problem is based on the Heath-Jarrow-Morton (1992) factor model which, though developed originally for interest rate instruments, seems very promising for commodity options.

All Monte Carlo algorithms depend on operating system supplied or other software in order to generate random drawings from a known distribution. Most software packages for numerical calculations contain programmes that generate random numbers. These programmes can also be implemented by any programmer who understands basic probability theory. Assuring the quality of pseudo-random number generators is critical to the implementation of simulation methods, as a poor random number generation can lead to incorrect results or poor convergence.

Chaplin (1993) suggests several tests that can be used for the verification of pseudo-random number generators. Press et al. (1992) give methods for improving system-supplied random number generators, and present stand-alone random generators; they also discuss methods for sampling from various distributions. Hammersley and Handscomb (1964) provide a good general reference for Monte Carlo methods, including discussions of random number generation and variance reduction techniques, and Schmeiser (1990) gives a more concise review of simulation methods, including pseudo-random number generation, random variate generation and variance reduction.

Binomial trees Binomial (trinomial, *n*-nomial) trees have become one of the most popular and widely used methods for pricing options. In a sense, the binomial tree approach occupies the middle ground between Monte Carlo simulation and finite difference methods; that is, while it can be described as "organised simulation", it can also be thought of as a special case of the finite difference method. In a tree method, the life of the option is subdivided into a number of time intervals. In each interval, the price of the underlying can move into a small number of states. For example, in the binomial tree method, the price in an interval can go up with a probability, say p, and go down with a probability $(1-p)$. The magnitudes and probabilities of the price shifts are determined from the stochastic process assumed for the price of the underlying by requiring that the distribution of the tree prices has the correct mean and variance at each time step (for example, Cox and Rubinstein, 1985; Hull, 1993; and Trigeoris, 1991).

Figure 1 illustrates a binomial tree along with the numerical assumptions used to construct the tree. The upward price movement is determined

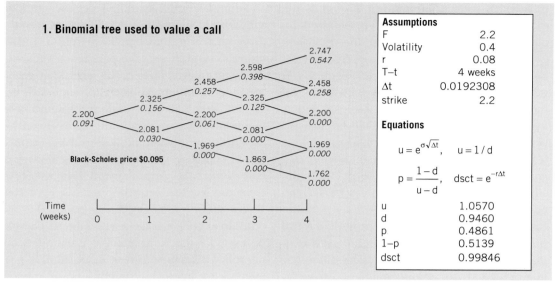

1. Binomial tree used to value a call

Assumptions	
F	2.2
Volatility	0.4
r	0.08
T−t	4 weeks
Δt	0.0192308
strike	2.2

Equations

$$u = e^{\sigma\sqrt{\Delta t}}, \quad u = 1/d$$

$$p = \frac{1-d}{u-d}, \quad dsct = e^{-r\Delta t}$$

u	1.0570
d	0.9460
p	0.4861
1−p	0.5139
dsct	0.99846

by multiplying the price at a given node by factor u. The downward movement is given by d, the inverse of u (d = 1/u). The top value at each node of the tree in Figure 1 gives the price of the underlying at that node. The lower, italicised number is the option value at the node. At horizon, the option payoff is computed for each of the terminal nodes. The option value is then calculated by means of a backward recursion, which takes the terminal payoffs back through the tree. The payoffs are discounted and weighted by the probabilities of the upward and downward price movements. The resulting discounted, probability-weighted average of the payoffs is an estimate of the option's value.

For example, a four-week European call option can be priced using the numerical assumptions shown in Figure 1. The option payoff at horizon is equal to the difference between the price and the strike, if this difference is positive, and zero otherwise. In Figure 1, the payoffs are equal to (from top to bottom): $0.547, $0.258, $0.00, $0.00, $0.00. The value of the option one week prior to expiration, at the top node, is equal to $0.398. The value at this node is calculated as follows:

Discount_factor × {Probability(up) × payoff(up) + Probability(down) × payoff(down)}

or

0.99846 × (0.4861 × $0.547 + 0.5139 × $0.258) = $0.398

Continuing backward through the tree to calculate values for all the nodes leads us to an estimate of $0.091 for the premium. For comparison, an application of the Black-Scholes formula produces a premium of $0.095. The discrepancy between the two values is due to the imperfect approximation of a continuous distribution of prices through a discrete distribution.

The accuracy of binomial tree pricing improves when the number of time steps used is increased. Using 30 time steps results in option prices which are within 1% of the Black-Scholes prices. Of course, using a very large number of time steps to produce very accurate prices has the drawback of requiring more calculation time. Hull and White (1988) demonstrate how control variate techniques can be used to accelerate the convergence of binomial option pricing methods.

Binomial methods afford great flexibility. They can be easily adapted to value American options, and have also been extended to evaluate options based on two underlying instruments (for example, Boyle 1988; Amin 1991).

Finite differences and numerical integration
Two approaches that price exotic options by numerically solving the partial differential equations governing the option prices are finite difference methods and numerical integration.

Finite difference methods were originally applied to option valuation problems by Schwartz (1977), and Brennan and Schwartz (1978), and were extended by Courtadon (1982) and Hull and White (1990). These methods start with the partial differential equation satisfied by the option price. A grid is constructed by discretising the time-price domain. In less technical terms, this means that a grid is constructed by dividing the life of the option into small time intervals and breaking the range of possible prices down into a number of intermediate discrete prices. (One may note the similarity to the binomial tree method.) The resulting grid of allowed time and price steps allows the differential equation to be approximated by a number of difference equations for which a numerical solution can be found. Dewynne and Wilmott (1993) and Wilmott, Dewynne and Howison (1993) discuss the application of finite difference methods to valuing exotic options. These methods are generally applicable when valuing options under Black-Scholes type price evolution, and may be computationally more efficient than other methods when valuing a large number of options (Geske and Shastri, 1985).

When the option valuation problem is reduced to an integral equation, the option value can be calculated by finding the expected payoff through numerical integration. We will give an example of the application of this technique in our discussion of spread options.

DETERMINATION OF INPUTS
Deriving a pricing formula for an exotic option is a necessary but not sufficient condition for the correct valuation and determination of risk parameters. Equally important are the inputs, notably volatility and, for options which depend on two or more underlying prices, correlation.

Volatility can be inferred from the observed prices of options in the market. One can simply use the option pricing formula and vary volatility until the quoted option premium is matched. Another approach is to use one of the techniques for solving a nonlinear equation, such as Newton-Raphson. One complication is that implied volatility is different for options at-the-money and options in- and out-of-the-money. This phenomenon, known as the "volatility smile", was noted in Chapter 6 and has recently received a good deal of attention in the literature. Derman and Kani (1994), Dupire (1994) and Rubinstein (1994) have independently developed option-pricing models which attempt to incorporate the implied volatility smile.

If quoted premiums are not available, or are not reliable, one can estimate volatility from historical data. This task is not trivial and requires a combination of careful econometric analysis and common sense. The standard procedure for estimating volatility as the standard deviation of the natural logarithms of ratios of historical prices is well known; further discussion on the subject can be found in Cox and Rubinstein (1985) and Leong (1992).

The price of a dual-commodity option depends on the correlation between the two underlying asset prices. Though correlation is one of the most widely used concepts in applied statistics, the use of this concept in the context of option pricing is quite difficult. First of all, correlation, like volatility, should be estimated within the framework of the assumptions made regarding the dynamics of the underlying assets' prices. Historical volatilities are estimated as the standard deviation of the natural logarithms of the price ratios, and the same approach can be taken in the case of correlations. Practitioners tend to overlook this fact, and sometimes use correlations based on levels of the prices.

A consistent estimator of correlation is given by

$$\rho = \frac{1}{n \times dt} \times \frac{1}{\sigma_1 \sigma_2}$$

$$\sum_{i=1}^{n} \Big[\ln F_1(i+1) - \ln F_1(i) \Big] \Big[\ln F_2(i+1) - \ln F_2(i) \Big]$$

(5)

where
n = the number of time periods sampled
dt = the time step between samples
σ_1 = volatility of asset 1
σ_2 = volatility of asset 2
and
$F_1(i)$ = price of asset 1 at time period i
$F_2(i)$ = price of asset 2 at time period i.

Historical correlations tend to be unstable over time. This may be a manifestation of permanent changes in the market structure, random shocks, or a reflection of seasonality. The

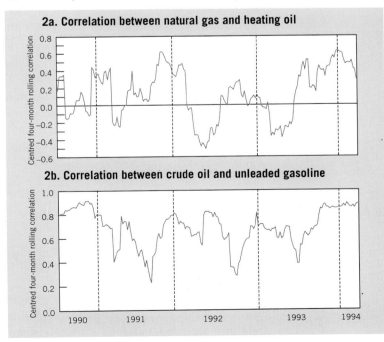

2a. Correlation between natural gas and heating oil

2b. Correlation between crude oil and unleaded gasoline

impact of seasonality is illustrated in Figure 2, which shows centred four-month correlation between crude oil and unleaded gasoline (Nymex prompt contracts) and correlation between natural gas and heating oil (Nymex prompt contracts). In the case of gasoline and crude, the correlation was affected by the Gulf War. In the case of natural gas and heating oil, correlation increases during the winter months when both prices are affected by the same underlying factor – namely, the weather.

One of the recent developments in the estimation of correlation and volatility is the application of the GARCH technology, which was originally introduced by Engle (1982). The term GARCH denotes a generalised autoregressive conditionally heteroscedastic econometric model. This term identifies the departures from the classical regression model given by:

$$y_t = \alpha + \beta x_t + \varepsilon_t \qquad (6)$$

where

α, β = regression coefficients,
y_t = dependent variable at time t,
x_t = independent variable at time t,
and
ε_t = random noise (error) term at time t.

In this classical regression model, the random terms are normally distributed and uncorrelated (that is, $\varepsilon_t \sim N(0,\sigma)$ for each t and $E(\varepsilon_i, \varepsilon_j) = 0$ for each i,j). The constant variance assumption for the normal distribution of random terms is known as homoskedasticity. This assumption is often violated in the case of financial time series, and special estimation techniques must be employed. The ARCH model postulates that the variance of the error term is time dependent and given, for the ARCH(q) model, by:

$$\sigma_t^2 = \alpha_0 + \alpha_1\varepsilon_{t-1}^2 + \alpha_2\varepsilon_{t-2}^2 + ... + \alpha_q\varepsilon_{t-q}^2 \qquad (7)$$

where α is a vector of unknown parameters. The GARCH(p,q) model, introduced by Bollerslev (1986), assumes that the distribution of the error term, ε_t, conditional upon information ψ_t available at period t, is given by:

$$\varepsilon_t|\psi_t \sim N\left(0,\sigma_t^2\right)$$

with

$$\sigma_t^2 = \alpha_0 + \alpha_1\varepsilon_{t-1}^2 + \alpha_2\varepsilon_{t-2}^2 + ...$$
$$+\alpha_q\varepsilon_{t-q}^2 + \delta_0 + \delta_1\sigma_{t-1}^2 + \delta_2\sigma_{t-2}^2 + ... + \delta_p\sigma_{t-p}^2 \qquad (8)$$

where α and δ are vectors of unknown parameters. Use of this model requires non-linear regression techniques and involves a relatively

high degree of econometric sophistication. It seems, however, that the GARCH technology is rapidly gaining acceptance in the dealer community.[4]

Path-dependent options

Path-dependent options have a payoff that is dependent on the price history of the underlying over part or all of the life of the option. Our review will be limited to Asian options, lookbacks and related contracts, and barrier options.

ASIAN OPTIONS

Asian options have payoffs that depend on an average of prices over a period of time. For a call, the payoff of an Asian option is given by max(avg(F) – K,0); for an Asian put the payoff is max(K – avg(F),0) where K is the strike price and avg(F) is the average price over the specified period.

The averaging period may correspond to the entire life of the option, or it can be shorter. Many contracts in the natural gas industry, for example, are based on the average closing prices on the last two or three days of trading of the first available Nymex contract. If an Asian option is traded when it is within its averaging period, pricing the option requires supplying the average-to-date price of the underlying. For such options, averaging effectively starts, from the point of view of the buyer, prior to the purchase of the contract. Averaging is typically calculated using an arithmetic average. A weighted average may be used to better fit the risk exposure of the option buyer. For example, a weighted average Asian may be used to hedge a series of planned fuel purchases which vary in volume. The weights may be chosen to vary inversely with the time until the option expires in order to give more importance to market conditions near expiration. An alternative to arithmetic averaging is to use a geometric average, defined as the nth root of the product of n prices. The latter is not usually used in the definition of option contracts, but may be very useful in numerical algorithms used for pricing.

The average-strike option presents another type of averaging option. An average-strike option has a payoff which is defined as max(F – avg(F),0) for the call and max(avg(F) – F,0) for the put. For this option, the average becomes a strike price which is compared against the underlying's price on the expiration date in order to determine the payoff. The comments made above regarding calculation of the average apply in this case also.

The volatility of an average price is lower than that of the underlying prices used in the calculation of the average. Because of this relationship, an Asian option at inception is much like a European option with a lower volatility. As a result, an Asian option will be less expensive than the corresponding European option, since premiums increase with increasing volatility. In addition to the lower cost, another advantage of Asian options is that their payoff is less sensitive to any extreme market conditions that may prevail on the expiration day (due to random shocks or outright manipulation).

Asian options are extremely important in the energy markets since, as we mentioned in our introduction, they were used long before the name and the pricing algorithms were invented. Asian options offer several advantages to both the producer and the consumer of energy products. Many buyers, such as utilities, are interested in hedging average fuel costs as the tariffs they charge to customers are based on average purchase prices. The producers are often interested in meeting budget targets that are based on average prices of energy products over the planning period. Asian options fit their risk profiles and allow them to achieve their goals at reduced costs, as these contracts are typically less expensive than the corresponding European options. From the point of view of the option writer, Asian options are preferred products because they are easier to hedge. Asian options with long averaging periods do not have the high gamma risk which may befall at-the-money European options near expiry. After the Asian option enters its averaging period, and the average begins to "set", the gamma risk of the option decreases and approaches zero near the end of averaging for options with reasonably long averaging periods. (If the averaging period is only two or three days, the gamma may still be sizable at expiration.)

Pricing algorithms for Asian options have received a great deal of attention in recent years. Asian options cannot be priced using the Black-Scholes formula since an average of prices will not be lognormally distributed even though the individual component prices are. Since there is no known closed-form solution for the distribution of the average, Asian options are priced using numerical solutions or approximations. A number of different pricing algorithms have been suggested over the last few years and we shall mention a few without going into details. Levy and Turnbull (1992) give a more comprehensive review of Asian pricing methods.

The Monte Carlo approach can be used to price almost any option, and it is natural to apply it to Asian options in the absence of better ideas. Numerical procedures can be made more efficient by using variance reduction techniques which allow reduction in the number of the simulations necessary for the desired precision. A popular approach is the use of control variates, suggested first by Boyle (1977), as a general option-pricing tool. This approach exploits, in this case, the fact that a closed-form expression, similar to the Black-Scholes solution, exists for pricing an option defined in terms of a geometric Asian payoffs. Enhanced simulation technology uses the history of prices for each path to calculate both the arithmetic and geometric Asian payoffs. The difference of these two payoffs is calculated and saved. At the end of the simulation process, the mean value of this difference is found and added to the known premium of the Asian option, defined in terms of the geometric average.

One can intuitively justify this approach by noting that the average difference between the arithmetic and geometric option payoffs is equal, in the expected value sense, to the difference between the corresponding premia. By adding this difference to the known geometric option premium, we produce an estimate of the arithmetic option premium. However, the variance of the estimated arithmetic premium is lower because the Monte Carlo estimates of the arithmetic and geometric averages are highly correlated. Numerical errors in the arithmetic and geometric payoff estimates tend to cancel one another.

An alternative approach, proposed by Levy (1991) and Turnbull and Wakeman (1991) among others, derives an approximation for the price of an Asian option. Levy's approach is based on the assumption that the underlying distribution of the arithmetic average is closely approximated by the log normal distribution. There is empirical evidence which supports this hypothesis. The authors used Monte Carlo simulation of geometric Brownian motion and tested the empirical distribution of the average for log normality, using a Smirnov-Kolmogorov test. This test shows that the assumption of lognormality of the average price is satisfactory when the averaging period is short (up to a year) and the volatility is below 40%. These results suggest that approximation methods should work well for short dated options, but become less accurate for Asians with longer tenors.

If we assume that the distribution of the average price is approximately log normal, we have to obtain more information about the shape of the postulated distribution. This information can be extracted from the dynamics of the price used in computation of the average. The first step is to derive the formulas for the first two moments of the distribution of the average, namely the expected value of the average, $E[avg(F)]$, and the expected value of the square of the average, $E[(avg(F))^2]$. Derivation of the formulas for the moments is a straightforward application of stochastic calculus, given the assumption that the price underlying the average follows a geometric Brownian motion process. Once the moments of the distribution have been estimated, one can easily determine the drift and the volatility of the process underlying the average.

An assumption of log normality of the average implies that its natural logarithm follows the normal distribution. This allows us to apply Wilkinson's approximation, which uses the moment generating function for a normal variable, to the natural logarithm of the average price at time T. The moments of the average price are expressed, under this transformation, in terms of the drift and volatility of the process followed by the average price. One can solve

for these two parameters and use them directly in the standard Black-Scholes formula.

Turnbull and Wakeman (1991) adopt a similar approach. Their approximation is more complicated and uses the Edgeworth series expansion to approximate the distribution of the average price.

Figure 3 compares the price of Asian options to that of Europeans. The figure shows the Asian premium as a fraction of the premium for a European option with the same strike, volatility and tenor. The forward price and the number of days until the start of the averaging period are represented by the two horizontal axes. The time to expiration is held constant at 365 days, and the end of the averaging period corresponds to the expiration date. The figure clearly shows that the Asian price converges to that of the European as the averaging period shrinks. For a given time until expiration, the discount of the Asian premium relative to the European widens as the options move out-of-the-money. Deep in-the-money Asian options have values that again approach those of European option values, since the price of both is dominated by intrinsic rather than time value.

LOOKBACK OPTIONS

A standard lookback call (put) option grants the right to purchase (sell) the underlying at the lowest (highest) price reached during the life of the option. Effectively, the best price from the point of view of the holder of the option becomes the strike price. The standard lookback call pays $(F(T) - min(F))$, and the standard lookback put pays $(max(F) - F(T))$. This means that the option always expires in- or at-the-money. The idea of the lookback option was introduced by Goldman, Sosin and Gatto (1979), and was explored further by Conze and Viswanathan (1991).

Conze and Viswanathan also discuss partial lookback options and options on extrema, which are similar to standard lookback options. Options on extrema are defined such that the put on minimum has a payoff equal to $max(K - min(F), 0)$, and the call on maximum pays $max(max(F) - K, 0)$. The call pays the difference between the maximum price reached over the life of the option and the strike. The put pays the difference between the strike and the minimum price.

In this paper we use the earlier definition of the lookback option. The standard lookback call is equivalent to the "put on minimum" plus a

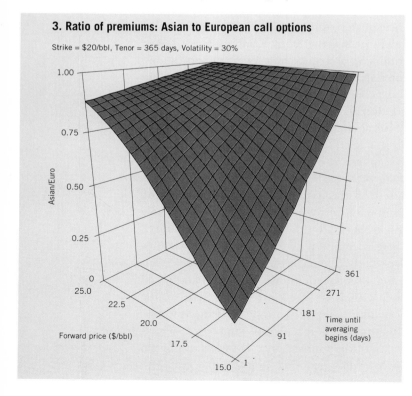

3. Ratio of premiums: Asian to European call options

Strike = $20/bbl, Tenor = 365 days, Volatility = 30%

long position in an ordinary call and a short position in an ordinary put, both with strikes set initially at-the-money. A similar equivalence holds for the lookback put and the call on maximum.

Another related option, a perpetual lookback, is called a Russian option. This option is an American-style lookback which "lives" forever, until it is exercised. To the best of our knowledge Russian options have not been offered in the market, but they are being investigated as an interesting theoretical problem.

The pricing and hedging of lookback options is explored by Garman (1989). Garman presents a replication strategy which consists of hedging a lookback call (put) using an option with a strike that is equal to the current minimum (maximum) price. At inception, this price is equal to the price of the underlying. When the underlying price establishes a new minimum (maximum), the option is sold and the proceeds are rolled into a new at-the-money contract. This roll results in a negative cash flow, since the new option is more expensive than the old one. This strategy, in the absence of transaction costs, will produce a payoff equal to that of the lookback option and therefore has the same value. At any point in time, the lookback option has a value that is equal to the current replicating option plus the option on the uncertain cash flows related to the replication strategy (which Garman calls a "strike-bonus option"). The value of the strike bonus option for a call, C_{sb}, is given by

$$C_{sb} = F\exp\left[-r(T-t)\right]\sigma\sqrt{T-t}\left[N'(d_L) + d_L N(d_L)\right] \quad (9)$$

where

$$d_L = -\frac{\ln\left(F/\min(F)\right) + 0.5\sigma^2(T-t)}{\sigma\sqrt{T-t}}$$

$\min(F)$ = minimum price attained to date during the life of the option, and N' denotes normal density function. Similarly, the strike bonus component of a lookback put is given by

$$P_{sb} = F\exp\left[-r(T-t)\right] \times$$
$$\sigma\sqrt{T-t}\left\{N'(d_H) + d_H\left[N(d_H) - 1\right]\right\} \quad (10)$$

where

$$d_H = -\frac{\ln\left(F/\max(F)\right) + 0.5\sigma^2(T-t)}{\sigma\sqrt{T-t}}$$

and $\max(F)$ = maximum price attained to date during the life of the option.

The formula above is the rule given by Garman (1989), modified for those cases in

which the drift, μ, is equal to 0. The other component of the lookback option price, in addition to C_{sb} (P_{sb}), is the price of an ordinary call (put) option struck at the minimum (maximum) price achieved over the life of the option.

This formula implicitly assumes that the sampling of the underlying price is continuous. In practice, price sampling is possible only at discrete time intervals, typically at the close of trading every day or on the publication dates of market newsletters. If this is the case, one can use the Monte Carlo approach or adjust the formula (9) or (10) for monitoring in discrete time.

The lookback option is clearly more expensive than the corresponding European option, as illustrated in Figure 4. This expense dampens the lookback's popularity in the marketplace; however, it is a useful instrument for those who wish to "buy volatility". The simultaneous purchase of a lookback call and a lookback put gives the buyer a combination of options which will pay off the difference between the minimum price and the maximum price attained over the holding period. While expensive, this strategy sometimes appeals to those wanting to speculate on high market volatility over a specific period of time. An example of a lookback option in action in the energy markets is provided by the oil put warrant offered by Bankers Trust in 1991. The warrant, known as U-Strike, gave the buyers the right to lock-in a strike price at the most favourable level reached by oil prices over an initial time period.

Even though the lookback is relatively unpopular in practice, the concept of the lookback is very useful as a building block for understanding other path-dependent options.

BARRIER OPTIONS
Barrier options were invented to reduce the ini-

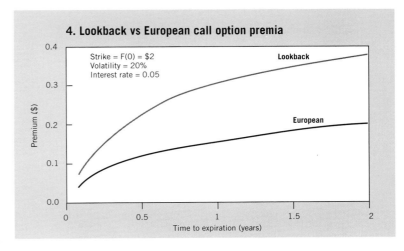

4. Lookback vs European call option premia

tial cost of hedging, and to allow the buyer to readjust the hedge when circumstances change. The barrier option either comes to life (is knocked-in) or is extinguished (knocked-out) under certain conditions. In practice, the event which activates or kills the option is defined in terms of a price level (barrier, knock-out, or knock-in price) that may be reached at any time during the life of the option. For a call or put, the following combinations are possible:

		Event	
		Out	**In**
Price	**Up**	Up-and-Out	Up-and-In
	Down	Down-and-Out	Down-and-In

The barrier option may be combined with a rebate. For a knock-out option, the rebate is paid when the option is extinguished as a compensation to the holder. For knock-in options, a rebate may be paid at the expiration date for options which have failed to reach the knock-in barrier.

A typical example of a barrier option is the "up-and-out put" purchased by an energy producer to hedge their natural long position. An up-and-out put may be an attractive alternative to the vanilla put option, as it is less expensive and provides the same price protection if prices move down from the current levels. However, if prices move upward, the increase in the underlying commodity's price reduces the need for downside price protection at the original strike. If the price moves up sufficiently to cross the barrier and extinguish the option, the owner may consider re-entering a hedge by buying another put at a higher strike price.

The up-and-out barrier put is less expensive than the corresponding European put because the underlying price may fall below the strike price after initially increasing and hitting the

barrier. In this case, the standard European put would expire in-the-money, but the owner of an up-and-out put would not receive a corresponding payoff. The up-and-out put holder has been compensated through the lower original cost of the option and, if applicable, the rebate.

Barrier options can be priced using closed-form formulae if we assume that prices are monitored continuously during the life of the option, and the option is knocked-out or knocked-in whenever the relevant condition is met. In practice, the option's barrier would be based on monitoring in discrete time (for example, using the closing Nymex prices) to reduce administration costs. Such an option could be priced more precisely using Monte Carlo simulation or by adjusting the continuous time formula to correct for discrete monitoring of prices.

Merton (1973) and Black and Cox (1976) were responsible for much of the early valuation of barrier options, and they derived closed-form solutions for some types of barriers. An important point is that a combination of an up-and-out call and an up-and-in call with the same barrier price has the same payoff as a standard call (assuming that all three have the same strike). Hence, knowing an up-and-out option price allows us to price a corresponding up-and-in option (and vice-versa), since we can price standard calls and puts easily. We provide pricing formulae for the various barrier options in Appendix B, and we would also refer the reader to Rubinstein and Reiner (1991a).

Figure 5 illustrates prices for an up-and-out put option as compared to a standard European option and illustrates the potential savings derived from replacing a European option with a barrier option.

From the point of view of the writers, barrier options may present formidable hedging difficulties. Benson and Daniel (1991) discuss some of the characteristics and hedging problems associated with options which have a knock-out level that is in-the-money.

Figure 6 illustrates the behaviour of the delta and gamma of an up-and-out put as a function of the underlying price and time to expiration. The put illustrated in Figure 6 has a knock-out level which is out-of-the-money. As one can see, the delta and the gamma undergo major change when the underlying price is close to the barrier price. This is because the option may be quite valuable or may be worthless depending on whether the underlying price crosses or stays below the barrier. The gamma actually

5. Up-and-out put vs European put option premia

Strike = Forward price = $2
Tenor = 6 months
Volatility = 20%

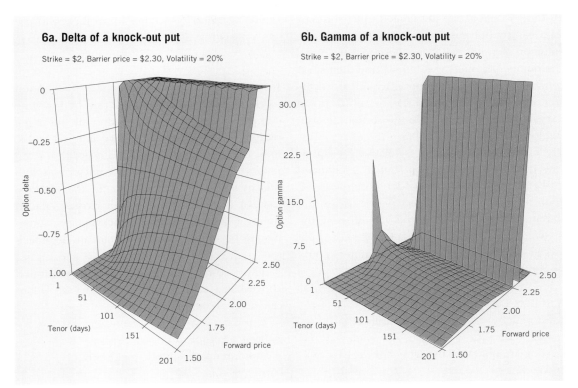

6a. Delta of a knock-out put

Strike = $2, Barrier price = $2.30, Volatility = 20%

6b. Gamma of a knock-out put

Strike = $2, Barrier price = $2.30, Volatility = 20%

becomes infinite *at* the barrier price, since the option's delta will suddenly change from a negative value to zero if the option is knocked out.

Barrier options should be written only by experienced derivative traders who are in a position to monitor closely the prices of the underlying instruments. Option writers who run a large book of barrier options can mitigate their risk by spreading barrier prices across different price levels.

LADDER AND CLIQUET OPTIONS
Ladder and cliquet options are two more options which belong to the family of path-dependent options. They can be described as discrete cases of a lookback option. The ladder option is structured so that a number of price levels guarantee minimum option payoffs if they are reached during the life of the option. If none of these levels is reached, then the payoff is the same as that of a standard European option. A ladder call option with two rungs has a payoff given by:

$$C_L(T) = \max[0, (F(T)-K), (L1-K, \text{ if } \max(F) \geq L1), (L2-K, \text{ if } \max(F) \geq L2)] \quad (11)$$

Figure 7a illustrates this ladder call option for two possible price paths over time. For price path number 1, the payoff is $F(T)-K$, as no rung has been reached during the life of the option. For price path number 2, the payoff is

equal to $L1-K$, as the rung $L1$ has been crossed by the price trajectory prior to time T, even though a standard European call would have expired worthless. An example of a two-rung ladder put option is shown in Figure 7b. The payoff for the two-rung ladder put is defined as:

$$P_L(T) = \max[0, K-F(T), (K-L1, \text{ if } \min(F) \leq L1), (K-L2, \text{ if } \min(F) \leq L2)] \quad (12)$$

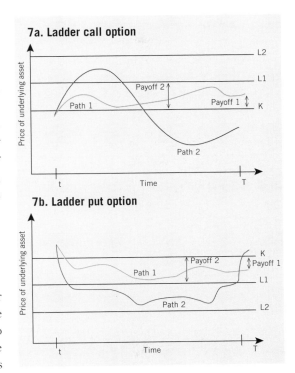

7a. Ladder call option

7b. Ladder put option

Ladder options are not limited to having only two rungs, but can be constructed with any number of rungs with any desired spacing. If the number of rungs was infinite and their spacing very small, a ladder option would effectively become the equivalent of the options on extrema discussed earlier in the section describing lookback options.

Pricing ladder options is relatively easy, as one can use the replication strategy mentioned earlier in this paper. A ladder option can be replicated as a combination of European and barrier options, and it can be valued using the software for those structures. For example, the ladder call option illustrated in Figure 7 could be replicated as follows:

1. Long a European call with strike = K
2. Short an up-and-in put with strike = K, barrier = L1
3. Long an up-and-in put with strike = L1, barrier = L1
4. Short an up-and-in put with strike = L1, barrier = L2
5. Long an up-and-in put with strike = L2, barrier = L2

A slightly different variation of the ladder option, which we call the "ladder-strike option", has received some interest from producers who are interested in protecting themselves from price declines. The two-rung ladder-strike put

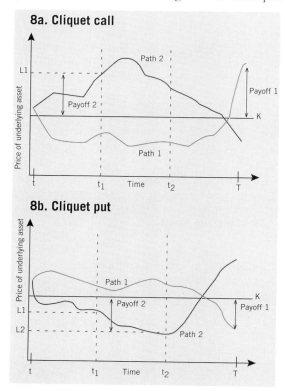

8a. Cliquet call

8b. Cliquet put

option is defined as having a payoff as follows:
$$P_{LS} = \max[0, K - F(T), (L1 - F(T), \text{ if } \max(F) \geq L1),$$
$$(L2 - F(T), \text{ if } \max(F) \geq L2)] \qquad (13)$$

If no ladder rungs are activated, this option pays off like a plain vanilla put option with strike K. If prices move up during the life of the option, the effective strike price is re-set to the level of the highest rung activated, and at expiration the option pays off as a put option with this new, higher strike price. In the extreme case of an infinite number of closely spaced rungs, a ladder-strike put struck initially at-the-money becomes equal to a standard lookback put.

The two-rung ladder-strike put mentioned above has a payoff that is similar to the ladder call, and can be replicated by:

1. Long a European put with strike = K
2. Short an up-and-in put, strike = K, barrier = L1
3. Long an up-and-in put, strike = L1, barrier = L1
4. Short an up-and-in put, strike = L1, barrier = L2
5. Long an up-and-in put, strike = L2, barrier = L2

Comparing the replication scheme for the ladder call option with the replicating portfolio for the ladder-strike put option allows us to find an equivalence relationship for these two options. The ladder call option is equivalent to a portfolio of options composed of long positions in the ladder-strike put (K, L1, and L2, same as for the ladder call) and a European call (strike = K) and a short position in a European put (strike = K).

In the case of a cliquet option, the price of the underlying is recorded for a series of points in time, and these price levels are subsequently used to determine the payoff at horizon. A cliquet call option with two cliquets at times t_1 and t_2 has a payoff given by

$$C_C(T) = \max[0, (F(T) - K), (F(t_1) - K), (F(t_2) - K)] (14)$$

An example is shown in Figure 8. The option payoff for the price path 1 in Figure 8a is equal to the payoff of the standard European call option, since the price of the underlying at times t_1 and t_2 is below the strike. For price path 2, the payoff is equal to L1 − K; the corresponding European option expires worthless. At time t_1 the underlying price is L1, and this price is used to determine the payoff. The underlying price at time t_2 is at a lower level and is, therefore, ignored.

A cliquet put option is defined similarly to the call. A cliquet put with two cliquets at times t_1 and t_2 has a payoff given by

$$P_c(T) = \max[0, (K - F(T)), (K - F(t_1)), (K - F(t_2))] \quad (15)$$

Figure 8b illustrates payoffs for two example price paths of the cliquet put option. Again, the option payoff for the price path 1 in Figure 8b is equal to the payoff of the standard European put option, since the price of the underlying at times t_1 and t_2 is above the strike. For price path 2 the payoff is equal to K − L2, though the corresponding European option expires worthless. At time t_1 the underlying price is L1, and at time t_2 the underlying price is at an even lower level, L2, which determines the final payoff.

EXPLODING OPTIONS

An exploding option is a single-contract version of a call or put spread which automatically liquidates if the conditions for maximum payoff are met. The call spread is a simultaneous position in two calls (one long, one short) with different exercise prices. An example is being long a call with a strike price K_1 and short a call with strike K_2, where $K_1 < K_2$. Thus if the price of the underlying is greater than K_1 but less than K_2, then the spread payoff will be $F - K_1$. If the price is above K_2, both options expire in-the-money and the net payoff is $F - K_1 - (F - K_2) = K_2 - K_1$, or the maximum possible payoff for the structure.

An exploding option is automatically exercised when the price of the underlying is at or above the cap (K_2) for a call spread, or when the price is at or below the floor (K_1) for a put spread. When this happens, the payoff to the holder is the maximum possible for the spread structure. In the case of the call spread described above, the exercise would take place whenever the price of the underlying touched or exceeded K_2. In the case of a regular spread, the price of the underlying could rise above K_2 and then, to the disadvantage of the option holder, decline so that the payoff at expiration is lower than the maximum possible.

An exploding option has an obvious advantage over a European spread option: it is always exercised under those terms most favourable to the holder, and allows that holder to take advantage of a significant change in market conditions which may or may not be sustained until the option expiration date.

Dual-commodity options

Dual-commodity options have payoffs that depend on the prices of two or more underlying instruments. Modelling such options may be quite complicated, as the premiums depend on the joint probability distribution of prices of two or more commodities. However, several types of dual-commodity options do have closed-form solutions, and Rubinstein (1991b) concisely reviews their valuation. For the options without closed-form formulae, Boyle (1988) and Amin (1991) suggest lattice valuation approaches, and Barret, Moore and Wilmott (1992) outline a numerical integration method which can be generalised to more than two underlying assets.

As we mentioned above in our general discussion of option pricing, using accurate volatility and correlation inputs is critical when pricing dual-commodity options. Option pricing is often executed using volatilities implied in the prices of traded options. Correlations can be inferred from market option premia as well.

Implied volatility can be determined from the price of a single option through iteration. Implied correlation can be found by using the prices of three options (of which, at least one must be a dual-commodity option) with similar terms by solving a system of three non-linear equations. The implied correlations and volatilities represent the market expectations of the price dynamics over the life of the option, interpreted in a risk neutral setting. If no implied values are available, one may resort to using estimates from historical prices.

SPREAD OPTIONS

A spread option is written on the difference between the prices, F_1 and F_2, of two commodities 1 and 2, with payoff defined as $\max(F_1 - F_2 - K, 0)$ for the call and $\max(K - (F_1 - F_2), 0)$ for the put. Spread options may be based on the price differences between:

❏ prices of the same commodity at two different locations (location spreads);
❏ prices of the same commodity at two different points in time (calendar spreads);
❏ prices of inputs to, and outputs from, a production process (processing spreads); and
❏ prices of different grades of the same commodity (quality spreads).

SPREADING THE CRACKS

Many companies in the energy industry are exposed to the difference in the prices of two related commodities, rather than to the price of an individual commodity. This type of exposure is generated when a company uses one commodity as an input to a process, which in turn produces another commodity. The difference between the input/output prices in such a case is known as a "crack spread".

The term "crack" refers to the technological process used in petroleum refineries; that is, the application of vacuum, heat and catalysts to break down larger, heavier molecules of hydrocarbons into lighter ones, with higher economic value. In the natural gas industry, a corresponding process consists of the removal of liquids from the gas stream through fractionation. The crack spreads are often classified as:
❑ heat spreads: the difference between the prices of No. 2 heating oil and crude;
❑ gasoline spreads: the difference between the prices of unleaded gasoline and crude;
❑ "resid" spreads: the difference between the prices of No. 6 fuel oil and crude;
❑ "frac" spreads: the difference between the prices of gas liquids (propane, ethane, butane, iso-butane, natural gasoline) and natural gas.

Market risks result from the volatile nature of both inputs and outputs, and from the imperfect correlation between the input and output commodity prices (due to the various independent fac-

tors affecting the feedstocks and products).

In addition to crack spreads, refiners are sensitive to the interplay of the spreads between various grades of crude, each of which may result in a slightly different mix of refined products, and the spreads between the market prices of the products themselves. The high volatility of some of these spreads can be explained if we consider that it is influenced by the volatilities of both underlying prices, moderated by their correlation (see equation 19 in the main text).

Refiners can hedge their exposure using a number of different approaches. One possibility is to use forward transactions to lock in prices of inputs and outputs. A second commonly used method is to purchase the input commodity under a netback agreement so that the price paid for the input is tied to the current level of prices commanded by the refined products. Another possibility is to enter into a basis swap under which a refiner pays a floating product price to a financial institution (a bank or a broker) and receives floating input price plus crack spread.

In the normal course of business, the refiner pays a floating price for the input and receives a floating price for the processed product. When these flows are combined with a basis swap, the floating price flows cancel out and a producer is left with a fixed crack spread. The figure opposite provides a detailed example of this type of transaction, as applied to a gasoline spread. This

Of course, there are no clear-cut distinctions between different types of spread options, and contracts may combine location, time and quality price differences.

An example of a location spread is an option on the difference between the prices of 1% heating oil at New York Harbor and at the Gulf Coast. The price difference may induce some traders to ship heating oil from one location to the other, but they run the risk of price change when the cargo is in transit. One way to mitigate this risk is to purchase a put option on the spread between the two prices.

Examples of time spreads are provided by options on the difference between average annual (calendar, in industry jargon) prices of natural gas (for example, the difference between the averages for calendar year 1995

and calendar 1996 gas prices), traded actively in the over-the-counter (OTC) market. Such options provide protection against reshaping of the natural gas forward price curve.

An example of a "processing spread" is an option on the difference between the prices of natural gas and of a basket of natural gas liquids (ethane, propane, iso-butane, normal butane and natural gasoline) which can be extracted from the natural gas stream at processing plants. Panel 2 provides a more detailed discussion.

Examples of "quality spreads" are the spreads between the prices of sweet and sour crude, or between the prices of different grades of heating oil (defined by their sulphur content).

There are several approaches to pricing spread options. One method treats the spread

arrangement can be applied to a basket of outputs designed to match the mix of products marketed by the refiner.

Although the approaches described above eliminate price uncertainty, they also eliminate any opportunity for additional gain should the crack spread widen. An alternative solution is to use a spread option. As the (unhedged) producers lose if the crack spread decreases – that is, if the price of crude (input) increases relative to the price of unleaded (finished product) – they can hedge by buying a put on the spread. The payoff of the spread put option is defined as max(K – (Price unleaded – Price of crude), 0), where K denotes the strike price. The table below provides some possible parameters for an option of this kind:

Tenor:	90 days
Forward price of unleaded:	$21.08/bbl
Forward price of crude:	$17.42/bbl
Strike (at-the-money):	$3.66
Volatility (unleaded):	25%
Volatility (crude):	24%
Correlation:	0.92
Interest rate:	5%
Put option premium:	$0.42

If the prices at expiration maintain their absolute spread, or if the spread widens, the producer lets the option expire worthless. For example, if the price of unleaded at expiration is $20.66 and crude falls to $14, then the option payoff is equal to max(3.66 – (20.66 – 14),0) = max(–3,0) = 0. The refiner allows the option to expire worthless, but benefits from the firmness of unleaded relative to crude. If the December spread narrows, let us say to $2.66, the producer

Crack spread swap

can recover one dollar (less the option premium).

Refiners often use an alternative option strategy. They sell long-dated crack spread straddles to financial dealers. A straddle is a combination of a put and a call with the same expiration dates and strikes. A buyer of a straddle hopes that the volatility of the underlying prices will increase, creating profit opportunities, or that the two prices will decouple. In other words, the buyer makes a bet on decreasing correlation or increasing volatility. However, the buyers of these options may have difficulty in re-trading the options to lock in a profit should the spread move their way. In fact the very poor liquidity in trading these options may oblige the purchaser to hold the options until expiration. In selling these straddles, a refiner can use the proceeds from the two options to offset changes in the crack spreads, as long as these changes are limited in size. The growing importance of spread options to the energy industry prompted Nymex to introduce heat and gasoline spread options to the exchange in late 1994.

between the two prices as a specific good; that is, as if it were traded separately from the two underlying commodities. This assumption may be justified in some cases. For example, in the natural gas industry an active market for the basis (ie difference) between two price indices, has developed in the last few years. The next logical step is to offer options on this special commodity.

The pricing of these options is complicated by the fact that, unlike a price, the spread can have negative values. The Black-Scholes formula cannot be used, since it is based on the assumption of a log normal distribution of prices at horizon, defined only for positive values. One can, however, assume that the spread has a normal distribution and use the pricing formula developed by Brennan (1979). This

approach is used by Wilcox (1991). A shortcoming of this approach is that the distribution of the spread is not necessarily normal or even symmetric. The obvious advantage of this method is the ease of computer implementation, as it produces a closed-form formula for option valuation.

Below, we show the formulae for call and put prices for a spread option. Note that the standard deviation of the spread, σ_A, is expressed in absolute, not relative, terms in this formula:

$$C = \exp\{-r(T-t)\}\left[(S-K)N(d) + \sigma_A\sqrt{T-t}N'(d)\right] \quad (16)$$

and

$$P = C - (S-K)\exp\{-r(T-t)\} \quad (17)$$

where

PANEL 3

BTU SWAPS

Many natural gas producers have shown interest in Btu swap contracts, under which the payments they receive for their gas are tied to the price of crude oil.[1] One reason for the popularity of these contracts is that they allow consumers to diversify across the energy markets without having to handle different physical commodities.

Another reason for entering into these contracts is the belief that the prices of energy commodities will tend to revert to certain historical relationships. When the long-term prices of crude and natural gas diverge significantly from their historical norms, Btu swaps can provide a way to profit from the expected reversion of the price ratios.

The figure shows historical natural gas prices expressed as a fraction of the cost of an MMBtu equivalent amount of WTI. The standard conversion factor for WTI of 5.826 MMBtu/bbl was used. The thin blue line in the figure illustrates closing prices for the prompt natural gas and WTI Nymex contracts, and the heavy black line shows the ratios of five-year swap prices between natural gas and WTI.

Near the beginning of 1994, spot gas prices were at historical highs relative to WTI, largely due to a weakness in the crude markets. The relative prices for five-year gas and crude swaps were less extreme, but still high relative to the average price ratio over past years. These high gas/crude ratios represented an opportunity for gas producers who believed that gas/crude prices would eventually move back closer to their historical norm. If crude prices recovered relative to gas, then producers holding Btu swaps were liable to realise above market prices for their gas.

Under a variation of the traditional Btu swap, a producer receives an initial cash flow that is equivalent to a loan. For example, for a time period prior to the beginning of the Btu swap, the pro-

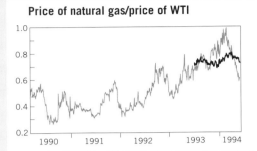

Price of natural gas/price of WTI

ducer receives payments that are based on a quoted index price plus an additional margin. Payment of the additional margin can be thought of as a series of loans made to the producer. During the Btu swap portion of the deal, the payments are set at a lower percentage of the crude price than for a stand-alone swap, so that the cash flows under this part of the contract repay the earlier loan amount.

Options can also be combined with Btu swaps to make them more attractive. As an example, consider a producer who wants to sell natural gas at prices that are tied to the price of crude oil. A market maker offers to purchase the natural gas at 65% of the price of crude on an MMBtu equivalent basis. The producer requires that the gas be sold at 70% of crude or better, so a new structure is proposed whereby options are granted to the market maker in exchange for a more favourable swap price. The options grant the buyer the right to buy an additional quantity of gas at the better of either 70% of crude price or a standard gas index price. This structure, a twist on the common "double-up" deal, can be implemented using options to exchange one asset for another. This method of adding value to the deal may help to satisfy the needs of the producer, and allow the transaction to be consummated.

1 Further discussion of Btu swaps may be found in Chapter 10

$$d = \frac{S - K}{\sigma_A \sqrt{T - t}}$$

S = the forward price of the spread, and
σ_A = annualised standard deviation of the spread price, S.

An alternative, and possibly better, solution is to assume that the two prices defining the spread follow a joint log normal distribution and to price the option as the discounted,

expected value of the payoff in the risk-neutral world. The expected value is then simply a double integral over a relevant integration region, dependent upon the forward price levels and the strike price. The specification of a joint log normal distribution requires the calculation of the two volatilities and the correlation coefficient between the underlying prices. The integral can be evaluated using standard numerical procedures. Ravindran (1993) shows how to reduce the double integral to a one-dimensional numerical problem. The risk parameters can be found by differentiating the integral equation, or can be approximated by re-pricing the option and using finite difference methods. The risk parameters include two deltas, two gammas, a cross gamma corresponding to the second mixed partial derivative, and a sensitivity with respect to the correlation coefficient. We propose that this sensitivity be called eta, η, as no Greek letter for this risk parameter has been suggested to the best of our knowledge.

OPTION TO EXCHANGE ONE ASSET FOR ANOTHER

This option, discussed by Margrabe (1978), gives the holder the ability to select the better of two assets. These options have, historically, been embedded in many futures contracts under which the short can choose the quality or type of commodity to be delivered.

For example, one can currently deliver any of 25 different types of Treasury bonds into the long Treasury bond futures contract that is traded by the Chicago Board of Trade. Given this option, the short will deliver the instrument that is the cheapest on the delivery date. In the energy markets, one possible application of this kind of option is a contract which allows the customer to buy natural gas at prices related to heating oil.

For example, if a utility is granted an option to buy one MMBTU of natural gas at 70% of the price of an MMBTU of 1% residual heating oil, it effectively has an option to exchange 0.7 MMBTUs of "resid" for one MMBTU of natural gas. This option gives the buyer the ability to lock in the economics of cheaper fuel, without necessarily investing in dual burner capacity or employing the specialised personnel necessary for handling two types of fuels. (Panel 3 provides an example of another use for this type of option.)

Energy users who elect to exclusively burn natural gas can also gain tax and "environmental" benefits. The reduction in emissions of pollutants can be monetised through a sale of emission credits, while in some states natural gas has a more favourable tax treatment than residual heating oil. Tax savings and the sale of emission credits can thus be used to defray the cost of purchasing exchange options.

The option to exchange one asset for another is actually a special case of the spread option, where the strike is set to zero. The pay-

off for the option to exchange commodity 2 for commodity 1 can be written as $\max(F_1(T) - F_2(T), 0)$. Although there is no general closed-form solution for pricing spread options, an analytical solution exists for this special case. The call option to receive commodity 1 by paying with commodity 2 is given by:

$$C = e^{-r(T-t)}[F_1(t)N(d_1) - F_2(t)N(d_2)] \quad (18)$$

where

$$d_1 = \frac{\ln\left(\frac{F_1(t)}{F_2(t)}\right) + 0.5\sigma^2(T-t)}{\sigma\sqrt{T-t}}$$

$$d_2 = d_1 - \sigma\sqrt{T-t}$$

$F_1(t)$ = Forward price of commodity 1 at time t, and
$F_2(t)$ = Forward price of commodity 2 at time t.

The volatility, σ, used for the inputs to expression (18), is derived from the volatilities of the underlying commodities and is given by:

$$\sigma^2 = \sigma_1^2 + \sigma_2^2 - 2\rho\sigma_1\sigma_2 \quad (19)$$

where ρ denotes the instantaneous correlation coefficient between the two prices.

The call option described above allows the purchase of commodity 1 by paying with commodity 2, if this is advantageous to the holder of the option. Equivalently, this option allows the holder to exchange commodity 2 for commodity 1. Using our earlier example, the buyer of natural gas can pay the price of 0.7 MMBtus of "resid" when this price falls below that of natural gas. The call, priced by equation (18), which allows the purchase of commodity 1 by paying with commodity 2, is equivalent to a put which allows the holder to sell commodity 2 and to obtain payments in terms of commodity 1.

Mark Rubinstein (1992) presents a binomial tree approach to valuing European- and American-type options to exchange one asset for another; a hybrid version of this type of option is discussed in Panel 4.

OPTIONS ON THE MINIMUM OR MAXIMUM OF TWO COMMODITIES

Options on the minimum or maximum prices of two commodities are closely related to the option to exchange one asset for another. For the special case where the strike price is zero, an equivalence relation is obtained:

$$\max(F_1(T), F_2(T)) = F_1(T) + \max(F_2(T) - F_1(T), 0) \quad (20)$$

$$\min(F_1(T), F_2(T)) = F_2(T) - \max(F_2(T) - F_1(T), 0) \quad (21)$$

USING HYBRID OPTIONS

The price of natural gas at the Permian Basin is one of the most volatile of the 60-plus locations where Enron Capital & Trade Resources (ECT) makes a market. The gas from this location traditionally flowed to California, where fluctuations in demand caused huge swings in the Permian index price. This instability resulted in a huge basis risk, basis being traditionally defined as the difference between an index and the average of the last three closing prices for the expiring Nymex contract.[1]

Recently, pricing of the Permian gas has been further complicated by changes in the pipeline system: a new interconnect has opened the northeastern and mid-continent markets to the production flow from this basin. In addition, the competitive situation in California was altered by the completion of the PGT (Pacific Gas Transmission) expansion, which opened this market to more Canadian gas from the Alberta region. These developments have created a new range of choices for the end-users operating in the Californian markets. (They also mean that historical volatilities and price correlations are now of limited use.)

Imagine the situation of a hypothetical California utility, GenCo, which is a large consumer of gas. GenCo is interested in a contract which would allow it to financially lock in the price of the cheaper of the two gas supplies on a monthly basis. This type of option would allow the company to contract for long-term transportation to California in order to eliminate its exposure to fluctuations in transportation rates, and would also allow it to negotiate for preferred rates under the long-term deal. However, under a long-term transportation contract the company would have to commit to buying gas from one source, and would thus incur "opportunity loss" if the gas from the other source proved to be cheaper.

GenCo therefore approaches ECT, which evaluates the factors affecting the prices of gas from both competing sources. The utility would like to maximise the benefit of having exposure to the relationship between the Permian and Alberta indices, which historically has been characterised by highly seasonal volatility and correlation as shown in the figure opposite. The two indices began to track each other much more closely in the autumn of 1993, when the PGT expansion became operational. Since the utility is a US company and its exposure is to the prices of Canadian gas translated into US dollars, correlation of the US dollar/Canadian dollar exchange rate with both prices is an additional factor which must be considered in the designing of the hedge strategy.

An option on the maximum of two assets, $\max(F_1,F_2)$, is equivalent to a long forward position plus the option to exchange F_2 for F_1 with payoff $\max(F_2-F_1,0)$. Similarly, a call on the minimum of two assets, $\min(F_1,F_2)$, is equivalent to taking a long forward position in F_2 and going short the option to exchange F_2 for F_1. Of course, we may be interested in valuing options on the maximum or minimum of two commodities when the strike price is non-zero. The solutions for these options, along with several interesting equivalence relations, were first published by Stultz (1982) and are reproduced, for the special case of commodity options, in Appendix B of the present volume. Johnson (1987) extended these results and derived solutions for pricing options on the maximum or the minimum of several assets.

Compound options

An option which allows its holder to purchase or sell another option for a fixed price is called a compound option. We will use the term "overlying option" to refer to the compound option, and the term "underlying option" to refer to the option which can be called or put by the holder of the compound option. For our discussion, the underlying options are options on energy commodity forward contracts. Typical cases of compound options include European-European options, which may be classified as call on a call, call on a put, put on a call, and put on a put. We shall use a call on a put as an illustration.

The purchase of a European call on a put means that the compound option buyer obtains the right to buy on a specified day (the expiration of the overlying option, T_o) a put option (the underlying option) at the overlying option's strike price, K_o. The underlying put has a strike of K_u and expires at an agreed time, T_u. At the overlying option's expiration, the holder can either:

❑ exercise the overlying option, ie purchase the

One solution is for the company to purchase index gas at Permian, where gas production is somewhat more reliable than the Alberta supply pool, and enter into the corresponding firm transport agreement. Then the company could purchase an option from Enron which would pay the difference between the effective US$ price of Alberta gas and the Permian price:

max(0, Permian (US$) – Canadian (C$) * FX (US$/C$))

where FX stands for the currency exchange rate. This option, a hybrid equivalent of an option to exchange one asset for another, allows GenCo to benefit should Alberta prices decrease significantly below the Permian index.

Pricing of this option is complicated by the fact that the price of one asset is a product of two related random variables. The following complicating factors must also be accounted for:

❑ the volatilities and correlations are likely to change in the future and will display a seasonal pattern which may be different from that observed in the past;

❑ all the relevant prices (the two natural gas indices and the exchange rate) are likely to undergo discontinuous jumps, the phenomenon known as "gapping" in derivatives industry jargon;

❑ hedging the option requires taking positions in three markets, two of which (the Permian and Alberta indices) have historically had very high

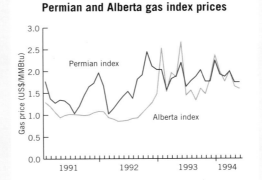

Permian and Alberta gas index prices

volatilities and an unstable correlation.

The provider has to be compensated for these risks, and this adds to the expense of this option. However, the attractiveness of purchasing this option ultimately depends upon the expectations of the buyer. If one expects that the prices of these two indices will continue to closely track one another, then the payoff from an option to financially exchange one index for the other will be negligible. If GenCo believed in this scenario, the company could go ahead with the simple purchase of index gas and live with the risk (perceived as small) of opportunity loss. On the other hand, if GenCo came to the decision that these two indices may again decouple in the future, then the option is very attractive.

1 For a case study of basis risk at the Permian index, see pp. 202–203 of Chapter 10.

underlying put, paying the premium equal to the strike of the overlying option, K_o; or

❑ allow the overlying option to expire worthless.

Compound options offer a method of locking in commodity price protection at an initial cost which is lower than that of the purchase of a cap or floor. These options are also useful for locking in the cost of price protection when the need for that protection is contingent on some future event (see Panel 5 overleaf).

Figure 9 shows the price of compound options (calls on puts) for three different overlying strikes. At the inception of the compound option, the premium of the underlying option is $1.06, so that for K_o=$1.06 the compound option has an at-the-money overlying strike price. When K_o=$2.00, the compound option is an out-of-the-money option, and when K_o=$0.50 the compound option is in-the-money with an intrinsic value of about $0.56. Figure 9 illustrates the typical behaviour of such an option. The

options lose value as they come closer to expiration, with the at-the-money and the out-of-the-money option values approaching zero for very short tenors.

The "European on European" compound options can be priced using the results of Geske (1979). These pricing formulae are reproduced

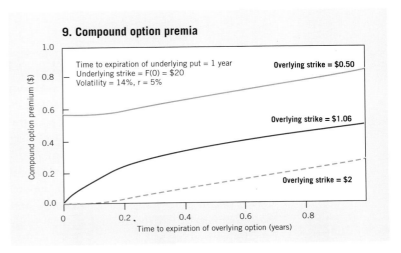

9. Compound option premia

Time to expiration of underlying put = 1 year
Underlying strike = F(0) = $20
Volatility = 14%, r = 5%

Overlying strike = $0.50

Overlying strike = $1.06

Overlying strike = $2

Time to expiration of overlying option (years)

COMPOUNDING THE OPTIONS

Recently, an independent exploration and production company, which we shall call Aggressive E&P, sought to purchase additional gas-producing properties. The banks providing credit for the purchase were convinced by the geological estimates of the available gas reserves used to back the loan, and were comfortable with the long-term cash-flow projections. But they became concerned that loan repayment could be jeopardised if gas prices fell, and they therefore stipulated that "downside" price protection be arranged.

Aggressive ruled out a fixed-for-floating swap, as they have a bullish view of the future and want to profit from any rise in gas prices. They then considered a zero-cost collar, constructed by trading a floor (a strip of put options) to Aggressive in exchange for the receipt of a cap (a strip of call options) of equal value. By using this "collar", Aggressive would preserve their exposure to price changes within the collar range (the range between the floor and cap levels), and thus preserve some of the "upside potential" – but the company eventually decided that the collar was too restrictive.

The company then considered the purchase of either vanilla European puts or Asian puts, but Aggressive faced a short-term cash constraint and decided that they really needed a structure with a smaller initial cash outlay. The purchase of a long strip of puts was unattractive for an additional reason. Aggressive expected its financial position to improve considerably over the next year, and it hoped that the banks would eventually relax the requirements for downside price insurance. In this case, the puts would not be required – but selling the puts after holding them for some time would mean the loss of the time value component of the option price and of the bid-offer spread.

Marketers at Enron Capital & Trade Resources looked for additional ways in which the bank's need for price insurance and the producer's desire for participation in a rising market could be satisfied. They found that a compound option structure of calls on puts could provide downside protection at a low initial cost.

Price protection was required over several years, so each compound option was structured as a call on a strip of 12 monthly puts. The series of 12 monthly puts provides price protection for one calendar year. Each call purchased by the producer expires in December of the year preceding the series of puts on which it is written. This structure allows the producer and its creditors to re-evaluate its financial position at each of these expirations, and to decide at that point whether or not to purchase the puts. To minimise the premium, the strike prices of the underlying puts were set at the lowest levels satisfactory to the bank creditors. In addition to setting the underlying puts substantially out-of-the-money, the strikes of the overlying call options were set out-of-the-money as well. The resulting structure allowed Aggressive to acquire the necessary price insurance for one-third of the cost of the outright purchase of a floor (floor level equal to the strike prices of the underlying put options).

The bank was satisfied that these options would provide a sufficient payoff to ensure the repayment of the loan, and the producer was comfortable with the level of the up-front premiums. Aggressive purchased the compound options, received funding from the bank, and completed their acquisition of the gas properties.

in Appendix B of the present volume. The pricing of a compound option becomes much more complex when the underlying or overlying option is an exotic. Such complicated structures are offered in the OTC markets by a few of the more sophisticated players. One example, an oil warrant, is an American option on an Asian option issued by Paribas Capital Markets Group Ltd in March 1991 (see Panel 6). Such options can be priced using numerical procedures, and the recommended approach is a binomial or trinomial tree procedure.

Digital options

Digital (or binary) options typically pay either a constant value or zero depending on whether the payoff condition is satisfied or not. Examples of such options are provided by cash-or-nothing options and asset-or-nothing options (see Rubinstein and Reiner, 1991b). A cash-or-nothing call on cash amount, X, pays X if F(T) is greater than its strike, K, or otherwise pays nothing. Similarly a cash-or-nothing put pays X if F(T) is less than K, or pays nothing. In other words, these options pay a fixed amount of

ASIAN MEETS AMERICAN

In March 1991, Paribas Capital Markets Ltd issued compound options on crude oil (January 1992 contract), with the unit size of the underlying commodity being equal to 50 barrels. The offering consisted of three separate parts with the following specifications:

1. Call on call. The overlying option was an American call with a strike of $2.00/bbl, expiring on September 27, 1991. The underlying call was Asian, with a price defined as an average of the 20 closing Nymex prices prior to December 10, 1991. The strike price of the option was equal to $21.00/bbl.
2. Call on put. The overlying option was American with a strike of $1.50/bbl and an expiry date of September 27, 1991. The underlying Asian put was based on the average price defined as in point (1), with a strike of $17.00/bbl.

The two calls described above were combined with a note floated by the issuer that had a par value equal to the strike of the overlying option. The note would be used to finance the purchase of the underlying option, should the compound option be exercised. If the call remained unexercised, the holders of the options would be refunded the note proceeds.

3. The third structure was an option with a payoff defined in the prospectus as 50bbl * max(0, 4 − IF − 19I). This translates into a European butterfly, with a long position of two European calls on futures (strikes of $15.00 and $23.00) and a short position in two calls on futures with the strike of $19.00/bbl. The expiration date was December 13, 1991.

The figure below shows that the third structure is effectively equivalent to a portfolio of options.

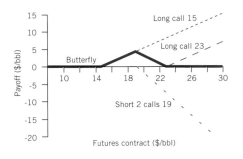

Butterfly structure

Some of these options (in and out-of-the-money options) are sold to the investors; at-the-money options are sold to the issuer by the buyers of the package. Valuing this "butterfly" structure is quite straightforward and is equivalent to pricing a portfolio of long and short European options on futures.

By using this butterfly structure, the issuer effectively bought options with a strike price of $19.00, which was close to the at-the-money level, and sold calls with strikes of $15.00 and $23.00. (The price of the January 1992 crude contract on Nymex fluctuated around $19.00 at the time of the warrant issuance; it was $19.17 on March 13, $18.64 on March 25, and $19.33 on March 28.) Investors purchasing the butterfly must have believed that the future volatility would be low, since holding this structure was a bet on price stability around the $19.00 level. At-the-money call options are much more sensitive to volatility than the in-the-money and out-of-the-money options which were sold by the issuer to the investors. This allowed the issuer to effectively "buy" volatility. As we will see in a moment, the compound option structures (1) and (2) above allowed the issuer to "sell" volatility. Thus the combined issuance of the butterfly structure and the compound option structures was really a volatility arbitrage. Paribas was marketing two different structures in an attempt to "buy" volatility at a low price and "sell" high.

Evaluation of the first and second investment structures offered by Paribas requires an algorithm to price a compound option involving two non-vanilla structures: American and Asian options. The technique we used employs a binomial tree with our proprietary Asian option valuation program attached to each node. The model developed for this panel has an additional feature which allows the use of different volatilities for the construction of the tree and for the valuation of the underlying Asian option. (We shall explain shortly why this is a useful feature.)

Once this was accomplished, the pricing of the options was a straightforward exercise. The table overleaf shows pricing of the call on call and call on put at different volatility levels as of March 25, 1991, using the closing Nymex price of the relevant contract on that date. We have ignored the note component of the warrant price as, on any given

Pricing the calls

Call on call

| Asian volatility | Tree volatility | | | | | |
	0.15	0.20	0.25	0.30	0.35	0.40
			Option value ($/bbl)			
0.15	0.020	0.087	0.208	0.367	0.549	0.762
0.20	0.020	0.090	0.211	0.370	0.554	0.765
0.25	0.022	0.094	0.216	0.376	0.562	0.770
0.30	0.026	0.101	0.222	0.384	0.573	0.777
0.35	0.029	0.108	0.235	0.395	0.587	0.787
0.40	0.036	0.121	0.252	0.415	0.604	0.809

Call on put

| Asian volatility | Tree volatility | | | | | |
	0.15	0.20	0.25	0.30	0.35	0.40
			Option value ($/bbl)			
0.15	0.030	0.106	0.225	0.372	0.545	0.721
0.20	0.031	0.108	0.229	0.375	0.548	0.723
0.25	0.034	0.114	0.236	0.383	0.552	0.732
0.30	0.038	0.122	0.245	0.394	0.560	0.744
0.35	0.045	0.132	0.256	0.408	0.574	0.758
0.40	0.054	0.148	0.275	0.425	0.595	0.775

Note:
Valuation date: March 25, 1991
Closing price, January 1992 Nymex contract on crude: $18.64
Interest rate: 5%

date, this would be a constant. Note that the option prices in the tables above are in $/bbl and must be multiplied by 50 to give the warrant values.

The volatility at the top of each table refers to the tree volatility, the volatility over the life of the compound option. The volatility at the side refers to volatility over the life of the underlying Asian option.

The warrants were registered on the Luxembourg Stock Exchange. It seems that there was no active secondary market for these structures, which we suspect was partly due to their pioneering nature. The techniques of financial analysis required to price compound options of a complex nature were not sufficiently disseminated in 1991 to allow a wide range of potential buyers to do their "homework".

But why was this structure offered at all? The answer probably lies in the special historical circumstances prevailing in 1991. In the aftermath of the Gulf War, price volatility was high by historical standards and its future course was uncertain.

Different groups of investors held diverse expectations regarding future price direction and volatility. The exotic options offered by Paribas allowed both camps to make directional bets. The compound option is really a leveraged volatility play: not only does a compound option have, *ceteris paribus*, high vega, but the use of American options as the overlying increases premium sensitivity to σ.

The issuer may have viewed this time period as an opportunity to "sell" volatility, expecting that the actual volatility over the life of the option would be lower than the current implied volatility level of the market. In March 1991, it seemed reasonable to expect that, by the time the underlying option was purchased (that is, by the time the overlying option was exercised), volatility would be much lower. This is why in our model we allow the use of different volatilities for the construction of the tree (average volatility over the period terminating on September 27, 1991) and for the life of the Asian option.

money if they finish in-the-money, and pay nothing when they finish out-of-the-money. The valuation of such an option is straightforward: its expected payoff at expiration is given by the payoff amount, X, times the (risk-neutral) proba-

bility that the option will finish in-the-money. This price is equal to $XN(d_2)$, using the symbols used in formula (2a), discounted to the valuation date.

The asset-or-nothing call will pay the value

of the underlying instrument if the option ends in-the-money, but nothing otherwise. Its price is equal to the expected value of the asset, conditional upon the price of the asset exceeding the strike at expiration. This conditional expected value is equal to $F(t)N(d1)$ ($F(t)N(-d1)$ for the put), again using the symbols as defined for formula (2a).

A "gap" call option is a binary option with a payoff defined as $F(t) - X$ if $F(t) > K$, and nothing otherwise. In other words, the payoff, if the option is in-the-money, is given by the difference between the value of the underlying $F(t)$ and a reference price X. The reference price is different from the strike price, K, which determines if the option ends in-the-money. For example, for a crude oil OTC call, the strike may be set at \$15.50/bbl and the reference price X at \$15.00/bbl. If the crude price at option expiration is \$16.00/bbl, then the payoff is \$1.00; if the crude price is equal to \$15.40, the payoff is zero as the condition for "in-the-moneyness" has not been satisfied. The "gap" put option can be defined similarly.

Some digitals are offered with the additional provision that no premium is paid for the option at inception. Cash settlement of these options occurs only if the option finishes in-the-money. Options expiring out-of-the-money require no payment by either buyer or writer. Such options are known variously as cash-on-delivery (COD), pay-later, or contingent options.

In the case of these options, the buyer does not receive the full payoff given by the difference $F(T) - K$ ($K - F(T)$) for a call (put). The amount deducted from the full payoff may be viewed as paying for the option – but only when the option ends in-the-money. The payoff is necessarily negative for some values of $F(T)$, making these options quite painful to the buyer on some occasions. For example, consider a three-month put on an October 93 natural gas contract with a strike of \$1.95/MMBTU, bought when the underlying price was \$2.20. The contingent premium to be paid at expiration was set at \$0.11. This means that if the natural gas price is \$1.90 at expiration of the option, the payoff for the buyer of the option would be negative \$0.06. If the natural gas price at option expiration is above \$1.95, no payment is made by the option writer or buyer.

COD options, like other binary options, are quite difficult to hedge. This is illustrated by the behaviour of the put option's delta and gamma, which are shown in Figure 10 as functions of the price of the underlying and time to expiration. The delta, which is used to determine the hedge position, is extremely sensitive to the price of the underlying when the underlying price is near the strike price K and the time to expiration is small. This extreme sensitivity of delta is reflected in the large gamma of this region. Small movements of the underlying price may require huge changes in the hedge position. Hedging these options would be sim-

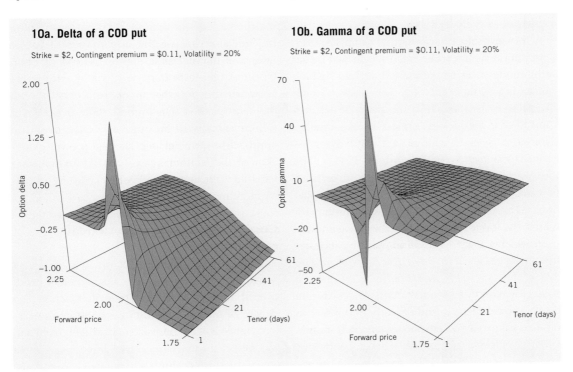

10a. Delta of a COD put

Strike = \$2, Contingent premium = \$0.11, Volatility = 20%

10b. Gamma of a COD put

Strike = \$2, Contingent premium = \$0.11, Volatility = 20%

ple if digital options were readily available in the marketplace – but they are not.

Turnbull (1992) discusses a method for hedging COD options using three types of European options. By using positions in three European options, a portfolio which is neutral in delta, gamma and omega can be constructed. (Omega is defined as the rate of change of gamma due to a small change in the underlying asset price.) The obvious drawback to this hedging strategy is the expense of carrying the long European option positions.

NATURAL GAS DAILY OPTIONS
One of the interesting features of the US natural gas industry is that monthly contracts on the physical delivery of gas in the following month are negotiated during a relatively short period of time at the end of each month (typically between the 20th and the 25th of each calendar month). The period when the sales/purchase contracts are negotiated is known as a bid-week. Contracts negotiated during the bid week traditionally had options embedded in them, long before the theory for pricing these options had been developed.

Take-or-pay contracts, discussed earlier, are an example of contracts with embedded options. Another type of option with a long history in the natural gas markets is the daily call option, which allows the buyer to take additional volumes of gas at very short notice (typically, one day). Such options have several interesting features, such as "forward start" and volume restrictions, which complicate pricing.

A forward start option written at time t_0, say, is an option with a strike price which will be set at-the-money at a later time $t_1 (t_1 > t_0)$ and which will expire at time $t_2 (t_2 > t_1)$. The price of such an option at t_0 is equal to the price of a corresponding at-the-money option whose time to expiration is $t_2 - t_1$, valued at t_1 and then discounted back to t_0 (eg Rubinstein, 1991a). The forward start feature means that the strike price is made equal to the gas index for a given location at the beginning of the delivery month for which the option is written. The price indices used for this purpose are compiled by industry newsletters such as *Inside F.E.R.C.*, *Natural Gas Week* and *Natural Gas Intelligence*, and are based on surveys of transaction prices during the bid week. These indices are published in the first issues of the newsletters in each month, and they closely reflect the market conditions prevailing at that time. With some qualifications,

we can assume that the options are at-the-money at their inception on the first day of the month. The buyer may exercise them whenever the daily price exceeds the strike.

Volume restrictions are defined in terms of the monthly and daily maximum and minimum volumes that the buyer can purchase. For example, the contract can require the buyer to take no less than 200,000 MMBTU, but no more than 310,000 MMBTU, of gas during the month, together with a daily maximum of 20,000 MMBTU and a daily minimum of zero. In some cases, the buyer can go from minimum daily quantity to maximum daily quantity and vice-versa in a number of finite steps, or ratchets. If the minimum monthly quantity is not taken, the buyer may be required to pay an agreed fine.

The volume restrictions give these options the flavour of American options, combined with path dependence. The decision to exercise an option depends on past decisions, which determine the remaining available volume, and on the number of days to expiration. If the number of remaining days is large, it usually makes economic sense to defer exercise of the option as the price could move even higher. On the last day, it makes sense to use the full daily volume available if the option is in-the-money and the monthly maximum has not been reached.

Exercise of these options presents a problem which is similar to deciding whether to call a bond. Interest rates could drop lower, increasing the benefits of retiring debt, but postponing the decision means the advantages of lower rates will accrue for a shorter period of time. Optimal timing will depend on the trade-off between the potential benefits of postponing the decision, and the shrinking time period over which they will be enjoyed. One possible approach to pricing such an option is an extension of the binomial tree with additional state variables; the authors have successfully implemented this approach.

Concluding remarks: practical considerations

This chapter is a product of our experience in structuring option-based risk management products at Enron Capital & Trade Resources. The degree of market penetration for the more exotic options is very uneven, and ranges from full acceptance in the case of the largest and most sophisticated companies, to very reserved, polite interest (with avoidance of any firm commitment) from many smaller energy companies.

Why are many producers and end-users so wary of using some risk-management products? One reason is that some of the products are relatively new and are insufficiently understood, and the pricing models are not readily available to many potential buyers. They are unwilling to use these products when they cannot replicate the pricing with a high degree of certainty. And, in the case of customised products, it can be difficult to obtain comparable, simultaneous quotes from multiple market makers.

Exotic options also present some formidable problems to the institutions that offer them. One obvious problem is that many exotic options are highly customised and require, in each case, a set of indicative data which does not lend itself easily to integration with the existing pricing and portfolio software. The "quants" attached to the risk management desks often struggle against time constraints to build a new and reliable option-pricing model, only to find from the risk systems manager that the new product cannot be captured and carried in the company's portfolio management system – and has to be hedged and marked-to-market in a spreadsheet.

The spreadsheet method is not a sound risk management procedure, and it violates the explicit policies of many companies. If option positions are dispersed in many different spreadsheets, it is difficult to monitor the risks and to rebalance the hedges in a timely manner. The "spreadsheet risk" is one of the more serious and unrecognised of the many dangers posed by exotic options. This risk may, of course, be amplified by "model risk" (flaws or approximations in the mathematical equations underlying the option-pricing algorithms), and by the risk that there is a "bug" in the computer code used to implement an otherwise solid theoretical construction.

One obvious question for any institution contemplating buying or selling exotic options is whether it should acquire commercially available software, or develop the necessary computer programmes internally. As exotic options become more and more customised, they demand a flexibility that is rarely available in commercially packaged software.

Another potential problem is that commercial software packages may be offered as black boxes; or, if the source code is offered, it may be prohibitively expensive. Such packages can be very useful for validating models developed internally, but we feel that most market makers need proprietary software. It is required not only for pricing, but also for hedging options and marking them to market. Using a black box is risky, given the high cost of even a minor mistake or interpretative error.

Another reason for purchasing source code, or generating the models internally, is accounting requirements. In most companies, options have to be marked to market daily, and the auditors are reluctant to rely on models which cannot be easily verified and explained. Of course, some of the smaller participants in the exotic options markets simply cannot devote the resources needed to build in-house valuation software. The "trade off" is that the packages they use will not be flexible enough to value some of the highly customised exotic products offered in the market.

Let us review some other complications. Typically, exotic options are conceived through an interaction between research groups and marketing personnel who work closely with customers. The extensive customisation of exotics results in products with prices which are difficult to verify by comparison with similar contracts available in the OTC market or with exchange-traded benchmark options. The lack of market information can also mean that it is difficult or impossible to obtain reliable estimates of implied volatilities and correlations from the available quoted option premia. In this situation, the trader must work closely with the research group to determine relevant inputs.

Econometric research, relatively unimportant in the option industry of the past, is vital in the case of exotic options. Many traders who understand implied volatility have had to familiarise themselves quickly with the arcane art of ARCH, GARCH and EGARCH estimators.

An additional complication, in the case of energy commodities, is that many of them have a strong seasonal pattern which may evolve under the influence of various market forces.[5] Traders typically use correlations and volatilities based on the historical data for the time period corresponding to the time interval for which the option is written. For example, if an option is written in June for December expiration of the same year, one would use the historical data for the same months in the past. This heuristic approach has a major shortcoming: it necessarily fails to use the most recent market developments, which may include information affecting the seasonality of volatility and the nature of the correlations.

Once an option is written and put into the portfolio, hedging the option becomes, in the case of many exotics, a real challenge. The difficulties arise for two different reasons. One source of problems is the definition of the option, which may result in dramatic changes of delta in some regions of the values of the underlying prices. High gamma risk is another way of describing the difficulty of maintaining a replicating portfolio which instantaneously hedges the option.

This risk may be amplified by a special property of the underlying prices. In the energy markets, prices often undergo a sudden and significant change – for example, the price changes brought about in the crude markets by political or military events in the Middle East. This property, known as "gapping", violates the underlying assumptions of the option-pricing models discussed in this chapter. Let us recall that the underlying assumption was that the prices follow geometric Brownian motion, which postulates continuous changes. In practical terms, a sudden, drastic change in price level causes a major shift in the delta of an option and requires a rebalancing of the hedge. The speed with which prices change can make it practically impossible to readjust the hedges in a timely manner. This problem is aggravated by the need to simultaneously rebalance the hedges for a number of underlyings when hedging multi-commodity options.

Additional challenges often arise when hedging in the energy markets due to a lack of market liquidity. Although several energy commodities enjoy respectable market liquidity, most of the trade volume is concentrated in a few nearby months. Of commodities trading on the Nymex, crude oil has the largest open interest, at around 400,000 contracts. Although there are

18 consecutive monthly contracts, plus four additional long-dated contracts, the three nearby contracts account for almost half of the total open interest for crude. So, even for the most active of the Nymex energy commodities, there is little liquidity beyond a time horizon of three to six months.

The Nymex natural gas, unleaded and heating oil markets also enjoy reasonable liquidity in the front months. But for some other commodities, such as propane, there is only a small contract volume even in the prompt month on most trading days. The *total* lack of liquidity in many markets, and the lack of liquidity beyond the nearby months in the more developed markets, give rise to risks that are essentially similar to the gapping risk discussed above.

Even when prices move in an orderly fashion within the energy markets, adjusting hedges for a large portfolio of options may be difficult due to the lack of market depth. This problem is, of course, exacerbated for longer-dated contracts. The limited liquidity makes hedging any type of option risky, but this risk is amplified for exotic options which have large gammas (such as barrier and digital options), as these lead to rapid changes in hedge ratios. Given this, it could be argued that only experienced market makers, who have a substantial book of business and thus a greater ability to diversify across the OTC markets, are in a position to construct and hedge exotics.

Another complication is that not only price levels, but also levels of volatility and correlation, may undergo rapid changes. Figure 11 illustrates the relationship between the correlation of price levels of crude oil and heating oil (Nymex prices, prompt month, six-month trailing) and the volatilities of both prices. One can see that not only does volatility change quite suddenly, but also that the changes in volatility are associated with changes in correlation – typically in the *same* direction. This phenomenon was particularly visible during the Gulf War, and can be explained by the sensitivity of both prices to a common factor. When this common underlying factor disappears, the relationship between the two prices grows weaker.

Derivatives specialists moving into the commodities arena should especially note this finding, as in many other derivative sectors any increased volatility in the markets typically coincides with *reduced* correlation.

There are no easy answers to the problems involved in hedging these risks. Some dealers

11. Crude and heating oil correlation and volatility

PANEL 7

STATIC REPLICATION OF A COD OPTION

The COD option, like all options incorporating digital components, provides a challenge for the option market maker who cannot "back-to-back" trades in CODs.

Simple delta hedging can be dangerous because of the extremely high gamma at the option strike. This danger leads naturally to the idea of creating a delta and gamma neutral portfolio, requiring the use of option products for the construction of the hedge. (Hedging using the underlying only can have no effect on gamma exposure, since the underlying has a gamma of zero.)

The hedger can incur substantial costs in rebalancing an options-based hedge, and will thus benefit from further immunisation against the risk of large market moves. This can be attained by constructing a portfolio which is not only instantaneously delta and gamma neutral, but for which the delta stays relatively neutral over an extended range of prices.

Turnbull (1992) suggests one approach to implementing such a hedge: choosing a portfolio of options which is delta, gamma and omega neutral when the forward price is equal to the COD strike price. (Turnbull defines omega to be the derivative of gamma with respect to price, that is, the omega is the "delta" of the gamma.)

To investigate the cost and performance of this replication method, take the case of a trader who sells a COD call option on natural gas with a strike price of $2.00/MMBtu. The trader receives a contingent premium of 16.5 cents if the option expires in-the-money. Constructing a portfolio which sets delta, gamma and omega to zero (instantaneously when the forward price = $2.00/MMBtu) requires the use of three hedging instruments. In this example, we will use as our hedge instruments European put and call options with a $2.00/MMBtu strike price and put options with a strike of $1.90.

In order to find the number of options required for hedging the COD (the hedge ratios), one must first calculate the values of delta, gamma and omega for the COD and each of the hedge instruments. The hedge ratios are then specified by the requirement that the total portfolio be delta, gamma and omega neutral. Finding the three hedge ratios which result in a portfolio with zero delta, gamma and omega presents the simple problem of finding the solution to three simultaneous linear equations with three unknowns.

For our example, we valued all the options in our portfolio using the following assumptions:
❑ 20% volatility;
❑ a 5% risk-free interest rate;
❑ that at the time the hedge is constructed all options are 90 days from expiration;
❑ and that the current forward price is $2.00/MMBtu.

To hedge our short COD call position, we found it necessary to purchase 0.9235 call options (strike = $2.00) and 1.7222 put options (strike = $2.00) and to sell 1.8831 put options (strike = $1.90). Setting up this hedge required a cash outlay of 13.76 cents (ignoring transaction costs). This value is the present value of the expected payoff of the three hedge options.

If we include the effect of the actual market bid/offer spread, the cost of creating the hedge will increase by about 0.25 cents to 1.0 cent, depending on the prevailing liquidity of the options and the volume being hedged. To recoup a 1.0 cent additional hedging cost, the trader must raise the asked-for COD contingent premium from 16.5 cents to 18.6 cents. The trader's expected profit increases only about half as quickly as the COD premium, since this premium is contingent on the option ending in-the-money, and the currently at-the-money option has about a 50% (risk neutral) chance of expiring in-the-money.

try to address these problems by trying to run a portfolio as a matched book of business, to the extent that this is possible. This policy, however, greatly limits the volume of business which may be taken into the book.

Another solution is to use sophisticated hedging strategies which employ a combination of options to replicate the behaviour of the underwritten option. (One example of such a strategy is discussed in Panel 7.) Finding an adequate portfolio of replicating options may require the use of optimisation techniques. The main shortcoming of the option replication strategy is the expense incurred when purchasing the replicating options. Other solutions proposed by practitioners, such as stochastic replication, are still in the early stages of development.

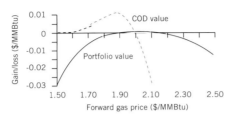

A. Value of naked and hedged COD options with 90 days to expiry

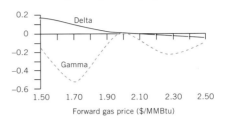

B. Portfolio delta and gamma with 90 days to option expiry

Figure A shows the value of the constructed portfolio (less the value of the cash outlay) over a wide range of forward prices. The constructed portfolio is amazingly stable, losing a maximum of only three cents over a range of forward prices from $1.51/MMBtu to over $2.50/MMBtu.

Even if the market gaps severely after the hedge is "put on", the exposure is very limited. Over a smaller range of forward prices, from $1.90 to $2.10/MMBtu, the portfolio changes by less than 1/20th of a cent per MMBtu. The effectiveness of the hedge is also illustrated by the small resulting delta and gamma values shown over a range of forward prices in Figure B . Although the portfolio is instantaneously gamma neutral at the forward price of $2.00/MMBtu, gamma is negative for other forward prices. This behaviour of gamma can be inferred from the decreasing portfolio value for both upward and downward movement of the forward price away from the $2.00/MMBtu level as shown in Figure A.

We also need to know how well the hedge performs over time. Figure C shows the portfolio value over a range of forward prices in a scenario in which the options have only three days remaining until expiration. Compared to the initiation of the hedge, the portfolio has considerably greater sensitivity to gas prices, as can be seen by the delta and gamma, shown in Figure D. Note that in this figure the plotted gamma values have been scaled down by a factor of 100. However, the maximum loss exposure is still less than five cents over the price range shown, and is modest compared to the unhedged COD.

Of course, we could adjust the hedge in order to further eliminate price exposure over the life of the contract, but each readjustment entails further hedging costs through the option market's bid/offer spreads. Selection of the optimum hedging strategy, including hedging costs, requires the use of stochastic optimisation techniques.

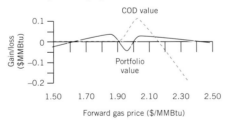

C. Value of naked and hedged COD options with 3 days to expiry

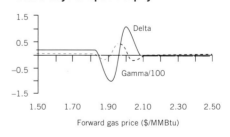

D. Portfolio delta and gamma with 3 days to option expiry

Many of the problems outlined above tend to be mitigated by the portfolio effect, which can be exploited to the advantage of large players in the market. This effect, the theory behind which is explained in more detail in Chapter 8, results from the natural self hedging which occurs between partially or totally offsetting contracts that are contained in the portfolio of a market maker who takes positions on both sides of a market. Managing a large portfolio of contracts – while avoiding excessive concentrations in any single series – provides the critical mass necessary to absorb the short-term price risks that arise out of new business; a large volume of business also helps to minimise hedging costs.

1 *We are grateful to the publishers of RISK for inviting us to contribute to this publication, and especially to Robert Jameson for his comments and patience demonstrated waiting for the final version of the manuscript. We would like to thank Darrell Duffie of Stanford University and Frédéric Barnaud of Elf Trading for their comments. We also received much support and feedback from our colleagues at Enron, including Jeff Skilling, John Esslinger, Joe Pokalsky, Jay Fitzgerald, Greg Whalley, Jean François Brault, Matt Hogan, Joe Toussaint, Pinnamaneni Krishnarao, Ellen Liu, Corwin Joy, Grant Masson, and Jennifer Modesett, and from Tom Costantino of Enron Oil Transportation and Trading.*

2 *MMBtu stands for million British Thermal Units (Btus). Btu is a unit of measure for the heat (energy) content of a fuel.*

3 *Bid-week is the period near the end of each month during which contracts are negotiated for the purchase and delivery of physical molecules of natural gas during the following month. See additional discussion of bid-week in Chapter 10.*

4 *Chapter 2 of this book compares several GARCH methods with historical and implied volatilities and finds that some types of GARCH estimates may be superior to simple historical volatilities.*

5 *In the case of natural gas, changes in availability of gas storage influenced by Order 636 are likely to change the seasonal pattern of natural gas prices in the future.*

BIBLIOGRAPHY

Amin, K., 1991 "On the Computation of Continuous Time Option Prices Using Discrete Approximations", *Journal of Financial and Quantitative Analysis*, 26 (December 1991), pp. 477-95

Barrett, J., G. Moore, and P. Wilmott, 1992, "Inelegant Efficiency", *Risk*, 5 (October 1992), pp. 82-4

Benson, R., and N. Daniel, 1991, "Up, Over and Out", *Risk*, 4 (June 1991), pp. 17-19 (also reprinted in: *From Black-Scholes to Black Holes*, Risk Magazine Ltd. 1992, London)

Black, F., 1976, "The Pricing of Commodity Contracts", *Journal of Financial Economics*, 3 (January-March 1976), pp. 167-79

Black, F., and J. Cox, 1976, "Valuing Corporate Securities: Some effects of Bond Indenture Provisions", *Journal of Finance*, 31 (May 1976), pp. 351-67

Black, F., and M. Scholes, 1973, "The Pricing of Options and Other Corporate Liabilities", *Journal of Political Economy*, 81 (May-June 1973), pp. 637-59

Bollerslev, T., 1986, "Generalized Autoregressive Conditional Heteroscedasticity", *Journal of Econometrics*, 31 (1986), pp. 307-27

Boyle, P. P., 1977, "Options: a Monte Carlo Approach", *Journal of Financial Economics*, 4 (May 1977), pp. 323-38

Boyle, P. P., 1988, "A Lattice Framework for Option Pricing with Two State Variables", *Journal of Financial and Quantitative Analysis*, 23 (March 1988), pp. 1-12

Brennan, M. J., "The Pricing of Contingent Claims in Discrete Time Models", *Journal of Finance*, 34 (March 1979), pp. 53-68

Brennan, M. J., and E. S. Schwartz, 1978, "Finite Difference Methods and Jump Processes Arising in the Pricing of Contingent Claims: A Synthesis", *Journal of Financial and Quantitative Analysis*, 13 (September 1978), pp. 461-74

Chaplin, G., 1993, "Not So Random", *Risk*, 6 (February 1993), pp. 56-57

Conze, A., and Viswanathan, 1991, "Path Dependent Options: The Case of Lookback Options", *Journal of Finance*, 46 (December 1991), pp. 1893-1907

Couradon, G., 1982, "A More Accurate Finite Difference Approximation for the Value of Options", *Journal of Financial and Quantitative Analysis*, 17 (December 1982), pp. 697-703

Cox, J., S. Ross and M. Rubinstein, 1979, "Option pricing: A Simplified Approach", *Journal of Financial Economics*, 7 (October 1979), pp. 229-63

Cox, J., and M. Rubinstein, 1985, *Option Markets*, Englewood Cliffs, NJ, Prentice Hall

Curran, M., 1994, "Strata Gems", *Risk*, 7 (March 1994), pp. 70-1

Derman, E., and I. Kani, 1994, "Riding on a Smile", *Risk*, 7 (February 1994), pp. 32-9

Dewynne, J., and P. Wilmott, 1993, "Partial to the Exotic", *Risk*, 6 (March 1993), pp. 38-46

Dupire, B., 1994, "Pricing with a Smile", *Risk*, 7 (January 1994), pp. 18-20

Engle, R. F., 1982, "Autoregressive Conditional Heteroscedasticity with Estimates of the Variance of United Kingdom Inflation", *Econometrica*, 50 (July 1982), pp. 987-1007

Garman, M., 1989, "Recollection in Tranquillity", *Risk*, 2 (March 1989) (also reprinted in: *From Black-Scholes to Black Holes*, Risk Magazine Ltd 1992, London)

Geske, R., 1979, "The Valuation of Compound Options", *Journal of Financial Economics*, 7 (March 1979), pp. 63-81

Geske, R., and K. Shastri, 1985, "Valuation by Approximation: A Comparison of Alternative Option Valuation Techniques", *Journal of Financial and Quantitative Analysis*, 20 (March 1985), pp. 45-71

Goldman, M. B., H. B. Sosin and M. A. Gatto, 1979, "Path Dependent Options: Buy at the Low, Sell at the High", *Journal of Finance*, 34 (December 1979), pp. 1111-27

Hammersley, J.M., and D.C. Handscomb, 1964, *Monte Carlo Methods*, New York, NY, John Wiley & Sons

Heath, D., R. Jarrow, and A. Morton, 1992, "Bond Pricing and the Term Structure of Interest Rates: A New Methodology for Contingent Claims Valuation", *Econometrica*, 60 (Jan. 1992), pp. 77-105

Hull, J., 1993, *Options, Futures and other Derivative Securities, 2nd edition*, Englewood Cliffs, NJ, Prentice Hall

Hull, J., and A. White, 1988, "The Use of the Control Variate Technique in Option Pricing", *Journal of Financial and Quantitative Analysis*, 23 (September 1988), pp. 237-51

Hull, J., and A. White, 1990, "Valuing Derivative Securities Using the Explicit Finite Difference Method", *Journal of Financial and Quantitative Analysis*, 25 (March 1990), pp. 87-100

Johnson, H., 1987, "Options on the Maximum or the Minimum of Several Assets", *Journal of Financial and Quantitative Research*, 22 (September 1987), pp. 277-83

Levy, E., 1991, "Pricing European Average Rate Currency Options", *Journal of International Money and Finance*, (October 1991)

Levy, E., and S. Turnbull, 1992, "Average Intelligence", *Risk* 5 (February 1992) (also reprinted in: *From Black-Scholes to Black Holes*, Risk Magazine Ltd. 1992, London)

Leong, K., 1992, "Estimates Guesstimates and Rules of Thumb", *From Black-Scholes to Black Holes*, Risk Magazine Ltd., London

Margrabe, W., 1978, "The Value of an Option to Exchange One Asset for Another", *Journal of Finance,* 33 (1978), pp. 177-86

Merton, R., 1973, "The Theory of Rational Option Pricing", *Bell Journal of Economics and Management Science,* 4 (Spring 1973), pp. 141-83

Press, W., B. P. Flannery, S. A. Teukolsky, and W. T. Vetterling, 1992, *Numerical Recipes in C, 2nd edition,* New York, NY, Cambridge University Press

Ravindran, K., 1993, "Low-fat Spreads", *Risk*, 6 (October 1993), pp. 66-7

Rubinstein, M., 1991a, "Pay Now, Choose Later", *Risk*, 4 (February 1991), p. 13

Rubinstein, M., 1991b, "Somewhere Over the Rainbow", *Risk*, 4 (November 1991), pp.63-6

Rubinstein, M., 1992, "One for Another", *From Black-Scholes to Black Holes*, Risk Magazine Ltd., London

Rubinstein, M., 1994, "Implied Binomial Trees", Finance working paper No. 232, Institute of Business and Economic Research, University of California at Berkeley (January 1994)

Rubinstein, M., and E. Reiner, 1991a, "Breaking Down the Barriers", *Risk*, 4 (September 1991), pp. 28-35

Rubinstein, M., and E. Reiner, 1991b, "Unscrambling the Binary Code", *Risk*, 4 (October 1991), pp. 75-83

Schmeiser, B., 1990, "Simulation Experiments", *Handbooks in Operations Research and Management Science Vol. 2: Stochastic Models*, D.P. Heyman and M.J. Sobel eds, North-Holland

Schwartz, E. S., 1977, "The Valuation of Warrants: Implementing a New Approach", *Journal of Financial Economics*, 4 (August 1977), pp. 79-93

Stultz, R., 1982, "Options on the Minimum or the Maximum of Two Risky Assets", *Journal of Financial Economics*, 10 (1982), pp. 161-85

Trigeoris, L., 1991, "A Log-Transformed Binomial Numerical Analysis Method for Valuing Complex Multi-Option Investments", *Journal of Financial and Quantitative Analysis*, 26 (September 1991), pp. 309-26

Turnbull, S., 1992, "The Price is Right", *Risk*, 5 (April 1992), pp. 56-7

Turnbull, S.M., and L. M. Wakeman, 1991, "A Quick Algorithm for Pricing European Average Options", *Journal of Financial and Quantitative Analysis*, 26 (September 1991), pp. 377-89

Wilcox, D., 1991, "Spread Options Enhance Risk Management Choices", *Nymex Energy in the News* (Fall 1991), pp. 9-13

Wilmott, P., J. Dewynne, and S. Howison, 1993, *Option Pricing: Mathematical Models and Computation*, Oxford, Oxford Financial Press

8

Cross-market Derivatives

Shannon Burchett and Christopher Turner
The Chase Manhattan Bank NA

Cross-market derivatives are an innovative class of instruments that gather assets from different markets into a group, and then treat that group as their underlying asset. Such a financial instrument can cope simultaneously with several of the disparate risks facing a corporation and limit, or reduce, their joint impact on the firm's bottom line. For example, an interest rate swap, with payments linked to energy prices, can be used to manage jointly a firm's exposure to energy prices and changes in interest rates. Another type of cross-market derivative might consist of a foreign exchange option with a strike price that is indexed to an energy price.

Strategies which make use of cross-market derivatives are often known as "integrated hedges", because they integrate and rationalise the various types of price protection undertaken by a corporation. The great advantage of using integrated hedges is that they offer comprehensive price protection at a reduced cost to firms that have exposures to financial prices in more than one market. This is because the movements of financial prices in different markets are frequently unrelated: changes in exchange rates, for example, are generally only peripherally related to oil price movements. The less related the hedged exposures, the cheaper an integrated hedge is likely be – an effect that is explained fully later on in this chapter.

As a result, those corporations that are faced with large, continuing and predictable exposures are the most likely to employ integrated hedges. Energy exposures, which tend to arise from the firm's most basic production technology, are especially likely to be persistent and predictable; furthermore, most firms with energy price exposures are also likely to be exposed to financial prices in other markets. It follows that firms with energy exposures have been among the first to explore the concept of integrated hedging.

Sceptics have suggested that these new structures are another example of "excessive innovation" within the energy markets. Derivative houses have been accused of employing innovation as a marketing tool – not as a response to a demand for new hedging vehicles. However, when properly designed, these new instruments rationalise a firm's hedging activities, so that a firm would only hedge its energy price risk after considering its interest rate and foreign exchange risks. Truly integrated hedges are thus necessarily custom built – and require substantial initiative, planning and interest from *within* the firm. Furthermore, although the initial outlay may be relatively high, these programmes should act to *reduce* overall hedging costs, without lowering the level of protection.

The greater initial cost of integrated structures is caused by the relatively higher planning costs that they incur. In addition, integrated hedges must be constructed, at least partially, with over-the-counter (OTC) instruments – which are more costly than exchange-traded derivatives. An economy of scale is necessary to offset these additional costs and, as a result, integrated hedging is most suited to managing large and long-term exposures.

There is also a less legitimate reason as to why integrated structures may tend to command premium prices: like any customised product, it is much more difficult for potential buyers to compare prices offered by different firms, and few end-users have the capability to deconstruct integrated hedges to examine the component prices. However, this is essentially a problem of user-education and market inefficiency rather than a fundamental criticism of the strategy.

This chapter will first examine how (and why) integrated hedging has evolved in the marketplace, and survey the use of complex hybrid instruments in integrated hedging programmes. We will then analyse how these programmes take advantage of the "portfolio effect", and compare the cost implications of integrated and more traditional hedges by means of a detailed simulation. In additional panels, we will look at three of the more common applications of integrated hedging.

Evolution of integrated hedging

The first attempts to cope simultaneously with different kinds of risk took the form of debt instruments combined with energy derivatives. These structures were used to protect the net income of issuing firms by relating their interest payments to energy prices. The Mexican state oil firm, Pemex, became the first company to make use of this tactic when it issued its so-called Petrobonds in 1973. This structure indexed the principal repayment to oil prices – the variable that most threatened the profitability of the firm.

In the 1980s, several companies launched debt issues that had energy derivatives embedded in them. Petro-Lewis and Standard Oil both sold notes that offered coupon payments which were linked to the price of crude oil. Standard Oil's issue, described in Figure 1, consisted of US$300 million in debentures, and US$37.5 million each of oil-linked notes due in 1990 and 1992, respectively. One commentator noted that in order for Standard Oil's notes to yield a return approximately matching an equivalent corporate bond, the price of West Texas Intermediate crude oil needed to rise from the prevailing price of US$13/bbl to about US$40/bbl by the time of its maturity.[1] By implication, because the price of crude oil rose at a much slower pace over this period, the firm's interest costs were lower than they would have been if it had sold a traditional corporate bond.

One of the more notable debt issues of this type was not issued within the energy markets; it was sold by Magma Copper Company in the late 1980s. This indexed note linked the bond's coupon directly to the firm's source of profits:

the price of copper. The coupon increased as the price of copper rose, and decreased as the price fell.

Many of these debt-linked structures (such as Magma's) were created to guard against the very real possibility of financial distress. In fact, the debt sales associated with the hedges would not have taken place had not the firm employed the hedge to reduce the likelihood of default. As noted in Chapter 12, firms in emerging markets have often used structures similar to these to gain access to the credit markets of the industrialised world. More creditworthy firms, although attracted to the idea of a net income hedge, tended to regard these hybrid debt issues as cumbersome and expensive.

More recently, corporations have begun to realise that by designing a hedge that is closely matched to their net income, a firm may actually reduce its hedging costs. This is because an integrated hedge will only intervene to hedge a financial price when doing so will have a positive impact on the firm's bottom line. This approach generally allows more movement in the underlying financial prices than do traditional hedges; it thus reduces the hedge's cost without sacrificing protection.

A detailed example of how integrated hedging can facilitate new investment by a corporate is described in Panel 1. Another example is where a refiner wishes to hedge its exposure to crude oil prices, petroleum product prices, and interest rates through an interest rate swap that is linked to the "crack spread" (the difference between the cost of crude oil and the revenue the firm receives from its slate of petroleum products). In its simplest form, this swap can be structured so that the refiner pays its market swap rate, plus a factor linked to the crack spread. If the crack spread is low, so that profit margins are low, this factor is negative and the firm pays a rate that is less than its market swap rate. If the crack spread is high, so that profit margins are high, this factor is positive and the firm pays more than the market swap rate – that is, the refiner agrees to give up some of the upside benefit of a rising crack spread by paying a slightly higher rate of interest. Note that the refiner will usually not have to pay anything "upfront" when entering into the swap; the slightly higher rate it may pay if crack spreads are high covers the cost of the hedge.

The integrated risk management programme described above is not merely a more efficient hedge. It also provides insurance against the

1. Standard Oil's issue, June 23, 1986

37,500 oil-indexed units
consisting of
$300,000,000 6.30% Debentures due 2001
$37,500,000 Oil-indexed notes due 1990
$37,500,000 Oil-indexed notes due 1992

The Debentures and Notes are being offered in Units, each of which consists of eight Debentures of $1000 principal amount each, one Oil-indexed note due 1990 and one Oil-indexed note due 1992 of $1000 principal amount each. The Debentures and Notes will be issues only in registered form and will not be separately tradeable until after July 31 1986, or such earlier date as may be determined by the Underwriters with the concurrence of the Company

Price: $7,976 per unit
plus accrued interest on debentures from July 1 1986

INTEGRATED SHIPPING FINANCE AND HEDGING

David Quarmby, Credit Lyonnais Rouse Derivatives

Cargo Co is a multi-national shipping company, which owns and operates several cargo vessels. Following increased demand for its freight services, it has taken the decision to expand its fleet. Cargo Co has, furthermore, successfully signed a new two-year fixed-price contract of affreightment with its most valued customer. Based on its established customer business, Cargo Co is confident that it can obtain financing in US dollars to purchase a medium-sized vessel for $50 million.

Cargo Co perceives two main threats to the profitability of the new vessel. Firstly, fuel oil prices could rise, thereby eroding the profitability of its fixed-price transportation contract. Secondly, higher US dollar interest rates could also reduce profitability by increasing the interest payable on the loan. In fact, interest rate rises also have a detrimental effect on the asset value of the vessel itself, as the charter's future cashflows are discounted by a greater amount.

It is calculated that approximately 25% of the new vessel's operating costs will comprise fuel oil purchases. This figure will increase as a proportion of operating costs when the price of fuel oil is high – and it is liable to be the most variable cost element as many of Cargo Co's other operating costs (wages, handling costs, etc) are known. Cargo Co has, however, set a conservative budget price for the vessel's fuel oil when bidding for the new freight contract. It is effectively "short" fuel oil at this budgeted rate.

Cargo Co's finance director would, traditionally, obtain US dollar financing at the most competitive rates available, whilst the bunker fuel oil purchaser would independently decide whether or not to hedge the fuel oil – either separately or as part of the company's overall fuel hedging strategy. This traditional approach, however, ignores several important cross-market synergies. Cargo Co therefore decides to explore an integrated approach to hedging its exposures whilst at the same time securing competitive financing.

The incorporation of commodity derivatives into a shipping finance package can present an almost infinite number of hedging and cross-market subsidy combinations, depending on the company's desired risk profile. In our example, the principal aim of Cargo Co is to lock in some of its profit margin in the pre-negotiated contract by hedging a proportion of the vessel's fuel oil purchases. Cargo Co is able to hedge the vessel's FOB Rotterdam high sulphur fuel oil consumption by the use of a two-year fuel oil swap. Cargo Co agrees to pay a fixed price and receive a floating price based on the price of HSFO 3.5% Barges FOB Rotterdam. The current swap market fuel oil fixed price for HSFO 3.5% fuel oil is below Cargo Co's budgeted fuel oil rates.

The fuel oil swap fixings settle on a monthly basis to coincide with the fuel purchasing contracts. The price source for the swap price is Platt's European Marketscan. The Platt's price source reflects Cargo Co's own actual purchasing of bunkers. It could have opted to settle against a number of different locations and/or fuel oil grades, for example, Singapore 380 centistoke, New York Harbor 3% CIF Cargoes or CIF Med 3.5% Cargoes.

A fuel oil swap is an off-exchange instrument. There is no exchange-traded contract that adequately hedges FOB Rotterdam HSFO. The IPE Brent crude oil futures contract has too large a basis risk to be effective as a hedge against fuel oil purchases, both in terms of product and location. The short-term and illiquid nature of the Simex Singapore fuel oil futures market makes hedging beyond one or two months very difficult. Fuel oil swaps provide a simple and effective method of hedging price risk for medium- and long-term periods (up to 10 years) on most major locations worldwide and for volumes tailored to suit ship owners' requirements.

By entering into a fuel oil swap at its conservative budgeted rate (ie higher than the HSFO swap market rate), Cargo Co not only removes the risk that fuel oil prices will rise above its budget rate, but creates a financing subsidy. The fuel oil is used to protect the borrower's cost of funds. In our example, Cargo Co, mindful of the possibility of higher US dollar interest rates, yet reluctant to pay the high fixed rate for the 10-year period, opts to put in place an interest rate cap and to pay a floating US dollar rate for its funds. Cargo Co decides that its new vessel's profitability is most vulnerable to a rise in interest rates over the first five years of the repayment loan – accordingly the cap's maturity is set at five years. The cap's strike price is set at the lowest interest rate obtainable using the fuel oil swap subsidy. The cap's notional volumes are matched to the outstanding balances of the repayment loan.

Of course, should Cargo Co successfully re-negotiate the fixed-price contract with its client at the end of the two-year period, it could once again lock in its fuel oil price with a swap. It may then be able to re-apply a subsidy to its interest rate hedging. For example, it may decide to extend the maturity of the cap, or perhaps reduce the margin payable over US$ Libor.

The agreed loan is a straightforward amortising 10-year facility, with interest paid semi-annually at a margin geared to six-month US$ Libor. The interest rate cap volume amortises to match the value of the underlying debt, and settles on the same matched, semi-annual basis (see figure below).

Overall, then, the fuel oil swap improves the operating economics of the vessel by removing the uncertainty of fuel prices for the pre-negotiated contract, whilst the interest rate cap sets a maximum interest cost over the five-year period. These

economic benefits are also supplemented by the reduced cost of integrating hedges on different markets (a concept explained in the main text).

From the lending and hedging institution's point of view, combining hedging within financing is also a logical progression. With known parameters for fuel oil and interest rates, earnings volatilities are reduced and the loan repayment becomes more secure. In preparing and sanctioning credit approval for the loan, the bank is also able to sanction hedging credit more easily, since the context is more certain. In addition, the integrated transaction will appear more attractive from a group earnings perspective, and this would be taken into consideration when setting the borrower's margin.

Depending on the structure employed, documentation of the fuel oil and interest rate hedging mechanisms can be incorporated into the financing itself, such that the package is fully integrated. This is important where security has to be taken, and is preferable as a means of avoiding definitional and legal risks as well as mismatches.

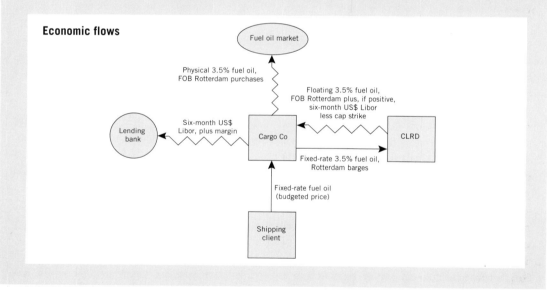

situation that is most dangerous to the vitality of a company: the combination of disparate risks. Bankruptcies often occur because of a combination of changes in commodity prices, foreign exchange rates, and/or interest rates; integrated hedges are adept at dealing with these "worst-case" scenarios.

An integrated hedge for an airline might cover two of its principal exposures, interest rates and jet fuel prices, through a swap designed so that the airline pays a fixed rate of 5% for as long as the price of jet fuel remains above, say, 45 cents per gallon. As described by

Figure 2, if fuel prices falls below the trigger, the company increases its fixed interest payment to 5.5%. This swap thus makes the firm's net income less sensitive to *both* interest rates and fuel oil prices. The hedge is likely to be cheaper than a simple floating-to-fixed swap because the airline is willing to give up some of its interest rate protection if jet fuel prices fall. If fuel prices fall, however, the higher interest costs will have less impact on the firm's bottom line.

While they are not traditional strategies, the integrated hedges for the refiner and the airline do not involve exotic or hybrid instruments –

they are actually just relatively simple combinations of standard instruments. The airline's swap, for example, is simply the sum of two fairly common derivatives. As illustrated in Figure 3, the hedge is based upon an ordinary floating-to-fixed interest rate swap in which the airline receives a floating rate and pays 5%. This derivative is added to a series of binary put options on jet fuel prices. The binary put options, which require that the airline pay a fixed amount if jet fuel prices move below the strike price (in this case, 45 cents a gallon), are designed with expiration dates that match the payment dates on the swap. As a result, at each payment date the airline will pay its fixed payment on the swap, 5%, plus the value of the matching put option expiring on that date. This option will be worth either 0 or 0.5%, depending on the movement of jet fuel prices. Note that when the swap is initiated, the airline will receive a payment for the options, and this will reduce the fixed payments on the swap.

Hybrid derivatives

Corporations in the energy sector have recently begun purchasing a new class of hedging vehicles that are ideally suited to integrated hedging. These derivatives, also known as hybrids, have a payoff that is dependent on the behaviour of several underlying assets.

Several different types of these multi-factor derivatives have already become familiar within the foreign exchange and interest rate markets. Rainbow options are characterised by a payoff that is linked to the "best" performing of a collection of underlying currencies. Diff swaps, also called quanto swaps, gather assets more subtly. These derivatives allow the exchange of interest rates that are denominated in a currency other than their "home" currency. For example, a firm might use a principal sum denominated in US dollars to swap Fibor (Frankfurt Interbank Offered Rate), usually denominated in Deutschmarks, for some fixed rate (again, paid in US dollars).

On a conceptual level, the simplest of the multi-factor options is the basket option, which is simply an option on the dollar value of a collection of foreign currencies. A cross-market variant of this derivative might have, as an underlying asset, a basket of several dollar-denominated assets that are exposed to interest rate and energy price risk. This hybrid derivative would provide the buyer with a given level of protection for the aggregate price movement on all the underlying assets.

Among the more common cross-market hybrid derivatives is an option on one asset that has a "knock-out" provision which is dependent on a second asset, often an energy price. If the price of the second asset hits a trigger level, the option evaporates. Panels 2 and 3 discuss interest rate and foreign exchange applications, respectively, for these structures.

In Panel 2, we consider a manufacturer who is "short" both natural gas and interest rates. To hedge these risks, the manufacturer employs a Libor cap which is "knocked-out" if natural gas prices fall below a specified trigger during the life of the option. As long as natural gas prices remain above the trigger, the company's interest rates remain capped. This hybrid derivative offers an optimal hedge for the natural gas consumer, for the hedger is only exposed to higher interest rates during periods of lower natural gas costs. At the same time, the firm has given up some of the upside potential of a favourable swing in energy prices, so that it is almost certain that the premium on this option will be less than the premium on an equivalent traditional interest rate cap.

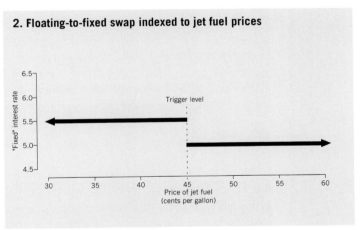

2. Floating-to-fixed swap indexed to jet fuel prices

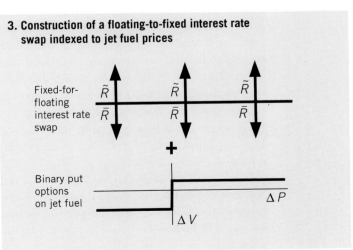

3. Construction of a floating-to-fixed interest rate swap indexed to jet fuel prices

2a3b
b5a2
3f41

8e97
c6d0
7b18
e49f
a2c5
d713
5fb6
0c8e
9d24
f1a7
64be
b830

154

CROSS-
MARKET
DERIVATIVES

PANEL 2

METAL INC'S LIBOR CAP WITH A NATURAL GAS KNOCKOUT

James MeVay, Chase Securities

Metals Inc purchases large quantities of natural gas, which it uses as a source of energy in its manufacturing process. The corporation finances its need for working capital by borrowing at a floating rate of interest.

To the extent that the price of natural gas and the rate of interest charged tend to rise together, their impact on the firm's bottom line is negative; to the extent that the prices tend to fall together the impact is positive. More interestingly, to the extent that interest rates and gas prices tend to move in opposite directions, each price's individual impact on the firm's profit margin is effectively neutralised. In other words, there is a *natural* hedge effect whenever this inverse relationship exists.

If this firm were to purchase a conventional interest rate hedge, such as an interest rate cap, the firm would be buying protection against interest rate movements without regard to gas prices. In this case, even when the movements in interest rates and natural gas prices tended to neutralise each other naturally, the firm would receive an "excess" or "windfall" payoff from the interest rate cap. In itself this might seem positive – but, in fact, the company would have spent money for protection that it has little need of.

A. Libor cap linked to natural gas

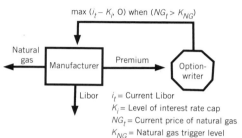

$$\max (i_t - K_l, 0) \text{ when } (NG_t > K_{NG})$$

i_t = Current Libor
K_l = Level of interest rate cap
NG_t = Current price of natural gas
K_{NG} = Natural gas trigger level

The institution selling the option, the option writer, receives the option premium and agrees to pay the manufacturer the difference between the interest rate cap, K_l, and the prevailing level of Libor, i_t, when Libor is greater than the cap. The option writer is only committed to make the payments, however, if the price of the natural gas hedge, NG_t, as determined by an appropriate price index, is greater than the natural gas trigger level, K_{NG}.

Alternatively, the company may choose a hedging structure that would tailor the protection more closely to its cost function: an interest rate cap with a payoff that is contingent upon the price level of natural gas.

One way to create such a hedge is through a gas-linked Libor cap, the mechanics of which are described in Figure A.

More specifically, the premium charged for the knock-out cap will partially depend on the probability of the cap's elimination; the more likely it is that the cap will be eliminated, the higher the savings. Thus, for any given trigger level, an increase in the volatility of natural gas prices will increase the likelihood that the cap will be eliminated, and decrease the option premium. Likewise, for any given volatility, any increase in the knock-out's trigger – the level of natural gas prices below which the cap will not be in force – will raise the probability that the cap will be eliminated and thus decrease the cost of the cap.

The cost of the manufacturer's knock-out cap will also depend on the interaction between the value of the Libor cap and the probability that the cap will be knocked out. The deeper in the money the cap, the more the option writer will

pay to eliminate it. Equivalently, the more valuable the cap the more the option writer will pay for any given increase in the probability of its elimination. From the perspective of the purchaser of the cap, this translates into a lower option premium on the cap.

The probability of a knock-out when the cap is valuable depends on the relationship between natural gas prices and interest rates. Let us suppose that natural gas prices and Libor tend to move together. When Libor rises, it is likely that gas prices will also rise. That is, when the cap is more valuable, it is less likely that natural gas prices will touch the trigger and extinguish the cap. Alternatively, let us suppose that gas prices tend to fall when Libor rises. In this circumstance, when Libor rises, making the cap more valuable, it is more likely that gas prices will fall, touch the trigger, and extinguish

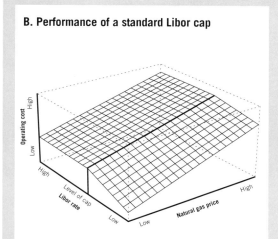

B. Performance of a standard Libor cap

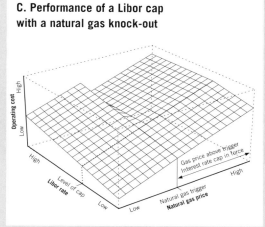

**C. Performance of a Libor cap
with a natural gas knock-out**

The payoff of this structure is the higher of spot interest rates minus the strike – but only when spot natural gas prices are in excess of a trigger level. In the case of this structure, a payoff occurs only when the hedger is exposed to the greatest harm, that is, an upward movement of both gas prices and interest rates.

Since the payoff of this structure is contingent upon the level of gas prices, the cost of the option will be less than one that is independent of the performance of a second asset.

The performance of the standard Libor cap is described in Figure B.

Here we see that, at low interest rate levels, the total operating costs rise as gas prices rise. However, with this product, interest costs are contained even at low levels of gas prices (when they

may well be affordable for the company).

This cost function is in contrast to that of the gas-linked cap, which is shown in Figure C. This instrument produces a similar cost behaviour to that created by the regular cap for various levels of gas prices, except that at low gas price levels the firm's interest rate cost is unconstrained. However, as gas prices rise, the interest rate cap is triggered and behaves in a manner similar to the conventional cap. When the price of gas is low, there is no cap on Libor; as a result, the lower portion of the cost surface depicted in Figure C depicts the firm's operating cost increasing with both natural gas prices and with interest rate costs. When natural gas prices are above the trigger, however, the firm's interest rate costs are restricted – as the diagram illustrates.

the cap. Thus, the more natural gas prices and interest rates tend move in opposite directions, the more likely that the cap will be knocked out when it is in the money, and the cheaper the knock-out cap is (relative to the standard cap).

The discussion above makes it clear that the relationship between the underlying asset prices is the key to understanding hybrid derivatives. This relationship is described by the correlation between the asset prices. (The mechanics of measuring correlation are described in Chapter 4.) Depending on how it is structured, a hybrid derivative will be cheapest when the asset prices are either perfectly positively or perfectly negatively correlated.[2]

The firm will structure its hybrid derivative as a mirror image of its exposures. In the context of the knock-out cap purchased by the corporation described in Panel 2, the firm is negatively exposed to increases in either interest rates or

natural gas prices; the hedge was thus constructed so as to protect against upward movements in both interest rates and natural gas prices. As a result, the more negatively correlated natural gas prices and interest rates – that is, the less likely they are both to simultaneously increase – the lower the premium of the option.

Conversely, consider a similar hybrid derivative designed for an energy producer. This hedge would guard against upward movements in interest rates and downward movements in energy prices. As a result, the more positively correlated energy prices and interest rates – the less likely energy prices are to fall when interest rates rise – the lower the premium of the option. The impact of correlation on the cap price is illustrated in Figure 4 as a function of two variables:

❏ the correlation between interest rates and gas prices; and

❑ the natural gas price trigger which must be reached before the cap is knocked out.

As we noted earlier, the higher the probability that this trigger will be reached when interest rates are high, the less costly the hybrid. It follows that the higher the negative correlation between Libor and gas prices, the less expensive the cap. Likewise, the higher the trigger level, the more likely the cap will be extinguished, again reducing the cost of the option.

The manufacturer could have employed a "knock-in" cap to create a similar hedge. This option is identical to a knock-out cap, except for the placement of the trigger, which is set *above* the current price of natural gas. The price of gas would thus have to rise above the trigger to initiate the cap. It is clear that this option will be less expensive than a knock-out option, as the trigger is, by definition, set higher. (Note that as the cap does not exist at the outset in the case of a knock-in option, any value that it

may have must be discounted.)

Instead of an option with a knock-in or knock-out that is dependent on the behaviour of a second asset, an option might have a "ratchet" provision that is linked to another asset. Instead of an option that evaporates should the price of a second asset trip a trigger, the strike price of the ratchet option will simply move to a new level. In fact, such an option would typically have numerous strike prices, each linked to a range of prices in the second underlying asset.

Consider, for example, the oil producer described in Panel 3. This producer, Oil Inc, hedged its sterling/dollar exchange rate exposure by means of a knock-out option, which linked the firm's foreign exchange exposure to the price of Brent crude oil. This firm could have created a similar linkage by using a ratchet option. This hedge would consist of a standard sterling call/US dollar put option with strike prices that varied with the price of Brent crude, as described by Figure 5.

By means of this hybrid derivative Oil Inc would not be exposed to sterling/dollar exchange rates that would be burdensome in the light of its cash flow from crude oil sales. At the same time, this firm, like the manufacturer in Panel 2, has given up some of the upside potential of a favourable swing in energy prices. As a result, this hedge will almost certainly be less expensive than a traditional option.

The extent of the savings accruing to Oil Inc for using the ratchet option will depend partly on the likelihood that the strike price will be raised. For any given set of trigger levels, an increase in the volatility of oil prices will increase the likelihood of an increase in the strike price, and thus reduce the price of the ratchet option relative to the standard foreign exchange option.

The ratchet option will tie Oil Inc's foreign exchange exposure more closely to the price of oil than the knock-out option that Sara Sullivan describes in Panel 3. Knitting the firm's foreign exchange exposure closely to its oil price exposures with a ratchet option would, in fact, be a sensible course of action for Oil Inc: the firm's overriding and continuing exposure is to oil prices. However, a firm with more variable exposures might find that a ratchet option ties its exposures *too* closely to oil prices.

As with the knock-out cap, the premium of the foreign exchange ratchet option will also depend on the interaction between the value of

4. Cost of Libor cap with a natural gas knockout

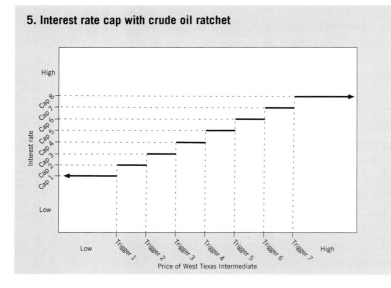

5. Interest rate cap with crude oil ratchet

PANEL 3

OIL INC'S KNOCKOUT OPTION

Sara Sullivan, The Chase Manhattan Bank NA

Oil Incorporated is a US multi-national oil producer with a number of overseas subsidiaries. One of its major international production sites is in the North Sea, where it has a number of rigs producing a significant volume of Brent crude. This subsidiary's operational costs are in sterling, whilst its revenues from the sale of the North Sea crude are in US dollars. As a result, the company wishes to hedge its foreign exchange exposure over a one-year time horizon, using an option-based strategy.

The traditional hedge would be to purchase a European-style sterling call/US$ put option, which would place a limit on the firm's exposure to a weakening dollar. The extent of the protection provided by this option is reflected in the cost of the option premiums.

The management of Oil Inc, while concerned to hedge their position, are unhappy with the cost of the traditional strategy. They decide to try and reduce the hedging cost by exploiting the firm's exposure to natural crude oil. This exposure means that the firm benefits from a rise in the price of crude, but suffers reduced dollar revenues should

the price of oil fall. The firm's direct sterling currency exposure is to a strengthening pound (weakening dollar), as the company's costs are fixed in sterling but will be financed from dollar revenues.

Table A illustrates the qualitative impact of market movements on these combined risk positions. The firm is most concerned about the cost impact detailed in the upper-right quadrant of this table, where crude oil price decreases are matched with a depreciating dollar.

To hedge its foreign exchange risk, Oil Inc needs to purchase a £ call/US$ put option. A standard European-style currency option will fully protect its foreign exchange exposure at a fixed upfront price. A knock-out feature could be added to the option in order to reduce the premium cost. Instead of a standard currency knock-out option,

Table A. Combined impact of oil price and US$/£ exchange rate movements on Oil Inc

	£ declines	£ rises
Crude oil price declines	*Neutral*	*Negative*
Crude oil price rises	*Positive*	*Neutral*

the option and the likelihood that a trigger will be touched. The probability of an increase in the strike when the option is in the money depends on the correlation between crude oil prices and the foreign exchange rate. Suppose oil prices and the sterling/dollar rate are *negatively* correlated. In this instance, if the sterling price of dollars is rising, bringing the option into the money, it is likely that oil prices will move downward, bringing down the strike prices, and pushing the option still deeper into the money.

Conversely, suppose oil prices and the foreign exchange rate are *positively* correlated. In this instance, when the sterling price of dollars is rising, taking the option into the money, it is likely that oil prices will also be rising; the option's strike prices will be ratcheted up, moving the option out of the money. Thus, the less correlated oil prices and the sterling/dollar rate, the more likely that the strike price will be increased when the option is expensive, and the cheaper the ratchet option is relative to the standard option. Regardless of the correlation between movements in the financial prices,

however, the premium on the ratchet option will never be higher than that on a standard sterling/dollar option.

All of these hedges also result in a lower *upfront* hedging cost than that possible when using traditional hedging structures. However, this disguises an important difference between different varieties of integrated hedges. The integrated hedges that we described at the end of the last section of this chapter, employed by the airline and the refiner, lowered costs solely by surrendering some of the upside benefit from beneficial swings in the energy price linked to the interest rate hedge. Although a portion of the cost savings from the knock-out cap and knock-out foreign exchange option described in Panels 2 and 3 are also attributable to the surrender of part of the upside, the remainder of the savings arises from the lack of coordination between movements of energy prices and financial prices.

As we have discussed, the savings available to users of integrated hedges depend on the willingness of the firm to sacrifice the potential benefit from a favourable swing in financial

Table B. Premium savings from inclusion of knockout in Oil Inc's foreign exchange option

Strike price	Price of European option	Cost of option including knockout. Correlation between £ exchange rate and oil prices		
		−30%	0%	+30%
1.47	598	341	421	491
1.50	472	263	332	391
1.55	308	165	216	259
1.60	191	98	134	163

Prices in US$/£; spot reference rate = US$1.48/£; Brent oil trigger set at US$18/bbl

Note: Each knock-out option has a 12 months expiration and an oil trigger set at US$18/bbl. The options are "touch" options, whereby the option contract will be terminated if the Brent Oil price trades at this level at any time over the lifetime of the option.

an oil barrier may be used to construct a cross-market knock-out structure. Should the price of oil rise and the barrier be breached, the currency option would be terminated, leaving the firm's sterling/dollar exposure unhedged. But in this circumstance the higher oil price would be beneficial to Oil Inc, increasing its dollar revenues.

The reduction in the premium for the knock-out option, relative to the traditional European option, will depend on: the level of the oil barrier; the volatility of the price of Brent crude; and the correlation between the price movements of crude and the dollar/sterling exchange rate.

The more volatile the oil price, the lower the currency option price, as there is a greater chance of the option contract being "knocked out". The more positive the correlation between movements in the prices of the two assets, the greater the likelihood that the price of oil will reach the barrier while the option is in the money – again reducing the premium of the currency option.

Table B compares the price of a £ call/US$ put option with an oil knock-out, against that of an identical option without a knock-out. It also charts the effect of different correlation scenarios on the price of the knock-out option. Note that the correlation between changes in the sterling/dollar exchange rate, and changes in oil prices, determines the extent of the saving to Oil Inc.

The setting of the oil trigger is the key to determining the overall effectiveness of the hedge. Obviously, if the option contract is terminated, then the unhedged currency risk needs to be fully offset by the gain in the dollar revenues from the higher oil price.

prices, and, if the hedge includes a cross-market derivative, the correlation between the firm's exposures to the hedged financial prices. The more benefit Oil Inc, for example, is willing to surrender from a favourable swing in the sterling/dollar exchange rate, through a lower knock-out, the less costly its hedge. Likewise, the more positively correlated the firm's exposures, the smaller the savings that will accrue to the firm.

Correlation is clearly the key to pricing hybrid derivatives; unfortunately it is difficult to measure. Many correlations, particularly those that cross markets, are not supported by strong causal connections. Further, apparently robust correlations may deteriorate despite apparently convincing rationale. Consider the Exchange Rate Mechanism crisis in Europe in 1993, when the correlation between the British pound and the Deutschmark went from positive to negative. Such regime shifts are not uncommon, and could lead to the mispricing of hybrid derivatives.

After the firm has purchased a properly constructed integrated hedge, however, it will not be faced with substantial risk from shifts in correlation. Correlation describes the probability of joint movements of two financial prices. A properly constructed integrated hedge, on the other hand, will protect the firm from actual joint movements in the financial prices. Oil Inc, for instance, will set the oil price knock-out on its foreign exchange option at a level such that any increase in revenues from higher oil prices will sustain the higher costs resulting from a sharp decline in the value of the dollar.

Portfolio effects and integrated hedging

The saving arising from the negative correlation described above is simply the local manifestation of an important concept in financial theory – the "portfolio effect". As described in detail in Panel 4, the portfolio effect tells us that the variance of the return on a collection of assets will nearly always be less than the variance of the return on any subset of the portfolio. Less technically, in a portfolio, a movement in the price of one asset is likely to be offset by a movement in the price of another asset, so that the average return on the portfolio will most likely be less volatile than the return on any of its members.

To see how the portfolio effect applies to risk management, imagine a Japanese shipper with exposures to residual oil prices and the yen/sterling exchange rate. This firm wishes to construct a hedging strategy that limits the maximum negative impact of these financial prices on its bottom line.

This hedging strategy could easily be implemented using traditional options. The firm need only purchase a call option on residual oil to guard against a rising oil price, and a sterling call/yen put option that would place a limit on the firm's exposure to a weakening yen. The cost of this hedge would simply be the sum of the option premium of the crude oil option and that of the foreign exchange option. These premia will be determined by the usual factors, including the volatility of oil prices and the yen-sterling exchange rate.

Alternatively, the shipper may implement an equivalent hedge by purchasing an integrated hedge consisting of a single basket option. One way to view this hedge is as a traditional option, with an underlying asset consisting of the combined yen value of the firm's exposures to oil prices and the yen-sterling rate. Again, the firm limits the maximum risk it faces from its exposures through the strike price.

The cost of the integrated hedge will simply be the premium of the basket option, which is determined by the volatility of the "return" on the underlying asset. The portfolio effect, however, implies that the volatility of the return on this asset will almost always be less than either of the volatilities of its members (that is, the yen value of the manufacturer's yen-sterling exposure or the yen value of its oil price exposure). As a result, the premium on this option will be no greater than, and almost certainly less than, the combined premia of the traditional options.

The extent of the saving available to the manufacturer will depend on the correlation between movements in the yen/sterling rate and those in the oil price. In any portfolio, if the movements in the prices of the constituents are perfectly negatively correlated, then the volatility of the portfolio will be less than the volatility of any of its members; conversely if the price changes are perfectly positively correlated, then the volatility of the portfolio will be more like an average of the volatilities of its members.[3] Thus, to the extent that movements in the yen/sterling rate and the oil price tend to offset each other, that is, to the extent that their correlation is less than one, the integrated hedge will be cheaper than the traditional option-based hedge.

Figure 6 describes the difference in the cost of the hedges more explicitly. It illustrates the cost savings, in per cent, for a hypothetical basket option over a traditional option-based hedge, and it plots these against the correlation between the changes of price in the underlying assets. (In this case, the firm is assumed to have equal exposures to both of the asset prices, and these prices are assumed to have equal volatilities.) The figure makes it clear that all of the cost savings in the basket option arise from the portfolio effect; when the asset price changes are perfectly correlated, there are no cost savings. Likewise, when the price changes are perfectly negatively correlated, the cost savings reach their maximum (in this case, 100%). Nevertheless, the figure indicates that the savings from the basket option are by no means zero, even when the asset price correlations are much larger than zero.

The correlation coefficients listed in Table 1 provide a rough indication of the correlations that integrated hedges may be designed to take advantage of. For example, over the past five years the correlation coefficients for interest rates and energy prices have been near zero. This suggests that, over the last five years, energy prices and interest rates were about as likely to move in the opposite direction as in the same direction – suggesting that portfolio effects which may be exploited by hybrid securities are readily available.

An important subsidiary point arises from the fact that interest rates and energy prices are about as likely to move in the same direction as in opposite directions. This is that the impact on

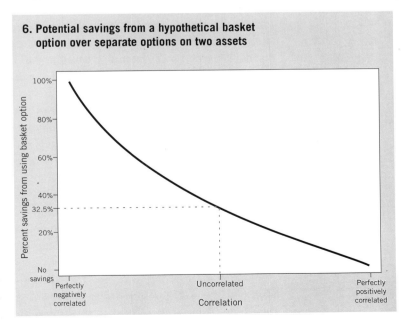

6. Potential savings from a hypothetical basket option over separate options on two assets

PORTFOLIO THEORY: AN ILLUSTRATION

Portfolio theory is a fundamental concept in financial analysis. It tells us that the variance of the return on a collection of assets will nearly always be less than the variance of the return on any subset of the portfolio. Less technically, in a portfolio a movement in the price of one asset is likely to be offset by a movement in the price of another asset, so that the average return on the portfolio will most likely be less volatile than the return on any of its members.

The portfolio effect has usually been illustrated by considering groups of equities. Instead, we may consider a portfolio consisting of "risks". Suppose a firm consumes 100,000 barrels of West Texas Intermediate crude per month. This firm also generates ¥200 million from the sale of goods in Japan — but it must repatriate the yen into US dollars. Over the period 1989 through 1993, the firm would, on average, have benefited as the price of WTI fell, at an annual average rate of 3.7% per month, while the dollar value of the yen rose, at an annual average rate of 3.1% per month. The volatility of oil prices over this period was about 116.3%, while that of the yen/dollar exchange rate was 35.9%.

It is tempting to suggest that the volatility of this portfolio of risks is simply the sum of the volatilities of the WTI oil price and the yen/dollar exchange rate, or 152.2% per year. However, this figure would be an over-estimate of the portfolio's volatility, as it does not take into account the likelihood that a change in the price of WTI will be offset by a change in the yen/dollar exchange rate. In fact, between 1989 and 1993, only 14 out of 59 months saw an appreciation of the dollar that coincided with an increase in the price of oil. Likewise, in only 17 months was there both a dollar depreciation *vis-à-vis* the yen, and an increase in the price of oil.

These facts suggest that movements in the exchange rate and oil price are largely uncorrelated; the estimated correlation coefficient between the two financial prices confirms this, as it is only about 0.1.

It is clear that an appropriate estimate of the

volatility of the portfolio must take into account the extent to which the financial prices move together. In general, the less positively correlated the exchange rate and the oil price, the smaller the volatility of the portfolio. The precise formula that represents this relationship makes this clear,

$$\text{(Volatility of portfolio)} =$$
$$\sqrt{\begin{array}{l} W_{WTI}^2 (\text{Volatility of WTI})^2 + \\ W_{¥/\$}^2 (\text{Volatility of } ¥/\$)^2 + \\ W_{WTI}W_{¥/\$} (\text{Covariance of WTI and } ¥/\$) \end{array}}$$

In this equation, W_{WTI} represents the proportion of the portfolio representing the dollar value of WTI crude oil, and $W_{¥/\$}$ represents the proportion of the portfolio representing the dollar value of the yen.

The covariance term is simply the correlation between the volatilities of the members of the portfolio, scaled by the volatilities themselves:

$$\text{(Covariance of WTI and } ¥/\$) =$$
$$\text{(Volatility of WTI)} \times$$
$$\text{(Volatility of } ¥/\$) \times$$
$$\text{(Correlation between WTI and } ¥/\$)$$

In this case, given recent oil prices and exchange rates, the firm's exposure to the yen/dollar exchange rate and the price of WTI crude oil are very roughly equal, so that $W_{WTI} = W_{¥/\$} = 1/2$. Given these "weights" and the volatilities of the financial prices themselves, the volatility of the portfolio is given by:

$$\text{(Volatility of portfolio)} =$$
$$\sqrt{\begin{array}{l} \left(\frac{1}{2}\right)^2 (116.3\%)^2 + \left(\frac{1}{2}\right)^2 (35.9\%)^2 + \\ \frac{1}{2} \times \frac{1}{2} \times 2 \times \text{(Covariance of WTI and } ¥/\$) \end{array}}$$
$$\text{(Covariance of WTI and } ¥/\$) =$$
$$(116.3\%) \times (35.9\%) \times 0.1 = 4.2$$
$$\text{(Volatility of portfolio)} = 62.4\%$$

Note that the smaller the correlation between the asset prices, the smaller the volatility of the entire portfolio.

corporate profits of movements in energy prices may often be offset by movements in interest rates even when no deliberate hedging is undertaken. That is, the firm *itself* may be considered to be a natural portfolio of business risks. It is likely, therefore, that a corporation

that hedges its exposures to interest rates independently of its exposures to energy prices is "over-hedging". In other words, the firm is buying insurance for changes in interest rates and energy prices that will often partially offset each other. An integrated hedge will take into

Table 1. Correlations between monthly changes in selected financial prices

| | US$ exchange rates | | | | Brent crude | Energy prices | | | Interest rates | |
	Gold	DM	¥	£		Gas oil	Natural gas	Jet fuel	Long-term treasuries	Six-month Libor
Alum.	0.133	−0.047	0.078	0.026	0.067	0.037	−0.044	−0.061	0.165	0.180
Gold		0.245	0.266	0.264	0.227	0.205	0.004	0.136	0.190	0.034
DM			0.678	0.758	0.069	0.191	−0.003	0.089	−0.221	−0.207
¥				0.587	0.001	0.132	−0.036	0.082	−0.153	−0.079
£					0.093	0.128	0.024	0.096	−0.132	−0.174
Brent crude						0.806	−0.050	0.235	0.106	0.172
Gasoil							−0.066	0.197	0.114	0.154
Natural gas								0.005	−0.143	−0.166
Jet fuel									0.073	0.160
Treasury										0.588
Libor										

Note: All correlations are based on monthly percentage changes in the financial prices between January 1985 and April 1994, except for the interest rates which are based on data from 1989 through April 1994

account the joint behaviour of the prices.

It is worth stressing that these portfolio effects exist even where asset price movements are fairly highly correlated. The correlation between the US dollar/sterling and the US dollar/yen exchange rates, for example, is somewhat larger than 0.5; yet over the past five years, the two exchange rates have moved in opposite directions for nearly a third of the time. It is likely that the impact of changes in the dollar value of the yen on the profits of a firm exposed to both exchange rates will fairly frequently be offset by changes in the value of sterling.

Integrated hedging versus conventional strategies: a simulation

To illustrate the difference between traditional hedging and strategies that make use of cross-market hybrid derivatives, we simulated their different effects on a firm that is vulnerable to energy price risk, interest rate risk and foreign exchange risk.

We imagined that a US airline (Airline Inc) depended on two factors, fuel oil and short-term debt (commercial paper), to produce "output" (passenger miles) that it sells in the United States and in Japan. Given the markets it operates in and its production process, the airline's net revenue is hurt by increases in jet fuel prices or interest rates, and benefits from any depreciation in the US dollar *vis-à-vis* the Japanese yen.

In the simulation, we generated prices for Airline Inc's output in the United States and in Japan; a price for jet fuel; a short-term interest rate; and a yen-dollar exchange rate. We manipulated these prices so that the firm was faced with environments that were characterised by

low, medium and high volatility (as illustrated by the figure in Panel 5).

Regardless of the state of volatility, the correlations between the movements in the asset prices were assumed to be constant. Jet fuel and interest rates were assumed to be mildly positively correlated. On the other hand, jet fuel and the exchange rate were assumed to be negatively correlated, as were the interest rate and exchange rate. (The technical details on which the simulation rests are described in detail in Panel 5.)

We chose this structure to best illustrate the firm's response to an environment characterised by a large, but not atypical, shift in volatility. We also wanted show the impact of correlation, but not to allow it to determine our results.

Given the simulated prices, Airline Inc must simultaneously choose its production level, the quantity of jet fuel it purchases, and the size of its commercial paper sale. Note that the firm can only control its use of foreign exchange by altering the number of passenger miles it produces, as the firm has no control over the proportion of domestic and Japanese purchases.

We noted above that any firm may be considered to be a natural portfolio of its business risks, so that a change in one financial price to which the firm is exposed will often be offset by a change in another price. But this model is simplistic – the firm is not a static group of assets. A better model of the firm would have at least an element of Schumpeter's creative destruction.[4] That is, it would imagine a firm constantly evolving, altering its use of cost factors and the production process to maximise its profit in the face of changing market conditions. A risk-management plan must take into account

TECHNICAL DETAILS OF THE SIMULATION OF AIRLINE INC'S HEDGING

In the extended example given in the main text, we assume that Airline Inc produces its output (passenger miles) by means that allow a constant elasticity of substitution (CES); this allows the firm some, but not perfect, substitution among the inputs to its production process.

Because the simulation has a very short time horizon, we assume that Airline Inc has control of only the quantity of jet fuel it consumes and its short-term indebtedness. It combines these factors with,

$$Q = \gamma \left(\begin{array}{l} \delta_1 D^{-\rho} + \delta^2 O^{-\rho} + \\ (1 - \delta_1 - \delta_2) \times \\ F^{-\rho} \end{array} \right)^{-\frac{1}{\rho}}$$

where D is the quantity of short-term debt the firm chooses, O is the quantity of fuel the firm chooses, and F are other fixed inputs that the firm has no control over in the short term. The parameter ρ describes the ability of the firm to substitute factors in producing output Q; the parameters δ_1 and δ_2 describe the relative importance of the factors in producing the output; and γ describes the efficiency of the production process.

We imagine Airline Inc to be a charter airline operating only between the US and Japan. The firm sells one third of its output in yen, and the remainder in US dollars. The airline receives different prices for its product in the US and in Japan. The company takes these prices as given –

Airline Inc's production has no impact on prices. Thus the airline's total revenue is given by

$$TR = \alpha P_{us} Q + (1 - \alpha) P_j fx_{j,us} Q$$

where α is the proportion of Airline Inc's sales in Japan; $fx_{j,us}$ is the yen-dollar exchange rate; P_j is the price of the airline's output in Japan, denominated in yen; and P_{us} is the price of the airline's output in the US, denominated in dollars. Given this model, Airline Inc's net revenue in any given period is given by

$$NR = TR - rF - P^0 O$$

where r is the short-term interest rate, and P^0 is the price of fuel oil. In each trial, the airline chooses its quantity of jet fuel and short-term debt to maximise net revenue, given foreign and domestic output prices, interest rates, exchange rates and fuel prices.

The simulation begins by drawing 5,000 realisations of three years of the various prices facing the firm: output prices, interest rates, exchange rates and fuel prices. For simplicity's sake, we model the prices at the monthly level and assume that each is generated by a simple random walk. The innovations to the random walk are assumed to follow a multivariate normal distribution with a known correlation matrix; the correlation matrix we chose has no relation to the actual relationship between jet fuel prices, short-term interest rates, and the yen/dollar exchange rate.

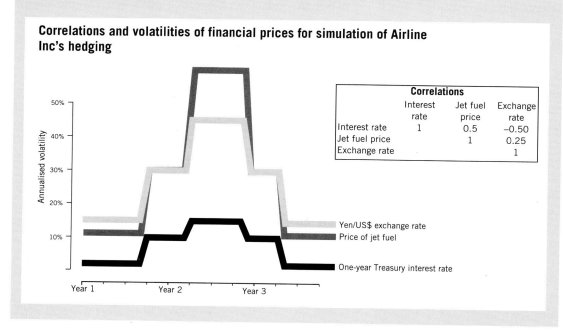

Correlations and volatilities of financial prices for simulation of Airline Inc's hedging

	Correlations		
	Interest rate	Jet fuel price	Exchange rate
Interest rate	1	0.5	–0.50
Jet fuel price		1	0.25
Exchange rate			1

Yen/US$ exchange rate
Price of jet fuel
One-year Treasury interest rate

We assumed that volatility is also known, though it varies from period to period for the interest rates, exchange rates, and fuel prices. The correlation and volatility assumptions are illustrated in the figure on the previous page.

For each realisation of the prices, Airline Inc's net revenue and its use of jet fuel, short-term debt and foreign exchange is calculated.

In the second stage of the simulation, the costs and benefits of hedging are calculated for the airline under two scenarios. In the first, Airline Inc is assumed to purchase separate options for each exposure. In the second, Airline Inc uses a basket option to hedge. In either case, the hedge ratios are based on the firm's usage of the assets over the last six months, and the strike prices are set 10% away from prevailing prices. For each realisation of the prices faced by the firm, the premia and pay-offs from the hedges are calculated for both of the hedging strategies.

Parameter settings employed in Monte Carlo simulation

$$Q = \gamma \left(\frac{\delta_1 D^{-\rho} + \delta_2 O^{-\rho} +}{(1 - \delta_1 - \delta_2) F^{-\rho}} \right)^{-\frac{1}{\rho}}$$

Parameter	Value	Description
γ	100	The efficiency of the production process, $0 < \gamma$
δ_1	0.2	The relative importance of short-term debt, D, in the firm's production process, $\delta_1 + \delta_2 \leq 1$
δ_2	0.2	The relative importance of jet fuel oil, O, in the firm's production process, $\delta_1 + \delta_2 \leq 1$
ρ	2	The ability of the firm to substitute factors in its production process, this parameter is bounded by $0 \leq \rho$
α	0.75	The proportion of Airline Inc's output sold in the US. The proportion sold in Japan is $(1 - \alpha)$

the firm's ability to substitute cost factors, or it will conclude by encouraging the firm to take out larger hedges than is efficient.

One of the main tasks of the "optimising" model of the firm presented here is to capture this aspect of risk management.

In our simulation we compared the firm's performance in three instances:
❏ no hedging;
❏ a traditional hedge which employs separate energy price, interest rate and exchange rate option contracts to hedge the firm's disparate exposures individually; and
❏ an integrated hedge which employs a basket option to hedge all of the firm's exposures simultaneously with one instrument.

The results of the simulation are illustrated in Figures 7–9 overleaf. These figures provide summaries of the distribution of percentage changes in net income and the proportion of trials where the firm incurred financial distress.

We examined the distribution of percentage changes in Airline Inc's net revenues by plotting the median and lower 95th percentile of the monthly distributions of each month's percentage change. These statistics, describing the distribution's middle and its extreme lower end, are plotted as bold lines in the figures. The histogram lying behind these lines indicates, for each period, the proportion of trials where the firm incurred financial distress, as defined by net income falling below some arbitrary, low, level.

In the simulation illustrated by Figure 7, Airline Inc is not engaging in any hedging. Note that during periods of high volatility, during the middle of the simulation, the median change in net revenue remains roughly constant at about zero, while the lowest 95th percentile change falls dramatically. Simultaneously, the proportion of trials where the airline entered financial distress soared, rising to nearly 3% of the trials as a whole during this period.

In and of themselves these facts mean little – Figure 7 is completely artificial. We can alter the lines and the histogram in the figure simply by changing a few key parameters. The purpose of this figure is to provide a point of comparison – a control – for when we allow the firm to hedge.

Figure 8 illustrates the result when Airline Inc adopts a conventional hedging policy. This policy allows the firm to hedge its interest rate, foreign exchange rate and fuel oil price exposures by using traditional options. We structured the firm's hedging policy so that, each month, the firm purchases a sufficient number of

164

options to hedge a six-month moving average of its uses of short-term debt, foreign exchange and fuel oil. These options have a six-month expiration and a strike price set at 10% above the current value of the financial price. The cost of this hedge is simply the sum of the option

premia, as illustrated in the bottom panel of Figure 8. We assume that the firm knows the current volatility of the foreign exchange rates, interest rates and energy prices, but does not know any of the future volatilities.

Note that the hedging costs rise markedly when the firm's environment becomes more volatile in the middle portion of the simulation.

The top panel of Figure 8 illustrates the change in the simulation result, if we allow Airline Inc to follow this simple hedging policy. While the median change in net revenue remains roughly unchanged, the "lowest 95th percentile" – the worst outcome for the firm – improves substantially for the hedged firm. In the unhedged case, during the period of highest volatility, this worst case results in a decline of about 20% in net revenue in a single month. In comparison, in the hedged case, the worst case is a 7% decline, but only during one month.

Likewise, the maximum proportion of trials where the airline fell into financial distress, described in Figures 7 and 8, fell from more than 3% per month for the unhedged example to roughly 0.5% per month for the hedged firm.

In our final exercise, illustrated in Figure 9, we allowed Airline Inc to implement a very simple integrated hedging programme. Rather than using individual interest rate, foreign exchange rate or energy price options, the airline employs a basket option to gather these risks together. This simple hybrid derivative treats the US dollar value of the firm's exposures to all of these financial prices as the asset underlying the option. The strike price of the option is equivalent to that employed in the traditional hedge; that is, it is the dollar value of the exposures at current financial prices plus 5%. The maturity of the option is six months, as before. Again, the firm's hedging policy is structured so that, each month, the firm purchases a sufficient number of the basket options to hedge a six-month moving average of its uses of short-term debt, foreign exchange and fuel oil.

The top panel of Figure 9 reveals that the performance of the integrated hedge in limiting the impact of volatility on the firm is very similar to the standard option-based hedge. The key difference is in the cost of the hedge. This cost is 25% less than the cost of the standard hedge at the beginning of the simulation. During the period of highest volatility, the savings increase so that the integrated hedge costs about 40% less than the standard hedge.

Of course, this simulation paints a highly

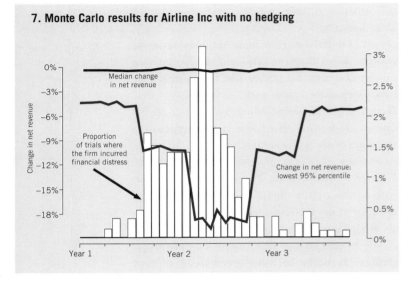

7. Monte Carlo results for Airline Inc with no hedging

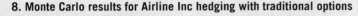

8. Monte Carlo results for Airline Inc hedging with traditional options

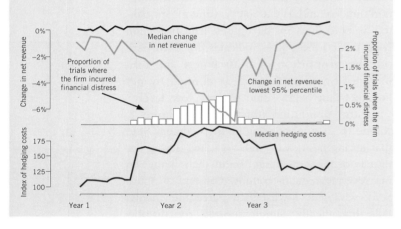

9. Monte Carlo results for Airline Inc hedging with a basket option

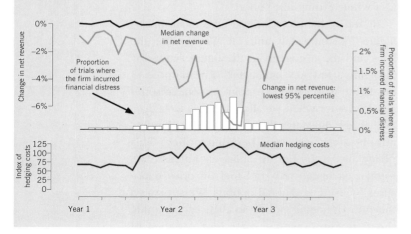

simplified picture of the hedging activity of a real firm. We have set a few simple rules for the firm's hedging programmes, for example in setting strike prices and notional amounts, which the programme follows slavishly. Further, our model of the firm's costs and production is extremely schematic. These simplifications do not, however, detract from the fundamental conclusion: that the conventional and the integrated hedge both succeed in managing the firm's net exposure; and that the integrated hedge offers a considerable cost saving.

Conclusion: from simulation to application

Given the advantages outlined above, it seems fair to ask why integrated hedging is not the norm among major international end-users of energy risk management, rather than a specialised sub-sector. There are, perhaps, two interrelated reasons for this.

Traditionally, many corporations have evolved so that decisions on commodity price risk management have been primarily the responsibility of operational management, rather than the treasury. But when structuring integrated hedges, such as interest rate swaps indexed against energy prices, it is essential that there is close cooperation between the central treasury and the management of the operating companies. In particular, the operational management must provide treasuries with the necessary technical information and expertise concerning energy and other commodity markets.

Another possible problem is that risk management teams responsible for managing risks within a company may see the integration of risk management as a threat to their role and function within the company.

It is important to consider these practical obstacles when implementing integrated hedges, but they do not negate the fundamental benefit: integrated hedging programmes, because they take advantage of the portfolio effect, can significantly reduce hedging costs, without decreasing the level of protection.

1 *Julian Walmsley,* The New Financial Instruments *(New York, 1988).*

2 *Perfect positive correlation implies that the asset prices tend to move in the same direction to a degree that reflects a constant proportionality between the relative price changes, while perfect negative correlation implies that the asset prices tend to move in the opposite direction to a degree that also reflects a constant proportionality.*

3 *In theory, if the members of the portfolio are perfectly nega-tively correlated, the weights of the assets in the portfolio can be arranged to give the portfolio zero correlation; unfortunately, firms do not have that much control over their portfolios of risks.*

4 *Joseph A. Schumpeter,* Essays on Entrepreneurs, Innovations, Business cycles, and the Evolution of Capitalism, *edited by Richard V. Clemence (New Brunswick, NJ, 1989).*

Classic and emerging markets

9

The Oil Market

Frédéric Barnaud and Jean Dabouineau
Elf Trading

The trading environment of the oil markets is inherently unstable. Geology, geopolitics, economics, law, taxation, finance, technology and environmental concerns are liable at any time to make a formidable impact on the evolution of the market structure. The fundamental factors that generate risk in the oil industry, such as geological risk – on which the risk-reward relationship of the pioneering epoch of oil exploration was mainly based – may be reduced by the use of modern techniques and technology, but they cannot truly be *managed*.

Instead, the management of risk in the oil industry has tended to focus on managing the relationship between *time* and *price*. To produce crude from an oil field requires several years and a huge investment; to bring oil from the well to the customer requires at least a few weeks and sound logistics (pipelines, cargoes, storage facilities, refineries, distribution networks). These logistical facts form the backdrop to the growth in risk management in the oil industry.

The main aim of this chapter is to provide a global and up-to-date analysis of how the structure of the oil industry and the oil markets impact upon the hedging strategies of the end-user (energy consumer), the oil company and the energy derivatives' provider. We will focus on three specific issues: locational risks and the role of fundamentals; price term structure and the role of storage; and crack, product and quality spreads and the role of refining. In our conclusion we will attempt to map out how the markets in oil derivatives are likely to evolve in the future.

Introduction: market perspectives

HISTORICAL PERSPECTIVE

The modern oil markets – spot, forwards, futures and derivatives – have evolved only over the past 20 years. In this period, the means of assessing and managing risks in a context of highly volatile energy prices have increased tenfold. Financial instruments and new techniques have turned wet barrels into paper and then video barrels.

The fundamental pricing environment for oil transactions has also undergone major changes since the large price jumps of the 1970s. The shift in the ownership of producing assets from major oil companies to producing countries and national companies, through different forms of nationalisation, marked the beginning of open markets. For most companies, this meant that they could no longer simply transfer risk and added value vertically along different steps of the logistic chain. Consequently, crude oil supply contracts have evolved from being relatively fixed to being relatively flexible (Fig. 1).

Another important element in the development of the oil markets has been the ambition of taxation authorities to transform the more or less arbitrary transfer prices for transactions among sister companies – for example from exploration and production to refining – into a more visible system.[1]

The physical oil markets now play a major role in creating the supply and demand equilibrium in local markets, and in global arbitrage. Oil companies and oil importing countries often consider the oil markets as a kind of dynamic counterweight to the dominance of producing

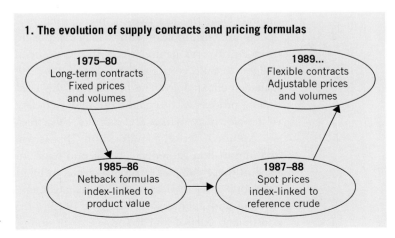

1. The evolution of supply contracts and pricing formulas

1975–80
Long-term contracts
Fixed prices
and volumes

1989...
Flexible contracts
Adjustable prices
and volumes

1985–86
Netback formulas
index-linked to
product value

1987–88
Spot prices
index-linked to
reference crude

countries or, more precisely, of OPEC.

Given the strong current of liberalism in the United States and in the United Kingdom since the early 1980s, the oil markets have become established as a genuine market, and as an adequate pricing reference. In particular, because of the increased flexibility in the contracts available to end-users, the oil markets have become a major factor in the pricing mechanism for short- to medium-term crude oil and refined products – a role which was dramatically revealed to the world by the Gulf crisis of August 1990–March 1991.

RISK MANAGEMENT AND THE END-USER
The first end-users to adopt hedging strategies used forwards, futures, options or swaps to fulfil very specific aims, such as protecting budgets, protecting stocks or as a tool in financing. But risk management is now also associated with strategic decisions, taken at board level, with regard to a whole range of business concerns.

Before taking any exchange or over-the-counter (OTC) position, each corporate end-user must examine the real objectives of its risk management strategy. The hedging programme should be fully integrated into supply flows and stock optimisation, and variable supply costs (and therefore cash-flows) must be constantly monitored. Nowadays, the move to risk management may well be forced by innovative initiatives from competitors. That is to say, it may be externally imposed rather than internally driven. In any case, senior executives must make an explicit decision as to the company's tolerance to oil market risks in terms of amount or volume, duration, diffusion and absorption.

For example, if we look for a moment at the Regional Electricity Companies (RECs) in the UK – described in some detail in Chapter 11 – it is not purely philosophical to ask whether these companies are essentially risk-averse or risk-neutral. Over the last two to three years, producers and distributors with a major exposure to electricity and natural gas prices have been obliged to take conscious decisions about risk management strategy. The first step of this continuing process was to gain a full understanding of the electricity market and its risks – in effect, an extended period of education, discussion and information gathering. The second stage for most of these companies was to create an internal group able to deal with risk management: contract and counterparty analysis, operational constraints, control and follow-up of positions,

liquidity and valuation principles (mark-to-market). Only then were the companies able to start properly managing their energy risk.

As well as understanding the external dynamics of the market, end-users must identify their internal risk component through an investigation of both financial and physical inflows and outflows: risk usually arises from asymmetries between fixed and floating exposures, and between short-term versus long-term exposures. As part of corporate strategy, risk management requires that clear objectives are set for the different aspects of the business:
❏ *physical:* storage and supply optimisation;
❏ *financial:* securing budgets and cash-flows, enhancing return on investment and debt-to-equity ratio;
❏ *marketing:* designing innovative marketing and tariff policies that offer a competitive advantage;
❏ *general:* gaining access to market information and arbitrage opportunities.

Difficult choices must be made when setting up oil price hedging strategies. It is not only a matter of choosing instruments, but also of integrating these with the business or trading environment. In particular, potential hedgers have to take into account:
❏ legal, accounting and tax considerations;
❏ operational handling and costs;
❏ information and processing systems;
❏ procedures for decision-making, authority and limits (volume or amount, maturity);
❏ procedures for reporting of positions (mark-to-market);
❏ procedures for following up positions (evolution of residual risks); and
❏ the impact of liquidity and of indexation mismatch.

Liquidity is a particularly important factor to consider, not only at the initiation of a transaction, but also through the life of the contract up until maturity. Industry indices, such as the Department of Trade and Industry (DTI) indices in UK natural gas pricing, are sometimes used for price escalation formulas. Writing derivatives on such indices is possible because of a good correlation (excluding domestic tax elements) with international oil prices (mainly Platt's assessments). However, their liquidity is still much lower than for direct Platt's-indexed derivatives and this may justify a limited premium. On the one hand, this locally indexed derivative better represents the company exposure, but on the other, the contract is not very liquid or easily transferable. The choice of index is thus an important decision, and should be made at an appropriate level.

Management must also be clearly aware of the possibility of opportunity losses – fixing the price of oil using a swap means that (unlike unhedged competitors) the company may not be able to take advantage of a reduction in prices. Most end-users are not market specialists, and it is in the interest of long-term players in the market to adopt an "educational" approach; in particular, companies should not be led into ill-adapted deals which yield a large residual exposure.

Choosing the right instrument is a crucial part of the hedging process. In Panel 1, we focus on one particularly active end-user market sector and tabulate the benefits and disadvantages of using particular instruments.

Finally, it should be stressed that in the oil market, more than in any other derivative market, an end-user's strategy will be affected by whether the market is in backwardation or in contango. The choice between a swap and an option depends not only on the option premium, but also on the market price level and structure, and on possible market scenarios.

RISK MANAGEMENT AND THE OIL COMPANY

Oil price risk has traditionally been at the heart of the oil business, and most oil companies have now adapted their vertical structure to the new challenges created by oil price risk trading and management. Risk management trading in oil companies can be divided into the three main areas of business outlined below:

❑ *System trading* This is aimed mainly at optimising the supply, import and export requirements of the oil group. It involves the systematic researching of the most profitable markets for the crudes produced by the group. The transfer of risks from the production sector of the company to the trading sector requires that the latter should be able to handle logistics and security matters, to offer contractual and financial guarantees, and to provide adequate hedging programmes against large price fluctuations.

The supply trading entity will also arrange physical supplies at competitive prices for the oil group's refining, distribution and chemical divisions. Furthermore, it will try to take advantage of any opportunities to profit from physical arbitrage: for example, the opening of export windows between the United States and North-west Europe (NWE).

❑ *Third party trading* This business sector handles trading crudes and products with large oil companies and traders. Such transactions are usually independent of direct supply concerns, but form part of global arbitrage strategies. They may also be associated with prefinancing and barter operations.

❑ *Risk management* The risk management desk monitors and manages price volatility, maturity and basis risks. It acts principally on behalf of the group itself, mainly for production, transportation, refining, distribution, chemicals and international trading. Risk management may also provide the distribution subsidiaries of the oil company with additional marketing tools, such as attaching price guarantees to physical deliveries.

At the same time, some oil companies have developed an independent portfolio of clients to whom they offer specific derivative instruments: for example, airlines, shipping and transportation companies, utilities and large industries, independent oil producers, refiners or traders, banks and financial institutions.

Thus, within an oil company, many elements take part in the risk management process. And a great variety of commercial opportunities may be considered. For example:

❑ the portfolio of equity crudes may be better adapted to the needs of the company's refining structure. An instance of this is the adjustment of the "sulphur balance" by buying low-sulphur crudes or by investing in hydro-desulphurisation;

❑ distribution networks may be reorganised around refineries and storage areas to enhance logistics;

❑ assets and acreage may be modified or swapped for those with better taxation or cost profiles.

In the next section we will look closely at the risk management strategy of refiners; in this introductory section we will investigate the risk management strategies of the other "fundamental" sector of the industry: exploration and production (E&P).

Oil exploration is a business with one of the highest R&D costs of any industry: the average cost of drilling oil is expressed in millions of dollars. Production also requires heavy investment, and has both a political and a strategic aspect. However, few producing companies or countries presently consider hedging their complete programmes; the reasons for this are discussed in

INSTRUMENT SELECTION IN THE AIRLINE SECTOR

Jet fuel represents, on average, about 15% of the direct operating costs of airlines, but because the price volatility is so high it can suddenly become a much more significant cost. Price rises cannot be easily transferred to customers because of tariffs and competitive pressures. For this reason, many derivatives providers initially targeted airlines as the "ideal" user of hedging techniques.

European and, to a lesser extent, Asian airlines have been the most active in the market; their hedging operations are now very professional, and are often run just like a trading desk. For example, most airlines are fully aware not only of the behaviour of related markets, such as IPE gasoil futures and jet kerosene derivatives, but also of the price term structure and of ways to interpret or to take advantage of it.

Even so, risk management is mostly designed to stabilise short- and medium-term cash-flows and to secure minimum profitability. Moreover, hedging proposals are frequently combined with physical tenders for airport supplies. Although one might have hoped that longer-term derivatives would start to be used as part of aviation financing, the peculiarities of the air finance sector are such that this is only happening to a limited degree.

The instruments used by airlines have evolved from simple swaps to more complex or exotic types. The choice between them depends on market level and structure, on trading habits, on budget settings and cash availability (in the case of an option-like premium). It is obviously important for airlines to understand the exact characteristics and potential effects (profits/losses, volume and maturity risks) of hedging instruments. Below, we attempt to tabulate the nature of the risks and benefits associated with particular instruments.

❑ *swaps* are tailor-made to minimise the basis risks on a fixed-floating transaction. When entering the transaction, the commitment between hedgers and providers in terms of future cash-flow is symmetric. However, airlines buying forward supplies at a fixed price risk an opportunity cost whenever spot prices decline during the contract period;

❑ *caps* (call options) may be purchased to hedge against the risk of a price rise, without risking the potential benefits of a drop in price. That is, caps

cannot incur any opportunity cost. This payoff is, of course, asymmetric, and is balanced by the upfront premium paid to the option writer;

❑ *collars* offer a hedge on the upside risk, just like caps, but the cost of this option is exchanged by assigning part of the downside to the writer. That is, collars usually have no initial cost, but entail a potential loss of opportunity (just like swaps, but at a lower level). In the past, some airlines have not fully recognised the potential impact of this opportunity cost, and found themselves in a difficult position, compared to unhedged or capped competitors, when the price of jet fuel dropped heavily;

❑ *double-ups* offer a swap-like instrument, but at a lower market price than the equivalent swap. This price benefit is offset by the fact that the provider may double the hedging quantity at the initial or a lower fixed price. In effect, the airline buys a swap and sells a put option on a similar swap (a swaption), which may later be exercised. This reduces the initial hedging cost, but the potential opportunity cost is doubled. Moreover, the implicit sale of a put does not provide enough protection with regard to the additional volume, should prices rocket upwards. Double-up strategies are therefore liable to have quite an impact if there is a large price move. Smaller or inexperienced airlines should be wary of entering into them, while airlines with large volumes to handle and a good trading organisation may find them more attractive;

❑ *combinations* between IPE gasoil futures and kerosene to gasoil spread hedging tend to be used by airlines that are very active in the market. For example, gasoil screen-hedging may be completed by the purchase of options on the kerosene-gasoil spread value over some future period. In that way, the correlation between both products is kept under control (at the expense of a limited premium), while hedging the absolute price risk is achieved by means of day-to-day operations on the IPE. Users should remember that this is a sophisticated strategy that needs careful monitoring.

The jet fuel sector is also discussed in Chapter 5, where a further panel describes the implementation of a differential swap.

more detail with reference to the emerging markets in Chapter 12. The taxation framework, and the risk-taking nature of the industry itself, are fundamental when assessing the potential market for E&P-oriented derivatives.

In the past, small US oil companies appear to have been more willing to use medium- to long-term hedging programmes than large North Sea producers, or national oil companies in South America, the Middle East or the Far East. However, some of these larger producers have hedged selectively, for instance, during the Gulf crisis or during periods of large contangos.

Ideally, an oil company's hedging programme should be designed to ensure the company's financial stability (repayment of liabilities); minimum profitability (distribution to shareholders); and the successful development of new projects (putting existing reserves on stream or discovering new reserves). The time duration and the payoff structure of such hedging transactions would depend on the exact needs of the company:

- ❑ profitability over one or more accounting year(s);
- ❑ duration of liabilities if debtors require guarantee of repayments;
- ❑ return on investment for long-term projects.

Short-term hedging is usually made on a cargo-by-cargo basis, and must be designed to take account of tax factors because there is usually an asymmetry between taxation on oil revenues and taxation on hedging (financial) revenues or losses. The structure of market oil prices can move violently between backwardation and contango (we explore this in detail in the next section) and these different structural contexts strongly influence the hedging strategies available to producers (as discussed in Panel 2).

One of the specific strategies suited to medium- to long-term hedging is the use of oil-linked debt to facilitate global financing. According to market circumstances, and the objectives of the strategy, the oil company can also construct an optimal combination of put options and swaps (Fig. 2). The swap (or forward sale at a fixed price) is used to reward third parties, shareholders and debtors, and ensures a minimum profit and liability repayment; the put option is set up on the remainder of the production volume to hedge the downside. The proportions of swaps and options relative to the field's production plan are adjusted according to initial market conditions, cost structure and the taxation framework. It is worth noting here that if the fixed payment for the swap is sufficient, then this will itself finance the initial premium on the option.

Our brief analysis of E&P hedging suggests that risk management for the oil industry is a complex process. This is particularly true in the case of an integrated company, which has the potential to take advantage of the size and variety of its own flows of risks. Yet, however sophisticated the trading, no company can afford to ignore the market fundamentals discussed later on in this chapter.

RISK MANAGEMENT AND THE DERIVATIVES PROVIDER

We would define the derivatives provider as the counterparty that bears the ultimate market risks embedded in any derivative. This may well be an oil company, as described above, an oil trader, a bank or an investment house (the so-called "Wall Street refiners"). On the one hand, the provider must develop its clientele. On the other, it needs to identify and quantify the exact residual risks in its portfolio. The derivatives' provider must pursue long-term objectives, and report and control its exposure in real time, while remaining dynamic enough to gain trading efficiency and technical advantages over competitors.

In recent years, the energy derivative market has attracted many trading companies. However, not many have been able to sustain a long-term engagement. Among these, even fewer are willing to keep and manage market

2. Two-year profitability of producing activities including optimal hedging (swap and put), costs, liabilities and profit scenarios

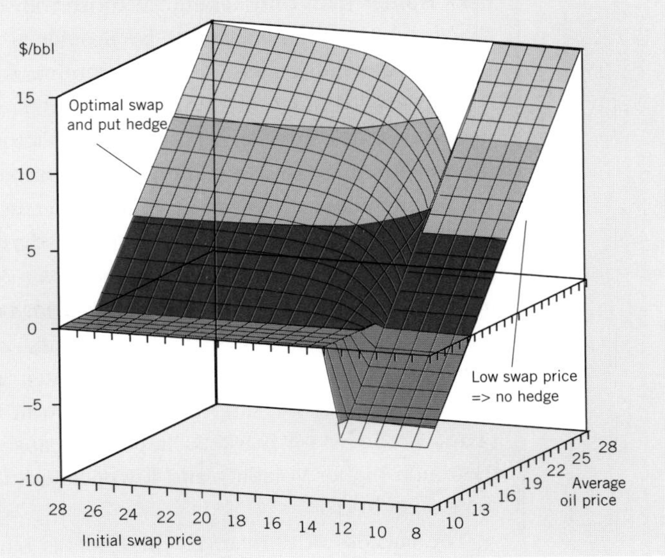

PRODUCER TACTICS AND MARKET STRUCTURE

Backwardation

In this market scenario, spot prices are higher than term prices, and there is an added value for physical crude oil. Producers will therefore tend to sell immediately, and thus will act to undermine the backwardation spread. Any hedging by a producer will be equivalent to forward sales below the spot price. This implies that hedging will entail a loss if market prices do not decrease during the contract maturity.

For instance, this situation obtained during 1989, when the market was in backwardation all year long, with a limited $3–4/bbl upside move. During such periods, producers are reluctant to hedge in the short term, except when market sentiment leads them to believe that a market move or structural reversal is expected.

Conversely, long-term hedging in this kind of situation can appear much more attractive. The proportional effect of backwardation is reduced, and there is the possibility that the market may move into a contango – making the transaction very profitable indeed. Thus, long-term analysis of the fundamentals may yield hedging opportunities, especially when strong backwardation has arisen as the result of a major crisis.

Contango

In this scenario, the market is over-supplied with physical oil, and spot prices are lower than term prices. The producer faces difficulties when selling crude, but can sell futures at an advantageous price. Providing that market prices are not increasing at the same time, any hedging strategy is liable to pay off. Thus the producer has an immediate interest in short-term hedging. Conversely, hedging long-term prices could be less advantageous – even if selling $3/bbl above the spot price looks very attractive. This is because strong contangos are often associated with poor *short-term* market conditions; so if the spot is very low, say $12/bbl, selling long term at $15/bbl should be regarded cautiously.

Trendy market

A market trend can sometimes be defined as an amplifier of the backwardation or contango phenomenon. That is, an upward trend may sustain or even increase the market backwardation, and a downward trend will have the same effect on a contango (for example March to June 1990, or the winter of 1993/94). Following from the descriptions above, the producer will be even more reluctant to hedge in backwardation when there is an upward trend, and even more tempted to hedge in contango when there is a downward trend.

Of course, every hedger will attempt to anticipate the reversal of the trend, or act just after this reversal when the market is at its peak or has bottomed out. However, the importance of trends in the market to the hedger relates strongly to the type of hedging contemplated (short, medium or long-term).

risks (rather than only taking on those they can "back-to-back"), and are able to provide a full range of derivatives across the different markets.

The involvement of commercial banks and financial houses has been an important factor in the development and liquidity of the market. It has been motivated by their clients' increasing demand for structured transactions, and by the prospect of higher margins – as well as contributing to a strategic diversification from their traditional business and risks (interest rates and foreign exchange). However, techniques and strategies cannot be simply translated from the financial to the oil markets, largely because of the much higher volatility and lower liquidity in the energy sector.

The success of derivatives providers is based on two major elements: marketing and dynamic hedging. Marketing is a long process of gaining a specific relationship with potential clients, either affiliates or external companies. Dynamic hedging is the constant monitoring and adjustment of the different risk portfolios. Both are intimately linked when initially pricing a transaction, but the subsequent hedging is quite independent of the origin of the risk.

Providers usually determine the price of an energy derivative by using trading models, and then by adding the bid-offer spread. The different components considered in the pricing of a screen-based swap are detailed in Table 1 (in this example, a WTI-indexed swap). In the case of "proxy hedges", there are additional risks in the relationship between the physical and the

Table 1: Fair price and bid-offer components of WTI-indexed swaps

Type	Component	Main characteristics
Trading decisions	Existing portfolio	Asymmetric
	Preferred direction	Asymmetric and speculative
	Long-term choices	Strategic, management decisions
	Competition on the deal	Information, marketing
Hedging actions	Liquidity on the Nymex	Term and volume related
	Forward rolling of positions	Term and volume related
	Floating component of settlement	Speculative
	Forward versus futures risk	Interest rates related
	Options versus underlying risk	Volatility and term related
Maths and models	Reliability of hypothesis	Structural stability of models
	Theory versus market bias	Simulation or history
Environment	Credit-default risk (forward)	Credit management
	Fungibility, transferability	Legal terms and clauses
Unavoidable	Commissions	Volume related
	Internal costs	Portfolio and organisation related

hedging indices. The obvious risk is the correlation risk, discussed in detail in Chapter 4. However, this is not only a technical problem, as coping with it demands an understanding of the behaviour of markets and oil fundamentals.

Because illiquidity and price gaps characterise most energy markets, the hedges actually implemented may be very different from those that were initially conceived. Compared to the "target" hedge, the actual hedge may not be well secured: it usually leaves a residual open position, and necessitates rolling contracts forward. The resulting side effects and costs, in terms of both the underlying risks and the additional hedging instruments that may be required to deal with the residual, must be anticipated when pricing and hedging derivatives. In particular, liquidity in the futures markets is often restricted to the first quoted months, and to specific hours (that is to say, when Nymex is open!).

Liquidity problems inevitably affect the choice of maturities and volumes when hedging. However, it should not be assumed that a hedge will remain illiquid in the long term. The structure of liquidity in a market evolves over time, and is affected by the changing habits of traders and hedgers. For example, the growth of energy derivatives is usually acknowledged to have created similar interest in long-term WTI positions. Fears of changes in tax regimes, or of further regulatory interference in paper markets, may also badly affect liquidity. In short, dynamic hedging depends on evaluating liquidity over time, managing price gaps, accessing all the available information on the market, and mastering any arbitrage opportunities.

In order to achieve profitable dynamic

hedging that is based on an understanding of the global markets, and which can take advantage of portfolio effects, an increasingly sophisticated set of techniques and systems are necessary. Computing the equivalence functions of different products and maturities is an essential art when devising a hedging strategy. For example, should a specific portfolio of refinery margins be created or should its different elements, oil products and crudes as well, be separated out? (In fact, both strategies are justifiable.) Another question might be: how can one extrapolate from Nymex WTI three-year forward prices in order to price and structure a 10-year deal? If the risks of this kind of transaction are not precisely identified and measured, they will certainly accumulate and lead to heavy losses. In Figure 3 we have attempted to represent graphically the dynamic equilibrium of different expertises needed by derivatives providers.

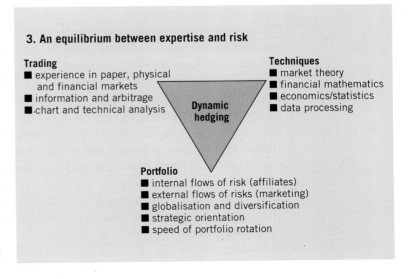

3. An equilibrium between expertise and risk

Trading
■ experience in paper, physical and financial markets
■ information and arbitrage
■ chart and technical analysis

Dynamic hedging

Techniques
■ market theory
■ financial mathematics
■ economics/statistics
■ data processing

Portfolio
■ internal flows of risk (affiliates)
■ external flows of risks (marketing)
■ globalisation and diversification
■ strategic orientation
■ speed of portfolio rotation

TRADING DERIVATIVES IN A MULTI-DIMENSIONAL WORLD

This chapter naturally focuses on risks that are specific and integral to the oil industry. But, of course, most companies have to devise strategies that take account of other kinds of risk as well.

Of these, one of the most important is foreign exchange rate risk. When hedging oil price risk, an exchange rate risk may be incurred, because most contracts are traded in or indexed to the US dollar. Many European end-users actually pay their energy supplies in local currencies, and may therefore be highly sensitive to any lack of correlation between currencies, and between the currency markets and the oil markets. This problem may be solved by the kind of integrated hedge described in Chapter 8, but some end-users prefer to keep a kind of Chinese wall between oil and financial hedging.

It should also be remembered that market behaviour is often driven by local considerations. For example, the demand in Germany for winter storage is largely related to the Deutschmark price per tonne of heating oil.

The main market risks affecting oil price risk management, including exchange rate risk, are presented together in Figure 4. However, even in the case of a pure back-to-back or a perfect hedge, the different actors in the physical oil and derivative markets are also subject to credit, counterparty and contract (cc&c) risks:

❑ *credit risk:* credit risk expresses the exposure of forward cash-flows and deferred payments to market risks. It must be considered with regard to: the risk components of the underlying index (for example, volatility, correlation, liquidity); the maturity and type of the instrument (for example, short-term versus long-term, buying versus selling, swap versus option); and the relative level of the market;

❑ *counterparty risk:* credit risk must be further specified in the light of a counterparty's ability to fulfil its obligations and contractual commitments. A measure of counterparty risk is obtained from internal and credit rating analyses of the client's creditworthiness; most traders then allot to each counterparty a set "credit line" (which may, or may not, take into account the counterparty's ability to deliver physically in the event of financial difficulties);

❑ *contract risk:* residual exposure of a balanced portfolio to changes in, for example, the regulation of the market, taxation rules, or changes in the indices.

4. Main oil market risks

time and maturity

quality

delivery and shipping terms

exchange rate

location

These risks are very much inter-related, and assessing them will require the opinions of credit, legal and trading managers; they will need to take into account the trading habits and the nature of any potential client or counterparty. For example, some oil companies with existing relationships in the physical markets may value each other for regularity and performance in physical trading, rather than solely relying on assets-related credit rating; this tends to accelerate authorisations in the case of short-term deals.

More and more frequently, and especially for medium- to long-dated transactions, specific trading conditions are negotiated around a master agreement – as discussed in a panel in Chapter 14.

The estimates of the value of derivative transactions at risk to "cc&c" are usually made using proprietary models. These are based on historical and market parameters, on the structure and maturity of instruments (swaps and options do not yield similar credit exposures) and on the possibility for risk reduction, diversification and netting of positions. Recently, there have been advances in the evaluation of credit risk using the mathematical framework provided by option theory, and credit risk quantification and management is liable to become much more sophisticated (and complex) over the next few years.

Finally, we should stress the importance, and difficulty, of gaining accurate information when trading in the over-the-counter energy markets. The importance of information to the efficiency of markets is well known, but the fact is that the over-the-counter oil markets, either physical, forward or derivatives, are characterised by a very poor visibility. Transactions are often private and confidential, and may be negotiated instantaneously or over the course of a few months at board or state level. Only large participants are able to get reliable and, more or less, complete information. For example, little is known about the deals made between some banks and their captive clientele, and this has sometimes led to an underestimate of this sector of the derivative market.

Conversely, some traders tend to exaggerate the number and quantity of their deals. Even public exchanges, despite their legal obligations, sometimes fail to provide their regulatory bodies with enough visibility and information on the behaviour of some large traders.

This lack of information impairs market efficiency, and creates apparent arbitrage opportunities. But converting these apparent opportunities into cash profits requires a careful appraisal of fundamental market factors, and we will focus on these in the following sections.

Derivatives, market phenomena and correlations investigated

LOCATIONAL RISKS AND FUNDAMENTALS

When trading world-wide and on all possible indices – Platt's assessments, for instance – it is dangerous to ignore the fundamentals of the oil industry, or the effect of the transfer mechanisms between the different consuming centres.

For example, developing countries are expected to initiate three-quarters of the growth in the global demand for oil up to the year 2000. In particular, as demand for oil in Asia rises by 3–4% per year over the 1990s, from a level already exceeding 15 million barrels per day (bpd) in 1992, the dependence of the region on oil imports should increase sharply (up from 8 million bpd in 1992 to nearly 12 million by the end of the decade). At the local level, China and, to a lesser extent, India will be responsible for much of this increase in demand. The map of trading flows in the region is therefore about to be redrawn. At the global level, the Asian requirements will certainly impact on shipping economics: a 150,000 bpd shift of West African crude shipments from the Atlantic Basin to Asian markets would require an extra 1 million tonnes of dead-weight shipping capacity.

Any trader must also integrate many fundamental elements, especially when measuring basis risk between similar grades. Geographical spreads usually reflect shipping terms and the different state of equilibrium obtaining in each market. A colder-than-normal period in the United States may have a stronger-than-normal impact on prices, depending on the level of

readily available stocks. Such local disruptions usually disconnect the US market from the European markets and, subsequently, create opportunities for moving heating oil or fuel oil cargoes to the East Coast (Fig. 5).

Besides the fundamentals, one must remember that oil markets are not homogeneous and are subject to different pricing principles and environments. In the Asia Pacific region, price or import controls on oil products are still endorsed in many countries, while other countries explicitly encourage free trade.

In the United States, markets are considered as highly open, but environmental regulations, import taxes and other constraints (such as logistics) vary greatly from state to state. For example, the California Air Resources Board (CARB), which imposes restrictive product quality and emission legislation on local refiners and marketers, has inspired new trading practices with neighbouring states, and with Canada and Asia.

Moreover, the different types of participants in the market behave quite differently from region to region. Typically, producer hedging is more present in the United States and, to a lesser extent, in the North Sea, than it is in other countries. Meanwhile, hedging for financial purposes is growing strongly in the Asia Pacific region. Some end-user groups may rely heavily on specific markets and introduce demand-led distortions: for example, European utilities strongly influence both high and low sulphur fuel oil, while the chemical industry focuses on naphtha.

Correlation maps, such as Figure 6 overleaf, are an effective way of illustrating the relative efficiency of price and information transfers in the global market in the past. In Figure 6, one can clearly see the importance of both the US East Coast/Gulf Coast and NWE/MED links for

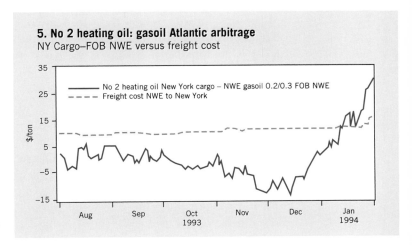

5. No 2 heating oil: gasoil Atlantic arbitrage
NY Cargo–FOB NWE versus freight cost

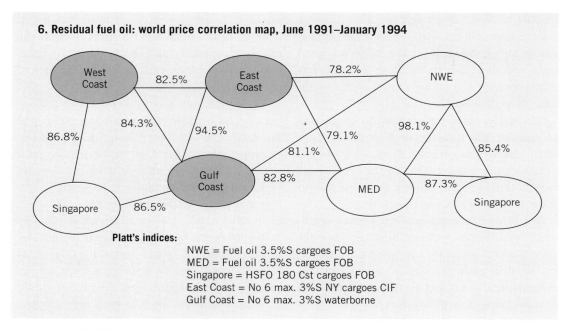

6. Residual fuel oil: world price correlation map, June 1991–January 1994

Platt's indices:

NWE = Fuel oil 3.5%S cargoes FOB
MED = Fuel oil 3.5%S cargoes FOB
Singapore = HSFO 180 Cst cargoes FOB
East Coast = No 6 max. 3%S NY cargoes CIF
Gulf Coast = No 6 max. 3%S waterborne

heavy fuel oil. The other links are, mathematically speaking, of a second-order; however, they must still be monitored by traders with global portfolio exposures.

In crude oil markets, the WTI-Brent spread is the leading indicator. The price relationship is either implicit, both products being international markers that sometimes compete in the same refining area (mainly the Gulf Coast), or explicit, for example through EFPs and the delivery procedures of the Nymex Light Sweet Crude Oil (WTI) contract. In the latter case, some Brent-related crudes may be substituted for WTI, which creates arbitrage opportunities, though these are not easily or frequently achievable.

Statistics and economics are important tools for investigating cross-correlations, basis and locational risks. Various mathematical techniques exist to distinguish market trends, market cycles and other fundamental characteristics from purely random walks. Once non-random behaviour is identified, residual risks contained in serial noise may then be evaluated using a more or less modified mean-variance approach. But traders cannot take decisions and market positions on the basis of statistics alone; they must interpret such patterns in light of their own analysis and information, their portfolio orientation and their existing market expectations. As illustrated in Panel 3, there are so many potentially influential factors, and these are so unstable in their relationship, that any formal model of a given trading situation would be too complex, and too quickly disconnected from trading reality, to be of any use.

MODELLING TERM STRUCTURE AND THE ROLE OF STORAGE

Term structure risks often arise from hedging choices and constraints, even when traders are writing a screen-indexed swap. For example, a three-year swap on Brent could be hedged on the IPE futures market. However, contracts are traded up to 12 months forward, and around 80% of both volume and open interest, in other words liquidity, are concentrated on the first three maturities. The traders' choice of maturity is bound to be compromised by both liquidity and the term structure of prices and volatilities. The resulting time-spread risks must be taken into account and managed. The process of pricing and hedging is therefore based upon a recursive process of evaluation, which itself must reach a satisfactory state of equilibrium before the transaction can be concluded, and which is constantly adjusted during the life of the transaction. (What we have just described is usually summed up as "dynamic risk management".)

Let us now investigate term structure models and related issues in the context of both physical and paper (futures and derivatives) oil markets. The notions of *price term structure* and *convenience yield* express the time component in the evaluation of crudes and products that we identified in our introduction as such a crucial factor in the energy markets. The traditional hypothesis is that the price for future delivery should reflect, on the one hand, the cost of financing and carrying physicals until the maturity date (see Panel 4) and, on the other hand, the aggregated expectations of economic agents

MARKET FOCUS: GASOIL IN NORTH-WEST EUROPE

Europe is an important refiner and consumer of middle-distillates. From a global perspective, it is a net importer. The markets in north-west Europe are integrated around three main trading centres: Amsterdam-Rotterdam-Antwerp (ARA), Le Havre and London. The two main functions of these markets are:

❑ *Inland supplies* ARA is a large refining, storage and trading area which supplies most of the requirements of the continent. The trade tends to flow inland along the river Rhine, supplying the Netherlands, Belgium, West Germany, eastern France and Switzerland. It is known as the "barges market".

❑ *Imports and exports* The market also copes with the need for incremental imports, especially from Russia and Algeria; conversely, sometimes there is an opportunity to sell cargoes profitably to the United States, Mediterranean or Asian markets. This market function centres around ARA and, more recently, around Le Havre, and is naturally called the "cargoes market".

The difference between barges and cargoes is more than just a matter of the unit size of the transaction (around 2,000 tonnes, as opposed to around 20,000 tonnes). For example, barge assessments are highly dependent on freight rates on the Rhine (see Fig. A), on the dollar to Deutschmark exchange rate, and on the level of both ARA stocks and German consumer heating oil stocks (which show a strongly seasonal pattern). External shocks, such as tax increases, may also impact on the demand side of inland markets, while supply squeezes influence the offer side.

Such fundamentals usually affect the cargoes markets to markedly lesser extent, if at all. On the import side, prices show an extreme sensitivity to political uncertainties in Russia and Algeria, and

to quality and volume availabilities. On the export side, external supply and demand imbalances may create opportunities, according to chartering conditions, freight rates and quality differentials. For example, growth in demand in the Asian markets regularly causes market tensions in the North-west Europe market (see Fig. B) and the Mediterranean market. On occasion, this phenomenon has been so strong that, combined with a decrease in European needs, the cargoes markets (ARA and Le Havre) have temporarily become dominant over the barges market. (Traders suspected that this was happening for some time, and the statistics bear them out.)

In contrast to the physical and forward markets, the paper markets are centred around the London IPE gasoil futures contract. Delivery procedures are tied to barges in the ARA area, but IPE gasoil is the price marker for all the European gasoil markets. For example, Russian cargoes are negotiated at a premium over IPE quotes. Any news or change in the market usually impacts first on the IPE gasoil contracts; only then is it translated into the price differentials between the IPE and the physical indices. In other words, the IPE provides the lead in improving the efficiency of the global markets.

The term structure of gasoil prices is also monitored and hedged through IPE time-spreads, though the forward markets can also be used for this purpose in the very short term. The correlation between the first IPE time-spread and the level of end-of-month stocks in the four ARA-related countries (the Netherlands, Belgium, Germany and Switzerland) is over 75%. A positive correlation, though smaller (due to the relative strength of the cargoes and barges markets), is also present between IPE time-spreads and freight rates on the Rhine.

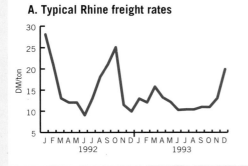

A. Typical Rhine freight rates

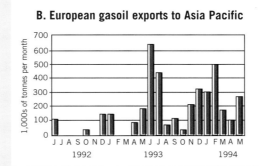

B. European gasoil exports to Asia Pacific

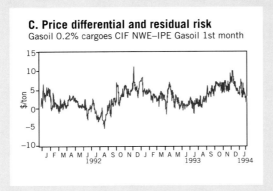

C. Price differential and residual risk
Gasoil 0.2% cargoes CIF NWE–IPE Gasoil 1st month

Despite these correlations, the paper and physical markets are structurally so different that hedging with IPE contracts may still give rise to a large basis risk (see Fig. C). Market participants who do not want to bear these risks, or who require more flexibility or longer maturities than those offered by the IPE, are inclined to enter into swaps and other OTC derivatives transactions. In these cases, Platt's assessments or IPE settlements comprise the possible indices for calculating floating prices.

about future oil prices. Seasonal or trend factors are usually considered as market expectations.

The theories of storage and of convenience yield provide additional insight on backwardation phenomena and on the instability of the term structure over time. Keynes first introduced the theory of *normal backwardation*, which implies that hedgers are net sellers in the medium-term market and need to pay a premium to speculators oriented toward the shorter term. Consequently, spot prices may be higher than forward prices. However, the theory is not completely descriptive of market facts:
❑ there is no real evidence of a downward bias in the pricing of futures;
❑ hedgers may be either net forward buyers or sellers, or indeterminate. For example, at the end of 1993 and beginning of 1994, prices were at a five-year historical low. Despite the prevailing contango, many end-users entered the market in order to hedge forward requirements at attractive absolute prices. In order to absorb such volumes, the term structure of prices

adjusted itself into a relatively higher contango. Hedgers, being mostly net buyers in the swap markets, amplified the contango resulting from a depressed spot market and developed a *normal contango* situation. This, of course, is the reverse of the situation described by Keynes;[2]
❑ traders who cover the hedging needs of exposed counterparts may not be speculating, but looking for portfolio diversification or partial covering of financial exposures to inflation. For example, portfolio managers took some preventive positions in oil markets during the Gulf crisis in order to anticipate any medium-term rise in the Consumer Price Index. In other words, trading in oil markets may have other objectives than strict hedging of physical risks or wild speculation.

In fact, short- to medium-term effects related to physical supply and demand imbalances must be taken into account. The modern theory of term structure introduces the "convenience yield", the yield which "accrues to the owner of the physical commodity but not to the owner of a contract for future delivery" (Brennan 1989). In other words, it is sometimes better to have the commodity at hand rather than a paper claim! Backwardation is the premium paid for earlier rather than later availability, for instance, to ensure that the planned refining operating schedule is not disrupted. In essence, normal backwardation represents the cost of holding minimum operating stocks in a just-in-time delivery environment.

Backwardation further expresses the risk of rupture or bottle-necking in the logistical chain from production to consumption. It may be linked to specific market issues like the 1989/90 winter squeeze in US heating oil markets (Fig. 7), or to general uncertainties such as the recurrent crises in the Gulf region or in Russia.

Derivatives providers are interested in devel-

7. Winter squeeze and the explosion of short-term backwardation
No 2 heating oil Nymex, October 1989–February 1990

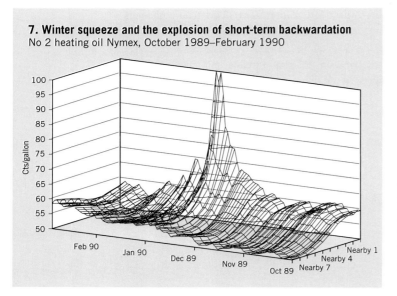

oping a truly representative theory of term structure so that they can use this to guide their tactics in pricing and hedging – especially for long-term OTC transactions. The convenience yield may prove useful, for it may be modelled as a source of randomness. Gibson and Schwartz (1990) developed a model of a stochastic and mean-reverting convenience yield which is correlated to a more classical model of stochastic spot prices. However, such an approach is rather difficult to interpret, given the fact that the convenience yield is not a traded asset. Elf Trading (1991) disclosed a class of term structure models more adapted to oil markets, with a bivariate stochastic process on both the spot and the long-term price behaviour of oil.

Arbitrage relationships along the forward curve provide the mathematical background to compute a flexible and maturity-dependent form of marginal convenience yield. Since the convenience yield is extremely sensitive to short-term factors, and less so to longer-term factors, the way in which the convenience yield is absorbed over time must, ideally, be incorporated in hedging strategies. (In the very long term, other economic elements, such as the marginal cost of renewable resources or of competing energies, must also be considered.)

In fact, the cost or benefit of rolling positions forward is directly dependent on movements in the term structure of prices. In other words, a volumetric hedge of a long-dated position in the shorter term may cover large absolute price moves (parallel shifts), but it will not provide cover for changes in time-spreads – as certain trading houses recently discovered. Maturity exposures require a kind of dynamic hedging that is based on two related concepts:
❑ the curvature of the forward price function; and
❑ volatility transfers and kinetics.

In addition to the above, it is worth stressing that any model used by traders will have some restrictive hypotheses, and should provide hedging advice based on simple market prices (generally speaking, spot assessments and futures settlement prices). The model needs to be mathematically stable, at the very least, and its relevance to the empirical world must be tested and constantly monitored.

Using a term structure model of the kind described above, and making use of computed evaluations, traders should be able to trade on bid and offer prices, using a cost function. This function is sometimes intuitive, and sometimes partly modelled; it is designed to take account of liquidity risk and the way in which certain hypotheses basic to the model may be violated over time.

In oil markets, the ability to price and hedge term structure risks represents an important part of the value added by derivatives providers. It clearly remains the most technical element of trading, at the frontier of general market and storage theories – and, indeed, of financial mathematics.

INDUSTRIAL SPREADS AND THE ROLE OF REFINING
For convenience, we will here refer to crack, product and quality spreads as *industrial spreads*. These are another piece in the oil puzzle and, as summarised below, have a substantial impact on the profit and loss accounts of many participants in the market:
❑ Refiners are subject to variation in the sum price of their products relative to that of crude oil; this variation is commonly referred to as a crack spread. Aside from fundamental factors, such as overall capacity and demand for oil products, crack spreads are the most important determinant of refiner revenues. Hedging refinery margins through the exchange and over-the-counter markets has thus become an established part of the corporate strategy of refiners.
❑ End-users and petrochemical companies may have large risks related to industrial spreads. For example, utilities that are capable of burning natural gas or fuel oil can quickly alter their policies according to relative or spread values. For chemical industries, the economics of steam-cracking are mostly based on the relative prices of naphtha, gasoil and LPGs, and then on the price differential from naphtha to ethylene and propylene. Even companies that are not very flexible with regard to feedstocks must

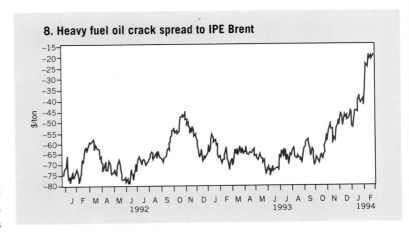

8. Heavy fuel oil crack spread to IPE Brent

CONTANGO AND THE CASH-AND-CARRY ARBITRAGE

When analysing the term structure of futures and swap prices, it is important to consider the cost of carrying the commodity, especially in contango situations. If the degree of contango exceeds the carrying and financing costs of storage, then low-risk but profitable transactions (known as "cash-and-carry" arbitrages) may be entered into (Fig. A). The trader buys the crude or oil product, and stores it, while at the same time selling futures or swaps of a given maturity and an equivalent quantity. The difference between the spot and the forward prices must cover the cost of financing and holding oil during the period of storage.

Generally speaking, the arbitrage is initiated whenever $F(T) - Spot > r + c$. Its horizon should be chosen in order to take full advantage of the market contango. At maturity, the paper settle-

ment usually offsets the proceeds from the release of stocks: apart from the convergence process between the paper and physical prices, all the financial implications of the deal are transparent when the deal is executed.

Let us develop a practical example, based on market gasoil prices for August 17, 1993 (Fig. B).

In this example, the total costs are $1.50/ton more than the revenues from the forward sale, and the arbitrage is theoretically unworkable. However, the trader may still consider it for two reasons:
❑ the physical premium, that is, the price differential between barges (spot) quotations and the first IPE traded month, is around −$2.50/ton. It is expected to move into a positive number (short-term backwardation) at some point during the coming winter season. Therefore the arbitrage seems to offer a limited downside risk — at least, according to estimates using historical data and market simulations;
❑ the cost of storage used in the calculation was an average cost for the ARA zone. However, the trader or the oil company may have access to less expensive storage capacities, for example, storage that has been in use for years and thus entails limited fixed costs.

Because of the opportunity for profit arising from excessive contango situations, one would expect that the size of contango should be limited

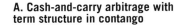

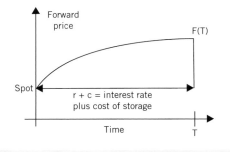

A. Cash-and-carry arbitrage with term structure in contango

consider product spreads, as competitors may take advantage of them.
❑ In the case of hedgers, industrial spreads arise out of the way in which they assume residual risk. For example, European shipping companies

willing to hedge their heavy fuel oil budget using IPE Brent futures would bear a large basis risk (Fig. 8), that is, the risk of variation in the price difference between the physical index and the hedging index. If, instead, they purchase cover by means of fuel oil swaps and options, then they effectively transfer this basis risk to the derivatives provider.

The underlying indices of industrial spreads are characterised by high volatilities and unstable correlations. Just like locational risks, industrial spreads are strongly dependent on fundamentals, for example liquidity, supply and demand, and refining economics.

Moreover, term structures are usually not homogeneous on both indices of a given industrial spread. Gasoil cracks integrate seasonal factors specific to gasoil, and not those specific to Brent. It can happen that the fuel oil markets are in contango, while the crude oil market is in

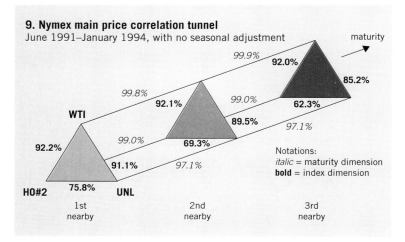

9. Nymex main price correlation tunnel
June 1991–January 1994, with no seasonal adjustment

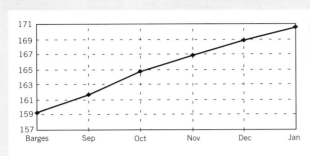

**B. Gasoil barges and
IPE prices
(Aug 17, 1993)**

Contango from spot to January contract =
170.25 – 159.25 = 11$/ton
Hypothetical cost of storage = 2$/ton/month for
5 months = 10$/ton
Approximate cost of financing = 0.50
$/ton/month for 5 months = 2.50$/ton

to cash-and-carry costs (including financing costs). It is therefore not surprising to find a correlation of around 70% between time-spreads and stock levels during contango periods (Fig. C).

But this theoretical limit is not always precisely representative of market realities. In particular:
❑ in reality, the marginal cost of storage is far from uniform for all actors;
❑ storage capacities may simply be full, with none left to initiate further cash-and-carry arbitrages;

C. Stock levels and time-spreads

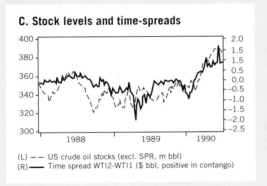

(L) – – US crude oil stocks (excl. SPR, m bbl)
(R) ——— Time spread WTI2-WTI1 ($ bbl, positive in contango)

❑ the premium between physical and paper prices may also impact on the economics;
❑ oil companies have an increasingly dynamic and market-oriented approach to stock valorisation and hedging – a phenomenon which must be taken into account.

The reverse of the cash-and-carry arbitrage is not workable, as there is no loan market for oil. Moreover, producing countries or integrated companies are often reluctant to release stocks when an exceptional backwardation occurs because of the high risk this strategy entails. (A large backwardation can rarely be characterised at the time as "exceptional" because it reflects unpredictable factors.)

As a result, unlike contango situations, there is no theoretical limit to the backwardation phenomenon – and the higher it is, the more unstable it becomes. Even so, some financial techniques, such as the monetisation of working or compulsory stocks, may take limited advantage of specific backwardation situations.

backwardation. Correlation tunnels (Fig. 9) are a useful way of illustrating the extent to which the price relationship between crude and products is dependent on maturity.

It is interesting to see how correlations between quite different indices tend to vary according to the time-horizon (although this may not be so true when looking at the long term, as some traders price products by taking positions on the crack spreads). Conversely, correlations between similar indices for different months tend to be both higher and more stable.

The observation above demonstrates that simple, or even robust, statistics are neither sufficient nor adequate to reveal and model the behaviour of term structures. They may shed light on physical and very short-term risks, but they are insufficient for the dynamic management of derivatives.

For refiners, the term structure of crack

spreads is also an important indicator of forward profitability and a factor when taking strategic decisions. In particular, an investment for an upgrade or a new unit may be combined with the medium-term hedging of crack spreads or refinery margins. Panel 5 examines hedging strategies for refiners in more detail.

The future: market developments and marketing strategies

The oil derivative markets have developed around two complementary axes: hedging the oil-price exposures of large companies, and the financing operations of the oil industry. Both of these have generated rapid growth for the OTC energy derivatives industry. Since 1987, the OTC market has also fuelled much of the growth in liquidity in the exchanges, especially for back-month trading (as discussed in Chapter 13). Below, we discuss some developments in the

STRATEGIES FOR OPTIMISING REFINING ACTIVITIES

For trading and risk management purposes, a refinery is often compared to a set of black boxes (or units) with a series of flows, and production flexibilities and constraints (Fig. A). Cracks spreads represent the refiner's risk/reward coefficient for each product; in aggregate they comprise the refinery margin.

One way for a refiner to protect the profitability of its activity is to fix the global refinery margin for some future period. The refiner is naturally short on crude and long on products; the index used in the margin swap is therefore the difference between the weighted sum of products and the value of a crude reference (usually dated Brent, WTI, Dubai or Tapis). Selling a refinery margin swap consists of selling an index (basket of products: crude) at a fixed price, based on refinery yields, and buying back at a floating price the average value of the index over a contractual period.

When the fixed margin is greater than the cost of refining crude, including some financing ele-ments, the refiner may enter an arbitrage with minimum risk and almost certain return: the "cash-and-refine" arbitrage is similar to the "cash-and-carry" arbitrage described in Panel 4, though it is more complex to initiate. If a yearly refinery hedge is considered, yields are adjusted to both winter and summer seasons. Such strategies may also be used to hedge processing agreements, and they do not preclude traders or refiners from profiting from physical and operational opportunities. For example, when hedging using an average value the hedger can optimise product delivery by selecting the most appropriate delivery dates.

Refinery risk management must also integrate a time dimension, first because of storage, and also because of the time required to transform crude into the refined product. Each product has its own price term structure, which means that refiner hedging is characteristically a multi-dimensional problem. The hedging strategy needs to be customised to the individual refiner's

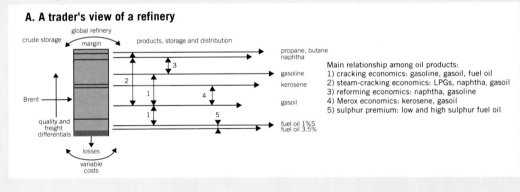

A. A trader's view of a refinery

markets for crude oil, and oil products.

CRUDE OIL

Crude oil is the largest and the most visible oil market. In the short term, it is the trendsetter for the other energy markets; for example, it is highly sensitive to OPEC rhetoric, to the general economic environment and to political events or uncertainties.

The main instruments are futures, forwards or swaps based on WTI and Brent indices. Using these, the North Sea producers and traders have created a very sophisticated trading environment. After years of evolution, behaviour in this market seems to have stabilised, and centres on hedging flat price risks with IPE

Brent contracts, and hedging price differentials using 15-day forward time-spreads and the recent, but active, contracts for difference (CFDs). The Brent market is particularly important, given that Brent is the main international crude marker for most crudes in the Atlantic Basin, and is of increasing importance in the Asia Pacific region.

Crude is also the index preferred by arbitrageurs and investment funds. The demand generated by investment strategists for derivative funds is growing at an impressive pace in terms of variety and volume. Investment transactions, which can be either private placements or public offerings such as warrants, allow financiers to take trading positions that are

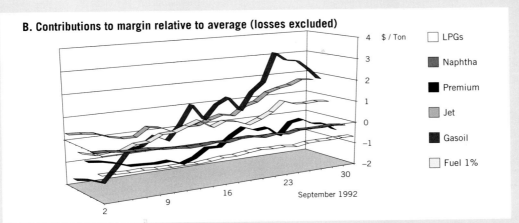

B. Contributions to margin relative to average (losses excluded)

accounting and valuation procedures, and to the various market conditions: refinery margins, crack spreads, product and quality spreads, crude and product time-spreads.

In fact, refiners may consider locking-in individual crack-spreads as well as their overall margin. This strategy tends to be adopted by refiners who are accustomed to the paper markets, and it may offer advantages if one product has a large contribution to the refinery margin. (Over the medium term, in particular, this strategy may outperform a hedge on the overall margin.) When choosing which products to hedge, refiners have to analyse the relative contribution of each product to the refinery margin. Figure B illustrates the change in the relative contribution of products to the refinery margin, using a simple ranking, over a one-month period. In this example, hedging gasoil and fuel oil crack spreads would appear to be the priority.

Options on industrial or crack spreads can also prove useful to refiners. Depending on market conditions, a refiner could gain a satisfactory cash premium by selling an option on the gasoil crack spread, and thus facilitating cashflow. For a trader with a processing contract, this premium could finance part of the processing fee. Moreover, any flexibility or constraint on the refining system may be valued and interpreted as an option or as a combination of options. For example, it is possible to increase or decrease the utilisation rate of some refinery production units. A truly sophisticated hedging programme would attempt to integrate such elements into a global risk management programme.

One final area of refinery risk management is the use of paper instruments to ensure physical delivery or distribution. On the supply side, refiners are sometimes willing to enter medium- to long-term crude oil swaps, or to use options, in order to gain a guaranteed paper access to crude. Such hedges provide financial security while enabling the refiner to optimise its supply channels.

On the distribution side, refiners and integrated oil companies may design marketing strategies which combine physical deliveries to the factory gate with derivatives that offer fixed prices (or price collars, etc.).

indexed to oil without the bother and risk of directly managing a commodities desk.

The market in long-term price management for financing purposes is dominated by natural gas (as described in the next chapter) and crude oil. Long-term price managment in crude oil was facilitated by Nymex's decision, in late 1990, to offer three-year contracts on Light Sweet Crude Oil. The OTC market trades longer maturities of up to 10 years, but specific risks are attached to such transactions.

For example, the production of both Brent and WTI is expected to decline quite rapidly, and therefore they may become less effective as representative markers; in particular, lower production rates might make prices easier to manipulate. The Brent and Ninian fields have already been mixed, with a limited loss of quality, to form Brent Blend. However, some traders are already pushing for the replacement of Brent by Forties, thereby introducing another quality change. Indeed, the output of Forties already usually exceeds the output of Brent, and a forward market for Forties is emerging. In the case of WTI, there is no real alternative crude. Companies with long-term derivatives indexed on WTI and Brent may have to negotiate indexation changes, and quality differentials, or make use of early termination clauses.

OIL PRODUCTS

The growth in the derivative markets for oil products has arisen partly out of the increasing desire of end-users to ensure the profitability of their operations by hedging their energy risk, and partly out of the growth recorded in refinery margins trading (as described earlier in this chapter).

There is a great range of companies for whom oil supplies represent a substantial part of their variable costs. For example, kerosene in the case of airlines; bunker for shipping companies; motor diesel for transportation fleets; heating oil and fuel oil for utilities; fuel oil for industries. For these end-users, derivatives provide tailor-made hedges with flexibility on maturity, pricing periods and indices. The indice may, for instance, take the form of a formula that weights indices for different geographical zones (for example, $^2/_3$ NWE + $^1/_3$ MED), or different products (for example, escalation formulas for natural gas prices in Europe).

The great potential of the OTC energy product market is that it allows fuel supply managers and financial officers to design a strategy that is exactly suited to their commercial strategies. Initially limited to the medium term (one, two or three accounting years), derivatives on oil products are now being proposed for long-term hedging. For example, an electricity or industrial company investing in cogeneration usually has to ensure a long-term natural gas supply contract partly or totally indexed on gasoil or fuel oil. Rather than hedging supply costs with WTI-related instruments, companies are increasingly negotiating long-term swaps or options on gasoil and fuel oil – and these may be written in local currency, such as the British pound.

The success of the energy derivative markets will, in part, be determined by their ability to create and sustain new sectors. For example, inside observers all agree that a spot market for (peak) natural gas is emerging in the UK (see Chapter 10). This market will certainly affect the way the electricity business operates, and may lead to futures contracts and to new generations of derivatives.

The strengthening of environmental legislation will also have an effect. The 0.3% sulphur quality for heating oil disappeared from Europe in October 1994, and a new 0.05% sulphur constraint will be introduced in 1996 for motor diesel. The former change is expected to be absorbed smoothly by the refining industry, but the heavy investment necessary to deal with the 1996 change is still under consideration. Of course, these changes are liable to have an impact on the swaps or options based on the relevant underlying indices. The problem is not only one of uncertainty: writing derivatives on the new quotations will also pose technical difficulties, because of the lack of historical data to evaluate the implied hedging risks. It is worth stressing that the lack of historical data means that traders in the "new" contracts will first have to make a precise analysis of the relevant economic and industrial fundamentals. Depending on the extent of new regulation, this is potentially true for all oil products, but is especially true for gasoil, gasoline and fuel oil.

In the US, derivatives are being marketed for hedging the sulphur differential from on-highway diesel oil to Nymex heating oil (although sales are limited at present). In Europe, the market for fuel oil has quickly grown around two main indices, low and high sulphur fuel oil. However, as we have stressed throughout this chapter, and as evidenced by Figure 10, choosing the right index can have a major effect on the bottom line.

Since 1993, physical traders have started to make substantial use of short-term derivatives based on indices such as gasoline and naphtha. However, the liquidity of these markets for long-term deals is still sporadic because traders often appear to have the same orientation – long or short – at the same time.

Risk management in the chemical industries is still very limited, and is restricted largely to naphtha supplies for steam-cracking. But this area of business has growth potential, especially when the chemicals business cycle moves to the "upside".

Derivatives on LPGs and, more precisely, on propane have also gained more liquidity. The

10. Price differential: low-high sulphur fuel oil NWE cargoes CIF

underlying physical market is growing because propane can sometimes be used as a clean alternative to fuel oil; the successful introduction of a daily price report by Argus has made traders less reluctant to enter LPG swaps in their books (the weekly Platt's report, used previously, was not representative enough).

Geographically speaking, marketing efforts have now switched to the Asia Pacific region. This is because the major part of the growth in demand for oil products is now coming from developing countries (Fig. 11), and particularly the developing Asian countries.

Singapore, the nerve centre of the Asian oil markets, is the third-largest refiner in the world, and is also one of the world's most important storage, shipping and trading centres. This said, the Asia Pacific region can be problematic for traders, and for other market participants. It is still oriented to short-term trading and, lacks widely accepted references. The pricing of crude in the region has not stabilised around a single marker, but is instead related to Dubai, Brent or Tapis, or is linked to an official or a market (APPI) index. Given its moribund gasoil contract, and the limited trading in fuel oil futures, the region's exchange (Simex) does not yet provide a strong base on which to develop OTC derivatives. However some paper markets, such as short-term forwards, are becoming more important.

MARKETING PACKAGES AND MARKET RISKS

The evolution of hedging strategies is guided by two considerations: the competitive need to propose increasingly customised packages to clients; and the need to be able to dynamically manage the market risks that arise out of these packages.

Marketing packages are often built to give more attractiveness to a strategy, for example by lowering a swap price or by limiting an option premium. However, end-users should remember that *any flexibility or constraint given or received on either maturity or volume is generally worth an option (swaption or compound)*. An embedded option may add substantial risks, and these must be fully understood by clients who seek to

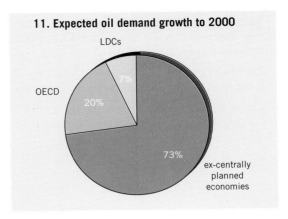

11. Expected oil demand growth to 2000

LDCs

OECD

7%

20%

73%

ex-centrally planned economies

hedge physical risks with paper strategies.

Marketing packages are increasingly being developed with reference to non-oil price risk variables: some put the emphasis on optimising taxation liability, on enhancing finance packages, or on physical delivery. For example, oil companies and distributors in the US, and now in Europe, have developed specific supply programmes which offer guaranteed prices for forward supplies at the client's gate (or wing, in the case of airlines). These contracts, constructed using futures, swaps and options, involve new types of risks, such as the possibility of non-performance on the physical side: the contractual agreement must closely tie together the physical arrangements and the paper arrangements.

The exotic character of marketing packages may also be limited by the fact that trading houses must be able to fit them into their existing portfolios and systems. Mathematical models must be flexible enough to adapt to a quickly changing trading environment. There are so many potential parameters that may impact on market risks that a sensible policy is to be able to fully understand and manage these before diversifying and creating more sophisticated instruments. In many cases, it may make more sense to "mix" proven instruments to fit a client's needs better rather than designing a completely new tool.

1 *Interaction between UK oil taxation and the growth of dated and 15-day Brent markets is discussed in Mabro et al. (1986) and Mabro and Horsnell (1993).*
2 *See Keynes (1930).*

BIBLIOGRAPHY

Barnaud, F., 1990, "In Search of Liquidity: Hedging and Speculation in Oil Futures Markets", WPM 13, Oxford Institute for Energy Studies.

Barnaud, F., and J. Dabouineau, 1992, Past Correction: the Volatility of Oil Prices, *Risk*, September 1992, vol. 5, no. 8.

Brennan, M. J., 1989, "The Price of the Convenience Yield and the Valuation of Commodity Contingent Claims, working paper, University of British Columbia.

d'Almeida, J., and F. Barnaud, 1993, "Mix and Match: Dynamic Hedging in Oil Derivative Markets", *Futures and Options World*, Energy Special.

d'Almeida, J. and P. Lautard, 1992, Elf Trading and Oil Derivatives, Pipeline Winter 1992, International Petroleum Exchange (IPE), no. 3, London.

Gabillon, J., 1991, "The Term Structure of Oil Future Prices", WPM 17, Oxford Institute for Energy Studies.

Gibson, R. and E. S. Schwartz, 1990, "Stochastic Convenience Yield and the Pricing of Oil Contingent Claims", *The Journal of Finance*, vol. xlv, no. 3.

Keynes, J.M., 1930, *A Treatise on Money*, vol. II, Harcourt Brace, New York.

Mabro, R., et al, 1986, *The Market for North Sea Crude Oil*, Oxford Institute for Energy Studies.

Mabro, R. and P. Horsnell, 1993, *Oil Markets and Prices*, Oxford Institute for Energy Studies.

Trabia, X., 1992, *Financial Oil Derivatives*, Oxford Institute for Energy Studies.

The Natural Gas Market

Jay Fitzgerald and Joseph T. Pokalsky
Enron Capital & Trade Resources

The North American natural gas industry has undergone a rapid process of evolution over the past 15 years. With annual revenues now totalling $94 billion, the market has emerged from the shadow of the crude oil market to become the leading growth sector of the US energy market.[1]

The market has not simply grown – it has also experienced radical change. Deregulation has forced market participants to compete in the wholesale, industrial and commercial sectors and, in some states, competitive forces are reaching the residential level. In this deregulated environment, market participants have found themselves increasingly exposed to price movements and to counterparty performance risk – and this has led to an exponential increase in risk management.

The most direct evidence for the growth in risk management is the success of the New York Mercantile Exchange (Nymex) natural gas futures contract: it has enjoyed the largest annual percentage volume gains of any contract launched in the history of that exchange. In 1994, the daily average volume of the Nymex contract exceeded 25,000 contracts, or over four times the average daily consumption of gas in the United States (55 billion cubic feet). Meanwhile the off-exchange, or over-the-counter (OTC), market generates a volume in structured products that is comparable to the volume traded on the Nymex. Industry experts estimate that well over 10,000 OTC transactions were completed in 1994 alone.

The rapid growth in risk management is partly explained by the nature of the North American gas industry – which is structurally quite different to that of the global oil industry as described in the previous chapter. Because of the handling and transport costs, very little demand for natural gas on the North American continent is met by importing liquefied natural gas (LNG) from overseas. The industry, being domestically-oriented and smaller than the global oil industry, offers participants fewer alternatives for placing or sourcing natural gas. Additionally, for technical reasons, the transport and storage capacities of the natural gas industry are relatively inflexible compared to those of the oil industry. It follows that the price elasticity of natural gas, demonstrated by its price volatility, is generally much higher than for other commodities, including crude oil.

Furthermore, compared to the oil industry, capitalisation is less concentrated and operations are less vertically integrated (see Panel 1). Producers, gatherers, processors, transporters, storage operators and marketers are often separate economic entities – a fact which is *increasingly* true in the deregulated environment. These disparate companies often lack the capital and the retail distribution networks that help to buffer the oil majors against adverse price movements.

The most fundamental reason for believing that natural gas risk management will continue to grow in the future is the strength of the underlying market: natural gas usage is expected to post healthy volume gains in absolute and relative terms in the coming years. The arguments for natural gas as the "fuel of the future" are compelling. Its delivered price is typically below that of most fuels on an energy-equivalent basis. Capital costs for new electricity generating units that burn natural gas are lower than those for oil-fired, coal-fired, hydroelectric and nuclear plants.[2] Increased concerns over the environmental impact of sulphur dioxide emissions from burning fossil fuels; an interest in decreasing the reliance on imported energy supplies; and the desire to rebuild domestic energy industries have provided the impetus to reduce regulatory and capital constraints on the natural gas industry.

The purpose of this chapter is to highlight the principal issues in risk management as the gas industry gears up to meet the energy needs

PANEL 1

MARKET STRUCTURE

In contrast to the vertically integrated nature of much of the worldwide oil industry, the North American natural gas industry consists of a chain of distinct market segments. The chain begins with a large number of natural gas producers, who are linked by discrete gathering, processing, transportation and intermediation functions to a diverse array of gas consumers.

Most natural gas production in the United States is developed from reserve basins in the Texas and Louisiana Gulf Coast (both onshore and in the Gulf of Mexico), in the Permian Basin of West Texas, the San Juan basin of New Mexico, the Hugoton/Anadarko basins of Kansas and Oklahoma, and in the Rocky Mountains region.

Significant amounts of gas are also produced in Alberta, Canada; with the recent expansion of pipeline capacity from Canada, approximately 10% of daily US demand is now met by Canadian gas. While in the past the United States was a small net exporter of gas to Mexico, over the course of 1994 Mexico became a net exporter to the United States. The market is thus truly a North American market.

Natural gas is transported from the production regions to the market areas through pipeline systems which traverse each of the lower 48 states. In 1994, an estimated average 55 billion cubic feet (bcf) was consumed daily in the United States.

There are over 5,000 active oil and gas producers in the United States, the vast majority of

Price differentials among major supply areas

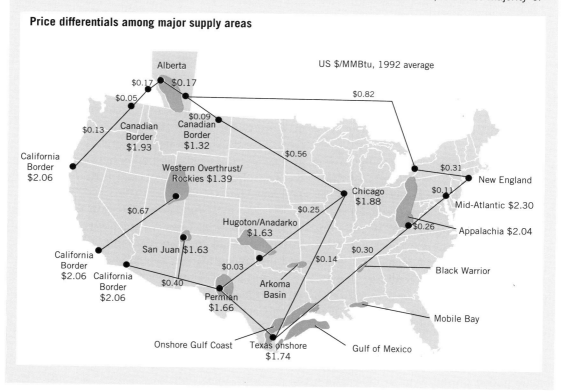

of the 21st century. We begin by describing how the market structure and regulatory history have impacted on the development of risk management in the natural gas industry. We then focus on the critical theme of risk-managing capital investment in the gas industry. The next section discusses in detail the tactics and instruments that are commonly used to manage the different kinds of gas price risk. We then discuss the role of the intermediary in risk management, and conclude by analysing how the

market may develop – both in the United States and the United Kingdom.

Market structure

A BRIEF MARKET HISTORY
Regulation has played a commanding, and often problematic, role in the evolution of the natural gas market. Government intervention in the natural gas industry dates back to the mid-1800s, but it is sufficient here to begin with the Phillips Decision of the United States Supreme Court in

191

**THE NATURAL
GAS MARKET**

Natural gas business segmentation

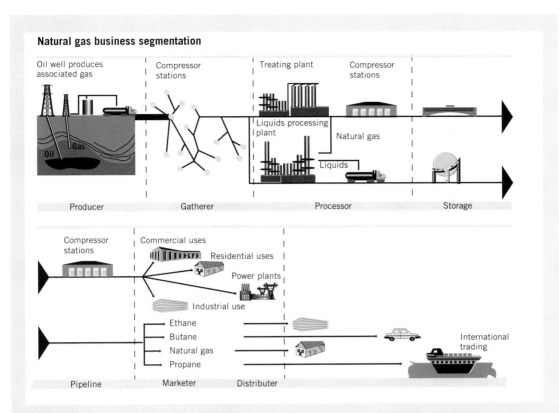

which are small independents. The top 20 public domestic reserve-holding companies produce less than 45% of total annual production, with the next 20 producing only an incremental 9%. The relatively small size of most natural gas producers means that they cannot justify the cost of in-house marketing and support of risk management activities. This has created a need and opportunity for natural gas gatherers and gas marketers, and has resulted in an active market for trading physical gas.

Gas processing plants are the next link in the chain. The raw natural gas stream, which is primarily composed of methane gas, is also rich in heavier molecules, including ethane, propane, butane and natural gasoline. These hydrocarbons are removed from the gas stream, and sold at a premium as natural gas liquids (NGLs). NGLs are used mainly for process and feedstock purposes in the chemicals industry or, in the case of propane, as an easily transportable source of energy for heating applications.

The gas processing plants are usually situated at the end of the pipeline systems which aggregate small volumes of gas into larger, more easily marketable gas pools. Generally, these processing facilities run full-time, extracting NGLs. However, at times, the price spread between natural gas and NGL prices narrows to a point which makes NGL production uneconomic; in this situation, to the extent operationally possible, the NGLs are left in the gas stream. With the emergence of longer-dated hedging markets in propane and, to a lesser extent, ethane, the forward price spreads between natural gas and the liquids stream are beginning to be actively traded and managed in

1954. In deciding the case, the Court held that the primary aim of the Natural Gas Act of 1938 was the "protection of consumers against exploitation at the hands of natural gas companies". The Federal Power Commission (FPC) acted to carry out the Court's interpretation by mandating a cost-oriented approach to wellhead price regulation on a case-by-case basis, just as they had imposed cost-of-service regulation on pipeline companies. (Cost-of-service regulation allowed pipeline companies, which in many instances acted as monopoly utilities, to earn only what was deemed a "fair return" on the asset, based on the cost of implementing and operating that asset.) When such focused regulatory oversight of each producer proved unmanageable, the FPC adopted a system of national wellhead rates based on the concept of "vintaging". The concept of vintaging was developed as a way of assigning different values to specific gas production based upon the date of well completion (and, in some cases, the

much the same way as oil refinery crack spreads.

Interspersed throughout the business chain are natural gas marketing companies, which buy, sell and trade the commodity. These marketers range from larger integrated players such as Enron, which markets over 10% of total US daily gas consumption, to very small shops which serve niche markets. The gas marketing business has consolidated in recent years, as some of the stronger independents (such as Access Energy and EnTrade) have been acquired by larger players (such as Enron and Tenneco) while many smaller, less well-capitalised players have shut down altogether. Competing with these gas marketing companies are the marketing arms of production companies, pipeline marketing affiliates, and local distribution companies (LDCs). Marketers add efficiency to the market by providing pooling, storage, balancing, financing and risk management services.

Next in the chain are pipeline companies. Pipeline capacity is sold on the basis of firm or interruptible service, and, in the last few years, a secondary market has developed to trade pipeline capacity. As discussed in the main text, interstate pipeline companies now act primarily as transporters, though many have non-affiliated gas marketing subsidiaries. In contrast, intrastate pipelines, not being subject to FERC authority, can act as both transporters and gas merchants. That is not to say that the intrastate pipeline companies have a monopoly or oligopoly power – the Texas and Louisiana Gulf Coast intrastate pipelines serve the most sophisticated, competitive markets in the United States, and therefore must compete strongly on price and, to a lesser extent, service. In total, approximately 110 pipeline companies control over 280,000 miles of natural gas pipeline throughout North America.

The largest part of the residential and commercial transportation function is handled by Local Distribution Companies (LDCs). LDCs typically serve industrial, commercial and residential needs for heat and energy. Much of the gas that is consumed in non-gas-producing states is provided by LDCs, but in gas producing states most of the supply to large industrial and electric utility concerns is served via direct pipeline connections. Generally, natural gas commodity, transportation and service charges are fully passed through to the end-consumer, with little or no price risk accruing to the LDC. LDCs, along with electric utilities, are generally overseen by state regulatory bodies such as Public Utility Commissions (PUCs), which serve to protect the public interest.

The chain ends at the natural gas burnertip. The largest end-use sector is the industrial market, which in 1992 consumed over 7.5 trillion cubic feet of gas, or approximately 40% of total annual consumption. Refiners, chemical manufacturers, ammonia and methanol producers, steel and aluminium manufacturers, and paper mills account for the bulk of industrial activity. On-site industrial electricity generation makes up a large part of the industrial consumption.

Combined residential and commercial consumption comprises rather under 40% of demand; residential gas usage is about double the requirement of the commercial sector. Electric utility consumption, combined with other uses, makes up the remainder.[1]

The vast majority of gas is used as a fuel source, although a considerable amount is used as feedstock for ammonia, methanol and other chemicals. The primary industrial markets for gas are in Texas and the Louisiana Gulf Coast region, while the primary non-industrial markets are California, the Great Lakes region of the Midwest, and the Northeast region.

1 *Natural Gas Trends: North America*, Cambridge Energy Research Associates, 1994, p. 38.

depth of the well). Gas wells that had been developed in certain regulatory eras sold gas at a maximum lawful price that was quite different to the maximum price of gas from wells developed at a different time; "deep gas" wells produced gas that could be sold at higher prices than gas produced from shallow formations.

Many observers believe that these price schedules eventually led to the severe shortages of the 1970s, since they encouraged consumers to use the relatively cheap fuel but did not pro-

vide any incentive to producers to replace reserves. To guard against shortages in the future, pipelines entered into take-or-pay (TOP) contracts with producers. The pipelines then resold the gas to local distribution companies (LDCs) at equivalent prices with "minimum bill" provisions that mirrored their take-or-pay contracts.

Congress intervened with the Natural Gas Policy Act (NGPA) of 1978, which was designed to address the supply shortage. The NGPA provided for the gradual deregulation of wellhead gas prices and for inducements to limit gas usage, particularly for industrial consumers. The process of deregulating wellhead prices for natural gas was eventually completed with the implementation of the Natural Gas Wellhead Decontrol Act of 1989.

Limitations on industrial gas consumption imposed by the NGPA, coupled with the lifting of price controls which in some cases resulted in gas being sold for over $10/MMBtu (million British thermal units) – about 50 times greater than some vintages – quickly reversed the supply shortage. By the early 1980s a gas surplus, the so-called gas "bubble", had been created that would linger until the 1990s. To make matters worse for the pipelines, in 1984 the Federal Energy Regulatory Commission (FERC), the successor to the FPC, issued Order No. 380, which declared "minimum bill" contracts between pipelines and LDCs to be invalid. Thus pipelines were faced with obligations to buy more gas than they could sell, at prices that were above market value.

In an effort to reduce their liabilities under their supply TOP contracts, pipelines began offering "special marketing programmes" through which they sold gas to non-traditional customers – typically, industrial end-users – at reduced costs. This increased sales, thus reducing the pipelines' liabilities under their supply TOP contracts. In 1985, however, the courts stopped this activity. They declared that the pipelines' practice of denying LDCs access to these lower-cost gas supplies was discriminatory. Nevertheless, this opened the door for the next step in deregulating the gas market – the unbundling of pipeline gas sales and transportation services. The first step in this unbundling process was FERC's Order 436, issued in 1985. In effect, this order required pipelines to provide open access to capacity on their systems, making it much easier for LDCs and other end-users to purchase their gas supplies directly at the wellhead and then contract separately with the pipelines for a transportation service only.

In 1987 and 1988, the FERC issued two more orders that further liberalised pipeline operations. Order No. 500 provided for the sharing of TOP contract costs, including contract renegotiations, buy-outs or buy-downs, among producers, pipelines and pipeline customers.

Order No. 490 removed the requirement that pipelines obtain FERC approval before terminating purchase agreements from producers. Under this new regulation, either the pipeline or the producer could terminate their arrangement upon expiration of the contract and 30 days notice. More recently, the FERC has taken a further significant step towards deregulating the natural gas market. Order No. 636, issued in 1992, requires pipelines to complete the unbundling of their sales and transportation services and to provide a system for resale of any firm capacity held by their customers. Figure 1 illustrates the history of these regulatory orders and the demand/supply balance for natural gas in the United States.

Order No. 636 has now been fully implemented, completing the evolution of the pipeline companies from "merchants" to "transporters". This transition has paved the way for greater competition amongst third-party service providers, and has also resulted in an active transportation-capacity trading market.

THE SPOT MARKET
The unravelling of long-term supply contracts and the initiation of open access for interruptible transport under FERC Order 436 encouraged the development of a market for short-term gas supply commitments. This market has come to be called the spot or cash market. Knowledge of this market is essential when initiating a gas price hedge, as any risk management structure needs to be properly integrated with the spot market.

Three types of spot market transactions are common: "firm", "interruptible" and "swing".[3] Firm transactions require counterparties to a transaction to perform according to the price and terms of the contract, short of a true event of *force majeure* (which is defined quite narrowly in most firm contracts). Firm transactions are usually executed under a Master Firm

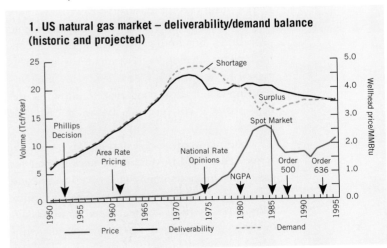

1. US natural gas market – deliverability/demand balance (historic and projected)

Purchase/Sale agreement, which includes make-whole provisions in the form of liquidated damages and includes financial penalty provisions in the event of non-performance.

Interruptible contracts can be interpreted more broadly, although the trend of most counterparties has been to define specific levels of interruptibility. These transactions also require performance as specifically stated, but usually on a "best efforts" basis rather than on an absolutely firm basis. Due to the risk of non-performance on the part of the producer, this type of transaction generally trades at a discount to firm gas.

Finally, swing sales are deals which provide for little in the way of obligation. Price and term are subject to renegotiation at any time. The swing market is highly volatile, and can best be characterised as a daily market. End-users tend only to use it for their daily pipeline volume "balancing" requirements.[4] Marketers and traders are the most active participants in the market for this gas, as they use swing transactions to balance purchases and sales, or for position trading.

The spot market mechanism has evolved into a highly institutionalised process for the active buying and selling of gas. Outside of the swing market, most gas is traded on a 30-day basis, with pricing generally negotiated near the end of each calendar month during what is known as "bid week". Bid week coincides with the nomination deadlines for monthly pipeline capacity. While the name may imply a leisurely period of time for pricing and trading, in practice, bid week periods for the majority of pipelines have been compressed into a very short time window. Some pundits now refer to bid week as "bid day" or even "bid hour". In fact, the majority of spot market trading occurs in the hours immediately following Nymex futures contract settlement. The settlement date procedures governing the Nymex futures contract were developed to coincide as much as possible with bid week and the various pipeline nomination deadlines, to allow for the best possible convergence between cash and futures.

While many producers and end-users remain active sellers and buyers in the spot market for gas, in recent years many have opted to sell and buy under long-term firm contracts or "index transactions" which are referenced to published monthly prices. Index prices, which are published for a wide variety of producing area gas pooling points and major consumption areas, are generated by polling participants in the spot market. The most referenced index is McGraw Hill's *Inside FERC Gas Market Report (IFGMR)*, although *Gas Daily, Natural Gas Week, Natural Gas Intelligence* and others are also frequently cited.

This process of polling and publishing the responses of market participants at various pipeline points differs greatly from the practice of aggregators posting prices for wet barrels of crude oil. Crude market postings are prices at which aggregators and refiners will actually transact for crude barrels at a specified location. The natural gas indices represent a much more informal survey of how people say that they transacted. These surveys do not distinguish between the various contract types, described below, under which gas purchases/sales are transacted. In addition, since a response to a survey is not an offer to transact, there is little control over survey responses, which sometimes leads to the published indices being unrepresentative of true market prices. This is one of the reasons why basis differentials are unstable and difficult to predict. (One reason for the difference in setting spot prices is that the concentration of buyers in the crude market is greater than in the natural gas market.)

The prices in the spot market reflect the ability of the natural gas delivery system to satisfy immediate demand and to consume available supply. Unexpected weather patterns, production problems, pipeline "outages" or shutdowns, or storage injections or withdrawals, can move prices up or down significantly. Severe price movements can be very localised, and may not be dampened by the price of gas in other regions or by the price of alternative fuels; this market inefficiency is caused by the limitations of the physical delivery system, and the time and costs involved in switching fuels.

Spot deals currently account for about 40% of the market, down from a high of about 70-80% in 1989. While the majority of the remaining gas bought and sold in the market is transacted under long-term index contracts, with monthly price resets, an increasing number of long-term contracts are arranged using different price-setting mechanisms. The most common of these are fixed-price contracts for specified terms, and "trigger" contracts whereby the buyer or seller sets their price at a differential to a transparent price source such as the Nymex.

EMERGENCE OF THE NYMEX CONTRACT

On April 3, 1990, the Nymex launched a natural gas futures contract. This contract brought risk management to the forefront of the natural gas industry by providing a standardised hedging vehicle and true price transparency. The delivery point for the Nymex Natural Gas futures contract is the Henry Hub gas processing plant of the Sabine Pipe Line Co at Erath, Louisiana. This delivery point was selected because it interconnects with twelve other pipeline systems: Acadian, Coastal (ANR), Columbia Gulf, Dow Intrastate, Koch Gateway, Louisiana Resources Co (LRC), Natural Gas Pipeline of America (NGPL), Southern Natural, Texas Gas, Transco, Trunkline and Texaco's gathering system.

As we noted above, this contract has been Nymex's most successful product launch to date in terms of rate of growth. The liquidity of the contract has allowed the over-the-counter (OTC) market to develop structured hedge transactions with their customers at narrow bid/ask spreads. Nymex, as well as OTC principals, have expended substantial time and resources to educate the market on the benefits and applications of hedging, and already there are a large number of gas industry companies active in the market.

The largest players are the natural gas marketing companies. Risk management capabilities have become a core component of their business, and virtually every gas marketing company has dedicated resources to providing risk management services to its customer base. It is estimated that over 80% of gas producers actively use risk management tools; and that somewhere between 60 to 80% of the larger industrial end-users of gas also manage their energy costs. Many of these companies already have experience in managing the risk of their interest rate and foreign exchange exposures, and are beginning to identify the parallels with their energy exposures. Gas and electric utilities tend to be far less active due to the regulatory restraints and uncertainty, but most have reviewed possible applications of energy risk management products in their business.

Capital investment at risk

In the late 1980s, significant investments were made in the exploration and production of natural gas. These projects, which came on-line in the early 1990s, were predicated on the common belief that prices would rise. When prices did not rise as predicted, the upstream natural gas industry realised revenues that were $3.5 billion below expected levels. This revenue shortfall acted to depress both domestic exploration and production budgets; funds were redirected to oil exploration and overseas ventures. In 1991, the top 40 gas companies replaced only 72% of their depleted domestic reserves, and in 1992 only 68% was replaced. The proven reserves-to-production ratio dropped to a decade-long low of 9.1 years, while the number of domestic rigs fell to an all-time low of 721 rigs in 1992, and was up only slightly to 754 active rigs in 1993.[5]

Nevertheless, the long-term future of the industry seems assured. There are more than 1,300 trillion cubic feet of recoverable domestic natural gas reserves – enough to meet anticipated demand for the next 70 years – that can be produced using today's exploration and production technology.[6] While independent and major producers are increasingly interested in recovering these reserves, doing so will require a great deal of capital. Capital is required not only for exploration and production, but also for the expansion of pipeline transmission and distribution systems, and for the development of facilities to burn the gas – specifically, gas-fired electrical generation plants. Obtaining this capital is challenging, given the risk embedded in investment projects which depend upon natural gas prices.

Since the removal of natural gas price controls in 1978, there have been wide swings in natural gas prices. These price fluctuations, the financial pressures resulting from deregulation, and large write-downs resulting from take-or-pay contract settlements, led to a severe drop in the creditworthiness of many pipeline companies in the 1980s and early 1990s (Fig. 2). The uncertainty over future price levels that was created by a large supply overhang, and by concerns over the viability of long-term contracts, led market participants to dramatically shorten the maturity of their gas supply contracts.

2. S&P senior unsecured debt rating

	1981	1994
Enron	A+	BBB
Coastal Corporation	A	BB+
Columbia Gas System	A	D
Panhandle Eastern	A	BBB–
Sonat Inc	A	BBB
Transco	BBB	B
United Gas Pipeline	BBB	n/r

Source: S&P Coastal - Michigan Wisconsin Pipeline

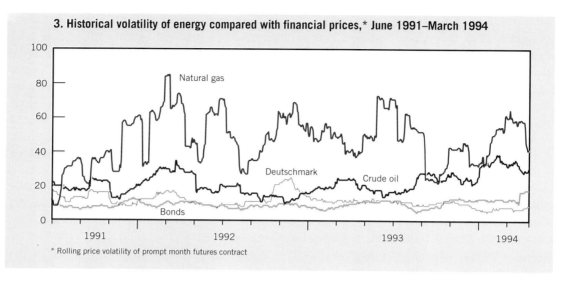

3. Historical volatility of energy compared with financial prices,* June 1991–March 1994

* Rolling price volatility of prompt month futures contract

Almost overnight, contract terms changed in duration from years to months, and the active "spot" market described above evolved to become the primary arena in which to sell and buy gas.

While dramatically shortening the maturity of transactions alleviated concerns about contract and credit risk, it also greatly increased the exposure of industry participants to changes in commodity price levels.

Natural gas volatility is dramatic – in fact, over the last three years, gas volatility has been significantly higher than that for crude oil, US Treasury Bonds and the German Deutschmark versus the US dollar (Fig. 3).

Over the course of 1992–93, natural gas futures exhibited the highest volatility of any commodity traded on the organised US futures exchanges. Weather events were largely responsible: an unseasonably warm winter season in 1991–92 drove the February Nymex contract to a $1.05/MMBtu settlement, while just seven months later Hurricane Andrew interrupted offshore Gulf Coast production, gathering and transmission to such an extent that gas prices rose to an October Nymex settlement of $2.60/MMBtu.

A late winter during the 1992–93 season meant that the May 1993 contract settled at $2.76/MMBtu, even though earlier in the year hopes that the winter would be mild had led to the February 1993 contract being settled at $1.63/MMBtu. Within two months of the May high, gas prices had fallen back to a more normal $1.92/MMBtu.

A hard winter during the 1993–94 season meant that the February 1994 futures contract settled at $2.47/MMBtu. From this peak, prices dwindled, due to a combination of new incre-

mental gas supply, accelerated storage injection schedules and a relatively mild summer: by the time the October 1994 contract settled, prices had sunk to $1.40/MMBtu.

From January 1992 through December 1993, the observed 30-day annualised volatility of natural gas was nearly 50%. Longer-term prices are also volatile. Over the same period, the one-year futures strip exhibited 30-day annualised volatility of about 20%. On some occasions, there were daily changes of around 2–5% in the 12-month Nymex average ("12-month strip").

Commodity price volatility of this magnitude greatly increases the variability of the returns to investment capital, and results in high risk premia being charged for any investment in the natural gas industry.

Other industries dependent on the price of a commodity commonly use long-term contracts that offer protection from price volatility as a way of lowering the cost of capital. For example, as described in Chapter 12 of this book, gold, silver and copper producers often hedge their production when arranging project finance. Furthermore, a statistical analysis of returns from firms that have issued hybrid, commodity index-linked debt shows that their equity betas declined after the debt issuance, indicating that shareholders recognise the benefits of commodity price risk management.[7]

The objective of commodity price risk management is to reduce earnings volatility and lower the probability of financial distress. A well-designed risk management programme should allow increased financial leverage and higher, less risky returns to shareholders' equity. The benefits to the company of such a programme are enhanced creditworthiness, higher market capitalisation, and a significantly lower

RISK MANAGEMENT AND INCREASED FINANCIAL LEVERAGE: AN EXAMPLE

Imagine that a natural gas production company enters into a fixed-price sale of its production for five years at an initial price of $2.00/MMBtu, escalating at 5% per year. Entering into the fixed-price agreement will remove much of the uncertainty concerning future revenues to the company, and thus allow it to increase its financial leverage.

Two detailed financial statements are presented overleaf. Financial Statement A represents a production company with a constant 50/50 debt/equity ratio. Financial Statement B represents the same company with a constant 70/30 debt/equity ratio. Assuming an original equity base of $4.5 million, the more leveraged capital structure allows the company to access $6 million more capital than can be accessed in the less leveraged structure.

This additional capital can be used to increase the size and the diversification of the company's production assets, thus reducing its exposure to reserve risk, as well as to commodity price risk. As illustrated in the financial statements, the earnings per share and the annualised cumulative five-year returns to equity, are higher for the more leveraged company (14.5% versus 11.5%). Moreover, there is no additional price risk for the shareholders since the company's commodity exposure is 100% hedged.

To illustrate the impact of commodity price volatility on the production company, the annualised cumulative five-year returns to shareholders' equity for various combinations of financial leverage and price hedging are obtained from simulation and shown in Figure A opposite. As can be seen from this graph, the probability of negative returns to equity increases significantly as commodity price exposure climbs. Also, when the commodity exposure is unhedged, the probability of negative returns to equity is greater when the company is more highly leveraged. When 50% of the price risk is hedged, the uncertainty in prices and the revenues is reduced, and the probabilities of negative returns to equity are more or less the same for both 50/50 and 70/30 leverage ratios. This is due to the assumption of economies of scale, which reduces the total operating cost per unit volume for the more leveraged case. Thus, the lower operating costs, combined with hedging the price exposure, help to offset the risks resulting from higher leverage.

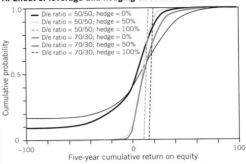

A. Effect of leverage and hedging on returns to shareholders

For this analysis, assumptions about the company structure and tax rates are the same as shown on the financial statements. The annualised forward volatilities for natural gas prices are assumed to be 22%, 20%, 18.5%, 17% and 16% for years 1, 2, 3, 4 and 5 respectively.

For instance, in the case of the production company with a 70/30 debt to equity ratio and no price hedge, there is a 35% probability of the five-year cumulative returns to the shareholder equity being negative; the probability of this occurring in the case of the firm with a 50/50 debt to equity ratio and 50% of its volume hedged is 5%. With a 100% price hedge, the probability is zero percent regardless of the capital structure.

The effect of financial leverage and price hedge combinations on the financial stability of the production firm are exhibited in Figure B.

For the highly leveraged capital structure and no commodity hedge, the probability of at least one net cash shortfall is 20%; this is reduced to zero with a 100% price hedge.

No two firms are exactly alike, but the approach outlined above can be adapted to model the sensitivity of returns to equity investment for a variety of capital structures that have different levels of exposure to commodity price fluctuations.

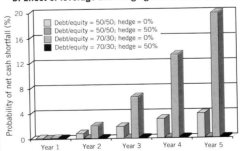

B. Effect of leverage and hedging on financial stability

For this example, the probability of a net cash shortfall is defined as earnings before interest and tax (with non-cash deductions such as depreciation and well amortisation added back) falling below fixed interest charges.

FINANCIAL STATEMENT A
PRODUCER X: 50/50 Debt Equity
STATEMENT OF INCOME
(In $ Thousands Except Per Share Amounts)

	End of 0th Year	1st Year	2nd Year	3rd Year	4th Year	5th Year
Operating revenues		3,650	3,951	4,321	4,778	5,350
Operating expenses:						
Lease and well		379	388	527	556	593
Exploration		238	261	289	322	358
Depreciation, depletion and amortisation		1,466	1,500	1,547	1,608	1,688
Other		1,218	1,251	1,161	1,189	1,221
Total operating expenses		3,300	3,401	3,524	3,675	3,861
Operating income		350	550	796	1,103	1,489
Interest income		273	294	322	359	409
Other income		229	229	229	229	229
Interest expense		338	363	397	444	504
Income before income taxes		515	711	950	1,247	1,622
Income tax expense		180	249	332	437	568
Net income		335	462	617	811	1,054

PRODUCER X: 50/50 Debt Equity
BALANCE SHEET
(In $ Thousands Except Per Share Amounts)

	End of 0th Year	1st Year	2nd Year	3rd Year	4th Year	5th Year
Current assets	3,645	3,916	4,290	4,790	5,447	6,301
Net oil and gas properties	7,898	8,485	9,295	10,379	11,802	13,652
Other assets	608	653	715	798	908	1,050
Total assets	12,150	13,054	14,301	15,968	18,156	21,003
Current liabilities	1,350	1,450	1,589	1,774	2,017	2,334
Long-term debt	4,500	4,835	5,296	5,914	6,725	7,779
Other liabilities	1,800	1,934	2,119	2,366	2,690	3,112
Shareholders' equity	4,500	4,835	5,296	5,914	6,725	7,779
Total liabilities and shareholders' equity	12,150	13,054	14,301	15,968	18,156	21,003

PRODUCER X: 50/50 Debt Equity
CASH FLOW FROM OPERATIONS
(In $ Thousands Except Per Share Amounts)

	End of 0th Year	1st Year	2nd Year	3rd Year	4th Year	5th Year
Net income		335	462	617	811	1,054
Depreciation, depletion and amortisation		1,466	1,500	1,547	1,608	1,688
Change in Current Liabilities		100	139	185	243	316
Cash flow from operations		1,901	2,101	2,350	2,662	3,059
Common stock shares outstanding		400	400	400	400	400
Earnings per share		0.84	1.15	1.54	2.03	2.64
Return on equity		7.17%	9.12%	11.01%	12.83%	14.54%
Return on assets		2.66%	3.38%	4.08%	4.75%	5.38%
Times interest earned		252.56%	295.95%	339.12%	381.20%	421.62%

after-tax cost of capital. Panel 2 describes a hypothetical case history of the impact of forward price hedging on the returns of a financially leveraged natural gas production company.

If risk management techniques were comprehensively applied, the cumulative savings to the industry from reduced capital costs on investment needed to develop reserves, build pipelines, and construct power generation plants to satisfy the projected demand for gas up to the year 2000, could be as much as $33 billion.[8] By means of risk management, the industry could increase its typical debt-to-equity ratios of 60/40 to 80/20 *without* increasing the probability of financial distress.

These financial principles are being put into practice at Enron Capital & Trade Resources through its Cactus Production Payment programmes and the Joint Energy Development Investments Limited Partnership (JEDI). Over the past three years, Enron has arranged through both Cactus and JEDI over $2 billion of financing to the independent oil and gas market – making the company one of the leading providers of capital to the industry.

Cactus is a senior/subordinated master trust that holds an interest in a limited partnership which acquires volumetric production payments (VPPs). A volumetric production payment involves the acquisition from a producer of a specified volume of gas and/or oil for future deliveries (the way in which Zilkha Energy used a VPP is explained in detail overleaf in Panel 3). The value of any given volume of production is obviously sensitive to changes in commodity

FINANCIAL STATEMENT B
PRODUCER X: 70/30 Debt Equity
STATEMENT OF INCOME
(In $ Thousands Except Per Share Amounts)

Assumptions
5% annual increase in prices ($2.00 start price)
50/50 debt/equity for all years
7.5% interest rate on debt
7.5% earned on cash balances
35% income tax rate

	End of 0th Year	1st Year	2nd Year	3rd Year	4th Year	5th Year
Operating revenues		5,366	5,909	6,635	7,635	9,060
Operating expenses:						
Lease and well		557	572	805	859	939
Exploration		250	367	390	426	476
Depreciation, depletion and amortisation		2,309	2,371	2,464	2,601	2,807
Other		1,695	1,769	1,743	1,912	2,080
Total operating expenses		4,811	5,079	5,402	5,799	6,303
Operating income		555	830	1,233	1,836	2,757
Interest income		456	489	540	614	724
Other income		289	289	289	289	289
Interest expense		787	846	932	1,061	1,252
Income before income taxes		512	762	1,129	1,678	2,518
Income tax expense		179	267	395	587	881
Net income		333	496	734	1,091	1,637

PRODUCER X: 70/30 Debt Equity
BALANCE SHEET
(In $ Thousands Except Per Share Amounts)

Current assets	6,075	6,524	7,193	8,184	9,656	11,866
Net oil and gas properties	13,162	14,136	15,586	17,732	20,922	25,709
Other assets	1,012	1,087	1,199	1,364	1,609	1,978
Total assets	20,249	21,748	23,978	27,280	32,187	39,553
Current liabilities	2,250	2,416	2,664	3,031	3,576	4,395
Long-term debt	10,499	11,277	12,433	14,145	16,690	20,509
Other liabilities	3,000	3,222	3,552	4,041	4,768	5,860
Shareholders' equity	4,500	4,833	5,328	6,062	7,153	8,790
Total liabilities and shareholders' equity	20,249	21,748	23,978	27,280	32,187	39,553

PRODUCER X: 70/30 Debt Equity
CASH FLOW FROM OPERATIONS
(In $ Thousands Except Per Share Amounts)

Net income		333	496	734	1,091	1,637
Depreciation, depletion and amortisation		2,309	2,371	2,464	2,601	2,807
Change in Current Liabilities		167	248	367	545	818
Cash flow from operations		2,808	3,115	3,564	4,237	5,263
Common stock shares outstanding		400	400	400	400	400
Earnings per share		0.83	1.24	1.83	2.73	4.09
Return on equity		7.13%	9.75%	12.88%	16.50%	20.53%
Return on assets		1.59%	2.17%	2.86%	3.67%	4.56%
Times interest earned		165.04%	190.14%	221.06%	258.15%	301.18%

prices, interest rates and currency exchange rates. But by hedging the value of these proceeds, they can be transformed into a series of known cash flows that amortise with the production profile of the financed reserves. This allows the master trust to be capitalised in the commercial bank and institutional investor markets at attractive risk premia. Producers which enter into these transactions are also able to access more debt than could be acquired via traditional non-recourse reserve-based financing. The result is a significantly reduced overall cost of capital.

JEDI is a partnership between the California Public Employees Retirement System ("CalPERS") and Enron Capital & Trade Resources, which was formed in 1993 to invest in natural gas related projects. Each partner has committed equity contributions of $250 million over a three-year period. The use of commodity risk management practices allows for greater leverage of the equity capital in these investments than would otherwise be possible. In virtually all its investments, JEDI has utilised a combination of commodity, interest rate and currency hedges to reduce the specific risks embedded in the transactions.

Risk management in practice
STRATEGIES AND TACTICS
The formulation of a clear company policy is the key to the proper use of risk management instruments. Is this financial technology going to be used to manage risk, to meet specific policy objectives, or to improve the company's competitive position?

VOLUMETRIC PRODUCTION PAYMENTS: THE ZILKHA ENERGY EXAMPLE

In developing its business, Zilkha Energy Company, a medium-sized independent producer based in Houston, Texas, focuses on rapid reserve growth. However, its use of 3D seismic exploration techniques in the Gulf of Mexico requires a great deal of "front-end" capital – capital which is difficult to raise by traditional means.

Historically, Zilkha has had two alternatives: selling existing producing properties or borrowing money. By selling its existing producing properties, Zilkha risked losing a significant source of future cash flow and reserve "upside". But the amount of money Zilkha could raise by borrowing money in the bank market against known reserves was limited, and severe restrictions would have been imposed on the use of the borrowed funds.

Through the application of risk management products, coupled with intensive geological surveys and Enron's ability to take physical gas as payment, Enron Gas Services (EGS – now Enron Capital & Trade Resources) was able to provide an integrated solution to Zilkha's needs. In May 1991, in the first of many transactions with Zilkha, EGS paid $24 million for a specified vol-

ume of Zilkha's proven reserves. This transaction, known as a volumetric production payment (VPP), allowed the company to pay down bank debt and secure additional working capital without having to sell acreage or borrow funds. It also entitled EGS to a designated amount of oil and gas production from specified Gulf tracts, free of the cost of production. The deal was structured so that EGS had recourse only to the physical production fields, and not to the company or its other assets.

Without known forward prices on the three components of financial risk in this transaction – natural gas, crude oil and interest rates – a deal such as this would be very risky for a financier. However, having determined a reserve production profile, EGS was able to carve out a specific portion of the reserves that it considered it could prudently finance through a VPP. EGS hedged the value of the natural gas and crude oil volumes through forward commodity and interest rate transactions. As a result of hedging the risk components of the deal, EGS was able to forward Zilkha a far larger payment than the company would otherwise have been able to negotiate.

In terms of the number of daily transactions, tactical hedging represents the vast majority of retail business executed. Typically 12 months or less in term, tactical trades are executed with the intention of protecting budgets, achieving minimum short-term cash-flow levels, controlling short-term revenues or costs, or protecting value differentials from location to location or between commodity prices.

Strategic hedging is much less frequent, but forms a significant fraction of the total volume of business completed. Typically longer than twelve months in term, these hedges are tied to strategic, financial or tax opportunities. Often, strategic hedging is transacted by means of a structured project financing such as a volumetric production payment (VPP), as discussed above and in Panel 3.

Commodity-indexation strategies can also help companies to meet long-term objectives. Capturing known margins, securing competitive advantages or financially altering a producer's production mix between gas and crude price risk are also frequent goals in strategic hedging

programmes. Although, so far, relatively few transactions have been completed in the natural gas sector to secure competitive advantage, a few players in pure commodity businesses (such as natural gas producers or bulk chemicals manufacturers) are starting to consider these strategies. Fixing cost/revenue spreads, locking in an advantageous gas price compared to a competitor, or expanding service offerings are all examples of using forward pricing for competitive purposes. Panel 4 describes how Reynolds Metals used risk management products to pursue this kind of strategy.

Purely speculative transactions make up the smallest portion of the deal spectrum. Most of these transactions are very short-term in nature, and reflect a producer or end-user's view of the direction of prices for the near month.

Many hedgers see in each deal, regardless of motivation, some speculative element. It is human nature to try to pick a market bottom or top at the same time as implementing a genuine hedge – tactical hedgers are the most likely to be tempted by this. As a result, many hedgers miss

HEDGING STRATEGIES:
THE REYNOLDS METALS EXAMPLE

Like most other metals companies, Reynolds Metals, a leading US aluminium producer, has a high degree of exposure to energy prices. Natural gas prices are no exception — fully one-third of Reynolds' production costs are related to gas.

However, because of the price volatility inherent in the US natural gas market, planning at the plant and corporate levels was always a frustrating exercise. With the emergence of the Nymex natural gas futures contract and the concurrent development of a liquid OTC market, Reynolds had the means to begin to take control over its price exposure.

Over the course of 1991, Reynolds set out to map a strategy for its energy portfolio. Securing a firm physical supply of gas was a central part of this strategy; financial swaps were then used to lock in the price of a substantial portion of this supply. Rather than devoting time and resources to develop an in-house futures-based hedging strategy, Reynolds went to the OTC market, which offered low-cost, highly customised solutions.

The company began by implementing a swap that hedged 12Bcf of annual consumption for a three-year time period, a quantity equivalent to about 25% of Reynolds' annual consumption. Rather than hedge its basis risk, the company chose instead to settle against Nymex. By not hedging the basis risk, Reynolds in effect went "short" on its basis exposure. The company believed that the price differential in the forward basis market was too high, and thus adopted a strategy that depended upon the basis in the spot market being lower than that quoted in the forward market.

For several months after Reynolds implemented the initial hedge, long-term prices continued to fall. This provided Reynolds with the opportunity to hedge 70% of its consumption.

In order to rationalise the gas purchases in terms of the company's overall position, Reynolds elected to restructure its swaps to better match the pricing cycle of the refined metals that the company produced. Since aluminium prices were at cyclical lows, Reynolds decided to "tilt" the swaps. This tilt provided lower fixed prices in the current year, with annual step-ups over the course of the next two years. Because this adjustment was designed so that the net present value of the position remained equivalent to the non-stepped net present value, the swap dealers were happy to oblige.

The timing of the swaps was fortuitous: over the course of late-1992 and through the summer of 1994, gas prices rose significantly. In fact, while the one-year Nymex strip traded as low as $1.33/MMBtu in late January 1992, by the end of 1992, it was trading at over $2.00/MMBtu; over the course of 1993 it averaged over $2.20/MMBtu. In Spring 1993, gas prices skyrocketed, and the strip reached nearly $2.50/MMBtu.

Once again sensing opportunity, Reynolds chose to dynamically manage its existing position. Rather than unwind the swap positions for substantial cash value, and expose the portfolio once again to floating gas prices, Reynolds chose to structure a reverse zero-cost collar around half of its existing position.

This new position allowed the company to benefit from falling gas prices below a predefined level, while exposing it to some upside risk should prices continue to escalate above a certain point. In either case, Reynolds would have a portfolio of fixed and floating price exposure at very attractive prices when compared with competitors which had not hedged. Because of the opportunistic timing and dynamic management of the transactions, with nearly one year of the transaction terms remaining, the company has already received more than $23 million in positive cash flow from its swap and option settlements.

their target opportunities. Both the short- and long-term markets can and do move very quickly. At or near the end of calendar years 1992 and 1993, the 12-month strip traded at seasonal lows. In each year, within one month of winter lows, prices increased 15% and 13%, respectively, leaving many would be end-user hedgers forlornly waiting for another "opportunity".

VARIETIES OF RISK

While many customised hedge transactions are sophisticated in design, and may utilise complicated contract structure, they can be disaggregated into their various risk characteristics. Setting aside certain generic risks (credit, contract, interest rate and currency risk), the risks facing natural gas market participants can be categorised as follows:

❏ *price risk* The risk of a movement in the absolute price of gas, as defined by the price of gas traded at the Henry Hub. This is the gas processing plant and pipeline interconnect point owned and operated by the Sabine Pipeline Company in Erath, Louisiana, which serves as an interconnect for pipelines delivering gas from supply basins in the Gulf Coast to pipelines serving the Northeast and Mid-continent market areas. It is also the delivery point for the New York Mercantile Exchange (Nymex) natural gas futures contract.

❏ *basis risk* The risk of movement in price differentials between two pricing indices. The most common price differentials quoted are those between the average of the last three days prompt month Nymex futures contract settlements and a specified *IFGMR, Gas Daily, Natural Gas Week* or *Natural Gas Intelligence* index.

❏ *physical risk* The risk that natural gas will not be delivered to, or transported from, the agreed location as required. Natural gas is transacted for under firm, interruptible and swing contracts subject to various price, production, transport and demand conditions.

❏ *cross commodity price risk* The risk that the price of natural gas will change relative to the price of other fuels, electricity rates, gas liquids

prices, and other commodities or products where natural gas is a primary cost component.

MANAGING PRICE, BASIS AND PHYSICAL RISK
A specific example will serve to clarify how risk can be effectively managed. Below, we describe alternative methods by which a producer selling its production into the El Paso pipeline system in the Permian Basin of West Texas could manage price risk.

The monetary and physical flows that occur under a firm physical transaction (executed under a Master Firm Purchase/Sale Agreement) are shown in Example 1. In this example, the producer is paid a flat $1.85 per million British thermal units (MMBtus) to deliver natural gas for a fixed term into the El Paso pipeline system. Both parties commit to gas delivery at this price regardless of factors that would cause a disruption in the flow of gas under an interruptible or swing contract. This transaction hedges both the seller and buyer from price, basis and physical risk.

If the producer wishes to decouple the physical sale from the price risk management component, it can enter into a financial swap. A financially settled, fixed-to-floating natural gas swap that can be executed under a Master Swap Agreement is shown in Example 2. In this example, the producer receives a fixed price and pays a floating price. Here the fixed price is $2.00 and the floating price is the average of the settlement prices for the last three trading days of the Nymex contract for the delivery month. Each month, the producer will financially settle the difference between $2.00 and the average of the last three settlement prices of the Nymex contract. In addition, it will sell its gas under a swing contract into the spot market in the Permian Basin. Comparing the $2.00 Nymex price swap to the $1.85 Permian price in Example 1 shows that the basis between the Nymex and the *IFGMR* El Paso Permian index in the forward market is −15 cents.

The hedge outlined in Example 2 is the most "accessible" hedge, since it can be executed on behalf of the producer by financial intermediaries who trade on the Nymex, or by the producer itself if it wants to manage a futures trading account. However, this hedge manages only price risk and does not address basis and physical risk.

Ignoring these risks can be disastrous, as was demonstrated in May 1993. The problems started in the spring of that year, when some producers were offered the opportunity to sell gas

Example 1. Firm physical purchase/sale of gas

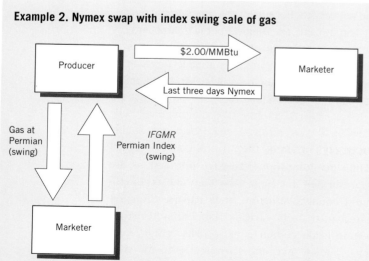

Example 2. Nymex swap with index swing sale of gas

Example 3. Nymex swap with basis swap and index firm sale of gas

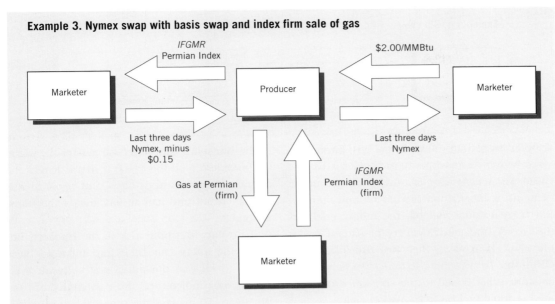

forward for May 1993 under a Master Firm Purchase/Sale Agreement for $1.85, or to receive $2.00 on a fixed-to-floating Nymex-indexed swap. These prices reflected the fact that the basis between the last three settlement prices of the May 1993 Nymex futures contract and the May *IFGMR* El Paso Permian index was being traded in the forward market with Permian at a 15 cent discount.

However, when the price of the futures contract increased to $2.70 at settlement, while Permian cash prices lagged behind at $2.20, the realised differential, or basis, between the last three days of Nymex and the *IFGMR* El Paso Permian Index widened by 35 cents to a 50 cent discount. Furthermore, as expected demand failed to materialise, prices for Permian gas were then traded down from the $2.20 first-of-the-month index price to $1.50. This meant that those spot market producers who hedged their price risk with a Nymex-referenced swap and who sold their production under a swing contract (where the price can change daily) were traded down to these levels, realising a loss of 70 cents from the first-of-the-month prices. This resulted in a loss of $1.05 from combined basis and physical risk and a realised sale price of just $0.80 per MMBtu. The experience taught natural gas producers that often the most important question is not *when* to hedge, but *how* to hedge.

A more robust, but complicated, hedge can be initiated by the producer to manage price, basis and physical risk simultaneously. This is shown in Example 3. At the same time as executing a fixed-to-floating Nymex swap, the producer enters into a financially-settled basis swap whereby the producer receives the floating Nymex index minus 15 cents and pays the *IFGMR* El Paso Permian index for the delivery month. In addition, the producer enters into a Firm Physical Purchase/Sale Agreement whereby the producer is paid the *IFGMR* El Paso Permian index by the counterparty that is purchasing the gas.

Example 3 achieves the same results as the physical gas contract in Example 1, but because Example 3 strips the risk into its various components and manages each separately it entails higher transaction costs. However, Example 3 may appeal to those who are less risk averse, and who wish to try to time the initiation of the price, basis and physical hedges in order to gain a greater, but more speculative, return.

MANAGING CROSS COMMODITY RISK

Cross-commodity price risk is also a concern. Investors in oil and gas production may want to synthetically shift production from one energy commodity to another. Utilities may find it attractive to invest in plants that burn natural gas – but if they do so they run the risk that the delivered price of natural gas may change relative to that of alternative fuels. These risks may be managed using a firm transaction (executed under a Master Firm Physical Purchase/Sale Agreement), whereby the price of one commodity is determined by that of another, or by means of a swap contract with financial settlements that are based on the difference between the published price indices of two different commodities.

In Example 4, a utility located in the Northeast region of the United States has

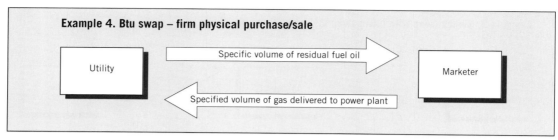

Example 4. Btu swap – firm physical purchase/sale

Utility

Specific volume of residual fuel oil → Marketer

← Specified volume of gas delivered to power plant

retooled its plant to burn natural gas, in order to comply with emissions standards set by the Clean Air Act. Instead of unwinding its current firm index-based contractual commitment to purchase residual fuel oil, the utility redelivers the "resid" and takes delivery of natural gas at the plant. It manages the price risk inherent in doing this by arranging to purchase natural gas at a price that is tied to the spot price of delivered residual fuel oil in its market area.

Alternatively, the utility could enter into a financial swap to pay a formula index, based upon a published price for residual fuel oil in New York Harbor, and receive the average of the settlement price of the last three trading days of the Nymex natural gas contract. This is called a Btu swap, and is shown in Example 5. Here the utility would sell its current "resid" purchase commitment to the spot market, take the proceeds from this sale and combine them with the proceeds from the financial settlement

of the Btu swap, and purchase gas for the plant. The problem with this tactic is that is leaves the utility exposed to both basis and physical risk on the "resid" and natural gas legs of the transaction.

To reduce the basis risk in the financial Btu swap, the utility can enter into financial basis swaps to lock in the difference between their market area indices and those referenced in the Btu swap. To manage the physical risk of its gas supply, it can enter into a Firm Physical Purchase/Sale Agreement whereby it pays the market area index it receives in its gas basis swap in exchange for a firm commitment to deliver gas. It will also have to enter into a firm contract to sell its "resid" stocks against the same market area index that is referenced in its "resid" basis swap. As demonstrated in Example 3, it is possible to hedge any combination of risks, though this flexibility may be achieved at the expense of higher transaction costs.

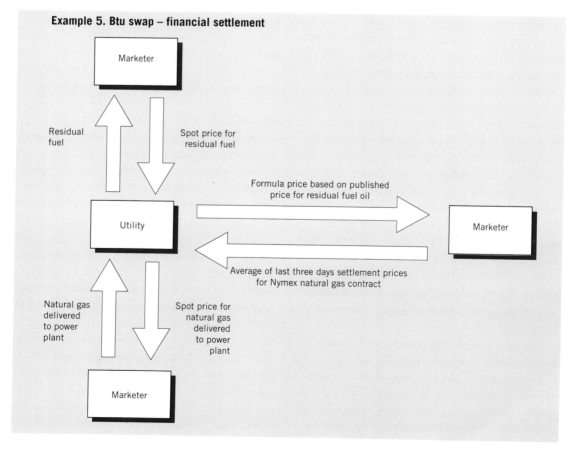

Example 5. Btu swap – financial settlement

Marketer

Residual fuel

Spot price for residual fuel

Utility

Formula price based on published price for residual fuel oil → Marketer

← Average of last three days settlement prices for Nymex natural gas contract

Natural gas delivered to power plant

Spot price for natural gas delivered to power plant

Marketer

OPTIONS

Market participants also use options to manage risk. Like fixed-price transactions, options may be entered into using a Firm Physical Purchase/Sale Agreement or a Master Swap Agreement. As with the above examples, an option may be settled either by actually delivering the commodity or by settling financially against a Nymex, *IFGMR*, *Gas Daily* or other index.

The reasons for using options are varied. Many market participants use options when they are taking a view on the market; the options act as insurance against adverse price moves while allowing the company to profit from the "upside" if the market moves in the expected direction.

However, many other uses exist. For example, firm fixed-price physical contracts often have monthly volumetric swing provisions embedded in them. These provisions give the purchaser a monthly option to "turn back" a portion of the contracted volumes if the contract price is above the market prices current at the time of delivery. These swing provisions may be managed by using options that settle monthly. Some fixed-price firm physical contracts have daily swing provisions in them; while it is relatively illiquid, there is a market in option strips that settle daily (see discussion in Panel 5).

Many options in the energy markets are Asian options. Asian options have a payoff that depends on the average of the reference index during a specified time period. For example, the payoff might be dependent upon the average of the last three settlement prices for the prompt-month Nymex natural gas futures contract. Another example is an option that settles against the daily average of a specified Gas Daily Index published for a delivery month.

Spread options are also prevalent in the industry. These options have a payout that is dependent upon the difference of two specified indices. One common use is to hedge the basis between two published *Inside FERC* market indices. This is known as an index spread option. Another is to hedge summer–winter price differentials with a time spread option.

An end-user may wish to have the option of purchasing its natural gas supply at the spot market price for either natural gas or residual fuel oil – whichever is the better. These options are often called "better of" options. Another alternative is to have the option payoff dependent upon a combination of referenced com-modity prices. These "basket" options may appeal to oil and gas producers who want to hedge the total revenue received for their production. A basket option with a payoff that is determined by the value of a combined oil and gas index would be cheaper than buying separate options to hedge the oil production and to hedge the gas production.

Caps, floors, collars, swaptions, participating swaps, extendible swaps and other hedge management structures can be created with the option types discussed above. A technical discussion of the kind of option structures used in the natural gas market, and the energy markets generally, is provided in Chapters 6 and 7 of this book.

THE ROLE OF THE INTERMEDIARY

The primary role of the risk intermediary is to provide its customer with instantaneous liquidity – for all transaction types, at all times. To do so requires an understanding of customer needs, in-depth knowledge of the products and the markets, and the ability to assume and manage the risks embedded in the customer transactions.

Many different types of intermediaries have entered the natural gas market in the last few years. Most numerous are those that intermediate in the spot market, where they match up the needs of producers and end-users. Some companies focus solely on financial hedge transactions, and offer no physical services, while others bridge the physical and financial markets.

When entering into a transaction, these intermediaries assume credit and contract exposure to the counterparty, in addition to market risks. Credit exposure is of paramount concern in the natural gas industry. A combination of industry conditions and high price volatility make it likely that market participants will be exposed to weak credit. To mitigate this exposure, and to allow customers to engage in prudent commodity risk management practices, a number of contract provisions are used by intermediaries. These include exposure collateralisation, termination of contract upon a material adverse change in the counterparties financial condition (MAC clause) and mutual termination, if desired, at agreed forward dates.

A risk intermediary depends upon its ability to price and manage the market risk of a complex transaction portfolio. Some companies attempt to minimise risk by running a "matched book" of transactions, but this means that they often can-

STORAGE AND NATURAL GAS RISK MANAGEMENT

The nature of natural gas storage has changed significantly during the last decade. Previously, most storage capacity was owned and utilised by the pipeline companies, who used it to secure the reliability of their supply. They needed to be certain that they could meet their regulatory obligations to end-users. Specifically, the pipeline companies used storage to help meet expected winter demand, to protect against unexpected production and transportation disruptions, and to supply peak demand during severe weather. A high premium was attached to storage because it insured the pipelines against the consequences of market disruption.

As deregulation of the natural gas industry has evolved, so has the need for storage. While storage facilities are still primarily operated by the pipelines, many of them are leased by third parties. Deregulation has also increased the number of independent storage operators, whose motivation is different from that of the pipeline companies before Order 636.

Following Order 636, the pipeline companies now function as contract carriers, offering various types of transport services to third parties. The obligation for surety of supply has thus shifted away from the pipeline companies to producer and pipeline marketing affiliates, marketing intermediaries, and to the end-users themselves. To meet these obligations, marketers and major end-users enter into various supply, transport and storage agreements.

The dominant form of gas storage is the reservoir storage facility, which cycles gas only once a year. These reservoirs require many months to fill, have inflexible withdrawal schedules, and use large amounts of cushion gas (that is, gas which saturates the physical reservoir and cannot be withdrawn). For many intermediaries and end-users, it is thus much more efficient to use the forward markets to create synthetic storage than to develop production area reservoirs or to acquire such storage facilities.

The forward markets can be used to manage seasonal price differences. However, until recently it was not possible to manage the exposure of intra-month price movements using financial swap contracts. Intra-month spot market price volatility is typically higher than that of the prompt month Nymex contract prior to its settlement. This intra-

Table A. Characteristics of natural gas storage facilities

Type	Cushion to working gas ratio	Injection period	Withdrawal period	Injection/withdrawal flexibility
acquifer	2:1	7–8 months	2–3 months	Low
reservoir	2:1	7–8 months	2–3 months	Low
salt dome	1:2	20–40 days	10–20 days	High

not respond to customer demands quickly or consistently. Dynamic portfolio management is the process of managing a "mismatched" portfolio of maturity, location, product and grade risks. It demands an understanding of the dynamics of the forward price curve of all those products for which the intermediary makes markets. The intermediary must also understand how exogenous factors may affect the curve, and the relationships between the curves.

For instance, location basis (price differential) risk between various pipeline indices is seasonally dependent, as the demand for gas varies significantly between market areas throughout the year. When pricing long-term transactions (that is, 10 years or more) where the basis risk is borne by the intermediary, market illiquidity means that the intermediary must consider the impact of pipeline expansions, reserve development, alternative fuels and electrical "wheeling". The relationships between the forward curves of energy products are not obvious: for example, natural gas liquids (NGLs) prices are more closely related to the price of crude products than they are to the price of natural gas. This means that an intermediary active in the NGLs market must have a good understanding of the crude and product market, and

month price risk is likely to increase in the future, as production and pipeline industries operate at higher and higher utilisation rates, making the marketplace more susceptible to pricing disruptions.

In order to meet the increasing need for flexibility in intra-month and intra-day gas supplies, facilities that store natural gas in salt caverns, known as "salt domes", have increasingly been developed – about 60% of new storage projects are of this type.

Salt-dome storage facilities can be filled and emptied up to 12 times a year, and require much less cushion gas than traditional facilities. The speed of the recycle period and the withdrawal flexibility mean that salt-dome storage can be used for meeting peak-day and even peak-hour demand.

Enron began offering financially settled swap and option contracts to protect customers against intra-month price swings in 1993. Two of these products are the Gas Daily Swap and Omicron. In the case of the Gas Daily Swap, the fixed price can be set well in advance of the beginning of the month, or it can take the form of a first-of-the-month index such as that published by IFGMR. The difference between the fixed price and the average of the reported daily prices for gas over the month is settled at the end of the month.

Omicron is the term Enron uses to define a strip of daily-settled options. Like the Gas Daily Swap, the strike price can be fixed and known well in advance of the beginning of the month, or the strike can be the first-of-the-month index. The customer can settle the contract financially, receiving the difference between the strike price and the daily price of gas, or they can settle physically by delivering or receiving gas priced at the strike price for the option. Omicron can also be structured as a series of contingent daily-settled options; the customer can exercise these on any day that they choose, but is limited to a known fixed number of option exercises during the month.

The shift in the type and location of storage facilities make it more difficult for risk managers to interpret the impact of changes in storage capacity, and calculations concerning storage utilisation, on the forward market. The development of salt-dome storage within market areas and the abandonment of production-area reservoir storage facilities means that total working gas storage capability will appear to be declining in volume. But, to the contrary, the ability of the natural gas delivery system to meet peak load demand will be growing.

Table B. Impact of salt-dome projects on daily deliverability of natural gas

Market areas	Salt-dome projects as % of new projects	% increase in daily deliverability of natural gas
Production area	75	75
West Coast	15	56
Northeast	50	75
Midwest	30	45

ideally run a crude and crude product desk.

When managing an options book, the impact of these factors is magnified. As detailed in Chapter 7, the intermediary must also understand how to manage its exposure to changes in volatility (vega), changes in market prices (delta and gamma), the passage of time (theta), as well as other risks. Effectively managing these risks requires large investments in personnel, accounting, control and risk management functions, as well as computer systems. High price volatility and low liquidity in the dealer market for more exotic options, such as location basis, time spread, basket and IFGMR-indexed

options, requires that a market maker be prepared to dynamically manage its book against an array of market factors.

The intermediary uses offsetting transactions to manage the portfolio of risks generated by its OTC business. The natural gas futures and options market on the Nymex is the most visible and active of the markets used. Marketers also transfer risk to and from each other on the OTC-brokered market for swaps and options. The OTC market offers a fair degree of liquidity in long-dated swaps, physical transactions and basis swaps, as well as options and exchange for physicals (EFPs).

EFPs constitute the exchange of a Nymex contract for the obligation to deliver or receive gas at a specified location under a firm contract at a specified differential to the price of the exchanged futures contract. In the exchange, the party delivering the contract receives the gas, and the party receiving the contract delivers the gas. This market becomes very active prior to and during bid week as market participants seek the most economical means to sell and buy their gas.

Market outlook

The combined efforts of marketers, swap counterparties and financiers in natural gas risk management have revolutionised the gas industry. Furthermore, there are strong fundamental reasons to suppose that the natural gas risk management sector will continue to grow:

❏ natural gas usage will increase because of environmental concerns and the relative economy of gas-fired combined cycle plants in electricity generation;

❏ open access in power transmission will increase competition and reduce margins, making commodity price risk management more important for utilities;

❏ volatility in prices will continue to be high, given the increasingly fine balance between supply and demand;

❏ access to development capital will be increasingly tied to sound price risk management practices; and

❏ market participants are becoming increasingly comfortable with risk management tools and techniques.

Other changes seem already to be underway:

❏ the industry will increasingly manage risk exposures through contract structure rather than by investing in and managing physical assets;

❏ regulatory changes will allow utilities and LDCs to increase their use of risk management products; and

❏ natural gas risk management sectors will start to develop outside the United States.

The rest of this section will discuss the first two of these changes in more detail, while Panel 6 examines the third.

One major effect of the development of liquid forward markets is that forward price contracts have begun to substitute for investments in (and management of) physical assets. For instance, a producer can now use the forward basis differential market instead of entering into a long-term transport commitment. Alternatively,

end-users can lock in a summer–winter price spread by using a monthly indexed forward price contract instead of purchasing storage. In addition, gas marketers are increasingly aware that they can monetise the monthly swing capability in any firm physical contract that they hold by selling financial options.

In the post-"636" era, the pipeline companies can no longer simply pass on capital expenditure for pipelines and storage. Decisions by pipeline companies and others to invest in these assets will be dictated by the level of real economic returns that the assets can generate. Proof of this structural change can be seen in the capacity brokering (the buying and selling of various types of transport capacity) that has recently started to take place. This developing market can be used to manage existing transport commitments, to provide alternatives in managing physical delivery commitments, and for price discovery and hedging when making capital investment decisions.

The nature of the storage business is also changing, as investment shifts away from production area reservoir facilities and towards market area salt dome facilities. As discussed in Panel 5, these storage fields are being developed to serve an important market need: peak load demand within market areas. This need will increase in the future as the industry operates at an ever-tighter supply/demand equilibrium.

In the current US regulatory environment, LDCs and utilities have little economic incentive to engage in risk management activities on behalf of their customers. It is widely held that if a programme was implemented that was not pre-approved by the appropriate regulatory authority, any "benefits" from hedging would accrue to ratepayers, while any "losses" would be borne by shareholders. However, over the past year, many state Public Utility Commissions (PUCs) have become more favourably disposed towards the use of risk management tools by regulated utilities. In California, San Diego Gas & Electric and Southern California Gas have each been approved for Gas Cost Incentive Mechanisms (GCIMs), which share the economic risks and benefits of purchasing performance between shareholders and customers; monthly spot-indexed prices are used as the performance benchmarks. A key component of these GCIMs is that the PUC has waived its right to make any "hindsight review" of gas procurement methodologies.

While the GCIMs are based on monthly spot

THE UNITED KINGDOM: A DEVELOPING MARKET

Louise Kitchen, Enron Capital & Trade Resources – Europe

The North American market for natural gas price risk management is by far the most advanced in the world. Outside North America, the gas market in the United Kingdom, which is in the process of being liberalised, offers the most interesting prospects for new risk management solutions.

The differences between the UK market and that of North America are immense: the UK consumes, on average, only about 6 billion cubic feet daily, compared to a North American consumption of at least 60 billion cubic feet. Futhermore, the United Kingdom consumption is served by about only 40 active producers, who supply almost exclusively from the UK continental shelf (predominantly the North Sea). The UK gas industry is presently undergoing a period of dramatic change brought about by the liberalisation of the on-shore natural gas market; these changes will bring with them increased levels of uncertainty and volatility.

Traditionally, to safeguard development capital, producers have entered into "life of field" (dedicated depletion) contracts at fixed base prices that escalate in accordance with a basket of indices, and which incorporate high levels of "take or pay" (that is, where the buyer agrees to pay for a quantity of gas, whether or not it is taken). Such indices have typically incorporated Producer Price Index (PPI) and the price of selected oil products, although the advent of new buyers in the market, particularly the power generators, has led to an increase in the use of wider baskets of indices (electricity, retail price index, etc)

As producers have tended not to develop fields unless the gas was already committed for delivery, they have not been heavily exposed to shifts in the future price of gas. Furthermore, both the producers indirectly, and users directly, gained a level of security (albeit with the inefficiencies that a monopoly controlled market provides) from British Gas which, as operator of the on-shore transportation system, acted as a supplier of last resort and provided a "balancing" mechanism for third-party shippers. (That is, British Gas used its supply portfolio to make sure that the input of gas into the gas transportation system matched the output.) As a result, no significant spot market has developed in the United Kingdom during the initial years of market liberalisation and, to date, no reliable gas index has evolved.

The Monopolies and Mergers Commission (MMC) would clearly like to see a more competitive market develop. The MMC report of October 1993 recommended a number of steps which needed to be taken in order to establish a competitive framework prior to the opening up of the entire UK natural gas market to competition. The envisaged date for the limited reduction of British Gas' residential franchise was April 1, 1997, with a review of the situation at the turn of the century. The reduction would allow a further tranche of the British Gas monopoly – those customers consuming between 1,500 and 2,500 therms per annum at a single site – to be opened up to competitive supply.

The MMC also recommended the divestment of British Gas' trading division. The President of the Board of Trade was keen to open the domestic market earlier, and proposed removing the monopoly threshold from April 1, 1996, with full competition for all non-domestic users and gradual competition for domestic customers. The intent is now to open a sample geographical area to full competition (equating to 5% of the residential market). The President also supported the need for divestment, but as this would interfere with the early opening-up of the market, British Gas was instead required to establish "Chinese walls" between its trading, and transportation and storage, divisions.

The MMC also recommended that a "Network Code" (the rules governing all shippers) should be implemented (the implementation date being October 1, 1995 at the time of writing) to ensure that an equitable operating regime is applied to all parties transporting natural gas through the British Gas transportation system. When the Network Code is implemented, those companies transporting gas will be required to match their system inputs (gas purchases) to their consumption on a daily basis at all exit points of the system (this is known as "daily balancing"). The balancing mechanism will provide a key stimulant for the market, as market players shall be able to bid in their available "flexibility" (additional gas supply, and interruptible gas demand). The list of those bids accepted will be published and could – theoretically – provide the market with a daily value for gas, although the primary purpose of the flexibility market will be to satisfy the operational requirements of the system on the day.

At the time of going to press, the exact nature of the balancing mechanism is being actively debated. According to British Gas proposals, the balancing mechanism will serve the sole purpose of balancing the system. A counter-proposal from within the industry, which has gained considerable support, maintains that while system balancing should be the primary objective of the flexiblility market, the role of the market should naturally expand to facilitate a variety of transactions including shipper-to-shipper trades. The idea behind this proposal is that both commercial trading and operational balancing markets could co-exist within the same framework.

The daily prices resulting from the daily balancing mechanism will not, however, produce forward prices for gas. (Indeed, one of the criticisms levelled at the British Gas proposal is that it will hinder the development of a forward market.) Transparent forward prices will only become available as gas market liquidity increases. With this increased liquidity, the need for and the ability to undertake risk management by marketers, producers and consumers will grow. The development of the US natural gas industry (see main text) illustrates that when liquid spot, forward and system-balancing markets have evolved it will no longer be necessary for markets to commit to dedicated field contracts, or for producers to secure investments through long-term take-or-pay contracts.

The continuing growth of the role of the gas marketing companies and other intermediaries in the United Kingdom, in terms of both the new transportation regime and the development of a spot market, means that it is likely that a forward market for natural gas will develop. The 30 or so active gas marketing companies in existence at the time of writing can be divided into four main groups according to their backers:
❏ producers;
❏ regional electricity distribution companies;
❏ those with electricity generator shareholdings (which would include Enron); and
❏ those companies which are independent.

Some market players doubt that a liquid forward market can develop in a market limited to the United Kingdom. However, an "interconnector" between the United Kingdom (at Bacton) and the Continent (at Zeebrugge, Belgium) is committed for start-up in 1998. This would generate greater supply security through supply diversity for the United Kingdom, but also increase market efficiency and facilitate the development of a more liquid spot market – especially when the Continental gas markets are liberalised.

Already, participants in the United Kingdom are actively hedging the risks inherent in the escalation factor of their gas contracts. For example, companies both on-shore and off-shore with fixed-priced contracts that escalate according to a formula including gasoil, can hedge the gasoil component of their escalation in order to remove a risk element from the gas price. Portfolio adjustments and enhancements regarding term and quantity weighting are also being pursued via a number of mechanisms (including physical swaps).

The risk of meeting the delivery requirements of their portfolio of customers on days of high national demand – which may expose companies to the price of gas supplied by British Gas as supplier of last resort ("back-up gas") – is also being addressed by some shippers. One way of managing this risk is to purchase physical option contracts: for example, a shipper would purchase call options and would be provided with additional flexibility on given days of the year.

These activities represent only a fraction of the risk that could face market players over the next few years. Whether the market develops out of a spot market based on daily prices discovered by means of the flexibility market, or by some more circuitous route, depends on discussions between the regulator, British Gas and industry participants during 1995. But it is clear that the changes will bring risk and volatility with them, and that tools will be needed to manage these changes – whether these are instruments familiar from other sectors of energy risk management, or some completely new strand of tools of both a physical and financial nature.

standards, a number of other LDCs and utilities are using intermediate- to long-term fixed-price gas contracts to build gas portfolios which lessen the effects of term volatility on their customers. In Texas, Houston Lighting & Power (HL&P) has been active in both short- and long-term fixed price transactions, using the well-reasoned argument that a disciplined portfolio approach to gas procurement is the most prudent approach. Many other LDCs, specifically in the Midwest and Northeast, are also actively building price portfolios by procuring physical supply packages which possess risk-mitigating pricing structures.

As regulators take a more enlightened approach to portfolio purchasing, these LDC and utility markets could become the largest users of natural gas risk management products. However, there is the risk that many PUCs will remain conservative in their views. If progressive views do prevail, there is still a risk that the PUCs will prefer a spot standard rather than a longer-term portfolio approach for procurement practices, which may artificially limit the term of any financial products that are used.

1 *1993 revenues for production, gathering, transportation, distribution and marketing. US DOE "Natural Gas Monthly", December 1994; AGA, "Gas Fax", 1994.*

2 *Energy Information Administration Annual Outlook for US Electrical Power, 1991.*

3 *Contractually, these transactions are termed Baseload Firm, Baseload Interruptible, and Swing. Market jargon is "firm", "baseload" and "swing", respectively.*

4 *Operations which purchase natural gas often vary in the amount of gas they actually need each day. However, the amount of gas entering a physical gas transportation system must be kept roughly equal to the amount being drawn out,* *or the integrity of the system is threatened. Thus "balancing" operations are used to adjust for the excess or underage of gas used.*

5 *"Natural Gas Trends: North America", Cambridge Energy Research Associates, 1994, p 23.*

6 *Enron Outlook, 1992.*

7 *"Shareholders Applaud Risk Management"*, Corporate Finance, *June/July, 1992.*

8 *Comments of Enron Gas Services Corp., Notice of Inquiry and Request for Public Comments: State Policies Affecting Natural Gas Consumption, US DOE.*

11

The UK Electricity Market

James Hoare
GNI Ltd

The unique physical attributes of electricity, and the heavy regulation of its supply and sale, have in the past prevented this form of energy from being traded in open markets. This situation is now beginning to change across the world – and the electricity market in the United Kingdom is in the forefront of developments. The aim of this chapter is to explain to an international derivatives audience how and why electricity derivatives have developed in the United Kingdom, and to look towards the role that these derivatives will play in a fully deregulated marketplace. We will also examine, in a separate panel, some parallel developments in the electricity markets of the United States.

The privatisation of the UK electricity supply industry (ESI) in 1990 resulted in a new market in physical electricity – the "pool" – in which generating companies, suppliers and large users buy and sell quantities of electricity. However, because of the difficulty of storing electricity, pool prices can vary substantially. There have been instances where prices have fallen to below £5.00 per megawatt hour (MWh) for short periods, while on other occasions prices have risen to over £250.00 per MWh.

The exposure caused by this volatility is managed through the use of over-the-counter (OTC) derivative instruments, in particular "Contracts for Difference" (CFDs), which are used extensively between the generators and the Regional Electricity Companies (RECs) who act as suppliers. The CFDs generally take the form of large, tailored swaps and cover approximately 75% of the current electricity consumption of England and Wales – equivalent to around £5 billion per annum.

Shortly after privatisation, the RECs saw a need to fine-tune the contract portfolio that the government had put in place. They realised that they needed a short-dated and more flexible instrument to manage their exposure to pool price, and the Electricity Forward Agreement (EFA) was designed to meet this need. EFAs offer standardised terms and may be used to hedge or trade pool prices; an EFA broker coordinates the trading, and a network of price screens helps to make trading EFAs more transparent than trading CFDs. The EFA market is primarily used by the generating companies, the RECs and certain large users of electricity, but it is open to any company that wishes to participate.

Structure of the electricity industry

When the electricity supply industry was privatised in 1990, the twelve area boards of England and Wales became the individual Regional Electricity Companies. Their role is to act as electricity suppliers and to maintain the low voltage networks in their region.

According to the original plan, the United Kingdom's electricity would have been generated by three separate privatised companies, but the difficulty in assessing the costs of de-commissioning nuclear reactors meant that all nuclear generation plant was withdrawn from the privatisation programme shortly before the flotation date. The majority of this plant is operated by Nuclear Electric, while British Nuclear Fuels, the nuclear reprocessing organisation, has two sites of its own. Both these companies remain in the public sector. The two major privatised generating companies are National Power (about 35% of generation) and Powergen (about 26%). A number of independent companies have entered the generating market since privatisation, and these are now contributing a significant proportion of generating capacity. Finally, the high voltage grid that links generating sets to regional centres of demand is run by the National Grid Company (NGC), which is owned by the RECs.

As described briefly above, a physical market for electricity, known as the pool, was established at the time of privatisation. This market is vital to the operation of the industry. All large generators are obliged to sell their output into the pool, while the RECs (and large industrial users if they wish) buy from the pool. The pool exists merely as a set of procedures and rules that enable the most economic generating sets to be operated to meet national demand at any one time. It also sets a market price for electricity for each half-hour of each day.

The industry is regulated by The Office of Electricity Regulation (OFFER), which has the task of encouraging competition in those areas of the industry where such competition will bring benefits to the users, such as generation, while protecting the interests of small electricity consumers in those areas where monopolies still exist, such as the RECs' franchise on distribution and retail supply. This task is difficult and has been further frustrated by the political need to support the UK coal industry, whose principal customers are the electricity generating companies.

In Scotland, the situation is different from England and Wales, as the industry is split between two vertically integrated privatised companies – Scottish Power and Scottish Hydro Electric – which each act as a generator, supplier and distributor. Scottish Nuclear remains in the public sector. This chapter will focus on the situation in England and Wales.

Supply and demand

Electricity demand varies according to many factors. Daylight loads are higher than night loads, while usage at weekends is less than during weekdays. There are also seasonal variations and occasional demand spikes caused by other factors, such as television schedules. In the longer term, upturns in economic activity are reflected in increased electricity usage. Peak national demand normally occurs during winter weekdays between 17:00 – 17:30 hours and can reach 48GW, while demand can drop to 16GW on a warm day in the summer (see Fig. 1). NGC forecasts that there will be a gradual increase in peak demand during this decade, and predicts a peak of 54GW by the year 2000.

To service the differing levels of demand, generators use plant that may be classified into three main groups. Continuously operating (or base load) plant is characterised by high capital costs, but relatively low running costs; plant with lower utilisation has lower capital costs, but progressively higher running costs; and plant that operates for only a few hours each year to service peaks in demand (known in the industry as "peak lopping plant") has the lowest capital costs but the highest running costs.

At present, total generating capacity exceeds 60GW, with a further 18GW of power generation projects notified to come on line by the year 2000. The majority of these new generating sets are combined cycle gas turbines (CCGTs), although a new PWR nuclear reactor of 1,254MW is scheduled to be commissioned shortly. It is probable that some of these projects will not be constructed and it should be remembered that National Power and Powergen are pursuing a programme of closure of older coal-burning plant.

The generating capacity in the pool is supplemented by supply connections with Scotland and France. These interconnectors provide for an exchange of power across these borders, but in practice, the flow is always *into* the pool as generating costs in Scotland and France are cheaper. (Hydro-electric power is plentiful in Scotland, while nuclear power is available at competitive prices from France.) The French interconnector is 2,000MW, and in 1995 the Scottish link will be upgraded to 1,600MW (from 850MW).

NGC also owns and runs two pumped storage sites in Wales with a total capacity of 2,088MW. These systems pump water into hillside reservoirs during periods of low-priced electricity; the water is then allowed to run back down the hillside, driving turbines, during periods of peak demand. The system is approximately 80% efficient and has an important balancing effect on pool prices. NGC Pump Storage bids and offers into the pool as a generator, but also acts as an immediate reserve to the system because of its ability to respond quickly in the event of a system failure.

Competition in generation over the four years since privatisation has substantially altered

1. Seasonal differences in daily demand profiles

the generating mix in terms of fuel type, as is illustrated in Figure 2.

The benefits of privatisation are percolating through to electricity consumers. A user of more than 100KW has been able to choose his supplier since April 1, 1994, and can negotiate an individual agreement. About 50,000 sites fall into this category, and these users can either accept the standard tariff from their host REC, negotiate an alternative fixed-price supply agreement with any other supply company or generator, or buy direct from the pool. Combinations are also possible whereby a user may agree to accept the pool price, but also negotiate a price cap with a supply company. In 1998, the RECs will lose their franchise customers and all users will be free to "shop around" for their electricity supply.

The electricity pool

The electricity pool was introduced when the industry was privatised in order to facilitate the bulk trading of physical electricity between generators and suppliers. In order to appreciate the mechanism, it is important to identify the key characteristics of electricity that set it apart from most other commodities. First, because electricity is difficult to store, it is necessary to constantly match generation with demand. Second, on an integrated system, it is not practical to trace the supply of electricity from particular generators to particular suppliers. Third, the variation in demand, together with the variation in generating capacity, gives rise to enormous volatility in price.

All of the electricity supplied in England and Wales is presently required to be traded through the pool, except when industrial users elect to generate their own electricity on-site.

Prices in the electricity pool are set 24 hours in advance for every half-hour of the day. The pool price consists of three principal components:
❑ System Marginal Price (SMP);
❑ a payment to reward capacity;
❑ and an uplift payment to cover transmission losses and sundry expenses (see below).

The generators' income consists mainly of the Pool Purchase Price (PPP), which is the SMP plus the capacity payment. Suppliers pay Pool Selling Price (PSP), which consists of the PPP plus the uplift payment.

The procedure for setting pool prices is complex, and begins with NGC forecasting the national demand for the day ahead (taking into

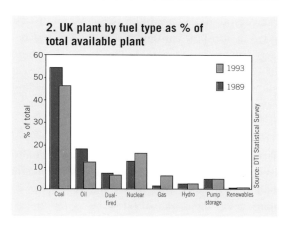

2. UK plant by fuel type as % of total available plant

Source: DTI Statistical Survey

account current weather patterns and historical data). Each generator then submits offers to the grid operator for each of the generating sets that it owns. The generator's offers detail the price at which it is prepared to produce power, the operating characteristics of its plant and the availability of that plant for the next 24 hours. (To avoid confusion, practitioners from other markets should be aware that this process of offering plant is known in the industry as "bidding-in".)

NGC then uses a computer-based algorithm to reconcile their forecasted national demand with the data received from the generators. This produces the "unconstrained schedule", which gives, in simple terms, the lowest price, or System Marginal Price, at which sufficient generation can be scheduled to meet demand for each half-hour of the day. In reality, the process is complicated, as the algorithm must accommodate the different characteristics of generating plants. A coal or nuclear set will have high start-up and shut-down costs, but will be relatively cheap to run. Conversely, an open-cycle gas turbine can be called on-line immediately for a low start-up cost, but will be expensive to operate. The computerised system must identify the most economic method overall of meeting national demand.

NGC also calculates the generating capacity of the pool for each half-hour, in order to provide the market with an indication as to the generating plant that will need to be constructed for the future. At times of low demand and high availability of generation, the capacity element is zero; it increases as demand rises towards the point where there may be insufficient generating capacity.

Capacity is calculated as:

$$LOLP \times (VLL - SMP)$$

Where LOLP is the loss of load probability calculated by NGC for each half-hour (a number between 0 and 1), and VLL is the Value of Lost Load, a constant currently set at £2,345 and rising with price indexation. The long-term value of capacity should be relatively stable, since it should represent the incremental cost of adding capacity to the system, but in the short term the pool value of capacity can be extremely volatile. The SMP plus the capacity provides the Pool Purchase Price; all generators who are required by NGC to generate to meet demand for any half hour receive this same rate, regardless of the level of their original offers.

The uplift element of the pool price is a cost designed to cover transmission losses, ancillary services, the cost of providing reserve generating capacity, and the differences entailed in scheduled and actual operation (for instance, overcoming constraints in the grid and responding to unforecasted demand). PPP plus uplift yields the Pool Selling Price, which is the cost of electricity ex-grid for a supplier. Uplift prices are not normally volatile – although they have moved noticeably over the last year as areas of the grid are upgraded. Uplift currently adds around 8% to PPP.

Pool prices are calculated on every day of the year and provisional prices are published in the national press. Settlement is a continuous process through NGC, and payments are due 28 days after the date of generation.

Figure 3 illustrates how the components of the pool price contributed to volatility during a typical winter weekday in 1992, while Figure 4 traces a weekly average price for continuous electricity consumption (baseload) since the pool began in April 1990.

The CFD market[1]

The Contract for Difference, or CFD, is in essence a simple arrangement. In return for an option fee, the seller of the contract agrees to pay to the buyer the difference between pool price and the contract exercise price in each settlement period (half-hour) when the pool price exceeds the exercise price. In many formulations the difference payments may also be made in the opposite direction, that is, whenever the pool price is below the exercise price. If a CFD operates at times when a generator is producing electricity for the pool, or a supplier has a demand for pool electricity, then the contract effectively swaps the pool price for the contract price.

As described earlier in this chapter, the market for CFDs was born out of necessity when the electricity supply industry was privatised. At March 31, 1990, virtually all of the expected output of the successor generating companies was hedged through CFDs that were negotiated bilaterally with the successor supply companies. Today, the position is somewhat different, and a small but significant proportion of electricity is traded through the pool without any associated hedging.

CFDs typically have a term of one or two years, but in cases where a generator has made a long-term fuel purchase arrangement then contracts can be for longer periods. The coal-backed CFDs put in place on March 31, 1990, when the electricity industry was privatised, covered a period of three years, whereas those recently concluded between the major fossil generators and British coal producers have a term of five years. For some newly established generating companies with CCGT (combined cycle gas turbine) plant, and associated gas purchase contracts and financing arrangements, the CFDs may extend for up to 15 years.

As financial instruments (and thus subject to the provisions of the Financial Services Act), CFDs can be traded independently of the production or consumption of electricity. Generating and supply companies have tended to use CFDs for hedging rather than specula-

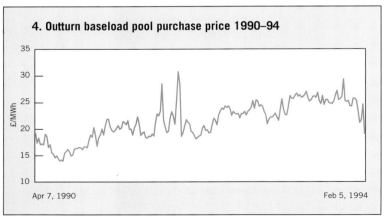

3. Components of pool price on winter weekday

UPLIFT
CAPACITY
SMP

£/MWh — Time of day

4. Outturn baseload pool purchase price 1990–94

£/MWh

Apr 7, 1990 — Feb 5, 1994

PANEL 1

THE HISTORY OF THE CFD AND EFA MARKET: SOME CRITICAL COMMENTS

Liz Wright, Southern Electric

When the generating companies first began to sell CFDs to the RECs in 1990 (see main text), these contracts bore little resemblance to a financial risk instrument. They were more akin to actual purchase contracts from specified generating plant. In effect, the CFDs passed on most of the fuel risk and operating risk of plants to the RECs.

Furthermore, PowerGen and National Power were the main source of these contracts, and thus were in a very powerful position. It followed that the contracts were large, inflexible and expensive and offered little scope for renegotiation. The situation was clearly a very lucrative one for the generators, but was unlikely to be sustained.

As most of the generators' income was guaranteed via CFDs, the level of the price in the pool was not critical to them. The pool was simply used as a means of despatch for generating plant, and the bid prices bore little relation to the cost of running that plant. With the overcapacity of plant in the electricity supply industry, it also became apparent that the pool capacity element (LOLP) would not remunerate the generators for the fixed costs of their older plant.

This meant that the prices that were being charged for CFDs would not be reflected in the pool. To counter this, the generators attempted to exploit shortcomings in the pool mechanism by bidding strategically so that their income was supplemented by the uplift element (see main text) in the pool price. As a result, the profile of prices in the pool bore little relationship to the demand for electricity. Even after this manipulation – which resulted in several referrals to the Regulator – pool prices fell short of the high CFD prices.

The RECs, meanwhile, remained convinced of the usefulness of CFDs, but saw an urgent need for more competition. They lobbied to set up a brokered OTC market based on a financial swap contract rather than an electricity purchase contract and, not wishing to be excluded, the generators agreed to cooperate.

The start of the EFA market was even slower than had been anticipated. One problem was that some RECs regarded the market as essentially speculative, and their internal procedures for those using the market were often more rigorous than those needed for the larger CFDs. Also, a number of RECs did not have systems in place which could analyse their demand requirements down to the four-hour timeslots used in the EFA market.

However, when Morgan Stanley, Phibro and Marc Rich joined, they competed with the generators, injected liquidity into the market, offered more flexible contracts, and introduced novel hedging techniques. With the arrival of these newcomers, the true potential of the market has become apparent.

At present, the volume of CFDs traded is relatively low. There are three main reasons for this:
❏ the regulatory formula for the RECs' remaining franchise market allows some of the pool price risk to be passed on to customers (within specified limits);
❏ the large volume of British coal-backed CFDs between the generators and the RECs has reduced the additional number of CFDs which needs to be traded;
❏ the generators recent undertaking with the Regulator on pool price levels in itself provides a partial hedge to pool prices.

However, all these considerations are due to disappear in 1998, when the EFA market will surely become the focus for a large proportion of CFD and derivative products trading.

The future of the EFA market is discussed in detail in Panel 3.

tion. Recently, however, some companies from outside the electricity supply industry have started to trade CFDs – an essential development if the market is to become more liquid.

At the moment, however, the vast majority of CFDs are negotiated bilaterally between generators and supply companies. These companies have looked to match the cover afforded by various forms of CFD to the envelope of exposure they face in the physical market known as

the pool. Contracts thus will relate to:
❑ the System Marginal Price (SMP);
❑ the capacity component of the pool price (LOLP × (VOLL−SMP));
❑ the uplift payment; or
❑ any combination of these.

In fact most CFDs relate to Pool Purchase Price (PPP), which is the sum of the energy (SMP) and capacity components of pool price, since this is the common risk shared by generators and suppliers. On occasion, uplift costs have also been included, so that the CFD becomes a hedge against the Pool Selling Price (PSP). In some formulations the components of PPP are treated separately because the incidence of LOLP is so uncertain that, for PPP contracts that have a low ratio of peak to average cover over the year, a common view between the contracting parties of the value and incidence of pool capacity may be difficult to achieve. In a PPP contract where the components are hedged separately, the capacity cover will equate with the peak SMP cover, but otherwise will usually be greater than the SMP cover provided.

CFDs can be considered in two generic groups: "stacking contracts" and "time-dependent" contracts. Stacking contracts rank the half hourly pool prices over the contract billing period in a "stack" of descending price order before the contract operates. Thus, if the contract applies only to a sub-set of the half-hours in the billing period, then these will be determined from their position in the stack. In this case it will not be apparent until the end of the billing period which half-hours have been covered by the contract. The entitlements in a time-dependent contract are simply a function of the time of day, day of the week, or season of the year. The contract's operation is thus apparent as time progresses.

The contracts put in place at privatisation were based mainly on stacking arrangements, but the financial consequences of unforeseen pool price glitches (short-duration price spikes), have led to the generating companies offering CFDs that are based predominantly on parameters linked to time. In practice, stacking contracts may be more appropriate for covering the output of generating plant that will only generate for short periods at times of highest demand, or the demands of suppliers with their own load management capabilities. For average utilisations the times of day variants tend to prove more effective in achieving a hedge.

One reason that stacking contracts may have fallen from favour for the majority of CFDs is their relative complexity. However, in some circumstances they offer more versatility than time-related forms. Their general features include monthly billing cycles, limits on the monthly and annual call that can be placed on the contract, and periods during which the contract operation is excluded. The first five subsections below describe some of the forms that have been employed in the new market, and then we move on to look at time-dependent and other forms of CFDs.

TWO-WAY STACKING CFD (FIG. 5)
The simplest of the stacking contract forms, this contract type stacks Pool SMP or PPP in descending order of price over the half hourly periods covered by the contract. The contract has an option fee, usually paid monthly, and an exercise price. The contract is "called" whenever the pool price is above the exercise price. Difference payments, calculated from the product of the contract amount in each half-hour period and the difference between the exercise price and the pool price, are paid by the seller to the buyer. Conversely, the contract is "put" when the pool price is below the exercise price. At these times the buyer pays the seller the difference payment. The contract can cover all hours or exclude certain periods such as nights and non-business days. The relationship between the option fee and exercise price is relatively arbitrary, since the total worth of the contract, which will reflect an expectation of future pool prices and any risk premium that is judged appropriate, will be the sum of the option fee and the exercise price.

ONE-WAY STACKING CFD (FIG. 6)
Similar in form to the two-way version, the one-

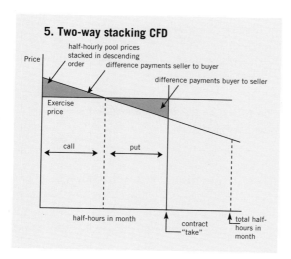

5. Two-way stacking CFD

way stacking CFD can only be called, and the associated difference payments made to the buyer, whenever the price in the stack is above the exercise price in the contract. The value of the option fee depends crucially on the level of the contract exercise price, and will reflect expectations about the level and distribution of the difference between the pool and contract exercise price.

MIN AND MAX TAKES (FIG. 7)

A composite of the previous two types, this arrangement has a minimum and maximum take that is identified with the contract period. The contract operates as a two-way option up to the minimum take, when the contract is either called or put in each settlement half-hour depending upon whether the pool price is above or below the exercise price. In half-hours identified as being between the minimum and maximum take, the contract will operate as a one-way option, allowing the contract to be called if the pool price is above the exercise price. In this configuration it is usual for a second exercise price to apply to this part of the contract period.

CAPACITY-ONLY CFD (FIG. 8)

Despite the fact that the capacity element of the pool price is the most volatile, and under certain circumstances could theoretically reach extreme levels, capacity-only CFDs have so far been employed only relatively infrequently. The apparent interaction between the level of pool LOLP and SMP bidding behaviour encourages suppliers to hedge both components of pool price simultaneously. Where they are required, capacity-only contracts can be structured as a one-way option against $LOLP \times (VOLL - SMP)$ with a zero exercise price. Essentially, the seller agrees to reimburse all the buyer's pool capacity costs in return for the option fee.

INVERTED STACKING CFD (FIG. 9)

Typically, this form of contract operates in the same manner as a two-way option against PPP, as described above, but excludes the periods in which the price is highest. It is assumed that in these hours the buyer will be able to interrupt their consumption of electricity, thus avoiding high pool prices, and hence the need for the cover.

TIME-DEPENDENT CONTRACTS (FIG. 10)

Generally, both generators and suppliers have

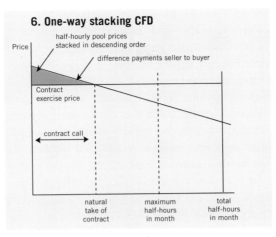

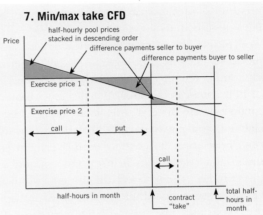

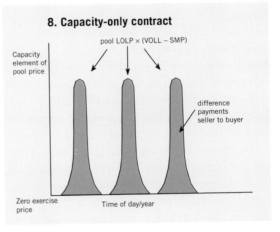

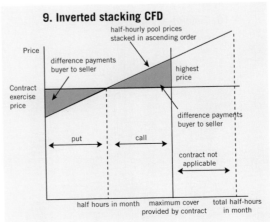

found it easier to predict the pattern of their electricity output and demand with reference to time than to the level of pool price, so that time-related contracts (Fig. 10) are the most commonly used.

The contract form is usually structured as a two-way option, with the difference payments being made in either direction depending upon whether the pool price is above or below the exercise price. In this fashion the contract effectively swaps the pool price for the contract price. The contract can operate either as a hedge against PPP or against SMP. In the latter case, a separate part of the contract will comprise an associated capacity hedge along the lines described above.

Typically, the contract quantities vary according to the season and the time of day. A separate option fee may be included, but in the case of PPP contracts the usual practice is to have a single exercise price. This is likely to have been derived from an expectation of the shape of pool price over the contract term, weighted by the contract quantities in each time period of the contract. Time periods in the contract can be based on standard intervals of time, perhaps the same as those in the EFA structure, or sculpted to reflect changes in the level of cover required.

PLANT-RELATED CFDS

Generally, there is no relationship between CFDs and the physical output of plant or the demand for electricity (other than that implied in the hedging policy a generator or supplier may be following). However, in the case of CFDs backed by the output from a single plant, the CFD may include clauses that link its application to the physical availability of the plant. In these circumstances the buyer is likely to impose conditions that increase the likelihood of the output being available at times when the highest pool prices are expected.

PRICE INDEXATION

Contracts of relatively short duration, say up to a year, are usually based on a single exercise price since the generator can predict costs within this timescale with reasonable certainty, or hedge them (in the case of certain fuels). For longer-term contracts it is often the practice to index the exercise price and option fees to underlying costs. This is invariably the case where the fuel the generator is procuring is linked to long-term arrangements.

In these circumstances, there is the inevitable risk that the indexation of the contract will cause the contract price to move out of line with prices in the physical market. The most common risk-sharing arrangements designed to overcome this are as follows:

❏ modifying the exercise price to move proportionately with the pool price. This arrangement is often accompanied by a floor on the exercise price, but has the effect of sharing an increase in the pool price between the two contracting parties (see Fig. 11);

❏ basing the exercise price in the contract on the pool price, unless it moves outside certain bounds set by the indexation of the initial price to underlying costs. If this occurs then the indexed price becomes the exercise price (see Fig. 12);

These types of arrangement are most appropriately applied to baseload contracts. For CFDs designed to offer cover to a generator only during peak periods (for example, the one-way stacking contract described above), the exercise price may be indexed to the fuel costs of the peak-lopping plant – such as distillate oil. The idea behind such an arrangement would be to ensure that the exercise price moved in line

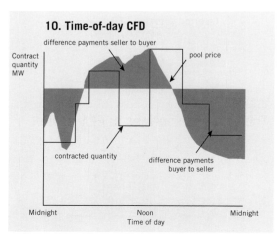

10. Time-of-day CFD

difference payments seller to buyer

Contract quantity MW

pool price

contracted quantity

difference payments buyer to seller

Midnight   Noon   Midnight
Time of day

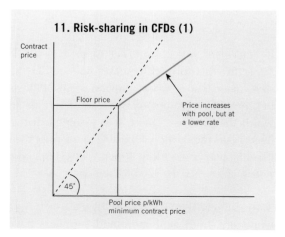

11. Risk-sharing in CFDs (1)

Contract price

Floor price

Price increases with pool, but at a lower rate

45°

Pool price p/kWh
minimum contract price

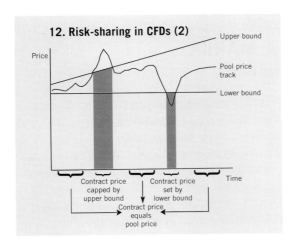

12. Risk-sharing in CFDs (2)

Price

Upper bound

Pool price track

Lower bound

Contract price capped by upper bound

Contract price set by lower bound

Time

Contract price equals pool price

with fuel costs, thus stabilising the volume of the contract. However, if the pool price at these times moves in line with fuel prices, because the bids made by generators reflect movements in their marginal costs, then such indexation will inadvertently create an exposure to fuel prices and to dollar exchange rates (which then may need to be hedged elsewhere).

The EFA market

As discussed in the previous section, the electricity derivatives market is dominated by bilateral agreements in the form of CFDs. However, soon after privatisation the industry began to feel that these instruments were too large and complex for the efficient management of price risk. A short-dated standardised mechanism would allow the fine-tuning of these large contracts, and also ameliorate any problems caused by the way in which each generator specified different contract terms on which to sell CFDs. Furthermore, those with experience in other energy markets realised that the transparency of a standardised OTC instrument would encourage interest from outside the Electricity Supply Industry, thus enhancing liquidity to the eventual benefit of all.

Discussions took place with GNI Ltd, the London-based derivatives broker, and a broking service in EFAs has been available from their offices since October 1991. Although the market is of particular benefit to the RECs and the major generators, EFAs may be used by any company to hedge or trade pool prices.

MARKET STRUCTURE

EFAs are basically swaps, and thus are similar to Contracts for Difference. They are normally two-way contracts and do not involve the payment of fees up-front. The buyer and the seller agree a forward price for the pool over a defined peri-

od in the future. If the price turns out to be greater than the agreed price, the seller compensates the buyer; if it turns out to be less, then the buyer compensates the seller. As envisaged at the outset, the majority of EFA trading (about 90%) has focused on PPP; the balance of transactions have used capacity or SMP as their reference variable.

In the EFA market, the year is divided into calendar weeks. Then, for each day forming part of a week, six four-hour trading slots have been designed to relate to the daily peaks and troughs in pool prices.

Table 1 delineates these EFA periods, and it can be seen that, because demand follows a different pattern, weekends are treated separately to weekdays. WD2 represents the low off-peak periods during a weekday between 03:00 and 07:00 hours, while WD5 covers the four hours in the early evening when demand is usually at its highest.

Contracts can be transacted to cover a minimum of a four-hour period for a whole week (20 hours) or weekend (8 hours) in units of at least 1MW, but in practice the relevant WD and WE periods are combined over a number of weeks to form larger and more effective contracts. Typically WD3, WD4 and WD5 are combined to provide daylight cover over a month (four or five weeks), the winter (weeks 40 to 13) or a whole year. Offpeak cover is also popular, usually designated in contracts covering WD1 and WD2. The EFA periods are now seldom transacted in isolation, and the framework should be viewed as a series of standardised "building blocks" with which market participants may construct the price cover that they require.

The purpose behind the concept of the four-hour EFA time period was to smooth out any very short-term spikes in the pool price, while retaining hedging effectiveness, and simultaneously condensing market activity into a manageable series of trading periods. This structure has proved successful and has been accepted throughout the industry.

Table 1. Time periods in EFA market

	Mon–Fri	Sat + Sun
23:00–03:00	WD1	WE1
03:00–07:00	WD2	WE2
07:00–11:00	WD3	WE3
11:00–15:00	WD4	WE4
15:00–19:00	WD5	WE5
19:00–23:00	WD6	WE6

USING THE EFA MARKET

Liz Wright, Southern Electric

Southern Electric regards the EFA market as a valuable tool when managing the risk that arises out of our use of the electricity pool. We know the number of customers we have, but the quantity of electricity that we sell depends on external factors such as the weather and the economy. As the year progresses, therefore, we usually want to adjust our CFD portfolio. With around £700 million a year spent on purchases from the pool, the potential swings in margins can be very high if pool price rises dramatically and remains unhedged.

The process of using the EFA market begins when we compare the hedging cover provided by the CFDs that we have entered into with our latest demand forecast. In one typical instance, the analysis revealed that we had incurred some exposure during the early night hours, around the morning peak, and especially during the early evening peak of 5.00–6.00pm.

After the analysis, we had to decide whether it would be prudent to hedge this exposure. We decided that we needed to hedge the early evening peak (which equates to time period WD5) – particularly during the winter months. But we also decided not to hedge the morning time periods (WD1 and 3) unless the cover was available at a good price.

We set about implementing these decisions by:
❑ purchasing annual baseload cover;
❑ selling summer baseload cover; and
❑ selling winter off-peak cover (WD2, 4 and 6).

The cover was eventually purchased at a price that was lower than an outright purchase of WD1, 3 and 5 in the EFA market, owing to the high volatility of prices expected at those times. Although four different counterparties were involved, by matching complementary cover and risk positions with the counterparties, a deal was constructed for peak slots at below the market price.

This was the first part of the strategy. It left us with a residual requirement, which we tried to put through the EFA market as an annually sculpted contract – that is, a contract with a customised demand profile, as opposed to a standard baseload contract. Unfortunately, the offers we received were higher than the price levels that we thought a contract of this shape was worth. We thus remained uncovered for this residual load.

As things turned out, the pool price was below both our bid and the counter offers received – so, on this occasion, remaining without cover proved fortuitous.

DOCUMENTATION AND SETTLEMENT

The "EFA Standard Terms" were agreed by the industry when the market commenced trading in 1991. These terms identify the characteristics of the transaction in general, the settlement arrangements, and procedures in the event of a default. They have not been amended or added to since that date, and they appear to be acceptable to new entrants to the market.[2]

The EFA Standard Terms provide for settlement of EFAs on a weekly basis between the two counterparties to the agreement. Settlement follows the procedures in the pool rules as closely as possible, and differences are paid 28 days after the last Friday of the relevant week. However, it is quite usual for counterparties to agree separately to a monthly settlement period, for ease of administration, on small or short-dated EFAs.

TRADING

Transacting business in the EFA market differs from agreeing CFDs, as EFA trading is conducted through a broker by telephone. Oral agreement is binding. The broker is assisted by a network of screens linked to participants on which he can broadcast details of bids and offers that are received, thus contributing to the transparency of the market.

Unlike the market in CFDs, trading in EFAs is essentially anonymous. All details to a transaction are agreed through the broker without the counterparties being aware of each other's identity during the negotiation. The trade is concluded when each party accepts the other's name as a suitable credit risk for the transaction. It is possible for a trade to fail at this late stage, although in practice the broker is usually aware of names that will not "match" and will not commence such negotiations. Upon acceptance of each other's credit risk, a contract is understood to exist between the two parties, and is settled bilaterally between them in accordance

THE FUTURE OF THE EFA MARKET: SOME CRITICAL COMMENTS

Colin Bryce, Morgan Stanley & Co International

The EFA market is – and probably always will be – a market on the margins of the electricity supply industry. This criticism will remain true for as long as the traditional "bilateral" lines of trade dominate the industry – that is, trade between generators and the regional electricity companies (RECs), and between both of these sectors and their end customers.

However, the existence of an EFA market, sending price signals from the sidelines of the electricity market, but also increasingly providing an arbitrage function, has forced the generators and the regional electricity companies to become more competitive – particularly on price.

Sending price signals – signals which the industry cannot ignore in the embryonic competitive environment – will continue to be the most critical function of the EFA market. In a market where "cost plus" has been the order of the day, the EFAs are whittling away the plus!

When the EFA market was created, it was not envisaged that it would develop in this way. As explained in the main text, its raison d'être was to provide a forum in which ex-cathedra contract cover could be fine-tuned intra-year and intra-slot. However, in 1992 and 1993, trading and risk management organisations such as Morgan Stanley, Marc Rich and Phibro Energy began to enter the market, and to make rather more dynamic assessments of value.

As a result, on more than one occasion, the EFA market has temporarily become a proxy for bilateral baseloads – and the tail has threatened to wag the dog. For example, it was via the EFA market that the first baseload trade for the 1994/5 contract round was concluded in July 1993 (at £27.25). This rapidly resulted in a further seven trades being concluded at this level on the EFA market, and a series of bilateral trades were subsequently concluded between generators and RECs. Trading and risk management organisations will continue to identify and execute transactions with a positive expected value, and thus will increasingly provide the market with value-driven liquidity.

The interesting question is whether the EFA market – in its current form as neither a futures nor a forwards market – can do more than this. The answer depends on two critical factors: one negative and one positive. On the negative side, the market is finite in size: it is a UK-based market with a small number of participants of a threshold size large enough to make meaningful trades. This will not change.

On the positive side, however, is the scope for improvement in the mechanism by which the market price is determined. Presently, price is not determined by the fundamentals. And, given this, it is difficult to contemplate managing electricity price risk on the basis of prevailing coal, oil or gas prices (even if all of these benefited from a liquid underlying market – coal and gas currently do not). However, as competition is introduced into prices on the generation side of the business, then one would expect a move away from prices based on "cost plus", towards prices more closely

with EFA Standard Terms.

Naturally, the counterparties remain confidential to the market after the transaction, and the broker merely reports to the market the price and the period covered, together with a cumulative weekly volume of trades that have taken place over the previous five days. The anonymity that the EFA market offers is becoming more important as EFAs establish themselves within the contract portfolios of RECs, generating companies, and other participants. Large generators are finding that they can act anonymously through the EFA market, whereas the face-to-face negotiations associated with CFD trading often influence the prices that they are able to obtain.

During the early history of the EFA market, trading was very subdued. The generators did not welcome the transparency that EFAs brought to trading in electricity derivatives, and chose to watch developments. The RECs exchanged small quantities of cover between themselves for individual four-hour EFA periods, but found that the volatility of the pool price, when assessed over such a short time-frame, resulted in wide differences between

reflecting short-run marginal costs (when a sizeable capacity margin exists) and long-run marginal costs (when capacity is tight).

It seems likely that there will be a moderate excess of capacity in the medium term, as plant closures will be exceeded by new CCGT capacity. It is difficult to prophesise much beyond this period, as whether further construction takes place depends on the price signal sent out by the market. At the present time, it would appear that the RECs – the traditional buyers of the long-dated contract cover that must be sold for new facility project financing to be completed – are viewing such cover almost as stranded investments. This is because the RECs have begun to worry that the termination of their legal franchise in 1998 will be more than a technicality, and that they may actually start to lose business. If they are exposed to competition, then the high-priced IPP contracts may become a millstone around their necks. The only surprise in all this is that it has taken price-capping action by the Regulator (described in the main text) to correct the price signal.

If the above forecast proves to be correct, then in the medium term we can expect electricity prices to reflect marginal operating costs more closely – perhaps with the addition, from time to time, of marginal outage costs. (These marginal outage costs approximate to the capacity element, as described in the main text.) Marginal operating costs will largely be a reflection of fuel prices, and as the market focus moves from coal towards gas, the ability of the risk manager to offset price risk in the other energy markets will be enhanced. In this circumstance, more players from outside the industry will be attracted to the EFA market, and will improve its liquidity. Eventually, expected-value trading will give way to relative-value trading.

While the market may become more attractive to players from outside the industry, it will remain a market of limited size. This is likely to prevent the electricity market becoming submerged by speculators and money managers, as has happened in the crude oil market. It also means that the EFA market is unlikely ever to dominate the electricity industry – which may be no bad thing.

The predictions outlined above are based on certain critical assumptions:
❑ that the pool will remain in its present form;
❑ that the RECs will remain in the supply business;
❑ that regulatory intervention does not become so prevalent as to be unmanageable at a realistic risk premia;
❑ and that non-captive customers will continue to want to pay a risk premium for the elimination of volatility.

Of course, certain changes in the nature of the EFA market are almost inevitable. In particular:
❑ the need for finer tuning may lead to a requirement for half-hourly (rather than four-hourly) cover facilities; and
❑ options may well become more popular as the price of short-term volatility declines.

The second prediction is based on the idea that, as volatility declines, the price of options will become more acceptable, and as prices begin to reflect short-run marginal costs, buyers will want to retain downside flexibility while protecting themselves against the risk of marginal outage costs.

It is surely true that, within the UK's particular form of real-time electricity pricing, there will be an increasing need for a liquid risk-transference mechanism. And it follows that over time this will manifest itself in a tradable term structure of prices in a limited and marginal – yet still valuable – EFA market.

bids and offers.

Gradually, the individual periods were combined to construct strips of cover over longer periods; this flattened out the volatility and gave rise to a more worthwhile contract.

Transactions then began to emerge in which all the EFA periods were taken together to form a 24-hour continuous load, which might be extended for a month, a quarter or – more typically – a year. Substantial business was achieved in these annual "baseload" contracts, and this in turn attracted the hitherto reluctant generators to the market, together with some international trading companies who use EFAs in a similar manner to other energy swap products.

More recently, the EFA market has explored other structures. Various options have been transacted – usually call options against peak periods. Options have proved to be attractive to those RECs with a residual exposure to peak pool prices, as well as to industrial users hoping to benefit from cheap prices by buying direct from the pool while at the same time looking for some insurance against volatile peak prices. Some more elaborate collar and swaption structures have been discussed, and a limited num-

THE EVOLUTION OF ELECTRICITY DERIVATIVES IN THE UNITED STATES

John Woodley, Morgan Stanley & Co

On April 1, 1988, an electric swap contract was assigned to a customer of Niagara Mohawk Power Corporation in New York. It was assigned under an innovative new pricing scheme that ensured that the customer would continue to pay the revenues stipulated by US regulation, yet faced monetary incentives to change their pattern of demand for electricity in response to hourly price signals.

On March 31, 1990, a power pool came into being in England and Wales. The retailers faced changing half-hourly price signals from the pool, but were assigned contracts for differences, or swaps, that allocated to them a portion of the cost of supporting coal price subsidies.

The two pieces of recent history outlined above seem to illustrate a common truth. Wherever competition or other forms of pricing pressure intrude, commodity pricing displays a consistent pattern: long-term contracts, a spot market and markets for intermediate term contracts. The spot market quickly becomes volatile, sometimes manifesting dramatic price movements in order to ensure that supply equals demand at all times. Meanwhile, the contract markets evolve from being a means of ensuring both certain supply and a known price, into a means of protecting both consumers and producers against the risk of spot price changes. Finally, the intermediate and short-term contracts become more and more standardised, bringing greater efficiency to the market.

As described in the main part of this chapter, the electric market in England and Wales has leapfrogged that of the United States. The stan-

dardisation of intermediate term contracts is well under way, and calls are intensifying for that most standardised of all contracts: a futures contract. In the United States, a less dramatic, but no less profound, change is in progress. The destination will be the same, even if the path is different.

The US electric market transacts 2,797TWh per year,[1] as compared with the 267TWh in England and Wales. However, the relative size of the markets in geographic terms is such that this translates to 288MWh per square km[2] in the United States and 1,767MWh per square km[3] in England and Wales – even though the United States uses twice as much electricity per person. Why is this significant? Well, one of the most intractable problems of the England and Wales pool has been the price component called "uplift". As described in the main text, this captures and allocates the costs of transmission constraints and other costs – and it has more than doubled since the pool's inception.[4] This uncontrolled rise of the uplift price component is the result of the inaccurate pricing of transmission in a geographically small area. Consider, then, the magnitude of this problem in a country the size of the United States. It is not surprising, therefore, that transmission pricing is currently consuming most of the legislative and regulatory effort devoted to restructuring the US industry.

Further frustrating restructuring efforts is the fact that most of the electricity supply industry in the United States is in private hands, and is vertically integrated. Nationalisation, restructuring and

ber have been concluded.

It should be stressed that the EFA market is still not sufficiently mature for option-modelling techniques to be employed with any degree of reliability.

In addition to generators and RECs, who use the EFA market to fine-tune and enhance their CFD portfolio, EFAs are also now being used by Independent Power Producers (IPPs). These companies own and operate generating sets, usually combined-cycle gas turbines. In order to secure finance for construction, the IPPs negotiate long-term natural gas purchase agreements for their feedstock fuel and agree corresponding-

ly long-term CFDs for the sale of their electricity with an REC. It might be assumed that this arrangement isolates an IPP from exposure to the pool price, but the plant operators look to the EFA market to buy-in cover for periods when maintenance or breakages prevent the set from generating. In effect, the existence of a short-term market enables the IPP to schedule the down-time of their plants more economically.

The future

The privatisation of the UK Electricity Supply Industry was an ambitious project. At the outset, the Government stated the dates upon which

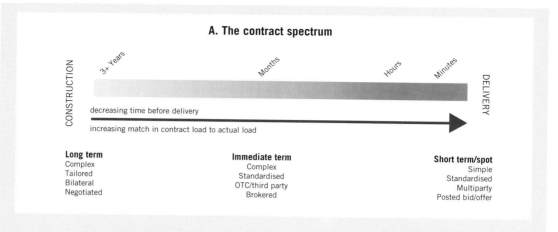

A. The contract spectrum

CONSTRUCTION

3+ Years   Months   Hours   Minutes

DELIVERY

decreasing time before delivery

increasing match in contract load to actual load

Long term
Complex
Tailored
Bilateral
Negotiated

Immediate term
Complex
Standardised
OTC/third party
Brokered

Short term/spot
Simple
Standardised
Multiparty
Posted bid/offer

reprivatising is just not an option! So, what path is the United States electricity industry likely to follow as it reshapes itself to resemble other commodity markets?

First, as I hinted in my opening sentence, we should not underestimate the extent to which the market already demonstrates derivative-like structures. For example, in 1979 the Southern Company instituted coal-by-wire sales to neighbouring oil- and gas-based utilities in response to the oil crisis. The pricing was calculated using "cost of service" criteria, as allowed and enforced by US regulations. (That is, the capital costs of the plant were passed on as a fixed cost, and each kWh sold was priced according to the unit's operating cost.) As the oil crisis passed, the pressure on prices inspired some changes. The buyers approached Southern, requesting that they should be able to replace the energy from the coal-fired plants with less expensive energy from other Southern Company plants whenever this was available. This concession was made, followed fairly quickly by a concession that allowed customers to replace the energy with *any* lower-priced energy available in the region. Diagrams B and C tell the

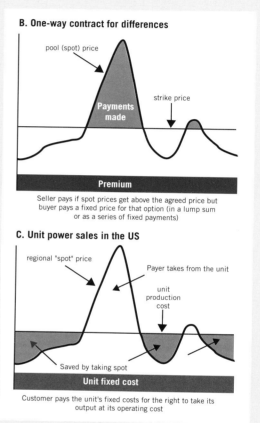

B. One-way contract for differences

pool (spot) price

strike price

Payments made

Premium

Seller pays if spot prices get above the agreed price but buyer pays a fixed price for that option (in a lump sum or as a series of fixed payments)

C. Unit power sales in the US

regional "spot" price

Payer takes from the unit

unit production cost

Saved by taking spot

Unit fixed cost

Customer pays the unit's fixed costs for the right to take its output at its operating cost

each size of electricity consumer would be free to choose their supplier. As discussed earlier, users of over 1MW were able to choose their supplier immediately after privatisation in 1990, while 100KW customers have only been able to negotiate freely since 1994. The whole market will become open in 1998, and there are various opinions about the degree of loyalty of domestic users to their host REC.

So far, this timetable has been achieved, but the market has required more regulation than was envisaged. In the early years, the pool did not operate satisfactorily, and the major generators influenced prices by taking advantage of

their dominant share of generation. This resulted in no fewer than four enquiries by the Regulator into the behaviour of pool prices and, in 1993, National Power and Powergen were on the verge of being referred to the Monopolies and Mergers Commission. In February 1994, the Regulator capped the 1994/5 and 1995/6 pool purchase price as follows: time-weighted £24.00 Mwh; national demand weighted £25.50 Mwh (at October 1993 prices).[3]

It has been difficult to establish electricity derivatives, and in particular EFAs, in a market so easily influenced by the large generators, and so vulnerable to regulatory decisions. However,

story. This highly cost-based regulated pricing structure looks suspiciously like a one-way electric forward agreement (EFA). In exchange for paying for the fixed cost of the plant, the customer has the ability to buy, at a preset price, the unit running cost, but otherwise purchases electricity at the regional economy exchange price. The unit capital cost is the equivalent of the premium attached to a one-way EFA, while the unit variable cost equates to the strike price of the one-way EFA, and the regional economy exchange price simulates the pool price. Of course, unlike EFAs, these American contracts are not tradeable.

Does it follow that the United States is but a step away from electric contract markets, derivatives and a formal futures market? Many significant players in the electricity supply industry believe this is so. At the time of writing, Nymex is planning to launch a futures contract – and their working group has already largely designed it. More than 35 potential electric brokers have registered with the Federal Energy Regulatory Commission.

In addition, the Market Management Research Program at EPRI, often at the forefront of market developments, is working with Pacific Gas & Electric on the development of electricity options contracts to facilitate the efficient trading of electricity. The initial focus of experimentation with these electricity systems will be in the Western Systems Power Pool. In April 1994, the California regulators proposed ending monopoly rights to supply electricity to large customers in the state – a move which would clear the way for new market participants.

What will the outcome be? The US gas market may provide some clues. While the Nymex natural gas futures contracts are priced at the Henry Hub in Louisiana, other hubs are priced differently. Further, a participant in the market can price, or offer to price, relative to Henry Hub or any of the other delivery points in the gas network. To offset the price risk, contracts are beginning to be offered to cover the price differentials between hubs. This suggests that, in the case of the electricity market, one should expect the creation of a localised electric power price and contracts which begin trading against a publicly available or transparent clearing price. Some substation within the Western Systems Power Pool seems a likely first candidate. Other pricing points will follow. The efficient pricing of transmission demands that power pools, separated by fully loaded transmission lines, will clear at different prices. As these markets become more robust, market makers will offer protection against the price differentials that arise between the various pools. The links between prices in each separate pool will become more transparent. New transmission and generation will be built to erode the price differentials – and the price linkages will become even more transparent.

This is speculation. But we *do* know that the infusion of competition in commodity markets creates downward pressure on prices; that heightened market activity leads to more transparent spot prices; and that, as the world's commodity markets have developed, each has spawned contracts that are of an essentially similar structure.

1 *EEI Pocketbook of Electric Utility Industry Statistics (39th edition, published 1993).*

2 *Statistical Yearbook of the United States, 1993.*

3 *Courtesy of James Hoare of GNI Ltd.*

4 *Paper by Nick Winser presented on April 14, 1994.*

the structural stability that is emerging as the market matures, and the pressure on margins brought about by competition among suppliers and generators, has seen volumes grow in the EFA market.

The catalyst to further growth in UK electricity derivatives will be the development of a similar instrument for natural gas trading. This would produce a truly integrated energy derivatives market in the UK, providing real benefits in risk management to generators, suppliers and consumers.

1 *"The CFD market". This section was kindly contributed by David Tolley of National Power.*

2 *Herbert Smith, the London-based law firm, drafted the original terms. The trading of the EFAs falls within the jurisdiction of the Securities and Futures Authority (SFA).*

3 *The indications in the first half of 1994 were that both generators were bidding plant into the pool in line with the Regulator's targets; pool prices seemed also to be exhibiting a more predictable pattern, although they remained volatile within the day.*

12

Emerging Regional Markets

Stijn Claessens and Panos Varangis
The World Bank[1]

Many developing countries, whether energy producers or importers, could benefit from improving their energy price risk management. Their traditional methods of managing exposure to energy prices have not proved satisfactory and, in the past, developing countries have made little use of energy derivatives. However, new evidence suggests that developing countries have now started to employ exchange and over-the-counter (OTC) energy risk management instruments – and that they will do so increasingly in the future.

The purpose of this chapter is to review this evidence, to state clearly the benefits that market-based risk management instruments offer to developing countries, and to analyse the main impediments to their use. We will also discuss the strategies that can be adopted to neutralise these impediments and, in various panels, describe specific instances in which derivative instruments have been successfully used to solve energy risk management problems. In our conclusion, we will try to highlight the opportunities and challenges for derivatives providers implied by the growth in emerging regional markets.

Oil price exposure in developing countries

The great majority of developing countries suffer from large energy price exposures on either exports or imports. In several developing countries, oil and fuels account for more than 90% of total export earnings. For 20 out of the 21 developing countries listed in Table 1, the oil and oil products category is the number one export-revenue earner, while for 15 countries energy exports account for over 60% of total exports.

While the dependency of several developing countries on oil exports is well documented, the significance of oil in the import bill of developing countries is less well known. Import totals

are often also influenced by energy prices, because oil and fuels account for a large share of the import bill incurred by many developing countries – particularly in the low-income group. It has been estimated that oil and products together account on average for around 12–14% of total import expenditures in developing countries. In at least 19 developing countries, oil imports accounted for 20% or more of the total import bill over the period 1984–88. Moreover, in periods of relatively high oil prices, such as during the early 1980s and during the Gulf War, oil imports accounted for over 25% of the total import bill in many developing countries (Claessens and Varangis, 1991).

The reliance on energy products in many developing countries has created a number of problems, not only for local oil export and

Table 1. Share of oil and oil products in total export revenues: selected developing countries

Country	Share (%)
Algeria	77
Colombia*	23
Congo*	73
Ecuador*	37
Gabon	60
Indonesia	17
Iran	98
Iraq	99
Kuwait	93
Libya	65
Malaysia*	6
Mexico*	32
Nigeria	98
Oman*	97
Papua New Guinea*	40
Qatar	91
Saudi Arabia	91
Syria*	47
Trinidad and Tobago*	75
United Arab Emirates	89
Venezuela	85

Source: IMF/International Financial Statistics, various issues
*Signifies non-OPEC members

import companies, but also for governments. State budgets are often heavily influenced by oil prices and, as these prices tend to be volatile, budgetary problems have arisen. In Nigeria, for example, the direct and indirect cost of the oil price decline during the early 1980s is estimated to have been equivalent to over 70% of non-oil GDP; the indirect cost alone amounted to over 20% of non-oil GDP in one year (see World Bank, 1994). For Indonesia, the ratio of debt service to exports rose from 8.2% in 1981 to 27.8% in 1987, with nearly two-thirds of this resulting from the dollar depreciation after 1985 and the fall in oil prices after 1986.

In Venezuela, oil-related revenues accounted for 78.5% of total government revenues in 1991. In addition, it was found that a 10% change in oil prices translates into a 6% change in total government revenues (see Claessens and Varangis, 1994). In the case of Trinidad and Tobago, oil-related revenues accounted for 41% of total government revenues in 1990. Here, a 10% change in oil prices translates into a 3.4% change in total government revenues. Mexico, Nigeria, Costa Rica, Brazil and Chile, among others, are also very exposed and faced enormous problems in dealing with oil price uncertainty during the period of the Gulf War (for oil importers) and during the period immediately following the Gulf War (for oil exporters).

The traditional methods used by developing countries to manage their energy price risk have not, by and large, proved successful (see World Bank, 1994; Arrau and Claessens, 1992; and Deaton, 1992). These methods include:
❑ domestic price stabilisation funds;
❑ contingent finance;
❑ reserves management; and
❑ export diversification.

Either as complements or substitutes to these approaches, market-based financial risk management techniques (such as futures, options and swaps), may significantly assist developing countries to hedge energy price risks.[2] Of course, the use of oil derivatives cannot immunise state budgets and economic plans from the impact of long-term falls in oil prices. But the effects of temporary, short-lived increases and falls in oil prices can be adequately mitigated. And even in the case of long-term movements in energy prices, oil derivatives can assist state planners to adjust to new oil price levels.

Furthermore, developing countries can link their exposure in energy prices to the form of finance used to obtain loans or to finance pro-

jects, and thus obtain this finance at more favourable terms. For example, developing countries, and companies in such countries, could sell call options on oil to reduce nominal interest costs.

In the past, some developing countries have hedged energy price risks through the use of traditional short-dated market-based instruments (futures and options). But very few developing countries have had access to the long-dated derivative instruments – such as oil swaps, long-dated options, and oil-linked bonds – which would permit a more comprehensive strategy.

Why do so few countries attempt to manage their energy price risk in this way?[3] Most importantly, the capacity to hedge has been hindered by domestic restrictions concerning access to international financial markets (mainly due to domestic institutional and legal barriers); cash-flow problems; and the low credit standing of many developing countries in global financial markets. These factors will be discussed in detail later on, as will subsidiary constraints such as:
❑ a lack of familiarity with derivatives and their strategic uses;
❑ misconceptions that confuse hedging with speculation;
❑ in the case of companies, the lack of appropriate internal controls and accounting systems;
❑ in the case of large producers, a lack of liquidity when implementing longer-term hedges; and
❑ imperfections in the correlation between spot prices and futures prices (basis risk).

Developing countries and the oil markets
The use of commodity derivative markets by developing countries is not new. Coffee and cocoa producers, for example, have used futures and options contracts extensively over the last 10–15 years (see Laughlin and Falloon, 1990). The wave of deregulation and privatisation which is spreading across developing countries, however, is bringing significant changes to the way in which commodity risk is allocated among, and managed by, the various parties in the domestic economy. Although, as Table 2 shows, the open interest in US commodity exchanges attributed to developing countries is still very small as a percentage of the total open interest, there is a growing acceptance of swaps, options and futures as tools to manage risk, and as devices for tapping new sources of finance. Among developing countries, the largest users of the US futures exchanges are Latin American countries.[4]

Table 2. Percentage of reportable developing country open interest over total open interest in US futures exchanges for selected commodities (1991)

Commodity group	Asia (developing)	Middle East and North Africa	Sub-Saharan Africa	Latin America
Grain and soybean complex	0.19	0.12	-	1.21
Livestock products	-	-	-	0.39
Foodstuffs	0.30	0.18	0.68	2.09
Industrial material	-	0.14	0.03	1.58
Metals	0.07	0.90	-	1.19
Crude oil*	-	-	-	1.40
Financial instruments	0.01	0.20	-	2.04
Currencies	-	0.27	-	3.17

*Total for all developing countries is around 1.6%.
Note: The data were compiled from CFTC "01" report forms, which are filed daily by futures commission merchants, clearing members and foreign brokers. (-) signifies values less than 0.05. For more detail, see Claessens and Varangis (1992), Tables 1–3.

The New York Mercantile Exchange (Nymex) estimates that, in 1993, developing countries accounted for only 1.6% of crude oil futures contracts,[5] and for only 0.2% of the natural gas futures contracts in 1992. However, developing countries also participate indirectly in oil exchanges through the OTC market. Some of the swap-related open interest can certainly be attributed to developing countries, although unfortunately there are no data to quantify this properly. In both exchange-traded instruments and the OTC market, most of the interest from developing countries has focused on crude oil derivatives. However, recently their interest in heating oil and gasoline has been growing.

The interest of developing countries in the oil derivative markets grew very significantly after the Gulf War, and the proportion of that interest finding its way onto the OTC market has also expanded rapidly. According to the Bank for International Settlements, the total amount of commodity-indexed swaps and options rose to about $40–50 billion immediately after the Gulf War, compared with $7–10 billion before. The largest portion of the commodity swap market, as much as 80%, is made up of oil-related transactions;[6] in early 1993, it was reported that the market for energy swaps was at least $25 billion per annum. Since the Gulf War period, Mexico's use of the oil derivative markets to hedge its oil export revenues has been widely reported (see Panel 1).[7] On the import side, Chile, Brazil and El Salvador reportedly used the oil derivative markets during the Gulf War to lock in, or set a ceiling on, the price of their oil imports.[8]

Following the Gulf War, Mexico, Brazil and, more recently, Chile, are reported to be regular users of the oil derivative markets. Mexico set up PMI, an affiliate of Pemex, specifically to increase the flexibility of its commercial oil operations (including the use of derivative markets, as described in Panel 2). Other developing countries known to have occasionally used the oil derivative markets include Algeria, Ecuador, China, Argentina (various private oil companies), and several companies in Asia (notably in Hong Kong, Korea, Singapore and Thailand). Asian airlines are known to be significant users of jet-fuel swaps (see Panel 3).[9] There is now a long list of countries reportedly considering the use of oil derivatives, including: Venezuela, Nigeria, Colombia, Costa Rica, Indonesia, Trinidad and Tobago, Uruguay, Saudi Arabia, Peru, Kuwait and Iran.

Among the developing countries, Latin American countries are the main users of US energy exchange traded derivatives. Data for the first quarter of 1994 show a significant increase in the open interest of Nymex's energy futures contracts attributed to Latin America (see Table 3).

The increase in Latin America's share of open interest in energy futures can largely be attributed to the following four factors:

Table 3. The share of open interest in Nymex's energy futures contracts attributed to developing countries (January–March 1994)

	Latin America	Rest of developing countries
Crude oil	3.1	0.4
Heating oil	2.2	0.3
Unleaded gasoline	3.1	0.2
Natural gas	0.2	na

Source: Nymex

MEXICO'S EARLY OIL HEDGING

In late 1990, and during the first half of 1991, Mexico started to use financial risk management to protect its earnings from crude oil exports (roughly 1.3 million barrels a day) against a price drop. The three-part strategy covered a significant part of its export earnings over this period. Mexico bought put options at different exercise prices, sold oil futures and used short-dated (up to one year maturity) oil swaps to hedge its oil price risk. Buying put options guarantees a minimum price; and oil futures contracts and swaps guarantee the seller – and the buyer – a specified price at some future date. By using these contracts, Mexico effectively ensured a minimum price for part of its main export earner in the short term. In addition, Mexico established a special contingency fund to protect against any long-term decline in oil prices.

Mexico's overall strategy ensured that it received at least $17 a barrel – the price used as the basis for its 1991 budget. Mexico's participation in the futures markets reassured investors that, regardless of oil price movements, the economic programme and the budget would be sustained. The strategy was successful for Mexico; oil prices fell significantly in early 1991. Not only did Mexico achieve more certainty *ex ante* about its oil earnings, but also it profited *ex post* as the gains (from a minimum price) exceeded the initial costs of buying the put options. Since then, Mexico has continued its programme of hedging its most important export (see Panel 2).

❑ ongoing economic liberalisation and privatisation programmes, which have made governments and companies more responsive to market forces;

❑ the fact that Latin American companies buy and sell crude oil and oil products at prices based, to a large extent, on US prices (which means that their basis risk is relatively low);

❑ an increasing expertise in derivatives (the proliferation of financial instruments in the rapidly growing Latin American stock markets have had a spillover effect on the commodity markets);

❑ the removal of legal barriers and controls, such as foreign exchange controls, that previously impeded the use of hedging instruments;

❑ the proximity to the United States, which has advantages in terms of trading hours and the physical trade patterns for crude oil and oil products.

The share of open interest in Nymex's energy futures attributed to the rest of the developing countries is insignificant. Far East Asian and Middle Eastern developing countries still account for less than 0.5% of the open interest in Nymex's energy futures contracts. Differences in trading hours, in patterns of energy trade, and in the physical characteristics of crude oil and oil products traded may account for the lack of significant growth. Developing countries are also users of IPE energy contracts, as indicated by Table 4.

Far Eastern and Middle Eastern developing countries seem to be using the IPE, as Table 4 illustrates, although their share is still small. In Table 4, Far East includes Japan, but we would estimate that developing countries in the Far East account for 65% of the Far East's share, that is, about 2% of the total trades placed through the IPE. We would also estimate that around 65% of the "Other" category in Table 4 may be attributed to Latin America; thus, Latin America accounts for around 0.5% of trades placed through the IPE.

One reason why the IPE is used by a number of Far Eastern and Middle Eastern countries is that they use Brent crude as a pricing benchmark. It is also known that some Latin American oil companies use Brent crude in their pricing formulas (Petrobras and several Argentinean oil companies, among others).

The countries of the Commonwealth of Independent States (CIS) are the biggest users of the IPE outside the industrial economies of Europe and the US. Their share grew from

Table 4. IPE client base by geographic location in 1993 (% of trade placed through the IPE)

United Kingdom	39.3
Europe	28.4
United States	23.6
Middle East	0.67
Far East	3.06
CIS	4.25
Other	0.75

Source: IPE

PANEL 2

SETTING UP AN OIL RISK MANAGEMENT PROGRAMME: THE PMI EXAMPLE

PMI is an affiliate of Pemex (Mexico's state oil company), created in the early 1990s to handle Mexico's international trade in crude oil and oil products. (85% of PMI is held by Pemex, with the remaining 15% held by the Mexican Development Bank and the Mexican Eximbank.) PMI was set up in order to increase flexibility in the commercial operations of Pemex. PMI effectively buys crude oil and oil products from Pemex, and sells them in the international market; it also sells oil products to Pemex. For operational purposes, there is a transfer pricing formula for crude oil and oil products between PMI and Pemex.

In order to secure profit margins from the oil trading operations, and take advantage of arbitrage opportunities, PMI decided to establish and implement a risk management programme. Before entering the oil derivative market, PMI implemented the following five steps:

1) Gathered information and analysed the oil derivative markets.

2) Identified the following price risks: production risk, refining risk ("crack-spread") and price risk due to trading.

3) Defined the objectives and goals of risk management (see table below).

4) Calculated the necessary capital for its operations, and defined limits for capital at risk in collaboration with the Central Bank and the Ministry of Finance. In addition, PMI established a mecha-

nism to revise these limits if necessary.

5) Established proper accounting and monitoring systems. More specifically, PMI created a system of checks and balances constructed jointly by the accounting, treasury and legal department.

It took PMI a total of three years to move from step (1) to actually trading in the oil derivative markets (trading began in 1992). Most of PMI's risk management activities fall into the "tactical" strategy defined in the table below.

Initially, PMI concentrated its trading volume in instruments of less than one month. It is now making more use of longer-dated instruments, but in the fourth quarter of 1993 rather more than half of PMI's positions were still less than one month, and about a fourth were more than three months – which indicates that PMI is continuing to concentrate on rather short-term hedges. However, the volume of trades have been increasing rapidly, and roughly tripled between 1992 and 1993. In terms of instruments used, PMI initially used mainly swaps and options. Subsequently, the volume of trades using swaps has remained about the same, with the volume of options doubling. However, currently, about half of the volume of trades is executed in the futures market. As experience is gained, the limits on capital-at-risk in terms of US dollars have been raised; the figure more than tripled between 1992 and 1993.

PMI's risk management strategies and their objectives

Strategic	Tactical	Speculative
Use of hedging instruments to decrease cash-flow volatility	Use of hedging instruments to increase flexibility in physical transactions	Take positions "outguessing" market trends
Main objective	*Main objective*	*Main objective*
Minimise risk exposure	Optimise profits while maintaining risks at "acceptable" levels	Optimise profits by increasing risk exposure

0.07% in 1992 to 4.25% in 1993.

In the pre-Gulf War period, users of oil derivative markets in developing countries dealt mainly in very short-term instruments. This was because the instruments were largely being used to hedge risk arising from the operational cycle: the period of about three months from wellhead to consumer (see, for example, the case of PMI described in Panel 2).

However, the Gulf War emphasised the benefits of longer-term hedges. The high oil price volatility, as well as the unpredictability of oil prices, created problems for state budgets and corporate planners in developing countries (whether oil users or producers). The increases in the liquidity of longer-dated oil futures contracts, as well as the extension of the maturity of oil futures contracts further into the future, is an

AN INTEGRATED HEDGE: KOREAN AIR
YEN-DENOMINATED JET FUEL SWAP

A jet fuel swap executed in June 1993 by Korean Air, reportedly with JP Morgan, provides an excellent example of an integrated energy hedge.[1]

The majority of swaps in jet fuel and other energy products involve both fixed and floating payments in dollars. According to market sources, however, Korean Air will pay a fixed yen price for its jet fuel, and receive a floating yen price. The starting point for such a swap is to fix the fuel's dollar price by reference to the Platt's benchmark, and then to agree the dollar/yen exchange rate for the fixed leg of the swap. In this case, the rate was reportedly fixed at the start of the deal, but in other swaps the rate can be refixed every month. The floating price is likely to be based on the monthly mean of Platt's Singapore jet fuel prices.

Korean Air thought that the yen was overvalued when it went into the swap, but the Japanese currency subsequently strengthened further against the dollar, and jet fuel prices continued to fall. As a result, dealers say, the airline is now paying out on the swap, although some analysts say it is likely to have had a separate currency hedge against the possibility of further dollar weakness.

The size of the Korean Air deal – reputedly 4.2 million gallons a month for a year – is indicative of the increased liquidity of the jet fuel swap market.

1 J Aron, Bankers Trust, Merrill Lynch and Morgan Stanley are also said to have offered non-dollar energy swaps.

indication of the increasing use of longer-term derivatives.

However, the majority of users of oil derivative markets in developing countries are still using only short-dated instruments. A major reason for this is the lack of longer-term strategies with regard to risk management. Most of these short-dated transactions are designed to increase the flexibility of the oil company in its physical transactions: buying and selling crude oil and oil products. This type of hedging may be designated "tactical hedging". Often, companies and governments in developing countries do not consider price variations beyond one year, as most of their financing and budgetary needs are considered within that period.

One pattern that has emerged is that first-time users of risk management instruments in developing countries tend to use OTC instruments. OTC instruments require less monitoring of positions, do not usually have margin calls, and may be customised to the particular developing country's needs (with regard to type of oil, contract expiration dates, etc). As experience with hedging instruments is gained, users in developing countries start to deal in exchange-traded instruments. This pattern can be seen in numerous instances: PMI in Mexico; several private Argentinean oil companies; the oil company and government in Ecuador and Chile; and Sonatrach in Algeria.

Even when users in developing countries gain experience in hedging, the OTC market may still be attractive. Small oil companies in developing countries, where trained personnel to staff a risk management unit are hard to find, or where the volume of trade is small, and/or the physical characteristics of the crude oil and oil products are different from those represented at the exchange, may favour the OTC market. Central American and African oil importers tend to fall into this category. Also, airlines in developing countries may be attracted to the OTC market in order to hedge their jet fuel expenses – as several Far Eastern airlines have already shown (Panel 3).

One interesting aspect of the oil derivative markets is the way in which energy swaps and options may be incorporated in structural loans. Most of these deals go unpublished, but several developing countries such as Algeria and Mexico are said to have negotiated them. The most widely cited deal is that arranged between Algeria's state oil company, Sonatrach, and Chase Manhattan, in 1989 (Panel 4).[10] Energy risk management instruments can provide an assurance to investors that a significant component of the project's risk – the oil price risk – is covered. As a result, developing countries can obtain financing for projects that without oil price coverage would not be considered by investors – and can also obtain that financing at more attractive terms. In the future, a number of projects involving the expansion of refining capacity in Latin America, particularly in Colombia, Trinidad and Tobago, and

PANEL 4

SONATRACH'S OIL-LINKED LOAN

Algeria's state-owned oil company, Sonatrach, entered into a loan agreement with a syndicate of international banks in November 1989. The loan, coordinated by Chase Investment Bank, London, consisted of a US$100 million conventional floating-rate loan (with a seven-year maturity and a four-year grace period) and a series of oil option transactions. The proceeds of the loan were used to replace expensive (4% above Libor) short-term loans, reducing Sonatrach's interest service costs. With this scheme, Algeria re-entered the medium-term syndicated loan market at a much-reduced cost. Sonatrach pays an interest rate of 1% above Libor over the life of the loan; without the scheme, the cost would have been 3–4% above Libor.

Two special features were added to the loan. First, Sonatrach sold Chase four call options written on oil,[1] so reducing the cost of funding. Under this arrangement, Sonatrach pays Chase a certain amount of cash if the price of oil rises above a specified ceiling (for instance, US$23 per barrel).

This does not significantly increase Sonatrach's risk, since its revenue also increases. But, by selling the oil options, Sonatrach traded some upside potential in its oil export revenues for an immediate reduction in the cost of funding.

The second feature was designed by Chase to bring other banks into the syndicate. Chase provided members of the syndicate with an opportunity for additional profits from oil price movements. Chase pays the syndicate an additional interest margin above Libor, if the oil price rises above or falls below a specified price range – in effect, 0.125% for a US$1 move in the price of oil, if the price moves substantially. This does not affect Sonatrach's payments, as the extra margins are provided by Chase. This could have increased Chase's oil price risk, but the risk was eliminated by complicated transactions in the options market (see figure below).

1 The maturities of the four options are 6, 12, 18 and 24 months.

Sonatrach/Chase transactions

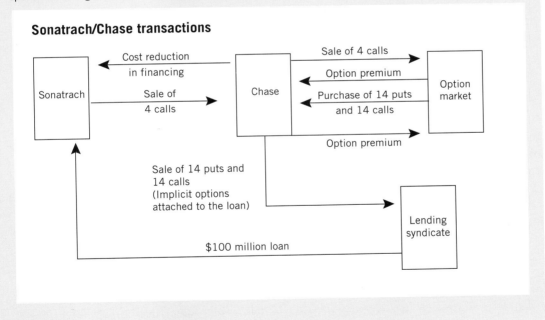

Venezuela, could benefit from using the oil derivative markets.

The structure of these deals is likely to vary widely, and in most cases it will be customised to the particular situation. For example, the repayment of a loan may be structured to be in barrels of oil, with either physical delivery or conversion to dollars at the time of repayment. In this way, the assets and the liabilities of an oil company may be matched. Another type of structure links the interest rate of the loan to oil prices. In Figure 1 overleaf, the Central Bank of an oil producing country pays less than the market rate when oil prices are low (say, below $20 per bbl) and pays more than the market rate when prices are high (say, above $20 per bbl). Structures such as this were used in the context of the Brady plan (see Panel 5).

PANEL 5

OIL-LINKED BRADY BONDS

Some of the new instruments issued under the Brady plan include recapture clauses based on oil prices. Under the Brady plan, the commercial bank debt of several developing countries has been restructured and debt has been converted into bonds which include collateral in the form of zero-coupon bonds and interest guarantee funds. In addition, these bonds may include recapture clauses which require additional repayments if the export receipts of the debtor country improve sufficiently. Mexico and Venezuela were the first to include such recapture clauses. In addition, Nigeria has included a recapture clause.

In the case of the restructuring of Mexican debt in 1990, the recapture clause stipulates that Mexico owes (from July 1996), 30% of the extra oil revenues it receives if the oil price rises above $14 per barrel (adjusted for US GDP inflation). This amount is in no year to exceed 3% of the face value of the debt exchanged.

In the case of Venezuela, the bonds created in 1990 include detachable warrants for an upside recovery of value that is tied to the real price of oil. The Venezuela recapture clause stipulates that banks converting their debt to certain discount bonds will receive, for every $1,000 of debt exchanged, five warrants. Each warrant provides semi-annual payments (beginning in the sixth year)

of the difference between the average price of oil exported during the preceding six months and the strike price. The first strike price is $20.50 multiplied by $(1.02)^{12}$. The next (48) strike prices will be adjusted by the US producer price index. Payments per warrant are capped at $3 per warrant.

For Nigeria, 30-year bonds were issued in 1992 which incorporated a Payment Adjustment Warrant. The warrant entitles the holder to receive additional cash payments on each interest payment date commencing November 1996, subject to a cap, on the basis of the difference between the actual price of Bonny Light oil (Nigeria's main export crude) at the time and an inflation-adjusted reference price, initially set at $28 per barrel.

In the case of Mexico, the decision to include a recapture clause as opposed to creating a straight oil-linked bond was in part motivated by the prevailing regulation in the US concerning commodity-linked instruments – which made the issue of standard commodity bonds difficult. Regulations also motivated the decision to make the recapture clauses undetachable initially. The other debt restructurings were largely based on the Mexican experiment, and have tended to follow a similar structure. However, since then, regulations in the United States have become more flexible (see Chapter 14 of this book for a full legal discussion).

Barriers to using financial risk-management tools

The data and the anecdotal evidence discussed in the previous section indicate that while the proportion is increasing, only a small amount of the energy exports and imports of developing countries is routinely hedged. Why do so few countries attempt to manage their energy price risk using the international energy derivative markets? There are a number of barriers that prevent countries from participating, and we will discuss each of these in turn.

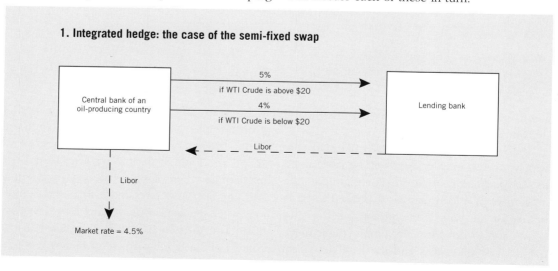

1. Integrated hedge: the case of the semi-fixed swap

BASIS RISK

From the point of view of many exporters and importers, the international markets for energy price risk management are incomplete. There often appears to be a mismatch between the characteristics of the energy exposure to be hedged and those specified in the hedging tools available. The mismatch may be with respect to maturity, or with respect to type. Maturities are generally limited to one to two years in the futures and options markets; long-dated, over-the-counter or capital market instruments are often not available at all for developing countries, or for the risk in question.

In principle, short-dated hedges can be "rolled over" (that is, renewed at maturity), so as to duplicate a long-dated hedge; in practice, developing countries often lack the expertise necessary to manage the basis risk arising from changes in the relationship between spot and futures prices (that is, roll-over risk). As a result, the protection offered by a roll-over will be considerably less than that of a long-dated instrument (where the financial intermediary often takes on the management of the roll-over risk).

Basis risk also arises from the differences in type or in the characteristics of the energy exposure to be hedged, and those specified by the hedging instrument. This is the risk that, over a given period of time, the price of the energy exposure to be hedged will not move in step with the price of the market hedging instrument. The reasons for this are the existence of many grades of energy exposures (for example, different grades of crude oil) and the limited number of liquid hedging tools.

For many energy exposures, however, both types of basis risk represent a relatively minor problem (see Table 5). In simulations of hedging of oil exports or imports, we found that using Nymex's short-dated crude oil futures (less than six months' maturity) could eliminate 75% to 85% of the near-term price risk over the period 1985–90 for most crude oils, implying a basis risk of 15% to 25% (Claessens and Varangis, 1991).[11] This level of basis risk is not high, considering the large variety of crude oils that we used in the simulations (the API varied from 25° to 40°). In particular, the crude oil prices of Mexico, Colombia, Ecuador, Saudi Arabia, Nigeria, Algeria and Libya tend to move together; they also correlate well with West Texas Intermediate (WTI) – the crude oil underlying Nymex's sweet light crude contract.

For other oil exporting countries the relationship was less close; but in these cases it was often their own pricing policies that tended to introduce the basis risk. Venezuelan crude prices, for example, do not follow any of the above prices very closely, even though Venezuelan crudes are close in quality to the other Latin American crudes. The resulting basis risk appears to be mainly due to the pricing policies adopted by Venezuela, and it follows that pricing policies that were more market-responsive would do much to remove this basis risk.

As the first column of Table 5 shows, the hedge ratios were not statistically different from one, with the exception of Bachaquero. This means that when hedging 1,000 barrels of oil, one needs to purchase/sell one futures contract of crude oil.

Table 5. Hedge ratios and basis risk for different crudes

	Hedge ratio	R-squared	Reduction from longer-term hedges
Istmo (Mexico)	1.08	0.88	0.69
Lagotreco (Venezuela)	0.85	0.69	0.35
Lagotreco (Venezuela)	0.92	0.78	-
Oriente (Ecuador)	1.01	0.77	0.67
Cano Limon (Colombia)	1.05	0.85	0.71
Bachaquero (Venezuela)	0.64	0.60	-
WTI (US)	1.03	0.97	-
Dubai (Abu Dhabi)	1.00	0.86	0.76
Brent (UK)	1.07	0.88	-
Alaska North Slope (US)	1.06	0.86	-
Es Sider (Libya)	1.09	0.84	0.81
Arab Light (Saudi Arabia)	1.01	0.80	0.67
Attaka (Indonesia)	1.03	0.80	0.66
Bonny Light (Nigeria)	1.08	0.83	0.82
Sahara (Algeria)	1.12	0.84	0.80
Khafji (Neutral Zone)	0.97	0.74	0.72

* Refers to the period August 1988–December 1990.
Note: The basis risk is 1–R squared. Thus, a high R squared means low basis risk.

When hedging longer-dated exposure, the basis risk introduced by maturity mismatches becomes more important. But this is still not a very large problem: our simulations showed that about 70% of price risk in excess of six-month horizons could be eliminated for most crude oils.[12] The third column of Table 5 shows these results for individual crude oils. Again, the crude oils of the exporting countries that followed more market-responsive pricing policies could be hedged the best.

We have also simulated hedging strategies for fuel exposures. While basis risk was not formally analysed for many refined products (due to the lack of data), an indication of the basis risk was obtained in the case of Venezuela (see Claessens and Varangis, 1994). An analysis of monthly data for 1990 shows that changes in the New York spot price for fuel oil, diesel and gasoline were closely correlated with Maraven's (Venezuela's refining sales subsidiary) price changes for these fuels. The coefficient of correlation was around 80% for all three of the fuels. The relationship is much less tight for weekly price changes, however. It appears that Maraven keeps its product prices fixed for a long time – sometimes up to eight to 12 weeks. This suggests that, in the short run, Maraven absorbs the price volatility. If Maraven makes its prices more market-responsive, the relationship to New York cash prices, and thus to the fuel futures prices, would increase. Thus, provided Maraven allows its product prices to become more responsive to international prices, one should not expect to find significant differences in the basis risk when hedging New York spot fuel prices and when hedging Maraven's fuel prices. For other developing countries, more statistical analysis is needed to establish the correlation between futures price changes and changes in fuel prices.

Basis risk, like liquidity, will nevertheless remain an important issue. One cannot expect that the markets for energy risk management instruments will develop sufficiently for all grades of oil and fuels, and constraints will remain quite severe at the longer end for some time to come.

LIQUIDITY

Even at the short end of the hedging spectrum, hedging by developing countries can be constrained by inadequate liquidity; this is relatively less true for crude oil, but more so for fuels.

Some figures may help to illustrate this fundamental problem. Currently, the futures/options market for crude oil is the most liquid of all commodity hedging markets. More crude oil is traded daily on the Nymex (the light sweet crude oil futures contract based on WTI crude) than the total world production of crude oil (about 65–80 million barrels in futures versus 60 million barrels of physical). And liquidity has expanded rapidly. In 1989 and 1990, the average daily Nymex crude oil futures contract trading volume was 55 million barrels and 63.4 million barrels respectively, compared to 22 million barrels in 1986. By the end of the first quarter of 1994, the trading volume in futures contracts exceeded 100 million barrels.

Options on Nymex's oil futures contracts account for an additional 25–30 million barrels, or half of world crude oil production. In addition, Brent crude oil futures contracts traded on the IPE have a daily trading volume of about 40–50 million barrels, and options on these contracts account for an additional 5–7 million barrels in daily trade. Thus, in New York and London, roughly three times the world's physical crude oil production is traded in futures and about one-half in options.[13]

The daily futures trading volume of heating oil (used to hedge diesel, jet fuel and fuel oil) is less, currently about 1.2–1.5 billion gallons; and there is about 50 million gallons of trades in options. Gasoline's daily futures and options trading volumes on Nymex are some 1.2–2 billion gallons and 150 million gallons, respectively. But these markets have been growing rapidly too. Since 1988, daily trading volumes in futures and options for heating oil have increased by over 50%, and they have more than doubled in the case of gasoline.

Measured in terms of open interest, most of the liquidity on the Nymex is concentrated in the short-run. While the maturities of crude oil futures contracts now extend beyond three years, the most liquidly-traded contracts are concentrated in the nearest nine to ten months. That is, about 75% of the open interest is concentrated in the first nine months. For Brent crude, most (up to 90%) of the open interest is concentrated in the first four to five months. The same holds true for Nymex's heating oil and gasoline futures contracts (78% and 90% of the open interest, respectively). In options, most of the interest is also concentrated in short-term maturities.

It would be wrong to ignore the market liquidity generated by the OTC market. This market is growing rapidly, and oil price swaps extending to seven or even ten years are now routinely used by entities in industrial countries.

The liquidity in the hedging markets can be compared to the total volume of oil exported (or imported) by developing countries. The total daily volume of oil exports by developing countries is about 30 million barrels. On the import side, the daily figure is about 7 million barrels. After comparing the liquidity in the hedging markets to the total volume of oil exported (or imported), it can be concluded that:

i) For short-term hedges, say up to six or nine months, the existing futures/options markets provide considerable and sufficient liquidity. Of course, on a single day, or even over the course of one week, there is not enough liquidity to cover all of the exports of all developing countries (or even those of a major country) for, say, six months (roughly 250–400 million barrels for a large developing country oil exporter) – but then, no one would advocate any country placing such a hedge over such a short period of time. The experience of Mexico (see Panel 1) proves that hedging large quantities in the short-term markets is entirely possible, provided that the hedging is executed *slowly*. During the Gulf War, Mexico hedged six months' worth of exports, or roughly 250 million barrels; it did so by spreading the sale and purchase of futures, options, OTC-options and short-dated swaps over a period of two months. Placing large hedges gradually can thus overcome many liquidity problems, and because doing so "locks in" prices over several trading days, rather than on a single trading day, it also achieves a smooth price path.

ii) For longer-term hedges (that is, more than a year), the use of exchange-traded futures/options contracts can only provide very limited coverage. Currently, all the open interest in crude oil futures contracts of more than a year is about equal to around 83 million barrels. This is roughly equivalent to two days' oil exports for all developing countries (or about two months of exports for a major oil exporter). In the case of refined products, longer-term futures/options hedges are able to provide even less coverage. Of course, the liquidity for longer-term hedges is much enhanced by the OTC markets, but access to, and terms offered by, this market depend critically on perceived creditworthiness (see below).

iii) There are few instances in which it is advisable to hedge an entire commodity price exposure. In most cases, partial hedges covering a fraction of the exposure are sufficient. The fraction of the exposure which should be covered is determined by the specific circumstances of the hedger, as well as:
❑ an analysis of the existing market circumstances;
❑ the amount of risk that is judged acceptable;
❑ the cost of hedging; and
❑ the possible offset between price and quantity fluctuations.

Because this analysis usually suggests that only a small fraction of energy exposure should be hedged, at least to begin with, it reduces the immediate problem posed by limited liquidity.

CREDITWORTHINESS
The credit standing of developing countries often prevents commercial banks and bond market investors from dealing with them. Of course, this does not really apply in the case of short-dated exchange-traded futures and options, which are subject to margin requirements that largely mitigate the credit risk. Also, if options are bought, they obviously represent no credit risk regarding the developing country.

However, forward, swap and option (if sold) contracts involve a consideration of the counterparty's creditworthiness. The longer the performance period (the length of the contract), the greater the credit risk. Since many developing countries are not judged to be very creditworthy, their access to long-dated energy risk management instruments is limited. In practice, most market participants are reluctant to offer entities in even the more creditworthy developing countries swap contracts that extend beyond one year.

A promising development is that private borrowers in several developing countries are now gaining better access to foreign finance (as witnessed by the rapid growth in portfolio and other private financial flows in recent years). To further enhance their creditworthiness, borrowers may be required to offer collateral or other forms of security (such as pledges of future receivables). For example, in the Mexicana de Cobre (MdC) deal of 1989, in order to obtain financing, MdC pledged an export contract to deliver 4,000 tons of copper to Sogem (a Belgian copper company) for 36 months. Sogem deposited the funds from buying the copper in an escrow account in New York. Only after the

CREDIT ENHANCEMENT: THE ASHANTI GOLDFIELDS CORPORATION LOAN

The Ashanti Goldfields Corporation (AGC) needed funds to finance an expansion programme that called for the construction of a new sulphide treatment plant. By using this plant and advanced mining technologies to develop medium-grade sulphide deposits, AGC expects to increase production by 50% (to a total of 1 million ounces per annum by the mid-1990s). AGC is Ghana's largest gold producer and one of the 20 largest gold-producing companies in the world.

In November 1992, the IFC, the private sector arm of the World Bank, announced the signing of a syndicated loan equivalent to US$140 million, as well as the establishment of a separate gold hedging facility for AGC. The loan may be drawn by AGC in either US dollars or gold. IFC will provide US$40 million and the rest, US$100 million equivalent, is to be syndicated between a group of nine international banks.

If AGC chooses to draw the loan in gold, payments will be made in US dollar equivalents of the gold amounts. The interest rate is a variable rate, set with reference to the London Gold Lease Rate. This arrangement helps to fulfil AGC's hedging strategy by creating a hedge equivalent to 10% of the annual output. It would also provide major cash-flow benefits to AGC, since the Gold Lease Rate – which is the difference between the US$ Libor and London Gold Contango (contango is the forward premium on gold) – tends to be around 1% per annum, compared with 5% per annum or higher for US$ Libor. Thus, the option of drawing the loan in gold links AGC's debt service to the price of gold. The advantage with the gold loan is that it provides a hedge for AGC's revenues, and provides financing at low nominal interest rates. If the loan is drawn in US$, the loan will be repaid as a conventional US$ loan, with the interest rate set with reference to US$ Libor.

At the same time, but independently of the loan, IFC arranged a 10-year hedging facility that will enable AGC to hedge between 30% and 50% of its annual gold production against gold price volatility. This is done through the use of commodity (gold) derivative products such as

---

lenders were paid, were the excess funds in the escrow account returned to MdC. Of course, the lender could only be sure that adequate sums would be paid into the account if the price of copper remained relatively healthy. To overcome this uncertainty, a copper swap was arranged with Paribas. Paribas received the variable price for copper (based on LME), paying into the escrow account a fixed price of $2,000 per ton.

Marked-to-market swaps are another way of dealing with credit risks, and in some ways are the OTC equivalent of the daily marked-to-market futures and options in the formal exchanges. As with futures and options, marked-to-market swaps require that the counterparty puts up a minimum margin.[14] Movements in prices over time can imply gains (or losses) for the party which is long in a swap transaction (or any other OTC derivative), and losses (or gains) for the party short in the transaction. When contracts are marked-to-market, these gains (or losses) are calculated at regular intervals (say, every six months) and settled with the counterparty. The amount of the gain or loss is calculat-ed on the basis of prevailing spot and forward energy prices.[15]

As a result of marking to market, the exposure of the party providing the swap to adverse changes in the creditworthiness of the counterparty is drastically reduced. The combination of an adverse change in the creditworthiness of the counterparty, and an adverse change in market prices, will still generate credit exposures, but only during the period until the next mark-to-market. Furthermore, as the time interval until the next calculation shrinks, the potential credit risk becomes less. In an extreme case, if the swap were to be marked to market on a daily basis, then credit risk would be virtually eliminated (as it is, in the case of exchange-traded futures and options).

The oil-linked bonds issued in the context of the Brady plan by Mexico, Venezuela and Nigeria dealt with credit risk by making the repayment obligations contingent on high export prices (see Panel 5).

Private entities involved in the energy business in some developing countries have started

medium-term gold swaps, gold floors (that is, the purchase of put options) and gold collars (that is, the purchase of put and the sale of call options, creating a price band). IFC will execute these transactions directly with AGC, and hedge itself in the gold derivatives markets.

Hedging gold price volatility is not new among gold producers. The majority of gold producers in North America, Australia and South Africa engage in hedging to protect their cash flows from gold price fluctuations. In 1991, about 75% of the annual production in these countries – about 1,000 tons – was hedged. Most of these hedging contracts have maturities of up to three years.

In developing countries, gold producers face a major constraint with regard to hedging. Almost all forms of hedging contracts require the market to assume the risk of non-delivery by the gold producing/hedging country. The international gold market is very credit-sensitive, and market participants are very limited in their capacity to assume the delivery risk of a producer in a developing country. In the case of AGC, the gold-linked financing deal avoids the logistical and security problems associated with the physical delivery risk of gold. This is because IFC has accepted the delivery risk as part of the credit enhancement it provided to AGC.

Instruments available under the Gold Hedging Facility arranged for AGC

Gold swaps During the life of the gold swap, AGC will receive a fixed price for a fixed amount of gold, and would pay a variable (market) price.

Participating gold swaps This instrument differs from the one above in that AGC would receive a fixed but lower price for a fixed amount of gold. With the sum generated by the price reduction, AGC would be able to purchase call options on gold covering a certain percentage of its production. These options would be exercised if gold prices rose.

Gold floors Through the purchase of put options, AGC would lock-in a minimum price for its gold production (all or part of it).

Participating gold floors Through the purchase of put options, AGC would establish a floor price for its gold production; simultaneously, through the sale of call options on a percentage of its production, AGC would participate in any rise of gold prices to the extent of the production covered.

Gold collars (or range forwards) These are very similar to participating gold floors. However, the upside potential is completely capped by selling calls. That is, the strike price of the calls is set so that the income from the calls exactly offsets the cost of the puts.

to use short-dated swaps for hedging purposes. For instance, export financing is reportedly often combined with energy swaps, so that the swaps provide a degree of price assurance for the future exports. The arrangements used in the MdC case, described above, offer one method of obtaining export financing.[16] Applying the idea to the energy sector is entirely straightforward: instead of copper, read oil. In addition, payoffs in energy derivatives can be structured so that any political fallout from selling at below market prices is minimised. For example, forward deals can be structured with a floor that will allow the country to benefit from some upside potential, while retaining the benefits of downside coverage.

In recent years, a number of ways of ameliorating the creditworthiness problem have been suggested. Several proposals have suggested the use of funds from international agencies to provide credit guarantees, thereby enhancing the leverage of developing countries in using longer-dated instruments to hedge oil export revenues, oil import expenses, raising pre-

export finance and finance for oil projects. For example, in 1992 the International Finance Corporation (IFC), an affiliate of the World Bank that deals with private sector projects, constructed a gold loan and provided a credit enhancement for Ashanti Goldfields Corporation (AGC), a private gold producer in Ghana (see Panel 6). The credit enhancement attracted a consortium of banks to provide additional funds for the expansion of AGC's capacity. Similar structures could be applied in the energy sector. For example, loans could be drawn in crude oil. In this case, a specific interest rate formula based on oil would need to be calculated, as oil moves from backwardation to contango (while gold is in permanent contango). The main problem in devising these deals is to find ways of guaranteeing the element of sovereign risk, while allowing the particular business risk to be assumed by the companies offering the derivative products. The international agencies are currently discussing a number of proposals aimed at addressing this problem.[17]

PREMIUMS AND CASH-FLOW

The up-front costs of certain risk management instruments can be a major concern for countries that already have problems in raising foreign funds. Purchases of options, caps and floors (that is, a series of options) require a significant premium up front – usually accounting for a significant portion of the amount of the underlying asset to be hedged. However, futures and collars can be implemented by importers (buying a call and selling a put) or exporters (selling a call and buying a put) at very low cost.

The effect on cash-flow of margin calls on futures positions can also be a significant problem. Meeting margin calls may suddenly require a daily injection of funds, perhaps at a time when foreign exchange is not readily available.

There are several ways that developing countries can manage the cash-flow problem. One way is take a stop-loss position: that is, for the entity in question to liquidate its position if it is short (long) and prices rise (fall) above a certain level. Liquidation, however, reduces the effectiveness of hedging. Another way is to avoid margins by buying call options. Of course, options cost premiums.

Because futures are still often the preferred instrument for hedging, we assessed the possible implications for cashflow by simulating the use of WTI-futures contracts over the period 1986–90 by an importer of crude oil (the analysis is similar for an oil-exporter).[18] At the beginning of each month, we posited that the entity bought 100 contracts of the second-nearest futures contract. For example, in January 1991, we posited that the importer bought 100 March 1991 contracts. One hundred contracts corresponds to 100,000 barrels per month or, on a yearly basis, 1.2 million barrels – a quantity representative of some of the smaller Central American and African developing countries. We assumed that the oil importer would hold these 100 futures contracts through each month and then sell them at the end of the month.

The initial margin requirement on a single futures contract is $2,000 (the minimum dictated by the exchange), and the maintenance margin is 75% of the initial margin, or $1,500. If prices were to fall and accounts be resettled, the importer could face a margin call. If the account falls below $1,500 per contract, the importer has to bring its account back up to the initial margin of $2,000 per contract. If, because of a price increase, resettlement leads to a margin account

above $2,000 per contract, the importer can withdraw the surplus.

Our simulations showed that the maximum margin call the importer would have faced on any single day from July 1986 to December 1990 on a total of 100 nearby futures contracts would have been $400,000. This extremely large margin call would have occurred on the eighteenth trading day of August 1990, when the futures price fell by $4 a barrel (from $30.91 to $26.91). The maximum withdrawal the importer would have been able to make over this period would have been $317,000 on the eighteenth trading day of October 1990, when the futures price increased by $3.17 a barrel (from $31.08 to $34.25). It is not surprising that the importer would have had the largest margin calls and withdrawals in the autumn of 1990, given the extremely high volatility in the oil market during that period.

For all other months during the period July 1986 to December 1990, the maximum calls and withdrawals were considerably less. Figure 2 plots the maximum calls and withdrawals per contract for each month in this period. (For 100 contracts the amounts need to be multiplied by 100.) The lower half of the figure shows the maximum call in each month, and the upper half indicates the maximum withdrawal in each month. The figure also indicates the average of the daily withdrawals and margin calls in each month. As can be seen, the autumn of 1990 was exceptional in having the largest calls and withdrawals. During almost all other months, the maximum withdrawal on any given day did not exceed $1,000 per contract.

On average over this period, the importer would have been able to withdraw money from its account as futures prices increased. The average withdrawal per day per contract over the period July 1986 through December 1990 would have been $28.44, or $0.028 a barrel. The largest average withdrawal over any month would have been in September 1990 – $610 a day per contract – because the futures price rose from $28.56 a barrel on the first of September to $39.51 a barrel at the end of that month; this represented a gain of about $10 a barrel, or $10,000 per contract. The largest average margin call would have been in the month of June 1988 – $122 a day per contract – because prices fell over that month from $17.72 to $15.16.

Overall, it can be concluded that margin calls and withdrawals would have been substantial,

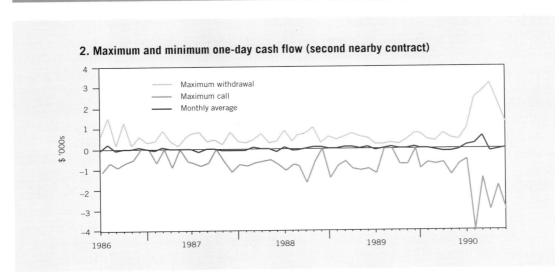

2. Maximum and minimum one-day cash flow (second nearby contract)

and that the importer therefore would have needed access to funds on very short notice. We estimate that for 100 contracts, the importer would have needed access on an almost daily basis to at least $500,000 for possible margin calls. Of course, the need for funds for margin calls would not have represented a cost to the importer, because the negative cashflow effects of margin calls would have been offset by lower bills on future oil imports. The need for funds implies only that the importer's cashflow position would have fluctuated over time. Nevertheless, margins can represent a serious constraint for developing countries in using exchange-based hedging instruments.

LEGAL AND REGULATORY BARRIERS

Many developing countries have exchange controls which prevent the purchase of the collateral required when using futures. Other developing countries have laws that completely prohibit access to the international futures markets. In Colombia, for example, laws were in place until recently which prohibited the use of external risk management instruments. Only after the Colombian government changed the legal framework was the private sector (including Ecopetrol, the oil company) allowed to hedge interest rate, energy price and currency risks.

Although foreign exchange controls can be a serious barrier, the trend in developing countries is towards a more liberal capital account regime. Many developing countries have now removed most of their foreign exchange restrictions.[19] In Latin America and East Asia, few countries still have serious foreign exchange barriers. And the barriers that do still exist are not always effective: in several countries which have formal foreign exchange controls, entities

exist (mainly in the private sector) which have used the hedging markets effectively.[20] This last statement is less true of oil companies in developing countries, which are mainly in the public sector and therefore have little chance of evading formal barriers.

INSTITUTIONAL BARRIERS AND GOVERNMENT INTERVENTION

Often, the exposure to energy price risk in developing countries is not very transparent. This usually arises out of:

❏ complex institutional arrangements (including taxation);
❏ market failures;
❏ distortions produced by political policies; and
❏ local regulations.

Consequently, the incentives for any party to engage in risk management may be poor, or the party least able to carry or manage the risks may be obliged to do so. In Venezuela, for example, the tax structure implied that the exposure of the state oil company to oil prices was quite different from the exposure of the government – and this substantially reduced the incentive to hedge. The usual result of this is that, in the case of imports, most of the risk is borne by the consumer, while in the case of exports, it is absorbed by the government budget.

Furthermore, in many developing countries, state enterprises face a "soft" budget constraint. As a consequence, they lack the main incentive of their counterparts in industrial countries – the threat of bankruptcy.

In some developing countries, government intervention also greatly diminishes the price risk incurred by the private sector. This intervention may be in the form of explicit or implicit domestic price stabilisation schemes, and/or fixed or regulated prices. In some circumstances, the tax system may present a deterrent against hedging, as net profits may be less exposed to external price risks than are gross profits. As a private company will only be interested in hedging net profits, its incentive to hedge will accordingly be less – implying that tax revenues, the difference between gross and net profits, are suffering the exposure to price risk.[21]

This means that the measurement of exposures and the need for hedging should not just be looked at from the viewpoint of the country as a whole, but should also take into account the perspectives of entities within that country: state enterprises, central and local governments, and entities operating price stabilisation schemes. In the case of energy risk, the distribution of risks and the interdependencies between risk bearers depends upon the institutional structures involved in energy production, processing, marketing and distribution. Hence, the design of a coherent hedging strategy can be a complex undertaking.

One example is Trinidad and Tobago, where the government receives royalties based on crude oil production from the state oil company Petrotrin, and a foreign subsidiary of Amoco. Amoco's production is exported in the form of crude oil, while Petrotrin's production is refined locally and exported as refined oil products. While the refinery has the capacity to hedge its exposure to the crack-margin using energy derivatives, the government of Trinidad and Tobago will still remain exposed to crude oil price risks. It may thus need to hedge its oil price exposure using the oil derivative markets. This implies that two hedges may be necessary.

A similar example, but from an import perspective, is Chile. Here, privately operated companies compete with the state oil company Enap on the importing of fuels and the refining of crude oil. All these companies only have an incentive to hedge the crack margin, which leaves Chile as a whole exposed to movements in fuel prices. At the moment, developing countries very rarely make use of integrated hedging strategies.

KNOW-HOW AND AWARENESS
Energy risk management requires a considerable knowledge of financial instruments, and an appropriate institutional framework within which to carry out hedging operations. Expertise is required in order to understand the risk structure of the company or economy, to identify appropriate risk management instruments, and to make and supervise hedging transactions. Furthermore, an institutional framework must be established to report, record, monitor and evaluate the mechanisms used, and internal control procedures must be implemented to prevent speculative transactions.

Many developing countries simply lack the necessary expertise for these operations, and a long-term training programme may be necessary. The experience to date in developing countries (as well as industrial countries), underlines just how complex an undertaking it is to develop adequate internal control procedures. The recent cases of Codelco, MG Corp (a unit of Germany's Metallgesellschaft AG), and Procter and Gamble Co have graphically illustrated the serious losses that can arise from a lack of proper monitoring.[22] It is notable that Codelco and MG Corp were already experienced users of commodity derivative instruments before their problems arose in the metals and energy sectors respectively.

Another important barrier to the use of energy price risk management instruments is a general lack of familiarity at the policy level with these instruments and their strategic uses; in particular, there is a tendency to confuse hedging with speculation. Many policy makers expect, for example, that energy risk management will lead to consistently higher profits, lower debt service payments, higher export prices or, conversely, lower import prices. The notion that risk management effects a trade-off between the assurance of predictable costs against *future* uncertain external price movements – which could produce either large windfall gains or losses – is not yet well accepted at the policy level. Similarly, the notion that risk management is an integral part of a company's operations, and should be pursued independent of market conditions, is not widely accepted.

The fact that policy makers are not aware that using risk management tools may entail "costs" – in terms of foregone higher revenues or lower expenses – can lead to successful hedging programmes being perceived as failures, or prevent potentially attractive hedging programmes from getting started. Political backlash has occurred several times. For example, when Brazil and Chile locked-in oil import prices towards the end of 1990, these prices were later considered to be too "high". In this respect, options can have advantages over the use of futures. With options, only the premium is at risk, and there is thus little chance of political backlash arising from having locked in a fixed price. For example, during the Gulf War, El Salvador purchased oil options to ensure a ceiling price for its oil purchases. When oil prices fell, El Salvador was able to take advantage of the fall, without political backlash, even though the option premium was "lost".

OTHER BARRIERS
Certain critical preconditions for the effective use of energy risk management instruments may not always be in place in developing countries. Technical factors such as transport, storage, time differences, data processing and, especially, communications can represent barriers.

One pertinent problem is that the organisation of oil companies in developing countries is often not suited to the use of energy risk management instruments. To remedy this, companies will need to set up a central risk management unit that collects inputs from various parts of the oil company (treasury department, financial and oil traders, and planning department). In summary, the various departments will need to:
❏ define the objectives and goals of risk management (given specific market conditions);
❏ set limits on the amount of capital at risk;
❏ institute mechanisms to revise these limits in line with an agreed policy on the company's appetite for risk.

These inputs can then be used to set up the appropriate risk management strategies. Presently, many oil companies in developing countries are anyway in the middle of internal reorganisations; the additional restructuring necessary for proper risk management is liable to take some time.

Conclusion: a developing market

We began this chapter by stating that many developing countries could benefit from improved energy price risk management. Experience, as well as theoretical work,[23] has shown that market-based financial instruments can offer considerable benefits when used coherently. We have spent much of this chapter outlining certain problems and suggesting possible solutions. We will conclude by briefly examining the potential effect that developing countries could have on the growth of the energy derivatives market, and by highlighting specific opportunities for derivatives providers that may arise out of this growth.

There is no doubt that developing countries are a potential source of growth for the oil derivative market. After all, developing countries account for 62% of world oil production, and only a small percentage of this production is currently covered by energy risk management instruments. On the import side, developing countries account for about a third of world energy imports, and projections show that their share will increase. Furthermore, the wave of deregularisation, and the higher reliance on market forces, in the energy sectors of developing countries is bound to accentuate the need for risk control.

Investment banks, oil trading firms, futures brokers and futures exchanges in developed countries have already targeted developing countries as a source of growth. The main opportunities and challenges in providing risk management instruments to the oil companies in developing countries, or to governments with oil exposures, are likely to be the following:
❏ The main limitation on the growth of the developing country market is credit risk. As discussed above, innovative companies can devise deal structures to alleviate this problem (marked-to-market swaps, pledges of future receivables, etc). In the future, international agencies may well provide specific credit guarantees intended to increase the use of commodity-linked loans and long-term swaps by developing countries.
❏ A market niche is developing for those companies prepared to assume or manage the differential risk between the spot market and the forward Brent or WTI prices. Many oil companies and governments in developing countries prefer not to manage the basis risk themselves.[24]
❏ Due to increasing environmental pressures in developing countries, the demand for less polluting sweet crudes is likely to grow. This implies a change in traditional oil shipping patterns and their associated price risks.
❏ As explained in more detail above, for small oil companies in developing countries, OTC instruments may be more attractive than exchange-traded instruments – at least in the initial stages of their hedging programme.
❏ Political constraints in developing countries make it difficult for oil producers to sell oil forward, because the producers may then be accused of selling their patrimony. When the oil markets are in backwardation, selling forward may mean locking in a price below the spot, which many developing country oil producers

are unwilling to do.[25] In many cases, oil producers seem to be seeking higher prices rather than stable prices. Given all this, options may be more palatable to policy makers in developing countries. Also, deals that combine financing and price-risk hedging components may also be better accepted in developing countries, because these deals can then be considered not as selling oil cheap, but as getting cheaper finance.

❑ Oil companies and governments in developing countries face a variety of risks, including currency and interest rate exposures. There is a need for structures that incorporate all these price exposures and thus provide an integrated

risk management strategy. For example, a number of Latin American oil companies and/or governments in oil producing countries have debt that is denominated in Japanese yen, while their revenues are linked to oil prices in dollars. Putting the two together, and hedging the net exposure (that is, the spread between the oil prices in dollars and the yen/dollar exchange rate) can be a more efficient way of hedging. An example of an integrated hedge is the yen-denominated jet fuel swap by Korean Air described in Panel 3; Chapter 8 of this book describes the technical aspects of integrated hedging in more detail.

1 *The views expressed in this chapter do not necessarily reflect those of the World Bank, its management, its Executive Board, or its member countries.*

2 *For example, for the case of Venezuela, Claessens and Varangis (1994) showed that the use of futures/options will increase the probability that an oil stabilisation fund will not go bankrupt. For other applications see Larson and Coleman (1994).*

3 *The limited use of energy (and other commodity) risk management instruments by developing countries motivated the World Bank to set up a programme of research and technical assistance (TA) in 1990. With regard to energy, the programme has given assistance in Algeria, Colombia, Costa Rica, Nigeria, Trinidad and Tobago, and Venezuela. It has focused on raising awareness of external exposures to oil prices; indicating to policy makers and the entities exposed the costs and benefits of using market instruments; and assisting them in the implementation of risk management strategies.*

4 *This could be due to proximity in location and to similar trading hours. Unfortunately, similar statistics for all commodities could not be obtained for exchanges in Europe and Asia.*

5 *Note that the percentage of open interest in crude oil contracts attributed to developing countries has remained the same between 1991 and 1993 at 1.6%. However, in absolute numbers, developing countries have increased the use of Nymex's crude oil contract, as the volume of contracts at Nymex has increased between 1991 and 1993.*

6 *See* Financial Times, *March 19, 1992. Because the OTC market is relatively new, and not as tightly monitored as the exchanges, no good data on liquidity is available. Data from ISDA indicates that this market had a (notional) principal amount outstanding at the end of 1992 of $15 billion in swaps and $5 billion in option-type instruments.*

7 *See also* Risk, *September 1991; and* Wall Street Journal, *March 11, 1991, among others.*

8 *El Salvador reportedly used money from an emergency fund at the Central Bank to buy call options.*

9 *In 1991 Asia accounted for about 20% of the commodity swaps.*

10 *Another well-publicised deal in developing countries, but having to do with copper, was that of Mexicana de Cobre (see* Risk, *September 1991).*

11 *Gemill (1985) and McKinnon (1967) present the framework for estimating optimal hedge ratios.*

12 *See Claessens and Varangis (1991).*

13 *We do not count two other crude oil contracts, Nymex's sour crude and Simex's Dubai, as they are not very liquid at present.*

14 *As with exchange-traded futures and options, the minimum margin which needs to be maintained will depend on the volatility of the underlying energy price and the creditworthiness of the counterparty. This minimum margin is negotiated between the counterparty and the party providing the swap.*

15 *The calculation involves deriving the replacement value of the swap using the then prevailing forward energy prices (obtained from futures exchanges and brokers dealing in energy swaps). This replacement value can be negative or positive, depending on whether the swap is out or in the money at the time of the calculation.*

16 *See also the case of the "prepaid sales contract" in JP Morgan & Co. (1991), pp. 80–83.*

17 *At the time of writing, Unctad is planning to organise a forum in which experts may exchange ideas on how to make developing countries more attractive to institutions offering derivative instruments.*

18 *See Claessens and Varangis (1991).*

19 *IMF Annual Report on Foreign Exchange Restrictions, 1993.*

20 *For example, private traders of coffee in Costa Rica and Colombia have used commodity (coffee) derivative markets to hedge their risks, even when formal legal barriers existed.*

21 *For industrial countries it is generally argued that the tax system provides an incentive to hedge as the tax schedule is convex (in the underlying commodity price). This is not generally the case in developing countries.*

22 *See front page articles in the* Wall Street Journal *of March 16, 1994 and April 14, 1994.*

23 *See Priovolos and Duncan, 1991; Claessens and Duncan, 1993.*

24 *Our point here regarding basis risk is especially clear in the case of jet fuel. There is no futures contract for jet fuel, and so hedgers are obliged to use gasoil. Jet fuel has traditionally been traded for an average differential of $25 to gasoil, with a high of $50. However, during the Gulf War, the spread increased to an average of $65 and a high of $186,* exposing many hedgers to a high basis risk. The increasing use of jet fuel swaps by airlines in developing countries, particularly in Asia, reflects the desire to avoid having to manage this basis risk.

25 *Of course, oil price backwardation provides an opportunity for oil importing developing countries to lock in below current spot prices for their future oil imports.*

BIBLIOGRAPHY

Arrau, P., and S. Claessens, 1992, "Commodity Stabilization Funds", PR working paper no. 854, The World Bank.

Claessens, S., and R. Duncan, eds., 1993, *Managing Commodity Price Risk in Developing Countries*, The World Bank and Johns Hopkins University Press.

Claessens, S., and P. Varangis, 1991, "Hedging Crude Oil Imports in Developing Countries", PR working paper no. 755, The World Bank.

– 1992, "Promoting Developing Countries' Use of Commodity Hedging", Paper presented at the seminar on "Risk Hedging Techniques and Operations", Bogotá, Colombia, November 19–20.

– 1994, "Oil Price Instability, Hedging and an Oil Stabilization Fund: The Case of Venezuela", PR working paper no. 1290, The World Bank, April.

Deaton, A., 1992, "Commodity Prices, Stabilization, and Growth in Africa", mimeo, Princeton University.

Financial Times, 1992, "Equity and Commodity Swaps: Techniques Find New Markets", March 19.

Futures Industry Association, *International Open Interest Report*, various issues.

Gemmill, G., 1985, "Optimal Hedging on Futures Markets for Commodity-Exporting Nations", *European Economic Review*, 27, pp. 2245–61.

JP Morgan & Co., eds. 1991, *Commodity-Linked Finance*, Euromoney Books.

Larson, D.F. and J. Coleman, 1994, "The Effects of Options-Hedging on the Costs of Domestic Price Stabilization Schemes", in *Managing Commodity Risk in Developing Countries*, S. Claessens and R. Duncan, eds., Johns Hopkins University Press.

Laughlin, T.J., and W.D. Falloon, 1990, "Catch-22 Solutions for Less Developed Countries", *Corporate Risk Management*, September, pp. 26–29.

McKinnon, R., 1967, "Futures Markets, Buffer Stocks, and Income Instability for Primary Products", *Journal of Political Economy*, vol. 75, no. 6, pp. 844–61.

Priovolos, T. and R. Duncan, eds., 1991, *Commodity Price Risk Management and Finance*, 1991, Oxford University Press.

Risk magazine, various issues.

Wall Street Journal, 1991, "Mexico's Move to Lock in Oil Prices in Gulf Crisis Means it Can Stay Calm Now as the Market Softens", Monday, March 11.

World Bank, 1994, *Global Economic Prospects and the Developing Countries: 1994*, Washington, DC.

MARKET ISSUES

13

Exchanges and the OTC Market

Alban Brindle
IPE

The markets in both exchange-traded contracts and over-the-counter (OTC) instruments have achieved consistently high levels of growth in the last five years, particularly in the period since the Gulf Crisis of 1990–91. The whole complex of energy trading now accounts for some 600 million to 700 million barrels of oil a day, or about 10 times the underlying physical base.[1] This growth is easiest to tabulate with regard to the exchanges (see Table 1). For example, in 1989 global exchange-based trading in energy futures and options amounted to 43 million contracts, while in 1993 it amounted to 70 million contracts – an increase of 62% in four years.

However, OTC instruments have experienced even greater growth. This is partly as a result of the extreme volatility experienced during the Gulf Crisis, which made most companies involved in the energy industry, whether upstream or downstream, much more aware of the effect that poor risk management could have on their profitability. Therefore, although futures and options trading on the three exchanges last year averaged just under 300 million barrels of oil equivalent a day, the forward and OTC markets are now estimated to trade a further 300 to 400 million barrels of oil a day.[2]

Table 1. Energy futures and options trading, 1986–94 (thousand contracts)

Contract	1986	1987	1988	1989	1990	1991	1992	1993	1994
Nymex									
WTI future	8,314	14,582	18,860	20,535	23,687	21,006	21,110	24,869	-
WTI option	135	3,117	5,480	5,686	5,255	4,969	6,562	7,157	-
Heating oil future	3,275	4,293	4,935	5,741	6,377	6,680	8,005	8,625	-
Heating oil option	-	144	126	298	407	863	1,248	803	-
Unleaded future	439	2,056	3,292	4,485	5,206	5,510	6,675	7,408	-
Unleaded option	-	-	-	332	436	574	860	661	-
Natural gas future	-	-	-	-	133	418	1,921	4,672	-
Natural gas option	-	-	-	-	-	-	81	346	-
Propane	-	15	24	15	39	56	51	45	-
Nymex total	14,780	25,735	34,316	38,490	42,459	40,787	47,212	55,412	
IPE									
Brent future	-	-	292	1,672	4,083	5,292	6,172	8,853	10,083
Brent option	-	-	-	61	153	234	792	1,059	532
Gasoil future	938	1,102	1,557	1,957	2,603	2,864	3,453	3,609	3,779
Gasoil option	-	1	16	35	102	91	199	218	137
Unleaded future	-	-	-	-	-	-	59	32	4
IPE total	943	1,107	1,865	3,729	6,946	8,513	10,676	13,770	14,534
Simex									
Fuel oil future	-	-	-	993	214	183	278	323	-
Gasoil future	-	-	-	-	-	-	26	-	-
Simex total	-	-	-	993	214	183	304	323	-
Total (all 3 exchanges)	15,723	26,842	36,181	43,212	49,619	49,483	58,192	69,505	-

THE ENERGY EXCHANGES

Nymex

Founded in 1872 as the Butter and Cheese Exchange of New York (renamed the New York Mercantile Exchange in 1882), Nymex has become the world's leading exchange for trading energy and metals futures and options contracts.

In 1978 Nymex pioneered energy futures trading with its heating oil contract. This contract rapidly gained acceptance, and since then the Nymex petroleum complex has grown to include unleaded gasoline (1981), West Texas Intermediate crude oil (1983) and propane (1987). Nymex also has active option contracts on crude oil (1983), heating oil (1987) and gasoline (1989). All energy futures contracts listed on the exchange are for 1,000 barrels (42,000 US gallons) and are listed in US dollars and cents.

Nymex West Texas Intermediate (WTI) crude oil has been the most actively traded futures contract on a physical commodity since it surpassed gold in 1987. By most measures, Nymex is the most transparent futures oil market in the world. In 1993, for example, Nymex traded 24,869,000 of its light sweet crude oil contracts, compared with 8,853,000 contracts traded by the equivalent IPE specification. In the same year, Nymex also traded 7,157,000 crude oil option contracts, versus 1,059,000 on the IPE.

The most recent success for the Nymex, however, has been the rapid growth in trading in natural gas, a contract initially listed in August 1990, but which has seen trading increase to almost 2 million contracts in 1993. In October 1992, the exchange also listed an options contract for natural gas, due to the increased liquidity in the underlying futures contract. In November 1994, Nymex also listed crack spread contracts between WTI crude oil and heating oil, and WTI and unleaded gasoline. Nymex currently ranks as the third-largest US futures exchange.

IPE

The International Petroleum Exchange of London (IPE) was incorporated on November 17, 1980, and is Europe's only energy futures exchange. The gasoil futures contract, with physical delivery by warrant, was the first contract to be launched on the exchange, early in 1981. In response to demands from the trade, this contract was subsequently changed to an FOB physical delivery contract in 1984. The early attempts to install futures contracts for gasoline, heavy fuel oil and Brent crude oil met with too little interest to create adequate liquidity.

However, in June 1988, a new Brent crude oil contract which utilised cash settlement was relaunched on the exchange, and this contract has progressively gained ground (particularly since the Gulf Crisis). It is based on the 15-day Brent crude oil forward market, one of the most widely traded forward crude oil markets in the world. Subsequent developments, particularly in the commingling of the Brent and Ninian crude oil production streams, have meant that the physical base for this contract has expanded, and this should improve the long-term prospects for the IPE's Brent futures contract.

Option contracts have also been introduced on both the gasoil and Brent crude oil futures contracts. These cover the first six months traded on the underlying futures contract. In January 1992, the exchange launched an unleaded gasoline futures contract which, it is hoped, will provide a viable hedging mechanism for the light end of the refined barrel in Europe.

Simex

Originally established as the Gold Exchange of Singapore in 1978, the Singapore International Monetary Exchange Ltd (Simex) was inaugurated in 1984 after its reconstruction in 1983. Simex established a mutual offset link with the Chicago Mercantile Exchange (CME) in 1984; however, the two exchanges are independently owned and operated, and maintain separate clearing houses. The CME/Simex link has, in effect, created a single trading floor between two separate exchanges in two different time zones. Energy contracts currently listed on the exchange include high sulphur fuel oil and gasoil. There are no options contracts for the energy products currently listed. The high sulphur fuel oil contract is currently the only liquid fuel oil futures contract listed on any exchange, and has so far had some success in servicing the needs of the fastest-growing bunkering (and oil-consuming) market in the world.

PANEL 2

TRADING ON THE EXCHANGES: A SUMMARY

Exchange-traded energy derivatives are traded under the rules and regulations of a centralised marketplace through a defined membership structure. Clients trade via an intermediary, who must be an exchange clearing member. These members have to fulfil certain criteria such as a minimum net worth, and are regulated by the appropriate self-regulating organisation or government body – normally the Securities and Futures Authority (SFA) in the UK and the National Futures Authority (NFA) and the Commodity Futures Trading Commission (CFTC) in the US.

Through the system of formalised performance guarantees extended to the floor clearing members, clearing of exchange-traded contracts (either by the clearing house or by the exchanges themselves) provides some degree of security to participants in the energy markets.

The London Clearing House (LCH), for instance, clears futures contracts in all the London futures exchanges. It is owned by the six major London clearing banks. When the clearing house becomes the central counterparty to all contracts registered on the exchanges, this removes bilateral obligations from the market, and allows certain offsetting trades to be cancelled out in the case of default by a clearing member. This allows for greater ease in offsetting an individual position, and increases liquidity within the marketplace.

Trading takes place competitively either by "open outcry" in pits or rings, or through electronic screen trading systems. Energy futures contracts rarely have formal market-making arrangements, although options trading through the exchanges may benefit from some kind of unoffi-

cial market-making undertaken by a group of specialist members. Through the pit trading system, trading is focused at all times on one standardised product, creating the liquidity necessary to provide narrow bid/offer spreads and the ability to accommodate large orders without moving the market price (and thereby minimising the "slippage" inherent in placing or removing hedges).

All energy futures contracts have the facility of allowing both the buyer and the seller to exchange a futures position for a physical position of equal quantity. This subject, and the Exchange for Swaps mechanism (EFS) available on the IPE, is discussed in detail in the main text.

All futures contracts tend to be designed along similar lines, employing either a system of cash settlement against an index, or physical delivery upon termination of the contract. All options are exercised into the underlying futures contract, and are American-style, allowing exercise at any time before expiry of the option. The months available to trade are all predetermined. On the Nymex and the Simex, there are certain pre-set price fluctuation limits, while the IPE has no price limits on any of its contracts, preferring to allow unlimited access to the markets irrespective of volatility.

Initial margins (that is, "good faith" deposits), usually between 5% and 15% of the underlying contract value, are normally set according to the historical volatility levels experienced in the recent past. Contracts on all three exchanges are Span margined, that is, the total margin requirement is calculated by estimating the risk of the entire portfolio of contracts on a particular market, and not by estimation of the potential risk on each individual contract.

The dominant view in the exchanges used to be that the two markets were in competition for a limited amount of business. In fact, of course, there is a great deal of interdependence between them: neither of the markets would have been so successful without the existence of the other. This chapter is intended to explore the nature of that relationship.

In the first section of this chapter, we will very briefly characterise some of the essential differences between exchange-based and OTC trading – that is, we will look at the traditional

competitive side of the relationship. We will then move on to look at the symbiotic part of the relationship: how the OTC players use the exchanges to hedge risk. We will examine some of the problems involved in using the exchanges in this way, and describe how the exchanges have started to respond to the relatively greater growth in the OTC market by introducing new mechanisms that are attractive to OTC users, and by planning new instruments that act in a complementary way to the OTC market.

COMPARISON OF OTC AND EXCHANGE MARKETS

Exchange	OTC
Centralised marketplace	Bilateral negotiation
Regulated	Unregulated
Open outcry	Telephone market
Access through exchange members	Occasionally broked
Standardised instruments	Tailor-made
Highly liquid	Variable trading
Wide range of market participants	Variable range of users
Ease of offset	No offset
Broker markets with commission	Principal market with bid-offer spread
Narrow range of products	Proliferation of products
Long development lead time	Constant development of new products
Clearing house as counterparty	Counterparty risk
Daily initial and variation margin collection	Monthly/quarterly settlement
Physical delivery/EFPs facilitated	Cash transfer only
Transparent market	Opaque market
Predetermined transaction costs	Indeterminable and variable costs
Ease of trading in "fast" markets	Market will dry up when highly volatile
Anonymity	Transparency when "getting out"

OTC versus the exchanges

The main characteristic of the OTC market is that it offers individually tailored instruments geared to match exactly the client's risk profile. This contrasts with the highly standardised nature of exchange-based instruments: the only elements that can be negotiated are the price and number of contracts. Admittedly, this distinction can become blurred: for example, because of the cash-settled nature of the IPE's Brent futures contract, some would argue that this futures contract is in fact a contract for difference (CFD).

Any potential user of either market must make a choice as to which instruments are most suitable for the management of a particular risk profile. I have attempted a summary list of the characteristics of OTC instruments versus exchange instruments in Panel 3 (arguably a little biased towards the exchanges point of view). But perhaps the clearest way of helping market participants to make a choice is to outline the main disadvantages. That is, in the case of exchange-traded derivatives:
❏ basis risk may exist between the exchange instrument used and the actual physical exposure; and

❏ rollover and management costs can be considerable.

On the other hand, OTC strategies:
❏ incur a credit and counterparty risk which can be both difficult to assess, and which may change rapidly; and
❏ may not be easy to exit from, and may involve implicit and variable costs over the life of the instrument (such as the in-built margin paid to the provider, and the costs arising from changes in the term structure of the market).

The fact that OTC instruments are tailored to suit an individual risk profile, and do not require constant monitoring and the infrastructure to cater for margin calls and position limits, holds great attraction for many users. Many firms simply do not have the necessary resources to successfully implement and sustain an exchange-based risk management strategy.

Of course, the basis risk incurred by the provider of an OTC transaction has to be covered by the margin that providers build into the terms of the swap; one problem faced by many end-users is that they cannot quantify this component of the cost. Furthermore, the final cost of the strategy will be obscure until the purchaser knows the average price of, say, Brent at

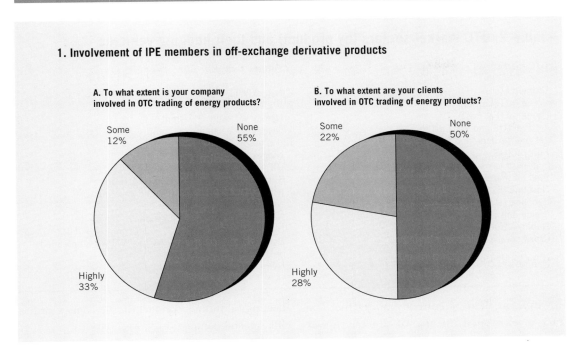

1. Involvement of IPE members in off-exchange derivative products

A. To what extent is your company involved in OTC trading of energy products?

Some 12%
None 55%
Highly 33%

B. To what extent are your clients involved in OTC trading of energy products?

Some 22%
None 50%
Highly 28%

the end of the transactional period. This contrasts with a strategy making use of futures: the transaction costs will be known as soon as the hedge is put into place.

It is true that some OTC instruments have become more standardised, and offer a relatively more transparent and liquid market. Examples of these markets are the jet-fuel swaps market and the 'dated to paper' or CFD market for Brent crude oil. However, the transparency in these markets is limited to those parties involved in the physical market on a regular basis, and it is facilitated through the use of specialist 'cash' market brokers which act as intermediaries. Therefore, the real-time price transparency and depth in these markets is still variable and limited. Moreover, participants are aware of each other's positions, which means that particular players can occasionally be 'squeezed'; this is especially true if most of the swap purchasers are taking similar market positions, or if one player is known to have a large position in a particular market.

Providers and the exchanges

As we noted above, the relationships that exist between these two markets are complex and rapidly changing. In the past, the exchanges have often taken the view that the OTC markets are in some sense 'unfair competition', and that they have detracted from the liquidity of the futures market. This attitude has now largely changed, as the exchanges have come to realise that much of the residual risk of OTC transactions, whether in terms of basis risk or position risk, is managed by the use of exchange-based futures and options contracts. Indeed, to some extent, the OTC market can be regarded as a channel through which risk flows onto the exchanges that, without the OTC market, would probably not have been managed at all.

The volume of trade generated by the OTC markets is difficult to quantify, but the pie charts in Figure 1 illustrate the answer to two questions we put to the members of the IPE in December 1993 in order to gain some idea of the importance of the OTC business on the exchange.

Those participants in the OTC markets who are most active on the futures markets tend to be the large OTC swaps providers. In the main, these participants are the energy risk management divisions of banks or those of oil trading companies, who are in turn providing risk management facilities for their end-user customers. Providers such as these have only two ways of offsetting the risk they assume from end-users: by selling an instrument to another party with a similar but opposing risk profile; or by managing this risk using appropriate exchange-based futures and options contracts. In fact, most of the residual risk will be managed by the provider either through trading forward oil markets or through the exchanges.

One of the most common forms of swap instruments in the energy sector is a jet fuel swap, whereby an airline, as the end-user, will purchase a fixed-price swap from an oil company or a bank. (This kind of arrangement is described in detail in Chapters 5 and 9.)

Table 2. OTC market sectors (by product) and their hedging vehicles

OTC market	Futures contract
Crude oil (US)	Nymex WTI
Crude oil (Europe)	IPE Brent
Crude oil (Far East)	Nymex WTI and IPE Brent
Jet fuel (US and Far East)	Nymex no 2 heating oil
Jet fuel (Europe and Far East)	IPE gasoil
Fuel oil (US)	Nymex WTI
High and low sulphur fuel oil (Europe)	IPE Brent
Fuel oil (Far East)	Simex fuel oil, Nymex WTI & IPE Brent
Gasoline (Europe)	IPE Brent and Nymex unleaded gasoline
Gasoline (US)	Nymex unleaded
Gasoil and jet fuel (Far East)	No 2 heating oil and IPE gasoil
Naphtha (Far East)	Nymex unleaded
Crack spread	Combinations: commonly Nymex WTI/No 2/unleaded or IPE Brent/gasoil
Natural gas (US)	Nymex natural gas

However, as there is currently no jet fuel contract in existence on any of the energy exchanges, the swap provider will look to the closest alternative, normally either the No 2

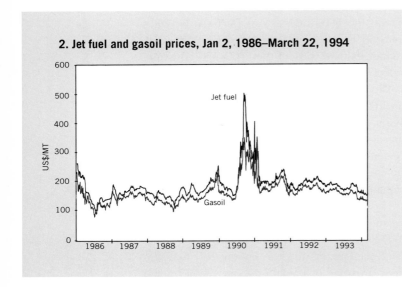

2. Jet fuel and gasoil prices, Jan 2, 1986–March 22, 1994

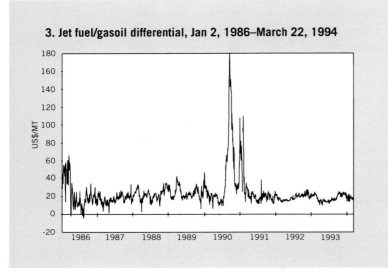

3. Jet fuel/gasoil differential, Jan 2, 1986–March 22, 1994

heating oil futures contract on the Nymex or the IPE's gasoil contract.

As can be seen from Figure 2, there is normally a close correlation between the prices of jet fuel and gasoil, as these two petroleum products are of a generally similar nature, and have overlapping boiling ranges as refined products. The basis, or differential, between jet fuel and gasoil normally lies in the range of $20 to $30 a tonne. Nonetheless, as Figure 3 helps to make clear, during the Gulf Crisis this relationship disintegrated rapidly over the space of a few months. In pricing a fixed jet fuel swap, one of the main considerations the swap provider would take into account would be an assessment of how the differential may change over the duration of the swap. Indeed, the main factor determining the price of the swap would be the provider's perception of the future volatility of the basis. Chapters 2 and 4 of this book examine in more detail the technical aspects of estimating volatility and correlations.

Table 2 provides a summary of the most popular OTC market sectors (by product), and the futures contracts which are commonly used as hedging vehicles for the management of the associated risk. However, this list is not comprehensive, as new markets often emerge as and when there is a need. Moreover, some futures contracts can become a better risk management tool at certain times, due to seasonal demand variations or short-term price aberrations.

Needless to say, there remain substantial risks to the OTC risk management provider, due to the potentially large basis risk between the instrument being offered and the exchange-traded contract which is used to hedge the position.

Environmental legislation, transport costs and geographical discrepancies can result in a highly volatile basis risk.

For example, when offering a fuel oil hedge to a utility based in the Mediterranean, the swap provider would normally hedge this position by using Brent futures on the IPE. However, as can be seen from Figure 4, the basis risk resulting from this action can be very high – and is sometimes greater than that arising from not hedging at all.

In the case of a gasoline swap based on north-west European prices, the position would probably be hedged by using either the Nymex unleaded gasoline contract or the IPE Brent contract. Considerations such as relative liquidity, structure of the market and potential basis movements over the duration of the hedge all have to be taken into account. Similarly, for a gasoil swap based on cargo quotations in north-west Europe, the swap provider may have to estimate the future differential between the IPE gasoil contract, based on the barge market in the Amsterdam-Rotterdam-Antwerp area, and the north-west European cargo market. The problems which can arise out of these considerations are discussed in more detail in Chapter 9.

Another problem is the duration of the OTC instruments on offer, which is often far greater than the maturities available on the exchanges;

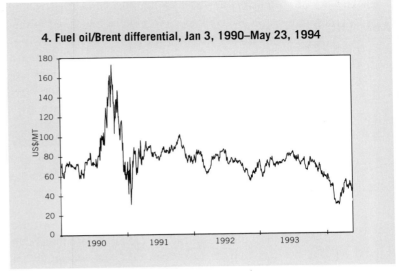

4. Fuel oil/Brent differential, Jan 3, 1990–May 23, 1994

the liquidity of exchange-traded contracts can be thin even beyond a few months into the future. For example, jet fuel swaps are now commonly offered as far out as two years forward – sometimes considerably longer – while the IPE gasoil contract only trades 18 months forward (and liquidity even that far ahead is poor). The Nymex contracts tend to trade further out, sometimes as far as three years forward; again, however, liquidity can be a problem when trying to "lay positions on" in these back months.

Often, the hedging technique will involve laying the position on in a month which has a

Table 3. Comparative maturities of exchange contracts used when hedging

Contract	Months traded
Nymex	
WTI future	18 consecutive months, plus 21st, 24th, 30th and 36th month
WTI option	Six consecutive, plus 9th and 12th month
Heating oil future	18 consecutive months
Heating oil option	Six consecutive, plus 9th and 12th month
Unleaded future	18 consecutive months
Unleaded option	Six consecutive, plus 9th and 12th month
Natural gas future	18 consecutive months
Natural gas option	12 consecutive months
Propane	15 consecutive months
IPE	
Brent future	12 consecutive months
Brent option	Six consecutive months
Gasoil future	12 consecutive months, plus 15th and 18th month
Gasoil option	Six consecutive months
Unleaded future	Six consecutive months
Simex	
Fuel oil future	Nine consecutive months
Gasoil future	Six consecutive months

reasonable level of liquidity, and then rolling over the contracts into months which are further out (once the month initially used comes near to expiry). For instance, instead of placing a hedge 12 months out, where there is insufficient market liquidity, the hedger will place the position into the six-month forward contract, then roll over this position once this six-month contract comes near to expiry. However, this technique sometimes erodes the efficiency of the hedge, and may substantially increase transaction costs if the market is in an adverse structure at the time of the roll.

Perhaps more important in the long term than the basis risk or trading costs inherent in providing a long-term OTC risk management service is the fact that the main crude oil streams being used to price these swaps have a limited lifespan.

The Brent crude futures contract is based on the 15-day forward market for Brent crude oil. The 15-day market, trading 500,000 barrel paper cargoes of Brent, has evolved into the world's most transparent and internationally traded forward market for crude oil. Nowadays, about 65 per cent of the world's crude oil is priced either directly or indirectly from the price of Brent. However, although the longevity of the Brent crude oil stream has been considerably prolonged as a result of the commingling of the Brent and Ninian crude oil streams in August 1990, production of Brent is predicted to start tailing off more rapidly beyond 1997.

This obviously has important implications for long-term swaps which are being priced according to Brent, some of which are now set to last considerably longer than the sustainable life of the field itself. At some point, a replacement benchmark crude will have to be found. So far, this looks likely to remain a North Sea crude oil, due partly to the lack of restrictions on export destinations. At the moment, the most likely candidate to replace Brent as the benchmark is Forties crude oil, a crude which is likely to remain in plentiful supply well into the next century. However, for the moment, forward trading in Forties is only a fraction of that represented by Brent.

The problem is much more marked in the case of WTI. The underlying physical base for this benchmark has been diminishing steadily over the last few years. This has led to a gradual drop in the level of physical trading in WTI, which has already had an effect on the price behaviour of this market.

Exchange mechanisms useful to providers

CASH SETTLEMENT ON FUTURES AND EFPS
The IPE's Brent futures contract is the only cash-settled energy contract offered by the exchanges; that is, no physical delivery of the commodity is necessary at expiry. Cash settlement is made against an index, published each day by the exchange, which represents an average of the previous day's trading in the underlying Brent 15-day forward market. All the outstanding contracts remaining open at expiry are marked-to-market against the index for the last day of trading, and a cash payment is either received or made within 48 hours.

Nonetheless, physical delivery can be made through the Exchange of Futures for Physical (EFP) facility, which is available on all energy futures contracts. There are three main types of EFPs, all of which involve exchanging a futures position for a physical position (and vice versa):
❏ The first involves liquidating a futures position. Via this mechanism, two users who are long and short of the same futures contract agree to liquidate the future and substitute a cash-market transaction.
❏ The second initiates a futures position. This is when a physical deal between two counterparties is "booked out" and at the same time the equivalent futures contract is inserted.
❏ The third involves the transfer of a futures position, where one party has a futures position and the other has a physical holding. Equal and opposite cash and futures transactions are initiated, resulting in the transfer of the futures and physical positions between the parties.

EFPs are offered by the exchanges as a way of increasing the flexibility of futures. They allow pricing to be separated from supply arrangements, and have a variety of practical uses:
❏ Delivery flexibility. Participants in the market can choose their counterparty and select a mutually convenient date, location and quality. They are typically executed between producers, traders and end-users in cargo-sizes, or fractions thereof.
❏ Out-of-hours trading. When the 'original' physical deal being closed out by an EFP is transacted at the same time as the EFP, the effect is to allow futures to be traded when the exchange is closed.
❏ Simultaneous transactions. A distributor who hedged his future purchases on the IPE could separately close out the future and purchase on the spot market. An EFP enables both legs to be

Table 4. An example of an EFP

Airline

August 3

Physical	Buys 3,000 tonnes of kerosene from refiner @ $192/t	($576,000)
The hedge	Sells Sep 30 gasoil futures @ $172	$516,000
The EFP	Long Sep 30 gasoil futures @ $146	($438,000)
Lost upside on physical	Spot kerosene price on receipt was $164	$492,000

Futures gain: **$78,000**   Physical loss: **$84,000**

September 2

Physical	Buys 3,000 tonnes of kerosene from refiner @ $160/t	($480,000)
The hedge	Sells Sep 30 gasoil futures @ $142	$426,000
The EFP	Long Sep 30 gasoil futures @ $114	($342,000)
Lost upside on physical	Spot kerosene price on receipt was $130	$390,000

Futures gain: **$84,000**   Physical loss: **$90,000**

October 6

Physical	Buys 3,000 tonnes of kerosene from refiner @ $119/t	($357,000)
The hedge	Sells Sep 30 gasoil futures @ $102	$306,000
The EFP	Long Sep 30 gasoil futures @ $111	($333,000)
Lost upside on physical	Spot kerosene price on receipt was $130	$390,000

Futures loss: **$27,000**   Physical gain: **$33,000**

Refiner

Firstly:

	Buys 30 gas oil contracts at	Agreed kerosene price is	Difference
August 3	$172	$192	$20
September 2	$142	$160	$18
October 6	$102	$119	$17

Secondly:

	Spot kerosene price on delivery is	Futures gas oil price	Difference	Gain from diff change
August 3	$164	$146	$18	$6,000
September 2	$130	$114	$16	$6,000
October 6	$130	$111	$19	($6,000)

Physical cost: $1,272,000   **Net gain: $6,000**

Key to table

Physical	The price the airline pays the refiner for the physical kerosene
The hedge	The airline hedges physical exposure against adverse price movements
The EFP	The price at which the airline sells gasoil futures to the refiner
Lost upside on physical	The spot price of kerosene, when airline receives physical from refiner. This is the price the airline would get if it immediately sold physical, and so it can therefore be considered as a credit (the opposite to the agreed long position)

transacted simultaneously, eliminating any risk of market moves.

Perhaps the clearest way of explaining the advantages of EFPs is a practical example.

Imagine that an airline wishes to buy jet kerosene from a refiner for its fleet of aircraft. The airline will require 3,000 tonnes of kerosene every month for the next three months (August/September/October). The date is July 17, and the spot price of kerosene is $200 a tonne.

The airline obviously needs a physical delivery at particular dates, but rather than pay a price for the kerosene that is dependent on those dates, the airline decides that it wants to have the flexibility of choosing the date and thus the price at which to pay. Therefore it is agreed that 3,000 tonnes of kerosene will be delivered at the start of each month, and the price is determined by the airline sometime within the first week of the delivery month. The refiner thus allows the airline to "trigger" the price of delivery on a day of their choosing, and the airline and the refiner agree to EFP on the day and at the price determined by the airline.

The airline will exchange gasoil futures contracts in return for the physical kerosene. This is agreeable to both parties since the products are of a similar nature.

On July 17, the jet fuel physical price is $200 a tonne. Table 4 tabulates the consequences of the agreement.

The "difference" column in Table 4 measures the difference between the kerosene price and the futures price (ie, the basis) at the same time, but under different circumstances. Firstly, it represents the difference between the futures gasoil price and the agreed kerosene price and, secondly, it represents the difference between the spot kerosene price and the futures gasoil price. The agreed kerosene price is determined by the airline, and the futures gasoil price is determined by the refiner.

In this example, the refiner makes a net gain of $6,000 due to the narrowing of the basis differential between the kerosene price and the gasoil price. However, the gain would have been even greater had the basis not widened in October.

The end result of these transactions is that the airline makes a net loss of $6,000. The total cost of engaging in these EFP transactions is $1,419,000. However, had the airline not engaged in these transactions, the kerosene would have cost it about $200 a tonne – which, multiplied by the 9,000 tonnes needed, equals $1,800,000. A saving of $381,000 was thus made because the airline was able to fix the price of kerosene for physical delivery at times (and prices) of its choosing.

It must be remembered that the airline would have lost financially if the spot had been lower than the price agreed. However, by adopting similar strategies hedgers always gain the certainty of a fixed price, as opposed to having to accept the market spot price. In the case of all EFPs, the exchanges require verification that the physical transaction actually took place between the two parties.

EXCHANGE OF FUTURES FOR SWAPS (EFS)

In addition to the EFP facility provided on all energy futures contracts, the IPE also provides the facility to exchange a swap position for futures contracts. This works in the same way as an EFP, except that it allows OTC contracts to be exchanged for futures.

The intention of the exchange in setting up this facility was twofold: firstly, to allow swap trades, whether they were using futures as part of the pricing structure or not, to be transferred from one party to another at an agreed transfer price. This increases the "transferability" of swap positions, and should eventually lead to increased liquidity within the off-exchange markets.

Secondly, the aim was to circumvent the problem of assessing counterparty risk. By allowing a transfer in or out of a swap position, resulting in a corresponding futures position, the swap transaction would benefit by coming within the umbrella of relative security that is extended to all contracts traded through the IPE. This should allow a wider range of potential users to access the off-exchange markets.

In short, the EFS mechanism allows swap traders to lock in a differential to a futures contract, or simply to exchange a swaps position for a futures position. As an example, let us take the most basic form of energy swap: a contract for price differences, in which cash differences are paid between a fixed price and a floating index price over the life of the agreement.

In these transactions, the swaps provider will typically provide the floating part of the transaction. Many providers were stung in the Gulf war, when a historically stable differential between jet fuel and its proxy on the exchanges (gasoil) began to rise to a level far above its normal range. Banks, and other providers, therefore began to offer hedging programmes which incorporated that differential. For example, an airline might buy the jet fuel from an oil company, whilst selling back an equivalent volume of gasoil through the use of futures contracts at a fixed differential to jet. EFSs allow for the integration of such deals to the futures market.

The futures component can be agreed at any time, whether the exchange is open or not, and then posted on the IPE up to one hour after the expiry of each contract. In this way, the transaction has been linked directly into a futures exchange; this means that the transaction gains the relative certainty of delivery associated with the futures contracts traded on the exchange.

Imagine a swap agreement in which, say, Morgan Stanley agrees to grant British Airways a 10,000-tonne jet fuel swap at $195 a tonne against Platts March 1993 jet fuel, CIF northwest Europe quote. This straightforward agreement is complicated slightly when the two firms agree a differential for jet fuel against the IPE's March gasoil contract of $24 a tonne, and agree to establish a March gasoil position. Morgan Stanley then becomes short of the jet fuel swap for March and long of 100 March gasoil con-

EFS example (stage one)

Morgan Stanley's position

Swap	*Futures*
Short 10,000t	Long 10,000t
Jet @ $195	IPE gasoil @ $171

British Airways' position

Swap	*Futures*
Long 10,000t	Short 10,000t
Jet at $195	IPE gasoil at $171

tracts at $171 a tonne. British Airways' position is long of the jet fuel swap and short 100 March gasoil futures at $171 a tonne.

The $171 a tonne gasoil exchange does not, however, depend on market price, but on the price of jet fuel and the basis (differential) between jet and gasoil agreed by the two counterparties. Both parties are now partially hedged by using the gasoil position, and their respective risk is limited to potential future changes in the pre-agreed differential between jet and gasoil of $24 a tonne. Morgan Stanley's risk is that the differential widens beyond $24, whilst British Airways' risk is limited to a narrowing of the differential below $24.

Both firms are now in a position to take advantage of trading opportunities. Morgan Stanley, for example, can grant a jet fuel swap to a refiner by agreeing to purchase jet fuel at an agreed fixed price, thereby matching the two positions back-to-back, and close out its futures position (preferably at a profit). British Airways, on the other hand, can either allow its position to run, or trade against it in a variety of ways.

In the same way, a swap contract, whether priced against a futures related price or not, would become transferable from one party to another.

Imagine that an airline has taken on a swap contract with its regular jet fuel supplier, fixing its price of jet fuel for the following six months. During the lifetime of the contract, the airline decides that it would like to get out of this agreement, as the market for jet has moved to a level below that of the fixed price, and the air-

line is now paying out money to the supplier. The airline could agree to sell the swap to another party at a pre-agreed transfer price, and exchange it for gasoil futures contracts which it can subsequently trade out of. As a result, the airline is able to abandon its swap position, transferring it to any player willing to take it on.

Other market participants may be willing to assume the swap position, either for a fee or because they have a different view of the market. For example, if the airline has locked in a jet swap at $200 a tonne and the market is now at $180, and the airline believes that it is likely to stay at that level for the duration of the swap agreement, then it may be willing to pay to get out of the position. Therefore, it makes contact with another airline through its IPE broker. This new airline takes the view that the jet fuel market will rise in the next few months to levels above $200. Therefore, the two airlines agree to transfer the swap at a mutually agreed price.

In this way, a market may eventually emerge whereby existing swaps might be traded on a "second tier" market. Standardised instruments, such as jet swaps, could be transferred more easily between parties with differing market outlooks or positions, thereby increasing the transparency and the liquidity in the OTC markets – and tying them more directly to the exchanges.

To sum up, by using EFSs, users can transform (usually with some basis risk or transactional cost) non-exchange products such as 15-day Brent, jet fuel swaps and OTC options into exchange-traded products. This gives three advantages to the market: firstly, it enables the

EFS example (stage two)

Morgan Stanley's position

Swap	*Futures*
Short 10,000t	Long 10,000t
Jet @ $195	IPE gasoil @ $171
Net Square Jet	Liquidate IPE @ $171 or above

British Airways' position

Swap	*Futures*
Long 10,000t	Short 10,000t
Jet @ $195	IPE gasoil @ $171
	? Remain long Jet swap
	? Increase/decrease IPE short
	position/EFS out of Jet swap

risk on OTC products to be traded with other counterparties; secondly, it provides direct offsets against any IPE contracts which have been used to hedge the OTC product; and it brings the trade within the cover of the clearing house security system.

For the moment, the EFS mechanism is used only rarely. However, as more players become familiar with the potential of EFSs, the IPE expects volumes to rise.

New contracts

Due to the limited range of contracts currently available on energy exchanges, there are many areas which are not yet adequately covered by the current contract complex. For example, recent developments within the gas industry, particularly in the UK, mean that the IPE is closely monitoring the potential for listing a natural gas contract on the IPE. Although the market in Europe is still controlled to a large extent by the respective national gas monopolies, it is generally accepted that this situation will change over the next few years, as greater competition for markets leads to a greater range of participation in the business, and a more diverse range of interests.

Although the UK has tended to lead the way in Europe in this area, with the recent break-up of the state monopoly British Gas into various constituent parts, and the development of gas distribution and trading interests by a variety of independent gas companies, as yet a spot market for gas has not evolved. However, once a free spot market for gas develops, then a forward and, ultimately, a futures market in this commodity will surely follow (see also Panel 6, Chapter 10).

In addition to natural gas, the exchanges are constantly monitoring the potential to list new contracts in other areas of the energy sector. As spot and forward markets develop, so futures exchanges can turn their attention to developing futures contracts which are based on these underlying markets. For example, the electricity market outlined in Chapter 11, once fully developed, will provide the necessary base for a very useful futures contract.

Returning to the petroleum complex, there are considerable areas of the refined barrel which are currently not covered by any successful futures contract. Heavy fuel oil, in both the North American and European trading zones, currently has no liquid futures market, although both the IPE and Nymex have both listed contracts in the past. Similarly, the light end of the refined barrel in Europe currently has no liquid exchange-based instrument available for risk management purposes. Similarly, no exchange has as yet managed to develop a successful sour crude oil hedging mechanism, although all three exchanges have listed their respective versions of this in the last three years.

The IPE is also currently in the process of developing a contract which would list the price of dated, rather than 15-day, Brent crude oil. The pricing of most physical crude oil is related to dated Brent, and not to the price of 15-day Brent (the market in which a futures contract currently exists). Therefore, an OTC market has sprung up in the last year which allows traders to control the risk of the very volatile price differential between the dated and the 15-day Brent markets. This OTC contract is currently known as the CFD or dated-to-paper market, and has experienced explosive growth since its inception. The IPE has therefore decided to list a contract which will emulate this OTC market very closely.

In this way, it is hoped that by emulating the success of the OTC markets, but offering the advantages that an exchange-traded market will provide, the overall size of the market will increase, and the unregulated OTC market will, effectively, be brought under the regulatory umbrella.

Indeed, if successful, this contract would eventually trade much further out than the few weeks that will initially be listed. It may go out as far as several months, and may even overtake the current IPE 15-day futures contract in terms of contract volume and importance as a pricing tool.

In the past, exchanges have regarded the OTC markets as unfair competition (due to their unregulated nature), and this has led them to suspect that the OTC markets have been detracting from the liquidity of the futures markets. However, it may be necessary to take a closer look at the reasons for the success of OTC instruments, and for the exchanges to play a more active role in providing a range of instruments which are better able to complement these markets, and cater more effectively for their needs. For example, the highly successful jet fuel swaps market has led many to consider the creation of jet fuel futures contracts.

In these relatively underdeveloped markets, two similar instruments are rarely able to trade successfully in the same time zone. For exam-

ELECTRONIC TRADING

Background

Historically, the best way to discover the current price of a market has been to have a presence on the floor of the exchange itself. As a consequence, major financial exchanges grew up with a trading floor as the central point, manned by intermediaries or brokers who would keep customers informed about what was happening.

The first automated execution systems appeared in the late 1980s. Systems such as the Swiss Soffex system and the German DTB system were created primarily to facilitate several financial centres within one country trading together at one time, whereas the Liffe APT system was initially conceived to alleviate a chronic shortage of space on the market floor. The Globex system was designed to provide a 24-hour trading capability to attract blossoming overseas business to the Chicago exchanges, whereas systems such as BEST and SAEF in the London securities market were designed to facilitate the explosion of small orders emanating from government flotations of utility companies during the 1980s.

Nearly all the 50 or so automated execution systems now in existence were implemented as a result of the worldwide trend towards deregulation of the financial markets. And whenever a government has been faced with the choice of starting a new exchange with a central trading floor or an electronic exchange where people can trade from their offices, electronic trading has won hands down. This is certainly due to the cost factor, which increasingly favours electronic trading. The cost of computers, software and communications is constantly reducing, whilst the cost of staff and the provision of major trading floors (some approaching 100,000 sq ft) is escalating.

Not all of the major financial marketplaces have plans to adopt electronic trading – in the long term, however, the shift seems likely to be universal.

New developments

The most notable foray into electronic trading systems in the energy world has been the introduction of the Nymex Access electronic trading system on June 23, 1993. The Access system has met with reasonable success, and other exchanges are currently researching the possibility of launching similar systems. So far, most trading has been concentrated in the WTI sweet crude oil futures contract, and a record of over 10,000 contracts traded in one day was set on April 4, 1994.

Several screens have now been installed in trading offices in London, and negotiations are currently taking place to allow screens to be installed in the Far East, either through the Simex or through the Sidney Futures Exchange. The most recent development has been the decision to list Nymex natural gas futures and options contracts on the system, and also to further extend the length of trading hours covered.

Prior to the launch of Access, it was not possible to trade the transatlantic arbitrage between London and New York, as the US markets were closed. However, with the advent of Access, London traders can lock-in differentials between the two markets, especially that between WTI and Brent, during the London trading morning. This further enhances liquidity during the non-US trading day.

---

ple, any jet fuel contract launched by the exchanges would be unlikely to be successful, as it would be in direct competition with the OTC market. However, a contract which traded the differential between jet fuel and gasoil might have considerable potential.

Similarly, over the last year, a liquid OTC market has emerged in Europe for heavy fuel oil. Currently, swap providers hedge their exposure either through laying off this risk through other players in the OTC markets, or by using currently available futures contracts – in this case, primarily, crude oil futures. Again, the listing of a differential contract, say between Brent and fuel oil, would match the needs of the market as a whole more appropriately than a contract in direct competition with the OTC market. Thus, in the future, we may well see the exchanges developing a whole range of "satellite" instruments.

Similarly, there is also potential in developing a range of satellite energy exchanges, effectively covering the 24-hour trading day, either by electronic means, or by facilitating the listing of the currently successful futures contracts on other exchanges. Recent developments in this area have included the launching of the Access after-hours electronic trading system by Nymex (see also Panel 4), whilst discussions are currently taking place to allow the listing of the Brent futures contract on Simex.

In the area of options, the IPE is currently considering the listing of average rate (Asian) options. Considerable business both in the physical and OTC markets is now transacted on the basis of monthly averages of prices, and it will be important for the exchanges to consider emulating these contracts if they are to provide the sort of risk management contracts that are relevant to the industry.

This does imply a change in attitude on the part of the exchanges. In the past, the impetus for listing new exchange contracts has often come from the physical trade. Thus the IPE, for example, would bring together a working party which would be representative of the underlying trade in order to formulate the framework for a new potential contract, and also to gauge its chances of success. The players who were most active in the OTC markets would not necessarily have been included in this consultation process – to the detriment of the exchanges. Exchanges are now likely to sound out OTC participants as well.

1 *A considerable proportion of this growth in energy risk management has come from outside the US, and much of it has been generated in Europe.*

2 *Trading volumes for the OTC and forward markets are difficult to estimate, as no official records are kept.*

BIBLIOGRAPHY

Clubbley, S, 1990 (second edition), *Trading in Energy Futures,* Hemel Hempstead

Hull, J, 1991, *Introduction to Futures and Options Markets,* New Jersey

Hull, J, 1993, *Options, Futures and other Derivative Securities,* New Jersey

Lofton, T, 1989, *Getting Started in Futures,* New York

Siegel, DR, and DF Siegel, 1992, *The Futures Markets,* London

Streit, M, 1983, *Futures Markets,* Oxford

14

Regulatory and Legal Issues

Kenneth M. Raisler and Alison M. Gregory

Sullivan & Cromwell

While various forms of commodity forwards, options, swaps[1] and commodity-linked hybrid products have
been in existence for years, their recent explosive growth has attracted the attention of regulators and raised questions regarding their
enforceability. The central issues are whether
the products are legal, and whether the market
participants are permitted to enter into them,
including questions about the criteria that may
limit participation.

To understand the legal issues that have
dominated the development of the derivatives
market in the United States, we will review the
historical division of jurisdiction between the
Commodity Futures Trading Commission
(CFTC) and the Securities and Exchange
Commission (SEC), as well as the role played by
the states in the regulation of this market. We
will analyse the recent CFTC releases on swaps
and hybrid instruments which provide guidance
on drawing a line between permissible and
impermissible products. In addition, we will
examine the issuances and proposals of other
regulators and legislators who are examining
the scope of proper participation in the derivatives markets.

Law and regulation in the United States

While both federal and state regulators and laws
are pertinent, the key regulator in the United
States on the issue of the legality of derivative
products[2] is the CFTC.

The CFTC is the regulatory agency empow-
ered under the provisions of the Commodity
Exchange Act (CEA) to regulate commodity
futures and options contracts as well as instruments with elements of futures or options.

The primary focus of the CFTC under the
CEA is the regulation of exchange-traded futures
and options contracts. Indeed, until amendments to the CEA were adopted in 1992 (see
below), all futures contracts had to trade on

CFTC-regulated exchange markets, and only
certain specific options could be traded outside
an exchange.

The possible characterisation of commodity
derivatives and hybrid products as futures or
options contracts subject to CFTC regulation,
including the exchange-trading requirement,
was largely ignored until 1987. As also mentioned in the introduction to this book, in 1987,
the CFTC commenced and settled an enforcement action enjoining a bank from issuing gold-
indexed certificates of deposit and threatened
enforcement action against another bank in
connection with its issuance of oil-indexed
swaps.[3] That same year, the CFTC released an
Advance Notice of Proposed Rulemaking with
respect to hybrid instruments which questioned
the legality of a full range of commodity derivatives under the CEA.[4]

Commodity derivatives, which contain elements of commercial contracts, financial contracts, and debt or equity elements with futures-
like and options-like components, are not easy
to differentiate in terms of the traditional regulatory authorities of the banking regulators, the
SEC and the CFTC. Not surprisingly, the 1987
Advance Notice met with considerable criticism
from the other regulators. In addition, the
Advance Notice, combined with the CFTC
enforcement actions, chilled development of the
business and drove much of it outside of the
United States. The CFTC made progress with
interpretations and rules issued in 1989 and
1990 (see below).

More significant progress was made with the
adoption of the Futures Trading Practices Act of
1992 and the adoption by the CFTC of rules in
early 1993 that broadly exempted swaps and
other derivatives from CFTC regulation. These
new rules go a long way to eliminate the threat
of CFTC enforcement action, as well as private
litigation or state enforcement action, to over-
turn a derivative transaction as being in viola-
tion of the CEA or state law.

However, as the growth of derivatives continues at a rapid pace, regulators and legislators continue to examine their role in this active marketplace. In addition to examining the nature of the products, which has largely been the activity of the CFTC, regulators have begun to focus on the role of the participant. Banking participants are subject to new guidelines. The derivatives-related activities of pension funds, insurance companies, mutual funds and municipalities, among others, are also subject to increased scrutiny.

JURISDICTIONAL REACH OF THE SEC AND
CFTC AND THE COMMODITY EXCHANGE ACT
In 1974, Congress passed the Commodity Exchange Act, granting the CFTC exclusive jurisdiction over transactions involving exchange-traded "contracts of sale of a commodity for future delivery" and commodity option contracts (exchange traded or not).[5] The term "commodity" is defined in Section 1a(3) as "wheat, cotton, rice, corn,..., and all other goods and articles, except onions..., and all services, rights, and interests in which contracts for future delivery are presently or in the future dealt in."[6]

Section 4(a)(1) requires that transactions in futures contracts be "conducted on or subject to the rules of a board of trade designated by the [CFTC] as a 'contract market' for such commodity." The CEA does not define the term "contracts for future delivery". However, case law and a CFTC Policy Statement have developed many of the elements of a "futures contract". The non-exclusive elements include that it (1) has standardised terms, (2) is usually offset, and (3) usually shifts the risk of a change in a commodity's value rather than transfers ownership.[7]

As mentioned above, the CFTC regulates commodity options. Options include "accounts, agreements (including any transaction which is of the character of, or is commonly known to the trade as, an 'option', 'privilege', 'indemnity', 'bid', 'offer', 'put', 'call', 'advance guaranty', or 'decline guaranty')."[8]

Although the CEA provides that the CFTC has regulatory powers with regard to futures contracts and options thereon, the CEA excludes or exempts certain financial instruments. First, forward contracts[9] are excluded from the CFTC's regulatory authority because the term "future delivery" does "not include any sale of any cash commodity for deferred shipment or delivery."[10] Although the distinctions between futures and forward contracts are

sometimes difficult to discern, the forward contract exclusion has provided an important basis for excluding many types of commodity agreements from the CFTC's jurisdiction and the provisions of the CEA.

Second, Section 2(a)(1)(A)(ii), often called the Treasury Amendment, excludes certain transactions, including "transactions in foreign currency".[11]

Third, CFTC Regulation 32.4(a) exempts instruments called "Trade Options". It provides that commodity option transactions (other than on agricultural commodities) "offered by a person which has a reasonable basis to believe that the option is offered to a producer, processor, or commercial user of, or a merchant handling, the commodity which is the subject of the commodity option transaction, or the products or byproducts thereof, and that such producer, processor, commercial user or merchant is offered or enters into the commodity option transaction solely for purposes related to its business as such" are generally exempt transactions.

The SEC and the CFTC have disagreed about the scope of their regulatory powers and the reach of their respective jurisdictions. One area of particular uncertainty involved the treatment of securities, indices comprised of securities, futures contracts on such instruments and options on such futures contracts.[12] To resolve uncertainties with respect to such instruments, the CFTC and the SEC specified which instruments were under the purview of the CFTC or the SEC in the Jurisdictional Accord of 1982.[13] In other cases, courts have resolved the uncertainty regarding the jurisdictional reaches of the CFTC and the SEC.[14] Those courts that have addressed the issue have unanimously concluded that Congress' grant of exclusive jurisdiction to the CFTC provides the CFTC with the sole regulatory authority to address products within its jurisdiction.

THE FORWARD CONTRACT EXCLUSION AND
TRANSNOR (BERMUDA) LIMITED V. BP
NORTH AMERICA PETROLEUM
The breadth of the forward contract exclusion for transactions involving "any cash commodity for deferred shipment or delivery" remains uncertain because futures and forward contracts often have similar features.[15] One United States District Court for the Southern District of New York decision, *Transnor (Bermuda) Limited* v. *BP North America Petroleum*,[16] illustrated and exacerbated this uncertainty.

Transnor, a Bermuda corporation, argued, *inter alia*, that the defendant petroleum companies violated the CEA because Transnor contended that 15-day Brent oil contracts (on which it had defaulted) were illegal, off-exchange futures contracts, not obligations falling within the forward contract exclusion of the CEA. In denying the defendants' motion for summary judgment, the Court concluded that such contracts were illegal futures contracts and were subject to CFTC regulation because, among other things, the "relatively standardized" oil contracts were "routinely settled by means other than delivery".[17]

This ruling posed a major threat to the oil trading market. It brought into question a large number of commercial transactions that were typically cash settled and that had not been considered to be subject to the CEA. That uncertainty and the ensuing clamours for relief prompted the CFTC to issue its Statutory Interpretation Concerning Forward Transactions (the "Statutory Interpretation").[18] In the Statutory Interpretation, the CFTC clarified the forward contract exclusion. The Statutory Interpretation explained that the exclusion applied to certain commercial transactions, including 15-day Brent oil contracts, notwithstanding infrequent delivery of oil, because (1) they "create specific delivery obligations", (2) any book-out or offset required "separate, individually negotiated, new agreements" (that is, not an "exchange-style offset"), and (3) the commercial parties, who transact "in connection with their business" and are capable of making or taking delivery, bore "substantial economic risk".[19] However, it was not certain that the CFTC's Statutory Interpretation, issued after the *Transnor* decision, would be recognised as binding by the courts or would eliminate the risk of private litigation.

In addition to the Statutory Interpretation, a decision by the United States Court of Appeals for the Ninth Circuit offered some comfort to certain market participants. In the Ninth Circuit's case, *In re Bybee* (*Krommenhoek* v. *A-Mark Precious Metals, Inc.*),[20] A-Mark transacted with a metals dealer named Bybee, who was transacting on behalf of customers. Bybee's customers did not know that Bybee purchased metals on margin and that A-Mark held a lien on the metals for purchase money owed. After the value of silver declined and Bybee paid A-Mark's margin calls, Bybee went bankrupt. A bankruptcy trustee (acting on behalf of Bybee's unpaid customers) sued A-Mark, alleging that it violated the CEA by transacting in illegal, off-exchange future contracts. Deferring to the CFTC's Statutory Interpretation, the Ninth Circuit determined that A-Mark was not liable because such contracts fell within the forward contracts exclusion. In reaching this conclusion, the Ninth Circuit determined that delivery was the "determining factor" and relied on the fact that the terms of the contracts included legal obligations to make or accept delivery (even if the parties routinely offset their obligations).[21] Because the Court concluded that certain types of commercial transactions in precious metals constituted forward contracts falling within the CEA exclusion, it implicitly rejected the reasoning of the Southern District of New York's *Transnor* decision.

Notwithstanding the comfort that the Statutory Interpretation, the *A-Mark* decision and case-by-case no-action relief provide commercial participants in the market for forward delivery of commodities, further clarification, discussed below, has been necessary.

STATE LAWS

In addition to CFTC regulatory issues, commodity transactions may also implicate the laws of the states. Because Section 12(e) states that nothing in the CEA "shall supersede or pre-empt...the application of any federal or state statute...to any transaction in or involving any commodity...that is not conducted on or subject to the rules of a contract market, or, in the case of any State or local law that prohibits or regulates gaming or the operation of 'bucket shops'...," off-exchange commodity transactions must comply with state laws, which often include various provisions that could pertain to commodity transactions.

For example, state "Blue Sky" laws may include anti-fraud provisions for transactions involving commodities. In addition, numerous states, including New York, have statutes prohibiting "bucket shops" or gambling. New York's gambling statute prohibits "all wagers, bets or stakes, made to depend upon...any lot, chance, casualty, or unknown or contingent event...".[22] Also, Section 225.00 of New York's Penal Law provides that anyone engaging in gambling when a person "stakes something of value upon the outcome of...a future contingent event not under his control or influence..." violates such Section. Arguably, numerous off-exchange commodity or energy derivative instruments could violate state statutory definitions of gambling because a party is risking "something of value" upon the outcome of a "contingent event" not under that party's control or influence (such as, say, commodity prices).

Similarly, off-exchange commodity or energy derivative transactions could violate statutes that numerous states, including New York, have which prohibit "bucket shops". Around the turn of the century, operations, called "bucket shops", existed that purportedly transacted in the commodity markets or exchanges. They accepted orders to purchase or sell securities or futures contracts and then, rather than executing them on an exchange or in a market, "bucket-ed" them. When prices moved against their positions, the "bucket shops" failed to honour their obligations and closed.

Sections 351 and 351-e of New York's General Business Law prohibit the operation of "bucket shops". Section 351 prohibits the making or offering of a contract "without intending a bona fide purchase or sale" of the subject matter of the contract and with the intent to settle such contract by referring to general "market quotations".[23] Arguably, "bucket shop" statutes, with very broad prohibitions, could prohibit certain types of off-exchange transactions, such as over-the-counter (OTC) instruments that do not receive CEA Section 4(c) exemptive relief,[24] and their existence threatens the enforceability of such transactions.

A few courts have addressed challenges to transactions based on "bucket shop" statutes. For example, the Fourth Circuit recently considered a lawsuit involving a wealthy and financially sophisticated individual, named Laszlo N. Tauber, who wanted to avoid the payment of many millions of dollars that he owed on foreign currency transactions based on, among other things, a "bucket shop" statute.[25] Tauber contended, *inter alia*, that such transactions were illegal because they violated New York's "bucket shop" statute. Rejecting Tauber's argument, the Fourth Circuit determined that the transactions constituted legitimate, "bona fide contracts, resulting in legal obligations to take delivery", rather than sham transactions that would have violated the "bucket shop" statute.[26] Similarly, New York courts have upheld other legitimate commercial transactions and rejected attacks against such transactions based on gambling or "bucket shop" statutes.[27]

Once again, lingering uncertainty has required that further relief, discussed below, be provided.

SWAPS POLICY STATEMENT

In 1989, the CFTC issued its Policy Statement Concerning Swap Transactions ("Swaps Policy Statement").[28] Although it lacked the force of a statutory interpretation or regulation, the Swaps Policy Statement did indicate that cash-settled swaps satisfying certain requirements would not be considered futures contracts or commodity options for the purposes of CFTC regulation.

In the Swaps Policy Statement, the CFTC stated that "most swap transactions, although possessing elements of futures or options contracts, are not appropriately regulated as such under the [CEA] and regulations", and that the CFTC, accordingly, would not take action against swaps, such as interest rate, currency and commodity swaps, provided such swaps qualified for its non-exclusive safe harbour protection. To qualify for the Swaps Policy Statement protection, a swap must have (1) individually-tailored and negotiated terms, (2) an expectation that the terms would be performed and would not be terminated absent counterparty consent, (3) an absence of the indicia of an exchange market, such as a mark-to-market margin or settlement system, (4) been undertaken in conjunction with the parties' line of business, and (5) not been marketed to the public. Due to recent developments, discussed below, the safe harbour created by the Swaps Policy Statement is relevant to only a small percentage of the swap transactions that it once covered.

FUTURES TRADING PRACTICES ACT OF 1992

To provide certainty with regard to the treatment of highly successful financial instruments such as swaps, hybrids and energy contracts, and in response to the mounting pressure for clarification, Congress amended the CEA with the Futures Trading Practices Act of 1992 (FTPA).[29]

In the FTPA, Congress, among other things, granted the CFTC the authority to exempt certain agreements, contracts and transactions from various requirements of the CEA or CFTC regulations, including the CEA requirement that transactions must occur on a designated contract market.[30] In assessing whether or not to grant exemptive relief, the FTPA and CEA Section 4(c) require the CFTC to consider the following: (1) whether the exemption is in the public interest and consistent with the purposes of the CEA, and (2) whether the agreement, contract or transaction (i) will only be entered into by "appropriate persons" and (ii) will not materially or adversely affect the CFTC or contract markets in discharging their CEA regulatory duties.[31] Before determining whether to issue an exemption, the CFTC was not required to find that the product to be exempted was governed by the CEA. The FTPA also amended Section 12(e) to give the CFTC authority to preempt state or local laws that prohibit gambling or "bucket shops" and to prevent the application of such laws with respect to transactions exempted by Section 4(c).

The Conference Committee Report accompanying the FTPA encouraged the CFTC to "use its new exemptive powers promptly upon enactment of this legislation in four areas where significant concerns of legal uncertainty have arisen: (1) hybrids, (2) swaps, (3) forwards, (4) bank deposits and accounts."[32]

Pursuant to its exemptive authority, the CFTC moved promptly in early 1993 to grant various exemptions for certain swaps agreements, hybrid instruments and energy contracts.[33]

SWAPS EXEMPTION
Although no determination had been made that swap agreements were covered by the CEA or fell under the purview of the CFTC, the CFTC approved final rules during January 1993 exempting certain swap agreements from almost all of the CEA and CFTC regulations, provided that the swap agreements meet certain criteria.[34] To qualify for an exemption, the swap agreement (1) must have been entered into by "eligible swap participants" (which resemble "appropriate persons" in Section 4(c) of the CEA and are entities of a certain size, certain individuals or entities – such as a futures commission merchant, floor broker or floor trader – or natural persons with assets exceeding at least $10 million);[35] (2) cannot be a fungible agreement with standardised material terms; (3) must have the creditworthiness or risk of its counterparties as a material consideration; and (4) must not be traded on or through a multilateral transaction execution facility.[36]

The exemption also requires that the agreement be a "swap agreement", which includes "(i) [a]n agreement (including terms and conditions incorporated by reference therein) which is a rate swap agreement, basis swap, forward rate agreement, commodity swap, interest rate option, forward foreign exchange agreement, rate cap agreement, rate floor agreement, rate collar agreement, currency swap agreement, cross-currency rate swap agreement, currency

option, any other similar agreement (including any option to enter into any of the foregoing); (ii) [a]ny combination of the foregoing; or (iii) [a] master agreement for any of the foregoing together with all supplements thereto".[37]

If the criteria are met, the "swap agreement is exempt from all provisions of the [CEA] and any person or class of persons offering, entering into, rendering advice, or rendering other services with respect to such agreement, is exempt for such activity from all provisions of the [CEA] (except in each case the provisions of Sections 2(a)(1)(B) [the Jurisdictional Accord], 4b and 4o of the [CEA (prohibiting fraud)] and § 32.9 as adopted under § 4c(b) of the [CEA], prohibiting fraud and the provisions of Section 6(c) and 9(a)(2) of the [CEA] to the extent these provisions prohibit manipulation of the market price of any commodity in interstate commerce or for future delivery on or subject to the rules of any contract market)...."[38] Also, such an agreement, to the extent it is covered by the terms of the exemption, would be exempt from state and local gambling and "bucket shop" laws, pursuant to CEA Section 12(e), as amended by the FTPA.[39]

HYBRIDS
Pursuant to its new exemptive authority, the CFTC also adopted rules exempting certain hybrid instruments from almost all of the CEA, including its exchange-trading requirement (the "Hybrid Exemption").[40] To qualify for the Hybrid Exemption's safe harbour protection, the hybrid instrument must be (1) an equity or debt security instrument according to Section 2(1) of the Securities Act[41] or (2) a time deposit, demand deposit or transaction account offered by an insured depository institution, insured credit union, or branch or agency of a bank that is federally or state regulated.[42]

Such hybrid instruments must also pass a "predominance test". It requires that, at the time of issuance, the "sum of the commodity-dependent values of the commodity-dependent components be less than the commodity-independent value of the commodity-independent component."[43] The commodity-dependent values are determined by decomposing the commodity-dependent components of the hybrid instrument into commodity options. For example, any forward-like commodity components of the instrument are split into long call options and short put options having the same strike prices. The commodity-dependent value is "the absolute net value of the put option premia with strike prices less than or equal to the reference price[44] plus the absolute net value of the call option premia with strike prices greater than or equal to the reference price, calculated as of the time of issuance of the hybrid instrument."[45]

The Hybrid Exemption does not exempt the hybrid instruments from the antimanipulation provisions or Jurisdictional Accord[46] provisions of the CEA.

ENERGY CONTRACT EXEMPTION

During April 1993, the CFTC approved a Final Order exempting certain energy contracts or energy-related derivative contracts. The CFTC's Exemption for Certain Contracts Involving Energy Products ("Energy Contract Exemption") responded to an application seeking legal clarity and certainty with regard to the off-exchange market for energy products that a group of crude oil and natural gas producers, processors and merchandisers filed and provides exemptive relief for certain energy-related contracts.[47]

The CFTC's Energy Contract Exemption granted relief from almost all of the CEA and CFTC regulations to certain contracts that involve transactions in crude oil, condensates, natural gas and natural gas liquids that can be used as an energy source regardless of whether the commodities are ultimately used as an energy source.[48] Also, the Energy Contract Exemption covers derivatives of these energy products, including gasoline, diesel fuel or heating oil, that are typically used as energy sources.

Only certain types of parties are eligible to qualify for the exemptive relief.[49] In addition, the energy contract must be an individually negotiated, bilateral contract between two eligible entities (or at least entities reasonably believed to be eligible) acting as principals. The contract cannot include a unilateral right to offset or settle by cash payment. Instead, the contract must include delivery obligations, although the CFTC recognised·that the parties may later negotiate another agreement to "book out" their obligations rather than to deliver the physical commodity.[50]

Energy contracts meeting the above criteria are exempt from all of the CEA except for the Jurisdictional Accord and certain sections prohibiting manipulation of the market price for the energy product. Thus, unlike the Swap Exemption's relief, the Energy Contract Exemption's relief includes relief from the antifraud provision of the CEA.[51]

Thus, the CFTC's Energy Contract Exemption clarified that energy-related contracts that qualified for relief were exempt from CEA requirements, such as the exchange-trading requirement, and provided legal certainty in the market for energy-related contracts. In providing this relief, the CFTC avoided the futures-forwards dichotomy altogether.

Enforceability

Determining whether the underlying transaction is legal in the jurisdiction[52] in which it is entered into is but one of several legal issues that needs to be examined.[53] Legal due diligence requires scrutiny of a number of elements of the transaction and the counterparties in assessing whether the derivative contract will be enforceable.

CAPACITY

At the outset, a party entering into commodity and energy derivative transactions should ensure that its counterparty has the capacity to enter into the transactions and, if capacity is present, that the signatory has the authority to bind the entity to the transactions.

The seminal case on this point is *Hammersmith and Fulham London Borough Council* v. *Hazell*, 2 W.L.R. 372 (1991).[54] In *Hammersmith and Fulham*, London local authorities had engaged in hundreds of swap transactions with swap dealers during the 1987–89 fiscal years. After the Audit Commission conducted an audit of the local authorities' activities and questioned the legality of the transactions, the Council's finance director closed any swap transactions that would result in losses to the Council, and the Council received an order from the Divisional Court of the Queen's Bench Division that the transactions were contrary to law. Swap dealers appealed, and the House of Lords determined that the applicable statute did not grant the local authorities the authority to enter into swap transactions. Because the local authorities lacked legal permission to engage in them, the transactions were *ultra vires* and, thus, void. This ruling caused the swap dealers to lose an amount that represents approximately one-half of the total losses incurred because of swap defaults since the beginning of the swap market.[55]

The capacity of any counterparty must, therefore, be analysed. Of particular concern are a range of constituents including governmental authorities, regulated utilities, insurance companies, pension funds and mutual funds. For example, local gas and electric utility companies in the United States are regulated by Public Utility Commissioners (PUCs). Because PUCs regulate many of the participants in the energy derivative markets, they oversee how such entities may permissibly contract to procure their fuel supplies. Some PUCs are currently examining energy derivatives and determining whether or not they will permit regulated utilities companies to use such instruments to hedge their exposure to changes in the price of fuel.[56] Unless PUCs approve the use of energy derivative instruments, many regulated utilities will be severely limited in how they engage in such transactions.

Similarly, insurance companies are another group of potentially significant derivatives end-users because of their interest rate and other exposures. Like regulated utilities, however, insurance companies face state regulation. Thus, their legal capacity to engage in derivatives activities remains uncertain without express authority from the applicable state laws and insurance regulators. Currently, the National Association of Insurance Commissioners (the NAIC), a quasi-regulatory association promoting uniformity among state regulators and comprised of the chief regulator of each US state or jurisdiction, is evaluating the use of derivatives by insurance companies. The NAIC has drafted a model statute authorising insurance companies to engage in derivatives activities within certain parameters.[57]

BANKRUPTCY

Congress amended the Bankruptcy Code with regard to "swap agreements".[58] These amendments offer considerable relief and certainty for market participants in such transactions. Parties to "swap agreements" can avoid Bankruptcy Code Section 362's automatic stay provision.[59] By avoiding the Code's automatic stay provision, parties to a master swap agreement can net their transactions, set off claims for settlement or collateral purposes and calculate one single close-out amount.[60] Based on the relief afforded by the foregoing amendments to the Bankruptcy Code, participants in derivatives markets with instruments qualifying as "swap agreements" under the Bankruptcy Code can liquidate their positions notwithstanding the filing of a bankruptcy petition and the imposition of the automatic stay.[61]

In addition, such transactions are exempt from the Bankruptcy Code's avoidance provisions, which might, for example, have permitted a bankruptcy trustee to treat some payments made within ninety days (or, possibly, one year) of the insolvent party's petition for bankruptcy as avoidable "preferences". Any payments received or collections made during the normal course of business with respect to such transactions cannot be avoided as fraudulent transfers or preferential transfers by a bankruptcy trustee.[62]

Bankruptcy trustees cannot choose to assume or reject any executory contract, including open positions in off-exchange commodity transactions, under Section 365(a).[63]

Also, relief from the automatic stay provision, coupled with the Bankruptcy Code's interpretation of a master swap agreement and its collateral agreement as a single agreement, make it far less likely that a bankruptcy trustee could "cherry pick" among transactions between an insolvent and a solvent swap counterparty.

In addition to providing relief to participants in the US swap markets,[64] the amendments to the Bankruptcy Code also clarified that forward contracts and options were afforded similar relief. The definition of "forward contract" for purposes of the Bankruptcy Code was expanded to include physical commodities that are not currently traded on US commodity exchanges and a "repurchase transaction, reverse repurchase transaction, consignment, lease, swap, hedge transaction, deposit, loan, option, allocated transaction, unallocated transaction, or any combination thereof or option thereon."[65]

Similarly, Congress has enacted certain other laws[66] that also increased legal certainty for US derivative market participants. Nevertheless, some uncertainty remains.[67]

NETTING

Counterparties in the OTC derivatives markets recognise that they reduce their risk by broadening the use of master agreements with bilateral close-out netting provisions and by working with their counterparties to ensure that such agreements and netting provisions will be legally enforceable in all of the jurisdictions in which they transact business. Although bilateral close-out netting arrangements are increasingly common in the OTC market and their use is recommended by most regulators, many market participants remain concerned about their enforce-

STANDARDISING DOCUMENTATION FOR ENERGY DERIVATIVES

Jeffrey Golden, Allen & Overy

Documenting energy derivatives may be conceptualised as having three distinct dimensions. First, there is the "sunny side" of the agreement, governing the parties relationship in the ordinary course and when it is not problematic. In this regard, the parties will wish to set out their understanding as to:

❑ the term of their contract;

❑ when and where payments, including premiums, will be made;

❑ if physical settlement is contemplated, the terms relating to the delivery of the underlying commodity (eg location, method of delivery, grading specifications, insurance, transfer of title);

❑ the quantity in relevant units of the commodity (eg barrels of oil);

❑ any fixed or strike price and the exchange, publication or other price source for any reference price that fluctuates or "floats" (including, if applicable, by whom it will be calculated and whether the relevant price will be the bid price, the asked price, the average of the high and low prices, the morning fixing or some other fixing and whether it will be based on the spot price or by reference to a futures contract);

❑ the pricing dates and, if appropriate, an indication of the time as of which the price is to be determined and the method for averaging prices when more than one price is determined in respect of a particular calculation period;

❑ if an option, the procedure for exercise, including whether automatic exercise applies for an in-the-money option and any requirement that telephonic notice of exercise be confirmed in writing;

❑ procedures for the giving of any other notices under the contract; and

❑ any rounding conventions or adjustments for payments or dates for exercise falling on non-business days.

Second, the parties must address the potential "dark side" of their relationship: what happens if a party does not pay or otherwise perform as expected (ie, defaults), or a new law or tax is introduced and, as a result, it becomes illegal or prohibitively expensive for one or both parties to perform. In that case, the parties will frequently wish to terminate early their agreement or, at least, the affected transactions, and to settle out on a lump sum or some other pre-agreed basis.

Triggering events for such termination need to be stipulated. They often reflect credit concerns such as:

❑ failure to pay or deliver;

❑ cross default;

❑ insolvency;

❑ merger protection; or

❑ loss of promised credit support.

In case a triggering event occurs, it is also essential to clarify:

❑ close-out procedures;

❑ the measure of any loss;

❑ the scope of any indemnification for that loss;

❑ netting and contractual set-off rights; and

❑ dispute settlement.

Finally, there is what the cartoonist, Gary Larson, might call the "far side" of the contract – the position of the parties should the weird and unexpected occur. Increasingly, market participants are concerned to address the consequences of unscheduled disruptions in the marketplace that may result in the unavailability of an agreed energy price, or make delivery of the underlying on the terms of the contract impossible.

A number of the relevant issues must be addressed for each individual trade: How many barrels of oil, how often and for how long? The questions, but not necessarily the answers, can be standardised. Some of the issues are peculiar to energy derivatives: Do we look to the IPE or to Argus or Platt's for our price? Others may be considered as a relationship matter between counterparties for all derivatives traded between them. Should there be cross-default protection? Should payments be made gross or on a net basis?

The evolution of standardised agreements

In the past, market participants varied considerably in their approaches to energy derivatives agreements – very often for no good reason and only because they chose different starting points. The result, a continuing "battle of the forms" in two-party negotiations, led in the early 1990s to calls for standardisation.

Documentation experts on both sides of the Atlantic attempted to develop an acceptable master agreement. Under the auspices of the International Swaps and Derivatives Association (ISDA),[1] a working group was established in New York in the autumn of 1990 to prepare a standard form master agreement to be used on a stand-alone basis for energy and other commodity-linked derivatives.

The task proved difficult, partly because market participants were anxious to preserve enough flexibility to accommodate cross-product netting arrangements and to address issues arising in respect of cross-border and, in some cases, multicurrency transactions. However, following a 20-month review of the netting and cross-border issues, as well as product-specific issues, by its working group, which reconvened in London with more international representation in 1993, ISDA published its Commodity Derivatives Definitions (the "ISDA Definitions").

In the same year, a stand-alone Master Energy Price Swap Agreement, designed primarily for dollar-denominated US domestic market energy derivatives, was published by the Energy Risk Management Association (ERMA).

One of the major obstacles to a general acceptance of standardised energy documentation is the difference in approach adopted by the financial institutions, on the one hand, with their emphasis on credit risk and netting (including netting for capital adequacy purposes), and by end-users, producers and refiners, on the other. This latter category tends to be more active in the physically-settled markets, where the tenor of the trade is often of a shorter maturity. Documentation in these markets has often been more product-specific and less detailed, with the parties taking a more "commercial view" and living with a measure of ambiguity about matters arising out of changed circumstances or in respect of legal uncertainty.

It seems possible, though, that the flexibility inherent in the latest ISDA documentation, which combines a short-form confirmation that sets out the terms end-users have traditionally agreed in the past, with the detail preferred by the financial institutions incorporated by reference, will provide a breakthrough. Certainly, the ISDA project is the most ambitious to date, and is supported by an educational programme, including workshops and commentaries, and a legal survey of key insolvency issues in respect of close-out netting.

1993 ISDA Commodity Derivatives Definitions

The ISDA Definitions cover a broad range of cash-settled commodity-linked derivative transactions, including energy price swaps, options, caps, collars, floors and swaptions. The definitions and provisions that are provided can be incorporated in whole or in part into the parties' contract and, together with the forms of confirmations provided, were designed primarily for use with, and to build on the modular architecture of, the 1992 ISDA Master Agreements.

A MODULAR APPROACH

The parties start with a core master agreement (multicurrency/cross border or local currency/single jurisdiction) that contains credit protection and other elements common to all derivatives.

Confirmations and related definitions designed for specific product types are then added on a "when needed, as needed" basis. When a client – say, a small oil company – calls a dealer to write an oil price swap, the dealer sends that client:
❑ a book of definitions (the ISDA Definitions) for commodity transactions; and
❑ the core agreement (a 1992 ISDA Master Agreement).

Then, as the client writes swaps with the dealer, the confirmations which describe the economic terms of each deal are stapled to the back of –and become a part of –the master agreement. From its point of view, the client has a simple "single product" master.

Now, let us suppose that the client has a business opportunity in a foreign market, and it needs to write an FX forward. The client can simply be sent the booklet of ISDA FX and Currency Option Definitions. The FX forward can be documented, and netted, under the ISDA Master. This is the *modular approach*: what appears to a counterparty to be a single product master becomes an effective cross-product netting tool as business expands.

Furthermore, the 1992 ISDA Master Agreement has a schedule that permits the parties to "fine tune" the core agreement without having to retype or deviate from the main printed form. (Most parties will put the forms of the confirmations on to their own systems as templates, and simply fill in the economic terms of particular transactions.)

The confirmations will usually break down into five principal sections (seven principal sections, in the case of an option):
❑ the introduction;
❑ general and economic terms;
❑ identification of the parties as fixed or floating price payers or as buyer or seller of the option, as appropriate;
❑ account details;
❑ the closing;
and, if an option or swaption:
❑ the procedures for exercise;
❑ cash settlement terms or the terms of the underlying swap transaction.

ENERGY REFERENCE PRICES

Among other things, the ISDA booklet provides approximately 75 price sources for roughly 20 commodities. Energy, metals, prices quoted on the Nymex, IPE and LME, prices published by the Financial Times, Platt's, Argus, Metal Bulletin are all present, while further price sources can be incorporated into the confirmations of trades by referencing short catch phrases such as "Oil-WTI-NYMEX". By referring to the ISDA Definitions, the user will find that "Oil-WTI-NYMEX", coupled with a specified price, such as "closing price", will suffice to establish a specific price per barrel of West Texas Intermediate light sweet crude oil on the New York Mercantile Exchange.

Also provided are "building blocks" that would permit parties easily to construct additional pricing sources for energy derivatives, including sources for prices for energy-linked products or markets that may inspire derivatives trading in the future. Not only energy swaps are covered. Standard forms for energy and other commodity-linked options, caps, collars, floors and swaptions are provided. Using these forms, and the ISDA Definitions that they incorporate, market participants will in many cases be able to fully document their trades using a confirmation of two pages or even less.

The technique of incorporating provisions by reference was designed to keep confirming documentation short, but flexible. As different conventions had developed among different market players, different products and different financial centres, any standard documentation had to be kept as "natural" as possible to avoid traders having to absorb a new language. Take "Calculation Periods", for example. What should be the relevant period for measuring price movements in determining a floating price payer's obligations? Some participants had set Calculation Periods using traditional "ISDA-speak": specifying "Period End Dates". The Calculation Period ran from, and including, one Period End Date to, but excluding, the other. Others specified actual dates, for example January 1 to January 31, intending to include all the days specified in the period: from, and including; to, and including.

As a potentially complicating factor, the ERMA document used ISDA-speak but redefined the terms! In that contract Calculation Periods ran from, but excluding, to, and including, Period End Dates. The approach reflected in the ISDA Definitions was aimed not so much at arbitrating as accommodating:
(i) if the parties specify all relevant dates they are inclusive;
(ii) if the parties specify "Period End Dates" and "ERMA" those dates are used as in the ERMA document; and

(iii) if the parties specify "Period End Dates" (but not "ERMA") the terms are used in the same way as they would be for ISDA documented interest rate and currency swaps.

MARKET DISRUPTION EVENTS

What happens if, on the stipulated pricing day, there is a "price source disruption"? Or a material "trading suspension"? What if, since the parties made their deal, there has been a material change in the content of the relevant commodity or the formula by which the relevant price had been calculated?

The booklet sets out a menu, and presumptions as to choice from the menu, of market disruption events and consequences resulting from them:
❏ go to a "fallback reference price"; *failing which*
❏ attempt to negotiate an alternative price source; *failing which*
❏ there will be a no-fault termination.

If the parties are happy with the presumptions, everything happens automatically. There is no need to provide details for the adjustments occasioned by, or even to address the issue of, market disruption events in the parties' confirmation. The presumptions relating to market disruption events are, however, all easily modified in a schedule to the parties' contract or, on a trade by trade basis, in the relevant confirmation.

CREDIT-RELATED PROVISIONS AND PHYSICAL SETTLEMENT

If the parties are using the ISDA Definitions and confirmations other than in connection with the 1992 ISDA Master Agreement, or any other master agreement, they should consider adding credit-related provisions to their confirmations. There is no provision in the confirmation forms for defined events of default, such as cross-default to third-party debt, or for early termination or settlement.

In addition, parties using the standard form documentation are advised to consider applicable local law issues, regulatory, tax and accounting matters, commodity exchange and any other issues not specifically addressed by the text included in the forms.

The ISDA Definitions were designed for use in the documentation of cash-settled commodity derivatives. Guidance and a list of issues to be considered in connection with transactions that settle by physical delivery of the underlying commodity can be found at Section VI, pp. 60-63, of the 1993 Edition of the User's Guide to the 1992 ISDA Master Agreements, published by ISDA.

---

1 Formerly the International Swap Dealers Association.

ability during bankruptcy in different jurisdictions.[68]

Some jurisdictions do recognise and enforce bilateral close-out netting arrangements. For example, as discussed below, the enforceability of such arrangements with United States counterparties in the United States is "almost certain" in insolvency proceedings involving derivatives.[69] While in other countries, such as England, Germany and Australia, that lack legislation expressly enabling a party to net derivatives obligations, such an agreement including certain provisions will likely be enforced. In France, the Parliament recently recognised that netting provisions covering derivatives payment obligations from "eligible transactions", that include commodity contracts, are enforceable if at least one of the parties is a "qualified institution"[70] and the eligible transactions are governed by a standard master agreement or were entered into on a regulated market. Similarly, such netting arrangements appear to be enforceable under Japanese law.[71] The lack of express authority in many jurisdictions, however, causes uncertainty when dealing with counterparties from certain jurisdictions and must be considered carefully.

Derivatives and issues before the regulators

Recently, Congress, various regulatory agencies, and institutional participants in the markets for commodity and energy derivatives have focused considerable attention upon some of the issues posed by these burgeoning markets. There has been much discussion about whether such instruments increase or reduce market risk and volatility. Some have studied these issues and released reports. Others have introduced bills, guidelines or standards attempting to govern the participants in the markets for these instruments.

GROUP OF THIRTY REPORT
The Group of Thirty, a group chaired by Paul Volcker and comprised of industry representatives, central bankers, bankers, and academics spent approximately nine months assessing global derivatives markets. Upon the completion of their review, the Global Derivatives Study Group released on July 21, 1993 a lengthy study entitled Group of Thirty Study on Derivatives: Practices and Principles ("Group of Thirty Study"), consisting of a Study and three volumes of appendices.

The Study offers an overview of the derivatives markets and proffers various recommendations. Twenty of them are designed to assist end-users and dealers with the management of their derivatives activities. Among them are recommendations that senior management approve overall risk management and capital policies for derivatives; that derivative positions be marked-to-market; that market risk and credit risk be independently and regularly analysed; and that credit risk be reduced by the use of multi-product master agreements with close-out netting provisions and by attempts to insure the legal enforceability of derivative transactions in different jurisdictions. In addition, dealers and end-users are encouraged to authorise only sophisticated professionals to execute transactions and to control and audit derivatives activities. The Study also recommends that dealers and end-users establish sophisticated management information systems to report accurately the value of derivative instruments and positions and to recognise the risks and exposures of a portfolio of positions.

The Study targeted four recommendations, intended to bolster the markets and infrastructure for derivatives, at legislators, regulators and supervisors. The Study recommends that legislators, regulators and supervisors remove legal and regulatory uncertainties with regard to derivatives instruments and markets; amend tax regulations that disadvantage derivatives; provide comprehensive and consistent accounting guidance; and recognise close-out netting arrangements and amend the Basle Accord to reflect the benefits of such arrangements with respect to bank capital regulations.

Working papers that provided the analysis and basis for the Study's recommendations are available in Appendix I. Appendix II analyses the enforceability of derivatives agreements in nine jurisdictions. Appendix III consists of the findings of a Price Waterhouse survey of industry practices.

OCC BANKING CIRCULAR 277
The Office of the Comptroller of the Currency (OCC) released Banking Circular 277 to guide national banks and federal branches and agencies of foreign banks with respect to their risk management practices for derivatives activities.[72]

For the most part, the Circular adopted recommendations of the Group of Thirty's Global Derivatives Study Group, such as recommendations that market and credit risk be regularly quantified, monitored and controlled; that auditors, operations and risk management systems be sufficiently sophisticated to manage derivatives instruments and activities; that netting arrangements and collateral agreements be considered to reduce risks; that banks ensure that counterparties have the requisite legal and regulatory authority to create enforceable agreements; and that positions and risks be marked-to-market. Similarly, the Circular, like the Group of Thirty Study, addressed legal, capital adequacy and accounting issues and emphasised the need for active supervision by senior management, and oversight by the Board of Directors to monitor the activities and authority and to control risks.

However, the Circular did not stop with the Group of Thirty recommendations. In particular, it stated that "[c]redit officers should be able to effectively analyze the impact of proposed derivatives activities on the financial condition of [the bank's] customer" and whether or not particular financial derivative instruments are applicable to managing the risk that the customer seeks to manage. According to the Circular, a national bank "approving officer" should be capable of "identify[ing] if a proposed derivatives transaction is consistent with a counterparty's policies and procedures with respect to derivatives activities, as they are known to the bank."[73] If the customer wants to proceed with the transaction, even though the credit officer (or approving officer) does not believe that the transaction would be consistent with the counterparty's policies and procedures, bank management should document its own analysis and any information provided to the customer.

This section of the Circular evoked a strong response from the banking community because many banks do not believe that such customer analysis or evaluations are appropriate when dealing with institutional counterparties. In addition, many banks remain concerned about the scope of their duty to assess the customer's risk, policies and procedures.

In part because of the strong response to this section of the Circular, the OCC released a bulletin to answer "the most frequently asked questions, and [provide] greater detail on the guidance" in the Circular.[74] After denying that the OCC adopted a suitability standard for the derivatives activities of banks,[75] it explained that the Circular's "appropriateness standard" applies to the transactions with "institutional customers", rather than transactions with dealers or, "in most cases, other market professionals".[76]

The Circular also authorised national banks to engage in physical commodity transactions in certain situations.[77] They must be undertaken to manage risks arising out of financial derivative transactions that are related to the physical commodity, and they must meet certain criteria. To fit within the Circular, the physical transactions must supplement the bank's current risk management activities, constitute a nominal percentage of such risk management activities and not be entered into for speculative purposes. National banks may engage in physical commodity transactions to manage risks arising out of permissible, customer-driven banking activities.[78] Also, the banks must submit a detailed plan to the OCC describing the proposed activity and receive approval before they may commence such transactions.

FEDERAL RESERVE BOARD GUIDELINES

The Division of Banking Supervision and Regulation of the Board of Governors of the Federal Reserve System (FRB) released its guidelines, entitled "Examining Risk Management and Internal Controls for Trading Activities of Banking Organisations" (the "Guidelines") to be incorporated in the FRB's Capital Markets and Trading Activities Manual. They are designed to guide FRB examiners in their evaluations of the internal controls and risk management policies and systems established for the trading of cash and derivative instruments.[79]

In large measure, the Guidelines follow the recommendations set forth in the Group of Thirty Study and resemble the OCC's Banking Circular 277. Like Banking Circular 277, the Guidelines highlight the oversight and management responsibilities of the Board of Directors and senior management;[80] the importance of managing market, liquidity, legal and operational risks; and the necessity of sufficiently sophisticated audit procedures and internal controls. "[W]ritten policies and procedures that clearly outline the institution's risk management guidance for trading and derivatives activities" are required. The Guidelines also state that, "[i]n general, a bank should not trade a product until senior management and all relevant personnel (including those in risk management, internal control, legal, accounting and auditing) understand the product and are able to integrate the product into the bank's risk measurement and control systems".

However, the Guidelines do not adopt Banking Circular 277's customer appropriateness standard, although the Guidelines do require a bank to take some steps to ascertain a counterparty's sophistication when recommending specific transactions to some counterparties. Specifically, it states that "where a bank recommends specific transactions for an unsophisticated counterparty, the bank should ensure that it has adequate information regarding its counterparty on which to base its recommendations."

HOUSE REPORT ON FINANCIAL DERIVATIVES AND RECOMMENDATIONS OF CONGRESSMAN LEACH

During November 1993, the House Banking Committee Minority Staff issued its report on financial derivatives. The Staff's two-part, 900-page report (the "Minority Staff Report") was the product of six months of work by the House Banking Committee's Minority Staff. In conjunction with the report's preparation, Congressman James A. Leach, the Senior Republican on and now the chair of the Committee, had sent numerous letters to the OCC, the FRB, the Federal Deposit Insurance Corporation (FDIC), the Office of Thrift Supervision (OTS), the SEC and the CFTC posing questions regarding derivatives. Some of these questions derived from the Group of Thirty's recommendations in its Study.

The responses received by Congressman Leach were included in Part I of the Minority Staff Report. Part I also included a discussion of the derivative markets that resembled the descriptions and discussions included in the Group of Thirty Study.[81] Part II of the Minority Staff Report is a general reference document with discussion and background on current policy issues with regard to derivatives.

In connection with the release of the Minority Staff Report, Congressman Leach released a list of his recommendations for regulatory and legislative reform with regard to derivatives. Congressman Leach's 30 recommendations do not necessarily comport with the body of the Minority Staff Report. They focus on regulatory standards pertaining to capital, disclosure, suitability and accounting. He also recommends that an inter-agency commission be established by statute. Such a commission would then be the agency responsible for coordinating with foreign authorities and establishing rules in the foregoing areas for all derivatives market participants. He recommends

imposing some form of uniform federal regulation on all derivatives participants, and that such participants be required to provide public disclosure of their derivatives activities and the risks inherent in such activities. He also recommends that federal banking agencies adopt guidelines similar to those customer appropriateness guidelines issued by the OCC. Congressman Leach's recommendations for extensive regulatory change and overhaul reflect his view that derivatives are "the new wild card in international finance" and "the most risk oriented part of the international financial markets".

GENERAL ACCOUNTING OFFICE REPORT

After a two-year study of derivative instruments and their associated risks, the General Accounting Office (GAO) released its report entitled *Financial Derivatives – Actions Needed to Protect the Financial System* (the "GAO Report").[82] The lengthy report details the significant benefits that market participants obtain from the use of derivatives for hedging and speculative activities.[83] In addition to recognising their benefits, the GAO Report also specified the market, legal, operational and credit risks associated with derivatives.

The GAO Report made various recommendations attempting to lessen the risks of derivatives, compel derivative dealers and end-users to disclose sufficiently the risks associated with derivative positions, and initiate the establishment of comprehensive federal regulatory and industry schemes that would require OTC derivatives dealers in the United States to adopt and comply with prudent risk management practices. The recommendations include (1) regulatory oversight of affiliates of securities and insurance companies, (2) the overhaul of the financial regulatory system, and (3) the adoption of sufficient accounting and disclosure standards. The GAO emphasised the importance of coordinating initiatives with the international community because, without international harmonisation of standards for examinations, capital, disclosure and accounting with respect to derivatives, US initiatives may create legal and regulatory incentives for moving desirable derivatives business outside the United States.

The GAO Report evoked quite a response. Congressional committees and subcommittees, including the Senate Banking Committee and the House Energy and Commerce Subcommittee on Telecommunications and Finance, have held numerous hearings at which distinguished members of the regulatory and financial communities have testified. For example, Alan Greenspan, the Chairman of the Federal Reserve Board of Governors, stated that "[t]he [Federal Reserve] believes that remedial legislation relating to derivatives is neither necessary nor desirable at this time [and that we] must not lose sight of the fact that financial markets are regulated by private parties."[84] In addition, the GAO Report elicited strong responses from some in the industry, including a Joint Statement of the Leading Financial Trade Associations in the United States of America which opposed the GAO's recommendations because they "would increase the cost and reduce the availability of these essential transactions".

LEGISLATIVE INITIATIVES
In the congressional elections of 1994, the American public elected a predominantly Republican Congress, producing a new leadership in the committees of Congress. Members of the new Congress have introduced various bills that would regulate, or enhance the supervision of, derivatives activities. The bills include a bill introduced by Representative James A. Leach, Chairman of the House Committee on Banking and Financial Services, and a bill introduced by Representative Henry B. Gonzalez of Texas, the Committee's ranking Democrat and Minority Leader. In general, the bills attempt to address the issues of capital, appropriateness and disclosure with respect to derivatives activities and their associated risks, although the bills differ in their approaches.

Congressman Leach's bill is entitled "Risk Management Improvement and Derivatives Oversight Act of 1995".[85] Among other things, it seeks to adopt recommendations that he made in connection with the Minority Staff Report (discussed above), including the creation of a Federal Derivatives Commission to "promote consistency in regulatory practices and to ensure progressive and vigilant supervision." In particular, the bill provides that the Commission shall "establish principles and standards for the supervision and oversight by Federal financial institution regulators of financial institutions engaged in derivatives activities and make recommendations to promote better risk management techniques and uniformity in the supervision of these financial institutions." The Federal Derivatives Commission would be chaired by the chairman of the FRB and comprised of the

heads of the CFTC, SEC, OCC and other financial regulatory agencies.

The Leach bill would also authorise the FRB to determine whether a self-regulatory association of derivatives dealers should be established for the supervision of derivatives dealers. Such an association would be registered as a national derivatives association and would set standards and procedures for the regulation of its members. Derivatives dealers, other than futures commission merchants or registered brokers or dealers of securities, would not lawfully be able "to effect any transaction in, or induce or attempt to induce the purchase or sale of, any derivative financial instrument, unless such derivatives dealer is a member of a national derivatives association...."

Representative Henry Gonzalez's bill is entitled the "Derivatives Safety and Soundness Act of 1995".[86] The bill, *inter alia*, requires enhanced supervision of the "derivatives activities" of "financial institutions". The term "financial institution" includes any depository institution, federal home loan bank, broker, dealer, government securities broker or dealer, investment company, investment adviser, futures commission merchant, floor broker, commodity trading advisor, commodity pool operator and insurance company. Any activities in which a financial institution is engaged in "derivative financial instruments" as either a dealer or active end-user would constitute "derivatives activities" for purposes of this bill.

Financial institutions that are end-users or dealers of derivatives must have written management plans approved by the institution's board of directors to ensure that derivatives activities are "conducted in a safe and sound manner", are consistent with the institution's risk management policy, and have appropriate oversight by a board with directors who understand the risks of derivative instruments, the institution's credit exposures, and the institution's activities with, and exposures to, various derivative instruments.

The bill also proposes various amendments to existing statutes, including certain amendments to the Federal Deposit Insurance Act to expand the list of derivative instruments covered by that Act's provisions. The bill provides that the United States promote greater coordination of regulation and supervision among the international regulators. It also directs the GAO to conduct a new study of derivatives. The new GAO study would examine the extent to which financial institutions use derivative instruments for speculation and whether margin and collateral requirements would curb any such speculation.

At this time, it is unclear which, if any, of the derivatives-related bills will proceed or finally be adopted. Frank Newman (Acting Secretary of the US Treasury), Alan Greenspan (Chairman of the FRB), Mary Schapiro (Chairwoman of the CFTC) and Arthur Levitt (Chairman of the SEC) stated that no new legislation was necessary at a Congressional hearing in January 1995 on the topic of derivatives.[87] The regulators oppose the bills on various grounds. Meanwhile, the regulators are working with members of the derivatives and financial industry to, among other things, reduce risk and increase disclosure without new legislation. For example, various industry groups have been developing standards for sales practices and codes of conduct. It is expected that many of these new sales practices and codes of conduct will be embraced by much of the derivatives industry.

Conclusion

Given the complexity of certain commodity and energy derivative instruments and the evolving regulatory landscape, participants in derivatives markets must weigh the legal and regulatory implications of their transactions carefully.

First, participants must consider the legality of the derivative product in light of the CEA, CFTC regulations, pertinent judicial or CFTC interpretations of the foregoing, and applicable state or local laws. Second, participants must assess the enforceability of any agreements involving derivative transactions. This assessment should include an evaluation of the legal capacity of the counterparties entering into the transactions and the laws of the applicable jurisdictions. Third, participants in the markets for derivatives must carefully monitor and manage their derivatives business. Even those entities not covered by the OCC's Banking Circular 277 or FRB Guidelines should consider comparing their activities against those guidelines and those of the Group of Thirty Study.

Finally, derivatives dealers and end-users must be mindful of the changing regulatory landscape. These changes go beyond traditional concerns about the legality of derivative transactions. Any entity engaging in, or planning to engage in, commodity derivatives transactions must consider the spectre of additional regulation, as well as the other legal and enforceability concerns.

1 *A swap is a bilateral agreement requiring each party to make periodic payments to the other party, the amounts of which are usually determined by netting the payment obligations of the parties. In such cases, neither party actually pays the notional principal amount during the term of the swap, and, on each scheduled payment date, the amount required to be paid by one party is netted against the amount required to be paid by the other party and only this net amount is paid by one party to the other. With some types of swaps, however, the parties exchange gross payments (such as gross payments in different currencies in the case of some currency swaps), not net payments.*

2 *Derivatives are instruments that derive their value from the value of underlying assets, including commodities, securities, interest or currency exchange rates, or indices of the foregoing. Derivative products include forwards, futures, options, swaps, swaptions, caps, floors, collars and other similar instruments. For the purposes of this chapter, the term "derivative" refers only to instruments traded off of an exchange, such as forwards, swaps and swap-derivatives. For a detailed discussion of exchange-traded futures and options on futures, see* Regulation of the Commodities Futures and Options Markets *by Thomas A. Russo (Colorado Springs, 1983) and the Second Edition of* Commodities Regulation *(Boston, 1989) by Philip McBride Johnson and Thomas Lee Hazen.*

3 *The CFTC acted against Wells Fargo Bank, in connection with its gold-indexed certificate of deposit programme and threatened to act against Chase Manhattan Bank, in connection with its issuance of oil-indexed swaps. See Robert B.* Hiden Jr. and Donald R. Crawshaw, Hybrids and the Commodity Exchange Act, *22 The Review of Securities & Commodities Regulation 233, 237 (Dec. 20, 1989).*

4 *Regulation of Hybrid and Related Instruments, 52 Fed. Reg. 47,022 (1987) (Advance Notice of Proposed Rulemaking, dated Dec. 11, 1987).*

5 *The CFTC received "exclusive jurisdiction [except for certain specified exceptions] with respect to . . . transactions involving contracts of sale of a commodity for future delivery, traded or executed on a contract market . . . or any other board of trade, exchange or market . . . ". CEA Section 2(a)(1)(A)(i); see also Section 4c(b).*

6 *See also CFTC Reg. 1.3(e). The definition of the term "commodity" includes everything except onions (including securities) provided that it involves contracts for future delivery.*

7 *See, for example, In re Stovall [1977-1980 Transfer Binder] Comm. Fut. L. Rep. (CCH) ¶ 20,941 (Dec. 6, 1979); Policy Statement Concerning Swap Transactions, 54 Fed. Reg. 30,694 (July 21, 1989) (also printed at Comm. Fut. L. Rep. (CCH) ¶ 24,494).*

8 *CEA Sections 2(a)(1)(A)(i) and 4c(b).*

9 *The CFTC has listed some of a forward contract's traditional indicia, which include the following: (1) commercial counterparties that can make or take delivery, (2) commercial transactions related to the business in that commodity, (3) privately-negotiated transactions among principals that cannot be assigned without consent, and (4) the absence of a clearing house or exchange-style offset. Statutory*

Interpretation Concerning Forward Transactions, 55 Fed. Reg. *39,188 (Sept. 25, 1990), at 39,191.*

10 *Section 1a(11).*

11 *Section 2(a)(1)(A)(ii) provides that "[n]othing in [the CEA] shall be deemed to govern or in any way be applicable to transactions in foreign currency, security warrants, security rights, resales of instalment loan contracts, repurchase options, government securities, or mortgages and mortgage purchase commitments, unless such transactions involve the sale thereof for future delivery conducted on a board of trade."*

12 *The treatment of swap-derivative instruments with elements of options on securities was addressed in an administrative action brought by the SEC against BT Securities Corporation ("BT Securities"), a subsidiary of Bankers Trust New York Corporation, in connection with certain swap-derivative instruments that Gibson Greetings Inc, ("Gibson") purchased from BT Securities. Some of the derivative transactions sold to Gibson had payment characteristics that related to, or were "linked" to, the prices or yields of debt securities issued by the US Treasury Department. Due to changes in interest rates, Gibson was liable to make large payments to BT Securities on these instruments, prompting Gibson to sue BT Securities and prompting several regulatory agencies to commence administrative proceedings against BT Securities. BT Securities settled Gibson's lawsuit and the proceedings with each of the agencies.*

The SEC settlement determined that certain of the swaps were securities. In particular, the SEC order dated December 22, 1994, deemed certain transactions involving individually negotiated, cash-settled OTC options on debt securities or groups or indexes of securities to be securities. Simultaneously with the issuance of the settlement, the SEC issued an exemptive order exempting swap dealers engaged in derivative transactions that were deemed by the SEC to be securities from the broker-dealer registration requirements of the Securities Exchange Act of 1934, provided that (1) the instruments satisfied the requirements of the swap exemption issued by the CFTC (17 C.F.R. ¶ 35) and (2) the instruments were documented as swap agreements.

See also note 38, infra, discussing the simultaneous CFTC order.

13 *See, for example, Section 2(a)(1)(B).*

14 *See, for example,* Chicago Mercantile Exchange *v.* Securities and Exchange Commission, *883 F.2d 537 (7th Cir. 1989),* cert. denied, *496 U.S. 936 (1990).*

15 *See note 9 and text accompanying note 7, supra.*

16 *738 F. Supp. 1472 (S.D.N.Y. 1990).*

17 Idem *at 1491. In this regard, the Court "conclude[d] that even where there is no 'right' of offset, the 'opportunity' to offset and a tacit expectation and common practice of offsetting suffices to deem the transaction a futures contract."* Idem *at 1492.*

18 *55* Fed. Reg. *39,188 (Sept. 25, 1990).*

19 Idem *at 39,191-92. One Commissioner dissented. He concluded that the oil contracts "do not sufficiently resemble forward contracts".*

20 *945 F.2d 309 (9th Cir. 1991).*

21 Idem *at 313, 312-15. Some courts have upheld forward contracts that are offset by adopting a different position. Instead of emphasising the delivery obligation and the necessity of creating a subsequent, separate transaction to offset the forward contract, they state that "[a] set-off is in legal effect a delivery."* Board of Trade of the City of Chicago *v.* Christie Grain & Stock Co., *198 U.S. 236, 250 (1905). See also* Salomon Forex, Inc. *v.* Laszlo N. Tauber, *8 F.3d 966, 978 (4th Cir. 1993).*

22 *N.Y. GEN. OBLIG. LAW §5-401 (McKinney Supp. 1993).*

23 *N.Y. GEN. BUS. LAW §351 (McKinney 1988).*

24 *See text accompanying note 30, infra.*

25 *See* Salomon Forex, Inc. *v.* Laszlo N. Tauber, *8 F.3d 966, 978 (4th Cir. 1993).*

26 *Interestingly, the court also noted that the transactions were not intended to be settled by reference to the dealings of others. Instead, they would be settled by offsetting transactions entered into by the parties.* Idem.

27 *See, for example,* Liss *v.* Manuel, *296 N.Y.S.2d 627 (Civ. Ct. 1968);* Holberg *v.* Westchester Racing Association, *53 N.Y.S.2d 490 (App. Div. 1st Dept. 1945).*

28 *54* Fed. Reg. *30,694 (July 21, 1989).*

29 *P.L. 102-546, 106 Stat. 3590.*

30 *See CEA Section 4(c); see generally* Thomas A. Russo & Marlisa Vinciguerra, Financial Regulation and Title V of the Futures Trading Practices Act of 1992, *Futures Int'l Law Letter (Nov.-Dec. 1992).*

31 *See CEA Sections 4(c)(1), 4(c)(2) and 4(c)(3).*

32 *H. Rep. No. 102-978, 102nd Cong., 2nd Sess. (1992), at 81. See also CEA Sections 4(c)(5)(A) (regarding hybrids) and 4(c)(5)(B) (regarding swaps).*

33 *See Parts 34 and 35 of the CFTC Regulations; 58* Fed. Reg. *5580 (Jan. 22, 1993); 58* Fed. Reg. *5587 (Jan. 22, 1993); and 58* Fed. Reg. *21286 (April 20, 1993).*

34 *58* Fed. Reg. *5587 (Jan. 22, 1993); see generally* A. Robert Pietrzack and Michael S. Sackheim, CFTC Exemption Procedures for Novel Derivative Transactions, *Securities & Commodities Regulation at 121-24 (July 1993).*

35 *"'Eligible swap participant' means, and shall be limited to, the following persons or classes of persons:*

(i) A bank or trust company (acting on its own behalf or on behalf of another eligible swap participant);

(ii) A savings association or credit union;

(iii) An insurance company;

(iv) An investment company subject to regulation under the Investment Company Act of 1940 (15 U.S.C. § 80a-1 et seq.) or a foreign person performing a similar role or function subject as such to foreign regulations, provided that such investment company or foreign person is not formed solely for the specific purpose of constituting an eligible swap participant;

(v) A commodity pool formed and operated by a person subject to regulation under the Act or a foreign person performing a similar role or function subject as such to foreign regulation, provided that such commodity pool or foreign person is not formed solely for the specific purpose of constituting an eligible swap participant and has total assets

exceeding $5,000,000;

(vi) A corporation, partnership, proprietorship, organization, trust, or other entity not formed solely for the specific purpose of constituting an eligible swap participant (A) which has total assets exceeding $10,000,000, or (B) the obligations of which under the swap agreement are guaranteed or otherwise supported by a letter of credit or keepwell, support, or other agreement by any such entity referenced in this subsection (vi)(A) or by an entity referred to in paragraph (i), (ii), (iii), (iv), (v), (vi) or (viii) of this section; or (C) which has a net worth of $1,000,000 and enters into the swap agreement in connection with the conduct of its business; or which has a net worth of $1,000,000 and enters into the swap agreement to manage the risk of an asset or liability owned or incurred in the conduct of its business or reasonably likely to be owned or incurred in the conduct of its business;

(vii) An employee benefit plan subject to the Employee Retirement Income Security Act of 1974 or a foreign person performing a similar role or function subject as such to foreign regulation with total assets exceeding $5,000,000, or whose investment decisions are made by a bank, trust company, insurance company, investment adviser subject to regulation under the Investment Advisers Act of 1940 (15 U.S.C. § 80a-1 et seq.), or a commodity trading advisor subject to regulation under the Act;

(viii) Any governmental entity (including the United States, any state, or any foreign government) or political subdivision thereof, or any multinational or supranational entity or any instrumentality, agency or department of any of the foregoing;

(ix) A broker-dealer subject to regulation under the Securities Exchange Act of 1934 (15 U.S.C. § 78a-1 et seq.) or a foreign person performing a similar role or function subject as such to foreign regulation, acting on its own behalf or on behalf of another eligible swap participant: Provided, however, *that if such broker-dealer is a natural person or proprietorship, the broker-dealer must also meet the requirements of either subsection (vi) or (xi) of this section;*

(x) A futures commission merchant, floor broker, or floor trader subject to regulation under the Act or a foreign person performing a similar role or function subject as such to foreign regulation, acting on its own behalf or on behalf of another eligible swap participant: Provided, however, *that if such futures commission merchant, floor broker, or floor trader is a natural person or proprietorship, the futures commission merchant, floor broker, or floor trader must also meet the requirements of subsection (vi) or (xi) of this section; or*

(xi) Any natural person with total assets exceeding at least $10,000,000." CFTC Reg. 35.1(b)(2).

36 *CFTC Reg. 35.2.*

37 *CFTC Reg. 35.1(b)(1). This definition is a quote of that provided in 11 U.S.C. 101 (55) (defining the term "swap agreement" for the US Bankruptcy Code).*

38 *CFTC Reg. 35.2. The exceptions to the exemption are provisions of the CEA that set forth the SEC-CFTC Jurisdictional Accord delineating the jurisdictional reach of the two agencies (see text accompanying note 13,* supra*) or prohibit fraud and manipulation.*

One such exception to the exemption, Section 4o of the CEA, was addressed in the CFTC order dated December 22, 1994, accepting BT Securities' offer of settlement. Among other things, the order explained that BT Securities violated

Section 4o, which prohibits commodity trading advisors from engaging in fraudulent activities. The order finds that BT Securities, while acting as a commodity trading advisor (CTA) to Gibson, made material misstatements and omissions in its offer and sale of swap agreements and materially understated the value of such agreements when Gibson requested valuations for the purpose of evaluating its swaps.

In order to be a CTA, one must give advice as to the value or price of futures or commodity options. In charging BT Securities with CTA fraud, the CFTC did not identify any specific transaction as being a future or commodity option. However, the CFTC's conclusion raises questions as to whether it believes swaps generally or any specific swaps may be futures or commodity options. Also, it is interesting to note that, historically at least, swap dealers have not considered themselves to be CTAs because swap agreements are typically described as privately negotiated bilateral agreements between two counterparties. The CFTC's determination, based on the facts available regarding BT Securities' dealings with Gibson, that an advisory relationship had been established raises concerns that a dealer may have fiduciary duties to its counterparty in specific situations.

See note 12, supra*, discussing the simultaneous CFTC order.*

39 *See text accompanying notes 22-27,* supra.

40 *See Part 34 of the CFTC Regulations; 58* Fed. Reg. *5580 (Jan. 22, 1993).*

41 *For example, in 1986, The Standard Oil Company launched a public offering of Oil Indexed Units. At maturity, the Units paid Unitholders principal plus a contingent payment, if at that time oil prices surpassed a strike price. See Hiden & Crawshaw,* supra *note 3, at 236-237.*

42 *Wells Fargo Bank's gold-indexed certificate of deposit programme is an example of such a hybrid instrument. See idem.*

43 *CFTC Reg. 34.3(a)(2).*

44 *The term reference price is defined to be the "price nearest the current spot or forward price, whichever is used to price the instrument, at which a commodity-dependent payment becomes non-zero, or, in the case where two potential reference prices exist, the price that results in the greatest commodity-dependent value." CFTC Reg. 34.2(g).*

45 *CFTC Reg. 34.2(e).*

46 *See text accompanying note 13,* supra.

47 *58* Fed. Reg. *21,286 (April 20, 1993).*

48 *The CFTC determined that the exemption did not rely on a subjective test of intent (that is, whether the energy-related product was intended to actually be used as an energy source). Idem at 21,289.*

49 *"[T]his order is limited to (A) commercial participants who, in connection with their business activities: (1) incur risks, in addition to price risk, related to the underlying physical commodities; (2) have a demonstrable capacity or ability, directly or through separate bona fide contractual arrangements, to make or take delivery under the terms of the contracts; (3) are not prohibited by law or regulation from entering into such Energy Contracts; (4) are not formed solely for the specific purpose of constituting an eligible entity pursuant to this Order; and (5) qualify as one of the following*

282

REGULATORY
AND LEGAL
ISSUES

entities: (i) a bank or trust company; (ii) a corporation, partnership, proprietorship, organization, trust, or other business entity with a net worth exceeding $1,000,000 or total assets exceeding $5,000,000, or the obligations of which under the agreement, contract or transaction are guaranteed or otherwise supported by a letter of credit or keepwell, support, or other agreement by any such entity or by an entity referred to in subsections (A), (B), (C), (H), (I) or (J) of section 4(c)(3); (iii) a broker-dealer subject to regulation under the Securities Exchange Act of 1934 (15 U.S.C. 78a et seq.); (iv) a futures commission merchant subject to regulation under the Act; or (B) any governmental entity (including the United States, any state, any municipality or any foreign government) or political subdivision thereof, or any multinational or supranational entity or any instrumentality, agency, or department of any of the foregoing...". 58 Fed. Reg. at 21,294.

50 Idem *at 21,294.*

51 *One Commissioner dissented from the CFTC's determination not to apply its anti-fraud jurisdiction.* Idem *at 21,295. In addition, former Representative Glenn English of Oklahoma, while he was Chairman of the CFTC's oversight committee, introduced a bill to amend the CEA "to ensure the continued application of the [CEA's] anti-fraud and anti-manipulation protections" to all exemptions that the CFTC issues. H.R. 2374, 103rd Cong., 1st Sess. (1993).*

52 *Different jurisdictions have different laws affecting the legality of the derivative transaction. For a discussion of the applicable laws of nine countries with significant participation in the derivatives markets, see Group of Thirty Study on Derivatives: Practices and Principles (hereinafter "Group of Thirty Study"), Appendix II. In Australia, for example, it is possible that derivative transactions could constitute violations of laws prohibiting illegal gaming, wagering or insurance businesses. Moreover, many derivative transactions arguably fall within the broad definition of "futures contracts" under the Corporations Law, as several unfavorable Australian court decisions have recently demonstrated.* Idem *at 2, 7-8. Recently, the Australian Securities Commission issued a derivatives "safe harbour" to provide legal certainty for derivative transactions. See ASC Policy Statement on Exempt Futures Market (proposing an "interim safe harbour" market under Corporations Law Section 1127(1) for individually-negotiated transactions between sophisticated parties). Uncertainty about the gaming and wagering laws of Canada also raises questions about the legality of derivative transactions in that jurisdiction.* Idem *at 86. Under English law, derivative transactions for bona fide business purposes should constitute legal "investments", rather than voidable "gaming or wagering contracts".* Idem *at 169. The German Exchange Act and interpretations define "futures transactions" so broadly that swaps and other off-exchange derivative transactions are covered. Such transactions are unenforceable unless both parties to the transactions qualify under the Act.* Idem *at 211. Japan also has some laws that raise questions about the legality of derivative transactions. These include the Commodity Exchange Law and Securities Exchange Law's anti-gambling provisions that prohibit off-market speculating on the indices of securities or commodities.* Idem *at 220. In Singapore, speculative derivative transactions may be voidable under the Civil Law Act's gaming and wagering prohibition.* Idem *at 283-85. France, on the other hand, has acted to provide greater legal certainty for the derivatives market. The French Parliament recently* amended Article 1 of the Law of 28 March 1885 to recognise the legality of certain derivatives transactions, including transactions on securities, goods or commodities that are cash-settled, and to exclude them from the article of the French Civil Code prohibiting gambling contracts, provided that one of the parties to any cash-settled derivatives transactions is a credit establishment or other financial institution.

53 *In addition to the legal issues discussed in this chapter, numerous other legal issues, including tax issues, must be examined.*

54 *A similar issue has been raised in a recent lawsuit filed in connection with the Orange County bankruptcy. Orange County has brought an action against Merrill Lynch and Co., Inc., for restitution of the money lost on certain obligations it purchased from or through Merrill Lynch and other types of equitable relief, claiming,* inter alia, *that such transactions were* ultra vires. See In re *County of Orange, No. SA 94-22272 (Bankr. C. D. Cal. filed Jan. 12, 1995).*

55 *Group of Thirty Study, at 51.*

56 *See, for example, Catherine Good Abbott, "Rethinking Prudence: Is the Spot Gas Market too Speculative?",* Cambridge Energy Forum; *Adam B. Jaffe and Joseph P. Kalt, "Oversight of Regulated Utilities Fuel Supply Contracts: Achieving Maximum Benefit From Competitive Natural Gas and Emission Allowance Markets" (The Economics Resource Group: April, 1993).*

57 *See Draft Investments of Insurers Model Act; see also Richard A. Miller, Michael P. Goldman and Adam C. Cooper, "The Insurance Industry's Use of OTC Derivatives: Developments - Special Concerns",* Institutions and Derivatives or Spring Training for Rotisserie Baseball *(American Bar Association Section of Business Law, Committee on Futures Regulation, Feb. 3-5, 1994) at 6.*

58 *11 U.S.C. § 101(55). Section 101(55) of the U.S. Bankruptcy Code defines the term "swap agreement" as: "(A) an agreement (including terms and conditions incorporated by reference therein) which is a rate swap agreement, basis swap, forward rate agreement, commodity swap, interest rate option, forward foreign exchange agreement, rate cap agreement, rate floor agreement, rate collar agreement, currency swap agreement, cross-currency rate swap agreement, currency option, any other similar agreement (including any option to enter into any of the foregoing); (B) any combination of the foregoing; or (C) a master agreement for any of the foregoing together with all supplements." See also Section 101(56) of the US Bankruptcy Code (defining the term "swap participant").*

59 *It would otherwise bar counterparties to such transactions from setting off amounts due from amounts owed to the debtor and would keep the counterparties waiting during a lengthy bankruptcy proceeding to ascertain whether any moneys remain to pay them amounts they are due.*

60 *See 11 U.S.C. § 362(14).*

61 *See 11 U.S.C. § 560.*

62 *See 11 U.S.C. §§ 546(g) and 548(d)(2).*

63 *See 11 U.S.C. §§ 362 and 365.*

64 *Appendix II of the Group of Thirty Study discusses the bankruptcy laws of nine jurisdictions. For example, under*

Australian law, the bankruptcy law should be clarified to avoid a possible interrelationship between Section 86 of the Bankruptcy Act of 1955 and Section 16 of the Banking Act 1959 that may occur if one party to a derivative transaction is a bank. Until the law is amended, the parties may seek to avoid the potential problem by entering into a master netting agreement with certain remedying provisions. Group of Thirty Study, Appendix II at 4, 24, 29, 46. Otherwise, Australia's bankruptcy law is similar to that of the United States in that it authorises set-off and a netting mechanism does not create a voidable preference unless the solvent party was aware of "an available act of bankruptcy". Idem at 24-26. In Canada, the most problematic law with respect to insolvency termination under a master agreement involves the Companies' Creditors Arrangement Act because it arguably allows courts to grant a stay precluding the termination of contracts. Idem at 138-42. France recently passed legislation authorising close-out netting with regard to "eligible transactions" provided that at least one of the parties qualifies as a "qualified institution" when a party to the agreement is insolvent. See note 50, supra. While German law does not address the enforceability of terminating and close-out provisions during insolvency or bankruptcy-related events, the general enforceability of netting provisions under German law lead many leading commentators to believe that they are enforceable during such events. However, a pending bill for a new Insolvency Code is before Parliament that does expressly provide that executory contracts, like swap agreements, may not be terminated upon the commencement of insolvency proceedings. Group of Thirty Study, Appendix II at 209-10. Under Japanese law, it appears that a terminating close-out provision would be deemed valid during a bankruptcy or reorganisation. Idem at 271. Although Singapore also lacks express authority on this issue, payments made "in the course of ordinary commercial trading [that] are unlikely to be motivated by any desire to improve the position of the counterparty vis-a-vis other creditors of the defaulting party" would not be deemed voidable preferences. Idem at 287-88.

65 See 11 U.S.C. § 101(25) (Supp. 1994).

66 Congress enacted FIRREA in 1989. In addition to expanding the powers of the Federal Deposit Insurance Corporation (FDIC), it provided that most banks or savings institutions that are parties to "qualified financial contracts" (which include swap agreements and commodity contracts) can, among other things, offset or net obligations and exercise contractual rights to terminate or liquidate such contracts. See 12 U.S.C. § 1821(e)(8); Group of Thirty Study, Appendix II at 300-01. Then, Congress enacted the Federal Deposit Insurance Corporation Improvement Act (FDICIA) in 1991. It ensures the enforceability of a "netting contract" between two "financial institutions", "notwithstanding any other provision of law" and notwithstanding any "stay, injunction, avoidance, moratorium or similar proceeding or order, whether issued or granted by a court, administrative agency, or otherwise." The term "financial institution" includes a registered or licensed broker or dealer (and certain affiliates), a depository institution, a registered or licensed futures commission merchant or certain other institutions. 12 U.S.C. § 4402(9). FDICIA defines the term "netting contract" to mean a valid US contract between financial institutions that provides for netting present or future payment obligations or payment entitlements (including liquidation or close-out values relating to the obligations or entitlements) among the parties to the agreement...". 12 U.S.C. § 4402(14). See Group

of Thirty Study, Appendix II at 302-03.

67 Congressman Leach introduced a bill proposing various amendments to bankruptcy provisions to clarify remaining uncertainty with regard to the applicability of automatic stay provisions with respect to derivative transactions. Also, it would amend the Federal Deposit Insurance Act by restricting a party's right to liquidate or terminate a contract when or after the FDIC becomes a receiver for a depository institution. See text accompanying note 84, infra.

68 See Group of Thirty Study, Appendix II at 139 (July 1993); OCC Banking Circular No. 277 [Vol. 5] Fed'l Banking L. Rep. (CCH) ¶ 58,717 (October 27, 1993) at 36,466. In addition, netting also significantly reduces the risk posed by derivatives because counterparties have much smaller exposures to each other. Accordingly, many have requested that the reductions in risk offered by netting agreements be recognised in the capital reserves requirements and standards. Group of Thirty Study, Appendix II at 139 (July 1993).

69 Idem; Appendix II at 304.

70 "Qualified institutions" means French banks and other credit institutions governed by the Banking Law of 1984, insurance undertakings governed by the Insurance Code and licensed stockbrokers "or non-resident entities having a comparable status". Article 2 of Law of 28 March 1885; see ISDA Memorandum of January 10, 1994 (distributing Notice of French New Legislation on Netting by Linklater & Paines). The reference to a "comparable status" will likely require that non-resident entities be subject to institutional supervision in their domestic countries. Idem

71 Idem at 271.

72 OCC Banking Circular No. 277 [Vol. 5] Fed'l Banking L. Rep. (CCH) ¶ 58,717 (October 27, 1993) at 36,459.

73 Idem at 36,462.

74 OCC Bulletin 94-31 [Vol. 5] Fed'l Banking L. Rep. (CCH) ¶ 58,717 (May 10, 1994) at 36,473.

75 Idem at 36,478. The Bulletin explained that the Circular's section is similar to a suitability rule "in that it presumes, consistent with safe and sound banking practices, that a bank dealer will not recommend transactions it knows, or has reason to know, would be inappropriate for the customer on the basis of available information". Idem at 36,479. However, it then states that the Circular's section "requires only that the bank's credit officers determine that a proposed derivatives transaction is consistent with a counterparty's policies and procedures with respect to derivatives activities, as they are known to the bank" and that, "[if] the bank believes that a particular transaction may be inappropriate for a customer, and that customer insists on proceeding, the bank need only document its analysis and the information it provided to the customer". Idem.

76 Idem at 36,479. See generally idem at 36,478-80.

77 Financial derivative transactions involving precious metals such as gold, silver and platinum are already permitted and are not subject to the Circular.

78 Fed'l Banking L. Rep. 58,717 at 36,466.

79 "This guidance specifically targets trading, market making, and customer accommodation activities in cash and derivative instruments at State member banks, branches and *agencies of foreign banks, and Edge corporations. The principles set forth in this guidance also apply to the risk management of bank holding companies, which should manage and control aggregate risk exposures on a consolidated basis, while recognising legal distinctions among subsidiaries. Many of the principles advanced can also be applied to banks' use of derivatives as end-users." Letter from Richard Spillenkothen, Director, Division of Banking Supervision and Regulation, Board of Governors of the Federal Reserve System, SR 93-69 (Dec. 20, 1993) at 1.*

80 *Boards of Directors "should regularly re-evaluate significant risk management policies and procedures with special emphasis placed on those defining the institution's risk tolerance...".* Idem *at 3.*

81 *During October 1993, the CFTC issued a* Study of Swaps and Off-Exchange Derivatives Trading *(the "CFTC Study") to provide Congress with any information necessary to assist it in ascertaining the need, if any, for future legislation relating to the market for over-the-counter derivative products. See H. Rep. No. 102-978, 102nd Cong., 2nd Sess. (1992). The CFTC Study was prepared in consultation with the Board of Governors of the Federal Reserve System and the SEC. The CFTC Study included descriptions and conclusions with regard to the derivatives market's size and scope and con-*

cluded that, at this time, no fundamental regulatory changes were necessary with regard to over-the-counter derivatives.

82 *GAO/GGD-94-133 (May 1994).*

83 *For example, the GAO Report declared that: "Derivatives serve an important function in the global financial marketplace, providing end-users opportunities to better manage financial risks associated with their business transactions. The rapid growth and increasing complexity of derivatives reflects the increased demand from end-users for better ways to manage their financial risks and from speculators for lower cost ways to potentially profit from market volatility."* Idem *at 123.*

84 *Testimony by Alan Greenspan, Chairman, Board of Governors of the Federal Reserve System before the Subcommittee on Telecommunications and Finance of the Committee on Energy and Commerce, US House of Representatives, May 25, 1994, at 23.*

85 *H.R. 20, 104th Cong., 1st Sess. (1995).*

86 *H.R. 31, 104th Cong., 1st Sess. (1995).*

87 *Testimony before the Committee on Banking, Housing and Urban Affairs, US Senate, January 5, 1995.*

APPENDIX A

Chapter 3: Valuing Energy Derivatives

IN THIS APPENDIX, we derive the stochastic differential equation for the futures prices (equation 38 in the main text) when the convenience yields are stochastic. We begin with the cost-of-carry relation:

$$F(t,T) = S(t)\exp\left[\int_t^T (r(u) - z(t,u))du\right]$$

Substituting the stochastic differential equation for $z(t,u)$, we obtain:

$$F(t,T) = S(t)\exp\left[\int_r^T r(u)du\right]\exp\left[-\int_t^T \left\{z(0,u) + \int_0^t \beta(v,u)dv + \int_0^t (v,u)dW_2^*(v)\right\}du\right]$$

Writing in differential form,

$$d\log F(t,T) = d\log S(t) + r(t)dt + z(0,t)dt - \left[\int_t^T \beta(t,u)du\right]dt + \left[\int_0^t \beta(v,t)dv\right]dt$$

$$-\left[\int_t^T \delta(t,u)du\right]dW_2^*(t) + \left[\int_0^t \delta(v,t)dW_2^*(v)\right]dt$$

Since equation (34) implies that:

$$z(t,t) = z(0,t) + \int_0^t \beta(v,t)dv + \int_0^t \delta(v,t)dW_2^*(v)$$

$$d\log F(t,T) = -\left(\sigma^2/2\right)dt + \sigma dW_1^*(t) - \left[\int_t^T \beta(t,u)du\right]dt - \left[\int_t^T \delta(t,u)du\right]dW_2^*(t)$$

For the expected futures price change to be zero, the drift of the log of the futures price must be equal to minus one half the variance of the log of the futures price. To derive the condition, necessary to ensure this relationship, rewrite the previous equation as:

$$d\log F(t,T) = \left[-\left[\int_t^T \beta(t,u)du\right]dt + (1/2)\left[\int_t^T \delta(t,u)du\right]^2 dt - \rho\sigma\left[\int_t^T \delta(t,u)du\right]dt\right]$$

$$+\left[-\left(\sigma^2/2\right)dt + \sigma dW_1^*(t) - \left[\int_t^T \delta(t,u)du\right]dW_2^*(t) - (1/2)\left[\int_t^T \delta(t,u)du\right]^2 + \rho\sigma\left[\int_t^T \delta(t,u)du\right]dt\right]$$

Therefore, to ensure that the futures price has zero expected increment, the following must hold:

$$-\int_t^T \beta(t,u)du + (1/2)\left[\int_t^T \delta(t,u)du\right]^2 - \sigma\rho\int_t^T \delta(t,u)du = 0$$

that is,

$$\int_t^T \beta(t,u)du = (1/2)\left[\int_t^T \delta(t,u)du\right]^2 - \sigma\rho\int_t^T \delta(t,u)du$$

By taking the derivative with respect to T on both sides, we obtain:

$$\beta(t,T) = \delta(t,T)\left[\int_t^T \delta(t,u)du - \rho\sigma\right]$$

Therefore, the futures price evolves according to:

$$d\log F(t,T) = \sigma dW_1^*(t) - \left[\int_t^T \delta(t,u)du\right]dW_2^*(t) - \left(\sigma^2/2\right)dt - 1/2\left[\int_t^T \delta(t,u)du\right]^2 dt + \rho\sigma\left[\int_t^T \delta(t,u)du\right]dt$$

or

$$dF(t,T)/F(t,T) = \sigma dW_1^*(t) - \left[\int_t^T \delta(t,u)du\right]dW_2^*(t)$$

QED

APPENDIX B
Chapter 7: Exotic Options
Formulae for Option Pricing

THROUGHOUT THIS APPENDIX, the following definitions apply:

t = valuation time,

$T - t$ = life of the option in years,

r = risk-free interest rate,

K = strike price,

$F(t)$ = forward price at time t, sometimes abbreviated F, and

$N(.)$ = cumulative normal distribution function.

A.1 Vanilla options

The premium for a call option on a forward contract is given by

$$C = \exp[-r(T - t)][F(t)N(d_1) - KN(d_2)] \, , \tag{A.1}$$

and the premium for a put option on a forward contract is given by

$$P = \exp[-r(T - t)][-F(t)N(-d_1) + KN(-d_2)] \, , \tag{A.2}$$

where

$$d_1 = \frac{\ln(F(t)/K) + 0.5\sigma^2(T - t)}{\sigma\sqrt{T - t}} \, ,$$

and

$$d_2 = d_1 - \sigma\sqrt{T - t} \, .$$

A.2 Barrier options

The equations (A.3) through (A.8) are for pricing barrier options which have no rebates; barrier options with rebates can be found in Rubinstein and Reiner (September 1991).

These equations are for knock-out options. Knock-in options can be priced using the parity relationship that holds between knock-in, knock-out and vanilla options with the same strike price. When all three options have the same strike and the knock-out and knock-in options have the same barrier price, then the knock-in call (put) premium plus the knock-out call (put) premium is equal to the premium of a standard call (put) option.

Down-and-out call option (B<K)

$$C_{dao(B<K)} = \exp[-r(T - t)]\{[FN(d_1) - KN(d_2)] - [BN(z_1) - K(F/B)N(z_2)]\} \tag{A.3}$$

Down-and-out call option (B>K)

$$C_{dao(B>K)} = \exp[-r(T - t)]\{FN(x_1) - KN(x_2) - BN(y_1) + K(F/B)N(y_2)\} \tag{A.4}$$

Up-and-out call option (B<K)

$$C_{uao(B>K)} = \exp[-r(T - t)]\{[FN(d_1) - KN(d_2)] + [BN(-z_1) - K(F/B)N(-z_2)]$$
$$-[FN(x_1) - KN(x_2)] - [BN(-y_1) - K(F/B)N(-y_2)]\} \tag{A.5}$$

Down-and-out put option (B<K)

$$P_{dao(B<K)} = \exp[-r(T - t)]\{[-FN(-d_1) + KN(-d_2)] - [BN(z_1) - K(F/B)N(z_2)]$$
$$+[FN(-x_1) - KN(-x_2)] + [BN(y_1) - K(F/B)N(y_2)]\} \tag{A.6}$$

Up-and-out put option (B<K)

$$P_{uao(B<K)} = \exp[-r(T - t)]\{-FN(-x_1) + KN(-x_2) + [BN(-y_1) - K(F/B)N(-y_2)]\} \tag{A.7}$$

Up-and-out put option (B>K)

$$P_{uao(B>K)} = \exp[-r(T-t)]\{[-FN(-d_1) + KN(-d_2)] + [BN(-z_1) - K(F/B)N(-z_2)]\} \qquad (A.8)$$

Where we use the following definitions:
B = barrier price level;

$$d_1 = \frac{\ln(F/K) + 0.5\sigma^2(T-t)}{\sigma\sqrt{T-t}} \;;\; d_2 = d_1 - \sigma\sqrt{T-t} \;;$$

$$x_1 = \frac{\ln(F/B) + 0.5\sigma^2(T-t)}{\sigma\sqrt{T-t}} \;;\; x_2 = x_1 - \sigma\sqrt{T-t} \;;$$

$$y_1 = \frac{\ln(B/F) + 0.5\sigma^2(T-t)}{\sigma\sqrt{T-t}} \;;\; y_2 = y_1 - \sigma\sqrt{T-t} \;;$$

$$z_1 = \frac{\ln(B^2/FK) + 0.5\sigma^2(T-t)}{\sigma\sqrt{T-t}} \;; \text{ and } z_2 = z_1 - \sigma\sqrt{T-t} \;.$$

A.3 Compound options

For the valuation of compound options, we use the following additional definitions:
F = F(t), the price of the underlying at time t.
F* = underlying price which makes the underlying option price equal to K_o at time T_0. F* must be found by solving equation (A.1) or (A.2) with the premium set equal to K_o, with T = T_u, and with t = T_o.
K_o = strike of the overlying option
K_u = strike of the underlying option
T_o = time of expiration of the overlying option
T_u = time of expiration of the underlying option
r = risk free rate
σ = annualized volatility
M(x,y,ρ) = bivariate cumulative normal distribution function.
ρ = correlation coefficient

Call on a call:

$$C_C = \exp[-r(T_u-t)]\{FM(x_1,y_1,\rho) - K_u M(x_2,y_2,\rho)\} - \exp[-r(T_o-t)]K_oN(x_2) \qquad (A.9)$$

where we have additionally defined

$$x_1 = \frac{\ln(F/F^*) + (\sigma^2/2)(T_o-t)}{\sigma\sqrt{T_o-t}}$$

$$x_2 = x_1 - \sigma\sqrt{T_o-t}$$

$$y_1 = \frac{\ln(F/K_u) + (\sigma^2/2)(T_u-t)}{\sigma\sqrt{T_u-t}}$$

$$y_2 = y_1 - \sigma\sqrt{T_u-t}$$

$$\rho = \sqrt{\frac{T_o-t}{T_u-t}}$$

The additional type of compound options are given in a very similar fashion. A put on a call is given by

$$P_C = \exp[-r(T_u-t)]\{K_uM(-x_2,y_2,-\rho) - FM(-x_1,y_1,-\rho)\} + \exp[-r(T_o-t)]K_oN(-x_2) \qquad (A.10)$$

Similarly the value of a call on a put is

$$C_P = \exp[-r(T_u - t)]\{K_u M(-x_2, -y_2, \rho) - F M(-x_1, -y_1, \rho)\} - \exp[-r(T_o - t)]K_o N(-x_2) \qquad (A.11)$$

Finally, the value of a put on a put is given by

$$P_P = \exp[-r(T_u - t)]\{F M(x_1, -y_1, -\rho) - K_u N(x_2, -y_2, -\rho)\} + \exp[-r(T_o - t)]K_o N(x_2) \qquad (A.12)$$

A.4 Options on the minimum or maximum of two assets

For options involving two assets, we use the following definitions:

F_1 = Forward price of commodity 1 at time t,

F_2 = Forward price of commodity 2 at time t,

σ_1 = volatility of commodity 1

σ_2 = volatility of commodity 2

ρ = correlation between commodity 1 and commodity 2, and

$M(x, y, \rho)$ = bivariate cumulative normal distribution function.

We further define

$$\sigma^2 = \sigma_1^2 + \sigma_2^2 - 2\rho\sigma_1\sigma_2$$

$$y_1 = \frac{\ln(F_1 / F_2) + (\sigma^2 / 2)(T - t)}{\sigma\sqrt{T - t}},$$

$$y_2 = \frac{\ln(F_2 / F_1) + (\sigma^2 / 2)(T - t)}{\sigma\sqrt{T - t}},$$

$$a_1 = \frac{\ln(F_1 / K) + (\sigma_1^2 / 2)(T - t)}{\sigma_1\sqrt{T - t}},$$

$$a_2 = \frac{\ln(F_2 / K) + (\sigma_2^2 / 2)(T - t)}{\sigma_2\sqrt{T - t}},$$

$$b_1 = a_1 - \sigma_1\sqrt{T - t},$$

$$b_2 = a_2 - \sigma_2\sqrt{T - t},$$

$$z_1 = \frac{(\rho\sigma_2 - \sigma_1)}{\sigma},$$

and

$$z_2 = \frac{(\rho\sigma_1 - \sigma_2)}{\sigma}.$$

Having made these definitions, we can now express the premium of a call on the maximum of two commodities or cash (in the amount K) as

$$C_{max(F,F,K)} = \exp[-r(T - t)] \{F_1(N(y_1) - M(-a_1, y_1, z_1)) + F_2(N(y_2) - M(-a_2, y_2, z_2) + K M(-b_1, -b_2, \rho)\} \qquad (A.13)$$

and the value of a call on the maximum of two commodities is simply given by

$$C_{max(F,F)-K} = C_{max(F,F,K)} - K \exp[-r(T - t)] \qquad (A.14)$$

If the strike price is zero, then this formula reduces to

$$C_{max(F,F)-0} = \exp[-r(T - t)]\{F_2 + F_1 N(y_1) - F_2 N(y_1 - \sigma\sqrt{T - t})\} \qquad (A.14B)$$

The purchase of call on the minimum of two commodities is equivalent to buying vanilla calls on the two individual commodities and selling a call on their maximum, ie

$$C_{min(F,F)-K} = C(F_1, K) + C(F_2, K) - C_{max(F,F)-K} , \qquad (A.15)$$

where $C(F_1,K)$ and $C(F_2,K)$ represent plain vanilla calls on F_1 and F_2 with strike price K.

A put on the maximum of two commodities can be valued as holding a call on the maximum of two commodities (with strike = K), being short a call on their maximum (with strike = 0), and holding a loan of the present value of the strike price.

$$P_{max(F,F)-K} = K\exp[-r(T-t)] - C_{max(F,F)-0} + C_{max(F,F)-K} \qquad (A.16)$$

Finally, a put on the minimum of two commodities (strike = K) is equivalent to having a call on the minimum (strike = K) and a loan of the present value of the strike price and being short a call on the minumum of the two commodities (strike = 0).

$$P_{min(F,F)-K} = K\exp[-r(T-t)] - C_{min(F,F)-0} + C_{min(F,F)-K} \qquad (A.17)$$

GLOSSARY

ADP *see* Alternative Delivery Procedure

Alternative Delivery Procedure (ADP) is the provision made in certain futures contracts, whereby buyers or settlers may make or take delivery under circumstances which differ from those stipulated in the contract

API or American Petroleum Institute

API gravity Industry-standard scale devised by the American Petroleum Institute for expressing the specific gravity of oils

Asian options have payoffs that depend on an average of prices for the underlying commodity over a period of time, rather than the price of the commodity on a single date. The averaging period may correspond to the entire life of the option, or may be shorter. Many contracts in the natural gas industry, for example, are based on the average closing prices on the last two or three days of trading of the first available Nymex contract

ASTM, or American Society for Testing Materials. The quality of a petroleum product may be described using ASTM specifications

ATK, or aviation turbine kerosene, is a medium-light fuel consumed in jet and turbo-prop aircraft engines

back-to-back Deal in which an intermediary is able to offset the price exposure generated by a derivative contract sold to one party with the price exposure of a contract undertaken with another. Ideally, a back-to-back transaction would leave the intermediary with no market risk at all, although it may still be exposed to other risks (notably credit risk)

backwardation Term used to describe an energy market in. which the anticipated value of the spot price is lower than the current spot price (the market is inverted). That is, when a market is in backwardation, market participants expect the spot price to go down. The reverse situation is described as contango (qv)

barrel (bbl) is the standard measure for oil and oil products. One barrel = 35 imperial gallons, 42 US gallons, or 159 litres. In energy units, one barrel = 5.8 million British Thermal Units (BTU)

barrier options are exotic options which either come into life (are knocked-in) or are extinguished (knocked-out) under conditions stipulated in the option contract. The conditions are usually defined in terms of a price level (barrier, knock-out, or knock-in price) that may be reached at any time during the life of the option

baseload electricity This term is used in the United Kingdom for the electricity produced at relative-

ly low cost by continuously operating (or base load) plant

basis risk Basis risk is the risk that the value of a futures contract (or an OTC hedge) does not move in line with that of the underlying exposure. For example, a natural gas producer which sells its gas production into the Permian Basin spot market in West Texas will be exposed to basis risk, if it hedges using futures contracts on the Nymex (in New York). This is an example of "locational" basis risk. Other forms of basis risk include "product basis", arising from mismatches in type or quality of hedge and underlying (eg hedging jet fuel with gasoil) and "time" or "calendar" basis (eg hedging an exposure to physical prices in December with a January futures contract)

basis swap Basis swaps are used to hedge exposure to basis risks, such as locational risk or time exposure risk. For example, a natural gas basis swap could be used to hedge a locational price risk: the seller receives from the buyer a Nymex settlement value (usually the average of the last three days closing prices) plus a negotiated fixed basis, and pays the buyer the published index (qv) value of gas sold at a specified location

bbl *see* barrel

b/d, B/D Abbreviation for "barrels per day". Also written as bpd/BPD

benzene Derived from petroleum, benzene is one of the most important feedstocks in the chemical industry. It is the simplest aromatic (hydrocarbons with a ring structure) compound

binary options *see* digital options

bpd, BPD Abbreviation for "barrels per day". Also written as b/d, B/D

Brady bonds Instruments issued under the Brady Plan that were used to restructure the debt of developing countries; some of these instruments include recapture clauses based on oil prices

break Sudden downward movement in futures prices on an exchange

Brent Blend Crude oil blended from the output of the Brent and Ninian fields in the North Sea

BS&W, or Bottom Sediment and Water, describes the wastage often found in crude oil and residual fuel

BTU, or British Thermal Unit. Standard unit of energy signifying the quantity of heat required to raise the temperature of one pound of water by one degree Fahrenheit. It is equivalent to 0.252kcal and 1.055kJ

BTU swap Commodity swap under which the floating price of one commodity is calculated as a percentage of the price of another commodity, both prices being expressed in terms of MMBTU (million BTU) equivalents

bunker fuel Term used to describe the heavy fuel oil purchased by shipping companies

buy-back price is the price that an oil company pays to a state for

oil that the company has produced but which is owned by the state

"calendar" or time spreads describe the price differential, or spread, that may arise between differently dated futures contracts. For example, the price difference between contracts for first and second month Brent offered on the IPE. Time spreads can be mitigated by purchasing options on the difference between average annual prices. In effect, such options provide protection against a reshaping of the forward price curve

CCPG, or Combined Cycle Power Generation *see* Combined Heat and Power (CHP)

CEA *see* Commodity Exchange Act

C&F, or Cost and Freight, indicates that the quoted price/contract includes freight

CFTC or Commodity Futures Trading Commission (United States)

charm describes an option risk parameter which measures the amount that delta (qv) will change due to the passage of time

CHP *see* Combined Heat and Power

CIF, or Cost Insurance Freight, indicates that the price/contract includes freight and insurance, but excludes customs duties

combination hedging describes the use of a combination of hedges to construct a risk management strategy. For example, a hedging strategy for jet fuel price exposure might make use of IPE Gasoil futures combined with a options on the kerosene/gasoil spread value over the risk-managed period

Combined Heat and Power (CHP), is used to describe power generation where fuel is burnt to produce both electricity and heat (or steam), both forms of energy being used to power the host industrial site. If the heat is not used on-site it can be used to generate further electricity using steam turbines, in which case the process is called Combined Cycle Power Generation (CCPG)

Commodity Exchange Act, or CEA, was passed in 1974 by the United States' Congress, granting the Commodity Futures Trading Commission exclusive jurisdiction over transactions involving exchange-traded "contracts of sale of a commodity for future delivery" and commodity option contracts (exchange traded or not). However, see also Futures Trading Practices Act (FTPA)

compound option An option which allows its holder to purchase or sell another option for a fixed price. For example, the purchase of a European "call on a put" means that the compound option buyer obtains the right to buy on a specified day (the expiration of the overlying option) a put option (the underlying option) at the overlying option's strike price

contango Term used to describe an energy market in which the anticipated value of the spot price in the future is higher than the current spot price. When a market is in contango, market participants expect the spot price to go up. The reverse situation is described as backwardation (qv)

contracts for difference, Contracts for Difference This term is sometimes used (uncapitalised) as an alternative to the term swap. In a more specialised sense, CFDs are the OTC derivatives (again, usually swaps) used extensively by generators and suppliers in the UK electricity market to manage their exposures. For example, in return for an option fee, a contract seller may agree to pay a contract buyer the difference between UK electricity "pool" price and the contract exercise price in each settlement period (half hour) when the pool price exceeds the exercise price

"convenience yield" The modern theory of term structure introduces this concept to describe that yield which "accrues to the owner of a physical inventory but not to the owner of a contract for future delivery". It represents the value of having the physical product immediately to hand, and offers a theoretical explanation (of limited predictive value) for the predominance of backwardation (qv) in the energy markets

"cracking" describes the technological process used in petroleum refineries; that is, the application of vacuum, heat and catalysts to break down larger, heavier molecules of hydrocarbons into lighter ones, with higher economic value

crack spread describes the difference in the prices of two or more commodities, where one of the (unrefined or input) commodities is used to produce the other (refined or output) commodity(s). Crack spreads are particularly important to refiners, as their profit margin is dependent upon the price differential between unrefined crude oil and a basket of refined products

cross-market derivative Derivative instrument designed to manage simultaneously price exposures generated in different markets. For example, an interest rate swap, with payments linked to energy prices, can be used to

manage jointly the firm's exposure to energy prices and to changes in interest rates

crude spreads The price difference between different varieties of crude. For example, the difference between the price of the May WTI crude oil futures contract on Nymex and the May Brent crude oil futures contract on the IPE

cubic foot Standard unit for measuring gas. 1 cubic foot = 0.0283 cubic metres

curve-lock swap Swap which "locks" the counterparty into an existing price relationship in the forward curve, with the aim of benefiting from any shifts in the forward curve eg between backwardation and contango

daily call option The daily call option, which has a long history in the natural gas markets, allows the buyer to take additional volumes of gas at very short notice (typically one day)

delta Option risk parameter which measures the sensitivity of an option price to changes in the price of the underlying instrument

demurrage Sum paid as damages for delay in loading or discharging cargo from a chartered ship

depletion control Any restriction placed on the speed with which oil or gas can be extracted from a given field

diff swaps are contracts to exchange the difference between a fixed differential (or "diff") between the price of two products, on the one hand, and the actual or floating differential over time, on the other

digital, or binary, options pay either a fixed sum or zero depend-

ing on whether the payoff condition is satisfied or not, eg cash-or-nothing options, and asset-or-nothing options

distillates Products of the refinery process, condensed out of crude oil during fractional distillation. They include naphtha, petrol, kerosene and gasoil

double-up swap This instrument grants the swap provider an option to double the swap volume before the pricing period starts; by granting this option, swap users can achieve a swap price which is better than the actual market price. The mechanism by which this is achieved involves consumers (who are buying fixed) selling a put swaption, or producers (who are selling fixed) selling a call swaption; in either case, the premium earned from the sale is used to subsidise the swap price

"downstream", as opposed to "upstream", activities include the refining and marketing of crude oil and oil products and, in fact, any activity after the crude oil has been produced and loaded

dual-commodity options have payoffs that depend on the prices of two or more underlying instruments

EFA *see* Electricity Forward Agreements

Electricity Forward Agreements, or EFAs, are standardised and brokered swap-like instruments used in the UK electricity derivative market to hedge or trade pool prices. Regional Electricity Companies and generators use EFAs as a means of fine-tuning their CFD (qv) transactions

E&P Abbreviation for "Exploration and Production"

exploding option Single-contract version of a call or put spread which automatically liquidates if the conditions for maximum pay-off are met

extendable swap The extendable swap is constructed on the same principle as the double-up swap (qv), except that instead of doubling the swap, the provider has the right to extend the swap, at the end of the agreed period, for a further pre-determined period

feedstock Raw material used by any processing unit. For example, crude oil is a feedstock of oil refineries and petrochemical plants

"fixed-for-floating" contracts. Alternative name for a swap

FOB, or "Free on Board", indicates that the price/contract includes delivery of crude or product on board a transporting vessel, but that the responsibility for transporting and insuring the cargo resides with the purchaser

forward contract Contract by means of which one counterparty agrees to sell to another counterparty a specified amount of a commodity for a certain price at a designated date in the future

"frac" spread Difference between the price of natural gas and of natural gas liquids (eg propane, ethane, butane, iso-butane). The equivalent term in the oil industry is "crack spread" (qv)

FTPA *see* **Futures Trading Practices Act**

fuel oil Heavy distillates produced during the refining process and used as fuel for power stations, ships, etc

futures contract Similar to a forward contract, a futures contract is

an agreement to buy or sell a commodity for a certain price at a designated time in the future. Unlike forward contracts, futures contracts are usually traded on an exchange which specifies standard terms for the contracts and guarantees their performance. Exchanges normally require that margins (qv) are posted by holders of open contract positions

Futures Trading Practices Act, or FTPA, of 1992. By this Act, Congress granted the CFTC the authority to exempt certain agreements, contracts and transactions from various requirements of the CEA or CFTC regulations, including the CEA requirement that transactions must occur on a designated contract market

gamma Option risk parameter which measures the sensitivity of the option delta to a change in the price of the underlying instrument. It is thus a "second derivative" of the option price with respect to the price of the underlying

gasoil Medium distillates produced in refineries during the fractional distillation of crude oil. Gasoil is burned in central heating systems, and is used as a feedstock for the chemical industry; it is also used to produce diesel fuel

gasoline spread The difference between the price of unleaded gasoline and crude oil

GOR, or Gas-to-Oil Ratio, expresses the volume of gas/volume of oil produced from a given well

heat spread Jargon used to describe the difference between the price of No. 2 heating oil and the price of crude oil

heavy crude Crude oil that possesses a high proportion of heavy hydrocarbon fractions (and a low

API gravity)

HSFO Abbreviation of High Sulphur Fuel Oil

index Published indices are often agreed upon as the price references for energy derivative contracts. For example, in the US natural gas industry, indices provide an average price of contracts for delivery during the calendar month at a given location. The average is based upon a survey of prices transacted during "bid week" (typically, the 20th to the 25th of the month). The best known indices are published by *Inside FERC, Gas Week, Natural Gas Intelligence* and *Gas Daily*

index swap In the natural gas market in North America, index (qv) swaps are often used to hedge against location price risk (a form of basis risk). The seller receives a fixed, or otherwise determined, price and pays the buyer the published index value for natural gas from a specified location

IPE, or International Petroleum Exchange. The IPE, based in London, is one of the world's leading energy futures exchanges

kappa *see* vega

kerosene Medium-light product of the fractional distillation of crude oil, used for lighting, heating and the manufacture of jet fuel

ladder options can be described as discrete cases of a lookback option (qv). The ladder option is structured so that a number of price levels guarantee minimum option payoffs if they are reached during the life of the option. If none of these levels is reached, then the payoff is the same as that of a standard European option

lambda *see* vega

light crude Crude oil that possesses a high proportion of light hydrocarbon fractions (and a high API gravity)

"limit up" The maximum move that is allowed in the price of an exchange contract, as specified in the United States by the CFTC (qv)

LNG, or Liquefied Natural Gas, is natural gas that has been liquefied by cooling to about -161 degrees Celsius at atmospheric pressure. Liquefied gas is hundreds of times denser than natural gas and much easier to transport

location spread Differential between the prices quoted for the same commodity at two different locations, eg between the price of 1% heating oil at New York Harbor and at the Gulf Coast

lookback option A lookback call (put) option grants the right to purchase (sell) the underlying energy commodity at the lowest (highest) price reached during the life of the option. Effectively, the best price from the point of view of the holder of the option becomes the strike price

LSFO Abbreviation for Low Sulphur Fuel Oil

margin Cash or securities that must be deposited with the clearing house of a broker or exchange for security against any losses which could result if the investor should fail to honour the obligations of any open futures position

margin swap *see* refining margin swaps

MTBE, or Methyl tertiary butyl ether, is a gasoline additive used to reduce pollution

naphtha Term used to describe a range of distillates from the heavier gaseous fuels to the lighter varieties of kerosene. Naphtha is used as a feedstock in the manufacture of petrol, and in the chemical industry (as a feedstock for ethylene, etc)

natural gas liquids, or NGLs, are the hydrocarbons extracted from the natural gas stream at processing plants by means of fractionation. The liquids include ethane, propane, normal butane, isobutane and natural gasoline

NGL *see* natural gas liquids

NWE Common abbreviation for the oil market in North-West Europe

Nymex, or New York Mercantile Exchange, is the largest energy exchange in the world

off-market swap In this type of swap, a premium is built into the swap price to fund the purchase of options or to allow for the restructuring of a hedge portfolio. Off-market swaps are generally used to restructure or cancel old swap/hedge deals: essentially, they simulate a refinancing package

OIP, or Oil in Place, signifies an estimate of the actual amount of oil present in a reservoir; only a proportion of OIP is likely to be recoverable (for technical and economic reasons)

OPEC, or Organisation of Petroleum Exporting Countries

open interest The sum of all the long positions (or short positions) taken in a given futures contract

option Contract that gives the purchaser the right, but not the obligation, to buy or sell the

underlying commodity at a certain price (the exercise, or strike, price) on or before an agreed date. With European-style options, purchasers may take delivery of the commodity only at the end of the option's life. American-style options may be exercised at any time over the life of the option. Most exchange-traded options are of American type; most OTC energy options are Asian (qv) options

OTC An "over-the-counter" or OTC deal is a customised derivative contract usually arranged with an intermediary such as a major bank or the trading wing of an energy major, as opposed to a standardised derivative contract available on an exchange. Swaps are the commonest form of OTC instrument

participation swap Similar to a regular swap in that the fixed price payer is fully protected when prices rise above the agreed (fixed) price, with the difference that the client "participates" in any price decrease. For example, a participation swap agreed at a level of $80/mt for high sulphur fuel oil, with a 50% participation, would offer full protection against prices above $80/mt. But the buyer would retain 50% of the savings generated when prices fell below $80/mt

path-dependent options have a payoff that is dependent on the price history of the underlying over all or part of the life of the option. The commonest form of option in OTC energy risk management (the Asian option) is a path-dependent option, as are lookback and barrier options

peak-lopping plant Term used in the United Kingdom for the electricity produced at relatively high cost by plant that operates for only a fraction of each year to service peaks in demand

PPP, or Pool Purchase Price, is a term used to describe a component of the pricing formulae used in the UK electricity supply industry

pre-paid swap By means of a pre-paid swap, the fixed payments that form one side of the cashflows generated by a standard swap, and which are normally paid over the life of the swap, are discounted back to their net present value and paid as an immediate cash sum to one of the swap counterparties. That counterparty will then make floating price payments over the life of the swap, just as in a standard swap. Pre-paid swaps are often used as a source of project finance or pre-export financing

"processing spread" is a general term for an option on the difference between the price of feedstock and products. For example, the difference between the price of natural gas and of a basket of the natural gas liquids (ethane, propane, iso-butane, normal butane and natural gasoline) which can be extracted from the natural gas stream at processing plants

PSP, or Pool Selling Price, is the price paid by suppliers to the UK electricity industry "pool", consisting of the PPP (qv) plus an "uplift" payment

"quality spreads" describe the price differential between different qualities of the same energy product. Examples are the spreads between the prices of sweet and sour crude (also known as "crude spreads"), or between the prices of different grades of heating oil (defined by their sulphur content)

RECs, or Regional Electricity

Companies, are the recently privatised electricity supply companies in the UK electricity industry

refining margin swaps simultaneously hedge the price of the products (or output) of a refinery, and the price of the crude oil feedstock (or input). That is, the products are sold, and the crude is bought, for equivalent forward periods. Refinery margin swaps effectively "lock-in" the profitability of a refinery

"resid" spread Difference between the price of No. 6 fuel oil and the price of a benchmark crude oil

residual fuel oil Non-volatile heavy fuel oils produced in refineries from the residue of the fractional distillation of crude oil

rho Option risk parameter which measures the sensitivity of the option price to the risk free interest rate

sculpted or shaped contracts Terms commonly used in the UK electricity industry to describe contracts with a customised demand profile, as opposed to standard baseload contracts

shaped contract *see* sculpted or shaped contracts

Simex, or Singapore International Monetary Exchange, the principal energy futures exchange in the Asia-Pacific region

slippage Difference between the price of a commodity or contract at the point of the decision to buy (sell), and the price at the moment of execution. The more volatile the commodity market, the more significant slippage becomes

SMP, or System Marginal Price, forms part of the pricing formulae

of the UK electricity supply industry

sour crude Crude oil with a high level of hydrogen sulphide or mercaptans

spread options are options written on the differential between the prices of two commodities. Spread options may be based on the price differences between prices of the same commodity at two different locations (location spreads); prices of the same commodity at two different points in time (calendar spreads); prices of inputs to, and outputs from, a production process (processing spreads); and prices of different grades of the same commodity (quality spreads)

"stacking contract" is the generic term for a type of Contract For Difference used in the UK electricity market

straddle Combination of a put and a call with the same expiration dates and strikes. A buyer of a straddle hopes that the volatility of the underlying prices will increase, creating profit opportunities

strip Industry jargon for any series of transactions with consecutive settlement or expiration dates. For example, an annual strip of futures denotes a purchase/sale of 12 consecutive futures contracts on the same commodity

swap Agreement whereby a floating price is exchanged for a fixed price over a specified period. It is an off-balance sheet financial arrangement which involves no transfer of physical energy; both parties settle their contractual obligations by means of a transfer of cash. The agreement defines the volume, duration and fixed reference price. Differences are settled in cash for specific periods – monthly, quarterly or six-monthly.

Swaps are also known as "contracts for differences" and as "fixed-for-floating" contracts

swaption Option to purchase (call swaption) or sell (put swaption) a swap at some future date

sweet crude Crude oil with a low level of hydrogen sulphide or mercaptans

"take-or-pay" is a description of a certain type of contract historically prevalent in the US natural gas industry. Under such a contract, the buyer agreed to purchase natural gas at a fixed price up to an annual maximum, but became subject to deficiency payments if the volume bought dropped below a minimum amount

theta Option risk parameter which measures the speed of time decay of the option premium

time spreads *see* calendar spreads

"trend" Term usually applied to movements in the short-term (spot) prices, where these are not thought to imply any change in the term structure itself. An upward trend may thus sustain or increase the market backwardation, and a downward trend will have the same effect on a contango

ULCC, or Ultra-Large Crude Carrier, is a tanker of over 300,000 tonnes deadweight

"upstream" All oil industry activities prior to the delivery of crude oil to the production terminal, eg exploration and production. The opposite of "downstream" (qv)

vega Option risk parameter which measures the sensitivity of the option price to changes in the price volatility of the underlying instrument. Also known as kappa or lambda

"vintaging" In the past, the regulated natural gas market in the United States used the concept of "vintaging" to assign different permitted maximum prices to gas produced from specific wells, based upon the date of well completion and, in some cases, the depth of the well

VLCC, or Very Large Crude Carrier, is a tanker of over 200,000 tonnes deadweight

INDEX